Frege

A Philosophical Biography

Dale Jacquette

CAMBRIDGE
UNIVERSITY PRESS

University Printing House, Cambridge CB2 8BS, United Kingdom

One Liberty Plaza, 20th Floor, New York, NY 10006, USA

477 Williamstown Road, Port Melbourne, VIC 3207, Australia

314–321, 3rd Floor, Plot 3, Splendor Forum, Jasola District Centre,
New Delhi – 110025, India

79 Anson Road, #06-04/06, Singapore 079906

Cambridge University Press is part of the University of Cambridge.

It furthers the University's mission by disseminating knowledge in the pursuit of
education, learning, and research at the highest international levels of excellence.

www.cambridge.org
Information on this title: www.cambridge.org/9780521863278
DOI: 10.1017/9781139033725

© Cambridge University Press 2019

First published 2019
Reprinted 2019

Printed in the United Kingdom by TJ International Ltd, Padstow, Cornwall

A catalogue record for this publication is available from the British Library.

Library of Congress Cataloging-in-Publication Data
NAMES: Jacquette, Dale, author.
TITLE: Frege : a philosophical biography / Dale Jacquette.
DESCRIPTION: New York : Cambridge University Press, 2017. | Includes
bibliographical references and index.
IDENTIFIERS: LCCN 2017019189 | ISBN 9780521863278 (hardback)
SUBJECTS: LCSH: Frege, Gottlob, 1848-1925. |
Philosophers – Germany – Biography. | BISAC: PHILOSOPHY /
History & Surveys / General.
CLASSIFICATION: LCC B3245.F24 J33 2017 | DDC 193–dc23
LC record available at https://lccn.loc.gov/2017019189

ISBN 978-0-521-86327-8 Hardback

For Tina

The work of Frege, which appears to be far less known than it deserves . . . abounds in subtle distinctions, and avoids all the usual fallacies which beset writers on Logic.

Bertrand Russell, The Principles of Mathematics *(1903), Appendix A.*
"The Logical and Arithmetical Doctrines of Frege," §475, p. 501

The question "What is a number?" is one which has been often asked, but has only been correctly answered in our own time. The answer was given by Frege in 1884, in his *Grundlagen der Arithmetik*. Although this book is quite short, not difficult, and of the very highest importance, it attracted almost no attention, and the definition of number which it contains remained practically unknown until it was rediscovered by the present author in 1901.

Bertrand Russell, Introduction to Mathematical Philosophy *(1919),*
Chapter II, p. 11

Contents

Figures

Acknowledgments

I am grateful to my editor at Cambridge University Press, Hilary Gaskin, for her enduring patience, to Beatrice Rehl, and to a succession of previous editorial assistants, during the long incubation period this book uncharacteristically required. I thank Tina M. (Trass) Jacquette for graphic design of logical symbolism and diagramming. Special thanks are due to my research assistant for this project at the University of Bern, Pascale Lötscher, who brought together and annotated sources of relevance to Frege's biography identified for each chapter planned. The inclusion, interpretation, and use of these references are in every instance entirely my responsibility. Rian Zuberi, Pascale's successor as my research assistant during the later phases of the work, tracked down elusive materials and prepared the book's concluding list of references. Rian's successor, Andreas Freivogel, third in line as research assistant in this extended project, aided in the final stages of the book's preparation by offering valuable proofreading support and help compiling the index. I was pleased to offer much of the content of the book to participants in my Bern seminar on Frege, during the spring semester of 2015, where I benefited in final rewriting of the text from the input, comments, questions, and criticisms of the extraordinarily talented and enthusiastic students who participated in the course.

References to Frege's Writings

The convention of referring to Frege's books using their original German titles or obvious abbreviations is followed throughout, whereas the titles of Frege's essays, published or unpublished, are generally given first in German with English translations, and thereafter cited using just the English equivalent.

Readers should expect to encounter references in German to Frege's *Begriffsschrift, Grundlagen der Arithmetik, Grundgesetze der Arithmetik*, and the planned (but unpublished in his lifetime) *Logische Untersuchungen*, with an explanation of each title's meaning in English. An essay such as "Über Sinn und Bedeutung" is introduced in its original German, and referred to thereafter in the text under the essay's English name "On Sense and Reference." Frege's "Funktion und Gegenstand," after suitable introduction, is afterward referred to consistently throughout as "Function and Object."

Where translations of any of these sources are quoted in the text, references in the notes are generally given to a preferred English translation and edition, cited using their English titles in full or abbreviated form, or indicated as my translation. This convention is frequently adopted in English-language commentary on Frege's writings. There is an additional reason behind the distinction between German for titles of books and English for essay titles in the body of a lengthy biography concerning Frege's life and works. Beyond aiding the reader to keep track typographically of Frege's books as distinct from essays, the convention is meant to facilitate reading and comprehension. Frege wrote comparatively few books, but many articles. His books are more easily recognizable in German than in their English titles. Longer German essay titles are more jarring for average English readers, who may stumble as they mentally translate the entire phrase every time the essay is named. It is easy under such circumstances to jumble up Frege's "Funktion und Gegenstand" with "Funktion und Begriff," or others of his frequently mentioned writings. The hope is that this linguistic division of references to Frege's books and essays will not appear as an unprincipled conflation of reference styles, but will rather be a sensible reader-friendly compromise among competing literary and scholarly choices.

Chronology of Major
Events in Frege's Life

- **1848, 8 November** – Frege born in Wismar, Grand-Duchy of Mecklenburg-Schwerin (House of Mecklenburg residing in Schwerin) (Germany)
- **1852, 31 March** – Birth of Frege's brother and only sibling, Cäsar Friedrich Arnold (known as Arnold)
- **1854–1869** – Attends the Große Stadtschule Wismar, through Gymnasium and Matura Examination
- **1866, 30 November** – Frege's father, Karl Alexander, the co-founder and headmaster of a local girls' school, dies in Wismar
- **1869** Summer Semester to Winter Semester **1870/71** – Studies mathematics in Jena
- **1871** Summer Semester to Summer Semester **1873** – Studies mathematics in Göttingen
- **1873** – Earns PhD in mathematics (geometry) in Göttingen. Thesis title, *Über eine geometrische Darstellung der imaginären Gebilde in der Ebene* (*On a Geometrical Representation of Imaginary Figures in a Plane*)
- **1874, 16 May** – Writes and defends Habilitationsschrift (post-doctoral thesis required for appointment to a university teaching post) in Jena. Passes writing and exam requirements and is appointed unsalaried student-fee-paid lecturer in mathematics. Thesis title, *Rechnungsmethoden, die sich auf eine Erweiterung des Größenbegriffes gründen* (*Methods of Calculation Based on an Extension of the Concept of Quantity*)
- **1879** – Publication of *Begriffsschrift: eine der arithmetischen nachgebildete Formelsprache des reinen Denkens* (*Concept-Writing: A Formula-Language for Pure Thought Modeled on Arithmetic*) – Promoted to *außerordentlicher* (Associate) Professor or Professor Extraordinarius in mathematics at Jena
- **1884** – Publication of *Grundlagen der Arithmetik* (*Foundations of Arithmetic*)
- **1887, 14 March** – Marries Margarete Katharina Sophia Anna Lieseberg
- **1891** – Publication of "Funktion und Begriff" ("Function and Concept")

- 1892 – Publication of "Über Sinn und Bedeutung" ("On Sense and Reference") and "Funktion und Gegenstand" ("Function and Object")
- 1893 – Publication of *Grundgesetze der Arithmetik I* (*Basic Laws of Arithmetic*, Volume I)
- 1894 – Review of Edmund Husserl's 1891 *Philosophie der Arithmetik*
- 1896, 26 May – Awarded the position of *ordentlicher Honorarprofessur* (Honorary Full Professor) in Jena
- 1898, 16 October – Frege's mother, Auguste Wilhelmine Sophia Bialloblotzky, dies in Jena
- 1902, 16 June – Letter from Bertrand Russell to Frege in which what later came to be called Russell's paradox is announced
- 1903 – Publication of *Grundgesetze der Arithmetik II*, with a last-minute *Nachwort* (Afterword) in response to Russell's paradox
- 1904, 25 June – Frege's wife, Margarete, dies in Jena
- 1908 – Accepts wardship of Alfred Fuchs (b. 30 July 1903), who was then aged six
- 1911, 1912 – Visits of Ludwig Wittgenstein
- 1914–1918 – WWI. Cordial mathematical and philosophical correspondence with Wittgenstein and others
- 1918 – Retirement from Jena. Assisted financially by Wittgenstein, Frege makes a permanent move to Bad Kleinen in Mecklenburg. Publication of "Der Gedanke. Eine logische Untersuchung" ("Thoughts: A Logical Investigation") and "Die Verneinung. Eine logische Untersuchungen" ("Negation: A Logical Investigation"), essays intended for a book-length collection, unpublished in Frege's lifetime, to be titled *Logische Untersuchungen*
- 1919–1923 – Germany's post-WWI Great Inflation. Frege's unsavory right-wing and anti-Semitic tendencies are seen in his political activities and private diaries
- 1921–1922 August – Legally adopts 18–19-year-old ward Alfred Fuchs as his son
- 1923 – Publication of "Gedankengefüge" ("Compound Thoughts"), third and last completed chapter of the projected *Logische Untersuchungen*
- 1925, 26 July – Frege dies in Bad Kleinen.

Prelude to the Afternoon
of a Paradox

A LETTER ARRIVED. It was brought to the university, then taken from the mail cubicle to the mathematician-philosopher's office. He received it at his desk with the usual triage of correspondence. He may have brought it back to the house with him as particularly interesting and requiring more concentrated attention. He had a rough idea of what it was about. He looked it over later in the day in the garden or at his sun-streaked table where he sometimes wrote. He needed to think more about what exactly it was supposed to mean.

Aged fifty-four years, Gottlob Frege was on the threshold of publishing the crowning conclusion to his lifetime's research in the logicist foundations of arithmetic. He had the usual doubts about some parts, but had worked everything out vigilantly, and in the end the whole package seemed fully in order. It was a significant accomplishment, a contribution to mathematical knowledge and scientific philosophy. Mathematics was shown to be, as Plato thought, independent of the vagaries of subjective thought, but, as only Frege expected to prove, planted on rock solid foundations in pure logic. Having begun with arithmetic, and having devised an exact logical notation for the expression of basic mathematical ideas, he was satisfied that elementary arithmetic could be reduced to logic, that it was nothing more or less than pure logic applied to a purely logical concept of number.

True, he was publishing the second volume of his 1893 master-work, *Grundgesetze der Arithmetik, begriffsschriftlich abgeleitet* (*Basic Laws of Arithmetic, Derived using Concept-Writing*), out of his own pocket in the next year, 1903. The demand for heavy-duty texts full of formal symbolisms that no one else working in logic or mathematics was interested in using or had any facility reading at the time was not encouraging. Printing books was a business like any other that must earn its keep. Technical writings no less than novels, travelogues, poetry, and libretti need at least to break even at the cash-drawer. The publisher, having already produced the author's first volume, and having been underwhelmed with sales, was unwilling to take the same risk again for the second volume without subsidy. A reasonable conclusion from a profit-driven rather than philosophical motive. Who would want volume two, having not already bought volume one?

Committed as he was to the philosophical project of presenting the complete reduction of arithmetic to logic, the scholar reluctantly paid the publisher's costs to see the work in print. He could do no more than present his ideas as he had rigorously painstakingly developed them. He was obligated to see the project through and have copies of his completed logic placed on library shelves. Perhaps he wanted to see the finished project in print, to hold in his hands what he had never doubted to be a major contribution to the foundations of knowledge. Then, too, his research had been supported by a large optical corporation, and they would want to see concrete results for their investment in his ideas, time, and labor. He could hope for a more appreciative reception from more knowledgeable discerning opinion when the whole work became available. It might take years, but the certainty of eventual success could not be doubted.

He knew, reflecting on the matter, that mathematical philosophy was ripe for a formally exact theory of the logical basis of arithmetic. There were already gratifying signs of positive recognition, of respect for and interest in what he had done, if not quite the revolution in philosophy of mathematics he endeavored to ignite. Unfortunately, recognition came so late, when certain important things could no longer be done. There were many misunderstandings. There was much to correct in how philosophy thinks of mathematics in its relation to a minimally adequate pure sym-bolic logic for the formally exact expression of arithmetical truths. Mathematical proofs are always matters of logical inference. It was a technical problem to discover and fit the right logic of functions to the inferences made in mathematical reasoning. Firmly convinced of the rightness of the approach, the author knew that it might nevertheless take time, many years perhaps, for the work to find its proper place at the end of a line of predecessors who had also sought to define the most basic concepts of mathematics and reconstruct the logic of mathematical reasoning.

What was required of the foundations of mathematics was first and foremost an adequate language for the expression of mathematical ideas. Frege's *Begriffsschrift, Concept-Script* or *Concept-Writing*, was designed to provide a syntactically univocal notation that in meaningful expressions referred and could only refer to individual existent objects, dynamic or abstract, belonging to the logic's reference domain, to the extensions of predicates in the language by which instantiated properties are truly or falsely ascribed to existent entities. The logic secondly introduced deductively valid inference mechanisms, the syntax and formal semantics of proof, whereby the theorems of mathematics, beginning with all the essentials of elementary arithmetic, could be rigorously derived as logical consequences of basic intuitive logically supportable axioms. If it were successful, then in this sense, for the first time in the history of mathematics and philosophy, everything in arithmetic from top to bottom would be tightly fastened down to a surveyable choice of formal logical principles. The same principles differently expressed turned out to be essentially those needed for what today is known as an algebraic second-order propositional and predicate-quantificational logic or general functional calculus. Such a system, the mathematician-philosopher's *Begriffsschrift*, differently expressed in equivalent syntax and with essentially the same existence-presuppositional extensional semantics, remains in contemporary applications one of the most widely adopted and adapted logics. It is the logic that in more linear sentential notation is still considered the standard classical first- and second-order logic. More, it is the basis, the *Urgrundplan*, for almost all variations into greater logical exotica for specialized applications of nonclassical logics, the port of call from which they depart and with which they are inevitably formally compared.

The postmark was from England. He did not recognize at first glance the handwriting of the correspondent. He had heard before, sometimes in critical but always most respectful terms, of the aristocratic philosopher Bertrand Arthur William Russell. He knew him to be working in a similar way on the logical foundations of mathematics. Russell was more directly inspired by the logical arithmetic of Giuseppe Peano, and as a result more comfortable with logic written in linear sentences, like most formalisms, rather than in Frege's diagrammatic two-dimensional *Begriffsschrift* notation. Russell read everything through the lens of Peano's mathematical logic. Peano was interesting, important. A good technician, which was not said lightly. Turning the envelope from front to back and back to front again, satisfied that the author had been identified, Frege withdrew two pages written in Russell's near native-perfect German, acquired from the German-speaking nanny of his privileged childhood. Frege opened the envelope again, unfolded the pages. He began to read the letter that had taken only a few days to cross the English Channel, to reach him in the heart of Thüringen, marked Friday's Hill, Haslemere, 16 June 1902.

Introduction: Logic, Thought, and Thinker

I AM DELIGHTED TO offer these reflections on the life of Gottlob Frege for Cambridge University Press's distinguished series of biographies of great philosophers. Frege is one of the founding figures of modern analytic philosophy. His contributions to logic and to the philosophy of mathematics and language set the stage and continue to shape lively research agendas for generations of analytic thinkers working in areas pioneered by Frege that today are well-established fields of theoretical philosophy.

This book is meant to answer three related interpretive questions concerning the meaning of Frege's lifework. Anyone interested in Frege's life, in addition to seeing how the basic documentable facts of his chronology can be fit together into a likely depiction of his life, can be expected to share a desire to know, in the seasoning of Frege's philosophical development, the best answers to the following philosophical–biographical questions. (1) What exactly did Frege hope to achieve in his mathematical and philosophical writings? (2) Should Frege's efforts be considered to have succeeded or failed, and in either case for what reason and in what sense? (3) What meaning should Frege's success or failure be understood to have for his significance in a wide-screen panorama of the history of logic and newly emergent analytic philosophy?

A final assessment in pursuit of answers to these interpretive questions must wait until Frege's biography in these pages is in one sense closed, if not completed, by the event of his death. The answer to question (3) requires assessment from a vantage point many years after Frege's passing, as appreciation of his accomplishments and applications of his methods finally begin to gain the attention that during his lifetime he was mostly denied. Much that is distinctively Fregean – and that was revolutionary in Frege – is taught and shared in philosophical education, but, owing to the sometimes subterranean nature of his influence, is largely taken for granted today.

This biography of Frege aims at telling a plausible story about his life and the unfolding of his philosophical thought. It connects the dots and data points representing what is definitely known concerning Frege's family background, upbringing, and education in a way that is meant to add dimension to Frege the mathematical logician and philosopher as son, sibling, student, teacher, husband, and adoptive father. These thematically chosen facts in historical sequence are integrated with chronological and ideological interrelations between the distinguishable components of Frege's philosophy as he crafts, presents, and refines his ideas. Of necessity, given Frege's perceived importance in the history of philosophy, attention is devoted to the extended period of Frege's philosophical maturity, dating from the time of his 1874 University of Jena Habilitationsschrift until his death in 1925. Frege's significance is explained as his conception and pursuit of a highly innovative systematic philosophical research program in the philosophy of arithmetic, for the sake of which everything else in his legacy serves in different ways as a means to that singular end. This period, following after Frege's childhood and adolescence, through his pre-Habilitation university education and including his Göttingen PhD dissertation in mathematics, covers the greatest part of his active life and is accorded the most attention.

Almost everyone working in analytic philosophy knows or thinks they know that Fregean logicism lost out mathematically in the first round to Russell's paradox, and later to more sophisticated self-non-applicational ("diagonal") constructions in logical metatheory at the hands of Kurt Gödel (1931) and Alonzo Church (1936), among other giants of classical metalogic. Even this judgment is partly true and partly false, and when considered in detail presents a more nuanced picture than at first appears. Philosophers often want their historical explanations oversimplified, something interesting on which to build their own reasoning. Effectively, the preference is for a just-so story with a metaphilosophical moral. In trying to understand the person and the world Frege knew as background to his writings, a different method is followed here. The ideal is to link together a selection of significant moments in Frege's life from historical sources. These incidents provide the scenery for a running narration about the main events of Frege's philosophical as well as personal drama. Frege's personality is evident in his writings, when considered in their entirety in chronological succession alongside supporting historical facts. It is there that Frege reveals what little of himself he wants the world to know. The impact of Frege's thought on the subsequent history of logic and of the philosophy of mathematics and language depends on whether and in what sense Frege's philosophy is rightly considered a success or failure, rolling the book's three primary questions into one. After considering the historical progression of philosophical development in Frege's life and thought, it becomes clear that Frege's philosophy succeeds not only despite but precisely because of its highly instructive philosophical failures, and because of Frege's exemplary clear-sighted grasp of philosophical problems and uncompromising standards of truth and proof in seeking their solutions.

Beyond this, the account of Frege's life disagrees with many standard accounts of where and how Frege's project falters. Further defects are found in the usual explanations of exactly how Frege's efforts may have succeeded in spite of themselves, and how the relevant episodes in Frege's project and its critical reception should feature historically as factors contributing to the evolution of contemporary logic. It is argued that Frege's logicism does not fail as a consequence of Bertrand Russell's game-changing 1902 paradox. It is argued instead that Frege could have capably answered the challenge of the Russell set without compromising his original intuitive 1893 unconditional extensionality principle for the identity of concepts interpreted as unsaturated functions in Axiom V in *Grundgesetze I*. Frege could have appealed to Axiom V, usually blamed for Russell's paradox, in order to prove that in *Grundgesetze* logic the Russell set does not satisfy concept–function identity conditions. Consequently, the Russell set does not exist and cannot support a logic-threatening paradox.

That is by way of glancing preview. Frege's importance is timeless, independently of the fate of his bid to reduce the theorems of elementary arithmetic to those of pure logic. His fame depends on the kinds of questions he asks, the methods of rigorous conceptual analysis and theory building that he personally embodies as he hones to practiced perfection a distinctive systematic approach to philosophical inquiry. What shines through in his personality as a writer is his uncompromising honesty, even when for good reasons he sometimes gets things wrong. These enduring philosophical qualities that have positively shaped the later course of analytic philosophy are among the notable unqualified successes of Frege's philosophy. They are not merely those in which Frege may have in some watery sense succeeded despite suffering more literal global failure in his philosophical work. The details of Frege's efforts to establish purely logical grounds for the basic laws of elementary arithmetic are the pulsing epicenter in terms of which the portrait of his revolutionary philosophy of logic, mathematics, and language turns, by reference to which all other philosophically relevant facts of Frege's life and thought are understood. The history of these events in rational progression reflects the fact that Frege, in his dedicated focus on the specific single-minded goal of establishing purely logical foundations for arithmetic, generally follows the logical course of action he devised in pursuit of this purpose. Frege acted deliberately. He mostly knew what he was doing, although he also made what in retrospect appear to be some stunning miscalculations. He is not tossed about on the stormy seas of countervailing contemporary mathematical and philosophical opinions. He perceived what he was up against when he was on the offensive, and chose his targets strategically.

For such a scientific model in applied logic and philosophy there can only be the same potential for theoretical explanatory success or failure of good hypotheses as is expected everywhere in science. Provided that something previously unknown is learned, even when a cherished hypothesis is shown to be false, there is always forward progress. If that is how the fate of Frege's logicism is understood, then in his lifetime Frege learned and taught the world something invaluable about the bounds of symbolic logic. Unfortunately, he did not have the time, or sufficient motivation and energy when he still had the time, to unravel the problem posed by Russell's paradox in the *Grundgesetze*. Receiving Russell's paradox letter of 16 June 1902 was the crucial moment of Frege's work in mathematical logic. If Frege's logicism is construed as a hypothetical exploration of the possibility of grounding arithmetic in pure logic, then a demonstrated failure of the hypothesis succeeds in taking philosophy another important step closer to the truth. It justifies philosophy in positively disregarding what might otherwise have seemed an attractive theoretical development, narrowing the original field of possibilities.

After lengthy consideration of the evidence in support of another popular myth about Frege, the biography explores the image of Frege as a disappointed, dispirited man after the announcement of Russell's paradox in 1902, and especially after the death of his wife, Margarete, in 1904. It is time to be skeptical about this personality sketch of an embittered elder Frege. Within about a year of suffering the buffetings of 1902–1904, Frege was active again, albeit continually stymied by his perception of the damage inflicted by Russell's paradox on his arithmetic in the *Grundgesetze*. In 1908, after the death of his wife, he took on the wardship of Alfred Fuchs and raised the boy as his own child. He wrote some of his most powerful essay-length expositions on the conceptual foundations of logic during this time, and carried on an extensive correspondence with contemporary logicians and philosophers. These are not obviously the actions of someone who had become soured to life because of difficulties in his professional work.

Although Frege's importance in the history, folklore, and contemporary practice of analytic philosophy is indubitable and he is widely acknowledged as its *éminence grise*, there has been no sustained biography of Frege that engages philosophically with Frege's ideas. If we want to understand the life of a mathematical logician and philosopher, we must gain a sense of the concepts, methods, ideologies, and controversies with which the thinker was preoccupied. A logician like Frege works with principles of logic. The reader of Frege's biography needs just as much to know something of what logic means as to know where Frege was born, how he was schooled, and the facts of his family life and death. The assumption here is that Frege can be known only through his work in symbolic logic. There is a burgeoning body of secondary literature on Frege's philosophy that continues to expand coverage in terms of close critical textual interpretation and consideration of philosophical applications of Frege's vision for the philosophy of mathematics and language. Archival biographical data recently made available will be subject to increasingly insightful discriminating interpretation. There is always much work for historical scholarship on Frege's philosophy, with new discoveries and interpretations to advance, all of which relate directly to his biography. The challenge is to weave together many of these disparate facts as among the defining moments of Frege's biography with an expanding appreciation of the merits and defects of his philosophical ideas as they developed and matured chronologically from beginning to end. To undertake a philosophical account of Frege as mathematical logician and philosopher, on the basis of original sources and interwoven with essential details of historical record and philosophical dispute, is the guiding impulse throughout this exposition offering a comprehensive perspective on what precious little is known about Frege's life.

I

Early Life (1848–1854)

F RIEDRICH LUDWIG GOTTLOB FREGE was born 8 November 1848 in the harbor town of Wismar on the Baltic Sea, in the northern German state of Mecklenburg-Schwerin. He was born into an educated middle-class Lutheran German–Polish family, in which he seems to have enjoyed a normal stern nineteenth-century European upbringing. He was an introverted boy in an introverted household that encouraged, rewarded and materially supported intellectual ambition and achievement.

Frege's Family Portrait

Frege's father was Karl (sometimes spelled Carl) Alexander Frege. He taught at several private girls' schools, eventually founding his own. Frege's mother, Auguste Wilhelmine Sophia Bialloblotzky Frege, was a teacher at the school, too, and took over its administration as headmistress when Frege's father died in 1866. The family was joined in 1852 by the younger son, Cäsar Friedrich Arnold, known simply as Arnold, who was four years younger than his brother Gottlob.[1]

A later family photograph taken around 1860 shows the apparently humorless couple with their two sons.[2] Being photographed was not a

---

[1] I take here the opportunity to express my indebtedness throughout this study to Lothar Kreiser for the historical documentation relating to Frege's life assembled in his comprehensive volume *Gottlob Frege: Leben – Werk – Zeit* (Hamburg: Felix Meiner Verlag, 2001). See Kreiser, *Gottlob Frege*, pp. 1–19.

[2] Kreiser reproduces the *c.* 1860 Frege family photograph in *Gottlob Frege*, p. 2. See also Kreiser, 'Die Freges aus Wismar' in *Gottlob Frege – ein Genius mit Wismarer Wurzeln: Leistung – Wirkung – Tradition*, ed. Dieter Schott (Leipzig: Leipziger Universitätsverlag, 2012), p. 81. The uncatalogued photograph seems to be in the possession of the Institut für

laughing matter, nor was the service generally provided for free. Subjects of the early lens all over the developed world sat rigid in their history-making poses, dreading the possibility that posterity might perceive them as being frivolous. Early photography required its subjects to remain still, holding their breath for a duration of exposure of a chemical plate's negative to instreaming light of several seconds. Unblurred portraits could be obtained only by holding the subject's head and shoulders fixed in a clamp. That point in the development of the art of photography was in the distant past by the time the Frege family portrait was made. The only explanation might then be that these were serious people for whom having their photograph taken was a serious occasion (except perhaps for the young Arnold). The image, if you were to exchange the faces with those of some of their neighbors, would look very much like the photographs of other respectable Wismar families seen at the photographer's studio. They were upright pillars of the local upper middle class, like any others of that class at the time having their images immortalized.

Gottlob's younger brother, Arnold, stands in a Slavic belted shirt with his legs hidden behind the voluminous folds of his seated mother's silk or satin dress. She, Auguste, wears a bonnet. Karl Alexander is hatless. Arnold sports a slight mischievous smirk on his face, looking more ironic than Gottlob. The older boy is framed in this moment between his grim-visaged parents. He wears a tailored suit cut to size, his hair neatly trimmed and his handsome young face tapering like a triangle to a narrow pointed chin. The eyes look almost defiantly directly at the camera. The boy's mouth is virtually a perfect straight line, bowing downward at both ends only slightly, almost imperceptibly, as though drawn with a straight edge and a sharpened piece of charcoal. The mouth reveals no thought or feeling, certainly no joy or anger, unless it is a moment of boredom and impatience at the process of assuring for posterity that we could one day see the young logician, mathematician, and philosopher Gottlob Frege as a melancholy lad.

From the photographic evidence, it is tempting to imagine dour nights of dutiful romance between Auguste and Karl Alexander in heavy linen night garments. By grudging or joyous fulfillment of an obligation before God they produced first Gottlob and then Arnold. Life was hard, and one

mathematische Logik und Grundlagenforschung der Universität Münster, with photo credit to Christian Thiel, Erlangen.

was not meant to treat anything lightly, nor appear immodest or above one's station in life. There were social proprieties that it was both politic and God-pleasing to observe, values projected forcefully enough to register with natural lighting on the photographer's plate. Together, Karl Alexander, Auguste, Gottlob, and Arnold could have been any respectable European family in similar financial and social circumstances at the time.

Wismar Baltic Harbor Town

Wismar in Frege's youth was still a flourishing trading port, albeit no longer as active as in its heyday during the rise of the Hanseatic League. Wismar's fortune was founded on the advantages of its natural harbor, protected by a projecting promontory where originally single-masted and later two- and three-masted ships, tall ships with deep draw, could safely dock and load and unload their goods. It was also strategically located to service a profitable trade, especially in salt and salted fish, amber, furs, wool and woollens, lumber and wooden manufactures, textiles, and every imaginable exchangeable good for people in the region.[3]

The merchants of the Hanseatic League not only sailed the seas transporting cargo, but also developed ports and markets for their goods. Elsewhere they kept offices and warehouses, called *Kontore*, in an expanding network that produced significant wealth in northern and especially northeastern Europe, from the Middle Ages to the late sixteenth century and beyond, until, having evolved through less centralized forms, that which remained of the League was completely and officially dissolved in 1862. The Hanseatic League brought trade to previously commercially innocent parts of northern Europe and the Baltic northeast, and helped put the inhabitants of those regions in touch with what was rightly called one kind of progress in their lifetimes. They usually had valuable raw materials or coveted craftwork for sale or barter, and they could regularly and reliably trade with officials of the Hanseatic League. The usual barrage of exceptions that did not affect the company's overall

---

[3] The volume edited by Schott, *Gottlob Frege*, is a useful source on Wismar in Frege's century. Wismar's history as a late Hanseatic port city is discussed in Christine Decker, *Wismar 1665: Eine Stadtgesellschaft im Spiegel des Türkensteuerregisters* (Berlin: LIT Verlag, 2006). A classic study is Franz Schildt, *Geschichte der Stadt Wismar bis zum Ende des 13. Jahrhunderts* [Wismar 1872] (Charleston: Nabu Press, 2013).

reputation notwithstanding, the League achieved the cultivation of a high level of corporate trust among its clientele. In exchange, merchants wanted *Bar*, cash money in a visibly valuable metallic form that they could spend back home. If necessary, they wanted to be able to melt the coins down to their indestructible malleable real convertible substance that could be fixed in market price on a true weight scale. If not coin, *Specie*, the Baltic traders wanted a wide range of goods and manufactures that, even with their pockets sagging with silver and gold, they could not readily purchase at any price when they returned to their native land. There was a lot of trading to do and a lot of money to make, and Wismar was very well situated for an active if not predominant role in the lucrative Hanseatic partnership.

The ships that docked for more than four centuries at Wismar during the Hanseatic period were primarily cogs. Long outmoded by Frege's time, there may still have been some relics in evidence as curiosities. There would in any case have been wooden models of them in public buildings, schools, or shop windows. These may have fascinated a young earnest boy with interests in mechanical things. All the design details of the famous Hanseatic cogs would be visible in a well-made cut-away miniature. A boy or girl at a display case with enough time to be absorbed in the object could envision exactly how and why it must have been built in just the way it was. This would not amount to a special sign of genius, but would just be how mechanically minded children of that age might have liked to occupy some of their time and exercise their imaginations about their hometown's past. The cogs, compact single-masted vessels designed in the tenth century, served as the work-horses for sea transport from the Middle Ages until after the collapse of the Hanseatic League and the ceding of Wismar to Sweden at the conclusion of the Thirty Years' War. Slowly, with the increasing presence of the Dutch, after their effective withdrawal from the Hanseatic League, and later the English, there came to Wismar's harbor seafaring trading ships with three and more masts, until they were phased out in turn centuries later by the rise of steam-powered shipping. Capable of carrying a two-hundred-ton cargo and extraordinarily stable in rough water, cogs were also considered ideal until the early eighteenth century for transporting troops in time of war. The favorable situation and enterprise of the people of Wismar had made the city of Frege's youth into one of the most important *hanseatische Städte*, where Frege was nurtured by his family and made his first acquaintance with mathematics and natural science, where you could always smell salt and seaweed in the air.[4]

A History of Frege's Birthplace

In 1259 Wismar entered a loose confederation with the northern German cities of Lübeck and Rostock in order to further its commercial shipping and marketing interests. By this means, the three cities formed the original core of what was to become the Hanseatic League. The Hansa bargained collectively for favorable treaties and tax exemptions, and organized themselves for insurance purposes and for protection against pirates. Wismar was a *hanseatische Stadt*, even a founding member of the League, but *not a freie und hanseatische Stadt*. It was nonetheless a wealthy and bustling port city for that part of the world during most of its history. The free and Hanseatic cities were limited to Hamburg, Bremen, and Lübeck, among forty-one official Hanseatic League cities, plus twelve *Kontore* or major shipping depots in cities that were not officially in the Hansa, but included active commercial centers such as Berlin and London. There was no tax exemption for Wismar from the Duchy of Mecklenburg, although, to this day, Wismar by tradition shows its independence among cities in the modern federal state of Mecklenburg-Vorpommern by proudly, perhaps even defiantly, flying its own distinctive flag.[5]

The word *freie* in *freie und hanseatische* city meant that citizens were free from the obligation to pay taxes to, and serve in the military of, the ruling state or royal family of the principality or grand duchy in which

---

[4] There are many excellent sources on the history of the Hanseatic League. For the variety of topics covered in a convenient format and as a place to begin, a useful recent text is Donald Harreld, ed., *A Companion to the Hanseatic League* (Leiden: Brill Academic Publishers, 2015). A valuable illustrated coffee-table interpretation with historical perspective is provided by Johannes Schildauer, *The Hansa: History and Culture* (Erfurt: Edition Leipzig, 1985).

[5] The Wismar city flag from 1918 until 1995 was a complicated mixture of symbols. There is in the *Stadtwappen* of those years a red boat at sea with three large silver-colored fish arranged beneath it below lapping blue scallop-shaped waves. On the bow of the boat a white dove or similar bird is perched, and on the single mast topped by a gold ball and cross there is a four-striped white and red banner. (These were the colors of Wismar as a Hanseatic city.) There is a crow's nest and an oversized shield featuring a bull with white horns, wearing a gold crown and with a tongue as red as the boat protruding downward from its gaping mouth. The bull is seen in all variants of the flag, sometimes cut in half to share the shield with the white and red stripes of the Hansa.

their city was geographically located and under whose jurisdiction and tax prerogatives it would otherwise belong. These cities were free in other ways also, in writing and enforcing many of their own laws, and maintaining their own armies that could also be pooled together for a common purpose in time of need among the Hanseatic cities. It was a formula that made the city in which Frege was born vastly wealthy in its time and independent in spirit. Wismar's success, and more importantly its strategic situation, saw the turnover of Wismar from German to Swedish ownership at the conclusion of the Thirty Years' War (1618–1648), in the treaty ending hostilities known as the Peace of Westphalia. Sweden, understanding the harbor's commercial and strategic value, sold the city back to Mecklenburg for a tidy sum in 1803. The Hanseatic League, by virtue of its self-interested foresight, was an early formidably successful corporation. It enjoyed special privileges that went with a highly profitable sea-going traffic. While it lasted, it patronized and encouraged the arts in comparison with other non-Hanseatic cities and towns in the same Germanic- and Slavic-speaking Baltic, Westphalian, and Netherlands states and provinces, whose cities may have been served by, but did not belong to, the Hansa.

Metallic skies over the Baltic Sea shroud Wismar's outlet onto the northern German coastline. Iron and copper from Hungary, the basic materials for making armaments, a vital necessity for Sweden as it flexed its war muscles in this era, were actively exchanged as commensurable necessities with other trading partners in the Hanseatic League. Business was especially brisk with Hungary and other eastern markets. Can it be coincidental that the Thirty Years' War began approximately when the Hanseatic League was starting to show signs of weakness and old age, of having peaked and outlived its prime usefulness, while at roughly the same time near the end of the Renaissance Swedish arms, especially muskets and cannon and the will to use them against southern neighbors, were gaining prominence and extending Swedish influence far into northern Europe? Could it be that the ostensibly religious motivation for the Thirty Years' War, namely to bring Protestantism more quickly and forcefully to the lower German-dialect-speaking provinces, was a mere pretense and that the real aim was to gather up the loose ends of an imploding organization for the sale and movement in this part of the world of goods on which Sweden's military supremacy depended, which it became possible to do precisely as the Hansa began to falter?

War spreads cynicism about religious and national authority when governments fight over what individuals within their geopolitical boundaries ought to believe. Whether the population believes anything about a postulated supernatural entity at all is surely only a matter of conscience in their free hearts. That was a good measure of the original impetus for Protestantism, making Sweden's efforts to impose Lutheranism on Catholic Europe something of a historical contradiction in terms. It is strategically wise for aggressors not to honestly declare that they are asking others to fight for material interests that they and their families are unlikely ever personally to share. Religion makes an excellent banner if the Inquisition terrorizes protestants, and protestants, a loose splinter coalition of non-Catholic Christians, want to show Catholics that they are prepared to put a halt to the torture and murder of non-Catholic Christians as far south in Europe as God's guidance of their hand would permit them to reach.[6]

The city of Frege's birth and childhood has been listed as a UNESCO World Heritage Site since 2002. It remains an off-the-beaten-path tourist destination in the former East Germany. It was rebuilt following years of neglect during Soviet occupation after World War II. When Frege lived and was schooled there with his family, Wismar was an active thriving community of about 12,000 persons. It had doubled in size by the turn of the nineteenth to the twentieth century, and today has a population of about 45,000. Wismar enjoyed a relatively rich cultural life, with the usual amenities, namely libraries, music halls, and theaters, of a nineteenth-century northern German city. It was not Berlin, Frankfurt am Main, Dresden, or Leipzig, but neither was it a bleak artistic or intellectual backwater. It provided a variegated stimulating counterbalance to Frege's awakening scientific and philosophical interests.[7]

---

[6] An authoritative history is presented by C. V. Wedgwood, *The Thirty-Years War* [1938] (New York: New York Review Books, 2005). For a slightly more recent discussion of relevant aspects, see Tryntje Helfferich, ed., *The Thirty Years War: A Documentary History* (Indianapolis: Hackett Publishing, 2009). The Hansa is usually mentioned only tangentially as marginal background to the war. See also Peter Harnish Wilson, *The Thirty Years War: Europe's Tragedy* (Cambridge: Harvard University Press, 2009), pp. 433–34. Wilson, pp. 431–32, emphasizes the interpretation of the Thirty Years' War as a response to the breakdown of Hanseatic League trade agreements.

[7] See Philip M. Parker, ed., *Wismar: Webster's Timeline History, 1348–2007* (San Diego: ICON Group International, 2010); and Gerd Giese, "Frege und Wismar: Orte der Erinnerung," in *Gottlob Frege*, ed. Schott, pp. 98–111.

Strategic Medieval City

To see Wismar today in aerial view is to appreciate the city's medieval somewhat misshapen oval layout, typical for defensive purposes at the time. The city in its *Altstadt* still features the grand bourgeois gabled architecture especially favored in the seventeenth century, influenced by Dutch, Polish, and endemically German practical styles. Many of the original buildings are still lavishly ornamented with grotesques and their original *Schilder* or crests for guilds or tradesman's signs of the family residing or conducting business there. Properties may have been built or inherited, or the proud inhabitants may have bought a home for themselves from previous owners in a competitive real-estate market, there being only so many plots of land within the city's walls for everyone who wanted to live in Wismar.

There were warehouses and guild centers, mostly of red brick and some with copper dome roofs. A few buildings were perched precariously over the city's main surviving canal that carves its way past the cathedral through the upper third of the town. The canal changes its name as it passes from the east, starting out as the Frische Grube (literally, Fresh Ditch or Pit), crossing at what is now a paved thoroughfare, running north as Hinter dem Chor (Behind the Choir), and continuing south, under the name Schweinsbrücke (Swine Bridge), to the west. There the canal becomes the Mühlengrube (Mills Ditch, Ditch or Pit of the Mills). At one time, as one can see by consulting the map of Swedish Wismar in 1716, and presumably before that time, there was also a waterway that ran alongside the city's defensive walls all around the periphery of the fortifications, hooked up to the main canal. It remains geographically like an upside-down version of the Grand Canal in Venice, which divides that still grander city in two, pouring out also into the sea, the Adriatic in that instance rather than the Baltic.

It is an attractive town, one with its own self-conscious sense of complex trading and military history and a rhythm of exuberance that comes from living by the sea and experiencing the constant arrival and departure of vessels from all over the world. It is not an overwhelming place; its confinement within the original medieval bastions makes it snug and human-sized. There is a sense of always knowing where you are when you walk around the old city of gabled buildings, lighted by torches in iron cages, with the skyward tower of the Evangelical Lutheran cathedral of the Domgemeinde Schwerin acting almost like a lofty lighthouse, a landmark to orient the walker or bicycle rider joggling over bricks and cobblestones. The Freges worshipped more modestly at the evangelisch-lutherische Kirchgemeinde St. Marien, or Marienkirche, in Wismar, where baby Gottlob was also baptized on 11 December 1848.[8]

The baroque, seventeenth-to-eighteenth-century city of Wismar, much of which was still intact during Frege's boyhood, was a masterpiece of Swedish military engineering and fortification. The 1716 map shows the city ready to take on attackers from any direction. The fried-egg shape of the inner city was enclosed within a nearly perfectly circular ring of bastions, set edge to edge without break except in one place to let ships into the city's heavily guarded main port. The triangular-shaped defenses were intended primarily to offer every strategic cross-firing angle needed to pick off invaders trying to make their way in from outside the garrison town. The bastions were offset two-deep, a higher one above a lower one, with the points of upper bastions overcovering the angled space between any two lower projections. The tiered bastions overlooked a city-encompassing moat flooded directly from the harbor that any aggressor, after having cleared the inlet's blockade chains and explosive mines, would need to cross while under heavy fire from multiple slings, crossbows, and later a succession of types of gunpowder weaponry, including cannon deployed before the time of the Swedish occupation.[9]

The canal both divided the northern third from the lower two-thirds of the town and, in more important ways, united the two parts. It was the main artery within the city for the rapid transport of whatever needed to be

---

[8] Kreiser, *Gottlob Frege*, pp. 1–2. The Marienkirche in Wismar was virtually destroyed by bombing in April 1945 in WWII and then torn down at the behest of the East German government in 1960, despite numerous protests. Only the eighty-meter-high brick Gothic tower still survives today, although there is a sculpture garden park in the area where the church once stood, around the tower, where an unpretentious bronze bust of former parishioner Gottlob Frege appears among the monuments. See Giese, "Frege und Wismar," pp. 108–109.

[9] Schildt, *Geschichte der Stadt Wismar*. The original German edition contains maps of old Wismar for comparison with the urbanography of the seacoast town today. An interesting juxtaposition aligns the original copperplate engraving of Wismar in 1694 made by Nicholas de Fer (1646–1720) with the transitional Karl Baedeker guide, *Northern Germany as Far as the Bavarian and Austrian Frontiers: Handbook for Travelers*, revised edition (New York: Charles Scribner's Sons, 1910), p. 164. The town layout and architecture of Wismar today still look more Swedish than German, suggesting that the renovations were locally accepted as civic improvements.

moved. The canal was not difficult to cross, the brackish water being usually calm and still. It was the main means of transport for goods in and out of the city, and was serviced by a network of carts pulled by men, horses or donkeys across a relatively efficient layout of streets. Flatboat channels linked any address on any street with any light shipping to be brought up from or down to the water. The bastions were broken on the northeast to connect the city of Wismar with the Baltic Sea, where ships first appeared in the seaway and then anchored and tied up at the city's wharf to transact their commerce. So it was still in Frege's time, albeit perhaps on a lesser scale than in the halcyon days of the Hanseatic League, as Wismar continued to play a diminished role in maintaining and expanding previously established shipping and trading routes.

What Little Is Known

Into this marvelous unassuming city Frege was born. Regarding Frege's early life until he entered the Große Stadtschule von Wismar from 1854 to 1869, there are no telling anecdotes about major character-forming events in his childhood. We know that his parents were both mid-level educators, which may have played an important formative role in Frege's personal homelife and intellectual development. We know that the family was evangelical Lutheran, and we understand that, to the extent that Frege's environment conformed to what was typical for the time, this would have meant a significant emphasis on pious duty in work and prayer.

The devout lay culture embraced a life of serious religious consecration as preparation for an afterlife. The promise of eternity was made only to the narrowly circumscribed faithful believers who do not merely recite *Luther's Small Catechism* from memory, and do not merely believe it, but belong to the right Lutheran synod and congregation. None of this was to be taken for granted. It was not luck, but God's plan, that someone like Gottlob should have been born into a family among the elect. Salvation was achievable only provided that the boy availed himself of grace by devout actions and acquired a correct understanding of the fragility of his salvation, for the sake of which reminders of mortality and how easy it was to sin played a central role in the worldview reflected in a traditional Lutheran *Weltanschauung*. When he was four, Gottlob met his baby brother, Arnold. We can surmise that they had a normal sibling relationship of dedication to and competition with one another, agreements and disagreements, and differences of aptitude for the family niches that each was able to fill.

What is perhaps of significance in this respect is the fact that we do not have a stock of archetypal stories about Frege's boyhood. There is no counterpart to the tale of a falling apple inspiring Isaac Newton's theory of universal gravitation. There are no reflections of teachers indicating a first spark of virtuosity that was later to culminate in some of the most insightful contributions to nineteenth-century logic, philosophy of mathematics, and the foundations of arithmetic, semantic theory, and philosophy of language. We are free to think of Frege as a normal northern German boy with a normal northern German father and Polish-descent mother growing up like so many other boys his age. The twist is only that both of his parents taught in the family-owned and -operated girls' school, meaning that both of his parents attached value to learning. Such expectations may have given Frege an appetite for intellectual pursuits already at home, even before he entered the Great City-School of Wismar at the age of six.

Frege, however ordinary many aspects of his childhood and upbringing seem to have been, was understood from an early age not to be of robust health. The concern of his parents and his need for convalescence from frequent illnesses are said to have intensified his natural inclination toward introversion and solitary activities. When we read in due course the commentary of those who knew Frege later in life, we see the lonely thinker, as though looking back upon him from the future, perhaps between the illnesses that sapped his strength and isolated him from others more than his temperament would predict. The state of mind is prefigured in the early family photograph. We cannot do better in summary than to offer this translation of Lothar Kreiser's observation of Frege's early life in relation to Wismar, in Kreiser's compilation of archival facts surrounding Frege's early life, *Gottlob Frege: Leben – Werk – Zeit*: "The city [Wismar] formed his character [*Wesen*, nature]. Modest but strict, clear of contour, tenacious perseverance, grim, not meek patience and defiant confidence in his own strength."[10]

Frege's Childhood, Boyhood, and Youth

Let's imagine the young man Gottlob Frege was to become. If we rely on the impressions of those who knew him, we can form a picture to

---

[10] Kreiser, *Gottlob Frege*, p. 20.

complement the 1860ish photograph of the Frege family. Young Frege's inclinations were shaped by a home environment that not only respected but actively promoted education, by Lutheranism, and by the harsh lessons taught a person of his age by bouts of illness. Outside the maritime fortified city of Wismar, Frege was unsurprisingly influenced by his parents, his teachers, his reading and conversation, the progressive scientific *Zeitgeist* or spirit of the times, and his own genius, to speak in one word of his highly individualized, independent thinking. This is not the place to inquire too deeply into the question of whether Frege's capabilities are attributable more correctly to his DNA or his environment, or to opt for the reasonable but not very informative compromise conclusion that Frege was the product of his genetic endowment in dynamic gene-expression interaction especially with his family, church, and school, and the inhabitants and social institutions of the once-Hanseatic Swedish fortress city of Wismar.

Looking ahead to Frege's adult years, after Frege had completed his second book-length post-dissertation study, comments made by Hans Sluga confirm the impression Frege had made years earlier in the family photograph: "With the completion of the Habilitationsschrift," Sluga wrote, "the path cleared for Frege's appointment as instructor of mathematics at Jena and Abbe saw to it that the appointment was made as quickly as possible. Back in Jena, Frege now joined the intellectual circle led by Snell and Abbe which met every Sunday afternoon at their house to discuss scientific, political, and above all philosophical issues ... Frege, who attended those meetings, was known even then as extremely introverted and quiet."[11] We can play it safe by suggesting that it was Frege's DNA, his home environment, the expectations of the confession in which he was raised, and the fact that the gray Baltic skies over Wismar did not improve his predilection for somber introversion and reflection that convergently made young Frege a Goethean Werther-like specimen. We further stipulate that these were the dispositions of someone likely to appreciate the higher reaches of abstract mathematical and philosophical inquiry to which Frege eventually ascended. We can consult the meagre sources among those who knew Frege and formed an opinion of his personality and intellectual capacities, recounting what they recorded

---

[11] Hans Sluga, "Gottlob Frege: The Early Years," in *Philosophy in History: Essays on the Historiography of Philosophy*, ed. Richard Rorty, Jerome B. Schneewind, and Quentin Skinner (Cambridge: Cambridge University Press, 1984), p. 341.

about the impression made by their encounters with Frege. Frege as a boy was by all accounts quiet, modest, reserved, given to his own thoughts, and in physical control of his feelings and actions. The said virtues nevertheless did not prevent Frege later in life from lashing out at dialectical opponents in his writings, denouncing what he perceived as the incompetence of colleagues, and engaging in vitriolic reviews of work he considered inferior contributions to the fields he cultivated.

We may provisionally suppose that Frege was like that. With no more than hearsay evidence, we are not going to get closer to him historically than a reasonable interpretation of the relevant surviving documents will allow. Because we want some kind of plausible image of young Frege developing into a logician, mathematician, and philosopher with which to begin, let us accept the bored young prodigy photographed that day around 1860 with his family. Perhaps there should be added to the list Frege's sense of his own superiority over rivals in his chosen intellectual activities. That Frege should have nourished any of these somewhat disagreeable traits, and that the roots of these later propensities may or even must have had their origin in Frege's character, surfacing from time to time in his interactions with others, does not mean that he was wrong in concluding that his colleagues later at the University of Jena or in the academic mathematical world more generally were not in fact technically competent to judge the quality or importance of his research. With minimal encouragement he quietly but determinedly prepared the ground for what would only later become a posthumous revolution in logic, the logical foundations of arithmetic, and the philosophy of language. The reverberations of Frege's philosophy continue to ripple indefinitely into the foreseeable futures of these subjects. However, it is unsurprising that at their time of origination, in what might have been Frege's time, his ideas were not adequately valued or even rightly understood.

We can tweak the image progressively into sharper focus as we learn more facts about Frege's life on which to build an interpretation. Frege's legacy can in retrospect, with no undue paradox intended, be characterized as in one sense partly Fregean and in another sense partly non-Fregean. Contemporary logic wants to have its Fregean cake and eat it too. Mainstream mathematical logic largely accepts the general logical and semantic framework Frege provided as a prerequisite to his logicism, in the course of his efforts to articulate a conceptual analysis of the laws of elementary arithmetic in purely logical terms. Logic today wants to detach these amenities from Frege's systematic thought, and many can be, and may even have been, designed for independent application, without taking on as doctrinal baggage the specific unqualified contents of Frege's formally insupportable conclusions, beginning with Frege's logicism. The fact that reducing arithmetic to pure logic in the sense entertained by Frege and such contemporaries as Peano and Russell writing with Alfred North Whitehead is no longer considered feasible should not distract us from understanding the history of Frege's project in its own terms as Frege seems to have conceived it, with its theoretical limitations and fatal faults undisguised.[12]

Accomplished Ancestors

If we are telling the life story of Gottlob Frege, who was to become a world-renowned logician, mathematician, and philosopher, then we should begin as is customary with the family tree.

We look back to Frege's grandparents, to Karl Alexander's father, Christian Gottlob Emanuel Frege, for whom our Gottlob was named, and, before him, Christian Gottlob Frege (1715–1781), who was a bank director in Leipzig. Christian Gottlob Emanuel Frege (1779–1811) was a short-lived businessman and Counsul of Saxony in Hamburg, where Frege's father Karl Alexander first saw the light of day. Christian Gottlob Emanuel married Frege's grandmother, Henriette Charlotte Prinz, and they had three children, two boys, one of whom was Frege's father, and one girl. The brother was Cäsar Emmanuel Frege (1802–1874), Gymnasium teacher in Wismar, after whom Gottlob's younger brother, Arnold, received his second name. The sister was Pauline (1808–1866), who in this family of achievers became a physician at a time when few women were expected to choose such demanding professions outside the home, if indeed they were to have any profession at all.[13]

Cäsar Emmanuel had the most progeny of the three. His children were all bank directors and attorneys, mayors and doctors. It should be

[12] See Michael Dummett, *Frege: Philosophy of Mathematics* (Cambridge: Harvard University Press, 1991); Michael D. Resnick, *Frege and the Philosophy of Mathematics* (Ithaca: Cornell University Press, 1980); and also the papers collected by William Demopoulos in *Frege's Philosophy of Mathematics* (Cambridge: Harvard University Press, 1997).

[13] Kreiser, *Gottlob Frege*, pp. 1–19; Kreiser, "Die Freges aus Wismar," pp. 71–83.

needless to mention that being born into such a prominent family had implications for Gottlob's aspirations and expectations of himself, of what was assumed in his taking a place among his relatives, who expected his success in some worthwhile area of endeavor and would be disappointed by anything less. If there is such a thing as inherited ability, then Gottlob would have fallen far from the family tree had he not found his way into a respected career. To say which is obviously to subtract nothing from Frege's own intelligence, energy, ingenuity, dedication, and hard work in realizing his ambitions. Signs of these tendencies were already visible in Frege's advanced school days, in his choice of courses, study of difficult scientific subjects, concentration on mathematics, physics, and chemistry, along with the usual language, history, and literature units, and his measured gravitation away from the natural sciences toward an appreciation for exact thinking in the humanities. Scientific studies left their mark ingrained on Frege's patterns of thought, as was the case for many of his contemporaries. Somewhat later in his education there began an increasing inclination toward philosophy, and especially the philosophy of mathematics and language, the important innovations of which he was destined to develop and take to new heights.

Karl Alexander Frege (Father)

Gottlob's father, Karl Alexander, did not enter into pedagogy for girls lightly or accidentally. He married Auguste on 18 July 1844 in the family Lutheran Marienkirche. In 1833, at the tender age of 24, Karl Alexander had already opened a private girls' school, which unfortunately had to be closed not long thereafter for financial reasons. In 1840, he entered into partnership with a staff of female teachers and opened a more successful girls' secondary school (*höhere Töchterschule*). The designation meant that it was literally higher in the sense of an advanced "daughters' school". The institution was announced as a *Bildungsanstalt für Mädchen* or education opportunity or situation for girls. Karl Alexander was headmaster there until his death.

The school continued even afterward to offer young women education in a range of subjects. Gottlob's father is thought to have died of typhus complicated by a lung infection, on 30 November 1866. Typhus was one of the great scourges of the nineteenth century, along with tuberculosis, cholera, syphilis, and clumsy horses. Karl Alexander was an author, and it must have provided a model for Gottlob to know that books were being written at home. Karl Alexander's publications were prepared for largely pedagogical purposes, but reflected his interest in history. He published first, in 1847, just before Gottlob's birth, his *Übersicht der Weltgeschichte* (*Overview of World History*). Later, in 1862, when Gottlob was fourteen, Karl Alexander published his *Hilfsbuch zum Unterrichte in der deutschen Sprache für Kinder von 9 bis 13 Jahren* (*Guidebook for Education in the German Language for Children from 9 to 13 Years*).[14] Finally, in 1866, the year of his death, Karl Alexander published his most theological–philosophical–anthropological treatise, *Die Entwicklung des Gottesbewußtseins in der Menschheit in allgemeinen Umrissen dargestellt* (*The Development of the Consciousness of God in Humanity Represented in General Outline*).[15]

Given Gottlob's age when the book appeared, it is conceivable that he may have served as test subject for some of Karl Alexander's efforts to offer helpful direction and supervision in teaching German to primary school children. His intended subjects would have included, but presumably not been limited to, the girls in his school's care. When he died, Karl Alexander's widow, Auguste, took over management of the school, and the family business continued under her administration until Easter 1877. Gottlob would have turned eighteen when his father passed away, and still had three more years to go to complete his studies at the Große Stadtschule (Gymnasium) Wismar, before leaving for university and setting out on his own.[16]

Auguste (Mother)

Frege's mother, Auguste, was born 12 January 1815, and lived to the ripe age of eighty-three, dying on 16 October 1898 in Jena. She moved there from Wismar to live with Gottlob in part of a duplex house she built there at Forst 29 for herself and Gottlob, joined in the year of their marriage by Frege's wife, Margarete. Auguste took up her first position as teacher in Karl Alexander's girls' school in 1843, and taught in the family-run academy for many years alongside Karl Alexander, continuing to teach until she sold the school, long after Karl's death. Auguste's mother was

---

[14] See Kreiser, *Gottlob Frege*, pp. 4–10.
[15] Published in Wismar 1866. See Kreiser, *Gottlob Frege*, pp. 176–82.
[16] Kreiser, *Gottlob Frege*, pp. 2–10, 16–18, 52–60, and 176–84.

Maria Elisabeth Ballhorn (dates not known for certain), and her father
was Johann Heinrich Siegfried Bialloblotzky (1757–1828), a pastor.
Gottlob's mother is usually assumed to have been Polish or of Polish
descent. Gottlob would then have been, roughly speaking, one-quarter
Polish and three-quarters German. Michael Dummett says guardedly
that Frege's mother was *perhaps* of Polish origin.[17] Bynum writes that
"Her maiden name may indicate Polish extraction; though it is also
possible that, like many people in the area, the Bialloblotzky's were
related to Slavonic peoples who had inhabited the Mecklenburg region
since the sixth century A.D."[18]

Given Wismar's close proximity to Eastern Pomerania and West
Prussia, with Poland just to the southeast, and centuries of intermingling
of Slavic and Germanic peoples at these ethnic crossroads, it would be no
surprise were Slavic background in Frege's mother's family to be
reflected like a relic of the past in her family's name. The heritage may
extend back to the noble Polish house of Ogonceyk, with ancestors
settling in Seehausen (Wittenberg an der Elbe) in the seventeenth century.[19] The grandmother's genealogy in particular seems to derive from a
Goedecke (numerous spellings) line, originating in the Netherlands, and
related to the great Dutch Renaissance humanist and protestant religious
reformer Philip Melanchthon. Frege is reported to have been extremely
devoted to his mother.[20] As Frege scholar Anthony Kenny further
observes, "During his education and early academic career, he depended
for financial support on his mother, who had succeeded her husband as
principal of the girls' school."[21]

If we want to know what they were all like at home during this time, we
must use our imaginations. On the basis of what can be known about the
general material culture in Wismar at the time, and the few facts about
the family in our possession, we can make some reasonably intelligent
projections. There were books in the house, no doubt, and music.

---

[17] Dummett, "Gottlob Frege," *Encyclopaedia Britannica* 2015, www.britannica.com/
   EBchecked/topic/218763/Gottlob-Frege.
[18] Terrell Ward Bynum, ed., *Frege: Conceptual Notation and Related Articles* (Oxford:
   Clarendon Press, 1972), p. 2.
[19] Nikolay Milkov, "Frege in Context," *British Journal for the History of Philosophy*, 9 (2001),
   pp. 557–70.
[20] *Ibid.*
[21] Anthony Kenny, *Frege: An Introduction to the Founder of Modern Analytic Philosophy*
   (London: Penguin Books Ltd., 1995), p. 1.

Auguste and perhaps Karl Alexander as well in this era would have been expected to play the piano, at least well enough to lead the family and students at the school in some of Luther's more stirring hymns and Schubert's *Lieder*. There would have been games with young Gottlob and the younger Arnold, in between Gottlob's bouts of illness, with wooden tops and puzzles and ball games and marbles on the carpeted floor in the family house at Böttcherstraße 2 in Wismar. Did the boys play cowboys and indians, or Cossacks and Hussars? One may imagine a family cat, and perhaps even a frisky dog for Karl Alexander to walk as he collected the newspapers, while thinking about the school and enjoying a smoke. When Karl Alexander died, the guardianship of both boys, Gottlob and Arnold, was assumed not by Auguste, but by Karl Alexander's brother, the boys' uncle and Cäsar Arnold's namesake, Cäsar Emmanuel Frege, who was a Lutheran pastor in Ahlden.[22]

(Cäsar) Arnold (Brother)

Frege's brother Arnold was born 31 March 1852. He too was educated at the Wismar Große Stadtschule, but, whether by inclination or because of a lack of qualification, did not complete the Gymnasium program. Arnold's journey at school was to take him from the Septima in 1858, via the Sexta in 1859, to the Quinta from 1862–1863. Six years later he had concluded his formal education, advancing no further than the level of Tertianer in 1869, but completing a merchant apprenticeship. Thus, after having followed a comparatively compact course of practical studies, extending from 1858 until his departure in 1869, Arnold left the school in precisely the same year as that in which Frege graduated. Arnold later became a business teacher, a more mundane pursuit than his brother Gottlob's eventual choice of mathematics and philosophy.

Arnold may have published some writings of his own later in life, after having moved to Neudamm at Stettin. The evidence for this is as follows. He was listed in legal documents involving entanglements with Frege after the latter's retirement from the University of Jena and the selling of his home there, which had been built by their mother. There was a promise of an annuity to be paid to Arnold through Frege from the proceeds of the sale, as "jetzt Schriftsteller" (now published professional

---

[22] See Kreiser, *Gottlob Frege*, pp. 2, 10, and 17–18.

author). Arnold, it must be said, never attained anything remotely approaching his brother Gottlob's eventual fame as thinker and writer. Arnold's publications, assuming that the information is accurate and complete, nevertheless remain interesting testimony supporting the inferences previously made concerning the intellectual climate in the Frege household, and the naturalness with which it seems to have been assumed that at least the men in the family would write for publication.[23]

We do not learn much more about Arnold until the two brothers have a less than entirely cordial exchange of letters over the aforementioned sticky property and contractual matters in 1924, the year preceding Frege's death in 1925.

The two Frege boys, Gottlob and Arnold, were perfect examples of how the divided-track system of German education separating university-directed from non-university-directed students functioned without class or social isolation on behalf of an independent pedagogical ideal. We should not lose sight of the fact that in Frege's part of the world the political model deeply etched into the cultural psyche was aristocratic rather than democratic. There were kings and counts, queens and countesses, and many grades of educational accomplishment within the academic pyramid during the time when Gottlob was considered an exceptional candidate for higher theoretical investigations, whereas Arnold was regarded as more pragmatic and vocationally oriented. Frege was on his way to becoming an academic prince of some kind, while Arnold remained a shopkeeper.

It is also possible that the family needed to hold back for financial reasons on any desire for both sons to continue toward a university education. Gottlob was never found wanting the family purse as he pursued his mathematics degrees, but it is possible that only one sibling could have been thus endowed. We can imagine Frege as he was just about to enter the Prima in 1866 shortly after his father's death to study for the examinations he would take in 1869. He had one foot on the final step leading to the university, and he was doing very well. How could he turn away from everything he had prepared for, and how could he, the eldest son in a traditional hierarchical Lutheran German household, however educated and progressive-thinking, be asked to do so, after having been awarded a First Grade? Arnold may have lived in

[23] *Ibid.*, pp. 2, 4, 17–18, 508–509, 567–70, and 625–28.

Gottlob's academically successful shadow long enough to see Gottlob as having set the bar so unattainably high that he could only embarrass himself by comparison. Sibling competitions of this kind sometimes lead talented people to occupy different complementary cornices in the family dynamic. One is an athlete, so the other is a scholar. One is a scientist, so the other is a musician. It may also have reflected a simple economic necessity, with Gottlob away at university in Jena, with a four-year head start on Arnold, for Arnold to curtail whatever higher educational ambitions he might have had. It is of course also possible that Arnold did not share requisite abilities and aspirations with his older brother.

For whatever reasons of disposition or finance, Arnold did not follow Gottlob's academic journey. He left the Große Stadtschule Wismar before advancing to the next tier in the chain of courses Gottlob had taken. It was prior to the first of three three-year study programs, the Obertertia, followed in the normal course of things by the Unterprima and then the Prima, culminating finally in the Matura at the threshold of university studies. Arnold effectively truncated the length of Gymnasium education Gottlob had undertaken by a total of six years. He opted for a vocational program within the Gesamtschule in Wismar. We do not have enough information to judge whether or not it was his choice. Writing on business-related matters later in life was a part of his career path for which time at university was not necessarily an advantage. University training and employment was only one conduit to personal creative fulfillment. It may have been made-to-measure for Gottlob, but apparently not for Arnold.[24]

Frege Aged Six

Gottlob was now a boy of six. He had been seriously ill as a child, but survived the onslaught of bacteria and viruses. The experience appears even years later to have left him introverted, somber, and reflective, as though forever brooding thereafter on his mortality. These were qualities that in many ways throughout the remaining seventy years of his life Frege sublimated but never completely outgrew. He was born in comfortable circumstances in a northern German and Polish-background family. He was raised in an environment that appreciated learning. He

---

[24] *Ibid.*, pp. 176–81.

was part of a family circle that in its wider reaches included modestly accomplished men and women in a variety of capacities in education and public service locally in Germany over several centuries. His parents were teachers in the girls' school that Frege's father had founded, and they were good Lutheran parishioners in regular attendance at the Marienkirche. Frege had a sometimes interesting and sometimes annoying two-year-old brother, just learning to walk and talk, the exact point of which may have been sometimes hard for Frege to grasp.

Frege at six began to take his first steps in education outside the home. He was taken by the hand to the courtyard of the Große Stadtschule Wismar. Pupils assembled outside the entrance among a scattering of trees and gaslights. The separate classroom and administration buildings were made of whitish brick, connected together by monastery-like arches and covered walkways. As though for meditation, hands were held behind waistbands as beards and glasses consulted beards and glasses about the truths of mathematics and the natural sciences. Frege studied in these ivy-covered halls for the next fifteen years in different parts of the Wismar academy, crossing its perimeters many times. Education was an important opportunity, not to be wasted. The values of applying oneself at school and the rewards it could bring did not need to be preached. They had been assimilated from an early age in Frege's life at home, as they naturally suited his disposition and sensibilities. No longer holding mama's hand, Frege was about to embark on an educational obstacle course that on its own timetable would take him beyond Wismar to Jena, then to Göttingen, and back to Jena for the remainder of his university career. He started then on the first day of an educational program that would prepare him intellectually for work in pure and applied symbolic logic, eventually to earn him an honored place in the history of mathematics and philosophy.[25]

---

[25] An excellent compact overview of Frege's historical significance is given by Joan Weiner, *Frege Explained: From Arithmetic to Analytic Philosophy* (LaSalle: Open Court, 2004), pp. 159–67.

2

Education through University Days (1854–1874)

WITH ACCOMPLISHED RELATIVES and a precocious younger brother peering over his shoulder, Gottlob entered the Wismar City School. He was six years old when he began Kindergarten. He would remain a student there for most of the next fifteen years. He took temporary leave when his father died. He was probably needed to help the disorganized family regroup, and he may have been ill himself. Beyond that, Frege's second home until he was ready to leave the city of his birth for Jena was at the Wismar Große Stadtschule.

Wismar City School Years (1854–1869)

Student life for Gottlob must have been sufficiently rewarding to have been tolerable for this duration. By comparison with contemporary American standards, it would have been the equivalent of studying in the same school, progressing through different levels of program from Kindergarten through high school and two years of college. A similar comparison could be made, with appropriate terminological adjustments, for the modern European system, in the case of a student passing through Gymnasium, which was a self-contained component of the Wismar Große Stadtschule. Frege's education was all conducted more or less under one roof, through a succession of highly motivated and scientifically trained instructors. There seems to have been nothing second-rate about the education Frege received in Wismar, and one hardly expects that his parents would have been willing to settle for less.

The choice was not entirely theirs. Frege would need to meet the school's admission requirements. He would have to be perceived as a promising student. His examinations and teachers' opinions would verify his qualifications. Above all, he would need to show signs of fulfilling that promise, of wanting to be schooled. What was the German educational system that young Gottlob at the tender age of six was about to enter? What was the fifteen-year Wismar Große Stadtschule conveyor belt on which he was about to step? It was at one level of description a progressive educational structure. There were five categories of education in the traditional German educational system. Pupils were tracked into one of three kinds of preparation beyond the primary. For university education, potentially university-career-oriented students normally studied at Gymnasium. Others underwent vocational education in a Realschule, as Gottlob's brother, Arnold, later did, for which they could be certified in other ways at the Hauptschule. These institutions had different objectives, but could be as demanding of students' attention and energy as any other. The expectations placed on students, as we will see in some detail in Frege's case, were by no means trivial or inconsequential.

Frege was apparently tracked from the beginning for Gymnasium and university studies. There could be movement of students from one of the categories Hauptschule, Realschule, and Gymnasium to another under explicit candidacy requirements. Perhaps this kind of relocation occurs more frequently today than in Frege's time, but it was certainly possible even then. Otherwise, a student who continued to show promise was directed toward improvement exclusively along one of three pathways, if not for academic pursuits, then for workplace training and vocational prospects. The system might seem elitist to an uncompromising democratic eye. As a pedagogical choice, it can be defended on the grounds that students with aptitude for a certain kind of career, as these things are best assessed in the wisdom of those with professional experience and judgment, can receive maximum educational preparation when the attention they need is not expended on students who show aptitude for a categorically different kind of study and training.

Whatever their drawbacks and advantages may have been, it was the divided programs for vocational and university students that Gottlob was about to enter at what was effectively the Gesamtschule, the Große Stadtschule Wismar. Of the variety of programs for students at Wismar, in the terminology of the day, Gottlob would not have been channeled into *das klassische Gymnasium*. This branch was specialized in the study of Latin and classical Greek or Hebrew, with modern languages in addition, as background to a career in the humanities. Rather, Frege would have undertaken courses in what in German educational parlance generally was known as the *Realgymnasium* or *Oberrealgymnasium*. The Realgymnasium in Frege's time focused on Latin and modern languages, science, and mathematics, while the Oberrealgymnasium offered modern languages, without the Latin, with emphasis especially on mathematics and the natural sciences. Gottlob eventually set his sights on mathematics and the sciences, particularly physics and chemistry. We know from historical records the exact courses he took in Wismar, and even the grades and comments he received in his performance record at the city Gymnasium.[1]

Days of Structured Learning

These eventualities were still far in the future when at the age of six Gottlob first entered the Wismar school. At Michaelmas 1854 Gottlob registered for the Septima at the Große Stadtschule. Kreiser, in his meticulously researched 2001 documentation of Frege's student days, explains that the Septima was designed primarily not for the teaching of facts but rather for the inculcation of cooperative skills that pupils would need as a foundation for the remainder of their primary education. He notes that pupils, including young Gottlob at the time, would have embarked on a program that required weekly eight hours of reading and writing, speech, and thought exercises (*Denkübungen*, about which it would be interesting to know more), four hours of calculating, literally accounting and elementary arithmetic exercises, two hours of singing, and four hours of child-appropriate (*an die Kinderwelt anknüpfende*) religious instruction.[2]

The impression is that of a well-thought-out program for pupils to occupy their hours as the state-regulated statutes expected, while integrating learning with related play activities to reinforce cooperative social interaction, especially with peers. Some limited reading and writing was expected even on the first day, which was perhaps not much to ask of six-year-olds coming mostly from educated homes. At Easter time, officially 15 March 1856, Gottlob at the age of eight graduated and transferred

---

[1] Relevant documentation is collected in the Gottlob-Frege-Zentrum der Hochschule Wismar. See Kreiser, *Gottlob Frege*, pp. 30–51; and Giese, "Frege und Wismar," pp. 105–107.

[2] Kreiser, *Gottlob Frege*, pp. 36–37. See also Kreiser, "G. Frege 'Die Grundlagen der Arithmetik' – Werk und Geschichte," in *Frege Conference 1984: Proceedings of the International Conference Held at Schwerin (GDR), September 10–14, 1984*, ed. Gerd Wechsung (Berlin: Akademie-Verlag), pp. 13–27.

from the Wismar Septima to the Sexta program. For Gottlob to proceed along this educational pathway, there were now weekly six hours of Latin, consisting primarily of declining nouns and conjugating verbs by a standard grammar school text, four hours of German, in precisely the category of primary school study for which Gottlob's father Karl Alexander later wrote and published a textbook, two hours of religion, four hours of natural science and history, six hours of mathematics (*Rechnen*), and four hours of calligraphy.

One imagines the calligraphy hours. After practicing single letters over and over again many times, mastering the pencil or feather and quill with a bottle of blue–black ink, pupils were presumably allocated sentences of morally and religiously edifying content to copy out as they trained their fingers, trying to govern initially unruly movements of the pen nib with sympathetic twistings of their tongues. Unlike many of his classmates, Frege apparently had no difficulties as a student with either the subject matter or the time spent seated in a classroom absorbing the highly structured learning on offer. He was not only a good pupil but also a natural one.

The next step was from the Sexta to the Unterquinta, to which Frege graduated on 2 April 1857. The boy was now nine years old. With similar distributions of class time for increasingly advanced topic areas and subject matters within those areas, the educational carpet ride now whisked Gottlob off to the Quinta 2. Abteilung (second division), extending from Easter to Michaelmas 1857. From the Quinta, Frege advanced in a steady progression to the Unterquarta in March 1858, when he was about ten, and then on to the Quarta at Michaelmas 1858. Half a year later again, at Easter time, 30 March 1860, Gottlob graduated to the Tertia, after having turned twelve. There then followed in steady succession Gottlob's graduation to the Obertertia two years later at Easter, 11 April 1862, again with all its requirements for particular numbers of weekly hours of literature, religion, history, science, and mathematics. Three years later, Gottlob advanced to the Unterprima at Easter 1865, when he was seventeen. This is the rough timeline of his pre-Gymnasium education at the Wismar Große Stadtschule.

It was proper development for a boy of six on his way to becoming a young man of seventeen. Gottlob had battled against and survived illness. He had met the demands of a difficult program in which he participated with his parents' encouragement. It is no accident that the Lutheran background of Frege's family should go together with their appreciation for and contributions to education. Martin Luther actively promoted universal education so that everyone could read the Bible, if only in Luther's own landmark German translation. Education has a way of getting out of hand, leading some liberated thinkers to question conventional social authority. This is, unsurprisingly, why those with more interest in power often try to oppose its free development. It was with good reason that Friedrich Nietzsche, whose father was a Lutheran minister, declared that Luther's promotion of education had sown the seeds of free-thinking atheism, that the great cathedrals of Europe were rapidly becoming God's costly ornate religious mausoleums.

Whether or not the Catholic hegemony, with the selling of indulgences for sins and other objectionable practices of the Roman Church in Luther's day, had it right that it was better for people's souls not to be educated, to reserve the Bible as the privileged text of an upper priesthood, the Reformation swept through especially northern Europe largely on the promise of making the word of God directly available to an increasingly literate public. In so doing, the Reformation fueled one of Europe's bloodiest and most sustained conflicts, the Thirty Years' War. As we have already seen, the long war, fought primarily by protestant Sweden against lower European Catholic regions, ostensibly on religious grounds but arguably more as a means of attaining economic dominance, had significant implications for Wismar, Frege's city of origin.

Wismar Große Stadtschule

At school, with so many programs in progress under one city education system, Gottlob discovered a world where he could begin to exercise the intellectual skills which were then powerfully awakening in him. He turned naturally and positively to the demands of an intelligently calculated step-by-step enrichment of his thinking. He responded amicably to the structured learning agenda, as his curiosity and desire to know led him through early stages of increasingly challenging study on the road toward a scientifically backgrounded secondary and university mathematical education. The boy becoming a seventeen-year-old young man was working steadily toward greater things at university, in which he made strong satisfactory progress and continued to refine his confirmed, enlarged, and newly discovered abilities.

The courses were laid out in explicit regulations. Gottlob had to take a succession of lessons and do well in them, once he had chosen or been funneled into a particular sequence of studies. There were few electives for personal artistic enrichment or poetic exploration. He had chosen to learn mathematics, physics, and chemistry. There were next to no options in the matter, and there was likely to be a pragmatic payoff further along for a solid Gymnasium scientific training. Young Frege was exposed to Latin and German as formal preparation, together with other modern languages and world history. Some of this was no doubt compulsory, but the program must have also gratified Gottlob's natural curiosity. The level of interest depended, as such things always do, on the teacher for the term. Gottlob was drawn by inclination to science rather than the humanities, to *Naturwissenschaften* rather than *Geisteswissenschaften*. Natural science was intrinsically fascinating. The scientific laws of physics and the structural diagrams of atomic and molecular structures in chemistry especially fascinated Frege. Two-dimensional pictures of the physical components of matter and exact chemical interrelationships made an impression on Frege in his early studies that was later to influence his understanding of logical interconnections. Structural diagrams of chemical compounds may have inspired Frege's efforts eventually to graphically picture the internal structures of truth-dependences in spatially two-dimensional diagrams.

What was brilliant in Frege's studies, assuming that good teachers were employed, was the organization of the assembly-line programs. Students were directed from one achievement, completion of requirements, and demonstration of competences to the next. There was a gradation of steps that were rewarded by appropriate acknowledgment and new opportunities, each paving the way for more demanding challenges for which students by then should have been well prepared. Understanding the stages of the program is essential to appreciating the exact kind of education Frege received in Wismar. At the beginning, advancement transitions were paced at twice yearly, roughly at Christmas and Easter. There was close monitoring of performance on these occasions, and opportunities to improve students' efforts, and to correct bad habits before they became permanent. Instructors worthy of the name would reward and encourage students for what they were doing right, offering advice and practical counsel to help them achieve their goals efficiently. Then, as a student matured and acquired more confidence, the rate of transfer from one plateau of study to the next in succession was halved to promotion at one-year intervals, after which the interval stretched over two years for several intervening phases, and finally three for the standard final two advancement steps. Expectations were increased as students committed themselves to longer sequences of increasingly intense study, and were prepared by what had gone before to absorb more theoretical knowledge while drawing interesting connections between several branches of a single area of learning.

Particularly important in Frege's studies in the Wismar City Gymnasium program were his classes with Gustav Adolf Leo Sachse. Sachse, born in 1843, was only five years older than Frege. At Easter 1868, as the calendar in German universities was measured at the time, Sachse was appointed *ordentlicher Lehrer*, the top rank of teachers within the Gymnasium system, analogous to a university-level Full Professorship. He was promoted to teach mathematics and natural sciences both at the Wismar Gymnasium and at the Realschule. He offered an incredible range of courses in mathematics and in calculation methods, which could have included or even featured accounting in the sense of financial bookkeeping, but focused on arithmetical methods generally, together with chemistry, geography, minerology, zoology, and drawing. When the time came for Frege to consider leaving Wismar in order to enter the next stage of his education, Sachse made a special appeal to Frege's mother to permit her eldest son to seek his fortune at the university in Jena, which at the time must have seemed so far away.[3]

Father's Death (1866)

Life changed for Frege during the first year of his enrollment in the Wismar school Unterprima. On 30 November 1866, Frege's father Karl Alexander died at the age of fifty-seven. There must have been surprise, shock, and grief at the Frege house. The blow to the family and presumably to Gottlob seems nevertheless to have made only a temporary dent in Frege's progress toward the degree he sought for entrance to university. Life always continues, even, and sometimes especially, in the face of death. The consequences for the family of Frege's father dying

[3] Kreiser, *Gottlob Frege*, p. 55. Gustav Adolf Leo Sachse (1843–1909) is considered significant enough to have a street where the Fachschule is located named after him in Jena. Sachse was a poet whose greatest claim to fame in the present history is to have encouraged Frege to continue his studies at the Universität Jena. See Kreiser, *Gottlob Frege*, pp. 55–58.

when Frege was just eighteen years old were immediate and long-
lasting.[4]

Academic Accreditation Aims

We know next to nothing about Frege's personal relations with family
members, especially in the early period of his life. It would be unsurprising
if the loss of Frege's father were one among several factors, including his
own ill health, that increased the time taken for Frege's graduation and
completion of the Prima to four and a half years rather than the expected
three years. Something interfered. Frege, despite the delay, graduated in
the top echelon of his class at Wismar. He successfully negotiated the
university entrance examination known as the Matura at Easter time 1869.
He passed his Prima examination with an evaluation of First Grade,
indicating that the student had to have very good knowledge (*sehr gute
Kenntnisse*) of all subjects taught in the opinion of all teachers.

Why did Frege take as long as he did, in the end an extra year and a half,
to complete his pre-university degree program? Frege's personal pique and
sense of perfectionism, perhaps the death of his father, bouts of illness, and
other factors have been plausibly cited to explain the fact. A reasonable
account, if each of these possible contributing causes were substantiated,
might invoke a convergence of factors rather than relying on any single
factor to explain the postponement of Frege's sitting for the Matura. Frege
was in the Wismar city school system for fifteen-plus years. Without a
better sense of the activity there, illuminating the attractions and opportunities for students to naturally engage their involvement, the experience
sounds rather like being condemned to the galleys. A hard-working student
normally completed requirements terminating in the Matura in fourteen
years; the most highly motivated could, in principle, graduate in thirteen.

Frege's fifteen and one-half years in the program leading to the Prima,
the final stage before the Matura examinations, was therefore only slightly
above average. Kreiser reasonably argues that Frege's delay in completing
the program could not have been due to learning difficulties, or he would
not have advanced to that level in the first place. It is interesting that

---

[4] Kreiser, *Gottlob Frege*, pp. 16–19. I do not tag each fact mentioned in the following retelling of
Frege's school days and family life, but it should be understood that I rely on Kreiser's
meticulous research tracking Frege in the first instance, especially through his education at the
Wismar Große Stadtschule. See Kreiser, *Gottlob Frege*, pp. 30–51.

Kreiser, by delving into these questions in written records, managed to determine that the interruption's duration of one and a half years was precisely the same as that of a similar deferral experienced by Gottlob's younger brother, Arnold, in his parallel vocational program, which occurred during precisely the same period.

A plausible explanation is that the boys decided, or their mother decided for them, that, as soon as they could, they would take a breather from the competitive world at school. For both brothers the interruption came in 1867–1868, when it might be expected that turbulence in the house following Karl Alexander's death would have mostly settled down, making room for realistic practical anxieties to compete with the emotional turmoil surrounding the loss of a loved one. That, anyway, is one glass through which to look at the facts occasioned by both Gottlob's and Arnold's timeout from school in the year-plus following their father's death. It is not unreasonable to imagine them taking a break, as even the most gifted students sometimes need to do, until they had regained the heart to get back on the next full cycle of the persistently grinding treadmill.

However, Kreiser concludes reasonably that the most likely explanation of Gottlob's and Arnold's withdrawal from study is that both brothers succumbed to an unidentified virus epidemic ravaging Wismar at exactly the time. It appears that in 1868 even the boys' mother, Auguste, was taken out of action by illness. She was unable to teach or run the girls' school as she had been doing in the previous several years since Karl Alexander's death. It is not out of the question that a hiatus imposed by illness, if Kreiser has correctly inferred its effect, on top of the loss of his father, may have contributed to the depletion thereafter of any desire Arnold might otherwise have had to further prolong his Gymnasium studies.

The remarks accompanying the evaluation of Frege's mathematical matriculation Matura examination which Kreiser reproduces are of historical significance. They presage the role Frege eventually played in logic and the philosophy of arithmetic. His instructors remarked that Frege's mathematical acumen did not particularly surpass that of many of his classmates, nor was it different in kind or degree. They were surprised, if anything, by the fact that Frege solved all the calculation tasks set by the exam without comment, and exclusively by means of symbolic formulas ("... *der sämtliche Aufgaben ohne Kommentar und ausschließlich mittels Formeln löste*").[5] The

---

[5] *Ibid.*, p. 49.

point they were making was presumably that Frege did not demonstrate any particular inventiveness, insight, or originality in solving exam problems. He applied appropriate formulas, rather than thinking parts of the problem out conceptually or explaining his reasoning in a descriptive solution sidebar. Interpreting the same facts more generously paints a different picture of Frege as proceeding only with the utmost formal rigor and minimal economy of derivation. We learn from these documents that he displayed this Fregean trait even during his pre-university days.

Frege applied himself assiduously at the Große Stadtschule Wismar. Upon returning to his studies after his father's death and his own hypothetical illness, Frege earned the highest awarded evaluation, entitling him to a place at the German university of his choice. He could not have done better than this, looking backward on this moment from the perspective of later mixed triumphs and defeats. It was then that the doors to the houses of learning throughout Germany were opened to qualifying middle-class students, including Frege.

Frege's degree as he proceeded to graduate from the Prima was listed simply as Science, and his destination the University of Jena. What did he pack with him besides his books and clothes when he traveled from Wismar to Jena? Jena was a city of art, music, and literature on the Saale river in Thuringia. It belonged to south-central Germany, not too far southwest from Leipzig, and closer to Weimar and, further still, Erfurt directly west. Frege went to Jena to study mathematics for the next step in his upward academic ascent for the qualifying degree of PhD. The university was famous well before Frege's time as the place where Friedrich Schiller had been appointed professor of history and philosophy in 1789. It was in Schiller's honor that the university was later renamed for its world-renowned poet, philosopher, historian, and playwright.[6]

University Preparations Complete

Gottlob was then twenty-one years old, a fully formed young man about to set sail for university life. Not only had his appetite been whetted for still more advanced concentrated study, for which he must have believed

---

[6] See Karl Schön, *Friedrich Schiller in Jena 1789–1799: Seine Lebens- und Schaffensjahre in Jena* (Munich: BookRix GmbH & Co., 2014).

he had prepared himself sufficiently and at great pains, but also he was about to begin the adventure of studying at university away from what had been his home for all his previous life in Wismar.

The once-Hanseatic and more recently Swedish garrison harbor fortress city, under the terms of its sale back to Mecklenburg, maintained a right of return or redemption for 100 years. During much of Frege's lifetime, the city's sovereignty was on loan from Sweden, even though the monarchy, including its military, had otherwise closed up shop in the immediate region. As a consequence Wismar was not officially represented in the Mecklenburg council until the Swedish crown finally relinquished its rights to the port in 1903. Sweden could negotiate from a position of strength after having been deeded indefinite title to the city after the 1648 Treaty of Westphalia. There must have been a faction in Sweden that thought they should never give it up, that they would be fools to surrender any foreign territory at any price, especially after investing so much time and effort in rebuilding the city's seventeenth- and eighteenth-century fortifications to state-of-the-art Swedish defensive standards.

Like the ships breezing out from the inland city harbor to the Baltic, Frege would soon be leaving Wismar, even if by carriage and train rather than picturesque sailing vessel. He would go to where his higher-educational pursuits would later seem like destiny calling him. He was traveling to his second home base, where the roots of his adult life and professional academic and research career would soon be planted, where he would remain active for most of his philosophically fruitful years. The distance of 350 kilometers between Wismar and Jena was not insignificant, but a journey of several days at best. Unfortunately, Frege's father did not live to see the successful matriculation of his eldest son, whose First Grade Matura evaluation would undoubtedly have made the Mädchenschule teacher proud, as it surely did Frege's now adrift and less financially secure mother, Auguste.

From Wismar to Jena

Virus downtime, if that is the explanation for the interruption of his studies, did not long dampen Gottlob's enthusiasm for studying mathematics and natural science. As we have seen, despite or perhaps because of the delay, he completed his work with top evaluations. He went to Jena, and although at the Große Stadtschule Wismar his field of study had been listed more generally as Science, at Jena he enrolled on 20 April 1869 as an undergraduate mathematics student.

Frege had seen something of interest and importance. He may have caught a glimpse of the kind of research he wanted to undertake as a lifetime course of inquiry. He may have thought the key to his future intellectual growth and development lay in the formal sciences, in pure mathematics, as a foundation for work in the natural sciences, if nothing else. He followed the normal course of studies in applied mathematics in physics and chemistry and other rigorous scientific disciplines, which he continued at Jena. He was offered thereby an invaluable opportunity to understand something of how mathematics was done and how it was expected to be integrated expressively and methodologically, explanatorily, into the fabric of the theoretical natural sciences and their practical applications.

Frege, through this engagement with scientific theory and its dependence on mathematics, readied himself to investigate the most fundamental conceptual issues in the foundations of pure mathematics in his first years at Jena. He earned a bachelor's degree in the subject at the conclusion of his studies from 1869 through 1871. He would now encounter questions that he would discover were really philosophical, rather than narrowly intrinsically mathematical. He may have been as surprised as anyone to arrive at the knowledge that he was a philosopher in the making, that he was interested in specifically philosophical questions.

Why did Frege decide on Jena, which was relatively far from home by the transportation standards of the day, to study mathematics at university? His pre-university examination scores would have allowed him to study anywhere, at any university of his preference in Germany. The choice of mathematics for Frege was most likely a combination of perceived ability and the advice of university-educated family and friends. There is evidence to suggest that Sachse, who had studied at the University of Jena, both recognized Frege's mathematical potential and was in a position to recommend him personally to faculty members he knew there, where Gottlob could no doubt expect to have an advantageous introduction. Sachse's Jena teacher Kuno Fischer would become one of Frege's instructors at Jena, with whom Frege studied the philosophy of Immanuel Kant. Sachse in time-honored tradition sent his best pupil on to study with his own advisor. As a graduating student who had lived all his life in the relatively insular environment of Wismar, who did not necessarily know where to apply for university study when the time came, it was easy to fall in with the considered opinion of a respected teacher at his own institution. What more responsible chain of advice could be exploited? Sachse knew Karl Snell and Hermann Schäffer in the mathematics department at Jena. In light of the attention their work in applied mathematics had already received, there came to be almost a sense of inexorability that Frege should make his first move in the world beyond Wismar by enrolling for the mathematics undergraduate degree at the University of Jena.[7] It was all the reason Frege might have needed, with no countervailing pressures inclining him elsewhere, to have chosen Jena for the next phase of his advanced higher learning. Despite his father's recent death, Frege, supported by the estate and his mother's goodwill, is said not to have been in especially poor financial circumstances during his early years studying mathematics at Jena.[8]

Frege's Mathematics Program

What did Frege study at university? Relying once again on Kreiser's archival excavations, in this case from Jena university records, we find the following list of courses and instructors with whom Frege studied by year of enrollment. These are the titles of the courses Frege took at Jena, their meaning being mostly so obvious in the original German as to require only occasional translation into English:

1869 (*Sommersemester*)

Analytische Geometrie – Hermann Schäffer
Experimentalphysik – Hermann Schäffer
Mathematische Theorien der Gravitation, der Elektrizität und des Magnetismus – Ernst Abbe
Allgemeine Chemie (General Chemistry) – Anton Geuther

[7] After Kreiser, see also Torsten Heblack, "Wer war Leo Sachse? Ein historisch-biographischer Beitrag zur Frege-Forschung," in *Frege in Jena: Beiträge zür Spurensicherung*, ed. Gottfried Gabriel and Wolfgang Kienzler (Würzburg: Königshausen und Neumann, 1997), pp. 41–52; and Gabriel, "Leo Sachse, Herbart, Frege und die Grundlagen der Arithmetik," in Gabriel and Kienzler, eds., *Frege in Jena*, pp. 53–67.
[8] Frege's financial state as a student expecting to study in Jena is detailed by Kreiser, *Gottlob Frege*, p. 53: "But Frege was not poor. The financial means flowing to him through his mother allowed good accommodation and an adequate income on which to live."

The fascinating aspect of Frege's curriculum is the extent to which it appears that he was directed in the first instance primarily toward mathematics, naturally, as his declared subject of concentration, but also in a systematic study of applied mathematical natural sciences. Looking at the roster of lecture and laboratory work Frege undertook at Jena, one can see almost exactly how his interests slowly gravitated from applied mathematics toward increasingly more theoretical and pure forms of mathematics. There was barely a hint of Frege's eventually awakening philosophical curiosity. Frege's natural interests would later bring philosophical questions about logic and mathematics into sharp focus, against an educational background of sustained natural scientific inquiry.[9]

Kreiser, in introducing these facts about Frege's study plan at Jena, makes an important point that might otherwise be overlooked. Frege appears to have deliberately chosen more theoretical courses even in the natural sciences, in preference to practical, applied scientific subjects intended for students aiming at an engineering or experimental science career. Combing the university catalog for similar alternatives Frege could have taken instead, in which he chose not to enroll, assuming the courses had not been overbooked, Kreiser makes a strong argument in support of Frege's presumed more purely theoretical mathematical preferences. The choices Frege might have made instead, at least in combination with his first semester's schedule, prominently included the following: Praktische Geometrie, taught by Schäffer; Mathematische Übungen (Mathematical Exercises), also presented by Schäffer; Organische Chemie, taught by Geuther; and Praktisch-chemische Übungen, offered again by Geuther.

The interesting and biographically telling exceptions in Kreiser's list of courses that Frege did not take in his first semester at Jena, without speculating as to his exact reasons in this sudden higher-educational land of milk and honey, were Carl Snell's course in Höhere Geometrie (Advanced Geometry), and most significantly, perhaps, and also, interestingly, taught by Snell, Philosophische Schöpfungslehre und Anthropologie (Philosophical Creation Theory and Anthropology).[10] The latter was an odd catalog listing for a university mathematics professor. If Frege's soon-to-be-soaring interest in philosophy had not yet taken wing, it is easy to understand that, and perhaps actually to situate on the calendar roughly

---

[9] Kreiser's archival collations are especially detailed in the category of Frege's itinerary of lecture courses in mathematics.
[10] Kreiser, *Gottlob Frege*, p. 61.

when, a serious preoccupation with philosophical questions about the formal sciences may have had its beginnings in Frege's ripening intellect. Perhaps, after all, Frege thought it important to be thoroughly grounded first in the natural sciences. Snell's sideline course may have smacked too much of philosophical theology to have aroused Frege's interest, given his scientific orientation, even though the course was being taught by an acknowledged expert in analytic geometry. If philosophy were to enter into Frege's curriculum, it would most probably need to be offered from a more rigorous theoretical standpoint.

Did that exist at Jena during Frege's time? Perhaps Frege went to university, like so many young people, thinking he knew what he wanted to do and the kinds of courses he should take. Then, being open-minded, he may have begun to shift toward a different set of subjects as his real lifelong enthusiasms began to emerge in the nourishing environment of university life. At a world-class university far enough away from Wismar for the first time, Frege must have been nearly intoxicated with new impressions and new ideas. The cross-fertilization of pure mathematics and theoretical natural science in Frege's syllabus came to fruition as a powerful combination in his later thought. For the moment, Frege was acclimatizing himself to the culture of higher education at Jena. He was starting to feel fulfilled, starting to have his cravings for the most advanced scientific knowledge available at the time partially satisfied, during the height of prominence of the great German universities. The more he learned, the more he wanted to learn, and the more secure he must have begun to feel pursuing his interests wherever they chanced to lead.

In the next semester, Frege's program at Jena continued to reflect a pure-mathematical and theoretical scientific emphasis:

1869–1870 (*Wintersemester*)

Anwendung des Infinitesimalkalküls auf die Geometrie (Application of the Calculus of Infinitesimals to Geometry) – Snell

Analytische Geometrie des Raumes (Analytic Geometry of Space) – Snell

Algebraische Analyse – Schäffer

Telegraphie und andere durch Elektrizität bewegte Maschinen (Telegraphy and Other Electrically Powered Machines) – Schäffer

Galvanismus und Elektrodynamik – Abbe

According to one authoritative source, Frege may have also undertaken practical chemistry exercises taught by Geuther in the winter term of 1869–1870.[11] Was it recommended that Frege build on the strengths he had developed the previous semester by enrolling in these specific courses? Despite the title of the course on application of calculus taught by Snell, the subject matter was clearly theoretical, involving a study of the mapping of abstract functions and numerical values in calculus onto equally abstract purely theoretical geometrical spaces. This would be a challenging problem for mathematics that would occupy Frege for much of his early university training.

The title may perplex, since the calculus of infinitesimally tiny ratios between changing values is geometrical. Mathematical analysis is dedicated to the problem of trying to determine the exact area beneath a given curve in two-dimensional space, as well as coping computationally with phenomena that can be geometrically pictured as involving continuously changing values. Newton and Leibniz independently discovered mathematical analysis in the seventeenth century. They did so partly out of necessity, due to the inadequacy of the then-available methods for determining areas obtaining under continuous physical progressions. The desired formal instrument for an expedient was generalized from the problem of quadratures. It was the quintessential mathematical challenge of projecting irrational real numerical values onto rationals. Precisely managed approximations in proceeding from circles to squares were anticipated. There were unlimitedly many useful calculations, as mathematical physics grappled with difficulties inherent in making geometrical analogies to the movement of continuously displaced projectiles, including those studied in astronomy, dynamic flow, and other continuous curve-charted processes. Applications of the calculus of derivatives and integrals, the formalism's *raison d'être*, had always been an essential part of its teaching, even as a theoretical subject. The pattern of Frege choosing theoretical rather than applied subjects in mathematics and the natural sciences was thus renewed and reinforced in his second semester program at Jena.[12]

---

[11] Werner Stelzner, "Ernst Abbe and Gottlob Frege," in *Frege in Jena*, ed. Gabriel and Kienzler, p. 16.

[12] Carl B. Boyer, *The History of the Calculus and Its Conceptual Development* (New York: Dover Books, 1959); and C. H. Edwards, Jr., *The Historical Development of the Calculus* (Berlin: Springer-Verlag, 1979).

Applied Mathematical Electrodynamics

The more interesting development in this time frame was Frege's unexpected interest in electromagnetism as a theoretical application of mathematics to physical phenomena. The choice smacks rather more of the practical than of the theoretical, although the basic physical forces investigated in this branch of mathematical physics were still a far cry from applications in anything like the engineering sense. They were highly mathematical, even when taught as theoretical background to the design of specialized machinery, such as that involved in the new technology of telegraphy.

Frege need not have enrolled for the telegraphy course out of any special interest in this recent mode of electrical communication. The application was listed as only one subject of the course, even if, as the first-mentioned item, it may have received the most attention. Professors with an eye on future occupations for their students may have thought that the telegraph would need skilled applied mathematicians to refine the technology for the future of commerce and long-distance information exchange of every kind. This was precisely what happened in Great Britain and the United States. It was the mathematician Carl Friedrich Gauss, the inspiring wellspring of so many advanced research programs, who with physicist Wilhelm Weber had built the first functioning telegraph at Göttingen in 1838.

With twenty–twenty hindsight, looking back from Frege's later career as a founder of modern, now so-called classical, propositional, and predicate-quantificational symbolic mathematical logic, it is easy to read into this classroom exposure to the dots and dashes of telegraph transmission an appreciation for the potential expression of all propositions as exclusively either true or false. Such was then the optimistic expectation that a bivalent system of propositional values in a fully algebraic functional calculus would meet the requirements of G. W. Leibniz's seventeenth-century proposal for a *characteristica universalis*, just as the telegraph, from its invention in 1836 onward, transmitted across an electrical wire messages that were coded in exactly two binary values, • (dot) and – (dash) in Morse code and its variants. The telegraph cable singing electrical signals from station to station was a syntactical way of transforming colloquial speech and writing into a two-valued symbolic dispatch.

There was a new age of communication flickering on the horizon as Frege attended lectures at Jena. Applied mathematics in theoretical electrodynamics, beginning with Gauss, took a professional interest in the rising telegraphic technology that mathematical natural science had made possible. The important breakthrough of telegraphic communication had been predicted and brought into being by a collaboration of mathematics and physics that a new generation, with Frege seated in the front row, was now called upon to refine and perfect.[13]

Did this early course in the new technology of telegraphy suggest to Frege, or later independently bolster, the classical logical proclivity toward treating every sentence expressing a proposition as exclusively true or false? Could one consider all propositions as referring, if they had referential meaning at all, exclusively to the True or the False, as Frege would later maintain? The binary long and short clicks and clacks of the telegraph key manifestly reduced the expressive capabilities of ordinary language to ordered sequences of dots and dashes, punctuated by complementary conventions. Had this fact hinted at anything of greater philosophical interest to Frege? The possibility is intriguing, but the hypothesis remains unconfirmed without testimony of some kind on Frege's part, which unfortunately the historical record lacks.

Telegraphy, despite its novelty at the time, seems a peculiar choice for Frege in his second semester at Jena. Perhaps the lecture period fit his schedule better than the alternatives on offer. Perhaps his general interest in electrical theory at the time was encouraged by some of his teachers. He may have been advised to follow up some of his initial curiosity by pursuing the subject at an advanced level. Perhaps the name of Gauss, echoing loudly especially in the mathematics halls at Jena where several of his circle were placed, had been invoked. The course description may have been invented to attract students with engineering interests in telegraphy. It led the description of topics to be covered, but by no means exhausted what students were promised in

---

[13] See George Prescott, *History, Theory and Practice of the Electric Telegraph* (Boston: Ticknor and Fields, 1860). A less technical, more readable history of the invention and its proliferation is provided by Tom Standage, *The Victorian Internet: The Remarkable Story of the Telegraph and the Nineteenth Century's On-Line Pioneers* (London: Bloomsbury, 2014). In the United States, telegraphy is generally associated with the refinements of Samuel B. Morse. Significantly, the invention of the first functioning electromagnetic telegraph with a broadcast distance of approximately 1,700 meters is credited to Göttingen mathematician Carl Friedrich Gauss and physicist Wilhelm Weber in 1838.

signing up for the lectures. Perhaps Frege was beginning to consider himself a student of Schäffer's, and became interested in studying whatever the professor was inclined to teach. Perhaps the course was the best alternative and the closest to Frege's developing scientific pursuits.

Kreiser lists for comparison some notable courses that Frege could have selected at Jena in his second semester, which he appears by default to have opted against. They are Theorie der Bewegung fester Körper (Theory of the Movement of Solid Bodies), taught by Abbe, and Differential- und Integralrechnung (Differential and Integral Calculus) and Populäre Astronomie, both taught by Schäffer. Whatever else Kreiser's listing shows, it suggests that Frege did not sign up for the course on telegraphy and electrical machines exclusively out of a general desire to continue studying with Schäffer, who had two other possibilities on offer. If Frege wanted to study with Schäffer, he might have chosen, without any special focus on telegraphy, the latter's electrodynamics course as the best alternative to Schäffer's lectures on popular astronomy and differential and integral calculus, for which Frege was already too advanced.[14]

Mechanics, Optics, Chemistry, and Mathematics

Frege now moved into his third semester, more at home with the university's palette of opportunities and expectations. During that semester he elected to attend the following lecture courses:

1870 (*Sommersemester*)

Analytische Mechanik – Snell
Lehre von der Brechung des Lichts (Theory of the Refraction of Light) – Snell[15]
Theorie der Funktionen komplexer Variablen (Theory of Functions of Complex Variables) – Abbe
Ausgewählte Kapitel aus der Mechanik und Physik (Selected Topics in Mechanics and Physics) – Abbe
Praktisch-physikalische Übungen – Abbe
Chemisches Praktikum – Geuther

[14] Kreiser, *Gottlob Frege*, p. 61.
[15] According to Kreiser; according to Stelzner, "Ernst Abbe and Gottlob Frege," the published title of the course was Optik.

The words Praktisch, Übungen (exercises), and Praktikum now entered Frege's schedule for the first time. This fact requires an effort at providing a plausible explanation without supporting historical documentation. We do not know in Frege's own words why his course load shifted in this direction. We can provisionally rule out interpreting Frege's program in his penultimate semester leading to the mathematics degree at Jena as representing a turn in his interests from theoretical to practical.

There are similar degree requirements in every program in the German-language university system even today. What might be significant is that Frege seems to have chosen to delay taking these obligatory exercises and practica until he had virtually completed his program in the semester before his final term and was firmly grounded in theory. Whether on advice, following general practice, on account of his own judgment and inclination, or largely by accident, Frege's timing of these courses was not necessarily premeditated. There are good reasons for a student to delay exercise and practica courses. We can think of some for Frege, beginning with the desire to work with certain mathematicians as their schedules would permit.

Exercise courses require lots of homework problems, but solving proofs and applying theorems by formula can be a holiday from theoretical mathematics. An application confronts the mathematician with a concrete problem to solve by invoking the right theorems and equations in appropriate ways. A solution is confirmed in practice when the problem has satisfactorily been solved. Theoretical mathematics is more cognitively demanding by virtue of involving properties of imperceivable objects. The action is on the page, symbolizing and managing inferences of mathematical theorems. The languages are syntactically complex and proof steps are sometimes murky. Thought must grasp the existence of abstract mathematical entities, intuiting their properties and pure relations to which they belong, with no theoretically admissible practical check on whether progress is being made toward logical consistency or absence of contradiction as the only criterion of truth. Listed as *Übungen* or not, Frege, like his classmates, in order to remain *au fait* would have needed to do weekly written derivations in advanced mathematics classes. There may have been no special advantage for Frege in scheduling exercise and practica courses later rather than earlier in his prospectus. He may have chosen to delay his exercise and practica courses as a natural reflection of his greater interest in pure mathematics and philosophical prioritization of pure over applied mathematics.

German university education in Frege's time ran a tight ship. Students did not have a lot of say about how they would like to structure their itinerary, once they had committed themselves to a university program and declared a major. As in most institutions of higher learning in the nineteenth century, and those in Germany were among the very best internationally, entering students were expected to know or decide soon why they were there and what it was that they wanted to achieve. What is more important than following an initial objective to an originally unforeseen end, especially when one's intellectual interests are still fluid, is that a student have a flexible plan and become part of a program, to get started in studies with a sense of direction. After that, it is possible, even if not always administratively easy, to adjust coursework to changing intentions within a degree program or even move about laterally. The nineteenth-century German university, especially at an academy like the University of Jena with its international reputation, justly proud of having had Schiller among its eighteenth-century faculty, was a place of serious advanced study and degree accreditation in relatively fixed programs of courses. When we examine Frege's calendar from semester to semester during his time at Jena, we do not see the well-rounded liberal arts education of a typical undergraduate student in Germany today.

In the framework of the program he had decided to follow, Frege was *ohne Wahl* (had no choice) within the rigid requirements at least as to categories of courses to be taken each term in order to satisfy the *Reglemente* (regulations) for the degree. Students, having earned the qualification, could then point to the program of studies by which they had acquired their diplomas, and the rigorous demands they had capably satisfied. It would be set in stone, printed on lambskin with a seal and ribbons testifying implicitly that the student had successfully completed these particular courses taught by these particular instructors, with these evaluations backed up by performance on established forms of examination concerning these particular questions. It would mean something definite. All of it would be subject to review. Such educational administrative dependences are largely taken for granted today, but were pioneered at the first universities in the Middle Ages. They were further improved in explicit thoroughness of statute coverage, if not overwhelming adaptability, during the rise of the first great scientific German universities of the nineteenth century. Frege received his higher education in this cultural atmosphere, where he prospered by playing by the institution's rules.

Frege had his program of study in mathematics with the *Dozenten* whose names continually reappear almost entirely and by category mapped out in advance at Jena by virtue of choosing mathematics as his field of study. The *Dozenten*, including *Professoren*, were all men at the time when Frege went to study mathematics at Jena. Women were allowed to attend lectures at German universities for the first time only in 1891.[16] We know from Kreiser's course listings the choices Frege could have made in some of his semesters. The fact that he was able to opt against them implies that not absolutely every moment of his lecture and study time at Jena was devoted to a predetermined set of specific courses. What was predetermined for Frege was the categories or ranges of courses that he needed to take as each semester progressed, in order to advance in good order toward the degree.

Frege's carefree days of German literature, modern languages, Latin, history, theology, and a dash of philosophy among his secondary education diversions were mostly behind him now. He might have been just as glad. To meet the program we see taking shape in his courseload at Jena, Frege must have sufficiently enjoyed what he was learning and how he was developing intellectually. He was now at university. It was understood that he would methodically track a well-chosen program from start to finish. That would demand dedicated concentration. The expectations would be notched up, but in other ways it would be much the same routine as he had followed in his fifteen years of academic training at the Wismar Große Stadtschule. The palpable difference in graduating from Wismar Gymnasium to the University of Jena for Frege was that, until he completed his degree requirements in 1871, he was doing mathematics in one form or another almost exclusively, with only one fascinating and potentially revealing exception, to which we next turn our attention.

Philosophy in Frege's Mathematics Curriculum

As the last semester of his mathematics degree program at Jena drew to a close, Frege chose an interesting slate of courses. He made a selection

[16] See James C. Albisetti, *Schooling German Girls and Women* (Princeton: Princeton University Press, 1988), pp. 163–66.

outside the narrow compass of mathematics offerings at Jena on this one
occasion, in order to hear a widely respected professor with whom Frege
had not previously studied. Frege's agenda as he completed his formal
pre-dissertation bachelor's degree coursework at Jena contained first the
following items that we may have grown to expect in his program:

1870–1871 (*Wintersemester*)

Die Fundamentallehren der mechanischen Physik (Fundamental Principles of
    Mechanical Physics) – Snell
Mechanik der festen Körper (Mechanics of Solid Bodies) – Abbe
Chemische Übungen (Chemistry Exercises) – Geuther

What, if anything, bears comment is that, for whatever reasons, Frege
did not choose to take Abbe's course on solid bodies when it was offered in
the previous 1869–1870 winter semester, under the title Theorie der
Bewegung fester Körper. Frege instead took the descendent of that course
by Abbe, which may simply have been roughly the same lecture material
retitled Mechanik der festen Körper, or may have been intended to build
upon the material covered in the previous year's winter term. Frege
probably considered himself already sufficiently knowledgable about the
first course to delay further work in the field. He took this final opportunity
also to satisfy his chemistry exercises requirement. Werner Stelzner proposes that Frege signed up for Chemische Übungen with Geuther in
Wintersemester 1869–1870.[17] That would be an anomaly in the structure
of Frege's overall educational program at Jena in his first semesters,
especially because it seems firmly established that Frege took Geuther's
Chemisches Praktikum only in Sommersemester 1870. Even if there
is confusion regarding the exact details of Frege's total study plan, important as they are historically, it is appropriate to conclude with this picture of
how Frege occupied much of his time at the university. The more conspicuous feature of Frege's last choice of courses is this:

Das System der kantischen oder kritischen Philosophie (The System of Kantian
    or Critical Philosophy) – Kuno Fischer

It is the one and only time that Frege took a course outside of mathematics and the applied mathematical natural sciences curriculum at Jena.
Some of his later semesters were so packed with lectures that one almost

---

[17] Stelzner, "Ernst Abbe and Gottlob Frege," p. 16.

wonders whether he harbored a secret desire to study philosophy all along. He may have wanted to make sure that he would have time in his schedule for at least some philosophical lectures outside his mathematics degree program. Kant was in Frege's time, and still is today, an absolute staple of German philosophical education. Kreiser explains that it was essential for Frege to have attended some lecture course in philosophy, because Frege's final degree requirements at the university would include an examination in the faculty of philosophy. The course on Kant given by Fischer (1824–1907) would have been attractive to Frege in several ways.

Whether primarily by inclination, to satisfy a long-suppressed curiosity, or as a tactical way of meeting a regulation toward completion of his university degree, Frege chose Fischer's lecture course on Kant's Critical Idealism in his 1781/1787 *Kritik der reinen Vernunft* (*Critique of Pure Reason*, or First *Critique*). Kreiser reports that, during the period when Frege was at Jena, Fischer offered instruction on logic and the metaphysics of scientific principles, as well as introductory lectures on the history of medieval and modern philosophy, that Frege did not choose to attend. Or at least he did not officially enroll. Fischer must have been a fiery teacher. He lost his position at the University of Heidelberg in 1853 for theological–political radicalism, which did not prevent him from being appointed *ordentlicher* (full) Professor at Jena in 1856. After 1872, shortly after Frege had taken Fischer's course on Kant, Fischer returned to Heidelberg, where he spent the rest of his career. He was a tireless writer, publishing treatises on aesthetics, logic and metaphysics, Schiller and the comic stage, Lessing, Francis Bacon, and Goethe, and an extraordinarily comprehensive ten-volume set on the history of philosophy. Fischer's history ranges from classical times through Kant, Hegel, and Schopenhauer, along with an influential biography of Kant interlaced with critical discussions of Kant's philosophy. The series went through two editions in Fischer's lifetime.[18]

At this point in his education, Frege had taken only one university-level course in philosophy. From this fact alone we cannot determine whether he did so by inclination, out of sublimated philosophical interests, or in deference to the diploma requirements of the mathematics program at Jena

---

[18] Frege's philosophical relationship to Kant is explored, *inter alia*, by Michael Dummett, "Frege and Kant on Geometry," *Inquiry: An Interdisciplinary Journal of Philosophy*, 25 (1982), pp. 233–54; John MacFarlane, "Frege, Kant, and the Logic in Logicism," *The Philosophical Review*, 111 (2002), pp. 25–65; and Delbert Reed, *The Origins of Analytic Philosophy: Kant and Frege* (London: Continuum, 2007).

on which he had set forth, to maximize his chances of doing well in the philosophical final examination. Nor do we know anything concerning what Frege thought about Fischer's course on Kant's transcendental idealism. If Frege applied himself as diligently in this minimal exposure to philosophy in his first university years as he did to his courses in mathematics and the exact natural sciences, then it is conceivable that Frege was more deeply influenced by his encounter with Fischer than might have been evident even to those who knew him well at the time. It could be that Fischer's explanations of Kant held forth for Frege's consideration the image of someone asking precisely the right kinds of questions that Frege's mathematical studies had awakened in his thought. It may have planted a seed that would not begin to send forth tendrils until Frege was ready to make the next major step in academic qualification. The dramatic philosophical turn in Frege's thought seems to have occurred even while he was engaged in mathematics research for the doctoral dissertation. This he eventually completed two years later in the summer of 1873, under the supervision of Ernst Christian Julius Schering at the Georg-August-Universität Göttingen.

Extramural Mathematical Activity

Frege's mathematical skill and dedication to study were noted by his instructors. His commitment was evident in the fact that he was one of only a handful of students who was able and sufficiently interested to attend and follow Abbe's courses. By reputation Abbe's lectures were among the most difficult and technically demanding in the mathematics curriculum at Jena, complicated by the fact that a speech defect reportedly made his lectures hard to understand.[19]

Frege reveled in the challenge. In one semester he was one of only two students working with Abbe on the theory of complex functions. In another class he made up part of a contingent of exactly five students sitting for lectures with Abbe in an otherwise untenanted university auditorium. Sachse tried to warn Frege about Abbe, as Frege transitioned

[19] Kreiser, *Gottlob Frege*, pp. 59–60. Abbe was known as a social reformer as well as an optical mathematician and physicist. His work at the Zeiss Corporation and management of Carl-Zeiss-Stiftung funding was perceived as contributing toward making Germany independent of foreign optical instrument makers, and his contributions led in particular to significant improvements in the design of achromatic microscopes.

from Wismar to Jena, but Frege understood the importance of what Abbe was teaching. He was determined to overcome any obstacles for the sake of advancing his understanding of rigorous mathematical concepts and demonstrations. Abbe in turn appreciated Frege's mind and philosophical mathematical ambitions, and was later one of his strongest and most influential supporters, both at the university and at the Jena optical instruments corporation Zeiss, parent company of the Carl-Zeiss-Stiftung that later supported Frege's work in logic. The institute, seemingly on faith, willingly supported mathematical research. Its directors at Zeiss handsomely financially underwrote developments in theoretical mathematics without asking too many questions, first for Abbe and finally also for Frege and others on Abbe's recommendation.[20]

However reserved he may have been, Frege was not too shy to present the results of his mathematical reasoning publicly to experts even during his Jena student days. He gave several lectures in 1870 and 1871 at the Mathematical Society of Jena. The society had been founded by Schäffer in 1850. Frege joined in 1870. Abbe was a frequent attendee, having been a member of the society since 1857. It was the first quasi-professional mathematical interest group to which Frege sought membership. Although the society itself was informal and had no official standing, Frege's participation indicated a genuine involvement in the advancement of mathematical knowledge beyond the momentary practical concerns of earning his university degree.[21]

The titles of Frege's talks are worth considering in the context of his evolving mathematical education. In 1870, Frege offered two talks at meetings. The first was "Über das Unendliche" ("On the Infinite"). He also presented thoughts about theoretical physics in an address given in the year of his joining the mathematical society, on the topic "Über Ampères elektrodynamisches Gesetz" ("On Ampère's Electrodynamic Law"). In 1871, the exact dates of presentation having been apparently lost to time, Frege spoke again on Ampère, in a series of lectures under the title "Vergleichung der elektrodynamischen Theorien von Ampère und Grassmann" ("Comparison of the Electrodynamic Theories of Ampère and Grassmann").[22]

---

[20] See especially Kreiser, *Gottlob Frege*, pp. 52–62.
[21] Karl-Heinz Schlote and Uwe Dathe, "Die Anfänge von Gottlob Freges wissenschaftlicher Laufbahn," *Historia Mathematica*, 21 (1994), pp. 185–195; here p. 186.
[22] Kreiser, *Gottlob Frege*, pp. 62–65 and 293.

It is interesting to compare Frege's choice of topics. He lectured about a subject of pure mathematics, and in a way philosophy of mathematics or cognitive groundwork of the concept of infinity. This was followed later by an exploration in three related topics in applied mathematical physical science, in the general area of electrodynamic phenomena, in which he had apparently not lost interest.[23] The protocols or minutes of the Mathematische Gesellschaft zu Jena still exist, but do not contain exact information as to when Frege offered his talks. It would have been a standard kind of university affinity group, intended to promote interest in specialized technical subject areas, with an opportunity for faculty and sometimes students to display their work and share their ideas, allowing them to benefit from one another's criticisms, without the dampening effect of exclusively faculty supervision. It was a forum that was run by and for both faculty and students, offering an opportunity to learn from each other in peer encounters, in which Frege actively participated during his two years' membership.

Advanced Mathematical Study

Frege, through his studies, was preparing himself at Jena for his academic career of choice. This was initially not to become a university lecturer and researcher, as was eventually to occur, but rather to become a schoolmaster like his father. Once again, characteristically, more modestly and less self-aggrandizingly, with more sense of his likely prospects in a competitive environment where family connections often meant more than they probably should in securing a university professorship, Frege envisioned entry at some lower tier of the educational hierarchy.

Perhaps he would return to teach and direct his family's girls' school that his mother, Auguste, had overseen since Karl Alexander's death. Perhaps he would teach somewhere else, even at the Große Stadtschule Wismar, where he had graduated with such excellent marks only five years previously in 1866, should there be an opening. In any case, he would be prepared to teach mathematics and natural sciences, especially physics and chemistry. For the plan to come to fruition, Frege would need a still more

[23] The content in overview of Frege's lectures is collected by Irmgard Kratzsch, "Material zu Leben und Wirken Freges aus dem Besitz der Universitäts-Bibliothek Jena," in *Begriffsschrift – Jenaer Frege-Konferenz* (Jena: Friedrich-Schiller-Universität, 1979), pp. 534–46. See also Kreiser, *Gottlob Frege*, pp. 469–79.

advanced degree, a doctorate or PhD, to begin which process he applied to the Göttingen mathematics institute on 2 May 1871. To qualify as a teaching headmaster, within the rigid structure of rules and regulations that had been designed to assure quality education and competent training of teachers and researchers throughout the German pedagogical system, Frege needed to pass the examination of a scientific evaluation committee, which was not to be organized in Jena until 1874. Frege, in consequence, strange to say, could not be qualified for secondary school teaching for at least another three years.[24] The bureaucratic policy is not easily justified. Frege missed the cutoff. Was this, somewhat ironically, an oversight or arithmetical miscalculation on Frege's part? Or was it the very opposite?

Since nothing was to be done about obtaining the teaching certificate for the time being, Frege chose to continue his mathematical studies in Göttingen. It was precisely in Göttingen that so many famous German mathematicians had taught and worked, in a golden age that had concluded prior to Frege's experience there, centering on the mathematics of Gauss, Johann Peter Gustav Lejeune-Dirichlet (1805–1855), and Bernhard Riemann (1826–1866), who had written his Habilitationsschrift under Gauss's direction in 1854, and became Ordinariat (Full) Professor at Göttingen in 1859. Riemann, who was internationally known for his discovery of what later came to be called non-Euclidean Riemannian geometries, had happened upon these formal systems unintentionally. They were discovered in the attempt to prove whether or not Euclid's fifth axiom or parallels postulate in the *Elements* was logically independent of the other four axioms. The fifth axiom states that through a point outside a line there exists exactly one distinct line parallel to the first. By denying the fifth axiom and checking it against logical consistency or logical inconsistency with the remaining four axioms, it was possible to judge whether or not the fifth axiom was logically dependent on, implied by, or inferentially independent of the remaining four axioms. The fifth axiom was shown in the event to be logically independent of the remaining four. As a dividend, a non-Euclidean geometry, consisting of Euclid's first four axioms and a contrary fifth axiom, was discovered in the undertaking. The denial of Euclid's fifth axiom permits no parallel lines in one category of non-Euclidean geometries and in another category infinitely many

---

[24] See Kreiser, *Gottlob Frege*, pp. 64–65; Kreiser, "Freges Universitätsstudium – warum Jena?," in Gabriel and Kienzler, eds., pp. 33–40; and Schlote und Dathe, "Die Anfänge von Freges wissenschaftlicher Laufbahn," p. 186.

parallel lines to that fixed in curved Riemannian rather than rectilinear Euclidean space. Riemann's death in 1866 marked the end of the most interesting era in mathematics at Göttingen, although it was still a vibrant and important center for the formal sciences when Frege went there to pursue more ambitious mathematical research five years later in 1871.

Göttingen remained a magnet for mathematicians. It was a valuable institution from which to gain a more advanced degree for someone with Frege's virtually inexhaustible desire to expand his mathematical knowledge. It is worth reflecting on the course that history took in Frege's development. Had the University of Jena had in place a scientific examination committee by which Frege could have been tested for his qualifications as a schoolmaster, he might have taken advantage of the opportunity, most likely passed with flying colors, and earned himself a position as a schoolmaster teaching mathematics to at most secondary education Gymnasium students for the rest of his life. That would not have been a miserable existence, although it is doubtful whether he would have ever had the leisure or inclination and occupational motivation to make what would later turn out to be some of his greatest signature contributions to logic, mathematics, and the philosophy of mathematics and language.

To monitor Frege's progress at Göttingen from summer semester 1871 to summer semester 1873, we take note of Frege's courses leading to his dissertation in mathematics, which he defended at the end of term in 1873.[25] When Frege attended lectures at Göttingen and was preparing to write his PhD dissertation, the mathematics department was in relative decline. Its energy had been sapped by disagreements over, and a resulting failure to find, adequate replacements for its leading lights of past years. There was no longer a well-defined agreed-upon research agenda as a framework for mathematical investigation at Göttingen. The institute, through death, retirement, and professional relocation, was effectively decapitated as remaining institute members lost heart. When Frege arrived for doctoral degree work at Göttingen hopes were pinned on the mathematician Alfred Clebsch (1833–1872), some of whose lectures Frege attended. Clebsch died at the young age of thirty-nine, unfortunately, even before Frege had completed his Göttingen degree, leaving his early promise unfulfilled.[26]

[25] Kreiser, *Gottlob Frege*, pp. 86–112.
[26] Rudolf Friedrich Alfred Clebsch, to cite his full name, was a mathematician at Göttingen who made contributions especially to algebraic geometry and invariant theory. In collaboration

There were historical reasons for Frege to have chosen Göttingen as the next stop in his mathematical education. There were nostalgic motivations of familiarity, since both of Frege's esteemed Jena instructors, from whom he had learned so much, Abbe and Snell, were products of a Göttingen mathematics program. The trouble for Frege was that those mathematicians were no longer alive or active at Göttingen. The next best thing would then be to drink in the same environment, to be a part geographically of somewhere that had seen the most productive years of some of Germany's greatest mathematicians.

An Embarrassment of Mathematics Riches

Not waiting for the grass to grow under his feet, Frege found himself the very next semester after graduating from Jena enrolled for an advanced degree in mathematics at Göttingen. He did not, as he presumably could have done, simply rent rooms in the vicinity and write his dissertation in consultation with an advisor or *Betreuer*, in this instance, a *Doktorvater* – or, in principle, but not at Göttingen in 1871, a *Betreuerin* or *Doktormutter*. Frege the Lutheran bourgeois seemed to appreciate what was opening before him as a rare opportunity. It would have gone against home values not to have taken full advantage of the educational access he was being granted, owing everything to his family back home in Mecklenburg.

Frege attended as many carefully chosen mathematical lecture courses and applied practical exercise courses as he could. Relying again on Kreiser's authority:

1871 (*Sommersemester*)

Analytische Geometrie (Analytic Geometry) – Alfred Clebsch
Abbildung der Flächen bei demselben Funktionen compl. Variablen
(Representation of Surfaces Defined by Corresponding Functions of Complex
Variables, in my free translation) – Alfred Clebsch
Funktionen compl. Variablen (Functions of Complex Variables) – Ernst Schering
Religionsphilosophie (Philosophy of Religion)– Councillor Lotze
(*Hofrat*, advisor)

---

with Carl Neumann at Göttingen, Clebsch founded the technical research journal *Mathematische Annalen* in 1868.

1871–1872 (*Wintersemester*) and 1872 (*Sommersemester*)
Experimentalphysik (Experimental Physics) – William Weber

1872–1873 (*Wintersemester*)
Mathematische Theorie der Elektrizität (Four-hour practicum) – Eduard Riecke

1873 (*Sommersemester*)
Variationsrechnung (Calculus of Variations) – Ernst Schering
Ausgewählte Teile der Elektrodynamik (Selected Aspects of Electrodynamics) –
    Eduard Riecke
Ausgewählte Kapitel der höheren Geometrie (Selected Topics of Higher
    Geometry) – Aurel Edmund Voss[27]

As Frege relocated from Jena to Göttingen he undertook a program of studies similar in main force to those he had previously followed. It was of course wise counsel to get to know most if not all of the professors where you were going to write a dissertation. There was always much to learn, to reinforce the lessons of the past and extend one's mathematical knowledge, understanding of theoretical concepts, ideals, proper methods, meaning, and metaphysics. Mathematicians often do not agree even on such elementary matters as these. Electricity and electrodynamics had not faded away from Frege's attention, as he migrated from Jena to Göttingen, although chemistry, unlike physics, appears to have been outdistanced by the time Frege began researching his Göttingen dissertation.

Despite the comparative downturn in the Göttingen mathematics institute's fortunes, there were some prominent mathematicians and excellent teachers of mathematics among its still illustrious faculty. The unfair thing is having to contrast mathematics at Göttingen during any later period with the run from Gauss to Riemann. Many of the mathematicians at Göttingen were known by Frege's Jena teachers Snell and Abbe. Between them there must have been sporadic contact over the years, an exchange of recommendations and other professional correspondence. They were still active, and Frege advanced his knowledge of mathematics considerably by joining their group as a dissertation student. Weber was considered to be one of the

---

[27] Kreiser, *Gottlob Frege*, pp. 87–88, indicates that the otherwise unknown Dr. Webb was the instructor, citing the Universitätsarchiv Göttingen, Sekretariatsakten, Abgangszeugnisse 1873, Nr. 342, Abgangszeugnis Gottlob Frege. See Bynum, "On the Life and Work of Gottlob Frege," in *Frege: Conceptual Notation*, pp. 3–4, note 4. A compact and accurate biographical sketch of Frege is given by Milkov, "Frege in Context."

leading physicists of his time, and Eduard Riecke had begun establishing a commanding research profile. Ernst Schering, who would supervise Frege's dissertation in 1873, was the editor of Gauss's papers. He was another significant influence from the standpoint of following Frege's branching interests in pure mathematics and the applied physics of electromagnetic phenomena. Schering completed his dissertation, titled "Zur mathematischen Theorie elektrischer Ströme" ("Toward a Mathematical Theory of Electrical Currents") in 1857. His Habilitationsschrift was a thesis also close to the second main chamber of Frege's beating mathematical heart, on the Gaussian topic "Über die konforme Abbildung des Ellipsoids auf die Ebene" ("On Conformal Mapping of the Ellipsoid onto the Plane").[28]

There was something that appealed fundamentally to Frege in this balance and interplay of pure and applied mathematics. The reason could be as obvious as the fact that pure and applied mathematics are caught up in a kind of dialectic, whereby pure mathematics is tested by the success of its applications, and applications rely increasingly on conceptually more refined abstract mathematical theorems. The interaction is more complex than that, and the uses of mathematics are often too differentiated to fall under an easy formula. Mathematics always has a specific kind of work to do, and can be understood only from that perspective, even when its work is highly abstract. If we lose sight of the practical, the theoretical is unmoored. It can set itself adrift in any direction that logical consistency without regard for facts can randomly assume. Sound policy, experienced educational theory, generally combines the theoretical with the practical, a formula Frege may have imbibed from his first pedagogical role model, Karl Alexander. A backup plan, rooted in practical applications of theoretical ideas, was essential. One cannot simply count on a position in life dispensing abstract concepts. The more uses of theory one masters, the more possibilities exist for making one's way through life's demands in a flexible variety of ways, adapting to circumstances and an uncertain market economy by taking the most reasonably determined decisions. It is also the best way to understand the strengths and weaknesses of even the most abstruse theoretical constructions. Kreiser,

---

[28] Ernst Christian Julius Schering (1824–1897), who was a student of Gauss, made few original contributions to mathematics, although he lent his name to the Gauss–Schering lemma, by which he generalized Gauss's lemma in the Jacobi symbol system for any odd positive integer.

hunting through archival library records at the University of Göttingen during Frege's sojourn there, discovered that Frege took out for loan from the university library only one book, a text on electrodynamics.[29]

Lotze's Seminar on Philosophy of Religion

Interesting also is the fact that in his first semester at Göttingen Frege signed up for a course in philosophy of religion that was at least nominally taught by the internationally famous philosopher and logician Rudolf Hermann Lotze. Lotze was interested not only in cultural philosophy, but also in symbolic logic. He had published an important, controversial, and hence much-discussed book under the title *Logik* in 1843, as well as poems, works on metaphysics, philosophical psychology, history of German philosophy and other traditions, and much else besides.[30]

It may have been for vocational reasons that Frege chose to attend Lotze's Göttingen lectures on philosophy of religion in the summer term of 1871, ten years before the Berlin philosopher's death. Lotze's discussions would have been fascinating. Lotze was listed in the Göttingen catalog for the Sommersemester as *Hofrat*, which means that he could have in some very loose sense supervised the actual teaching of the course by assistants without devoting much of his personal time to the lecture podium. In principle, it could even imply as little as that Lotze's name would have appeared on the registrar's records as awarding grades, although Lotze would not actually be doing the teaching. That was unlikely, perhaps, but

[29] Kreiser, *Gottlob Frege*, p. 90.
[30] Hermann Lotze (1817–1881) is sometimes described as having negotiated the turn from post-Kantian idealism to scientific philosophy. As such, he would have been an ideal role-model for Frege, regardless of the fact that Frege took only one course announced as offered in Lotze's name. Frege's contemporary and sometime correspondent, later publisher, Bruno Bauch, gave a critical evaluation of Lotze's logic in Bauch, "Lotzes *Logik* und ihre Bedeutung im deutschen Idealismus," *Beiträge zur Philosophie des deutschen Idealismus*, 1 (1918), pp. 45–58. See Gottfried Gabriel, "Frege, Lotze, and the Continental Roots of Early Analytic Philosophy," in *From Frege to Wittgenstein: Perspectives on Early Analytic Philosophy*, ed. Erich H. Reck (Oxford: Oxford University Press, 2002), pp. 39–51. See Michael Potter, "Introduction" to *The Cambridge Companion to Frege*, ed. Michael Potter and Tom Ricketts (Cambridge: Cambridge University Press, 2010), also on Lotze's influence on the young Frege, especially pp. 2–3. G. Gabriel argues in "Frege als Neukantianer," *Kant-Studien*, 77 (1986), pp. 84–101, that Frege ought to be thought of as a Lotze-influenced neo-Kantian. For some curious insights into Lotze, read for pleasure George Santayana, *Lotze's System of Philosophy* (Bloomington: Indiana University Press, 1971).

the *Hofrat* category was subject to abuse even in the well-organized nine-teenth-century German university. It is reasonable to suppose that students who had registered to hear Lotze heard and saw him in the flesh during at least an appreciable part of the semester. The same goes for *Hofrat* Weber's courses as listed, and without further documentation or first-hand observa-tional reportage, we cannot for the moment know more.[31]

Having had even casual contact with Lotze might have been inspira-tional for Frege's later work in mathematical logic, as it was for Edmund Husserl and many other mathematically inclined philosophers and philo-sophically inclined mathematicians at the time. Lotze argues that logic is independent of individual subjective psychology, that there are mind-independent laws of logic that it is logic's business to discover and codify. Lotze serves as yet another link in Frege's infrequent academic exposure to professional philosophy personified by a small number of its influential contemporary practitioners. Lotze, whose father was a physician, had also earned a medical degree, and was unusually well versed in the natural science of his day. Together with his strong background in biology, these qualifications would have made him an appropriate potential bridge figure for Frege, even in a course of lectures on philosophy of religion, linking logic with the mathematical natural sciences. It is a matter entirely of how questions of religion were identified and approached – the methodology to be applied to a relevant database after it has been properly recognized and defined. Whether the subject is the existence of God or a theorem in mathematics, Frege came increasingly to appreciate the fact that there was a scientific way of thinking about these things that served as a model for all reasoning. He concluded, as have many philosophers, that philoso-phy should begin by cleaning its own house, bringing the methods of hypothesis development, testing, and refinement to philosophical theorizing.

The method is obvious when put into words. It is something few contributors to the advance of knowledge would deny. What Frege says almost always has the ring of the expected, the inevitability of naïvely

---

[31] *Hofrat* can be translated literally as Counselor, a social–administrative and sometimes honorary rather than academic title. Frege as a Jena *Hofrat* could in principle be called upon for consultation in matters of interest to the royal house and its governing bodies. The title is sufficiently important to appear in Frege's legal name after this occasion before any of his later academic titles such as Honorary Ordinarius, Extraordinarius Professor Dr. See Kreiser, *Gottlob Frege*, pp. 461–69.

grasped and elegantly expressed truths. If he had the clarity to put into words what everyone should already know, what afterwards seems obvious, that can hardly be held against either the truth or the usefulness of his reminders. The difficulty was not in understanding and being able to recite Frege's methodological strictures, but in actually following the method. Writing about logical relations is much like working in a laboratory. It was his practical background in mathematical physics, chemistry, and electrodynamics that provided Frege with an understanding of the relations in meaning between an applied mathematical theorem in kinematics or fluid dynamics and the existent physical reality of which relevant laws were supposed to hold true. It looks toward the point of contact between applied mathematics and physical reality that soon after offered Frege a glimpse of pure logic and the purely logical foundations of basic laws of elementary arithmetic.

Lotze would have confirmed certain aspects of Frege's sense of procedure in philosophical inquiry. What are the relevant property-bearing objects to be considered? This preliminary question must first be asked, and then others follow. What are the objects' properties? Does God exist? If so, what is God's nature? Grandiose as such investigations may appear, if Lotze is right then the inquiry makes the only right use of scientific thinking in philosophical theology. Frege eventually asked in similar terms what we can know about the properties of invisible mathematical entities. The widely prevalent default Platonic metaphysics of mathematics considers mathematical entities to be abstracta that transcend the spatiotemporal order of phenomena, existing imperceptibly and mind-independently beyond the limits of phenomenal experience. What are the truths of arithmetic? What are they about? What makes them true? How can we know in the practice of mathematics whether or not a given proposition is true? The cascade of questions on a topic other than the foundations of mathematics, dealing instead with the fundamental problems of religion, at this impressionable age, even while he was still a Göttingen mathematics dissertation candidate, may have triggered Frege's own parallel reflections about the meaning and truth-conditions of logical and arithmetical expressions. There are interesting interconnections between theology and especially infinitary mathematics.

If we could talk with Frege it would be illuminating to know exactly what he thought of Lotze. What did he take away from these lectures, assuming them to have been delivered by the philosopher? What, if anything, made a lasting impression on the development of Frege's philosophical thinking when he heard Lotze? The lack of evidence of Frege's reaction to Lotze at the time of attending his lectures on philosophy of religion has not prevented plausible interpretations and projections from being proposed, drawing thematic associations between Lotze's philosophy of logic and mathematics and Frege's formally rigorous non-psychologistic logicism as his writings began to reflect advanced philosophical insights.

Dissertation Form and Content

In 1873, Frege was awarded a PhD in mathematics from the University of Göttingen. Frege's dissertation, written under the supervision of Schering, was titled *Über eine geometrische Darstellung der imaginären Gebilde in der Ebene* (*On a Geometrical Representation of Imaginary Figures in a Plane*). Frege's thesis developed Gauss's previous suggestion for establishing imaginary and complex numbers as existent mathematical entities by representing them as points on a plane outside the real number line.

Complex numbers are expressed by means of the general formula $a + bi$. What makes the number complex is not merely that it involves addition or multiplication. Numbers reducible to this form are called complex because they combine real numbers with the imaginary number i, where $i^2 = -1$. Normally, in elementary arithmetic, there is no natural number whose square is equal to any negative number. Nor, outside the realm of imaginary numbers, is it possible to take the square root of any negative number. No number times itself will ever equal a negative number, but only a positive number. There are negative roots of every number, such that, for example, $-2 \times -2 = 4$, just as $2 \times 2 = 4$. The square root of 4 function, accordingly, needs to cover both possibilities, of positive and negative values, 2 and -2 in this case. An equivalent restriction is marked by means of a device indicating the absolute value of a number so calculated, whereby conventionally $|\sqrt{4}| = 2$ and $|\sqrt{4}| \neq -2$.

Imaginary numbers were remarked by the Greek mathematician Heron of Alexandria, but are usually said to have been discovered or invented, depending on one's point of view in philosophy of mathematics, by Rafael Bombelli in 1572, around the time of the Protestant Reformation. They are so designated because they are supposed to be merely a way of completing the mathematical symbolism that does not correspond to any real number value. There was rightly thought to be no place on the number line extending infinitely in both directions from a common origin at 0 (zero) where imaginary numbers could conceivably be situated, although the real number line is not the only place for numbers to congregate in orderly assignment. Working with imaginary numbers requires special conventions for equation conversions, algorithms in which imaginary numbers at risk of contradiction are handled first before other operations. Frege's thought working toward his Göttingen PhD complements that of William Rowan Hamilton, mathematician and physicist, who extended the concept of an axis of imaginary numbers in a plane to a three-dimensional space of what were then named *quaternion imaginaries*.[32]

The basic idea in Gauss that Frege develops in his 1873 dissertation is that of mapping imaginary and complex numbers onto a vertical axis of a number plane, orthogonal to the horizontal reserved for real numbers. Imaginary and complex numbers, despite an anomalous limit case point of contact, are represented as perpendicular or orthogonal to rather than part of the real number axis. The axis vertical to a horizontal real number line in the standard geometrical interpretation, metaphorically speaking, can go up or down relative to the horizontal, to numerically distinguishable points of which both positive and negative numbers are univocally associated. It is the lower axis for negative number values where imaginary and complex numbers find their home representationally in the geometrical imaging of imaginaries in Frege's analysis. Are imaginary numbers merely a fancy, a stereotopic use of mathematical symbolism that is more a part of what Quine in the twentieth century refers to as "recreational mathematics"?[33] Do they have any applied mathematical role to play in the natural sciences? Imaginary numbers earn their keep in Fourier analysis, and in Euler's brilliant and applications-thirsty trigonometric formula $e^{ix} = \cos(x) + i \sin(x)$.

[32] A useful resource for non-specialists such as myself is Paul J. Nahin, *An Imaginary Tale: The Story of $\sqrt{-1}$* (Princeton: Princeton University Press, 2010). William Rowan Hamilton (1805–1865) was an Irish mathematician, physicist, and astronomer who perceived the usefulness of imaginary numbers in his theory of *quaternions* and discovery of the *quanternion group* extending complex numbers' geometrical mappings beyond the two–dimensional plane.

[33] W. V. O. Quine, "Reply to Charles Parsons," in *The Philosophy of W. V. Quine*, ed. Lewis Edwin Hahn and Paul Arthur Schilpp (LaSalle: Open Court, 1986), p. 400. Quine refers there to the higher reaches of set theory as a "mathematical recreation . . . without ontological rights."

Frege was familiar with a large range of practical uses for imaginary and complex numbers in his applied mathematical studies of heat flow and electrodynamic signal processing. Today a wide variety of applications of Euler's complex number featuring the imaginary value i includes data compression and image processing, among numerous useful computer algorithms. There is an enormous body of discussion about the practical applications of the so-called Taylor series, introduced into the mathematical literature by Brook Taylor in 1715, that represents a function approximated as an infinite sum of terms calculated from the values of the function's calculus derivatives fixed at a single point.[34]

Frege's dissertation has not made much of an impact on the history of mathematics, or more particularly on the theory of imaginary and complex numbers. One does not see his name or dissertation frequently mentioned as a milestone in the mathematical literature. Part of the reason is that subsequent mathematicians who continued to make lasting contributions to this field, especially Hamilton, five years before Frege was born, among others, superseded Frege in the history of this specialized field of mathematical research. Frege did essential work, but it does not appear that his heart was in it. He taught the material for many years after gaining a lectureship position at Jena, and he wrote occasional short papers on arithmetical–geometrical projections. He also gave lectures on the subject to local mathematical and natural science societies. However, he never again devoted serious sustained attention to it.

Arriving at principles for the geometrical mapping of imaginary and complex numbers onto a plane was not the sustained focus of Frege's energies in mathematics. His interests evolved rapidly in the direction of developing the first fully algebraic mathematical logic. He applied the logic to a purely logical explication of the concept of natural number in developing a purely logical reconstruction of the basic laws and theorems of elementary arithmetic. Frege did not keep his name in the air concerning this specific topic in number theory, but moved on shortly thereafter toward other interests in symbolic logic and the philosophical foundations

---

[34] The classic source for the calculus of finite differences is Brook Taylor, *Methodus incrementorum directa et inversa* [Direct and Reverse Methods of Incrementation] (London: William Innys, 1715) (Proposition VII, Theorem 3, Corollary 2), pp. 21–23. See also George Boole, *A Treatise on the Calculus of Finite Differences* [1860], ed. J. F. Moulton (New York: Chelsea Publishing Company, 1872); and D. J. Struik, *A Source Book in Mathematics 1200–1800* (Cambridge: Harvard University Press, 1969), pp. 329–32.

of mathematics. His later work is deemed so monumental and ground-breaking that he is often remembered primarily for the single achievement of discovering/inventing the functional calculus or predicate-quantificational logic, first showcased in his 1879 *Begriffsschrift*. The Göttingen dissertation is seen in retrospect as merely an academic exercise and preparatory inquiry for Frege that turned out not to be directly related to his long-lasting objectives.

Historians of logic and philosophy, looking for foreshadowings of Frege's later virtuosity in his student and graduate-student days, sometimes emphasize the fact that Frege's dissertation involved the extension of concepts of arithmetic into pure geometry, with an emphasis on how one branch of formal study can be linked to another. Michael Beaney in this spirit suggests that "Despite being a work in pure geometry, Frege's dissertation nevertheless hints at the subsequent direction of his thought. For he is clearly concerned with how results in one area can be extended into another."[35] That is true enough, as far as it goes, although much the same could be said of almost any dissertation written by young scholars with no further similarities to Frege's interests and subsequent career in logic and philosophy of mathematics. Who could have known from Frege's Göttingen PhD that he would soon be revolutionizing the field by creating the discipline of mathematical logic, as the first in a long series of extraordinary innovations to redefine the formal philosophical foundations of logic and mathematics?

Imaginary Numbers Acquire Geometrical Respectability

If there was a solid link to be forged between Frege's 1873 Göttingen dissertation and his later investigations in the foundations of arithmetic, it may be more accurately considered as Frege's preparatory exploration of the conceptual, and one might even say logical, foundations of geometry. Thus,

Frege completed his studies in Göttingen in 1873 with a [previously mentioned dissertation] thesis . . . This work dealt with a topic which was a subject of discussion among the geometers of this period, and it contains links to ideas of C. v. [Karl Georg Christian von] Staudt, F. [Felix] Klein, and O. [Otto] Stolz. Most striking about his

---

[35] Michael Beaney, "Introduction" to *The Frege Reader*, ed. Michael Beaney (Oxford: Blackwell Publishing, 1997), p. 2.

first work is that Frege tried to lay certain foundations for a portion of geometry. The motivation for solving his problem apparently came from the mathematics itself. Interpreting the theorems of geometry as synthetic a priori, the few philosophical remarks made by Frege in the thesis correspond to the views of Kant and of Frege's teacher in Jena, K. [Kuno] Fischer. Motivated by the mathematical content, Frege generalized the conception of visualization to comprehend geometrical objects.[36]

The judgment seems historically accurate and insightful, although it does little to assuage the sense that Frege's research at Göttingen was more a preparation for than a stepping-stone along the route leading toward his later logicism.

Frege was admitted to the dissertation defense on 6 August 1873 by the Dean of the Faculty of Philosophy, Ernst Ludwig von Leutsch. There was an oral defense or *Rigorosum* of the research, for which Schering and Weber were the examiners. Frege requested that the examination be conducted in German rather than Latin, which may have come as a relief to all. The very fact that such choices were on offer testifies to the extent to which PhD students were expected to have proficiency in the preferred classical language of the German universities. We are told that already in Frege's time it was quite common for doctoral candidates in the sciences to make this petition, and for it to be granted *pro forma*.[37] Imagine otherwise having to defend in Latin in order to receive your hood a doctoral dissertation on the representation of complex functions involving imaginary numbers in a two-dimensional geometrical plane, using concepts and words that did not even exist in Roman times. Luckily, Frege, who may never have advanced beyond declinations and conjugations from a classroom exercise folio, escaped the indignity of dredging up his Wismar Latin for the occasion of defending his Göttingen PhD dissertation. Frege was granted the degree of Doctor of Philosophy on 12 December 1873.

Frege's dissertation research reinforced an attitude toward mathematics that had started taking hold in his thought already during his Gymnasium secondary education at Wismar. Frege began increasingly to realize that what was important in mathematics was the *mode* of proof and demonstration, of precisely how the mathematician reasons from assumptions. These can range from axioms, where mathematics has been axiomatized, to the logical derivation of arithmetical theorems. Frege expected an exact sequence of precisely formally regulated steps by which inferences in

---

[36] Schlote and Dathe, "Die Anfänge von Gottlob Freges wissenschaftlicher Laufbahn," p. 185.
[37] *Ibid.*, p. 193.

mathematics were made as mathematical truths were discovered, verified, and communicated. The dissertation brought the early formal days of Frege's mathematical education to an impassive close. Learned experience is usually hard-earned experience. When in his philosophically creative period hereafter Frege had occasion to speak about formal proof and logical demonstration, of the logical structures of many different styles of mathematical reasoning comprehended by his logic, he was able to draw on years of experience working directly with a wide array of pure and applied mathematical inferences and theorem proof methods. He made their acquaintance at first hand not only in extensive classroom exposure, but also by direct involvement in his dissertation investigations. The end result of Frege's Göttingen doctoral studies was a mathematically sophisticated investigation of one of the decade's most rigorous and formally ambitious arithmetical–geometrical challenges.

3

Post-Doctoral Research and Teaching (1874–1879)

F REGE HAD BY now not only earned a PhD in mathematics, but thrived, academically and more importantly intellectually, in an environment of the most difficult mathematical study on offer at Wismar, Jena, and Göttingen. Taken collectively and in sequence as Frege did, this wayfaring offered a fair sampling of what German mathematics institutes at the time expected of their best degree candidates.

Many wilt at the thought of semester after semester of concentrated attention to mathematics and applied mathematical natural science. Those who do not love it and have no natural knack for abstract and formal syntactical relations cannot successfully undertake this kind of work. They will not be able to make themselves. The program is not for everyone, but for the best persons with special talents. Other programs, often equally demanding, are for students who are better at something else. The argument that justifies division of students after primary school into university-bound and non-university-bound programs also supports the narrow focus of mathematics degree students almost exclusively on mathematics. There is much to learn. The subject makes its own demands on students, whether enforced by institutional decisions or as a result of student choice. Inclination rather than oppressive degree requirements may have played an equal hand in Frege's scorecard of mathematics achievements, climbing a stairway of progress in the formal sciences from Jena through Göttingen.

Frege the Boy as Father to the Man

He was quiet, hard-working, seldom satisfied with himself, critical but always forward-moving. By seeking and internalizing reactions from all his teachers to transform into his own lacerating self-criticism, Frege inched toward self-improvement and the greater perfection of his thought, just as he worked through the bulletin of requirements for mathematics degrees at his succession of schools. What was Frege thinking, and what would he say when he considered it his turn to speak? He had tried his wings at the Jena Mathematical Society, offering lectures and discussion to its members, as other students presumably did. It is rumored that some of his first philosophical writings had already been composed before he completed his degree at Göttingen.[1]

Frege knew that his progress was being observed. At home, certainly, he would not have wanted to disappoint his mother and his brother. There was a spreading network of teachers in Frege's wake, who had been impressed with his mathematical abilities and had done him the enormous honor of recommending him for study with their own teachers at the institutions where they had earned their degrees, on whom Frege's Lutheran conscience could not allow him to bring shame. Mathematics is hard work. The ideas are usually not difficult, once the relations a mathematical theory is trying to formalize and how the symbol transformation rules are supposed to work have been understood. The rest is all complicated and sometimes ingenious manipulation of signs in your head or on paper. It gets into your blood, if you have the aptitude, as Frege did from the outset. For Frege, learning new things by trying out the syntax combinations of a mathematical language, axioms, and deductively inferred theorems was the fun part and most interesting aspect. Running up sharply against the expressive scope and limits of a symbolic language, one sees plainly what the symbolism can and cannot do.

Frege was proving himself worthy, and his mother, Auguste, believed in him. She may have imagined in his academic success something of the desire to which she knew Karl Alexander had aspired. Her dutiful husband, Auguste could perhaps also clearly judge, lacked Gottlob's

---

[1] Prior to completing his 1874 Jena Habilitation, Frege published three works. The first two were *Über eine geometrische Darstellung der imaginären Gebilde in der Ebene*, Inaugural-Dissertation der Philosophischen Fakultät zu Göttingen zur Erlangung der Doktorwürde (Jena: A. Neuenhann, 1873) and *Rechnungsmethoden, die sich auf eine Erweiterung des Größenbegriffes gründen*, Dissertation zur Erlangung der Venia Docendi bei der Philosophischen Fakultät in Jena (Jena: Friedrich Frommann, 1874). These were his dissertation and Habilitationsschrift. A successful candidate for promotion to PhD and Habilitation was expected to publish these theses, usually with presses specializing in this category of texts, and often at the student's own expense. Frege published also a one-page notice, "Rezension von: H. Seeger, *Die Elemente der Arithmetik*," *Jenaer Literaturzeitung*, 1(46) (1874), p. 722. English translations can be found in Gottlob Frege, *Collected Papers on Mathematics, Logic, and Philosophy*, ed. B. McGuinness (Oxford: Basil Blackwell, 1984).

God-beloved capacities that she would joyfully do her part even in late widowhood unstintingly to support. Eventually, the girls' school in Wismar would be sold. Auguste would commission the building of a duplex two-family house near the woods surrounding Jena, Forst 29, to which she and Gottlob would move in 1887. At that time Frege had just been appointed associate (*Extraordinariat, Außerordinariat*) Professor of mathematics. Arnold was making his own way in Wismar, minding family interests in Bad Kleinen on the headland opposite the Baltic, where Frege would eventually retire.[2]

Frege's natural mathematical abilities and passion for the subject, if he found it sufficiently absorbing rather than a four-and-a-half-year torture, are fact rather than legend. Frege was good enough, the record shows, to have been one of a handful of noted students able to follow some of the most difficult mathematical lecture courses at Jena. He kept pace with the subject matter of complex functions and their mapping into a two-dimensional real and imaginary number plane. The topic had been handed down from Gauss and his circle at Göttingen, some of whom decades later became Frege's teachers there, as also at Jena. From these teachers with exemplary academic pedigree Frege received appreciative recommendations from floor to ceiling. If the mathematics in the programs Frege completed came easier to Frege than it did to some of his colleagues, we should not lose sight of the fact that the seamless sequence of mathematics studies Frege successfully completed, however exhilarating he may have found the subject, could not also have failed to be cognitively absorbing. To an understanding of Frege's psychology we can add the pressures of what must have been an inherently stressful experience for a small-town Wismar boy being offered a wonderful chance to follow his star. He would take advantage of every moment. He would give satisfaction to his gifted hard-working family, and to the exponentially growing backcloth of academic advocates, sponsors, and well-wishers, not to mention his immediate teachers and colleagues, at each successive plateau of university study.

Imaginary and Complex Numbers

The idea of situating a one-dimensional linear number *Lauf*, in German mathematical parlance, the line or run of real numbers, in a two-dimensional

[2] See Kreiser, *Gottlob Frege*, pp. 565–70.

plane onto which imaginary and complex numbers can be one–one mapped, the assumption, the hypothesis that this could be done, was not a new idea. It was a suggestion going back at least to the mathematical imagination of Gauss,[3] who had taught at Göttingen from the late eighteenth into the nineteenth century. Frege evidently had no opportunity to study with the great mathematician in person.[4] Instead, he worked in the tradition of mathematics Gauss had started at Göttingen, with some of Gauss's most gifted students, among others who had been influenced by his thought.

Plotting imaginary and complex numbers orthogonally in a plane, in which the real number line is embedded as but one among infinitely many similar Euclidean elements, almost puts these peculiar syntactically recommended and practically useful but otherwise anomalous numerical values on a par with the natural numbers (including zero, 0), counting numbers (the same basic number line, but beginning with 1 instead of 0), and real numbers generally, rational and irrational. Why, after all, should all numbers appear like soldiers in linear formation, even metaphorically speaking, when the one-dimensional line itself is embedded geometrically in the model within an infinitely more comprehensive two-dimensional plane? Finding a place and laying down rigorous conditions whereby imaginary and complex numbers can be associated with something geometrical, bringing them one step closer to familiarity with the mathematical dimensions of space, making them real so that they can be named and otherwise referred to, counted, quantified over, more like ordinary real numbers, domesticates these imaginary constructions, even if they are quite literally out of line.

Frege became part of the movement of researchers following the path initiated by Gauss, and published his Göttingen dissertation in mathematics in that tradition. Along the way he accumulated a wealth of first-hand knowledge of mathematical reasoning. He gained a lifetime's reflection on

---

[3] At Göttingen Gauss (1777–1855) made important contributions to the foundations of arithmetic. See his thesis, written in Latin, *Disquisitiones Arithmeticae (Arithmetical Investigations)* (Leipzig: Gerhard Fleischer, 1801), and *Disquisitiones Generales circa Superficies Curvas (General Investigations on Curved Surfaces)* (Göttingen: Dieterichianis, 1828), on "intrinsic" differential geometry. After Wilhelm Weber had joined the Göttingen physics department in 1831 Gauss became increasingly interested in applied mathematical physics and especially electromagnetic phenomena.

[4] Gauss would have been dead sixteen years when Frege arrived at Göttingen in 1871. His presence may still have been felt in the mathematics department when Frege went there to study.

the logical structures of mathematical proof, as they are actually put into practice. Judging by how quickly he took the first step in his succession of publications, Frege must already in his Göttingen years have grasped a ground plan of the applied logical structures of basic arithmetical laws and logically derived theorems. It is the common underlying structure that unites all formal sciences under a single logical framework, beginning with a fully algebraic functional calculus or logic of concepts, on which basic laws of elementary arithmetic are superimposed. After that, Frege's logicism would be unstoppable. All of mathematics pure and applied must fall under a single set of purely logical laws and an analysis of natural number as a purely logical concept. At some point in his studies, probably no sooner than his time at Göttingen, Frege began to think of elementary logic and elementary arithmetic as conceptually interjoined, of elementary arithmetic as an extension and special application of pure logic. It was the vision of a unified logic and mathematics that Frege pursued throughout the rest of his intellectual life.

Logic and Göttingen Mathematics

What is interesting to later philosophy about Frege's calendar of university lectures is not only his concentrated coverage of advanced mathematics, with all but two exceptions for philosophy courses, but also reflection on what subjects he did not study in his programs at university. Naturally, every mathematics departments has its own focus and subjects for which its style of doing mathematics and the associated results are known. Usually this is because of an overwhelmingly important research figure or a cluster of mathematicians who cook up interesting work between them for a time.

Frege was climbing his way back up the chain of descent from Sachse and other Wismar well-wishers to Abbe, Snell, and Schäffer, and on especially to Scherring, with whom Frege seems to have enjoyed a special mathematical empathy. Ultimately, the trail would lead Frege to the Göttingen hotbed of Gaussian studies in the geometry of imaginary and complex numbers, where Gauss had relatively recently still been active. It was a plan that Frege seems to have fallen into quite naturally, but one that made perfect sense and that he exploited admirably for its opportunities to increase his acumen at every stage of a well-designed mathematical education.

The average catalog of subject listings in mathematics looks very different today than in Frege's time, even at Jena and Göttingen. Choosing Jena for a little online spying, only because Frege attended Jena first after having graduated from Wismar Gymnasium, one finds listed for the required Vorkurs Mathematik WS [Wintersemester] 2014/15, the following rather different topics from those greeting Frege on his entrance to either Jena or Göttingen: *Wichtige Schlussregeln der Logik* (Important Inference Rules of Logic); *Elementare Mengenlehre* (Elementary Set Theory); *Prinzipien für Beweise* (*direkter Beweis, indirekter Beweis, Beweis durch vollständige Induktion*) [Principles for Proofs (Direct Proof, Indirect Proof [*reductio ad absurdum*], Proof by Means of Exhaustive Induction)]; *Funktionen; elementare Kombinatorik* (Functions; Elementary Combinatorics); *Nachweis von Gleichungen und Ungleichungen, wie sie insbesondere auch für die Informatik relevant sind* (Proof of Equalities and Inequalities, Particularly as Relevant for Computer Science).

There was no comparable course in logic or set theory for Frege in his time. Needless to say, there were also no computers or *Informatik* as a new branch of mathematics. There were no information engineers professionally recognized as such. Boole's *The Mathematical Analysis of Logic* was not published until 1847, just one year before Frege's birth, and Boole's *An Investigation of the Laws of Thought on Which Are Founded the Mathematical Theories of Logic and Probabilities* did not appear until 1854.[5]

---

[5] George Boole, *The Mathematical Analysis of Logic: Being an Essay towards a Calculus of Deductive Reasoning* [1847], with a new introduction by John Slater (Bristol: Thoemmes Press, 1998); and Boole, *An Investigation of the Laws of Thought on Which Are Founded the Mathematical Theories of Logic and Probabilities* [1854] (New York: Dover Publications, 1958). Secondary resources are catalogued in Dale Jacquette, *On Boole* (Belmont: Wadsworth Publishing, 2002). Frege's two unpublished essays comparing the *Begriffsschrift* with Boole's algebraization of a four-term Aristotelian–Victorian syllogistic term logic in the above two major works are available in Frege's *Nachlaß*. See Frege, "Boole's Logical Calculus and the Concept-Script" (pp. 9–46) and "Boole's Logical Formula-Language and my Concept-Script" (pp. 47–52), in *Gottlob Frege, Posthumous Writings*, ed. Hans Hermes, Friedrich Kambartel, and Friedrich Kaulbach (Oxford: Basil Blackwell, 1979). Boole shunned propositional negation when he wrote in his *Mathematical Analysis of Logic*, pp. 18–19, that "The expression of a truth cannot be negatived by a legitimate operation, but it may be limited." Boole had in mind especially such legitimate "limiting" operations as probability qualifications by means of comparative acceptability values. The expression of truth can also be limited by predicate-complementation in speaking for some property *F* and its complement of being *non-F*.

Students in Frege's day were expected to have learned Aristotelian syllogistic logic and the subsyllogistic square of opposition at Gymnasium, if they bothered to learn it at all, after which this mostly worthless antiquated apparatus was seldom mentioned again among professional mathematicians. Without a symbolic logic adequate to their needs, mathematics students were supposed to have an intuitive grasp of the distinction between deductively valid and invalid mathematical reasoning before they applied to study university mathematics. There was nothing much to syllogistic logic, nothing much to study there. If logic was syllogistic term logic, then for very specific reasons there was naught to excite mathematicians. They knew that they seldom, if ever, reasoned according to the rigid framework of deductively valid syllogisms. Aristotelian logic was dismissed as having little if anything to do with mathematical inference in demonstrations of lemmata and theorems.[6]

Most proofs, even in classical times, beginning with Euclid's famous argument that there is no greatest prime number (evenly divisible only by 1 and itself), are instances of *indirect* reasoning or *reductio ad absurdum*. The method is to assume the negation of the proposition to be proved, and then to show by derivation from other given assumptions that a contradiction follows, literally reducing the assumption to an absurdity. This mode of reasoning cannot be properly expressed in Aristotelian syllogistic term logic, because it does not support the *negation* of any proposition as *reductio* hypothesis. It makes do instead with predicate complementarity in an object's having property non-*F* as an internally "negated" distinct term. Contradictions do not follow logically from true propositions, so the hypothesized negation of an assumption made for *reductio* purposes must be false, implying that the proposition to be proved is true. Q.E.D. *Quod est demonstrandum*. Thus it is demonstrated. In Euclid's proof, roughly speaking, we hypothesize that there *is* a greatest prime number, which we call *N*. Euclid then shows that, if we take all of the primes from 1 to *N*, multiply them together, and add 1, then the result is either prime and greater than *N*, or not prime. If the constructed number is prime, then there is an immediate counterexample to the assumption that *N* is the greatest prime number. A constructed number

---

[6] See, for literature and explanation of the canonical square of opposition, among numerous scholarly sources, Jacquette, "Thinking Outside the Square of Opposition Box," in *Around and Beyond the Square of Opposition*, ed. Jean-Yves Béziau and Dale Jacquette (Basel: Springer-Verlag, 2012), pp. 73–92.

greater than N cannot fail to be prime, because then there would need to be a prime number factor that evenly divides the difference between N and the larger number constructed from N. The absurdity that follows from the *reductio* hypothesis that there is a greatest prime is that N both is and is not the greatest prime number, proving that there is no greatest prime.[7]

Aristotelian syllogistic logic does not even indirectly enter into the inference structures of Euclid's reasoning. Nor does it help mathematicians to understand the underlying deductive validity of formal derivations of this kind. It is awkwardly made to do so only by the most contorted efforts to fit propositions and inferences of mathematics into a rigid and expressively limited syllogistic framework of three categorical propositions satisfying requirements for the distribution of repeated terms between exactly two assumptions and a single conclusion in the standard syllogism. That is not the informal logic of mathematical reasoning, not only in Frege's nineteenth-century German university lecture rooms, but already in Euclid's ivy-festooned times. If someone wants to study Aristotelian logic, which is not to say that Frege ever did, the advice would certainly have been to consider the philosophy department down the hall, or the classics department in the next building. Mathematically inclined students at the time were not usually thought to need any deeper consideration of logic, unless, which was almost unheard of, it was their chosen specialized subject matter. They would learn what constitutes good mathematical reasoning by directly studying approved mathematical proofs.

We know from Kreiser's invaluable data summaries that such courses were not taught. Within the typical range of choices among categories and Frege's narrowly prescribed options, logic and set theory were not offered, although it was presupposed that an informal understanding of the relevant concepts and relations of logic would have been acquired,

---

[7] Euclid's argument appears in *The Elements of Euclid, with Dissertations* (Oxford: Clarendon Press, 1782), Book IX, Proposition 20, p. 63. The proof assumes for purposes of indirect proof that there are at most only finitely many primes, the greatest of which is N. It then considers a number G greater than N constructed as the product of all the prime numbers $\leq N$, $+ 1$, for which the following dilemma is posed: either G is prime, in which case there is a prime number greater than N, contrary to the hypothesis; or G is not prime, in which case G is evenly divisible by some prime factor P that also evenly divides N, a factor in the construction of G, from $N + 1$. That is to say that prime factor P must evenly divide the *difference* between N and $N + 1$. However, the difference between N and $N + 1$ is exactly 1, a number that no prime number evenly divides.

more or less intuitively, in preparatory Gymnasium lectures. Set theory in Frege's time is another topic. The historian must look to Georg Cantor in the later part of the nineteenth century and early twentieth century for a more extensive blossoming of this mathematical meadow. The subject had changed very much since Frege's time as a student when, several years later, writing his 1884 text *Die Grundlagen der Arithmetik*, Frege was able to dismiss the proposal that the number 0 might be a null *set*, and the number 1 a singleton *set*, on the grounds that "sets" properly so-called, like tea china, are always assumed to contain at least two members. When only one chipped cup survives we do not call it a set, although we might say in special cases that it was once part of a set.[8]

Logic was only beginning to stretch its limbs. What bold first steps it was destined to take occurred largely through Frege's writings after 1879. By then Frege was thirty-one and giving lectures of his own at Jena. He was past the point where he could wind back the clock and take the courses in logic and set theory with the syntax and interpretations for which he must have sensed the need. He had to work these things out for himself. Jena university mathematics today, totally Fregean in its contemporary *Vorkurs*, emphasizing logical inference, proof methods and principles, set theory, combinatorics, and related topics, was not available when Frege studied for his university mathematics degrees. Nor is that any cause for astonishment, except in reflecting on how powerful an impact Frege and other like-minded mathematicians in roughly this timeframe only later came to exert. The practitioners notably included

[8] That sets in Frege's day had to have ≥2 members is clear from Frege's unwillingness in his *Grundlagen der Arithmetik* to reduce numbers to sets as doing so would seem inadequate in particular to define the natural numbers 0 and 1. See Frege, *The Foundations of Arithmetic: A Logical–Mathematical Investigation into the Concept of Number* (New York: Pearson/ Longman, 2007), §28 on "Number as Set," p. 42: "Some writers [Frege mentions his Jena colleague Carl Johannes or J. Thomae by name] define number as a set, multiplicity or plurality. There is a difficulty that occurs in this connection, through which the concept excludes the numbers 0 and 1." Georg Cantor, taken literally in this connection, imposed a similar implicit restriction of set membership to sets of minimally two members, excluding the null and singleton sets. Cantor, "Beiträge zur Begründung der transfiniten Mengenlehre," *Mathematische Annalen*, 46 (1895), p. 31: "Unter einer 'Menge' verstehen wir jede Zusammenfassung M von bestimmten wohlunterschiedenen Objecten m unsrer Anschauung oder unseres Denkens (welche die 'Elemente' von M gennant werden) zu einem Ganzen." I translate the opening passage of Cantor's essay, with emphasis especially on the implied *plurality* of "wohlunterschiedenen Objecten m" as follows: "By a 'set' we understand every collection M of particular properly distinguished objects m of our perception or of our thoughts (which are called the 'elements' of M) as a whole."

Frege's contemporaries Ernst Schröder, David Hilbert, Boole, Giuseppe Peano, and Bertrand Russell. The revolutionary subjects in mathematical logic that Frege discovered, invented, and in any case popularized in mathematics could not be studied then, although they are now regularly featured at colleges and universities throughout the world. Frege had not yet crystallized, discovered/invented, or published his system of symbolic logic that in other notations is now considered classical.[9]

A Simplified Frege Retrospect

One finally comes to consider, especially with historical hindsight rather than an appreciation for his ongoing personal and career decision-making in its historical context, that Frege's intense study of mathematical and rigorous natural science subjects, physics and chemistry at the beginning, trending toward electrodynamics through the final lectures he attended at Göttingen, was ultimately a means to another end.

Frege's university education was not yet complete. There was still the Habilitationsschrift to write and orally defend. It was the second book-length dissertation to be completed before Frege could be considered a university-level maximally degreed journeyman of mathematics. Frege composed, presented, defended, and published his Habilitationsschrift in 1874 under the title *Rechnungsmethoden, die sich auf eine Erweiterung des Größenbegriffes gründen* (*Methods of Calculation Based on an Extension of the Concept of Quantity*).[10] The book-length manuscript was a dress rehearsal for his 1879 *Begriffsschrift*. The "Concept of Quantity," to which the title of his Habilitationsschrift made reference, was formalized in Frege's general functional calculus in quantifications over existent objects satisfying and belonging to the extensions of concept-function output values when specific inputs are introduced. They were for Frege in every instance concept-functions applied to a specific choice of existent argument-objects.

For individuals involved in strenuous technical research, with practical applications already established throughout so much of applied mathematical natural science, the importance and intrinsic interest of the

---

[9] See Dummett, *Frege: Philosophy of Mathematics* (Cambridge: Harvard University Press, 1995), especially pp. 1–9 and 307–21.

[10] A detailed survey of the relevant events and documentation surrounding Frege's Habilitation at Jena is provided by Kreiser, *Gottlob Frege*, pp. 112–30.

discoveries being made is enough to explain their enthusiasm. These were exotic numbers geometrically reclaimed. Imaginary and complex numbers proved themselves indispensable for applied mathematical physics and engineering. Giving them a respectable address geometrically outside the real number line contributed to higher mathematics on the ontic presuppositions of its default stock-issue Platonic abstract realist metaphysics of mathematical entities. There were new refined methods of mathematical analysis. Identity relations between mapping functions and their imaginary and complex number inputs and the output values of specific locations on the number plane outside the real number line needed to be rigorously defined. It was solid responsible technical mathematical research. Frege nevertheless seemed to lose interest in the whole business after having come to believe that he had thought it all through by the time he finished his PhD.

Frege saw the project as far forward as his native fascination carried him. It was another great thinker's research program, and Frege had been a willing soldier in the Gauss battalion. If he were going to be a great thinker himself, he seemed to have realized at the time, then he would need his own research program, something designed by himself as a reflection of his own vision of things. He was bringing this part of his mathematical study to a close. The dissertation virtually capped this line of inquiry in Frege's professional career. Frege was already preparing for his first independent steps in mathematics, leading toward fully formalizable transparently proof-structured logical foundations of mathematics.

The work must have begun already at Göttingen. Assessments of the progression of his thought at the time cannot be made purely on the basis of his choice of lectures in mathematics or eventual dissertation topic. That vital experience was only one part of Frege's intellectual development. The scholar in him, with so many obligations and grateful to so many supporters along the way, was also a philosopher with his own ideas and constructive tasks in mathematics to undertake. Frege's studies in mathematics, to put things a bit dramatically, judging from what happened next, had wound him up a bit like a watchspring. The spring was about to be released with all the stored-up energy of everything Frege had learned about how rigorous mathematical demonstration proceeds and his sense of how it was supposed to function. He knew something of the mechanism of proofs from books, lectures, and his own efforts to derive theorems showing conclusively that certain mathematical propositions were true. The question was, as the spring uncoiled in Frege's productive mathematical imagination, what kind of energy would it release, and in what directions?

From Mathematics to Philosophy

It was approximately at this time that Frege's philosophical instincts began to assert themselves in his mathematical research. This makes it natural to inquire what, if any, impact his two university courses in philosophy, as previously noted, one by Fischer at Jena, on Kant's critical philosophy, and another by Lotze at Göttingen, on philosophy of religion, may have had on Frege's thinking at the time. We do not know exactly what Frege made of either set of lectures from surviving written records, and know only something of their content.

Fischer's course on Kant's philosophy at Jena in the winter semester of 1870–1871, for which Frege registered, has been considered by Frege scholars to have marked the beginning of Frege's lifelong fascination and confrontation with Kant's Critical Idealism. The influence of Kant on Frege is supposed to have been so extensive, according to one frequently repeated version of events, that he paid tribute to Kant's concept in the Transcendental Aesthetic section of the *Critique of Pure Reason* by agreeing with Kant that the transcendental ground of our cognitive ability to understand geometry is the pure form of our spatial intuition or perception (*Anschauungsvermögen*).[11] This is a Kantian teaching that Frege is often said to have accepted throughout his mathematical–philosophical career. Frege, in contrast, according to the same oft-told fable, disputed throughout his working life Kant's parallel proposal that the transcendental ground of our ability to understand arithmetic is the pure form of temporal intuition experiencing the passage of distinct moments of time.

Given that Frege was intimately conversant with translations from arithmetic into geometry and from geometry into arithmetic, he might have concluded on further reflection that there can be no firm and fixed distinction between these major mathematical subdisciplines. The posited inter-expressibility of arithmetic and geometry caused the downfall of Kant's philosophy of mathematics, rather than his more frequently

---

[11] Immanuel Kant, *Critique of Pure Reason* [1781 / 1787] (Cambridge: Cambridge University Press, 1998). The Transcendental Doctrine of Elements, First Part, The Transcendental Aesthetic.

mentioned decision to hitch transcendental reasoning in the metaphysics of perception to Euclid and Newton, who were later supplanted in the history of mathematical physics by Riemann and Einstein. Kant's transcendental method is more flexible with respect to data application than the objection acknowledges. The method was meant to apply to anything given to experience or judgment, asking what must be true in order for something given to be possible. A resurrected Kant could apply the method of transcendental reasoning just as effectively to Einstein's or Heisenberg's physics as to Newton's.

Frege substituted logic as explanatory ground of arithmetic in place of Kant's pure form of perception of physical objects in time. It was the objective that defined his research program after he had completed and published his Habilitationsschrift in 1874. One can only conclude from Frege's timeline that he had already written a substantial part of his Habilitationsschrift before he left Göttingen to begin post-doctoral research, when he returned to complete this part of his Jena credentialing. A mere five years later, Frege's *Begriffsschrift* was unveiled. Even Frege's reference in the *Begriffsschrift*'s subtitle to the concept of "pure thought" retained a distinctive Kantian ring. Purity for Frege, in this context, as for Kant, meant being uncontaminated by empirical and especially contingent *a posteriori* occurrent psychological factors. Kant wanted to eliminate emotions, especially happiness and pleasure, and the avoidance of pain and unhappiness, from the foundations of ethics. Frege similarly wanted to eliminate psychological events from pure logic at the foundations of arithmetic.

Regardless of the extent to which he could be justly labeled a Kantian on the basis of his choice of technical language, and independently of the value of such labeling for thinkers as independent as Frege soon proved to be, Frege found in Kant a giant of the *deutsche Aufklärung*, the German Enlightenment, with all the patriotic implications Kant's prestige had for nineteenth-century world philosophy. More importantly, Kant provided a starting-place for Frege's proposal to rebuild the philosophy of mathematics in a way that contrasted with its greatest theoretical competitor in Kant's Transcendental Aesthetic. Frege pit Plato against Kant, Platonic abstract realism against Kantian Critical Idealism. He opposed a mind-independent realm of mathematical entities, relations, and propositions, thoughts or *Gedanken*, as Frege categorized them in defiance of their psychological connotations, in contrast with subjective embodiments of the pure form of intuition in subjective perceptual experience of physical entities in space and time, in order to explain respectively the metaphysics of the once diametrically divided branches of mathematics in geometry and arithmetic.

Kant's writings provided touchstones in a common philosophical language of interrelated concepts exhibiting under analysis a clear well-defined structure (more or less). Within this architectonic, Frege discovered and expressed philosophical problems that with increasing urgency and persistence were starting to perplex him in his conventional mathematical research. Kant also served, if not as an antipode for Frege, although in some areas he was certainly that, then more vitally as a sparring partner, a worthy opponent, from whom Frege could learn valuable lessons, and on whose philosophical foundation Frege might once have believed he could constructively build, even if it implied showing that the Königsberg savant had gotten some important things desperately wrong. The lecture course on Kant's philosophy by Fischer was no doubt not Frege's first brush with Kant's thought. He would have heard Kant's name from some of his Gymnasium *Dozenten*, and possibly also from Karl Alexander. Fischer's course seems to have encouraged Frege's interest in Kant, who in the German academy remains a pillar of philosophical understanding.[12]

In the Göttingen lectures that Frege attended, Lotze maintained at the outset, although we do not know whether or how well he argued his case, that, like a scientific theory, a doctrine of religious belief should be rationally justified. Frege's interest in the general nature of inferential reasoning may have responded viscerally to this assertion of Lotze's. Lotze dedicated part of his first lecture to a discussion of proofs for the existence of God. Frege could not have avoided comparing the logic of religious reasoning with the inferential structures of mathematical proofs. The comparison might have been actively encouraged by the logician Lotze. If the existence of God can be validly deduced from the right

---

[12] Kant's importance in the later German academy, especially in nineteenth-century philosophy, is emphasized in Andrew Bowie, *Introduction to German Philosophy: From Kant to Habermas* (Oxford: Blackwell, 2003). A useful chronology of Kant's accomplishments is provided by Manfred Kuehn, *Kant: A Biography* (Cambridge: Cambridge University Press, 2001). See Kuehn, "Kant's Critical Philosophy and Its Reception – The First Five Years (1781–1786)," in *The Cambridge Companion to Kant and Modern Philosophy*, ed. Paul Guyer (Cambridge: Cambridge University Press, 2006), pp. 630–64. See also Tom Rockmore, *In Kant's Wake: Philosophy in the Twentieth Century* (Oxford: Wiley-Blackwell, 2006).

choice of true premises, then, just as in mathematics, belief in the existence of God, whatever its relation to the believer as an article of faith, could be scientifically upheld on general grounds of good reasoning. It was the promise of deductive inference and what it might entail that gradually gained hold in Frege's limited but influential university philosophical education.[13]

The question of whether there might not be a commonality between mathematical demonstrations and efforts rationally to prove the existence of God would have been treasure enough for Frege to take away from Lotze's 1871 summer semester lectures on the philosophy of religion. We see in hindsight once again how subtle stimuli played a significant role in Frege's intellectual growth. Lotze was at that time already an internationally respected philosopher. Despite his claim that in principle the truths of religion could be established as rigorously and rationally as those of any science, Lotze, in his later *Grundzüge der Religionsphilosophie* (*Principles of the Philosophy of Religion*),[14] staunchly opposed anything like René Descartes's style of rationalist argument for the existence of God in Meditation III of Descartes's 1641 *Meditations on First Philosophy*. There, God, characterized as the only possible origin of a correct if inadequate idea of God, is made the basis of a proof for the existence of God as the concept's necessarily divine origin. *Ex nihilo nihil fit.*[15] Nothing comes from nothing, and, since the idea of God is something, it also cannot derive from nothing. It must come from somewhere, and Descartes argued at length that only God outside the order of our ideas could be the source of our idea of God.

Lotze maintained on epistemic grounds that identifying the source of an idea can never establish its correctness, let alone prove a positive correspondence to anything specific or unified as the idea's existent cause. The further criticism is that what Descartes described in Meditation III is merely Descartes's mind connecting one set of ideas of God, including the idea of God's properties being essentially unified in a single entity, with an idea of God's being the existent cause of the idea of God. It is not as though we can will unity any more than existence into being for any of

---

[13] Kreiser, *Gottlob Frege*, pp. 99–103.

[14] Lotze, *Grundzüge der Religionsphilosophie* (Leipzig: S. Hirzel, 1884).

[15] René Descartes, *Meditations on First Philosophy, The Philosophical Writings of Descartes* (Cambridge: Cambridge University Press, 1984), Volume 2, Meditation III, pp. 24–36. See Kreiser, *Gottlob Frege*, pp. 99–100.

the mind's ideas, even for much less fantastic ideas than Descartes's idea of God.

Whatever the substance of Lotze's lectures on the philosophy of religion, Frege may have found the very different cultural dialectical environment of philosophy lectures a refreshing balm to the demands of computing, calculating, integrating, differentiating, geometrizing, and formal modeling on his overworked synapses. That philosophy could offer a different approach to some of the conceptual questions nagging Frege concerning the nature of mathematical objects and inferential structures of mathematical reasoning and deductive proof, involving topics regarding which Frege would later quench his curiosity, may have provided encouragement for his budding philosophical interests. Lotze had supposedly rigorous demonstrations for the existence of God up his sleeve, which were meant to be taken more seriously by students at his lectures than those he criticized. Like mathematics, insofar as mathematicians concern themselves with metaphysical questions of ontology, God for Lotze's philosophical theology exists in an abstract order that transcends space and time. For Frege, this was another telling correspondence, one that he may not have previously considered or reflected on so fully and thoughtfully before hearing Lotze lecture. The mathematical objects of theorems are equally imperceptible, Platonic ideal or abstract entities transcending space, time, and causation.

As Frege matured in his mathematical outlook, as he developed confidence in his ability to latch onto an interesting problem and advance solutions of his own, he began to realize that the writings of Kant and the recent genealogy of mathematicians he had studied, and to whose scientific work he had now produced a contradiction, were for him philosophically superficial. Kant, and all of philosophy, mathematics, and science, had a message for Frege, if he could only decode its contents. They were speaking to him, sometimes through writings from the past, sometimes in the lecture theater. He was going to learn whatever he could from them, and use what he could from the stockpiles of their ideas, where they were deposited as though on call. Some of the voices from the university lectern spoke directly to Frege, as he began to craft his own systematic mathematical–philosophical ideas. Professors offering lectures with secular knowledge were like ministers delivering sermons from the pulpit. The good boy, now a dashing hirsute man of uncommanding presence, excitable without showing it, knew exactly why he was there. He sat politely and listened intently but critically to every word from which he hoped to benefit.

Jena Habilitation

First, the final piece in the jigsaw puzzle of Frege's advanced degree accreditation needed to be set in place. For this he returned to Jena for post-doctoral studies as a *Privatdozent*. He must write, submit, and defend his Habilitationsschrift. When the last step was complete, Frege would have achieved the capstone of a brilliant university student academic career.

Frege equipped himself with one of the most impressive mathematical educations available at the time. He lifted himself from humble beginnings to academic distinction. At every stage, he demonstrated a notice-catching solid dependable work pattern. It was an ingrained cultural attitude astutely characterized by Max Weber in his monograph *Die protestantische Ethik und der Geist des Kapitalismus* (*The Protestant Ethic and the Spirit of Capitalism*).[16] Frege seems to have had that strength in abundance, once he was let loose on the German university world. He accumulated extremely valuable skills, and, more importantly from the standpoint of understanding his biography and attitudes to the systematically falling dominoes of degree requirements he had tipped over, he had something like the temper of entrepreneurial capitalism that was as alive in Germany as it was in all of Europe and North America at the time. True to Weber's model, Frege was himself a product of the Protestant ethos. He was steeped in the values of northern German Lutheranism in a family that had adopted Luther's rejection of the Catholic structural hierarchy and its abuses in the days of the early Reformation. Beyond questions of prevailing cultural trends, members of the Lutheran clergy were liberally interspersed among Frege's relatives, as we saw while tracing out some of Frege's kinship on noting the professions of his ancestors, contemporaries, and future generations of his father's and mother's family trees.

---

[16] Max Weber described the work ethic into which Frege and his family were born in his influential 1904–1905 essays, which were published first in the *Archiv für Sozialwissenschaften und Sozialpolitik*, 20 and 21, and later as a monograph under the title *Die protestantische Ethik und der Geist des Kapitalismus* (Tübingen: J. C. B. Mohr, 1934).

Frege loved mathematics. That is why he was there, what he was there to do. It was also the most practical option, with one foot realistically on the ground of practical applications and one in the lofty expanses of abstract theoretical philosophy. Nevertheless, when he was required to take at least one optional course outside mathematics during his mathematics degree programs at Jena and Göttingen, Frege, the record shows, seized the opportunity in both instances to attend philosophy courses. The fact obviously tells us something about Frege as an advanced graduate student, and his personality as a mathematician. There was an inevitability about how these episodes fell into place and positioned themselves as though directed from the future for the revolution that Frege the quiet achiever was systematically working to foment. He was acting for the good of both mathematics and philosophy, though we can appreciate this only once we know the trajectory of Frege's research beyond the Jena Habilitation. We understand today that it was something so fundamental and far-reaching that many years needed to elapse before the significance of his work could begin to be more fully appreciated.

For the history of mathematical logic, Frege's narrowly channeled preparation in the subject of his Göttingen dissertation was crucial. There were nevertheless other motivational factors that as Frege ripened may have changed in importance relative to his later post-degree lifework. They contributed in complex ways to his fashioning a pure logic of elementary arithmetic, in his efforts to secure what he believed largely to be the purely logical foundations of mathematics. If arithmetic could be shown to rest on logic, and there were freely available arithmetical mapping functions, then, since geometry and arithmetic could be modeled and mirrored in one another, we can recover all that remains of mathematics in geometry as functions on the natural numbers. The edifice exists; that is not the point. We know it exists because we have pieces of it, sometimes without understanding exactly how they are all interrelated, namely what depends on what and in what logically exact way. There is nothing for human thought manually to invent in mathematics, except the symbolic languages in which to express aspatiotemporally pre-existent mathematical predications, to arrive at efficient, gapless, transparent, and above all deductively valid derivations of theorems.

The object was to discover the edifice. To lay it out from the ground up brick by brick, with everything resting on pure logic. After that, it was only a matter of explaining how the entire structure fits together. It was a task for the philosophy of mathematics, or an essential philosophical undertaking in the foundations of mathematics, beginning with arithmetic. If we can do this, Frege glimpsed already at the time, then we will have explained the metaphysics of numbers, the basis for everything else in arithmetic. We will have unlocked the inferential structure of mathematical reasoning, and laid it open transparently to view, in order to ascertain its deductive validity or lack thereof. We can arrive, by employing the method, at an exact philosophical understanding of the concept of mathematical proof and the demonstration of mathematical truths as theorems validly deduced from surveyable intuitively true axioms. The basic laws of elementary arithmetic can then be put to work in an inferential structure that represents the mathematical relations Frege considered throughout his philosophical writings to involve real existent abstract entities, effectively a cross-section of unearthly Platonic Forms or Ideas.[17]

The Habilitationsschrift and Frege's Qualification
as a *Privatdozent*

Like the implications of Lotze's principle of inquiry in the philosophy of religion, Frege's ardent anti-psychologism boiled down to the intuition that a number was always one thing and our idea of it another. At a streetside level of common sense, it is hard to imagine how the philosophers of mathematics whom Frege castigated could have ever thought otherwise.

What was sometimes missing in Frege's attitude was compassion and commiseration for benighted theorists who did not already agree with his philosophical intuitions. Frege lacked appreciation of the fact that these theorists had made peace with some form of psychologism for the sake of avoiding the greater difficulties of available alternatives. Those alternatives, a good defender of a psychologistic philosophy of mathematics could contend, included Frege's solution when seen in their light. Frege always chose as his

---

[17] There is a substantial literature on the topic of Platonism in Frege's philosophy and especially in his philosophy of mathematics. Useful starting-places include Bob Hale, "Frege's Platonism," *The Philosophical Quarterly*, 34 (1984), pp. 225–41; and Crispin Wright, *Frege's Conception of Numbers as Objects* (Aberdeen: Aberdeen University Press, 1983). The picture is complicated, and some commentators find Frege's metaphysics more equivocal and less plainly Platonic. See Tyler Burge, *Truth, Thought, Reason: Essays on Frege* (Oxford: Oxford University Press, 2005), especially pp. 309–12.

starting-place basic laws and inference principles that he found *intuitively* unassailable – as did such theorists as Hilbert and Russell, who nevertheless disagreed with Frege. The question of which kind of theory, psychologistic or non-psychologistic, was philosophically preferable was a philosophically more intricate question than Frege recognized[18]. His rhetoric was nevertheless brilliant, entertaining, and instructive, matched in sparkling sharpness of wit only by Schopenhauer's occasional exuberance on believing that he had deservedly trounced a philosophical opponent.

Frege returned to Jena in 1873 as a *Privatdozent*. The category of *Privatdozent* in the German university system had a long evolving history. Originally it was a rank of instructor that offered no salary other than what the *Privatdozent* could secure by attracting students who would pay individually, when they could and finally did so, for the favor of the *Privatdozent*'s lectures. Often lectures by *Privatdozenten* were intended to prepare students for advanced courses or qualifying examinations. The *Privatdozent* was dependent on the interest, goodwill, and honesty of students who were sometimes in even worse financial circumstances than their instructors.

Becoming a *Privatdozent* was not a straightforward proposition. There were requirements to meet. It was usual for the status of *Privatdozent* to be awarded only to scholars who had completed their PhD at the same university. This clearly was not Frege's situation, since he had just defended his dissertation in mathematics at Göttingen. Frege would be required to defend the Göttingen dissertation once again in Jena on a formal occasion organized to make sure that his work in Göttingen was also up to Jena standards. This was known as a Disputation, or *Streitschrift*, in the statutes for *Privatdozenten* at Jena, where a candidate could be placed under close critical scrutiny with respect to quality of research and more especially teaching potential. There was a process for the evaluation of credentials, during which recommendations were bounced back and forth from the appropriate faculty and the university senate, which then

---

[18] The most authoritative study is Martin Kusch, *Psychologism: A Case Study in the Sociology of Philosophical Knowledge* (London: Routledge, 1995). Essays relevant to the subject are collected in the volume *Philosophy, Psychology, and Psychologism; Critical and Historical Readings on the Psychological Turn in Philosophy*, ed. Dale Jacquette (Dordrecht: Kluwer Academic Publishers, 2003), including Jacquette, "Introduction: Psychologism the Philosophical Shibboleth," pp. 1–19, Jacquette, "Psychologism Revisited in Logic, Metaphysics, and Epistemology," pp. 245–62, and also essays by Stelzner, Mohanty, and Kusch.

forwarded the package of papers to the local civic authorities, who considered, but were not bound by, the university's recommendation. Candidates for *Privatdozent* accreditation were also required to present a public showcase lecture in Latin or German on a topic relevant to the faculty in which entrance as a *Privatdozent* was being sought.[19]

The title of Frege's Habilitation study was, revealingly, *Rechnungsmethoden, die sich auf eine Erweiterung des Größenbegriffes gründen* (*Methods of Calculation Based on an Extension of the Concept of Quantity*). It offered a snapshot of the ongoing development of Frege's thought in mathematics and his increasing movement toward mathematical logic and the logical foundations of mathematics.[20] The generality of Frege's Jena Habilitationsschrift, when compared with that of his Göttingen dissertation, prefigured his development of the general functional calculus.

To highlight the stages of his advance, in Göttingen Frege completed the upstream progression from Wismar to Jena, to the source of Gauss's idea of correlating imaginary and complex numbers with specific locations uniquely specifiable in a geometrical plane outside the real number line. The number plane includes as only one of its dimensions the real number line within the plane. Positive and negative integers, and rational and irrational numbers, are already mapped onto that line, which by extension provided reference points for the rest of the plane. It was a topic toward which all of Frege's previous mathematical education inclined his further steps. It was that for the sake of which his mathematics teachers had passed him back up along the chain of descent to study with their own teachers. Since this was a highly specific, conceptually cutting-edge, topic in traditional mathematics at the time, Frege's research required a great deal of formal symbolic skill and mathematical imagination, moving from number theory to plane geometry, and understanding their common ground and formal functional interrelationships. Each distinct imaginary and complex number required a distinct geometrical address in the total real-plus-imaginary-plus-complex number plane, lest any be confused with any other. The mathematical conditions for the exact geometrical mapping correlations were not trivial to formalize.

---

[19] Kreiser, *Gottlob Frege*, pp. 112–30.

[20] There is surprisingly little secondary literature on Frege's Habilitationsschrift. For some discussion, see Mark Wilson, "Frege: The Royal Road from Geometry," *Noûs*, 26 (1992), pp. 149–80.

On returning to Jena to complete his Habilitationsschrift, Frege chose a more general topic. It was a subject of mathematical investigation in the widest sense of the term, one that reflected his later long-term project to develop a formal symbolic logic capable of representing the concept-functions and proof structures of all mathematical predications, inferences, and derivations of theorems from axioms. It was to be a mode of formal demonstration with no dodges or subterfuges, trapdoors or stage curtains, smoke or mirrors, with everything essential to the proof explicitly arranged and transparently open to view. This was a new idea that brought a higher level of theoretization to mathematics, which hitherto had been a duffle bag of unsystematically related formal results and proofs. Whereas Frege used the usual modes of computation in his specific researches on complex numbers and geometry, in the Habilitationsschrift he stepped back to reflect on what was logically required for any calculation or computation, and consequently in a sense for all mathematical reasoning as a special case.

It was in itself a noteworthy philosophical advance in Frege's thinking about the kind of logic needed for mathematical discovery. The Habilitationsschrift marked a first signal in Frege's written work of an independent shift from his degree-candidate studies. Innovations appeared precisely at the juncture between Frege's dissertation research and his Habilitation, moving away from conventional mathematical investigations in topology to the formal logical philosophical foundations of mathematics. It was historically that moment in the annals of symbolic logic when Frege first proceeded toward a lifelong pursuit of pure logicism in the philosophy of arithmetic. Frege's Jena Habilitation presaged the world's first fully algebraic functional calculus of quantity, of the subdomains of things, all or some, possessing a particular property. A concept understood as a function applies to and takes any existent object as an argument in the logic Frege first glimpsed while writing his Jena Habilitation. A concept-function saturated by an argument-object from the logic's domain of existent entities outputs as value-object an extension of existent entities with exactly those properties. The thought or propositional assertion that an object has the property would then be true or false, depending on whether or not the existent entity in question belonged or failed to belong to the concept-function's extension.

Two Freges

The interesting question, which is so intriguing partly because, without a coveted time-travel machine, it is unanswerable, is whether it was part of Frege's plan all along to maximize his preparation in conventional mathematics in order to strike forward in the direction of logicism and the formal and philosophical foundations of mathematics. Did the big picture appear to him all at once, beginning with a glimpse of purely logical arithmetic? Or did it come to him in stages, dawning on him gradually, until he slipped naturally and almost unnoticeably into its grip?

The record of events is that, after having completed and defended his dissertation at Göttingen in 1873, Frege finished and sat for examinations on his Habilitationsschrift upon returning to Jena the very next year. Advanced post-doctoral students in the German-language university community typically take three or four years to accomplish the same, and are sometimes granted as much as six. This raises the further intriguing question, which is equally unanswerable without the benefit of a time-machine, of whether Frege may have used his years at Göttingen to write a longer work that he then edited down to the dissertation. Perhaps he divided a longer manuscript into two *Nebenarbeiten*, one of which became the dissertation while the other, or the remaining part, was saved to be expanded and rewritten as the Habilitationsschrift the following year back in Jena. Otherwise, skeptics who disagree with the foregoing interpretation owe the more trusting among us an explanation of how Frege could possibly have written the technically formidable Habilitationsschrift from scratch in that diminutive length of time.

The difficulty here is perhaps one of the most important in Frege's biography. The historical issue is anthropologically engaging. It is like digging for remains of *Homo habilis* in order to discover something of our species' biological past. If we are active in, or interested in, analytic philosophy, then we may want to know exactly when Frege's logicism was first conceived. It is important not merely for the sake of being able to erect a historical shrine, but also in order to understand more fully the intellectual environment at the time when Frege first conceived of the idea of a general functional calculus. Whenever it was, this was the very moment at which a second–order predicate-quantificational logic and the forerunner of the principles of all classical formal symbolic logic took root in Frege's mathematical thought. It was equally the exact place and time where and when what was later considered analytic philosophy was first seen by Frege from afar. The point is not to honor the moment, but to attain a better grasp of Frege's philosophy in its historical context of development. It would be instructive for this purpose to know more definitely when this mythical moment took place, when more precisely Frege's inspiration for the future course of logic began to take hold of his imagination.

We have at least two different Freges. In interpreting his writings we may not know which best to choose, or whether to decline the choice altogether. Frege-1 was engaged before completing his mathematics PhD on the formal logical structure of proof methods. He may have worked out much of the material that was rewritten in the Jena Habilitationsschrift alongside his dissertation efforts to map complex numbers outside the number line onto a two-dimensional geometrical plane. The seed may have been sown even earlier in Jena. He may have reflected already at this early stage on the logical structures of the demonstrations required to prove positive correspondences between complex numbers and specific locations on the plane. Frege did not yet have his first book, the *Begriffsschrift*, recognizably in hand. At least, that is not suggested here. It is nevertheless what came almost immediately afterward, literally a handful of years after he had completed the Habilitation and had been admitted as a *Privatdozent* at Jena. The topic of Frege's Habilitation is nevertheless highly significant, marking his turn from purely mathematical research toward an increasingly philosophical engagement with algebraic logic, the nature of number, the truth of basic arithmetical laws, and the logical structure of mathematical reasoning.

Frege-2 completed his Göttingen PhD dissertation on mapping complex numbers onto a two-dimensional geometrical plane, returned to Jena, under just the same circumstances as Frege-1, and, needing to meet the Habilitation requirements, dramatically shifted the focus of his research in pure mathematics away from what it had been for the previous four and a half years. In less than half a year, over approximately four months in March 1874, after his defense of the Göttingen dissertation at the end of the summer semester of 1873, Frege-2, unlike Frege-1, wrote and defended a Jena Habilitationsschrift on completely new ideas about logical methods of calculation or computation based on a concept of quantity. It is effectively a disquisition on domain size, or what would later come to be known in the history of mathematics as the cardinality of a predicate's or concept-functor's extension. For Frege's purposes in the Habilitationsschrift, it was expedient to formalize quantification over relevant parts of a plane in which imaginary and complex numbers were mapped. That does not sound like the previously methodical Frege who had seen through all stages of a project in higher mathematics, encompassing pure number theory and analytic geometry. Frege-2 is not an impossibility, certainly not a logical impossibility, but the greater probability and plausibility undoubtedly belong to a more complete characterization of Frege-1.

The implication is that Frege was deflected from his four-and-a-half-year study of imaginary and complex numbers toward more general philosophical topics in the foundations of mathematics. He became especially involved in working out the logical structures of mathematical reasoning. The awakening of the mathematical logician alongside the mathematician in Frege must have taken place sometime before he finished his degree at Göttingen. Frege's *Begriffsschrift* was at least six years in the future. He shifted his attention from churning out specific mathematical results to inquiring into the metamathematical structure of mathematical methods of calculation, and by extension still more generally of all mathematical reasoning in discovery and proof.

Frege, in a sense, at this crucial pivotal moment in his philosophical development, if we have caught the character of his evolving thought correctly, even if only so crudely as to favor the existence of Frege-1 over that of Frege-2, was asking of himself in his Jena Habilitationsschrift what exactly he and his teachers had been doing for the previous four and a half years. He would soon come to appreciate that the question had many dimensions. He would chart for himself a research path by which he could approach as many of these fathomable philosophical difficulties as practicable with the precision and clarity that he admired in arithmetic and the applied mathematical natural sciences. He may also have wanted to emulate in the philosophy of arithmetic the open-ended systematic inquiring attitude that Lotze had brought to the philosophy of religion.

Here is an elegant mathematical proof. It is printed in a textbook, scribbled on the blackboard, and talked about informally over coffee. What is this thing called a mathematical proof, and how does it work? What would justify placing one's trust in the truth of its conclusions? Frege's teachers bombarded him with mathematical demonstrations, mathematical arguments for propositions deemed true as mathematical theorems. But they did not raise or try to answer philosophical questions about mathematics. Frege's instructors, unlike those observed in the Jena *Vorkurs* for mathematics majors today, did not seem to have had much interest in, or devoted much mathematical thought to, the problem of how mathematical proofs are able to expand knowledge of mathematical truth within a structure of rigorous formal mathematical demonstrations.

It was accordingly up to Frege to undertake the inquiry and set these elements in place. At some point, he saw that a thoroughly worked-out answer to philosophical questions about the nature, meaning, function, and truth of axioms and epistemic credentials of mathematical reasoning would explain all there was to know about mathematics. It would be a complete philosophy of the subject. It would be an important topic, a new area in mathematical studies, one that was later to revolutionize the field at the same time as raising questions and developing advanced methods of inquiry that have characterized a core concern of analytic philosophy in the twentieth and twenty-first centuries. The game was kicked off by Frege. As often implicitly as explicitly, Frege set the goals, defined the purpose, and identified the rules for what philosophers afterward have mostly wanted to talk about in trying to understand logic, arithmetic, mathematics more grandly conceived, and all aspects of the theory of meaning. All of these topics were considered by Frege. His logic remains modern logic or the base or point of departure for most of the research conducted in the field of mathematical logic that he founded. The mythical moment, whenever it occurred, when analytic philosophy was born, was presumably while Frege was still at university. It was at that moment that Frege realized that, however long it took, there was a need to show with full transparency and gapless inferential structures that the basic laws and derived theorems of elementary arithmetic are purely logical in form and concept. The insight should have been marked by an abrupt change taking Frege's work-in-progress in directions he had not immediately envisioned, concerning which he might not have previously approved.

The second interpretive hypothesis to add to the preference of some version of Frege-1 over Frege-2, assuming that Frege did not write his Jena Habilitationsschrift from scratch in less than half a year, is that Frege arrived at his understanding of the inferential logical structure of mathematical reasoning at a higher level of generality than he had been taught at Jena and Göttingen, higher even than he put into practice in his Göttingen dissertation research, sometime during his three years there.

The charmed moment might have occurred even earlier. It could have come when Frege was still at Jena for the first time, completing his first university degree. We can only conjecture that Frege's philosophical awakening is more likely, other things being equal, to have occurred during Frege's time at Göttingen, rather than before or after Göttingen during his periods at Jena. The possibility that Frege was made uneasy by unexplained logical concept-functions in mathematical reasoning the very first time he was presented with a proof cannot be ruled out. Although the question is among the most important to try to answer in writing Frege's biography, there is no documented source indicating when Frege began to turn his attention more fully to the logic of mathematics prior to announcing the topic of his Habilitationsschrift at the time of his post-doctoral return to Jena in 1873. What is fixed are the publication dates, dates for submission and defense of theses, and similar signposts scattered among relevant official documents, rather than the subjective passing ephemeral moments of inspiration that would later find expression in Frege's writings.

Bynum paints the following general picture of Frege's progress up to this point:

As soon as he received his Ph.D., Frege (probably sponsored by Ernst Abbe) applied for a teaching position at Jena. Among the several documents he submitted was a statement from his mother that she would support him, since the position he sought was unsalaried ["At this time a university lecturer (*Privatdozent*) received no salary. His only income from his university position was a meager standard fee that each student paid him to attend his course; but this was generally insufficient to live on."[21]]. At that time, she was already a widow; but apparently the income from the girls' school, which her husband had founded and which she was then directing, was sufficient to support herself and her son.[22]

Frege attached to his Habilitationsschrift the following brief and extremely rare autobiographical statement, corroborating the basic timeline of his studies up to his return to Jena in 1873:

I, Friedrich Ludwig Gottlob Frege, was born at Wismar on November 8, 1848. My father Alexander, who was principal of a girls' high school there, was taken from me by death in the year 1866. My mother Auguste, née Bialloblotzki, is still alive. I was educated in the Lutheran faith. After attending grammar school in my hometown for

---

[21] Bynum, "On the Life and Work of Gottlob Frege," in *Frege: Conceptual Notation*, p. 4, note 2.
[22] *Ibid.*, pp. 4–5.

fifteen years I graduated from it at Easter 1869 and spent two years at Jena and five semesters at Göttingen on mathematical, physical, chemical, and philosophical studies. In Göttingen I received the Ph.D.[23]

Hans Sluga, who extracted and translated the declaration, remarks that "This short statement, appended to Frege's Habilitationsschrift of 1874, is exceptional in his body of writing for its autobiographical character."[24] (It was in fact part of a required autobiography that every candidate had to submit.) Abbe offered an assessment of Frege's Habilitationsschrift to the Dean of Faculty at Jena, the illustrious Goethean evolutionary biologist Ernst Haeckel. The report was accompanied by a synopsis testimony of Snell's enthusiastic support. Snell described Frege as a very hardworking and ambitious young man (*sehr fleißiger und strebsamer junger Mann*), whom he was pleased to be able to recommend to the faculty (*der Fakultät zur Aufnahme empfehlen zu können*) for the teaching position that had become available.

We could hardly expect otherwise. Haeckel was none other than the famed naturalist, philosopher, physician, and graphic artist who investigated the physical structures of plants and animals, and noted and illustrated their formal similarities and evolutionary relationships. Somewhat in the spirit of Goethe's already antiquated concept of *Urpflanze*, Haeckel popularized illustrated biological taxonomies of plants and animals in branching, sometimes inverted, tree-structure organizations.[25] All three examiners were satisfied with Frege's demonstrated abilities. We have already heard from Snell. Haeckel's opinion as officiating chair of the committee was withheld. He was there to assure that formalities were properly observed and to officiate in executing the committee's will by preparing the necessary paperwork once a decision had been reached, in the making of which he would ideally have played no substantive role. Stelzner, in reviewing the committee's report, similarly noted that "Abbe's opinion is imbued with high regard for Frege's unusual mathematical talent, and the in-depth way of looking at fundamental problems in Frege's way of thinking, not satisfied with superficial, quickly accessible results. Already at the beginning of Frege's scientific

---

[23] Sluga, "Gottlob Frege: The Early Years," p. 329.   [24] *Ibid.*
[25] Stelzner, "Ernst Abbe and Gottlob Frege," pp. 17–18. The complete text of Abbe's *Gutachten* of Frege's Habilitation is reproduced by Kreiser, *Gottlob Frege*, Anhang 2.4, pp. 127–30.

career Abbe offers an assessment [of Frege's prospects] that characterized Frege's entire future œuvre."[26]

Things were looking good for Frege. The mathematics faculty wanted him badly on board. He had not blown in like a hurricane, but he was after all Frege. Everyone in mathematics at Jena knew him as such, knew what he was like in person, and must have sufficiently appreciated his good qualities to want him as a colleague. They were prepared in these early days to overlook what in retrospect must have been glaring warning signs of Frege's teaching deficits, preferring to see instead such virtues as serious deliberation in his social and pedagogical peculiarities, like his inability sometimes to answer even simple questions.

The Originality of Frege's Habilitationsschrift

Abbe described his former mathematics and natural science student's Habilitationsschrift as wearing "the signature of real originality and unusual innovative force in itself." He praised "the progress of the investigation, the general idea in the mathematical detail," which, he says, "expresses the ability of the writer to rise to an extraordinary level of abstraction while keeping its terms so fixed and determined that they still prove to be a powerful method of thinking."[27] Bynum reiterates that

In March 1874 Professor Ernst Abbe submitted to the University officials a report on this paper [Frege's Habilitationsschrift]. The report shows that the Jena mathematics faculty were most impressed by Frege's Schrift. Abbe found it to be erudite, clear, and to the point; bearing the mark of true originality and extraordinary creative powers; and containing novel points of view, sagacious explanations, and surprising relations among widely separate regions of analysis. He speculated that it might contain the seeds of a comprehensive new point of view which, when fully developed, would attain a durable significance for mathematical analysis. Thus, Abbe's report was a truly impressive recommendation and, as it turned out, a remarkable piece of foresight.[28]

With paper documentation and recommendations in proper order on Haeckel's desk, Frege was admitted to the prescribed oral examination of his Habilitation on 18 April 1874. Frege was now twenty-six years old, and about to complete the final tessera in the mosaic of his formal mathematical education. When it was set in place he would be qualified as a highly trained mathematician in his own right, an apprentice turned journeyman.

[26] Stelzner, "Ernst Abbe and Gottlob Frege," p. 17.   [27] Ibid.
[28] Bynum, "On the Life and Work of Gottlob Frege," in Frege: Conceptual Notation, p. 5.

It had not yet been a full year since his PhD defense at Göttingen on 6 August. (The doctorate was awarded by the university on 12 December 1873.) We do not need Frege's mathematical gifts to determine that the length of time between Frege's defending his PhD dissertation at Göttingen and defending his Habilitationsschrift back at Jena was a scant eight months, not to mention the fact that the Habilitation oral defense could not have been scheduled until Frege had finished or virtually finished writing the book-length text of the Habilitationsschrift. Else there would have been nothing on which he could be examined, nothing for him to defend.

The ideas that shaped Frege's most profound and lasting achievements in mathematical logic and the philosophical logical foundations of mathematics assumed definite form in Frege's mind as he prepared to face the Habilitation oral defense. The Habilitation was the bridge and first step in a new direction that Frege's research in mathematics would adopt, beginning in Göttingen and proceeding after a return to Jena through to the end of his active working life. It might be reasonably said, taking Frege's Habilitation lecture as starting-point, that he made the most decisive statement of his independence from conventional logic and mathematics when he returned to Jena, produced a Habilitationsschrift like a rabbit from a magician's hat in about sixteen weeks, and sketched the core of a fully algebraic general functional calculus of propositions, truth-functional negation, and material conditionality in one-way truth-dependences, with the quantities of existent entities in precisely specifiable reference subdomains. Frege's insights gained at Göttingen, whenever, wherever, and however they occurred, carried him forward over the next forty years of thinking about the problems of logic and the philosophy of mathematics. Eventually these were to include the semantics of names and propositions in the philosophy of language and the meaning and metaphysics of identity statements as in arithmetical equations such as $1 + 1 = 2$ and function (argument) = value constructions. Before any of these events could find their place in the history of mathematical logic and its philosophy, there was a grueling tribunal for Frege to undergo.

Frege before the Examiners

We do not know the demeanor of Frege's examiners that April Saturday. Attending the event were Frege, of course, Eduard Oscar Schmid, Geuther,

Moritz Schmidt, Eduard Strasburg, Carl Fortlage, Abbe, and Haeckel, the latter in his capacity as Dean of Faculty.[29]

The purpose of the Habilitation oral defense could be described as an investigation not so much into the fine points of Frege's research, but rather of his suitability as a potential *Privatdozent* to teach university-level courses in mathematics. Frege was fast-tracked into a teaching position at Jena out of desperation. Snell's illness and Abbe's commitments at the Carl-Zeiss-Stiftung had left the Jena mathematics institute seriously understaffed. The point of Frege's examination was primarily to satisfy the faculty that Frege could conduct himself competently in front of students, to communicate an interesting result intelligibly and answer questions with the normally expected facility of a university instructor. Candidates should at least be capable of fielding questions about their own recent research. It was considered a friendly place to start. Otherwise how could habilitated mathematicians teach something new to students? How could they be expected to satisfy their students' legitimate need for clarification and examples, with safeguards against counterexamples, this being the payoff, point, and purpose of mastering a syntactically challenging formal calculus?[30]

The committee could not have been much in doubt about Frege's ability. He had already presented several talks at the Jena Mathematical Society three or four years earlier. Abbe summarized the committee's findings upon examining Frege, indicating that, either ignoring the stated purpose of the defense, or as a way of satisfying the requirement, Frege was examined on the contents of his Habilitation, but more especially on the subject matter of his Göttingen dissertation. This topic was of interest to all the mathematicians gathered at his trial, many of whom had worked in the field themselves, so they asked questions concerning his thoughts especially about complex functions, which continued to feature in Frege's discussion of more general problems to do with mathematical methods. Abbe stated in his summary that Frege's opinions on very general questions, "*Fragen von sehr allgemeiner Art*," had been sought.[31] In conclusion,

[29] Kreiser, *Gottlob Frege*, p. 117.
[30] See Kreiser, *Gottlob Frege*, pp. 127–30, for the contents of Frege's Habilitation oral exam evaluations by Frege's soon-to-be colleague and *Habilitationsbetreuer* Abbe and the Dean of their faculty, the world-famous biologist Ernst Haeckel.
[31] *Ibid.*, p. 117.

the examiners were satisfied that Frege was proficient in his subject matter and had arrived at defensible views.

The committee members were less impressed by Frege's live performance than they had been by the written Habilitationsschrift. The report does not try to conceal the fact that some members apparently found Frege's replies "neither quick-witted nor fluent" ("*weder schlagfertig noch fließend*").[32] It was noted that Frege had not passed any exams specifically to judge his qualifications as a teacher of higher education, but specifically requested that the University of Jena not prolong or extend his time for this purpose.[33] Bynum recounts the outcome as follows: "Having sustained his oral examination, Frege was recommended by the committee for acceptance into the University. They requested speed in accepting him, because Professor Snell was not well, and Frege was willing to take over part of Snell's duties."[34] Haeckel prepared and submitted the Faculty report to the university senate the following day, 19 April 1874. Along with it was attached the request to admit Frege to an unsalaried *Privatdozent* position or *venia docendi* at the University of Jena. The appeal was supplemented by a petition from Jena University *Kurator* (trustee) Moritz von Seebeck to the Grand Ducal Ministry of State to appoint Frege to *Privatdozent* status quickly. Personal recommendations carried significant weight in the decision, and von Seebeck did not hesitate to mention not only that Frege had met with very positive responses to his Habilitationsschrift, but also, equally if not more importantly, since any number of mathematics candidates for such a position could say much the same, that Abbe knew Frege as his previous student, someone Abbe could say possessed "eminent talent for mathematical research in this science" ("*eminente Begabung für mathematische Forschung in dieser seiner Wissenschaft*"). The university *Kurator* added his "earnest advocacy" to the university faculty and senate recommendations for Frege to be taken on board as a *Privatdozent*.[35]

---

[32] My free translation and paraphrasing of Abbe quoted in Kreiser, *Gottlob Frege*, pp. 117–18.

[33] *Ibid.*, p. 120.

[34] Bynum, "On the Life and Work of Gottlob Frege," in *Frege: Conceptual Notation*, p. 5.

[35] Frege's reticence in answering questions put to him during the exam was noted with caution, but not considered a disqualification for the Habilitation. Frege's hesitations at his Habilitation defense, inferred from remarks even of his supporters who wanted to be able to hire him immediately thereafter to teach, could be seen as a didactic red flag and harbinger of his later disastrous classroom lecture presentation style.

Snell's persistent serious ailments and Abbe's administrative overwork and increasing involvement with the Carl-Zeiss-Stiftung meant that Frege was secured a position as a *Privatdozent* during the course of a significant lacuna in the teaching of higher mathematics at Jena. His former teachers, who knew and trusted him as a mathematician and active member and speaker at the Jena Mathematics Society, accelerated his progress through the Habilitation process. They did this with noted reservations, it is true. His responses to questions about his new work on mathematical computation methods based on the magnitude of a plane supporting projections of real, imaginary, and complex numbers, arithmetical functions of real and imaginary, were thought lacking in cleverness, verve, and fluidity.

No doubt the questions Frege was asked were good, difficult questions that reflected a thorough understanding of what he had attempted in the Habilitation. Frege may have vacillated, hesitated, dithered, or had to think his way through answers to unanticipated probings of his thesis. Frege was never to become a lecture showman, in the way that some teachers are said to have held lecture audiences entranced by their stage presence, character, and performance. A good question could bring everything to a standstill, as early as in the Habilitation defense, while Frege thought through all the possible channels of sources of a problem and their proper solutions. He would have judged a glib off-the-cuff answer to serious interrogation as frivolous, irresponsible, and worthless both mathematically and philosophically.

Still, the examination could have been worse. For one thing, it could have been conducted in Latin rather than German. The superable requirement might have existed not only for tradition's sake, but also to provide a good last-minute way to weed out candidates deemed unworthy of the Jena Habilitation by denying their request for a German as opposed to Latin recital. Frege and the committee were spared this. What happened instead on Frege's behalf, and that of the Jena mathematics institute, is that paper was moved at surprising speed and at the instigation of powerful sources within and outside the university in order for Frege to gain his unpaid position as a mathematics *Privatdozent*. His passion for the subject continued to be tested, and he survived with a roof over his head and bread to eat during this time almost entirely on his mother's generous maintenance. She may have suffered privations for Frege's sake, which Arnold seems later to have increasingly resented.

Frege was filling the mathematics teaching gap that Snell and Abbe had left open in the program. For the moment everyone was satisfied. However unfair the situation, there was presumably nothing more remunerative that the mathematics institute at Jena could have done for their own student returned to habilitate from Göttingen. They may have hoped that Frege could ascend to the level of an *außerordentlicher* (Associate) Professorship with a salary, and in time possibly even to the highest position of *ordentlicher* (Full) Professorship, and they may have shared their hopes with him. Frege seemed unperturbed when he was turned down for promotion from *außerordentlicher* to *ordentlicher* Professor later in 1896, on the grounds that promotion would bring with it a substantial burden of administrative responsibilities that he expected to interfere with the active pursuit of his research into the logical foundations of arithmetic. This meant that Frege never became a full-fledged member of the Faculty of Philosophy at the University of Jena. It never appears to have been his ambition. By then his university salary was being heavily supplemented by matching research assistance funds from the Carl-Zeiss-Stiftung, in the mutually rewarding academic–corporate optical design and manufacturing collaboration that Frege's teacher Abbe cultivated at the firm.

On 4 April 1874, further action was taken. To give a continuing idea of the number of hoops Frege still had to jump through, there remained successive stages of passing and ink-stamping or embossing of documents, all in order for the successful candidate to begin teaching without a salary at Jena. Upon satisfying his Habilitation requirements, the recommendations of the committee were expressed under Abbe's direction, then passed up the line to the university faculty, university senate, *Kurator* von Seebeck, and the Grand Ducal Ministry of the State of Saxony and sustaining provinces within the dukedom. There were letters from Abbe and Haeckel, along with supporting written attachments. With blinding speed by bureaucratic standards, the Ministry of State then informed the university on 1 May 1874 that Frege had been admitted to the university and habilitated as a *Privatdozent* for mathematics in the Faculty of Philosophy. It was in this faculty, not to be confused with an Institute of Philosophy where philosophy would be taught, that the mathematics department at Jena resided.

Frege was almost there, but not quite. On 6 May 1874, the university *Prorektor*, the mathematician and natural scientist Geuther, another of

Frege's teachers from his first university days at Jena, informed the
Faculty of Philosophy that Frege was now qualified as a *Privatdozent* in
mathematics, *provided* that he gave a public presentation and defense of
his research, *and* a satisfactory trial lecture to demonstrate that he could
competently lecture before university-level students. It was a marvelous,
almost unending-seeming, string of qualifications, and Frege patiently
held up under it all. These were the requirements for anyone in his
candidacy, and much of the proceedings took place behind the scenes
without stirring any anxiety, as paper changed hands and recommendations were written, collected, stamped as received, evaluated, and acted
on. All in all, it was not a process for the impatient or faint-hearted.

Frege's *öffentliche Disputation* (public polemical presentation and
defense) took place on Saturday, again, at 10:00 am, on 16 May 1874.[36]
Perhaps it was done on this day and at that time to assure that examining
committee members would be especially ornery in their relentless questioning of Habilitation candidates. The theses Frege chose to defend were
these five, which are open to interpretation also as reflecting Frege's
increasingly philosophical interests.

I.   The assertion that space is infinite is only relatively true.
II.   Figure belongs to things only insofar as they are objects of our attention.
III. The concept of number is not innately (originally, *ursprünglich*) given, but can be
      defined.
IV.   The axioms of geometry are not inductively known, but *a priori* truths.
V.   Quantity (magnitude, size) is not an intuition (*Anschauung*).[37]

What stands out for those who know what happens next in Frege's
philosophical progress is the topic of thesis III. It is precisely the definition by philosophical analysis of the concept of natural number that Frege
made the immediate target of his post-doctoral, post-Habilitation
research after his *Begriffsschrift* had been published in the technically
less demanding *Grundlagen*. When the *Begriffsschrift* failed to catch fire
among mathematicians and philosophers, Frege sensed the need to
pursue that plank of his large-scale project more informally and philosophically, although he may have done so for more strategic reasons than
has previously been appreciated.

---

[36] Bynum, "On the Life and Work of Gottlob Frege," in *Frege: Conceptual Notation*, p. 5, fn. 7.
[37] Kreiser, *Gottlob Frege*, p. 123.

The other main points Frege set forth include efforts to rebuff propositions that today would command little endorsement or enthusiasm, ironically perhaps because of Frege's later influence. The outdated suggestion that geometrical size can be understood simply as length, area, or angle, as a material perceptible object, which was still the subject of lively debate in Frege's time, is rejected as untenable, given the conclusions of Frege's investigations. Repeating Frege's argument in these more jaded times would today scarcely raise a logician's or philosopher's eyebrow, although it may have sounded young and revolutionary then. Having passed the Habilitation requirements at Jena, Frege stayed at the university for the remainder of his career until his retirement forty-four years later on 12 August 1918.

Appointment as Jena *Privatdozent*

It was firmly in the interests of mathematicians in the Jena faculty to hasten Frege's path toward teaching. Snell was prohibited from teaching by illness. Abbe had overwhelming administrative responsibilities, particularly connected with Zeiss's Jena work-station (*Werkstätte*).[38]

After five years of study, Frege was awarded *Privatdozent* status. The timetable was impressive, but not unheard of in the German university system for students writing extraordinary theses.[39] Frege was issued the Habilitation certificate (*Habilitationsurkunde*) officially on 18 May 1874, and began active teaching as a *Privatdozent* at Jena in the summer semester of that year. Now the future really did begin to seem wide open, with new untried responsibilities. Frege had in front of him a splendid opportunity to advance his mathematical understanding, to refine and extend the logic of mathematics in the previously underdeveloped field of algebraic symbolic logic. Bynum eulogizes in the following terms the moment of Frege's becoming a *Privatdozent* at Jena and its aftermath for Frege, logic, mathematics, and philosophy:

Thus, in the summer semester of 1874 Frege began his teaching career. His life during forty-four years at Jena was not so secluded and hermit-like as is commonly thought today. He was a member of the Deutsche Akademie der Naturforscher (Leopoldina), the Circolo matematico di Palermo (from 1906 to 1925), the Jenaische Gesellschaft für Medizin und Naturwissenschaft (from 1874 to 1917),

[38] Stelzner, "Ernst Abbe and Gottlob Frege," pp. 18–19.   [39] Kreiser, *Gottlob Frege*, p. 12.

and the Deutsche Mathematiker Vereinigung (from 1897 to 1925). He read several papers at meetings of some of these organizations. For three years – 1899–1901 – he was Assistant Treasurer (along with Johannes Thomae) of the last mentioned organization. He corresponded with many European scholars, including such important people as Husserl, Peano, Russell, Hilbert, Löwenheim, and Wittgenstein. He met Łukasiewicz, Wittgenstein, and Vailati (and, no doubt, many others). He published 40 works during his lifetime, including 4 books, 24 articles, 8 reviews and 4 comments and remarks. He also wrote a score of other works which did not appear before his death, but have recently been published in one volume.

The happiest period of Frege's professional career appears to have been the beginning, while he was a lecturer (*Privatdozent*). He was highly regarded by the faculty and the best mathematical students at Jena. He was young and vigorous, with great hopes for the future. During this busy five years Frege taught an extra-heavy load of courses and published three reviews, an article on geometry, and a little book (*Conceptual Notation*) on logic and mathematics that later scholars would come to recognize as monumental.[40]

Once again in Jena, this time as mathematics instructor rather than student, Frege had significant teaching duties as a new phase of mathematical and philosophical thinking began. From this time onward an emphasis on the logic of mathematical reasoning and the logical basis of mathematical concepts increasingly took root in his thought, which in another five years produced the *Begriffsschrift*. Frege's *Begriffsschrift* is an ideal formula language more precisely described in the book's subtitle, *eine der arithmetischen nachgebildete Formelsprache des reinen Denkens* – "an arithmetic-modeled formula language of pure thinking." Concept-writing or the conceptual notation was meant to provide the logical structure of mathematical proof as it had been practiced historically and was being practiced in contemporary applications. Frege now had the opportunity to develop in full the algebra of quantity he had first essayed in his Habilitationsschrift.

To pinpoint when Frege's philosophical turn took place, when modern analytic philosophy was in that sense conceived, the most responsible conjecture is perhaps that it was probably not during Frege's undergraduate years in Jena, but sometime before he departed Göttingen for his Habilitation and *Privatdozent* certification at his university *alma mater*. A mere five years later in 1879 Frege had not only written but also published the *Begriffsschrift*. At that point the die had been cast for all

---

[40] Bynum, "On the Life and Work of Gottlob Frege," in *Frege: Conceptual Notation*, pp. 6–7. See also Kratzsch, "Material zu Leben und Wirken Freges aus dem Besitz der Universitäts-Bibliothek Jena," p. 535.

his future research in logic, and the formal and philosophical foundations of arithmetic, in the significant body of work to which he dedicated the remainder of his career. Frege built a logically secure framework at this time to support the semantics by which the meaning and reference to truth-values of mathematical axioms, arithmetical equations in identity statements, and other interesting propositions were determined in the philosophy of language. Mathematics was interpreted as a formal technical language. Language was understood in a wider-ranging exploration of linguistic predication conditions that may have assumed preliminary shape sometime prior to Frege's first *Privatdozent* years at Jena.

It must have seemed like a natural progression to Frege. He was working systematically through these problems and observing from the inside his own growing sense of the fundamental unity of elementary logic and arithmetic. In his aspiration to achieve something worthwhile in mathematics, Frege had navigated a difficult program of studies at Wismar Gymnasium, Jena, and Göttingen, and had finally come to anchor at what became his lifelong academic homeport, Jena.[41]

---

[41] Consult for further resources related to Frege's time in Jena the "Bibliographie" to Gabriel and Kienzler, *Frege in Jena*, and the previously cited essays by Stelzner, Kreiser, Heblack, and Gabriel in that volume, pp. 5–32, 33–40, 41–52, and 53–67, respectively.

4

Frege's *Begriffsschrift* (1879) – An Ideal Logical Language

FREGE'S *BEGRIFFSSCHRIFT* WAS designed to provide the logical inferential machinery of mathematical reasoning. Its intended application, which was not fulfilled in this first book alone, was to deliver the essential formally expressive and deductive framework for explaining and reducing the basic laws and proofs of all theorems of elementary arithmetic to purely logical concept-functions and applied logical deductive structures. The logic inaugurated a program of sustained research in the philosophy of mathematics, with the formal foundations of arithmetic serving only as the first firm steps. Mathematics, it could then in principle be shown, was nothing other than an applied logical structure involving purely logical mathematical concepts.

Concept-Writing

Frege would do what he competently could in his lifetime to set the process in motion. He seems to have had a compelling sense of the direction logic and the philosophy of mathematics should take. He was inspired with a feeling of inevitability that the argument might be developed in a certain way from what his mathematical intuitions told him were the right starting-points. The project took shape in Frege's mind at Göttingen. The quantifier logic of the *Begriffsschrift* was embryonic in his Habilitationsschrift of 1874, which he presented to satisfy post-graduate degree requirements only months after having returned to Jena.

The fruits of Frege's investigations were now revealed in the publication of the *Begriffsschrift*. Frege eventually proposed reducing the basic laws and theorems of elementary arithmetic to purely logical principles and logically valid reasoning represented in an updated *Begriffsschrift* notation applied to the analysis of a purely logical concept of natural number. Higher mathematics was gained by applying functions to the objects of arithmetic, namely numbers and their pre-derived theorematic arithmetical interrelations. Mathematical invention on Frege's conception is facility in exactly defining functions to produce one formal logical construction or another, as Frege learned to do in mapping imaginary and complex numbers onto specific points in spaces orthogonal to the real number line in a geometrical plane. All of mathematics was supposed by Frege from the outset to be reducible to functions on the natural numbers and their arithmetical relations. He began with basic laws, the axioms and fundamental theorems of elementary arithmetic, supported in every instance by deductively valid logical inferences. The logic of the *Begriffsschrift*, despite being general in potential application, was dedicated from the outset in Frege's philosophy to the task of formalizing mathematical reasoning in accepted mathematical practice.

Kant was decently admired but refuted. Logic, rather than time as a pure form of perception, of intuition in Kant's Transcendental Aesthetic, was explicated as the ultimate ground of arithmetic and by extension all mathematics. It was a bold new idea, a hypothesis that deserved a young man of Frege's exceptional talents to give it the best imaginable run for its money. That was the routine Frege settled into after completion of the Jena Habilitation. Doing his ailing and overworked former professors' teaching for them, Frege lectured for more than five years from 1874 without the encumbrance of a university salary before being promoted to *außerordentlicher* (Associate) Professor on 2 August 1879. He barely scraped by. His private fee-paid lectures did not provide an adequate living even for a frugal bachelor. He must have felt used and exploited at this stage of his career, as indeed he was. He survived, as he had done during his school years, of which his apprenticeship university teaching at Jena was no doubt viewed by all concerned as an indefinite continuation, primarily through the generous support of his mother, Auguste.

Frege's groundbreaking *Begriffsschrift, eine der arithmetischen nachgebildete Formelsprache des reinen Denkens (Concept-Writing: A Formula-Language for Pure Thought Modeled on Arithmetic)* was published later in 1879. The *Begriffsschrift* is a fully algebraic formal symbolic concept-functional calculus. It is considered classical and even quaint today by those working on some contemporary far-reaching developments of the discipline Frege founded in 1879. The overlapping worlds of mathematics and philosophy at the time had never seen its like. Frege was an upstart. He thought he would be leading an army and turned around to see that no one was following or even understood his directions. Partly as a result of its novelty, to Frege's dismay the *Begriffsschrift* was neither enthusiastically received nor widely discussed. Although Frege was disappointed about the book's lack of impact, with the publication of the *Begriffsschrift* he had completed the first major step forward in a three-part explanation and defense of rigorous non-psychologistic logicism. The *Begriffsschrift* provided the formally expressive and deductively valid inferential tool by which Frege, in completing his philosophical design, graphically presented the underlying purely logical structures of arithmetical basic laws and elementary theorems. Let critics think and say what they will, with no sound objections raised, the logical machinery for Frege's logicism was now in place.

Algebraic Logical Structures

It is the *Concept-Script* or *Concept-Writing* in English. We rely on the German, as for Frege's other major works, and refer to it everywhere as the *Begriffsschrift*. We note that Frege's unprecedented choice of title was a declaration that something new and revolutionary lay between the book's pasteboard covers. Every language is a concept-script or concept-writing. We use ordinary or colloquial written language, German, English, Chinese, etc., to write about concepts. Frege had a special view of concepts (*Begriffe*), which he equated with functions (*Funktionen*), on formal constructive grounds, even as they appear in everyday language.

There is good reason to assume that Frege had been thinking for some time that logic was primarily a functional calculus of concept-functions. The evidence is that in 1879, when the *Begriffsschrift* was published, as its name significantly suggests, the logic was presented primarily as a logic not of objects, *Gegenstände, Entitäten, Objekte, Dinge*, but of concepts, *Begriffe*. Although individual objects and quantifications over objects distinguished by constants and several kinds of object variable made their appearance in Frege's logic from the outset, the formalism was designed predominantly as a calculus of incomplete, or "unsaturated" (*ungesättigte*), concept-functions that are not considered by Frege to be objects. The objects available for predication were not logic's direct concern, but were merely the existent entities comprehended in the logic's reference domain.

Frege's *Begriffsschrift* was an abstract formal logical language (*Formelsprache*, more literally formula-language) of pure thinking (*des reinen Denkens*), as Frege explained, modeled on arithmetic (*der arithmetischen nachgebildete*). The reference to "pure thinking" further suggested a Kantian influence that may have been part of Frege's background education, reinforced after his course at Göttingen with Fischer on Kant's Critical Idealism. Scholarly familiarity with Kant's philosophy seems in several ways to pepper Frege's logical and mathematical terminology, if not his thinking.

Frege's appeal to arithmetic as a model for the ideal formula language of the *Begriffsschrift* accounted for itself at least in part as an expression of his desire to apply a concept-writing in the first instance to an "elucidation" of the concept-functions of number and quantity, which are among the most basic ideas of elementary arithmetic. He offered the following summary:

> Arithmetic, as I said at the beginning, was the starting point of the train of thought which led me to my "conceptual notation." I intend, therefore, to apply it to this science first, trying to analyse its concepts further and provide a deeper foundation for its theorems. For the present, I have presented in the third chapter some things which move in that direction. Further pursuit of the suggested course – the elucidation of the concepts of number, magnitude, and so forth – is to be the subject of further investigations which I shall produce immediately after this book.[1]

Frege discerned nothing of methodological concern in the idea of using arithmetic as a *model* for a formal symbolic logic. The functional calculus of the *Begriffsschrift* was given safe harbor to pursue its reduction of the basic laws of elementary arithmetic to the concepts and inference rules of pure logic, without risking a whirlpool of explicit circularity. Perhaps no other logic, unless also modeled on arithmetic in another way, could possibly be adequate to the task of rigorously formalizing arithmetical rules and theorems as purely logical principles.

Was Frege's project nevertheless not committed from the outset to using and hence presupposing arithmetic? Did it not do so in order to explain arithmetic as resting entirely on concepts and principles of pure logic? Frege's logicism needed to rigorously prove that elementary arithmetic had the logical structure of elementary logic. It would turn out to be the logic of Frege's applied symbolic logical language that was "modeled"

---

[1] Frege, *Conceptual Notation* (Bynum's translation of the *Begriffsschrift*), p. 107.

on that of elementary arithmetic, by which Frege meant especially algebra. Frege's was a Platonist, analytic, and constructive rationalist endeavor in the cause of his signature style of logically–mathematically rigorous non-psychologistic philosophical logicism. It is perhaps unkind but nonetheless true to say that in the history of philosophy ideological rationalism has frequently been afflicted by fundamental circularities in its definitions and explanations, leaving its gravity-defying philosophical foundations capable of being upheld more by insistent will than by rigorous argument. We see something like this intransigence in Frege's case. He laid down rules. They were obvious to him. They were the spoil of his mathematical intuitions. We can like them or not. If we accept them, even hypothetically, even if only for the sake of argument, then he can teach us interesting things. If we do not accept Frege's rules, then he is powerless to persuade.

The publication of the *Begriffsschrift* in 1879 marked the first major advance toward bringing Frege's completed logicism into print. The great distinctive independent turning point in Frege's adult intellectual biography can accordingly be conservatively dated as early as 1873, possibly even before he had turned twenty-five, at least a year before he completed his Jena Habilitation while still at Göttingen. No one could have given him such an original idea, as was proved by the fact that virtually no one understood his major treatises immediately after their publication. In support of this historical hypothesis we can note that, at the time of production of his *Begriffsschrift*, Frege would have reached a realistic age for his maturing judgment skills and capabilities, and his assimilation of the mathematical training he had sought, to converge with life-shaping impressions, conversions, and commitments, in Frege's case to scientific philosophical and mathematical ideals. It could have been then that he knew what would be required of his abilities.

General Functional Calculus

The book was published in Halle, southern Saxony-Anhalt. Halle competed with Leipzig for much of the technical academic publishing in Germany at the turn of the nineteenth century. Frege could have done worse than have his first post-doctoral post-Habilitation book published by Verlag von Louis Nebert.

The printing of the text must have been extraordinarily demanding. It would have been a daunting technical challenge to prepare diagrams for Frege's two-dimensional logical expressions in a completely unprecedented formal symbolism. Today there are LaTeX editing tools for converting linear logical expressions to Frege's notation. In the steam-powered days before computer word and graphic image processing, Frege's obliging publisher and press would have had no previously set type on which to rely or that they could modify in producing the book. Almost everything in Frege's *Begriffsschrift* had to be specially built. The fonts for pages crammed full of symbols meant that each distinct logical pictogram in the logic had to be individually designed according to specific symbolic require-ments unique to Frege. Nearly as many lead type or copper plate inserts were needed to print the book's roughly ninety densely symbolic pages, assuming that entire pages were set with all logical formulas. The latter could have been individually cut and then assembled into sides, expediting the work if several hands were engaged in setting each page.

What logical notation did Frege propose? Frege's *Begriffsschrift* sym-bolism is unusual. It is easy to see why its spatially two-dimensional graphic display is sometimes compared with the pictorial representations of chemical structures, valences, attractions, forces, combinations, strength of bonds, and other items of theoretical chemistry that Frege would have studied at Wismar and Jena. The analogy between chemistry and logic is also remotely Kantian, and may have contributed to Frege's sense of the rightness of the formalism. It was Kant who in the eighteenth century, as the natural science of chemistry was beginning to emerge from its experimental alchemical origins, distinguished in philosophy between analytic and synthetic judgments on the model of the parallel division between chemical analysis and synthesis. As the names signify, analytic judgments are those whose truth-values can be determined by understanding the meaning of a proposition as one in which the concept of the predicate is contained and hence can be analyzed from or out of the concept of the predication subject. The hackneyed application, for which there does not seem to be a wealth of good alternatives, is that of a bachelor in one of its meanings being an unmarried male adult.

First came the numbers, then an arithmetic of numbers. The Fregean analysis of the concept of number and Frege's uniquely original concept-writing, expressions involving arithmetical functions predicated of numbers, was meant to set pictorially before the reader's eyes the incontestable fact so obvious to Frege that the foundations of arithmetic and ultimately of all mathematics were purely logical. Contrary to Kant, Frege maintained that the absolute presuppositional ground of arithmetic was not time as a pure form of perception or intuition, but instead pure abstract logic. He persisted in this expectation until the project failed with the same transparency as it had been intended to introduce to foundational abstract studies as Frege's methodological ideal in the philosophy of mathematics. Frege's logicism above all was not to be objectionably psychologistic, a limit that Kant's pure form of the *experience* of objects existing in time might be considered as exceeding. Frege found the conceptual grounds of elementary arithmetic instead in the objective purely abstract laws and inference structures of logic, and in a purely logical concept-function of number. The functional calculus was essential for Frege's philosophical purposes, because there must be functions applied to a single existent number successively to produce the entire run of natural numbers. We can begin with o or 1, providing we can show that they exist, building up all other numbers by means of arithmetical operations, all literally functional in the exact technical sense that Frege reserved for more detailed explanation in his 1891 and 1892 essays.

The *Bauplan*

In the first paragraphs of §1 of his *Begriffsschrift* Frege distinguished between constant and variable terms. He explained why as follows: "*I adopt this fundamental idea of distinguishing two kinds of symbols*, which unfortunately is not strictly carried through in the theory of magnitudes [quantities, extensions], *in order to use it for the more inclusive domain of pure thought in general.* I therefore divide all the symbols I employ into *those which one can take to signify various things* and *those which have a completely fixed sense.*"[2] Frege in note *) at the bottom of the first page of his *Begriffsschrift* significantly mentioned as examples the signs for an applied arithmetic. He singled out for emphasis the signs for the object 1 and Lim. (limit in the calculus), and the functions log (logarithm) and sin (the sine function in trigonometry).[3]

Frege's presentation of a symbolic logic of quantity in the general functional calculus, and its use in the expression of judgments, themes of traditional logic, began with an intuitively reasonable introduction of notation. He

---

[2] *Ibid.*, p. 111.   [3] Frege, note to the *Begriffsschrift, Ibid.*

unveiled the previously undocumented sign " $|$ —," which he explained as a combination of two simpler signs. The symbol features the *Inhaltsstrich* (content stroke) "—," which represents that a true or false assertion is to follow. If we did not already know that the proposition A (Frege's example) was being *asserted*, or if it was important for logical inferential or other reasons to make this explicit, then in Frege's *Begriffsschrift* we are expected to write — A. The second component sign attached is the leftmost bounding *Urteilsstrich* (judgment stroke) " $|$." It means that the proposition following the complete judgment + content stroke expresses the assertion that a proposition with the content of sentence A is true, $|$— A. A distinction between a proposition's being true and its being judged to be true was worked in this way into the logical-semantic fabric of Frege's *Begriffsschrift* from the outset. How Frege's choice did not bring psychologism in a form Frege himself later found objectionable in the writings of others, where it may be even more egregious, is a subject for further discussion that takes philosophical criticism beyond immediate biographical relevance. Writing $|$— A means only that A is judged true, asserted or pronounced true. Application of a truth assertion sign by itself cannot guarantee that what is said to be true is in fact true.

We can only judge as being true something that has propositional content. We must first know that a term "A," which in principle could conventionally designate anything, is an appropriate subject of judgment and of being judged true or false. Consequently, we never encounter " $|$ A" in Frege's *Begriffsschrift*, although by asserting that A has propositional judgment-worthy content in symbolizing — A we do not yet or thereby automatically pronounce judgment on the sign-content's truth, as we do by adding the *Urteilsstrich* to the *Inhaltsstrich*, in order to obtain $|$— A. Frege's use of these combined terms did not assert that A is true, and was not intended to do so, but only to assert that it is judged or asserted to be true. Frege's *Urteilsstrich* is literally a *judgment*-stroke, and nothing more. Wittgenstein understood this intended distinction correctly, which he then went on to disparage, in the parenthetical remark of *Tractatus* 4.442:

(Frege's assertion sign [Wittgenstein conflates the two parts and speaks only of the *Urteilsstrich*, which is admittedly the business end of the sign] " $|$—" is logically altogether meaningless; in Frege (and Russell) it only shows that these authors hold as true the propositions marked this way . . .).[4]

---

[4] Ludwig Wittgenstein, *Tractatus Logico-Philosophicus* (London: Routledge & Kegan Paul, 1922).

Naturally, one imagines Frege (and Russell) protesting that this does not make the sign *meaningless*. It is *unsinnig* only according to Wittgenstein's early picture theory of meaning in concert with Wittgenstein's general form of proposition in the *Tractatus*. Rather, Frege (and Russell) understood the sign as expressive of the judgment that a more deeply embedded sign ("*A*"), indicated by the *Inhaltsstrich* as possessing propositional content, is true in an application of *Begriffsschrift* logical notation. That is something that outside of Wittgenstein's *Tractatus* might well be either true or false (it is true or false that the sign with attached designation of its propositional content is judged true), and hence cannot be as Wittgenstein maintains "logically altogether meaningless."

Frege proceeded in §5 to explain "Conditionality" (*Bedingtheit*). The symbolism went on to spread its wings on the pages of Frege's text in spatially two-dimensional pictograms of increasing complexity and internal articulation. Whereas some propositional logics today prefer to begin with conjunction or disjunction, together with negation, which Frege's *Begriffsschrift* logic was also the first formalism fully capable of expressing, Frege began with what today is known as the material conditional. It is the proposition that links the truth-value of one proposition to its logical dependence on that of another in an if-then relation. The logical connection is expressed in ordinary language in such examples as "If B [is true] then A [is true]." Frege pictorially represented the logical structure whereby the truth of proposition A conditionally depends on the truth of proposition B, in a formula that in its entirety symbolizes the fact that it is judged true that if B is true then A is true.

The conditional gains entrance to logic on such an assignment of meanings to its component propositions exactly when it is judged (truly or falsely) that, if proposition B is true, then proposition A is true. Frege's *Begriffsschrift* symbolized the relation in a complete statement of the conditional form that Frege presented as his first two-dimensionally diagrammed logical structure of a basic conditional proposition, "If B then A," which is symbolized in *Begriffsschrift*:

Was Wittgenstein right to think that such an assertion is nonsensical or "logically meaningless"? Frege could say in his defense that not any and every sign had propositional content. This fact where it obtains must therefore be made explicit in an adequately expressive logical notation. Frege offered the counterexample of "house," for which the *Inhaltsstrich* formula "— house" would be false, and therefore not meaningless. Second, it is logically important, Frege would presumably maintain in defense of his *Begriffsschrift* logical notation, that, in order for the conditional, "If *B* then *A*," to enter into logical consideration, thought at least ideally or in the abstract must judge it to be true.

The conditional in and of itself is then expressed, without specifying what further propositions, if any, a molecular proposition *B* and a molecular proposition *A* might symbolize. By Frege's definitions of the basic truth-functions negation and material conditional, if either *B* is the proposition *C* and not-*C* (contradiction) or *A* is the proposition that it is not the case that both *C* and not-*C* are true (tautology), or both, then the conditional, If *B* then *A*, will be logically true. It will then be a tautology provable as a theorem of Frege's logic of quantity, in the propositional branch of the predicate-quantificational calculus. If, however, proposition *B* (shown in Frege's notation by the *Inhaltsstrich* sign to possess propositional content or *Inhalt*) symbolizes the proposition that "Grass is green," and *A* the proposition that "Snow is white," then the conditional, "If grass is green then snow is white," will not be logically true, even if it is materially true as a contingent fact about the world, and hence not a theorem of logic.

The above sample of basic concept-writing in Frege's logic says nothing other than is linearly expressible as the material conditional, "If *B* then *A*," or, in contemporary non-Fregean symbolism, $B \rightarrow A$ or $B \supset A$. The dependence of the truth-value of *A* on the truth-value of *B* in the diagram is represented by the fact that, in the judgment overall, reading from bottom to top, the propositional content of *B* comes before the propositional content of *A*. It is the same as in colloquial expression when we say, conventionally, mentioning *B* first or as having logical priority to *A*, "If *B* then *A*." We do not say by means of the expression that *A* is true *simpliciter*, but rather that *A* is true only *if* or *given* the truth of *B*. Insofar as the limited implications of the material conditional are concerned, the condition in proposition *B* might not after all be true, in which case the conditional as a whole is, by virtue of the definition of the operator, trivially true. The *Begriffsschrift* formula-picture shows graphically that the truth of *A* does not stand on its own, but materially depends on the truth of *B*.

The fact that Frege's logic required the *Urteilsstrich* to bring conditionals that are not *logically* true or false into the formalism's logical expression suffices to show that in his *Begriffsschrift* Frege did not limit himself to axiomatic systems of logic and mathematics alone. His ambition was to encompass mathematical reasoning, including those non-axiomatized inferential logics sometimes known today as natural deduction systems. Any proposition can be assumed true in Frege's logic, in order to determine what consequences may deductively follow, regardless of whether or not the proposition is an axiom, theorem, or tautology. *Reductio* reasoning generally requires an assumption of a proposition whose falsehood is determined when its implications contradict other more respectably adduced assumptions.

The Birth of Modern Logic

How did Frege carry algebraic logic forward into the late nineteenth century from the promising start but ultimately disappointing achievement of antiquated Aristotelian syllogistic term logic? An oversimplified but nonetheless accurate answer is that Frege created modern symbolic logic by his discovery/invention of truth-functional propositional negation.

Frege did so, moreover, in a way that in retrospect seems obvious. The essential idea was to interpret "not," in such propositions as "It is not the case that there is a greatest prime number," as a specific kind of *function* on propositional contents. Frege introduced the negation of the content of a meaningful sentence, along with a workhorse truth-function for the "if-then" conditional. The combination enabled logic to say "*If* it is *not* the case (*not* true) that there is a greatest prime number, *then* (it is true that) for any number there exists a method for constructing an even greater prime number." With truth-functional negation and the if-then material conditional, Frege covered all that can be expressed in what nowadays is denominated classical propositional logic. It is all that the underlying functional calculus of Frege's *Begriffsschrift* truth-functionally required. The same holds true for any truth-functionally equivalent or derivative logic based on the substructure of Frege's propositional logic, including all of classical logic from Frege's time to the present. Frege made all this available to the study of formal symbolic logic as early as 1879.

A term logic like Aristotle's and later developments is a system of logical structures that considers nothing more fundamental than the unanalyzable predications of instantiated properties to objects. Term logic takes as its terms in classical form predicational elements of the A–E–I–O categorical propositions of the canonical Aristotelian–Boethian square of opposition. The Aristotelian categoricals are (A) "All S is P," (E) "No S is P," or, equivalently, (E*) "All S is non-P," (I) "Some S is P," and (O) "Some S is non-P." The terms in all instances are S is P or S is non-P, in both universal and particular quantifications of predication subject S. The attribution of a complementary non-P property is equally a predicative term of the logic. Term logic terms are already given to logic, and the inference structures are rigid, making it a sometimes frustrating puzzle to fit actual reasoning and discourse to the syllogistic model.

A fully algebraic logic like Frege's in contrast treats its subject matter more combinatorially. There are as unlimitedly many constructions for logic to consider as there are in the algebraic formulations of elementary arithmetic. Frege's *Begriffsschrift* functional calculus combines proper names or constants for objects with predicates, representing concepts interpreted as unsaturated functions. The logic immediately comprehends predications of structurally unlimited internal logical complexity for all possible selections of objects and concepts, argument-objects and concept-functions, to a range of truth-functions and quantifier operations in vastly more possibilities than those afforded by three- or four-term predications in classical or Victorian syllogisms of three or more categorical propositions.

Concepts were functions for Frege, expressed in language by means of predicates. If we consider a concept-function like $\text{Red}(\underline{\ \ }) = v$, then we can complete the function by saying that some existent object a is red, $\text{Red}(a) =$ the True. There were functions in Frege's *Begriffsschrift* logic with specific input and correlated output, just as there are in arithmetic. A complete statement of functionalized predications relates the attribution of a predicate to an object as identical to some output value, $\text{Red}(\underline{\ \ }) = v$ and even $\text{Red}(a) = v$. Frege eventually identified predications with their truth-values, the True or the False. The employment of the same pattern for functional analysis and true or false predications of concepts interpreted as unsaturated functions to existent objects is the general manner by which Frege's *Begriffsschrift* was supposed to be a formula-language modeled on the algebraic combinatorics of elementary arithmetic. This is the sense in which the subtitle of Frege's first post-Habilitation book promised a logic formally modeled on the language of arithmetic.

Frege spoke from early on in this context of "thoughts" or *Gedanken*, where modern logic and semantics, in company with the present exposition, tend to speak of propositions, statements, or assertions. Frege afterward treated the relevant truth-values of thoughts referentially as reified entities, the True and the False. Negation as a truth-function in classical bivalent semantics takes a proposition's truth-value as input argument-object and outputs the one and only contrary truth-value. If a proposition p is true (refers to the True), then the negation of p, not-p, is false (refers to the False). Conversely, if proposition p is false (refers to the False), then the negation of p is true (refers to the True). Interesting intuitive results follow, as when we note that the negation of the negation of a proposition's truth-value is truth-functionally equivalent to the proposition's original truth-value. Double-negation equivalences are highlighted by Frege in the *Begriffsschrift* as among the system's logical axioms, collected also in the basic logical laws of Frege's 1893/1903 *Grundgesetze*.

Frege introduced propositional negation in the form of a negation sign to the history of logic in the following deservedly famous passages:

NEGATION

§7. If a small vertical stroke is attached to the underside of the content stroke [horizontal], this is to express the circumstance that *the content does not occur*. Thus, for example,

means: "*A* does not occur." I call this small vertical stroke the *negation stroke*. The part of the horizontal stroke to the right of the negation stroke is the content stroke of *A*; while the part to the left of the negation stroke is the content stroke of the negation of *A*. Here, as in other places in the "conceptual notation," without the judgement stroke, no judgement is made.

calls upon us merely to form the idea that *A* does not occur, without expressing whether this idea is true.[5]

In contrast, despite the algebraization of much of Aristotelian–Victorian syllogistic term logic by Frege's predecessor Boole, there was

---

[5] Frege, *Conceptual Notation* (Bynum's translation of the *Begriffsschrift*), p. 120.

no propositional negation in Boole. The omission was deliberate on Boole's part, because he knew, or at least intuited, sensed in his logician's heart, that, if propositional negation were included, then the logic would be subject to formal semantic paradoxes. Boole accordingly made do instead with predicate complementation, as Aristotle did in his original syllogistic logic, which was imitated by later adherents in modernized term logics.

Term logic distinguishes between the property F and its complement, the internally negated non-F, which is also sometimes written with a flat bar over the "F," neither of which, being a mere property term, has truth-value. The contrast in Frege's logic is with the true or false predication Fa and its truth-functional propositional or external negation not-Fa (or, it is not the case that Fa). An externally negated proposition, which Frege introduced to logic historically for the first time, unlike a predicate complement term, has truth-value. It is often formalized in contemporary symbolic logic by the "intensional" negation sign "$\neg$," as in $\neg Fa$, or by equivalents $-Fa$ or $\sim Fa$. Frege's logic recognized the truth-value of externally negated propositions, whereas the Aristotelian–Victorian partially algebraized logic of Boole worked with predicate complement terms that by themselves in non-F did not have truth-value and in complete predications of the form non-Fa had truth-values that were not systematically truth-functionally related to the truth-value of Fa.

Without propositional negation, Boole's algebraization of an extended system of syllogistic term logic was unable to provide logical foundations for the inferential structures of mathematical reasoning as mathematics is actually practiced. It could not formalize a logic whereby mathematical theorems were derived in proofs and demonstrations from mathematical axioms generally, and especially not those involving *reductio ad absurdum* reasoning. With propositional negation as a truth-function in hand, we can plausibly and powerfully reconstruct the reasoning of Euclid's proof that there is no greatest prime number by allowing the false hypothesis that there exists a greatest prime number to logically contradict the proposition that a greater prime number can always be constructed from any number assumed to be the greatest prime. Frege allowed truth-functionally defined propositional negation to carry the expressive and inferential burden of indirect reasoning.

Frege was interested in something more fundamental than Boole's algebra of logic. He wanted to arrive at logical principles of mathematical reasoning that also applied to the particularities of Boole's mathematical system. He was interested in logical thinking in the most general sense that could take mathematics under its wing along with inferences concerning any and every other specialized subject matter. Frege's logic right from its 1879 debut in his *Begriffsschrift* was importantly different from Boole's not only by virtue of including propositional negation among its essential innovations. The irony is that by taking this step, as Boole had foreseen, Frege not only made *Begriffsschrift* logic capable of directly representing the logical structure of *reductio* among other types of distinctively mathematical reasoning, but at the same time released into his system the viper that would make it vulnerable to the kind of formal logical paradox that Russell eventually discovered.

Frege braved the torpedoes, introducing a notational device for truth-functional negation. He thereby made explicit the denial of the truth of a proposition, which is otherwise designated in contemporary linear logics by a choice of symbolisms, typified by the dash "–," tilde "~," or intuitionistic negation, "¬." The last of these three symbols is considered more stylish today and is no longer used characteristically for, or associated exclusively with, specifically intuitionistic logics or mathematics. The negation of proposition A is alternatively standardly symbolized as "$-A$," "$\sim A$," or "$\neg A$," meaning in every case that it is not-(true that)-A, or that it is not the case that proposition A (is true). Frege accomplished this for the first time in the history of logic and mathematics, surpassing Boole in this important respect by offering a different algebraic logic than Boole's that still shared his inspirational purpose of replacing Aristotelian syllogistic term logic with a more flexible and universal logical algebra.

Frege's notational device, interestingly not revealed until *Begriffsschrift* §7, was to append a short vertical downward-hanging twig to the *Inhaltsstrich* marking the relevant propositional sign as assertible. Frege introduced his negation sign in the simplest possible case, for a sign whose propositional content and judgment was indicated, and the negation pendant to the *Inhaltsstrich* showed that the proposition that A is *not the case*. It was in effect the top line of the following *Begriffsschrift* formula, without the truth of proposition A being shown to depend logically in the judgment in question on the truth of proposition B. To refine the previous example, we choose the above conditional in Frege's notation to make the same point. We can write "It is not the case that if B then A," or, using the

arrow → (alternatively horseshoe, ⊃), in linear logical expression, ¬[B →
A]. Frege writes, in more graphically informative fashion,

Propositional negation, also in Frege's first use of the truth-function,
toggles a proposition's truth-value from true to false or from false to true.
If it is true that B → A, then it is false that ¬[B → A], and conversely.
Frege operates throughout in a classical bivalent or two-truth-valued
propositional logical system, like the telegraph's dots and dashes. Every
genuine proposition is either true or false, and no proposition is both true
and false. External or propositional negation reverses a proposition's
truth-value, denying what the unnegated proposition affirms.

With these two proposition-building operations in place, with diagrammatic features for representing the material conditional and truth-functional
propositional negation, the combinatorial possibilities are unlimited. Frege
could construct from these basic units endlessly many different logical
formulas expressing endlessly many corresponding different propositions
in a fully algebraic symbolic logic of propositions. If we think of these two
propositional items in every possible combination, then we have a sense for
the expressive capability of this part of Frege's *Begriffsschrift*.

It is left as an exercise to try writing out in Frege's notation the
following variations of original conditionals, and then translating the
following page of expressions from later in Frege's text into the symbolism of contemporary linear logic. Start with these: ¬B → A, B → ¬A,
¬B → ¬A, ¬[¬B → A], ¬[B → ¬A], and ¬[¬B → ¬A]. Then advance
to more complex formulas involving more than two propositions, related
to one another by the conditional and negation logical connectives,
adding C, D, and E. Finally, work from Frege's two-dimensional
tipped-over candelabra notation back to linear expression for the propositions Frege considered prior to *Begriffsschrift* §8, shown in Figure 4.1.

The Logic of Mathematical Reasoning

Mathematicians have always been unimpressed by syllogistic logic, as
much in its classical formulation in Aristotle's old-school version as in its
four-term enhancements in the so-called Victorian syllogistics centering

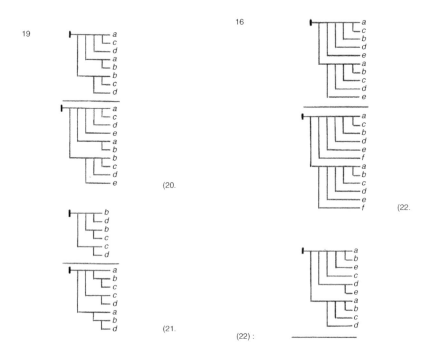

Figure 4.1 Some of Frege's Propositions

on the logic of William Hamilton.[6] It was the latter logic that Boole chose as the basis for his partial algebraization. Practicing mathematicians have also generally understood that their special forms of reasoning and proof structures presupposed some sort of logic. As of this late point in nineteenth-century logic and mathematics, no one until Frege had succeeded in developing an adequate symbolic model to formally represent the purely logical inferential structure of mathematical reasoning.

The four-term syllogistic, expanding on classical three-term languages, was a last-ditch effort to bolster Aristotelian term logic against

---

[6] See Ian Pratt-Hartmann, "The Hamiltonian Syllogistic," *Journal of Logic, Language and Information*, 20 (2011), pp. 445–74, on William Hamilton's efforts to improve traditional expressibility in a four-term Aristotelian syllogistic term logic. John Venn and others stretched the syllogistic to its limits, but still lacked a plausible formal representation of *reductio ad absurdum* inference in mathematical proof that for Frege was a *sine qua non* of an adequate symbolic logic. Franz Brentano similarly made limited unpublished contributions toward the four-term syllogistic. See Peter Simons, "Judging Correctly, Brentano and the Reform of Elementary Logic," in *The Cambridge Companion to Brentano*, ed. Dale Jacquette (Cambridge: Cambridge University Press, 2004), pp. 45–65.

its inevitable replacement by a fully algebraic logic that was formalized for the first time in the history of logic in Frege's *Begriffsschrift*. If logic were going to explain mathematical reasoning, it would need to surpass Aristotelian–Victorian logic. The time was ripe for the idea. It was catching on more or less spontaneously and simultaneously in Frege's Germany, Peano's Italy, Russell's England, and Peirce's United States, to mention only some of the best known protagonists and the countries in which they were working. Frege's *Begriffsschrift* logic, with its astonishing systematization and philosophical motivations, stands out in part because of Frege's determination and intellectual integrity. We know the craftsworker from his or her work, and in Frege's case we may feel that we can sometimes accurately discern the individual's personality characteristics in the scientific, philosophical, or literary productions to which their hand was turned.

Boole showed the way toward algebraization of a more flexible logic than the best the nineteenth century had to offer. His logical forms were still not fully combinatorial, and as such were not fully algebraic. They obeyed instead a slate of rules that remained wedded to the general structure of term logical syllogistic reasoning. Frege opened the door to expressive and inferential capabilities in logic with greater expectations for what a logical formalism ought to be able to do. He did so particularly, but of course not only or in the majority of cases, by adequately representing the deductively valid logical inference structures of indirect proof or *reductio* reasoning in mathematics. The only way to accommodate the *reductio* reasoning so prevalent in mathematical proof was to introduce a special rule saying that from "All S is P" and "Some S is non-P," to illustrate with the logically weakest form, any proposition follows deductively. If the proposition deemed responsible for the conjunction "All S is P" and "Some S is non-P" is that S^* is P^* or S^* is non-P^*, then we can certainly track deductive validity through an instance of *reductio* reasoning like that showcased in Euclid's proof that there is no greatest prime number. We do so unfortunately without guidance among the valid inference patterns in traditional syllogistic logic, and with no insight into the logical justification for inferring anything whatsoever from a contradiction, *ex falso quodlibet*.

The trouble that continues to disrecommend a syllogistic logic, consistently leading one to prefer Frege's to a purely algebraic remodeling of logical expression and inference, is that term logic considers only two permissible contradiction forms, for the A and O and E and I categoricals in the canonical square of oppositions, paired up as "All S is P" and "Some S is non-P," and "All S is non-P" and "Some S is P." These are the A–O and E–I cross-corner categoricals in the square. Mathematical reasoning, in contrast, sometimes involves contradictions of a more basic logical type, as when inconsistency turns on the conjunction that number N is the greatest prime together with its independently deduced absurd negation. We do not want to trivialize generality by allowing an interpretation whereby we speak of every number that is identical to N. It is not clear that such a conditionalization of categoricals is permitted in Aristotelian–Victorian term logic, even when partially algebraized as in Boole. Can we convert the hypothesis that number N is the greatest prime to "All S has property P of being the greatest prime number"? Whatever we may think of N, not everything can be the greatest prime number, because not everything is a number, not all numbers are prime, and not all prime numbers can be the greatest prime number, even if there exists a greatest prime number.[7]

That excludes the A–O contradiction in term logic, at least on the classical Aristotelian model. What then of the remaining E–I contradiction in the canonical square of opposition? For that suggestion to work, we need to begin with a much weaker I-form generalization, whereby we advance from N is the greatest prime number to the E-form, "All S is non-(Greatest prime number)." This internal term negation unsurprisingly contradicts the

---

[7] See John Corcoran, "Aristotle's Demonstrative Logic," *History and Philosophy of Logic*, 30 (2009), pp. 1–20; especially pp. 9–10 and 13. As Corcoran rightly observes, p. 9, "Since there are no 'truth-functional constants' [in Aristotle's syllogistic logic], there is no way to form negations, double negations, conjunctions, or any other 'truth-functional combinations' of categorical propositions. Aristotle took the *contradictory opposite* [A–O and E–I categorical pairs in syllogistic logic, shown at cross-corners in the canonical subsyllogistic square of opposition] of a proposition to serve some of the purposes we are accustomed to assigning to the negation." Corcoran's category of demonstrative logic, which he attributes to Aristotle's *Prior Analytics*, of demonstration as distinct from persuasion, is, as Corcoran acknowledges, a Socratic epistemic distinction that would likely not be congenial to Frege's anti-psychologism and desire for the mind-independence of logical concepts and inference. Corcoran's reconstructions of *reductio* arguments appear sound, but are not syllogistic. The indirect inferences are modeled on an ideal that Corcoran's reconstructions only imperfectly approximate, namely that of a fully algebraic general logic of concept-functions equipped with truth-functional negation. The task is to bring the syllogistic as near to a Fregean general functional calculus as the limits of Aristotelian logic permit. Corcoran's schema for *reductio* arguments involves stacking abbreviations of entire propositions that conceal rather than exhibit the internal logical structures by which deductively valid indirect inferences are supposed to proceed.

I-form, "Some S is the greatest prime number." If N is assumed to be the greatest prime number, then it is assumed that "Some S is the greatest prime number" (namely, N). That assumption already looks dangerous enough to support a contradiction. So it is, or should be, even to the untrained eye, but only in the right inferential framework. The question is whether a modernized classical term logic supports a contradiction with I-form propositions from a *reductio* hypothesis together with background assumptions in a deductively valid application of *reductio* mathematical reasoning, resulting in an E-form categorical. Even if such an ingenious explication could be devised, it would not do justice to the far simpler surface logical structure of *reductio* reasoning as it actually occurs in mathematics.

Moreover, in this application we need to state what the argument aspires to prove, and hence to reason in a blatantly vicious circle, where the E-form, if true, categorically excludes the possibility of there being a greatest prime number. That is not how Euclid's reasoning works. It is where the contradiction takes him after some effort, but it is certainly not the contradiction's starting-place. Nor is there guidance in traditional syllogistic term logic for handling contradictions once one has in hand the only two forms that can stand as contradictories, following out in *reductio* reasoning upon the falsehood of a hypothesis that is shown to contribute to implying a contradiction. These observations make it a travesty of formalization requirements to try representing the logical form of Euclid's proof in Aristotelian–Victorian term logic. Euclid assumed that there is a greatest prime number, and then showed how a greater prime number can be constructed given the hypothetical greatest prime number's position in the number line. Frege confronted the identical argument form for mathematical theorems many times in his work involving mathematical proofs, especially in analytic geometry. He accepted no pale substitute for a full-blooded explanation of the logical structure of indirect or *reductio* and other kinds of reasoning needed in logical derivations of mathematical proofs.

Frege anticipated applications of a symbolic logic adequate to represent the inferential structure of *reductio ad absurdum* or indirect proof reasoning when he continued as follows:

The same holds for negation. For example, in an indirect proof we say, "Suppose that the line segments AB and CD were not equal." Here the content – that line segments AB and CD are not equal – contains a negation; but this content, although it could be a judgement, is not presented as a judgement. Negation attaches therefore to the content, whether or not it occurs as a judgement. I therefore consider it more appropriate to regard negation as a characteristic {*Merkmal*} of an *assertible content*.[8]

Touching on psychology was already objectionable to Frege's ingrained enmity toward psychologism in the conceptual foundations of logic and mathematics. Boole's language sometimes slipped around, but for his defenders he never explicitly strayed into anything Frege could reasonably consider an objectionable form of psychologism. Boole admitted, here as elsewhere, that his project was *normative* in the sense that, in discovering the laws of thought psychologically, following a defensible empirical methodology in the only place where data could be found, the only place where the study of logic could begin, he discovered what are in fact *laws* of thought. The laws of thought offer prescriptions as to how thinking subjects *should* reason, rather than how they always or statistically in fact most often reason.

Classically, as in Frege's *Begriffsschrift*, a proposition is exclusively either true or false. The negation of a proposition is true if and only if the proposition is false. *Reductio* inference capitalizes on this toggling of truth-value from a proposition to its negation and back. We assume in *reductio* the negation of a proposition we are trying to prove, and we deduce from the hypothesis a contradiction, another proposition *and* its negation, on the strength of which we reject the hypothetically assumed proposition as false. The reasoning is semantically justified, once truth-functional propositional negation has been made available to logic. No true proposition, only a falsehood, can support the logically valid deduction of a logical contradiction or syntactical inconsistency. Contradiction is a clear sign of false assumption, and it is often the hypothesized negation of the proposition to be proved.[9]

It was the world's first such logic, as Frege well knew. It should have taken off like a rocket. Instead it fizzled and spluttered on the pavement. It was a disappointment to the publisher, and it was castigated by almost all reviewers, distinguished mathematical and philosophical experts alike, including some of Frege's Jena mathematics colleagues, the latter of whom, trying to be generous to a younger colleague, often could do no more than mention their expectations of worthwhile research from the promising newly appointed mathematician in the future. Their attitude

---

[8] Frege, *Conceptual Notation* (Bynum's translation of the *Begriffsschrift*), p. 114.
[9] See note 5 in Chapter 3, and note 28 below in this chapter.

was that there was no point in climbing all over him for his first effort, especially when his ideas were not very clearly understood. At the book-sellers, though not in tall stacks running the bookshelves' length, Frege's *Begriffsschrift* could now be purchased for just 3 Marks, were anyone sufficiently interested in possessing a copy.[10] There were internal and external reasons why Frege's 1879 logic did not light up the night sky.

The *Begriffsschrift* Square of Opposition

We turn now to the second major component of Frege's *Begriffsschrift* logic. It epitomized a development in which Frege's originality and logical insight were more fully exploited.

Frege had to find a way to talk about quantities of things. He needed a rigorous vehicle of expression for the numbers or magnitudes of objects to which properties can be predicated when taken as the arguments of formally well-defined functions. To press the comparison again for the sake of those more familiar with contemporary logical symbolism than with Frege's innovations, Frege needed, as did Aristotelian–Victorian syllogistic term logic, to be able to speak of *every* thing or *all* and *some* things having a property. He further had to be able to write out all syntax combinations formulable using the material conditional and negation. Aristotelian logic combines terms for properties, and establishes the range of their logical interrelations in four basic forms, known mnemonically as A–E–I–O cate-gorical propositions. The propositions are associated with those four vowels in the classic alphabetical device for displaying their subsyllogistic logical interrelations in the canonical Aristotelian square of opposition, where categorical A = "All S is P"; E = "All S is non-P," or, equivalently, "No S is P"; I = "Some S is P"; and O = "Some S is non-P."

Standard predicate-quantificational logic today for convenience uses two interdefinable quantifiers. They range over a domain of objects for which specific subsumption relations are supposed to hold. They imply that, if "All S is P," then every object in the domain included in the extension of predicate "S" is included also in the subdomain extension of predicate "P." The two convenient quantifiers are interdefinable as standing to one

---

another in a duality relation. Modern post-Fregean *Begriffsschrift* logic expresses the relation as the *universal quantification*, $\forall x[Sx \rightarrow Px]$. It says that everything in the logic's reference domain of existent entities is such that, if it has property S, if it is the subject of predication, then it has property P. *Existential quantification*, in parallel fashion, expresses the term logic quantification by which "Some S is P," standardly, $\exists x[Sx \wedge Px]$. The sentence means that something, at least one object belonging to the logic's reference domain of existent entities, is such that it possesses both property S and property P. It says that there exists something that has the property of being predication subject S and having additionally property P. The issue of whether Frege's transcriptions and efforts to map *Begriffsschrift* equivalents of these quantificational expressions onto the canonical Aristotelian square of term logic oppositions were correct will be addressed after explaining Frege's symbolic quantificational conventions.[11]

Frege provided in effect a typed logic of object, first- and second-order functional ("two-level") predicate logics. Each is marked by a distinct choice of Latin, Greek, and *gotische-Fraktur* (German "Gothic") letters of the alphabet in the semicircular depression wells or dimples that are inscribed along the content-stroke (*Inhaltsstrich*) or horizontal lines of *Begriffsschrift* generalizations. These variables function logically like their counterparts in linear *Principia Mathematica*-style quantificational logics. They bind orthographically identical occurrences of variables attached to predicates within their respectively distinguished scopes, delineated by the sometimes overlapping right-extending lengths of content-strokes. A quantifier-bound variable in an *Inhaltsstrich* depression binds any occurrence of the variable anywhere to its right proceeding along the same *Inhaltsstrich*. Frege's logic was a groundbreaking predicate-quantificational logical formalism, a second-order predicate logic, or, as Frege preferred, a two-level general functional calculus. It was a logic of concept-functions, existent objects, and second-level concept-functions of first-level concept-functions. Frege referred to the logic in the *Begriffsschrift*, and already in his Jena Habilitationsschrift, as a *Größenlehre*, translatable as a theory of magnitude or quantity, or more literally of size.

---

[11] A classic rewarding overview is that by Otto A. Bird, *Syllogistic and its Extensions* (Englewood Cliffs: Prentice-Hall, 1964).

It was by means of a quantificational logic, in which Frege could speak of all or some objects having this or that property or having this or that function applied to them, that Frege expected to ground mathematics in concepts and principles of pure logic. The logic was needed in working through the logical foundations of essential concepts, expression of basic laws, and derivation of elementary arithmetical theorems. Frege began with observations about the function of quantification in cognitive judgment:

§4 ... People distinguish *universal* and *particular* judgements: this is really not a distinction between judgements, but between contents. *They should say, "a judgement with a universal content," "a judgement with a particular content."* These properties belong to the content even when it is put forth, not as a judgement, but as an [unasserted] proposition. (See §2).[12]

Later, in §11, Frege turns to the topic of generality or quantification, which is effectively to say that of All or Every operations. Frege was familiar with the duality between basic quantifiers, whereby to say that "Every S is P" is logically equivalent to saying that "Not some S is non-P or is not P," as *Begriffsschrift* truth-functional negation allows. He introduces the basic concepts for this important part of his formal theory in the following terms.

GENERALITY [*Die Allgemeinheit*]

§11. In the expression of a judgement we can always regard the combination of symbols to the right of | — as a function of one of the symbols occurring in it. *If we replace this argument by a German letter and introduce in the content stroke a concavity containing the same German letter, as in*

$$\vdash\!\!-\!\!\underset{\mathfrak{a}}{\cup}\!\!-\!\!-\!\!-\Phi\,(\mathfrak{a})$$

then this stands for the judgement that the function is a fact whatever we may take as its argument.[13]

There follow the above-mentioned conventions on variables of several distinct types, adopted by Frege in the *Begriffsschrift* to express several different kinds of generalized predications. For his purpose, Frege

---

[12] Frege, *Conceptual Notation* (Bynum's translation of the *Begriffsschrift*), p. 114.
[13] *Ibid.*, p. 130.

introduces a shallow depression or well in the formula's *Inhaltsstrich* to accommodate a variable of the appropriate category. The logic is capable of expressing several kinds of quantifications. By means of the convention, Frege was able to say universally that *everything* is such that a certain description of conditions holds true. Scope ambiguities and quantifier collisions are neatly avoided in a visually lucid graphic way in Frege's *Begriffsschrift*. Let's have a look at a sample of Frege's use of his notation, combining the *Inhaltsstrich*, *Urteilsstrich*, truth-functional negation, and material conditional, together with a variety of variables for quantification over several kinds of objects. The Fregean formulas, looking like overturned candelabras, are reproduced in Figure 4.2 merely to show the visual appearance of Frege's notation in his *Begriffsschrift*, and the two-dimensional syntactical complications of which it is capable.

Begriffsschrift expressions began to look more complex at this stage. They became increasingly capable, in their intricacies, of doing justice to the kinds of mathematical relation among concepts for mathematical objects (the number 0 or 1, or the concept of the number 0 or 1, entering into the concept-script or concept-writing, for starters) and relevant mathematical concept-functions involved in Frege's plan to reduce all elementary arithmetic to the principles of pure logic. Frege's notation for quantification delivered the multiplicity of logical divisions he needed to express the elementary relations invoked in explaining the foundations of arithmetic. Although Frege's *Begriffsschrift* was meant to have all the generality and particularity of quantification over objects required to express the fundamental laws of arithmetic, and ultimately all mathematics, it was also supposed more generally to possess a capacity for expressing the logical structures "of pure thought" (*des reinen Denkens*), as the title of the *Begriffsschrift*'s second chapter declares, again in terminology reminiscent of Kant. In the book's third chapter, the underlying logic of a general theory of series, which is essential to the logical foundations of arithmetic as the natural number progression, is generated by iterative applications of the Fregean equivalent of a Dedekind–Peano successor function of the basic form $+1(\underline{\quad}) = n$.

Existent objects in this programmatic logical reduction and reconstitution of elementary arithmetic are caught like fish in the logic's reference domain, a net symbolically cast into the sea of entities by judicious

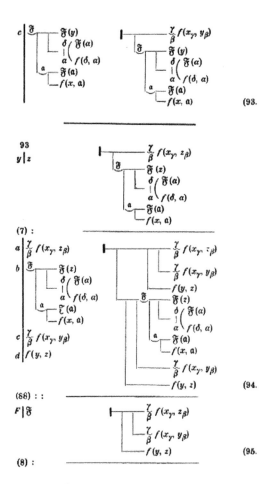

Figure 4.2 Fregean Formulas

formulation of universally generalized material conditionals. Quantifier duality involving negation permits all existential quantifications to be logically equivalently defined. Linear logic expresses the rule of quantifier duality more familiarly as $\forall x Fx \leftrightarrow \neg \exists x \neg Fx$. Informally, one hopes that an equivalent-sounding quantifier duality in this form, logically identical in meaning in many variants by contraposition and similar transformations, states that everything has property F if and only if there is nothing that fails to have property F.

Quantifier duality makes it possible in Frege's *Begriffsschrift* notation to make do in predicate-quantificational logic with only one of the quantifiers plus truth-functional negation. Frege for his purposes relied throughout his exposition of logical principles entirely on universal quantification. Truth-functional negation supports duality between existential and universal quantification, where the existential "Something is or has property f (or, as we prefer, F)" is written in the most basic application in original *Begriffsschrift* notation to say that it is not the case that for all objects it is not the case that the objects have property f (F). Not everything fails to have property f (F); something has property f (F):

$$\mathsf{T} \!\! \diagdown \!\! \mathsf{o} \!\! \diagup \!\! \mathsf{T} \!\! - f(a)$$

At the conclusion of the first chapter of the *Begriffsschrift*, Frege explained his logical notation in relation to the canonical Aristotelian square of opposition. The square was taught as part of standard logic instruction prior to Frege's new fully algebraic truth-functional logic of quantities. By exhibiting a *Begriffsschrift* version of the square, Frege may have hoped to make his symbolism accessible to old-fashioned syllogistic-logic-trained mathematicians, showing graphically how *Begriffsschrift* concepts matched up with the traditional Aristotelian ones. Whether or not Frege's early readers found it a satisfying transcription, there are several important mistakes in Frege's *Begriffsschrift* square.[14]

For comparison, Frege presented the canonical square of opposition, expressed informally or colloquially by means of A–E–I–O propositions at the corners of the square, in the manner shown in Figure 4.3. Without further preamble, Frege ended the chapter with his variation of the canonical Aristotelian–Boethean square, which is shown in Figure 4.4.

Frege made several misstatements in relating the four A–E–I–O categoricals reformulated in *Begriffsschrift* notation in the square. The errors are only partly compensated for by the existence restrictions implicitly presupposed in Frege's use of the symbolism, which have often been invoked by apologists for the *Begriffsschrift* square. The referential semantic domain of predication subjects to which

---

[14] *Ibid.*, p. 135.

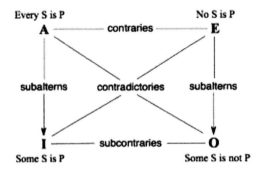

Figure 4.3 Colloquial Canonical Square of Opposition

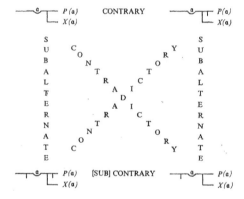

Figure 4.4 Frege's *Begriffsschrift* Square

Begriffsschrift predicates can meaningfully attach, over which quantifiers range, is limited to all and only existent entities. Even so, within their metalogical limitations, standard decision methods for predicate-quantificational logic do not allow A categoricals in the *Begriffsschrift* variant of the Aristotelian–Boethian square to stand formally as super-alterns to categoricals in Frege's square. The same is true of the relation between *Begriffsschrift* counterparts of classical categoricals E and O in the upper and lower right-hand corners of the square that Frege reproduced, and of that between A and E categoricals as contraries.

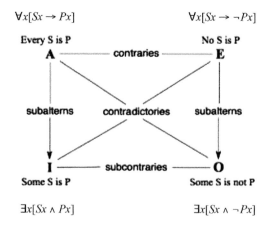

Figure 4.5 Transcription of Frege's Square into Contemporary Logical Notation

We shall overlook Frege's typo in making I and O categoricals contraries instead of subcontraries, as early editions of the *Begriffsschrift* published after Frege's death recommend. We offer Frege's retouched square in the notation of contemporary symbolic logic, in the form shown in Figure 4.5.

Frege's square in the *Begriffsschrift* and in contemporary transcription errs in several ways. It mistakenly describes I and O categoricals in his notation as "contraries" (abbreviated *conträr* in the lower line of Frege's original diagram), instead of "subcontraries." There is an important difference. Frege's lapse here may be a typesetter's fault, but it may also reflect the fact that Aristotelian syllogistic logic, which was then increasingly irrelevant to scientific study, was not taught enthusiastically at Gymnasium or university in Frege's apprenticeship years.

Contraries, like A and E categoricals in the canonical square, cannot both be true, but can both be false. That is not typically a situation encountered in mathematical proofs, although the possibility should not be discounted. However, subcontraries, as I and O categoricals are canonically supposed to be, are such that, although they cannot both be false, they can both be true. Frege's editors, in some later republications of his *Begriffsschrift*, noted the discrepancy. One of the editors of the second edition, the *zweite Auflage*, of Frege's *Begriffsschrift*, Edmund Husserl and Heinrich Scholz, added a footnote to the text: "[** Sollte offenbar 'subconträr' sein. Anm[erkung] d[es] Hrsgs [Herausgebers]," which translates as "Should obviously be 'subcontrary.' Editor's note."[15]

The correction is appreciated, but does not go far enough in resolving Frege's troubles in diagramming the *Begriffsschrift* square of oppositions. More important and logically interesting is the fact that A and E propositions in Frege's *Begriffsschrift* symbolization are not actually contraries. They could both be true, if, as in Frege's system, the conditional by which the universal quantifications in A and E propositions are true holds even when the antecedent (the if-part, B in the example "If B then A") of the conditional is false. Let A $= \forall x[Sx \rightarrow Px]$ and E $= \forall x[Sx \rightarrow \neg Px]$, then, if there exists no S, both Fregean algebraic A and E categoricals are true by default, further implying that they cannot be square-of-opposition contraries. A similar problem, usually interpreted as the result of an implicit existence presupposition in Frege's quantificational logic, namely that at least one object exists with property S in A-type categoricals, affects Frege's *Begriffsschrift* transcription of A-type categoricals, such as "Every S is P," and E-type categoricals, "No S is P" or "Every S is non-P." The categoricals are then written as A: $\exists x Sx \wedge \forall x[Sx \rightarrow Px]$ and E: $\exists x Sx \wedge \forall x[Sx \rightarrow \neg Px]$.

The *not* of modern algebraic propositional logic was introduced to the world for the first time in the history of mathematics in Frege's *Begriffsschrift*. Negation is univocally if unprepossessingly signified in *Begriffsschrift* notation by a vertical tag descending from appropriate positions along Frege's unique content-stroke or *Inhaltsstrich*. External propositional negation *not* supplements when it does not supplant the *non*-property complementation of traditional Aristotelian–Victorian syllogistic term logic. A new day dawned in symbolic logic from the moment Frege first dangled a truth-functionally defined negation sign from a propositional thought-content-stroke in *Begriffsschrift* notation. Frege functionalized the two opposed truth-values of thoughts (*Gedanken*) or propositions, namely reference to the True or the False. Truth-functional negation was new and unprecedented in the history of logic. It was the additional step needed to make logic fully algebraic.

Logic, in lieu of Frege's truth-functional propositional negation, relying only on predicate complementation for what is said not to be the case,

---

[15] Frege, *Begriffsschrift, eine der arithmetischen nachgebildete Formelsprache des reinen Denkens*, in Frege, *Begriffsschrift und andere Aufsätze. Zweite Auflage, mit E. Husserls und H. Scholz' Anmerkungen, herausgegeben von Ignacio Angelelli* (Darmstadt: Wissenschaftliche Buchgesellschaft, 1964), p. 24.

was incapable of adequately representing the inferential structure of such common forms of mathematical reasoning as *reductio*. Boole deliberately avoided the truth-value-reversing external negation of propositions in his logical algebra. It was Frege's daring insight to fully algebraize logic by interpreting negation truth-functionally.

"Purely" Logical Reduction of Arithmetic in a Logic Modeled on Arithmetic

If Frege's *Begriffsschrift* was modeled on that which it proposed logically to model, then logicism would seem to amount to nothing more than the proposition that there exists a logical model for an axiomatized elementary arithmetic. There is nothing obviously objectionable about that, although the deeper resonances of Frege's method in the *Begriffsschrift* are not thereby sounded. If all that Frege's logicism implied is that there was a logical model for an axiomatized elementary arithmetic, then it would be hard to see what all the fuss historically has been about. Surely there are logical models of everything, not all of which things will be said to be reducible in meaning consequently to the principles of pure logic. There must be a logical model of the sequence of events by which Napoleon Bonaparte in 1812 entered and left Russia, or of the eruption of the volcano beneath Mount Vesuvius in AD 72 that destroyed Pompeii and Herculaneum. These sequences of events may have, follow, or obey a logic, but that does not make them logical entities, concept-functions or properties.

Frege invoked the North Sea considered in objective terms, as contrasted with our subjective beliefs and opinions about the North Sea. He might have therefore appreciated the argument that being able to model something logically does not for that reason alone make whatever is modeled analytically reducible to the concepts or principles of logic. It is no objection to Frege's intended use of a later modified *Begriffsschrift* logic to represent the basic laws and derived theorems of elementary arithmetic to say that arithmetic is logic in the sense of being the logic of arithmetic. The logic used to model arithmetic is then a logic modeled on arithmetic. Arithmetic is presupposed in the supposedly purely logical analysis of arithmetic. If there is no circularity in this relation, it will take another occasion to unpack Frege's conclusions and make sure that nothing has been damaged or trivialized in transit. We must wonder about the philosophical acceptability of adopting a logical model of arithmetic in a language that is modeled, as

Frege openly stated, precisely on that of arithmetic. The integrity of the project depends among other things on exactly what Frege meant by "modeled on" (*nachgebildete*).

Pictorially, the conditional reigns supreme in Frege's notation. It has the most conspicuous formal representation in two-dimensional vertical linkages of unlimited iteration. The truth of one proposition is visually shown in Frege's hook-shaped material conditional to depend on the truth of another proposition. The connection of truth is like the passage of current in electrical wiring. Truth-value dependence in Frege's *Begriffsschrift* logic literalizes the German word *abhängig*, meaning hanging from, depending on something that is in some sense prior or superior, supporting, or sustaining. Here the priority ranking of propositions is truth-conditional. The material conditional, together with propositional negation truth-functionally defined, depicts the dependence of the truth of a conditional's consequent on the truth of its antecedent, the truth of consequent A depending on the truth of antecedent B, when $B \rightarrow A$. The hooklike spoke hanging from a content-stroke in Frege's *Begriffsschrift* depicts the truth of the proposition appearing at the forward end of the content-stroke as dependent on the truth of the proposition appearing at the end of the vertically lower bracket.

Nor is it obvious that there could be an alternative, however ominous the apparent circularity. A logical symbolism adequate to the analysis of the axioms of elementary arithmetic, Frege's natural anti-Kantian starting point in all of this line of inquiry, must certainly have the same constructive articulation as whatever formal structures the logic is expected to analyze. There must be a language with the same internal features needed to represent the expressive and inferential potentialities of whatever is meant to be logically modeled. Logic is effectively the logic of arithmetic, and by extension of all of mathematics reducible to the basic principles of arithmetic, together with a hefty assortment of freely available functions. A logic that is not modeled on the language of arithmetic could presumably not adequately represent the logical structures in arithmetical thought, expression, and reasoning, depending as always on how tight a connection there is supposed to be in Frege's arithmetical "modeling" of the functional calculus of concepts. This is the trouble all along with Aristotelian–Victorian syllogistic term logics. It is the reason why Frege found it necessary to leave syllogistic logic behind in favor of a fully algebraized general calculus of concept-functions.

Frege, importantly, did not propose to invoke arithmetical truths in the form of explicit mathematical theorems in the logic of his *Begriffsschrift*. He promised only to model the language of the new logic on the language of arithmetic, and more specifically algebra. The point, if only in part, is that Frege's *Begriffsschrift* logic was meant to represent the logical structures within mathematical proofs understood as logically deductive derivations of theorems from the basic laws of elementary arithmetic. Frege's logic was additionally required to do something of much greater philosophical moment. His *Begriffsschrift* needed to accommodate a correctly clarified concept-function that was relevant to Frege's interests in advancing the symbolism. The hungry *Begriffsschrift* general calculus of concept-functions needed to be fed an appropriate concept-function of natural number. When a purely logical concept of number snapped into place in Frege's symbolic logic, he believed that by implication all of elementary arithmetic from bottom to top is purely logical.

Frege needed the logical structure of the *Begriffsschrift* as a framework for the analytic presentation of concept-functions relevant to rebuilding arithmetic on truth-functional foundations from purely logical concept-functions in an application of his newly designed fully algebraic logic. Frege thought that, with the right starting argument and unlimited properly formalizable mathematical concept-functions at his disposal, all formulated in regimented *Begriffsschrift* logical notation, he could visually show the dependences of truths on other truths in elementary arithmetic. He proposed to demonstrate that the reconstruction of arithmetical theorems constituted a purely logical edifice. For Frege's logicism to succeed, he had to prove that the minimally sufficient axioms or basic laws of elementary arithmetic were purely logical, and that a correct proof of a theorem from an arithmetic's basic laws must preserve what is purely logical in deductively valid mathematical reasoning. The entire enterprise of elementary arithmetic was purely logical for Frege. Advanced arithmetic and higher mathematics in all its corollaries, Frege believed, would then be sure to follow. He may have been right, although it remains to be seen in what exact sense elementary arithmetic in Frege's analysis was supposed to be either pure or specifically logical, rather than at least partly metaphysical, partly mathematical, or something else again.

The line between logic and mathematics was not meant to be sharply drawn in Frege's logicism. That was finally the point. If Frege's logic was already mathematical, whether by virtue of being modeled on the language of arithmetic or in other ways, then there could be no philosophical incentive for Frege merely to "reduce" one algebraic formalization of arithmetic to another.

Axioms for a Language of Pure Thought

We must try to take Frege's description of his project literally at face value. Interpretation of Frege's logic is complicated by the fact that by *"Begriffsschrift"* Frege meant sometimes his book with that title, sometimes the logic itself developed in that book, and sometimes any formal logic or generic concept-writing or ideographic symbolism similar to that which Frege had proposed, such as Peano's later arithmetical logic or the once-trendy *Pasigraphie*.[16]

His *Begriffsschrift*, as the subtitle of Frege's book declared, is presented as a formula language of pure thought. It was not designedly in Frege the logic of all discourse, but only of that expressing thoughts that were in some sense pure. Frege considered pure thought in a Kantian sense to be uncontaminated by contingent psychological events or empirical exigencies, as Frege made clear many years later in his 1918 essay "Der Gedanke" ("Thoughts," as it is often translated, or more literally "Thought" in the singular). This fact emphasizes the continuity and completeness of Frege's early conception, which was pursued to its furthest implications in his lifework. The question of the viability of logicism in grounding the basic laws of arithmetic in principles purportedly of pure logic is thereby raised. If *Begriffsschrift* notation was modeled on that of arithmetic, then was Frege's logic not in some sense dependent on arithmetic and arithmetical structures, rather than the other way around, as Frege's logicism would have it, seeking to show instead that all of arithmetic is one-way dependent on logic? Apparently Frege did not put much weight on the phrase "modeled upon," and neither, perhaps, should his intended readers. It may mean, and need mean, no more than

---

[16] The term "pasigraphy" for a general theory of signs originates with Joseph de Maimieux's (1753–1820) *Pasigraphie, ou, Premiers élémens du nouvel art-science d'écrire et d'imprimer en une langue de manière à être lu et entendu dans toute autre langue sans traduction* (Paris: Bureau de la Pasigraphie, 1797). The connection to Frege is that in a pasigraphic language each symbol represents a concept. With talk of pasigraphy in the air, it is easy to see how Frege's logical ideography might be construed as a pasigraphy or a particular attempt at development of pasigraphy.

that Frege's logical symbolism in a general sense was structurally suggested by that of arithmetic and more narrowly algebra.

Frege's *Begriffsschrift* logical axioms, unlike those of the later
Grundgesetze system with which they overlap, were not drawn together
into one place in the text. The logic's inference rules were instead
presented informally over many pages. They were introduced as Frege
had occasion to make use of basic logical laws in explaining and developing the formal language. He proposed the following axioms of logic in
the *Begriffsschrift*, indicated here with their original numbering in Frege's
text. The first logical law is the first numbered theorem of Frege's
Begriffsschrift logic:

The most basic *Begriffsschrift* axiom is a version of the rule of *logical
addition*, $a \rightarrow [b \rightarrow a]$. The equivalent in a system of propositional logic
incorporating inclusive disjunction is $a \rightarrow [\neg b \vee a]$; hence also for
arbitrary proposition b, $a \rightarrow [b \vee a]$. If proposition a is true, then
certainly, if any other proposition b is true (or false), then a remains
true when disjoined to b (or its negation). Logically adding another
proposition to a in that case does nothing to change the resulting disjunction's truth-value from true to false. If a is already false, then the
condition with a as antecedent is (trivially) true by definition. There is
nothing logically impermissible in passing conditionally or inferentially
by Frege's axiom from a false disjunct to a true or false disjunction. Next
appears the axiom:

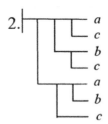

Equivalently, Frege's second axiom in logical theorem (2) is the
propositional tautology, $[c \rightarrow [b \rightarrow a]] \rightarrow [[c \rightarrow b] \rightarrow [c \rightarrow a]]$, which
is useful in countlessly many derivations.

8.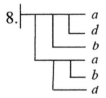

The principle in axiom (8) states the *Begriffsschrift* equivalent of the linear logical expression $[d \rightarrow [b \rightarrow a]] \rightarrow [b \rightarrow [d \rightarrow a]]$. The rule permits the truth-preserving intersubstitution of the antecedent on which the truth of a nested conditional depends with the nested conditional's antecedent. The theorem is useful to Frege in numerous logical derivations. He seems to have assumed, but did not try to argue, that the axiom is logically irreducible to more basic logical relations.

Skipping ahead numerically through other theorems proved along the way, again to the next basic logical law, Frege formalized the intuitive principle of *contraposition*. Linearly expressed, it is equivalent to $[b \rightarrow a]$ $\rightarrow [\neg a \rightarrow \neg b]$:

28.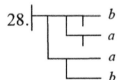

The basic laws (31) and (41) in Frege's *Begriffsschrift*, despite wide separation in the text, provide for double negation, which is more familiarly and economically written as $a \leftrightarrow \neg\neg a$:

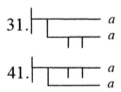

31.

41.

Frege conceivably overstepped the bounds of pure logic in the next axiom of the *Begriffsschrift*, with the introduction of the system's basic law (52). It treats a true identity statement as a logical tautology by attaching an *Urteilsstrich* to the proposition's *Inhaltsstrich*. The truth status of Frege's proposition (52) makes Leibniz's indiscernibility-of-identicals principles remarkably into a primitive axiomatic *logical theorem*. In Frege's formalization of the Leibnizian law of the indiscernibility of identicals, we find $c \equiv d \rightarrow \forall F[Fc \rightarrow Fd]$:

$$52. \quad \begin{array}{l} f(d) \\ f(c) \\ (c \equiv d) \end{array}$$

The rule is touted disputably again as an unconditional truth. It is presented as an axiom or basic law of pure *Begriffsschrift* logic, rather than a principle of mathematics or metaphysics, as Leibniz may have originally supposed. Frege offers an unconditional statement of the reflexivity of identity, for any existent object in the logic's referential semantic domain, $c \equiv c$:

$$54. \quad \text{——————} \ (c \equiv c)$$

The symbol "$\equiv$" used to represent the identity relation in Frege's *Begriffsschrift* was replaced for integration with standard arithmetical equations in the later (1893) *Grundgesetze*, where he explained the equivalent use of a more familiar identity symbol, "$=$." The axiom expresses the universal reflexivity of identity, expressible in contemporary symbolism as $\forall x[x = x]$, memorialized by Frege here for any constant term referring to any existent entity c as $c = c$.

Finally, in theorem (58), Frege presented a *Begriffsschrift* basic law for the application of universal instantiation, $\forall x, c[Fx \rightarrow Fc]$:

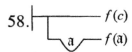

$$58.$$

The final law completed the muster of Frege's statement of eight seminal principles as purely logical *Begriffsschrift* axioms, originally scattered among theorems and lemmata in Frege's exposition. With the benefit of twelve or thirteen years' reconsideration, Frege eventually condensed the purely logical axioms for the applied arithmetical logic in *Grundgesetze* to six laws, including co-extensionality identity conditions for concept-functions, to complement which he also brought together principles of logical inference in a more convenient table. He included the deductively valid uniform substitution of co-referential terms and logically equivalent expressions in purely extensional contexts.

A casual glance at *Begriffsschrift* notation indicates, as previously suggested, that visually it resembles chemical bonding structures in two-dimensional representations more than it does the ordinary theorems or applications of arithmetic. *Begriffsschrift* logical notation in interesting complex applications also looks suggestively rather like electronic circuitry. It gives the appearance of a logic-switching circuit board laid out flat to display its signal-modifying connections. That was an application of mathematical logic that Frege at the end of the nineteenth and beginning of the twentieth century, with his interest in electrodynamics and telegraphy, might have already foreseen. Later, when *Begriffsschrift* logic was presented, Frege gestured toward some of the formalism's applications in only the most general terms. He emphasized again that the logic was intended to express the *contents* of *pure thoughts*. In *Begriffsschrift* Section III, SOME TOPICS FROM A GENERAL THEORY OF SEQUENCES, Frege explained it as follows:

§23. The following derivations are meant to give a general idea of how to handle this "conceptual notation," even if they do not suffice, perhaps, to entirely reveal the advantage it possesses. This would only stand out clearly with more complicated propositions. Besides, we see in this example how pure thought {*reine Denken*} (regardless of any content given through the senses or even given *a priori* through an intuition) is able, all by itself, to produce from the content which arises from its own nature judgements which at first glance seem to be possible only on the grounds of some intuition.[17]

In what exact sense, then, to revisit an unresolved question, was Frege's *Begriffsschrift* "modeled on" the formula language of arithmetic, and more especially of algebra? Frege inadvertently created a mystery as much as he illuminated the subject with the confusing pronouncements above, each of which seems to undo what the other says.

In the Preface to his *Begriffsschrift*, Frege explained his quest as that of uncovering the underlying logical structures needed for the deduction of theorems from arithmetical axioms. It was this otherwise concealed logic that he wanted to understand. He explained it properly only by writing down without exception absolutely everything that belongs to the complete algebraization of the logical inferences at work in mathematical proofs. The effort to accomplish his expository task amounted to the discovery/invention of a

---

[17] Frege, *Conceptual Notation* (Bynum's translation of the *Begriffsschrift*), p. 167.

formal language for the logical reconstruction of mathematics that was already mathematical in the most general sense of the word.

Frege understood the logic of a theorem's derivation only when he could look at it on paper, when he had fully articulated its principles and left nothing out of account. He was satisfied with nothing less than a symbolic logic that did justice to the deductive validity of all indispensable forms of mathematical reasoning. What else was there, after all, that could possibly validate acceptance of a mathematical theorem, if not the logic by which it was inferentially proved? Everything in mathematics, or rather, leaving geometry aside for the moment, everything in arithmetic, was the product of free-wheeling concept-functions applied to a baseline of natural numbers and the logically structured by-products of applications of other arithmetical concept-functions. It was, one hoped and supposed, an orderly enough affair befitting the prestige of mathematical truth. Frege, not satisfied with either reputation or pragmatic utility in the philosophy of arithmetic, demanded microscopic scrutiny of every theorem's inferential logic.

Frege assumed that anything as basic as elementary arithmetic was virtually upheaval-proof, except when it came to understanding its logical and philosophical foundations. The question was not whether it is true that $1 + 1 = 2$, but what the equation means and how its truth-value is determined. If there are alternative axiomatizations of arithmetic, then we must wait to see what is proposed and judge each reconstructive effort on a case-by-case basis. We should expect to consider not only formalisms other than Frege's ideal of arithmetic, but also radically different conceptualizations involving different axioms and rules of inference, among other distinguishing features, or exemplifying a different proof model entirely than the one he had anticipated. Anything else, without begging the question, any other axiomatically structured formal system, should be politely asked to get in the queue historically somewhere after arithmetic upon choosing another more suitably descriptive name.

Frege thought that when he had taken the purely logical foundations of number theory in hand he would be only a stone's throw away from having shown that all of elementary arithmetic and finally all of mathematics, presumably including at least analytic geometry, ultimately derived from concept-functions and inference rules of whatever he meant by pure logic. Frege prefixed his exposition of the *Begriffsschrift* logic with the following methodological addendum:

Now, while considering the question to which of these two kinds [of truths] do judgements of arithmetic belong, I had first to test how far one could get in arithmetic by means of logical deductions alone, supported only by the laws of thought, which transcend all particulars. The procedure in this effort was this: I sought first to reduce the concept of ordering-in-a-sequence to the notion of *logical* ordering, in order to advance from here to the concept of number. So that something intuitive (*etwas Anschauliches*) could not squeeze in unnoticed here, it was most important to keep the chain of reasoning free of gaps. As I endeavoured to fulfil this requirement most rigorously, I found an obstacle in the inadequacy of the language . . . From this deficiency arose the idea of the "conceptual notation" presented here. Thus, its chief purpose should be to test in the most reliable manner the validity of a chain of reasoning and expose each presupposition which tends to creep in unnoticed, so that its source can be investigated.[18]

Frege's intentions in the *Begriffsschrift* are difficult to put into words. He offers to explain the meaning of the book's title and his project to provide a formula language of pure thought in one stroke. He informs the reader at the outset that

In §3, I have designated by *conceptual content* (*begrifflicher Inhalt*) that which is of sole importance for me. Hence, this must always be kept in mind if one wishes to grasp correctly the nature of my formula language. Also, the name "Conceptual Notation" resulted from this. Since I limited myself, for the present, to the expression of relations which are independent of the particular state of things, I was also able to use the expression "formula language of pure thought." The modelling upon the formula language of arithmetic to which I have alluded in the title refers more to the fundamental ideas than to the detailed structure.[19]

The comment is nicely distancing at the same time, and perhaps for the same reason, as it is tantalizingly vague. The "fundamental ideas" of an arithmetical formula language would be *what?* They would be whatever was opposed to more complicated *Begriffsschrift* proof structures. Perhaps what Frege wanted to say is only what he had said before, namely that his *Begriffsschrift* was meant to be algebraic in the way of arithmetic, that his *Begriffsschrift* was meant to be a fully algebraic logic analogous to that of algebraic arithmetic. That would be more explanatory and might absolve Frege at least of any blatant circularity in his logicism involving applied *Begriffsschrift* logic. If that is what Frege meant by his *Begriffsschrift* being "modeled on" the established language of arithmetic, it is nevertheless not exactly what he actually said.

What should probably be taken without a grain of salt in trying to understand Frege's purpose in the *Begriffsschrift* is his explicit limitation of the

---

[18] *Ibid.*, p. 104.   [19] *Ibid.*

analytic task for the sake of which the logic had been designed. *Begriffsschrift* logic was not meant to be the all-purpose analytic tool for unpacking the underlying logic of all discourse. It had its limitations, although it turned out to have the necessary generality to cover many structural analyses beyond Frege's originally intended applications. The general functional calculus was dedicated instead to the specific errand of laying bare the conceptual and inferential logic of mathematical reasoning. Once this has been shown, a reader can see plainly on the page that the reasoning in such arguments as Euclid's argument to prove that there is no greatest prime number is nothing but purely logical concept-functions interrelated by purely logical connections. Frege further unpacked his rationale for the book's unprecedented purpose-built logic as follows:

> I believe I can make the relation of my "conceptual notation" to ordinary language {*Sprache des Lebens*} clearest if I compare it to the relation of the microscope to the eye. The latter, because of the range of its applicability and because of the ease with which it can adapt itself to the most varied circumstances, has a great superiority over the microscope. Of course, viewed as an optical instrument it reveals many imperfections, which usually remain unnoticed only because of its intimate connection with mental life. But as soon as scientific purposes place strong requirements upon sharpness of resolution, the eye proves to be inadequate. On the other hand, the microscope is perfectly suited for just such purposes; but, for this very reason, it is useless for all others.
>
> Similarly, this "conceptual notation" is devised for particular scientific purposes; and therefore one may not condemn it because it is useless for other purposes. Even if it fulfils its purposes in some measure, one may still fail to find new truths in my work. I would nevertheless take comfort in the conviction that an improvement in method also advances science.[20]

Immediately after having warned his readers that the *Begriffsschrift* is a specific tool for a specific logical job, Frege thus opened the doors to greater ambitions for the logic that the book had yet to reveal. The logic could be used, when properly developed, for application in many branches of knowledge. Frege mentioned by name only *philosophy*, but harbored high expectations for the system of logic he was about to unfurl, as much in theory-building in the natural sciences as in mathematics and philosophy. Thus, Frege wrote, again in the Preface to his *Begriffsschrift*,

> If it is a task of philosophy to break the power of the word over the human mind, uncovering illusions which through the use of language often almost unavoidably arise concerning the relations of concepts, freeing thought from that which only the nature of

---

[20] *Ibid.*, pp. 104–105.

the linguistic means of expression attaches to it, then my "conceptual notation," further developed for these purposes, can become a useful tool for philosophers. Certainly, it also does not reproduce ideas in pure form either, and this is probably inevitable for a means of thought expression outside of the mind {*bei einem äußern Darstellungsmittel*}; but on the one hand, we can limit these discrepancies to the unavoidable and harmless; and on the other hand, merely because they are of a completely different kind from those [discrepancies] peculiar to [ordinary] language, they provide a protection against a onesided influence of one such means of expression.[21]

Frege's remarks seem almost to anticipate Wittgenstein's diagnosis in *Philosophical Investigations* §593: "A main cause of philosophical disease – a one-sided diet: one nourishes one's thinking with only one kind of example."[22] Frege did not speak of philosophical ailments, but extolled the virtues of a formal symbolic logic like his *Begriffsschrift* because it presented a more highly regimented language in which logically and semantically confusing features of colloquial expression are avoided. Whether pathogenic or not, Frege early on prefigured the later Wittgenstein's concern about drawing all one's conclusions about the nature of language from limited samplings of colloquial expression, overlooking the unique characteristics of other languages that in some ways are stripped down to the basics of predicate expression, truth-functionality, quantification, and deductive logical inference.

Pros and Cons of Frege's Two-Dimensional Logical Notation

Why did Frege choose a printed-page-hungry spatially two-dimensional pictorial diagramming graphic for representing logical structures in his *Begriffsschrift*? The answer involves at least two convergent lines of reasoning, if we are not merely looking into psychological reasons to explain why Frege did what he did. Frege had definite mathematical and philosophical justifications for presenting logical formulas two-dimensionally instead of by means of linear expression, which he could also read, and as the history of logic later preferred.

The first consideration is that no one in the history of logic or mathematics had attempted what Frege achieved in his *Begriffsschrift*. There were no adequate models for him to follow. He was obliged to proceed intuitively, breaking new ground at every stage in discovering/inventing

---

[21] *Ibid.*, p. 106.
[22] Wittgenstein, *Philosophical Investigations* [1953] (Oxford: Blackwell Publishing, 2001).

the formal symbolic logic his logicism required. Given his background in chemistry, and more especially in pure and applied geometry, it came naturally and intuitively to Frege to represent logical relations in the new general functional calculus or predicate-quantificational logic as a structure of relations among arithmetical concept-functions capable of being pictorially fully laid open to view. After gaining familiarity with Frege's notation, something that even Russell seems not to have managed, it is relatively easy to see at a glance precisely what logical structures between concepts were expressed. There were no hidden factors, no compulsory under-the-table logical inferences at which to guess, regarding which one had to hope without knowing whether it was true that they were at work ensuring the deductive validity of a theorem's proof.

The linear inscription of logical formulas that more closely approximates a one-dimensional orthography has since come to enjoy greater popularity than Frege's *Begriffsschrift* notation. It did so already in Frege's time, first in Peano and then as modified only a few years downstream in Whitehead and Russell's *Principia Mathematica*. The heirs of those formal systems in contemporary symbolic logic have chosen to follow the linear inscription of Peano and of Whitehead and Russell, in admittedly more convenient but structurally less informative notations than Frege's. There are also disadvantages, despite their popularity, in non-Fregean logical symbolisms like Peano's and that of Whitehead and Russell. The formulas are standardly read from left to right. It is often necessary in the case of complex expressions to work back and forth several times. Exact scope delimitations need to be checked in the correct pairing of brackets or parentheses marking punctuation within a logical formula, parsing the sentence and reconstructing its meaning repeatedly if necessary. Frege's *Begriffsschrift* in comparison disambiguates quantifier scope graphically without much possibility of misunderstanding, permitting all essential logical relations to be scanned visually.

There remained insuperable typesetting difficulties in Frege's logic, in the days before computer text-processing. A glance through Frege's last two books, *Grundgesetze I* and *II*, shows what Frege's printers were up against. It would be an interesting experiment, which the present author regrettably is not at liberty to perform, to determine how long Frege's two volumes of *Grundgesetze* would be (in my printing with double columns in many of the technically mathematical parts of the text, weighing in at $253 + 266 = 519$ printed pages), if Frege's formulas were rewritten in linear Peano- or *Principia Mathematica*-style logical notation. Frege was later asked to do precisely this for a publication project by Louis Couturat that never saw the light of day. The simplest example for comparison is perhaps that of truth-functional conjunction or logical multiplication. Linear script reads $p \wedge q$, where Frege's logic requires significantly more consumption of wood pulp and ink for the logical equivalent, $\neg[p \rightarrow \neg q]$:

The second explanation of Frege's choice of a spatially two-dimensional symbolism for representing the logical principles of his *Begriffsschrift* is that it was essential to his purpose in these rock-bottom foundational excursa for the reader to be able to see more or less at a glance that there is nothing in disguise, nothing decisive at work beneath the logic's syntactical surface to validate the proofs of theorems from a handful of intuitively true axioms. Logical structures needed for inferences involving arithmetical predications especially in equations and concept-function input–output identity statements had to be visually inspectable, masking no logically unanalyzed inferential subterfuge, when arithmetical theorems were derived. Frege wanted the reader to be able literally to *see*, in a Kantian sense to intuit (*anschauen*), how mathematical concepts were built on logical concepts, how the concept-functional analysis of the number 1 as Frege's starting point was logically related to other concepts in a structure of logical laws, on which elementary arithmetic was logically inferentially reconstructable from intuitively accepted axioms.

There are more convenient linear logical languages, as Frege was aware. He developed *Begriffsschrift* symbolism with all its danglers, dimples, and drop-hinges for his own philosophical purposes. He modified but never abandoned the logic. *Begriffsschrift* notation offered something essential to Frege's intended application of the logic that linear symbolisms could not provide. Linear logics were dispreferred against Frege's desire to picture the logical roots and arithmetical branches of rigorous pure non-psychologistic logicism. The progression of logical theorems was meant literally to show that Fregean logicism was true. The derivation of arithmetical theorems in an updated version of the *Begriffsschrift* fourteen years later in the first (1893) volume of Frege's *Grundgesetze* would be the undeniable concrete demonstration of the truth of Fregean pure logicism. *Begriffsschrift* theorems could always be translated into contemporary symbolic logic. Small wonder, since Frege's logic was the starting-place for all propositional and predicate-quantificational logic today. Frege wanted conditional truth-dependences and truth-functional negations to stand revealed like dry bones in the definition of a concept-function and its true or false predication to any existent entity in the logic's reference domain.

The idea made terrific sense. Even if refinements were needed, Frege's *Begriffsschrift* by all rights should have been the talk of all logic, mathematics, and philosophy circles when it was published. It should have made his career; instead, in some ways, its damp reception undermined Frege's ambitions and dulled his confidence. Frege's optimism stumbled, no doubt, but he was never broken by his professional disappointments. He continued to write and publish logicism-related essays until his physical health began irrevocably to fail in the last two years of his life. More interesting for those outside his family and a few loyal friends at the time was the ongoing progress of his logical–mathematical–philosophical project. Frege may have perceived at least in hazy outline while writing his dissertation at Göttingen, if not before, the manifest concrete proof of logicism that he would pursue until Russell's paradox capsized Frege's *Grundgesetze*. At some early point Frege sensed the analytic and constructive work that would show with as much two-dimensional visual transparency as possible the content of axioms and the logical structures by which basic laws make possible the rigorous logical deduction of elementary arithmetical theorems.

For the sake of arranging all necessary reductions in Frege's logicism there must accordingly be sufficiently freely available arithmetical functions of many different kinds. They must be like colored candies in glass jars from which to choose, tracking every logically possible development of arithmetic, provided only that they are formalizable in Frege's *Begriffsschrift*. *Begriffsschrift* sentences must be syntactically consistent and semantically unambiguous. The analysis of the concept of number and specifically of the natural number 1 had to be purely logical in a sense acceptable to Frege if it were to play its intended part in Frege's logicism. Frege endeavored to build a case for all of these moments in his revisionary qualifiedly neo-Kantian analytic and synthetic constructive philosophical explanation of the whole of mathematics, including much, if not finally all, of geometry. Functions of descriptively specifiable domain and correlated range were free for the asking, and Frege was especially sanguine that the logical structures of all valid mathematical reasoning would be representable and reconstructible in *Begriffsschrift* notation.[23]

A Postmortem of Frege's Publication Fiasco

Frege's project so conceived was elegantly simple. It had a sense of the irrevocable, of belonging perfectly to the exact conceptual space it occupied, as though it had been prepared for it long in advance. It was as predestined as something normally encountered only in music and the fine arts. The music of Frege's *Begriffsschrift*, when once we know how to listen, makes everything appear precisely as it must. What, then, went wrong, when it went about as wrong as it could, as wrong as Frege must have imagined it would go right? Commentators on Frege's early publishing disaster are virtually unanimous, partly, one imagines, because

[23] A similar comparison of *Begriffsschrift* with standard linear logical symbolism is provided by Bynum, in *Frege: Conceptual Notation*, p. 23. He notes that for the exclusive disjunction Frege's two-dimensional formalism requires, for the standard logical expression, supposing it for simplicity to be an asserted truth, $[a \lor b] \land [\neg a \land \neg b]$, Frege must represent the *Begriffsschrift* equivalent of $\neg[[b \to \neg a] \to \neg[\neg b \to a]]$ in this lavish branching display of distributed truth-dependences and negations:

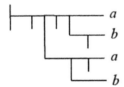

whereas, in Schröder's algebra, the expression for logical addition is the more space-saving $a_1b + a_1b = 1$. Boole's is, even more simply, $a + b = 1$. Frege must have had a special purpose in mind for the spray of conditional antecedents and consequents with negation in his *Formelsprache*, something that demands of logical relations in the foundations of elementary arithmetic that they be pictured, in such a way as to render them visually transparent and consequently susceptible to visual checking for inferential gaps or gaplessness in the reconstruction of arithmetical laws symbolized in *Begriffsschrift* logic. A useful recent guide to *Begriffsschrift* logical notation is provided by Edward Kanterian, *Frege: A Guide for the Perplexed* (London: Continuum, 2012), especially the greater part of the book, pp. 7–178. See also Gregory Landini, *Frege's Notations: What They Are and How They Mean* (London: Palgrave-Macmillan, 2012). Further insights on the uniqueness of Frege's *Begriffsschrift* two-dimensional notation in comparison with Peano–*Principia* linear formulas are provided by Danielle Macbeth, *Frege's Logic* (Cambridge: Harvard University Press, 2005), especially pp. 50–51. Frege himself in the *Begriffsschrift* explains the variables of his quantification theory beginning on p. 168 in the Bynum translation; see Section 11 of Part I.

they are cribbing a party line from one another about these historical matters. It is the difficult notation of the *Begriffsschrift* that is most often blamed for the book's sales and review-page failure. The spatially two-dimensional graphic notation of the *Begriffsschrift* unfortunately was not an optional feature for Frege, but essential, indispensable, and irreplaceable by any linear orthographic equivalent.

Short unappreciative one-page mentions of Frege's *Begriffsschrift* were published in 1879 by Reinhold Hoppe and Kurd Laßwitz. Laßwitz was an instructor at the Ernestinum Gymnasium in Gotha, and may have supported Frege's bid for promotion from *Privatdozent* to *außerordentlicher* Professor in 1879 when he seemed to have few supporters on his side. Further short notices were written by Paul Tannery and, in 1880, by John Venn and C. T. Michaëllis.[24] The list of those who came forward to criticize Frege's 1879 *Begriffsschrift* contains more or less the same names as can be found on the list of critics who published their appraisals five years later when his *Grundlagen* appeared for review in 1884. Nor had negative opinions of Frege's first work softened or subsided much in the interim, despite the ample opportunity for critics to further reflect on what Frege may have been trying to achieve in the first book. Michaëllis, Frege's colleague in mathematics at Jena, at least warmed his pen enough to remark, somewhat paternalistically,

We can say at the outset that, from a repeated study of Frege's writing, the diligence, incisiveness, and consistency with which he has worked out this system deserve

---

[24] Venn's review of the *Begriffsschrift* might have been the most disappointing to Frege. Compared with Reinhold Hoppe, Kurd Laßwitz, Paul Tannery, and C. T. Michaëllis, leaving Ernst Schröder out of the account for the moment, Venn was certainly the most prominent logician who looked at and commented on Frege's general functional calculus. Venn's one-page cast-off appeared in *Mind*, a publication that today would be considered the most respected among the other scientific and philosophical journals to carry notices of Frege's book. Frege himself would have been more concerned about Schröder's notice, the longest, most detailed, and most critical of the reviews, appearing in the prestigious *Zeitschrift für Mathematik und Physik*. Venn is condescending even in the first sentence, which sets the tone for the whole two-paragraph hatchet-job, "A Review of Frege's *Begriffsschrift*," *Mind*, 5 (1880), p. 297: "Dr. Frege's work seems to be a somewhat novel kind of Symbolic Logic, dealing much more in diagrammatic or geometric forms than Boole's." He appears at first to hold out an olive branch: "Symbolic systems are, I know, very difficult to judge by those unfamiliar with them; they will almost necessarily appear cumbrous and inconvenient to those who have been accustomed to make use of some different system." Then he goes in for what he seems to think is the kill, without argument or evidence that he has even read or considered the work carefully. "But, making all due allowance for these considerations," he condescends, "it does not seem to me that Dr. Frege's scheme can for a moment compare with that of Boole."

admiration; we wish for the author that his attempt may enjoy thorough study and more widespread dissemination among experts, and we do not doubt that his work, within the limits that he himself indicates, will find application and help to improve or better underwrite scientific method.[25]

Here there was an encouraging word. However couched in generalities, the comment stood weakly against the prevailing tide of criticism and neglect. It was like taping a bandaid over a deep wound gouged into Frege's sensitive self-esteem by the vast majority of less genteel reviewers.

Michaëllis was also to appraise Frege's 1891 essay "Über Funktion und Begriff," in 1894, and the first volume of the *Grundgesetze*, in 1896. Michaëllis to an extent was tracking Frege's intellectual development and the start of his professional career. While he had largely intelligent and sometimes supportive things to say about Frege's progress, contrary to his dilute praise for the *Begriffsschrift* in the 1879 review, when he returned briefly to the subject of Frege's *Begriffsschrift* in his 1881 *Jahrbuch über die Fortschritte der Mathematik* (*Yearbook on Advances in Mathematics*) report, Michaëllis was far less charitable toward Frege's brainchild. There Michaëllis flatly concluded that "it appears doubtful that mathematics will greatly benefit from the *Begriffsschrift* of Frege."[26]

Friedrich Wilhelm Karl Ernst (usually called simply Ernst) Schröder unleashed a more critical but also more extensive and searching fourteen-page review of Frege's *Begriffsschrift*.[27] The criticism indicated that Schröder had read the one-hundred-odd printed sides of Frege's text with care and discernment. Frege would later repay Schröder's compliment in kind when he reviewed the first volume of Schröder's *Vorlesungen über die Algebra der Logik*, which appeared in 1890.[28]

Even as Frege's most sympathetic technically adept reviewer, Schröder in the end did not understand what the *Begriffsschrift* was all about, and could not recommend the book to those seeking insight into algebraic logic.

---

[25] My translation of the passage in Michaëllis quoted in Kreiser, *Gottlob Frege*, p. 367.

[26] Asser, Alexander, and Metzler, "Gottlob Frege – Persönlichkeit und Werk," pp. 6–7.

[27] Ernst Schröder, "Anzeige von Freges *Begriffsschrift*," *Zeitschrift für Mathematik und Physik*, 25 (1880), pp. 81–94.

[28] Frege, "Kritische Beleuchtung einiger Punkte in E. Schröders *Vorlesungen über die Algebra der Logik*" ["Critical Elucidation of a Few Points . . ."], *Archiv für systematische Philosophie*, 1 (1895), pp. 433–56, English translation available in Frege, *Collected Papers on Mathematics, Logic, and Philosophy*, ed. McGuinness (Oxford: Basil Blackwell, 1984). Schröder was one of the few mathematicians at the time from whom Frege could have learned, just as he had taught Schröder what he thought the mathematician needed to know in developing his Boole-inspired logical algebra.

Schröder blasted Frege no less strenuously when he mentioned in his review a concern about "... multiple and partly serious issues" ("... *mehrfachen und zum Theil schwerwiegenden Ausstellen*") in Frege's book.[29] Despite all that, it was Frege's most serious notice. Schröder made an enemy of Frege, whose wrath he was later to feel, when in the same review he went so far polemically as to ridicule Frege's *Begriffsschrift* notation, oddly, for needing to be read from bottom to top in each hook-shaped material conditional, Schröder says, in the manner of Japanese calligraphy.[30] Following a different star, Schröder was soon to propose his own algebraic logic, distinct from Frege's and in Frege's judgment insufficiently rigorous and objectionably psychologistic in its conceptual foundations.[31] Schröder further complained, as had John Venn the previous year, that Frege did not compare *Begriffsschrift* logic with Boole's algebraization of Aristotelian syllogistic logic. The objection subtext was more that Frege had not simply followed Boole's algebraization of Aristotelian syllogistic logic.

Venn, in his highly condensed 1880 acknowledgment in the journal *Mind*, approximately one year after the book's publication, in keeping with normal one- or two-page journal notices at the time, packed into a casual mention after superficial examination in which one can virtually hear the pages of Frege's treatise fluttering through his fingers some of the most extraordinarily obtuse things said by anyone concerning the *Begriffsschrift*.[32] Disparaging words from a logician of Venn's stature could not have pleased Frege. The publication of his first book-length

---

[29] Asser, Alexander, and Metzler, "Gottlob Frege – Persönlichkeit und Werk," pp. 6–7.

[30] Schröder, "Anzeige von Freges *Begriffsschrift*," p. 91, compares Frege's *Begriffsschrift* notation with Japanese calligraphy that he supposes is written from bottom to top. The formulas in Frege's logic are perhaps analogously printed with their antecedents appendaged below, to conditionalize the truth of a main assertion or subconditionals or their negations. See Sluga, *Gottlob Frege* [1980] (London: Routledge, 1999), pp. 68–73 for a well-documented study of the Frege–Schröder feud.

[31] Ernst Schröder, *Vorlesungen über die Algebra der Logik*, three volumes (Leipzig: B. G. Taubner Verlag, 1890–1910). See Frege's review, "Kritische Beleuchtung einiger Punkte in E. Schröders *Vorlesungen über die Algebra der Logik*," pp. 433–56; Randall R. Dipert, "The Life and Work of Ernst Schröder," *Modern Logic*, 1 (1990–1991), pp. 117–39; and Volker Peckhaus, "Schröder's Logic," in *The Rise of Modern Logic: From Leibniz to Frege*, ed. Dov M. Gabbay and John Woods (Amsterdam: Elsevier, 1994), pp. 557–609. Frege in particular rejected the hierarchy of individuals required by Schröder's logic, lending support to the criticism that Frege would also not have accepted Russell's hierarchy of ordered syntax types in simple type theory as a solution to Russell's paradox.

[32] Venn, "A Review of Frege's *Begriffsschrift*," p. 297.

treatment of the formal instrument he would later adapt to reduce the axioms and theorems of elementary arithmetic to pure logic was not winning friends out of the gate. A big part of the problem was that Frege had not informed his readers what he wanted to do with the logic, that for which it was supposed to be good and useful. Michael Dummett summarizes the dismal situation in the following words:

> In 1879 Frege published his *Begriffsschrift* ("Concept-script"), in which, for the first time, a system of mathematical logic in the modern sense was presented. No one at the time, however – philosopher or mathematician – comprehended clearly what Frege had done, and when, some decades later, the subject began to get under way, his ideas reached others mostly as filtered through the minds of other men, such as Peano; in his lifetime there were very few – one was Bertrand Russell – to give Frege the credit due to him. He was not yet too downcast by the failure of the learned world to appreciate the *Begriffsschrift*, which, after all, discourages the reader by the use of a complex and unfamiliar symbolism to express unfamiliar ideas. He resolved, however, to compose his next book without the use of any symbols at all.[33]

Frege and Schröder, given their interests and mathematical preparation, were natural competitors and philosophical antagonists, as Frege was later to become with Hilbert, in their exchange of correspondence, and with Husserl, in reviewing Husserl's 1891 treatise *Philosophie der Arithmetik: psychologische und logische Untersuchungen*, in 1894.

When Schröder and Husserl came under fire from Frege's gun, it was primarily because of what Frege perceived as their unabashed psychologism and general lack of sufficiently expressive analytic and inferential rigor in the philosophical foundations of arithmetic. With Hilbert, Frege's disagreements centered primarily on the interpretation of axioms and their role in mathematical proof. Hilbert's formalism clashed diametrically with Frege's Platonic realism in mathematics. The latter was deemed philosophically insupportable by Hilbert, who substituted for Frege's commitment to the existence of subjectively intuited abstract mathematical truths the idea of mathematics as an objective rule-governed game of strictly meaningless symbol-token manipulations.[34]

In the Foreword to *Grundgesetze I* in 1893, Frege despaired of the dim reaction his *Begriffsschrift* had received. Looking back at the acknowledgments of his first 1879 book, he openly complained, as follows:

---

[33] Dummett, "Gottlob Frege" (*Encyclopedia Britannica*).
[34] See Risto Vikko, "The Reception of Frege's *Begriffsschrift*," *Historia Mathematica*, 25 (1998), pp. 412–22.

With this, I arrive at the second reason for my delay [between publishing the *Begriffsschrift* and the *Grundgesetze*]: the despondency that at times overcame me as a result of the cool reception, or rather, the lack of reception, by mathematicians of the writings mentioned above, and the unfavourable scientific currents against which my book will have to struggle. The first impression alone can only be off-putting: strange signs, pages of nothing but alien formulae. Thus sometimes I concerned myself with other subjects. Yet as time passed, I simply could not contain these results of my thinking, which seemed to me valuable, locked up in my desk; and work expended always called for further work if it was not to be in vain. Thus, the subject matter kept me captive.[35]

We can let Frege have the last word. He understood exactly what had happened. Some people speak of a mythical School of Hard Knocks. It is the experience of picking oneself up from life's challenges and learning from one's setbacks, moving on to better things. It is sometimes additionally meant as an alternative to conventional schools where subject matters are taught theoretically from books. Frege, to his distress, faced a fearsome combination of setbacks in both these senses. He was battered by a succession of seriously hard knocks within university academies, at home and in his personal life, and as a published writer in the review pages of technical and literary journals. When he was not being raked over the coals, he was ignored altogether by the mathematical philosophical guild. The *basso continuo* accompanying the melody line of Frege's pummelings is that for the vast majority of minds he was trying to reach with his first book it was almost as though he had never existed, as though he had never published his logic.

The repercussions of the lack of professional enthusiasm about Frege's *Begriffsschrift*, or even a ballpark-correct understanding of the book, were sudden and long-lasting. They were tangible later in the same year, when Frege was being considered for promotion from *Privatdozent* to *außerordentlicher* Professor at Jena. There was something nightmarish for a thinker of Frege's serious purpose. He heard that this or that *Zeitschrift* would be reviewing or at least offering a few columns' notice of his *Begriffsschrift*. The *Rezensionen* trickled in. The first one was negative, the second uncomprehending. Another wanted something that the book was never intended to provide. There was an occasional heartening word for the future. Some reviews were negative. It could not

---

[35] Frege, Foreword to *Grundgesetze der Arithmetik I* (Jena: Hermann Pohle, 1893); translated as Frege, *Basic Laws of Arithmetic, Derived Using Concept-Script*, by Philip A. Ebert and Marcus Rossberg with Crispin Wright (Oxford: Oxford University Press, 2013), p. xi.

be helped. Surely others would be positive. They would be enthusiastic, and they would understand what enormous potential the *Begriffsschrift* had, both as a general logic and for its intended applications in mathematical reasoning and the logical foundations of arithmetic and beyond. This is what Frege must have hoped. Unfortunately, the good reviews never arrived. Frege's *Begriffsschrift* made a dull thud in the back pages of virtually every journal that deigned to invite expert opinion on its merits.

The *Begriffsschrift* in Frege's Later Pedagogy

Frege published the *Begriffsschrift* in 1879. Unlike some scholars, Frege did not lecture in advance on the subject matter of the forthcoming text. He waited until the 1879–1880 winter semester at Jena, by which time the book would have already appeared in print. There was always the dread thought that after the book had already gone to press a fatal error would be found by an otherwise uncommunicative student with a lazy hand in the air.

Something else may have motivated Frege. Perhaps he thought the book would make more of an impact released without his offering in advance courses in the subject. Students might buy copies and come to his lectures to have the explicit but unconventional *Begriffsschrift* logic and implicit philosophy of mathematics explained. Interest among mathematics students at Jena would peak once the book had been published. That would have been a pleasant fantasy, and in the event nothing more. Frege offered lectures based on his logical system from 1883 until his retirement in 1918. The course was generally on the books for the winter semester, and, in an advanced treatment "beyond the summer term" as *Begriffsschrift* II. The exceptions were the semester after the winter semester of 1884, during which Frege did not teach any lecture or exercise course on topics in the foundations of mathematics, and the winter semester of 1902–1903, when Frege's course was not advertised, following the stunning receipt of Russell's paradox letter in June 1902. From 1889 to 1901, excepting 1897, Frege regularly offered summer semester lecture courses on the foundations of mathematics.

The first plank in Frege's pure logicism throughout all the theory's ups and downs remains the *Begriffsschrift*. We read in Asser, Alexander, and Metzler that

From 1902 this course appears only in the winter semester 1915/16, and is missing in the winter semester 1916/17, when a lecture was published in the summer semester in 1917 with the title "Foundations of Arithmetic" [*Grundlagen der Arithmetik*]. This shows that Frege never lost confidence in the ideas of his *Begriffsschrift*, although the failure of his logicist program caused him to look for new ways of substantive justification of the concept of number. In which direction he did, we can only suspect after the present fragments. It should also be noted that Frege's teaching was not confined only to logic and foundations of mathematics, he rather lectured in various areas of mathematics; the course catalogs include references to Frege's teaching: analytical mechanics, Abelian integrals, analytical geometry, differential equations, partial differential equations, function theory, definite integrals, algebraic equations, and number theory.[36]

Edward N. Zalta provides further evidence compiled from Kreiser's investigation of the university library at Jena in the following picture of Frege's teaching preparation for his assigned and elective courses. Frege knew the mathematics. Had he worked extensively on Abelian functions? As all new university instructors soon discover, it is one thing to have a strong grasp of a subject matter and quite another to be able to stand in front of students for several hours fourteen or fifteen weeks a semester and teach them the material with originality and animation, using fresh examples. Picking up in 1874 with Frege's first teaching appointment, Zalta writes as follows:

Library records from the University of Jena establish that, over the next 5 years, Frege checked out texts in Mechanics, analysis, geometry, Abelian functions, and elliptical functions ... No doubt, many of these texts helped him to prepare the lectures he is listed as giving by the University of Jena course bulletin, for these lectures are on topics that often match the texts, i.e., analytic geometry, elliptical and Abelian functions, algebraic analysis, functions of complex variables, etc. ... This course of Frege's reading and lectures during the period of 1874–1879 dovetailed quite naturally with the interests he displayed in his Habilitationsschrift. The "extension of the concept of quantity" referred to in the title concerns the fact that our understanding of quantities (e.g., lengths, surfaces, etc.) has to be extended in the context of complex numbers.[37]

The pressure on Frege to teach and thereby stanch the leak in the Jena mathematics curriculum was relieved somewhat in the following year

---

[36] Asser, Alexander, and Metzler, "Gottlob Frege – Persönlichkeit und Werk," pp. 13–14, my translation.

[37] Edward Zalta, "Gottlob Frege," *The Stanford Encyclopedia of Philosophy* (Winter 2012 Edition), http://plato.stanford.edu/entries/frege/. For the sake of emphasis, Zalta's references to the Kreiser and Kratzsch sources which have already been mentioned extensively throughout these notes have been replaced with ellipses.

when Johannes Thomae was brought back to Jena also to teach some of these kindred subjects.[38] When we consider the sheer number of advanced mathematics courses Frege was called upon to deliver after his Jena Habilitation, it is another tribute to his industry and capacity for compartmentalizing his research passions and lecturing responsibilities. Teaching occupied much of his time, energy, and attention; yet he was able to produce in the same five years, more likely three or four, the monumental logical theory of the *Begriffsschrift*.

Frege was active in other ways also during this time. In 1874 he published a review of Heinrich Seeger's *Die Elemente der Arithmetik* (*Elements of Arithmetic*) in the *Jenaer Literaturzeitung*.[39] He gave numerous lectures at meetings of the Mathematical Society of Jena, some of which dealt with topics tangential to the *Begriffsschrift*, especially quantification over the existent entities in a reference domain. Others were more of a purely mathematical nature, on relations between function theory and geometry, theory of curves, and "space curves" (*Raumkurven*).[40]

Frege was called up as a recruit for the military reserve over an eight-week training exercise in 1876. The normally scheduled summer semester courses in Frege's courseload as a result were canceled in 1876, so that Frege could meet his national obligation under Article 59 of the Constitution of the German Reich. As an able-bodied male citizen, he was required by law to serve off-and-on for seven years, generally from age twenty to twenty-seven. Since Frege was twenty-eight years old in 1876, he would not have been expected to enter the armed forces, but was placed on duty as a reservist for community service. He was nevertheless required to report for basic military training, including drill with firearms. Because of this technicality Frege held military rank as sergeant, although as a beginning university student at Jena, possibly because his father was deceased and he was the oldest surviving son, Frege had avoided involvement altogether in the Franco-German War of 1870–1871.[41]

---

[38] Thomae became *ordentlicher* Professor of mathematics at Jena in 1879, the year in which the *Begriffsschrift* was published.

[39] Frege, "Rezension von: H. Seeger, *Die Elemente der Arithmetik*, für den Schulunterricht bearbeitet," *Jenaer Literaturzeitung*, 1(46) (1874), p. 722.

[40] Frege's lecture "Einiges über Raumkurven" was presented to the Jena Mathematical Society at a meeting in 1876 (item 666). See Kreiser, *Gottlob Frege*, p. 126.

[41] *Ibid.*, pp. 480–84.

On the Verge of Unacknowledged Greatness

The brilliance of Frege's discovery is that, in developing a symbolism for a general function calculus aimed at formalizing the basic laws and derived theorems of elementary arithmetic, he advanced in the process a general application-non-specific formal system of logic. Frege's *Begriffsschrift* potentially supports indefinitely many applications beyond its role in constructively engineering a *de facto* proof of pure logicism.

Frege at thirty-one revolutionized logic and the philosophical foundations of logic and mathematics. He remained unacknowledged as having done any such thing for at least another half-century. His contemporaries to a cerebrum found his logic alien, as indeed it was and was meant to be. He did not anticipate that his readership would be so appallingly unqualified to recognize the value of something unprecedented in the technical literature. He miscalculated his reader-base and what they would bring to and take away from a work like the *Begriffsschrift*. He appears to have been genuinely astonished that others did not see things as simply and clearly as he did, that they could not at once grasp the utility of a general concept-functional calculus. The next stage was then to apply the general concept-functional calculus to an appropriate concept-function to concretely demonstrate the truth of pure logicism. If no one took the first step with him, then they would be unprepared for what was to follow.

The trouble was that Frege had not sufficiently explained the logic's intended purpose. Why precisely did he believe that the logic, with all its inherent difficulties, was needed and why, supposedly, would none other do? What were the innovations and problems that had motivated the formalization of Frege's logic in the first place, the significance of truth-value dependence and truth-functional propositional negation? How was the unwary reader to guess about these vital elements of the puzzle, when Frege had not condescended to explain himself more fully? Frege's answer, before experience cruelly taught him otherwise, might well have been that the universality of a fully truth-functionalized quantified functional calculus should be obvious and would recommend itself to all of logic and mathematics, to every thinking person in those fields. It would be love at first sight for some, and then the thing would begin to blossom and bear fruit. Philosophy would stand not far behind in the rear guard through time and familiarity, once the technical experts eventually came to agree and the symbolism gained currency. Logicians and mathematicians would not need to start using it; they would only need to learn to read and appreciate its syntactical merits, according to the projected reverie. It might even have happened, *if* the technical experts had agreed positively about its value in the early years of the *Begriffsschrift*'s unfortunate reception – which resoundingly they did not.

Frege's first published work in logic, despite the unsupportive reviews, was in a more important sense a tremendous mathematical–philosophical success, objectively speaking and in later historical judgment. At the same time, the book was a publishing and critical disaster for Frege in the court of professional but equally subjective academic opinion in the years 1879 through 1883. It must have hammered at Frege's ego to be confronted with rejection unsupported by correct interpretation and solid criticism in a disheartening succession of journal review pages, and even more so in the deafening silence that first shrouded the public unveiling of his new logic. With degree qualifications and a wealth of conventional mathematical preparation behind him, Frege made a bold unexpected break from his past staid research agenda in mathematics by publishing his *Begriffsschrift*. It was so new and unprecedented that it is no surprise in retrospect, however disappointing it must have been to Frege as events unfolded, that the circumscribed world of logicians, mathematicians, and philosophers of these subjects at the time was unreceptive and indifferent to Frege's first fully algebraic symbolic logic.

If Frege had traveled no further than this point in pursuit of his logical–philosophical goals, then by 1879 he would have already achieved the tremendous accomplishment of modernizing a fully algebraic truth-functional general functional calculus, a symbolic logic of concept-functions. He would have done so without accompanying fanfare primarily by injecting into a purely algebraic formalism a dangling vertical appendage for truth-functional propositional negation, and an exact notation for distinct overlapping restricted-variable quantifier scopes. Frege's introduction of truth-functional propositional negation made mathematical logic what it is today in its classical propositional logical undercarriage, fitted with a complex logic of generality over variable-trademarked subdomains within the logic's reference and true or false predication domain of all and only existent entities. What came next for Frege was to provide the purely logical inferential engine of his *Begriffsschrift* with fuel to turn its general concept-functional calculus wheels. The logic of concept-functions was later adapted to receive Frege's properly analyzed concept-function of *number*, focusing especially on the first natural counting number, 1.[42]

---

[42] Bynum, in his translation with biographical and critical commentary of Frege's *Begriffsschrift* as *Conceptual Notation*, endorses the stock explanation for the lack of formal symbolisms in Frege's *Grundlagen*, when in his introductory "On the Life and Work of Gottlob Frege," he writes, p. 24, "The poor reception given the *Conceptual Notation* taught Frege a hard lesson. In writing *The Foundations of Arithmetic* [*Grundlagen*] he was much more careful to prepare the reader for the new ideas that he would present and to make the book as easy to read as possible. This time, the text was written in bright, vigorous German; there were no special symbols to discourage the less tenacious reader. The scope and purpose of the book were clearly stated; and more than half of the text was devoted to a lively critique of relevant views of other scholars. . ." We have now seen that there is an alternative strategic methodological justification, rather than an emotional reaction to the reception of the *Begriffsschrift*, to explain why Frege temporarily abandoned the logical notation of the *Begriffsschrift* in writing the *Grundlagen*, before proceeding to the *Grundgesetze*.

5

From the Aftermath of the *Begriffsschrift* to the *Grundlagen der Arithmetik* (1880–1884)

> ... we are the victims of our own superiority. My music is beautiful, but when music passes from sensation to idea, it can have listeners only among people of genius, for they alone have the power to develop its meaning. My misfortune comes from listening to the music of angels and from believing that human beings could understand it.
>
> Honoré de Balzac, *Gambara*, from *The Unknown Masterpiece and Gambara* (1837), p. 134

W ITH THE 1879 publication of his *Begriffsschrift*, Frege believed he had established the expressive framework and inferential machinery for the large-scale purpose of reconstructing the purely logical foundations of elementary arithmetic. He was poised to formulate basic principles of arithmetic in the logical notation of his invented ideal language. He had made the first essential move in an effort to explain mathematical proof as deductively valid logical inference in his *Begriffsschrift* logic of concepts.

Unfortunately, Frege's first book was not well received. The standard account of what happens next is that Frege took to heart the advice of Brentano's student and later Husserl's dissertation director, the philosophical psychologist Carl Stumpf, to explain the goals of logicism in more informal terms than the formidable *Begriffsschrift*.[1] In 1884, according to the most frequently mythologized episode in Frege's philosophical

---

[1] See Wolfgang Ewen, *Carl Stumpf und Gottlob Frege* (Würzburg: Königshausen und Neumann, 2008), or the review of Ewen's book by Edward Kanterian, *Philosophical Investigations*, 34 (2011), pp. 312–17. Stumpf was Husserl's *Doktorvater* in philosophy, but Husserl's 1883 dissertation in mathematics was supervised by Leo Königsberger.

biography, Frege implemented Stumpf's suggestion by writing without demanding logical symbolisms his most widely read and admired second book, *Die Grundlagen der Arithmetik, eine logisch-mathematische Untersuchung*. He did so entirely without use of *Begriffsschrift* notation and employed only a few elementary arithmetical expressions, no more than the average educated reader would have known since grade school.

Logical Analysis of Numbers without the *Begriffsschrift* Formalization

The important features of Frege's *Grundlagen* did not require regimented formulation in a logical symbolism. Frege advanced the exposition of arithmetic as an extension of pure logic, and the analysis of natural number as a purely logical concept, without relying on *Begriffsschrift* notation. Among the main topics of interest are his interspersed methodological reflections, anti-psychologistic polemics, and self-conscious integration of the philosophy of mathematics with a philosophical semantics. These ideas seem to have been stewing for some time in Frege's thought, although he would not publish them for several years until the occasion of his second book. At least, that is how the story about the genesis of Frege's *Grundlagen* is often popularly explained.[2]

---

[2] Frege, *Philosophical and Mathematical Correspondence*, ed. Brian McGuinness (Chicago: University of Chicago Press, 1980), Letter XVI [xl]/1 of 9 September 1882. Stumpf writes, in the final paragraph, p. 172, "With regard to your work, to which I am looking forward with extraordinary interest, please do not take it amiss if I ask you whether it would not be appropriate to explain your line of thought first in ordinary language, and then – perhaps separately on another occasion or in the very same book – in conceptual notation: I should think that this would make for a more favourable reception of *both* accounts. But I cannot, of course, judge this from a distance." The editor and translator add to this their own note 4: "Frege followed Stumpf's suggestion by publishing [the *Grundlagen*] before [the *Grundgesetze*], thus dispensing at first with his conceptual notation." The present account offers a very different explanation, according to which publishing the *Grundlagen* before the *Grundgesetze* was methodologically necessary, rather than a pandering effort of what is called the Berkeleyan strategy, to make the same set of ideas more popularly accessible. (Note that the original *Briefwechsel* listing for correspondence with Frege is always indicated by means of the capital Roman numbers for the appropriate section of letters exchanged with a particular writer, followed by lower-case Roman numbers in square brackets for the corresponding listing when it has been chosen for inclusion in English translation, as above, in Frege, *Philosophical and Mathematical Correspondence*. There follows a slash and the number of the letter in exchange with Frege. "Letter XVI [xl]/1" means Letter 1 in German edition *Briefwechsel* volume exchange Section XVI, also listed in the English translation under its corresponding section, [xl].)

There is another dimension to the plain fact that Frege appeared to shy away from logical symbolism in his *Grundlagen*. Well-wishing friends like Stumpf are on record as having recommended a more informal and conceptual approach to the subject in his next book, in order to circumvent the incomprehension with which Frege's *Begriffsschrift* had been greeted. For Frege, however, the *Grundlagen*, just like the *Begriffsschrift*, had to be able to stand alone. Frege knew that he could not presuppose an average reader's familiarity with the *Begriffsschrift*. He would not have assumed this under the best of circumstances, and certainly not after the wretched sales and reviews the book had received. Next to no one was reading or talking about the new logic. The *Grundlagen* would have to promote the purely logical analysis of the concept of natural number therein on its own merits. The inquiry must be tested and judged by a critical readership interested in the concept of number, even if they had no penchant for *Begriffsschrift* pictograms. Frege knew that he could not explain the logic adequately in a few pages of the *Grundlagen* to make its formalizations sufficiently intelligible to justify any use of the *Begriffsschrift*'s formal symbolic notation in explicating the concept of number or criticizing the contending analyses he was proposing to supplant. His attention was fully focused on understanding the meaning of natural number terms 0, 1, 2, . . .

Without downplaying the disappointing notice Frege's *Begriffsschrift* received, there is a philosophical methodological explanation as to why Frege might have chosen in his *Grundlagen* to analyze the concept of number without the use of *Begriffsschrift* logical symbolism. The hypothesis opposes a popular myth as to why Frege kept *Begriffsschrift* logic underground in the *Grundlagen* until it re-emerged in *Grundgesetze 1* in 1893. It is an interpretation that can best be understood against the background of Frege's life. What was Frege's regular activity and professional development like during this time? How did publication of the *Begriffsschrift* affect his daily existence, intentions, and plans for the future, including writing and publishing the *Grundlagen*?

A Photographic Gallery 1874–1880

The previously described family photograph of the Freges rigidly posing for posterity shows Gottlob when he was about twelve and Karl Alexander was still alive, around 1860. There is a second photograph of

Frege alone taken in roughly 1874.[3] Frege as we see him here had successfully defended his Habilitation research at Jena. He could now be appointed to teach at the university, for the time being without salary, relying on student fees. He might be promoted should a position become available. The photo shows him as a young man in a dark coat, white shirt, and barely visible knotted tie. In the photograph of 1874, he looks remarkably like the American philosopher and logician Charles Sanders Peirce. Peirce is often mentioned alongside Frege as a coincidentally independent co-discoverer of a version of the general functional calculus that Frege was first to gesture toward in his Habilitationsschrift and publish five years later in the *Begriffsschrift*.

The image taken of Peirce looks to be that of a young man roughly the same age as Frege in his photograph.[4] Peirce was almost nine years older than Frege, so the photograph was certainly taken earlier. Like Frege perhaps a decade afterward, he wears an almost identical frock jacket, white shirt, and black bow. Both are clean-shaven, with long black hair almost reaching their shirt collars in back, parted on the left side and drawn unseverely away from the face, in the way that Frege would wear it all his life until his death in 1925, eleven years after Peirce's death in 1914. The next photos of Peirce we often see show him as having followed local fashion and parted his mop down the middle, experimenting with a variety of beard styles over the years. Frege, more austerely Lutheran in aesthetic attitude, might have found it an intolerable vanity, besides a waste of time and energy, to concern himself excessively with trivialities connected with physical appearance beyond hygiene and social present-ability. Peirce's hair in the early photograph charmingly covers half his ears. Frege's hair is combed slick more neatly behind these fully exposed auricles. The angle of jaw is similar, while Peirce's nose is more promi-nent, slightly more bulbous than Frege's finely sculpted features. Peirce's lips are also more sensuous-appearing than Frege's mouth, which is sealed in a perfectly horizontal line, as though in determination. The obvious, albeit accidental, difference is that whereas Peirce looks out of the plane of the photograph to a point beyond the viewer's right shoulder, his tie smartly knotted and plainly shown, Frege looks to the left far

---

[3] Photograph in the possession of Hildegard Intorf, Rostock. See Kreiser, *Gottlob Frege*, p. 646.

[4] Peirce's photograph has been dated to 1859, the year he graduated from Harvard University. The original photograph is in the Tuttle Collection, Institute for Studies in Pragmaticism, Texas Tech University (Lubbock).

beyond the three dimensions inhabited by the onlooker. He shows mostly the left side of his face with an intelligent arch of eyebrows as he gazes into the distance. He looks to his future, perhaps, serious and by now relatively accustomed to his social status, whereas Peirce in contrast wears a suggestion of cocky arrogance. There is only a hint of how Peirce's cravat is tied with black silk or similar fabric. He sits slightly backward, whereas Frege's physiognomy tilts somewhat forward. Frege looks straight across into unseen space, although his eyes themselves aim upward, while Peirce in his portrait looks to his side rather than straight ahead.

The differences and similarities are culturally interesting. Frege was in central Germany and Peirce in New England in the United States. They had both been credited with discovering predicate-quantificational logic, and of having other similar scientific interests, as well as educational coincidences favoring the engineering practicalities of applied mathematical physics. As to attributing further significance to the two photographs, who knows what their respective photographers asked them to do on the occasion, how they were directed to sit and look, or how many different images were taken in each case, how many light-sensitive plates were ruined by a premature sudden movement, or otherwise left discarded in a darkroom bin, how in general it transpired that these particular prints happened to survive for comparison today. The fact that Frege and Peirce should be partly united in their mathematical and philosophical interests, overlapping in their life histories a continent away over the greater part of their lives, makes it fascinating also to see in these portrait photographs how alike the two logicians, mathematicians, and philosophers appeared as young men. It is no exaggeration to say that, in the right light and at different times in their lives, it would have been easy even close at hand to mistake Frege for Peirce and vice versa.

In later years, Frege sported a thick bushy black beard and moustache, so dense and carpeting his face so fully below his slightly aristocratic nose and bright, piercing, faintly amused eyes that it can be wondered how a soup spoon could have ever found its way to his lips. It may have been the fashion, an eccentricity of Frege's, or an exigency born of the fact that Frege lacked time or money to visit the barber regularly. However much his pockets may have jingled with Saxony coin after securing his appointment as Associate Professor at Jena in 1879, out of necessity he might not have devoted much time to the vanities of personal appearance. However, it was not, for that matter, the case that Frege let himself go. He was following a minimal regimen of simplified dress and hairstyle that was in keeping with the times, at least for academics and intellectuals, by virtue of which he would have blended in with most of his non-manual-laboring contemporaries on the street, as well as many of the working-class citizens, at least on Sundays. As a reservist, Frege was keeping himself in soldierly trim, following a somewhat military regimen also in civilian life. The frequently reproduced later photograph of 1880 attests to a neat well-dressed middle-aged man encroaching on a gray-to-white-haired time of life, conducting himself with a sense of his hard-earned dignity and prestige as an Associate Professor at a university, framed by an extensive dermal cartography of scars acquired in the course of living through adversities. One does not survive repeated challenges as singingly as Frege did and not have the experience add to one's pride and feeling of advantage and ascendence.[5]

The Lutheran attitude in Frege's world was not merely to conceal but, further, to deny one's superiority. At the risk of arrogance and wrongful self-esteem, it remained an ideal to be pursued, even if it meant sometimes saying nothing, holding back, submitting to authority, or awaiting one's turn with unconditional patience. What was curious in Frege's statement made on the occasion of his Habilitation defense in 1874 was his declaration that he had been "educated in the Lutheran faith." It was a marvelous statement that, while perfectly true, said nothing definite about the path or current state of his beliefs at the time. To be educated in the tenets of a religion does not make one faithful. It implies only an ability to recite the right answers when called upon to do so. It proves no more than that the student knows what the believers in the particular religion into which the young adept is being indoctrinated accept as articles of faith. Belief in the truth of a doctrine, acceptance of the creed, is altogether another matter.

Answering questions of that type, in an adult life that had been shaped by preparation since the age of six for a rapid and unrelenting succession of examinations, was something for which Frege throughout his studies possessed an uncanny knack. Perhaps at some point during his first university

---

[5] Photographer unknown. The *c.* 1920 image of Frege is in the possession of the Universitätsarchiv Jena and the Archiv für Kunst und Geschichte, Berlin.

years at Jena, between physics, chemistry, and philosophical anthropology, Frege wondered, further fueled later by Lotze's lectures on the philosophy of religion at Göttingen, whether the propositions of a religious canon could be rationally justified. Perhaps at the Habilitation defense Frege was being deliberately ambiguous, leaving it open whether or not he had sustained his faith since the time of his boyhood education in its principles. Perhaps he considered it inappropriate to speak of his religious convictions, if any, since they were irrelevant when presenting himself for Habilitation at a more or less secular university's institute of mathematics.

We study the photograph of 1874 in vain for signs of these historical events in Frege's past etched into his face. The image shows only quiet confidence. At the time there were as yet no severe disappointments to read in his countenance. Frege had everything before him, plus the thrill of not knowing exactly what it would turn out to be. He was moving with workmanlike progress through his academic accreditation toward an unpredetermined future in which he would play a role in logicism's march to scientific philosophical respectability. Mathematics would finally have the most secure possible grounding. He was certain to make interesting discoveries along the way as he eventually firmed up his vision of the logical foundations of elementary arithmetic and divided the project up into three constructive components of the manifest proof of pure logicism appearing in print during his most active writing years from 1879 through 1903.

All this awaited Frege. His rapidly prepared Habilitationsschrift embodied a theory of quantity that anticipated the general functional calculus of the *Begriffsschrift*. In the 1874 photograph taken five years in advance of the publication of his logic, Frege does not engage the viewer but gazes at something in the distance. In historical retrospect it is tempting to read into the photograph the first summonings of Frege's mathematical intuitions in support of a rigorously developed non-psychologistic logicism. The photograph has the right approximate date to have recorded Frege on film at about the time when he first began to consider the logical–arithmetical relations that would engage and finally exhaust his energies over the remainder of his life.

Logic and Everyday Realities

Frege was hard at work teaching and vigorously pursuing his research plans at the Universität Jena from 1879 to 1884. His achievement in the

Begriffsschrift is all the more remarkable because he produced the book against the demands of heavy teaching responsibilities as a Jena university-unpaid *Privatdozent* during these first years of his appointment. Bynum makes the point eloquently:

> From the beginning, [Frege's] teaching load was unusually large, particularly in 1878, when Professor Carl Snell was very ill. Frege volunteered to take over most of Snell's work in mathematics and carry his own load besides. In so doing, he prevented an intolerable gap in the mathematical teaching programme until Johannes Thomae could be acquired a year later. His extra teaching certainly forced him to sacrifice much of his research time – and just when he was making great strides in logic.[6]

We recall the litany of qualifications Frege had to satisfy before being permitted to teach at Jena without regular pay. The pressures on Frege were considerable, as Bynum makes vivid. Frege offered yeoman service for many years at the university where he would ultimately spend the rest of his professional career. He was not making enough money from his unpaid position as a *Privatdozent*, relying as he must on payment of lecture fees by students. He continued at this time to be supported by his mother, Auguste, from the Wismar homefront. Bynum further adds to the picture as follows:

> Before the reception that greeted his *Conceptual Notation* [*Begriffsschrift*], Frege had every reason to be optimistic. He had established a good reputation at Jena, received a handsome promotion, and published his first book; but the joy and success that seemed assured were not to be. The happy years had ended, for the reception of Frege's book marked a turning point in his life. Henceforth frustration and tragedy were to haunt him. From 1879 to 1891 his works were ignored or misunderstood. From 1891 to 1901 they were slowly acknowledged; but this period was dramatically and ironically capped by Russell's recognition of Frege's greatness and almost simultaneous discovery of an antinomy in Frege's carefully laid foundations for mathematics. Even in his personal life sorrow and frustration plagued him; for after he was married to Margarete Lieseberg (1856–1905) of Grevesmühlen, the couple started a family only to see all the children die young. About 1900 they adopted a son Alfred; but Frege's wife died in 1905 and left him to raise the boy alone.[7]

Frege drew no salary, although his loyalty and willingness to shoulder more teaching responsibilities at the university than would normally have been expected of a *Privatdozent* were eventually rewarded by a regular salaried appointment as *außerordentlicher* or *extraordentlicher* (Associate)

---

[6] Bynum, "On the Life and Work of Gottlob Frege," in *Frege: Conceptual Notation*, p. 8.
[7] *Ibid.*, p. 20.

Professor. Frege was to hold that position at Jena throughout the rest of his career, *Honorary* Ordinariat notwithstanding, until his retirement from the university approximately forty-four years later in 1918.

At the age of thirty-one, when the *Begriffsschrift* was published, or aged twenty-six when he assumed his position and a heavy yoke of instructional responsibilities as a *Privatdozent*, Frege was an extraordinarily busy unpaid mathematician, teacher, and promising researcher, still dependent on his mother's goodwill and by implication the family's indulgence. Arnold got the short end of the stick from the beginning in this regard, sad to say, although in some sense he had had the same opportunity to demonstrate his talents and prove himself investable as his older brother. He seems eventually to have resented the favoritism shown the family's admittedly more promising, talented, and motivated first-born.

Frege had not been idle. To the contrary, he had worked extremely hard to get this far. He now had a book to show as a trophy alongside his lambskin degrees. While he filled in for his former instructors, who for different reasons were unable to meet their teaching responsibilities, he was doing that part of their work for them without institutional recompense, as his financially pressed widowed mother kept the rain from his head and sausage and fried potatoes on his plate.

Frege was living during this time at Kasernenstraße 12, formerly Upper Jüdengraben 505g, in the Gasthof zum Erbprinzen, not far from his colleague Thomae's residence. Later, he would move to the forest road outside Jena, Forst (or Forstweg) 29, where his mother joined him after selling the family-run girls' school in Wismar, and with the profits built a relatively large duplex house able to accommodate two families. There Frege and his mother, Auguste, lived in proximity, and, with paltry earnings coming in from Frege's position, lived within a sensible budget and frequently kept each other company. Gottlob had always been emotionally close to his mother. They may have become more united in spirit by Auguste's having nursed her oldest boy through the dangerous moments of childhood illnesses. Later in life he must have felt gratitude for his mother's moral and financial support of his scholarly scientific endeavors when his career was in its early stages.

Frege's *Begriffsschrift* was not published with a vanity press like so many Habilitationsschriften. This was a real, if somewhat diminutive, book, accepted and marketed by a real German book publisher for such dedicated products, which even then failed to live up to expectations. It was never imagined by Frege that his *Begriffsschrift* would become instantly popular. It was not that kind of book. What may have shocked his composure is the misunderstanding and indifference with which the technically trained mathematical readership reacted, that is, the very thinkers with whom he wanted to establish a rapport. Surely someone capable of reading Frege's pages would see the interest and importance of his new logical system. Once their appetite had been aroused, they would begin slowly to spread the word. There would be an upsurge of recognition and appreciation, and a rampage of applications for his logic in mathematics and the philosophical foundations of mathematics. There is a narrow window of opportunity for books to catch fire. Some good books never do so at all, and some gain an informed readership only long after an author's death. Frege's *Begriffsschrift* in those critical years must have seemed to Frege and his disappointed Jena mathematics mentors to be sinking immediately into miserable oblivion. It was a project based on an ideal in which Frege continued to believe, even when its most optimistic and intuitively appealing formulation had been logically discredited, as was eventually to be its fate.

Mathematical Activity

In addition to his teaching responsibilities and writing the *Begriffsschrift* in his first years as a habilitated *Privatdozent* at Jena, Frege had also been participating since 1874 in the Jenaer Gesellschaft für Medizin und Naturwissenschaft (Jena Society for Medicine and Natural Science). The society was organized in 1853 by professors of these two disciplines, who were later joined by the mathematicians Abbe and Schäffer. Judging from the Society's records, they probably did not manage to attract the prominent Jena mathematician Snell. The idea of the meetings, as with all such societies, was to exchange scientific information and promote collegial interaction, in this instance between the medicine and natural science faculties. Mathematics seems to have been admitted, at least officially, in a secondary capacity, as handmaiden to the natural sciences, including medicine.

After 1863, the society began publishing a professional journal. It remained productive in promoting the research interests of Jena colleagues in medicine and the natural sciences broadly construed until the end of WWII. The group met every three weeks at first, and then, as demand and attendance increased, every two weeks. The members would gather on Friday at 8:00 pm and adjourn for beer promptly at 10:00 pm. Kreiser reports that the society had only 36 members in 1878, but boasted 100 in 1893, and that the number of members thereafter fluctuated between 84 and 120 as late as 1917, the year before Frege's retirement.[8] It was an important point of intellectual, scientific, and expert technological contact in Jena for Frege. Frege throughout his life was a relatively sedentary homebody. The society offered an outlet and source of critical feedback as he continued his mathematical researches after the publication of the *Begriffsschrift*, leading to the completion of the *Grundlagen*. The text of the talk Frege gave on the *Begriffsschrift* to the society in the year of his first book's publication does not seem to have survived. Roughly every two years thereafter he addressed the group, generally on the foundations of mathematics, and as often cast explicitly in terms of the *Begriffsschrift*. Frege's total presentations to the society included at least the following talk topics, according to the society's minutes:

24 January 1879: Anwendungen der Begriffsschrift (Applications of the *Begriffsschrift*)

15 July 1881: Über den Briefwechsel Leibnizens und Huygens' mit Papin (On the Correspondence between Leibniz and Huygens with Papin)

27 January 1882: Über den Zweck der Begriffsschrift (On the Purpose of the *Begriffsschrift*)

2 November 1883: Über die Geometrie der Punktpaare (On the Geometry of Point Pairs)

17 July 1885: Über formale Theorien der Arithmetik (On Formal Theories of Arithmetic)

9 January 1891: Über Funktion und Begriff (On Function and Concept).[9]

It must have been a stimulating opportunity to share ideas and collect criticisms. Often it is the experience of making an argument public rather than anything that is actually said on the occasion that motivates renewed energy and pursuit of novel directions in a thinker's work. Since the Jena Mathematical Society, in contrast, was not mentioned after Frege's return for the Habilitation defense, it is likely that the society, which was never officially recognized at the university, either fell into neglect or continued informally and unofficially, perhaps only sporadically, thereafter. At roughly

---

[8] Kreiser, *Gottlob Frege*, pp. 473–79.   [9] *Ibid.*, p. 476.

the same time the Society for Medicine and Natural Science usurped the mathematical group's importance, even among Jena's mathematicians, and absorbed most of the Jena Mathematical Society's active membership.

All the more interesting from the standpoint of Frege's struggling finances, even after appointment as *außerordentlicher* Professor, is the fact that the society from 1884 to 1917 charged a membership fee of 6 Marks a year. Purchasing power actually increased in most of Europe during the nineteenth century, but this amount represented a minor hardship for Frege. Still, it must have been judged a worthy sacrifice in order for him to be able to meet with the group as a dues-paying member. Society provisions as of 31 October 1884 permitted participants who gave group lectures to publish their talks in the society's journal. It is noteworthy that Frege, who must have had other reasons for contributing verbally at meetings, did not take advantage of the society's publishing opportunity.[10]

The fact that the yearly membership dues for Frege in the Jena Society for Medicine and Natural Science were 6 Marks puts into perspective Frege's economic situation and the purchasing power of the Saxony Mark at the time. Its value was certainly greater than that of the Euro today or the Deutschmark as used throughout Germany during the years before the creation of the Eurozone, although it was still hardly a king's ransom. Frege's trifling 10 Mark honorarium for teaching three university-level courses in the summer semester of 1874 and winter semester of 1874–1875 offers an indication of the relative scale. Imagine beginning university professors being expected today to fork out three-fifths of their yearly teaching income in order to become active members of the Aristotelian Society, Mind Association, American or Canadian Philosophical Association, Australasian Society for Philosophy, or their counterparts throughout the world. Assuming reasonable proportionality, the comparison indicates more poignantly the merely symbolic nature of the payment Frege received for services rendered to the mathematics faculty at Jena. One can only hope that Frege's membership dues covered the fraternal glasses of beer with which each meeting was officially adjourned.

Frege began his *Privatdozent* position at Jena with a voluntarily augmented teaching load. He was working significantly beyond the usual

[10] *Ibid.*, pp. 469–79.

obligations for a post-doctoral recently habilitated entering *Privatdozent*. He took on some of his former teachers' instructional load, as well as the *Vorlesungen* (regular scheduled lectures) that came with the territory of his new position. During the summer semester of 1874, Frege taught the courses Über das Imaginäre (On Imaginary Numbers; literally, On the Imaginary) (for which ten students were registered as attending) and Anwendungen des Infinitesimalkalküls auf Geometrie (Applications of the Infinitesimal Calculus to Geometry) (two students), and in the winter semester of 1874–1875 he taught the course Analytische Geometrie nach neueren Methoden (New Methods of Analytic Geometry) (five students). For this service, although the position itself was officially unpaid, Frege received the aforementioned honorarium of 10 Marks. Perhaps it was just enough, when outstanding expenses had been met, for the luxury of having a photograph taken, something to commemorate completion of the Habilitation degree at Jena, to send his mother for a place of pride on the fireplace mantel shelf back in Wismar.

Frege in these days was scraping along collecting the standard charge at the time of 12 Marks *per capita* for his lectures as a Jena *Privatdozent*. At that rate, the most he could have earned in his early days was 132 Marks for the maximum enrollment of eleven students he was able to attract in the winter semester of 1878–1879. Students were sometimes permitted exemptions from payment of fees for reasons of privation; if such exemptions were granted, it was simply too bad for the *Privatdozent*'s pocket. It is noted by Kreiser, in this extensive section of his book, that, in that semester, nine of Frege's eleven students applied for relief from lecture fees. The consequence was that for his teaching at this time Frege received only 18 Marks. The economy was not in good order in 1879 when Frege came up for consideration to be promoted from *Privatdozent* to *außerordentlicher* Professor or Extraordinariat. Snell had ceased to teach altogether at this point, and there was internal pressure for Frege to be promoted to fill Snell's shoes. The trouble on the horizon was that whereas by 1884 Frege had also published his *Grundlagen*, when being evaluated in 1879 for the title-comparable position of Associate Professor, virtually his only piece of work to show for his time after the Habilitation at Jena had been the badly received, harshly reviewed, and even more apathetically ignored *Begriffsschrift*. He must have hoped that things would go better with the *Grundlagen*.

It was shaping up to be a promising year for Frege. His second book was released at roughly the same time as his promotion to Associate Professor status finally came through. There was not much unqualified praise or admiration expressed for Frege's little volume. Normally, one calls upon published reviews of a book to help reinforce a younger colleague's prospects for advancement. It was not as though no one had deigned to review the book. For such a technical subject Frege had a reasonable number of reviews and notices of his *Begriffsschrift* appearing in a variety of professional mathematical, scientific, and philosophical journals. With the exception of a few condescending gestures expressing the hope that Frege would continue doing logical and mathematical research, virtually all reviewers concluded with equivocal to negative remarks. Frege had staunch supporters in Abbe and Carl Fortlage, and, as outside evaluator, Kurd Laßwitz, who back in 1879 had published a two-page largely commendatory notice of the *Begriffsschrift* in the *Jenaer Literaturzeitung*.[11]

Frege at the Chalkboard

Kreiser catalogs Frege's teaching for all of his career at Jena in a goldmine of information, and there is no point in duplicating that carefully collected documentation.[12] There are interesting trends to discover in the courses Frege taught, and what he later offered after he had been promoted to Associate Professor. By then he had had ample opportunity to establish a reputation in his field for productive publishing, if not yet for widespread influence. With such recognition he may have slowly garnered more discretion as to course-offering options. Soon enough, beginning in the summer semester of 1886, Frege taught a split billing of three courses in the summer session and two in the winter semester, up from two in the summer and one in the winter. Frege's teaching thereafter stayed at 3–2 throughout the rest of his career, until 1901, when his salary began to be subsidized by the Zeiss Corporation. Thereafter, he taught only one course per semester, with supplementary lectures on the *Begriffsschrift* appearing more or less continuously from the time of its

---

[11] Kurd Laßwitz, "Rezension von *Begriffsschrift*," *Jenaer Literaturzeitung*, 6 (1879), pp. 248–49.
[12] Kreiser, *Gottlob Frege*, pp. 280–84.

publication in 1874. There were never many recorded attendees, and sometimes there were none at all.

Frege inherited a courseload from Abbe and some from Snell. It is interesting to ask which of these courses Frege may have been required to teach as a condition of his appointment, and which he chose to offer as a *Privatdozent*. The Analytische Geometrie nach neuren Methoden course seems to have been one of the program's staples, as were Frege's courses on Analytische Mechanik I and II in later years. It is reasonable to assume that analytic geometry was passed down to Frege to teach, perhaps from Snell, but more likely from Schäffer, in recent departmental history, which would mean indirectly from Abbe. It would have been an important course for all students at Jena, given that interest in imaginary and complex numbers and their geometrical mapping outside of the real number line was a Göttingen speciality. It was a grand research design issuing from the mind of Gauss, in which Frege and many of his teachers also played contributing parts. The Anwendungen des Infinitesimalkalküls auf Geometrie course fit directly the subject matter of Frege's Göttingen dissertation, and may have been the most substantial mathematics course on which Frege would have been comfortable lecturing to students at the time. Frege taught these courses, so presumably he could have chosen to teach them by his own prerogative. That fact suggests that it was a course Frege may have been bequeathed in his first semester teaching at Jena, the normal instructor for which was probably Snell. It may have been phased out immediately afterward or taken over by one of Frege's new colleagues, such as Thomae, being more suited to their backgrounds.

If these assumptions are correct, then Frege's chosen course was the remaining alternative, Über das Imaginäre. Offering a course on imaginary numbers, such as i, the square root of -1, which appears also in the complex number $a + bi$, would have tapped directly into Frege's previous sustained mathematical investigations of the Gaussian geometrical modeling of complex numbers. The choice of title seems more philosophical than purely technical. It advertises an inquiry into the concept of an imaginary number, a topic with which one imagines Frege is not only ready but eager at this time to engage mathematically and philosophically. The course title slings enticing bait for potential mathematics lecture enrollees. As collateral evidence, there are the sheer enrollment numbers for the three courses in the summer semester of 1874. Frege as *Privatdozent* snags ten curious students for the imaginary numbers course, a number which could be partly accounted for by their being inquisitive about what freely offered course the new instructor would teach. If his choice was either of the remaining two in Frege's first full year of teaching two consecutive semesters at Jena, then the comparatively small enrollments, half and one-fifth as many registrants as for the imaginary numbers course, would need to be explained in another way. It was also, significantly, a course that never again appeared in the university mathematics catalog as taught by Frege during his forty-four years lecturing in mathematics at Jena.

Applying information culled from Kreiser's compilation, Frege's *Begriffsschrift* lectures did not always command officially registered students. There may have been participants who had heard something of the new logic and foundations of mathematics the instructor had devised, who attended but did not officially enroll in Frege's logic and foundations of mathematics classes. We learn in this way that, in the winter semester of 1883–1884, Frege's weekly one-hour course on the *Begriffsschrift* enticed five students, but in the winter semester of 1884–1885, during which it was allocated two one-hour sessions per week, had zero enrolled participants. In the winter semester of 1885–1886, there were two students; for the winter semesters (as was generally the case for these offerings) 1886–1887, zero; 1887–1888, two; 1888–1889, 1889–1890, 1890–1891, and 1891–1892, again, a disappointing zero students registered for Frege's lectures on what in retrospect came to be judged one of the most important research trajectories in the history of logic and the philosophical foundations of mathematics. The situation improved in 1892–1893, when Frege had four students, with the number fluctuating thereafter between zero and roughly these highest numbers, with at most three students registered through to the winter semester of 1902–1903, whereupon, notably, eleven students darkened Frege's door, still hardly flocking to his podium, followed in 1903–1904 by a whopping twenty-one students signing up for the patient great grandfather of analytic philosophy's discussion of the logical foundations of arithmetic. Not even the publication in 1893 of the first volume of Frege's *Grundgesetze* seems to have made any impact on the dreary neglect of this work by one of the greatest minds of the century.

For comparison with interest in Frege's teaching after 1880, it may not have been until the publication of the second volume of the *Grundgesetze* in 1903 that there was a sudden upturn in Frege's *Begriffsschrift* lecture

enrollments, as Frege was slowly gaining slender international recognition. Later there would be a still paltry seven students for Frege (1905–
1906), and then nine (1906–1907). There follows a gap in the historical
record at Jena, at least in Kreiser's tally, in which there simply is no
information as to how many students wanted to hear Frege's exposition
of his revolutionary general functional calculus in the *Begriffsschrift*, or
learn about its advanced applications to the concept of number as
explained in the *Grundlagen*. The data then run dry, and we are left to
wonder whether Frege's popularity surged thereafter or dwindled. At
least one authority proposes that when a course failed officially to enroll
students, it was simply not taught, freeing more of Frege's precious time
for research, thinking, and writing. It may equally be true that Frege was
pleased or required to present the lectures if anyone was in attendance,
irrespective of whether or not they had signed in at the university
registrar.[13]

If we are looking to the reception of Frege's early publications as a clue
to the lack of students in his classroom, part of the explanation might be
found there. The remaining clientele available to mathematics offerings
at Jena, if we eliminate mathematics degree program candidates, would
have mostly been students engaged in the natural sciences. There was a
handful of these specialities for which Jena was known, a tradition to
maintain. For such young acolytes, a solid practical mathematical background was essential, especially in trigonometry and the calculus, but also
in the theory of imaginary and complex numbers, with their unlimited
theoretical and engineering applications. For these students mathematics
was an instrument, a tool to be mastered so that they could put it to good
use in physics, chemistry, civil and military engineering, even biology
and the developing subjects of sociology and political science, and unlimitedly many other rigorous natural scientific disciplines. Such students
would have had little interest in or perserverance for courses in abstract
logic or the philosophical foundations of elementary arithmetic, just as
for the more abstruse heights of pure mathematics. They had learned
elementary arithmetic already in primary school, with advanced treatment in their secondary training prior to coming to university. Why
would they return to that children's subject now? Like Frege, they had

[13] Rudolf Carnap, *Frege's Lectures on Logic: Carnap's Student Notes, 1910–1914*, ed. Erich H.
Reck and Steve Awodey (LaSalle: Open Court, 2004), pp. 2–3.

enrolled with specific purposes in mind that for them did not include a prior burning desire to discover how logic might support the basic laws of arithmetic. If the laws were correct and they worked in practice, why should mathematicians care any more about it? Who, in such a gathering of university scholars of demonstrated mathematical capability, could possibly get excited about the conceptual roots of elementary arithmetic?

The only answer is philosophers. Philosophy is viewed as a distraction from mathematics, a ruinous diversion and waste of time, certainly not something anyone needs to understand in order to master the relevant algorithms needed for practical theoretical and engineering applications.

Finally, there is the question of Frege's teaching style. We do not possess much in the way of anecdotal evidence, student evaluations of professors' performance being a phenomenon that is less than one hundred years old. Extrapolating backward from a later report on Frege's pedagogical technique by Rudolf Carnap in his "Intellectual Autobiography," we learn something of Frege's classroom presentation style and demeanor. As almost the sole source and recorded eyewitness of Frege's manner of lecture delivery, relatively late in his career, and assuming that Frege did not suddenly develop a lack of interaction with students, we are offered the following written reminiscence:

From 1910 to 1914 I studied at the Universities of Jena and Freiburg/i.B. [im Breisgau]. First I concentrated on philosophy and mathematics; later, physics and philosophy were my major fields. In the selection of lecture courses I followed only my own interests without thinking about examinations or a professional career. When I did not like a lecture course, I dropped it and studied the subject by reading books in the field instead . . . [T]he most fruitful inspiration I received from university lectures did not come from those in the field of philosophy proper or mathematics proper, but rather from the lectures of Frege on the borderlands between those fields, namely, symbolic logic and the foundations of mathematics.

   Gottlob Frege (1848–1925) was at that time, although past 60, only Professor Extraordinarius (Associate Professor) of mathematics in Jena. His work was practically unknown in Germany; neither mathematicians nor philosophers paid any attention to it. It was obvious that Frege was deeply disappointed and sometimes bitter about this dead silence . . . In the fall [Wintersemester] of 1910, I attended Frege's course "Begriffsschrift" (conceptual notation, ideography), out of curiosity, not knowing anything either of the man or the subject except for a friend's remark that somebody had found it interesting . . . We found a very small number of other students there. Frege looked old beyond his years. He was of small stature, rather shy, extremely introverted. He seldom looked at the audience. Ordinarily we saw only his back, while he drew the strange diagrams of his symbolism on the blackboard and explained them. Never did a student ask a question or make a remark, whether during the lecture or afterwards. The possibility of a discussion seemed to be out of the question ... Towards the end of the semester [only then!] Frege indicated that the new logic to which he had introduced us, could serve for the construction of the whole of mathematics. This remark aroused our curiosity.[14]

Carnap's later experience in Frege's classroom was in some ways typical, and, being Carnap, in other ways untypical. What stands out is the impression Frege made as a lecturer. Others lacking Carnap's motivations and philosophical preparation might not have been tolerant of Frege's eccentric teaching. According to Carnap's account, there were few students sufficiently able to learn much from Frege in that environment, given Frege's presentation persona. It could not have helped Frege's cause in this regard also that at his age he was only Extraordinariat and not fully promoted *ordentlicher* Professor. Reputation and standing in the mathematics faculty at Jena would not have gone unnoticed by students. When young scholars do not simply follow their interests as Carnap did, coming from a reasonably wealthy self-made small-ribbon-manufacturing family, considering himself free to do as he felt inclined, they may look to their instructors' academic status also as an index to those with whom, other things being equal in terms of their vocational prospects, it would be most worth their while to study. Frege did not rate highly when judged by students on this scale.

Carnap adds another note of explanation relevant to the sparse attendance at Frege's lectures during this later phase of Frege's teaching. Less than a decade before Frege's retirement and thirty-six years after he began his appointment as *Privatdozent*, Carnap made the following offhand comment: "The fact that the audience was so small was partly also due to the time: the lectures were at seven o'clock in the morning."[15] We do not know whether it was always Frege's policy to teach at this ungodly (or godly) hour, or the teaching schedule for his off-beat topic with which the increasingly suspicious and later openly hostile mathematics faculty at Jena may have saddled him. Conceivably, it was his choice deliberately to hold down the number of students with whom he had to deal, before whom he might have been embarrassed to speak, to risk the question that sees through the mask of classroom authority about things an instructor

---

[14] Carnap, "Intellectual Autobiography," in *The Philosophy of Rudolf Carnap*, ed. Paul Schilpp (LaSalle: Open Court, 1963), pp. 3–84.
[15] Carnap, quoted in *Frege's Lectures on Logic*, ed. Reck and Awodey, p. 20.

at heart may be altogether unsure about. Insofar as the number of students was concerned, he might have preferred having none at all. Interaction could have exposed his lack of wit, speed, and spontaneity of reply. His abilities in these areas were in doubt, as his Habilitation defense committee chair Abbe had already noted in 1874. Frege's reticence with regard to communicating directly and engaging in lively classroom conversation with students would have been a deterrent to many of his potential trainees in the new logic and arithmetic.

Who, reading these words, would have been sufficiently tempted and motivated to make the class bell by 7:00 am? Certainly there would not have been droves of students who could have profited from the content, if not the performance aspect, of Frege's lectures. Whether by choice, lottery, or uncongenial administration, perhaps to get an early start on his day, or have his teaching over with so that he could concentrate on writing, Frege had an early-bird special on *Begriffsschrift*-related lectures that would not have suited all students' personal schedules, not to speak of their late-night carousing from time to time, to which students worldwide are both prone and entitled. In a later manuscript, Carnap supplemented his portrait of Frege's personality thus: "I only lived in Jena until July 1919; after August of that year in Buchenbach near Freiburg. There I wrote *Der Raum* [*On Space*]. I only occasionally came back to Jena for a few days. Why did I not seek Frege out? I was too shy; he was after all very withdrawn."[16] Withdrawal being a doubtful strategy for winning large numbers of qualified students, not to mention Frege's lecture routine and their scheduled time, at least when Carnap attended, it is not astonishing that, on top of all the other difficulties Frege encountered as a result of his popularity, or rather lack thereof, in those days of his Jena Associate Professorship, he did not have many students.

If Carnap's experience was average, then students might have elected against Frege's elective lectures. It is interesting that Carnap appears to speak without acknowledging any special interpretation on his part of Frege as being considered neither mathematician nor philosopher in the conventional sense, but as a thinker working in the "borderland" between these fields. If this was Frege's general reputation at the time, if this was how he was perceived in the social climate of the Jena mathematics

---

[16] The relevant text is ASP/RC 088-80-01 in the Archive of Scientific Philosophy at the Hillman Library, University of Pittsburgh. The quotation is from *Frege's Lectures on Logic*, ed. Reck and Awodey, p. 10.

faculty and among philosophers also beyond Jena, then it comes as no surprise that mathematics majors would not have beaten down his lecture-room doors. Frege's clientele base was primarily natural science students needing to bolster their applied mathematics skills. However much they may have profited from other courses in Frege's Jena curriculum, Frege's *Begriffsschrift* was tangential to their essential requirements, to say the least. Neither the sleep-deprived pupils, nor certainly mathematically innocent philosophy students, would have attended, except out of curiosity, as Carnap remarks in his own case when recollecting his Jena University audit. We can extrapolate backwards from Carnap's later 1910 experience in Frege's classroom to the start of Frege's teaching career in 1874 a continuous degeneration of teaching ability that brought Frege from a promising start to what Carnap described thirty-six years later. The fewer students he had, the less he cared. The less he cared, the fewer students he had. There was no cycle discernible in the enrollment records for Frege's mathematics courses, only progressive descent and depreciation. The students did not show much interest, and for Frege the feeling was mutual.

There was word of mouth advertising for Frege, some of it positive. These recommendations had also reached Carnap, and he was sufficiently intrigued. Had this been Frege's demeanor all along, even from the first days of his *Privatdozent* appointment? If so, then there is no further mystery to be explained as to why Frege did not attract armies of enthusiastic logic, foundations of mathematics, or philosophy students to the blackboard he is reported as preferring to confront rather than the drowsy, sometimes uncomprehending, faces of Jena's pre-selected student population. Aside from these difficulties of acceptance and widespread interest, Frege was suffering the common fate of those who attempt to bring about innovations in thinking, namely that their proposals are likely to be misunderstood, neglected, rejected, incompetently dismissed, and ignored for a time before they gain recognition, if they are ever favored by history in this way. If Frege's professional colleagues did not understand or appreciate what he was developing, how could it be expected that an audience of students beginning university would find their way into such specialized previously unheard-of topics?

The early evaluation reports of Frege's teaching, in contrast with Carnap's later description, were generally positive. Was this whitewash, kind words to help ease Frege past the university committees that would need to judge his suitability to continue teaching mathematics at Jena? The faculty, at least at first, did not want to replace him. Or did Frege's teaching and engagement with students so severely decline in the time between his becoming a *Privatdozent* at Jena and the lecture course on his *Begriffsschrift* that Carnap attended? If the latter is the case, then Frege may have succumbed to pedagogical burnout at the lecture podium. Confronted by the combination of his general sense of dismay over the lack of sufficiently competent, prepared, and enthusiastic students with the general failure of his life's work to find acceptance, especially the critical hailstorm greeting his publication of the *Begriffsschrift* and the *Grundlagen*, Frege may have discovered himself going through the motions of teaching with little enthusiasm or expectation of any positive comprehending response.

A Guarded Journey of Ascent

Frege worked hard. He jumped through every hoop for academic advancement. He became Dr. at Göttingen, and then habilitated as a *Privatdozent*, and, looking ahead, *außerordentlicher* or Extraordinariat Professor, at Jena. He worked too hard not to be able to pursue his mathematical instincts wherever they might carry him. Why should Frege, after completing all his formal instruction and student-level training in mathematics, not have done whatever he wanted in his research? It was not until much later, in 1887, that his salary at the university was made substantial enough for him to support himself and a family. Since he was working mostly for free, he would do whatever he wanted in mathematics.

It was not *die Universität*, nor the good tax-paying citizens of Jena or Thüringen, or the royal house, that kept Frege's body and soul together, even as an *außerordentlicher* Professor. For a brief time during his Associate Professorship, in addition to his regular university duties, Frege was compelled to teach mathematics at a private boarding school for boys, the Pfeiffer Institut in Jena, which had been founded by Ernst Pfeiffer (1847–1917). Frege moonlighted there from 1882 to 1884. If Frege felt obligations to anyone or any institution other than to meet the bare-bones responsibilities of the contractual position he had accepted, it would undoubtedly rather be toward his loving supportive mother, Auguste.

Frege sought not merely to explain the logic of arithmetic, although he accomplished that task in exquisite detail, but rather to explain arithmetic as logic. The basic laws of logic are axioms that blossom inferentially in an explosion of derived logical forms of use in understanding the relation of elementary arithmetical axioms to derived arithmetical theorems. When the logic of concept-functions is applied to a purely logical concept of natural number, then elementary arithmetic as a whole can be perceived in *Begriffsschrift* notation to be purely logical throughout. Logical laws govern the application of arithmetical concept-functions to natural numbers 0 or 1 to produce all of the remaining natural numbers. A function for division on the natural numbers, on any two except for 0 as denominator, locates first all rational real numbers. Then, by means of functions equivalent to Dedekind cuts, all irrational real numbers, and hence collectively all real numbers, are situated along the real number line.[17] With the real numbers in hand, further functions provide all mathematical objects and relations needed for elementary arithmetic and geometry, including the calculus and extravagant higher-order mappings of real-number-transcending imaginary and complex numbers onto a two-dimensional plane. Effectively, if the project succeeds, all of mathematics before and after Frege will have been shown to rest upon purely logical foundations, and not, as Kant argued, on the transcendental ground of time as a pure form of perception, namely intuition or *Anschauung*.[18]

Frege would then have logically analyzed the concepts of arithmetic and introduced the general method of defining functions needed to prove within *Begriffsschrift* logic's expressive and inferential functional calculus all theorems deductively supported by a choice of mathematical axioms. As to prior off-screen selection of axioms, Frege had conservative ideas about their objectivity and the mind's ability to intuit abstract necessary truths. That the whole business was at some level subjective is indicated by the fact that not all mathematicians agree about the truth of basic laws

---

[17] Richard Dedekind, "I. Continuity and Irrational Numbers," in Dedekind, *Essays on the Theory of Numbers* [1901] (New York: Dover Mathematics Books, 1963), pp. 1–29, especially pp. 12–23. Dedekind might also have been rebuked by Frege for being psychologistic, especially in the essay's opening pages.

[18] See, among other useful sources, Carl J. Posy, ed., *Kant's Philosophy of Mathematics: Modern Essays* (Berlin: Springer-Verlag, 1982); A. T. Winterbourne, *The Ideal and the Real: Kant's Theory of Space, Time, and Mathematical Constructions* (Bury St. Edmunds: Abramis Academic Publishing, 2007); and Lisa Shabel, *Mathematics in Kant's Critical Philosophy: Reflections on Mathematical Practice* (London: Routledge, 2011).

of logic and arithmetic, as seen in Frege's disagreements with his contemporary and mathematical–philosophical rival Hilbert.[19] The logic's
graphic advantages were largely lost on Frege's readers, who did not
warm to his symbolism even with the greater passage of time. The
algebraic flexibility of Frege's functional calculus should have recommended the logic over the abstract symbolic representation of mutually
exclusionary or overlapping extensions of term logic predicates and
categoricals in Boole's logic as in two-dimensional Venn, Euler, or
Lewis Carroll diagrams.[20]

Criticisms and Practical Implications

In the meantime, Frege remained professionally active in other ways. He
joined the Jena Literary Museum (*Literarisches Museum zu Jena*) in 1879.
There he enjoyed access to numerous journals, magazines, and newspapers, as well as reference books of many different kinds that were
potentially useful to his work. There was a reading club, which Frege
often attended and to which he sometimes contributed lectures. He did so
regularly until 1912, and then again from 1914 to 1916, offering during
this time an unpublished lecture on "Logik" that was later included in his
Nachlaß (*Posthumous Writings*). Membership dues for the always cash-
strapped Frege with his material priorities properly in order were 5
Marks per quarter, 20 Marks per year. This is on top of the 11 Marks
he was already paying distributively to the Mathematical Society of Jena

---

[19] See William Demopoulos, "Frege, Hilbert and the Conceptual Structure of Model Theory," *History and Philosophy of Logic*, 15 (1994), pp. 211–25; Dummett, "Frege on the Consistency of Mathematical Theories," in *Studien zu Frege*, ed. Matthias Schirn (Stuttgart-Bad Cannstatt: Frommann-Holzboog, 1975), pp. 229–42; Michael Resnik, "The Frege–Hilbert Controversy," *Philosophy and Phenomenological Research*, 34 (1973), pp. 386–403; Stewart Shapiro, "Categories, Structures, and the Frege–Hilbert Controversy," *Philosophia Mathematica*, 13 (2005), pp. 61–77; Kai Wehmeier, "Aspekte der Frege–Hilbert-Korrespondenz," *History and Philosophy of Logic*, 18 (1997), pp. 201–209; and Frege, *Philosophical and Mathematical Correspondence*, correspondence with Hilbert, IV [xv]/1–9, pp. 32–52, especially Frege to Hilbert Letters IV [xv]/3 and 5, pp. 34–38, with what Frege seemed to think was a sting in the tail in the final paragraphs, and pp. 43–48.

[20] An entertaining early read on the logical diagrams of Euler, Venn, Lewis Carroll, and others is provided by Martin Gardner, *Logic Machines and Diagrams* (New York: McGraw-Hill, 1958). See also the more recently technically informed collections put together by Gerard Allwein and Jon Barwise, eds., *Logical Reasoning with Diagrams* (Oxford: Oxford University Press, 1996); and by Amirouche Moktefi and Sun-Joo Shin, eds., *Visual Reasoning with Diagrams* (Basel: Birkhäuser, 2013).

and the Society for Medicine and Natural Science.[21] Frege must have felt it an enormous privilege to be able to cultivate his thinking by acquiring membership in these associations and participating in their frequent meetings. It was a financial burden, but a way of remaining a student, of still being in school, where there was always so much more to learn, despite his now having become a professor.

What Frege discovered in the icy reception of his *Begriffsschrift*, in light of Stumpf's well-meaning advice, was not to popularize the next movement in the symphony he was energetically conducting to unhearing ears. Imagine Igor Stravinsky's *Firebird* being performed for the first time before an audience in Salzburg or Vienna in Wolfgang Amadeus Mozart's day. This is something like Frege's historical circumstance. He was so far ahead of his time, with no preparatory advances in the general mathematical and philosophical culture on which to lean, that he could not readily make his thought intelligible to those newly encountering his *Begriffsschrift*. Who among us even today, unless we have specialized interest and training, can painlessly read Frege's *Begriffsschrift* logical notation without first translating it into some more familiar kind of logic such as the Peano linear or Whitehead–Russell *Principia Mathematica* symbolism? Such translations were not available for the benefit of Frege's readers at the time. Lacking that guide, they were left to wonder why Frege wrote out his logic as he did, and why anyone should care.

Perhaps Frege thought that everyone would read the *Begriffsschrift* with Frege's own expertise and fatherly love for the book. They would wait like later eager cinema-goers at the theater after the last cliff-hanger to see what would happen to the villain, hero, and heroine in the next episode. Less anachronistically, he may have imagined that they would be captivated like those who read serial novels, like Charles Dickens's or Fyodor Dostoyevsky's at the time, fervently awaiting the next installment in order to find out the fate of the fiction's characters. Critics also wanted explicit comparisons between Frege's system and Boole's. They wanted to be able to take their bearings from something already known. In his penetrating but ultimately unkind review of Frege's *Begriffsschrift*, Schröder was particularly vocal in this respect. Frege missed the chance to offer what might have helped his audience better understand his large-

---

[21] Frege's professional society memberships and professional dues in 1879 and afterward are detailed in Kreiser, *Gottlob Frege*, pp. 469–79.

scale proposal by contrasting it with another, better-known, algebraic logic, namely Boole's extended four-term Hamiltonian syllogistic term logic.[22] Aside from typesetting difficulties inherent in his notation, editors and referees did not typically understand what they were looking at when scanning Frege's spatially two-dimensional logical formulas. They did not appreciate the usefulness of the strange ideography. Frege described his dilemma and the corner into which he had painted himself in a letter of 29 August 1882 intended either for Anton Marty, another Brentano student, or for Stumpf, explaining that "It is a difficulty for me to gain entry to the philosophical journals ... I am caught in an unfortunate circle: Before anyone will pay attention to the *Begriffsschrift* they want to know how it performs in applications, which I cannot demonstrate without presupposing an acquaintance with [the *Begriffsschrift* logical system]."[23]

A further point of note is that, as with his later essays on object, function, concept, sense and reference, thoughts in the sense of abstract propositions, negation, the conditional, quantification, deductive inference, and truth, Frege held back vital explanatorily useful discussions of what he must have considered side-issues in his logic, philosophy of mathematics, and theory of meaning. He deliberately refrained from juxtaposing his system with Boole's, and later with Schröder's supposedly objectionably psychologistic algebraic logic, both in the *Begriffsschrift* and in the *Grundlagen*. The topics instead were made afterthoughts in specialized essays materializing after his main works years after the publication of the *Begriffsschrift* and in between the *Grundlagen* and *Grundgesetze I*. The Boole essays never found a publisher during Frege's lifetime. If we are casting about for a flaw in Frege's explanations of his logical advances, it may well have been his failure to take into account the starting-place of his potential readers, who at the onset would not have understood, appreciated, or had much sympathy for his nonpareil formalisms. He offers no reason for readers to share his expectations about the positive value that might result when the logic is applied. Nor was Frege's name well known. There was no presumption by author recognition of something worthwhile likely to be going on between the volume's covers to help sell the book or recommend it positively to reviewers.

---

[22] See again Chapter 3 note 5 and Chapter 4 note 28.

[23] Kreiser, *Gottlob Frege*, p. 368, my translation. Also included in Frege, *Philosophical and Mathematical Correspondence*, p. 102.

Frege still had higher rungs of the academic ladder to climb. He would not merely survive being a *Privatdozent* at Jena after completing and defending his post-doctoral degree. He was determined to excel and make a career for himself. Most of all at this delicate stage of his work Frege wanted to answer the difficult questions that had troubled him almost from the outset in his program of mathematical studies, concerning the relation between logic and arithmetic. Frege wanted to investigate the relation between a correct general formal symbolic logic and the conceptual, expressive, and inferential ground of mathematics, beginning with elementary arithmetic.

Miscalculations

Frege could have forestalled some of the misunderstanding his work engendered. For reasons about which we can now only speculate, he did not see the value of doing so, or anyway did not act upon the insight if he ever considered the possibility. In consequence he paid a heavy price. He did so not only in terms of the immediate impression, or rather lack thereof, made by his first writings, but in terms of the frustration of his further academic ambitions, as he had been expecting to be promoted at Jena from *Privatdozent* to Extraordinariat Professor in 1884, roughly at the time of publishing the *Grundlagen*. It did not help much at the time, and may have even hurt his chances, although in chasing promotion he seems to have relied before the committee almost entirely on the strength, if that is the right word, of his *Begriffsschrift*.

When the promotion cycle came around again for Frege in subsequent years, and he would have been in principle eligible for preferment from *außerordentlicher* to *ordentlicher* (Full, with Chair) Professor, Frege was passed over in favor of others among his colleagues. Thomae was ranked first, followed by Aurel Edmund Voss, who had been one of Frege's teachers, second, and Jakob Lüroth in third place. These colleagues were all doing straightforward research in established branches of mathematics, rather than trying to revolutionize logic and the philosophical foundations of arithmetic. Frege, to adapt racetrack argot, did not show, did not even place. By then, Frege was able to more than compensate for the difference in salary with support from the cooperative relationship Abbe had bridged to the deep-pocketed Zeiss Corporation. As Abbe's protégé, Frege was also made a beneficiary of Zeiss patronage. By remaining at *außerordentlicher* status, voluntarily or by virtue of being passed over for his misunderstood mathematical hobby-horse, Frege limited his administrative duties and allowed himself greater time and flexibility for ongoing research in logicism. It would not be until 1896 that Frege was awarded an Honorary Full Professorship or *ordentlicher Honorarprofessur*, and that titular encouragement would not directly contribute to his university wages.

Abbe could not disguise his disappointment on Frege's behalf regarding the gamut of views ranging from lukewarm reception to undisguised animus that the *Begriffsschrift* attracted in the journals. Writing in support of Frege, Abbe still had to admit that the book would probably be thoroughly read only by a few, and that it would be understood and appreciated by still fewer. Laßwitz expressed qualified admiration for Frege's *Begriffsschrift*. His positive support may have literally saved Frege's appointment at Jena. Had Frege not been promoted to *außerordentlicher* Professor in 1879, it might have meant the end of his career as a professional mathematician at university rank. Naturally, Frege had many other teaching and research options open for a person with his skills and energy. It would nevertheless have marked a significant departure from where Frege had hoped his hard work and worthy ideas would carry him.

Remarkably, especially in view of what Carnap was much later to report of Frege's unengaging noninteractive teaching manner in 1910–1914, Frege's associates at the time praised his mathematics teaching, and especially his gift for exceptional clarity. As usual, Abbe's report was rewritten by the committee recommending Frege for promotion. Frege's teaching in particular was emphasized in such a way as to overshadow even Abbe's disappointment in the *Begriffsschrift*, and more trenchantly its appallingly bad press, which was predictable to everyone but Frege. According to Stelzner, "Concerning teaching effectiveness, Frege was evaluated very positively, which on later occasions was not usually the case . . ."[24] Frege had it in him to be a good teacher, unless the report was sheer fabrication to keep him on the payroll, implying that something demoralizing must have happened later to make him lose heart.

---

[24] Stelzner, "Ernst Abbe and Gottlob Frege," p. 20. See Sven-Ake Wegner, *Eine kurze Einführung in Gottlob Freges Begriffsschrift* (Wuppertal: Bergische Universität, 1979), pp. 1–2.

It was Fortlage more than Abbe who was convinced of the merits of Frege's promotion to Extraordinariat. The application, with all necessary documentation, was introduced by Eucken with the ailing Snell's support on 10 January 1879. The faculty decided the very next day, 11 January, to promote Frege to Associate Professor. The proposal went forward in the usual trail of pulp and ink to the *Prorektor* on 13 January. It was considered that the application had a good chance of success, not so much because of Frege's qualifications, as due to the external circumstances that Snell was too ill to continue teaching and Abbe was not seeking a permanent university position, in lieu of his private-sector employment opportunities at Zeiss. It was as if the argument from 1874, when, against the tide, Frege was appointed as a *Privatdozent*, had been fast-forwarded five years. This time, in 1879, when he was up for promotion to Extraordinariat, the committee's recommendation of 13 January stated that

Dr. Frege has continued his teaching beginning in the summer semester of 1874, meeting with considerable success and with increasing advantage for the university. Although he may not win much applause from the average student, he has by now acquired very valuable teaching effectiveness, and students are gradually becoming aware of what benefits his lectures offer. In fact, Dr. Frege possesses the virtue of great clarity and precision of representation, and, because of the deliberateness of his presentation, is particularly suited to introduce aspiring listeners to the most difficult matters of mathematical studies; his lectures on mathematicians with respect to the main points mentioned are totally exemplary.[25]

It is clear from the report and accompanying documents that it was Abbe who had attended Frege's classroom lectures. He was able from first-hand personal knowledge to report on Frege's abilities to the committee and finally to the university upper administration responsible for promoting Frege or dashing his hopes for academic advancement. It is not hard to read between the lines of these reports. Some evaluators called upon for their opinions were impressed neither with Frege's first line of research since the Habilitation, which had been crowned by the publication of the *Begriffsschrift*, nor with his teaching, and particularly not with the direction his teaching was likely to follow in pursuit of the embarrassments of his first slender, barely comprehensible, insufficiently motivated, mysteriously technical book. Others, particularly his teachers,

[25] Kreiser, *Gottlob Frege*, pp. 360–61, my translation.

who must have been scratching their heads wondering what Frege was up to with his scrolling filigree notation that the world had never seen before, wanted Frege onboard in the worst way, because he would minimally fill some of the gaping holes in their teaching calendar. Frege was someone they knew from reasonably long acquaintance who was after all, when he wanted to be, an excellent conventional mathematician and teacher of mathematics. Who knew whether or not he would discover something worthwhile on the unconventional road he was traveling?

In the meantime, as an Associate Professor, Frege would continue to teach the mathematics students and complete the program of studies to which their faculty was committed. Apologies concerning the *Begriffsschrift*, about what it was and what the outside world beyond and even within Jena's corridors was thinking of it, were also included in the committee's report. It would not do to pretend there was no elephant in the room. The beast had to be acknowledged and put in its proper perspective, to deprive it of the ability to derail Frege's promotion. What good could be said of it honestly was said. It was original. It discussed abstract logical and mathematical problems. It could not be expected to gain immediate understanding or attract a large following. It was peculiar, after all. The fact cannot be denied, but must be acknowledged without undue emphasis. There will not be many readers, the committee admitted, who will be capable of reading the work with understanding and a sense of its potential and logical–mathematical, not to mention philosophical, significance. The report concluded as follows: "In a word, Dr. Frege has been very useful to our university, he is much appreciated by his audience, and is an independent thinker."[26]

This was positive spin, for which there is sometimes a less flattering word. That Frege's work was ignored and maligned makes him "independent." The main point clearly outstanding was that he had already pitched in when needed as a *Privatdozent* and had filled the lecture niches which had arisen because of Snell's and Abbe's indispositions. That he was much appreciated by his audience in Jena mathematics classes by implication may be read as compensating for the fact that as a mathematical author he had not been much appreciated by his readers. Nor is it clear to what extent the committee, eager to retain Frege's teaching services and not understanding enough themselves about his

---

[26] *Ibid.*, pp. 361–62.

Begriffsschrift to praise or condemn the project with any confidence, and unwilling to go against the published opinions of experts in the field who had reviewed the treatise negatively, did not help Frege's cause by emphasizing as his forte the softest, most subjective side of his evaluation. He was a good teacher, especially. Those who wrote the report had seen him lecture; those who then read it had not. Frege's supporters could honestly say that they had come away from the experience with the sense that Frege's teaching was clear, solid, careful, and deliberate. Was this the same man Carnap later saw with his back to students at the chalkboard? What was needed by the Jena faculty of mathematics, they declared, was precisely such a teacher. Five years later, in 1879, as Frege faced another tribunal of internal promotion, they were prepared to overlook the scorn with which the *Begriffsschrift* had been greeted. As the paperwork was passed along from one university administrative office to a succession of desks, and finally to the Grand Ducal Ministry of Culture on 17 June 1879, the opinions about Frege's merits for promotion were at best guarded.

There was no great momentum to catapult Frege from his post-Habilitation *Privatdozent* position to Extraordinariat, but nor were there serious obstacles. It was probably seen as advantageous for the university because it was advantageous for the mathematics faculty. Ironically, *Kurator* August Freiherr von Tuercke remarked, on the one hand, that hardly anyone was going to be in a position to read and be able to comment authoritatively on Frege's *Begriffsschrift*, while on the other hand observing that on a number of grounds the book suffered from "a prominent lack of precision." Was he really competent to describe the *Begriffsschrift* as imprecise? Surely a reader cannot judge whether or not a book lacks precision without being capable of working through the symbolisms with sound understanding, something the average university bureaucrat was perhaps not chosen to do. The conclusion the committee reached is that, in light of Frege's significant academic qualifications, his project, whatever it was he was trying to do, might be expected to lead to worthwhile results, noting the lifesaving positive review of the *Begriffsschrift* by Laßwitz. Such judgment, tepid as it was, could anyway not be held against Frege.[27] The appointment went through after all this white-knuckle paper shuffling, and the Grand Ducal Ministry in the end appointed Frege *außerordentlicher* Professor

[27] *Ibid.*

(Extraordinariat) von Mathematik mit Spezialität. Frege's appointment was qualified as a special concentration (*Schwerpunkt*) as opposed to the general qualifications reflecting mastery of the field expected of an *ordentlicher* Professor or Ordinariat. The promotion was approved on 16 July 1879, and officially recognized in the university senate by the Vice-Rector of the University of Jena. The deal was sealed a few weeks later on 2 August.

At last Frege had a modest regular stipend. He began to draw a salary by which to plan his adult life and ease the burden his academic quests had imposed on his mother back in Wismar. She would now join him in Jena. After selling the girls' school, sometime in 1879 or 1880, she would build a double house in Jena at Forst (Forstweg) 29, which was completed in 1887. Thereafter, we read of Frege collecting 300 Marks annually, and, as the semesters pass, teaching fees of 162 Marks, 114 Marks, 108, 16, 84, 48, 30, 20, and so on, depending on enrollments, on top of his regular salary. Bynum offers the following detailed synopsis:

The promotion was granted on the strength of a recommendation by Ernst Abbe, who apparently was Frege's best friend and strongest supporter at Jena. Abbe cited the fact that Frege had given the University five years of excellent teaching, had carried an overload, and had taken on the work of the ailing Professor Snell. Then, in discussing the publication of the *Conceptual Notation*, Abbe made some perceptive comments. The book contains, he said, very original ideas that reveal unusual mental powers. He speculated that mathematics "will be affected, perhaps very considerably, but immediately only very little, by the inclination of the author and the content of the book." He noted that some mathematicians "find little that is appealing in so subtle investigations into the formal interrelationships of knowledge," and "scarcely anyone will be able, off hand, to take a position on the very original cluster of ideas in this book"; thus, "it will probably be understood and appreciated by only a few."

Abbe's speculations were remarkably prophetic . . . Abbe's pessimistic prediction that the Conceptual Notation "will probably be understood and appreciated by only a few" proved to be an understatement. For years, virtually no one but Frege understood the Conceptual Notation and no one important appreciated it.

Part of the responsibility for this unfortunate state of affairs was Frege's. He presented in his book many new and profound ideas; but they were abstract and difficult, at best, for the unprepared reader to grasp; and Frege did not prepare his readers well. He did not thoroughly explain the purpose of his symbolic language; he did not make it clear that his notation was a device to ensure correct reasoning in proofs of mathematical propositions. Also, he did not explain why the notation had an unusual two-dimensional form, or why existing notations (he probably did not know about them) such as those of Boole and Schröder would not suffice for his purposes. For these reasons it was a very difficult book to read; and because of all the symbols it was a bit frightening at first sight.

As a result, many readers misconstrued the aim of the book, and it was misjudged and rejected by those who should have welcomed it. This was tragic, for Frege, an exceptionally lucid lecturer, was adept at introducing complicated mathematical notions to beginning students; and it is a mystery that he failed to exercise his rare talent in his book.[28]

What Frege learned in writing the *Grundlagen* was not that he should take what he had written in his *Begriffsschrift* and reclothe it in ordinary prose. Even a casual survey of the *Grundlagen* reveals that Frege is not simply undertaking a prose rehash of his *Begriffsschrift*. No one can look at Frege's first two short monographs and come to the conclusion that he was trying to rewrite the first book in a second without using symbolic logic. The topic is new and different. Frege had not stalled or gone backward, but taken the next step forward in his systematic program to establish the logical foundations of mathematics beginning with elementary arithmetic. What he gained, possibly taking Stumpf's advice into account in his own way, was that an essential purely logical concept of natural number was needed as input to the general concept-functional calculus. He could, and there are good independent reasons why he should have done so, take this next vital step informally rather than in *Begriffsschrift* notation. That further development would come only later in the *Grundgesetze* with a fully articulated reduction of the basic laws of elementary arithmetic to concept-functions mentioned in the basic laws of pure logic. For the moment, *Begriffsschrift* logical symbolism was not only inessential, but potentially a hindrance to a purely logical analysis of the concept of natural number.

Battered but Not Defeated

Frege was unquestionably wounded by the weak reception of his *Begriffsschrift*. The present interpretation of the basic facts surrounding the history of Frege's writing and publication of the text, and the deafening silence and misaimed criticisms the project attracted, is not, as has sometimes been asserted, that Frege sought to rewrite the basic tenets of logicism in ordinary prose for the mathematically challenged or conventionally entrenched. That was not the reason for Frege's writing his *Grundlagen* without logical symbolism.

---

[28] Bynum, "On the Life and Work of Gottlob Frege," in *Frege: Conceptual Notation*, pp. 16–17.

Frege, if his admirers are candid, even in retrospect, did not do much to prevent misapprehension and mystification about his purpose. Frege's motivation and his expectations of applications for *Begriffsschrift* logic as an ideal language for the expression of concept-functions, truth-functions in particular, and inferential relations among true or false predications and molecular truth-functional compound propositions remained largely undisclosed. He did not openly share his sense that the logical interrelations of the most fundamental mathematical concepts would eventually be presented naked to the eye on the pages of his completed treatises, on turning from one diagrammatic proof to the next. The problem was partly one of Frege's demand for a thorough step-by-step gapless transparent inference structure for the theorems of arithmetic. Like the steps needed for mathematical proof, Frege glimpsed the project in its entirety. He had to put everything required for the demonstration in place *seriatim*, one major building block at a time, and only when previous inquiry had prepared the way. He took the necessary first steps first, laying out the logical system by which the most elementary concept-functions of elementary arithmetic could be explained.

If *Begriffsschrift* logic and the *Grundlagen* analysis of a purely logical concept of natural number were to have legs, Frege might have thought, his approach would have to establish its credentials entirely on its own merits, rather than because of its imagined utility in philosophically grandiose theory-building. We may be tempted to look the other way when problems arise if we think that we need these components for something of commanding value if those theories are set in place. The logic and analysis of natural number can be misjudged in light of what they are supposed to enable the philosophy of mathematics to accomplish, especially if interesting dividends are paid in other branches of these disciplines. That is a potential source of faulty reasoning based on wishful thinking that should be avoided. Frege's logic and analysis of natural number had to make their own way in the world before they could be effectively put to further use mathematically and philosophically. They could not be trusted for such an urgent task until they had first stood the test. Frege may have wanted their participation in the progress of pure logicism to draw fire on them. Then, only if they emerged unscathed, would he try to bring them together in the production of a rigorous pure non-psychologistic logicism.

The phantom question haunting most of the negative press that Frege's first book received, setting the tone also for later responses, is one that Frege himself could easily have answered. Assuming his grasp of how the parts were meant to contribute in a later phase to the philosophical objectives of a rigorous non-psychologistic logicism, he could have simply let his readers in on the secret. He could have done so as easily as any author trying to make a new contribution in a well-established field, if something had not psychologically, philosophically, or methodologically prevented him. He was paying the price for the oversight in the exposition of his early ideas, whether it was accidental or deliberate. He would continue to do so throughout his career until late in his retirement, Russell's notices notwithstanding. Frege's reputation and proper recognition surged, as he deserved, only many decades after his death.

Logicism Phase One-and-a-Half

All of the above led to the writing and publication of Frege's second book during this period of his life, the condensed discursive *Grundlagen*. Frege had already officially joined the ranks of initially under-appreciated intellectual innovators. He knew it at the time. If Carnap was right in his reading of Frege's attitude, the ignorance and neglect of Frege's work made a profound impact on the already-introverted Frege, exacerbating his lack of public self-confidence.

Nonetheless, it did not stop Frege from pursuing the larger plan of his logicist reduction of the basic laws of elementary arithmetic. He continued to work away at what he knew in his heart to be the right constructive logical analysis of the theorems of elementary arithmetic. He kept his aim on what he consistently judged the wave of the future for potential developments in logic and the philosophy of mathematics, as he would ultimately in later published phases of the program for selected topics in a general semantics and philosophy of language. He studied the critical notices of his writings as they appeared. He was satisfied that no one as yet had found a serious flaw in the program, albeit largely because no one had gone to the trouble to understand and correctly interpret, or even take a very close look at, what he was trying to argue.

Frege throughout this time remained his own harshest critic. He was philosophically driven to work out his ideas against relevant objections, but unconcerned about their critical reception in the sense of popularity or lack thereof. The validation and ultimate trial, the external standard his logical foundations of mathematics must first meet, was to put his thoughts into such a form that they could be published and exposed to approval or criticism. Frege's publication choices suggest that he understood mathematics and philosophy alike from an epistemic standpoint as dialectical processes. He wanted to make the two fields enter into productive dialogue, partly by positively developing his own logic and formal logical foundations of elementary arithmetic. He did so only after having effectively criticized major alternatives among recently active authors writing on similar questions concerning the concept of natural number. The satisfaction was partly in seeing how things worked, and partly in explaining how logical and logic-grounded mathematical structures fit together. A critic cannot take the measure of the extent to which a thinker's theory may be correct until its definitions and arguments have met with and overcome powerful ideological or methodological objections. If a criticism is decisive, then its target's author will at best have learned something invaluable and otherwise unobtainable.

Releasing a philosophical text in this sense is like performing a scientific experiment. It is done to see what will happen, to confirm or disconfirm an explanatory hypothesis. If an author receives genuinely bad objections, then they can be ignored, or mentioned only to be dismissed with a sentence or two, according to taste. If they are among the legion number of bad objections that can be made to look good, that could mislead other readers and commentators, and that misrepresent the author's mathematical–philosophical program and the extent to which the author is carrying it forward successfully, then it may become necessary to get in the ring and reply polemically. Frege, though he was sometimes diplomatic, was never reluctant to do this whenever he felt called upon to join an ongoing controversy or start a new one. It can be a valuable preliminary step to clear the ground of false contenders that may have useful but wrongly or incompletely developed suggestions. Frege found in the first half of the *Grundlagen* that his competitors in offering a correct analysis of the concept-function of number, who were expending their energies in contrary directions, did not arrive at a satisfactory definition. He strengthened the case for his analysis of a purely logical concept of natural number, presenting a positive constructive alternative analysis, after first explaining why received alternatives were unacceptable and why they stood in need of a preferable replacement. The book interweaved polemical criticisms of Frege's antagonists in the struggle to understand the conceptual foundations of mathematics with his own proposal for solving the problems he had identified, with an ascent at the end of the book to a properly clarified purely logical concept.

From the *Begriffsschrift* to the *Grundlagen*

The mathematical juggernaut of Frege's logicist program to reduce the laws of elementary arithmetic to concepts and expressive and inference structures of pure logic at this time continued to roll forward. Lacking a solid properly informed criticism of the *Begriffsschrift* in the sparse commentary available about his work, and hence having no reason to rethink the project from a scientific as opposed to popularity standpoint, Frege must have planned all along to follow his *Begriffsschrift* with an analysis of a purely logical concept of natural number. The purely logical concept of natural number, together with freely available concept-functions, would enable Frege to reconstruct all of elementary arithmetic as an application of pure logic.

The *Begriffsschrift*, the first pincer movement in Frege's plan to conquer arithmetic with logic, was never intended by Frege as an end in itself. It was a means to another long-term end. It was built by Frege as an indispensable tool primarily on its own general terms, and only secondarily in the particular application he intended all along when it was able to receive as input to the calculus a purely logical concept of natural number. With a purely logical calculus of concept-functions applied to a purely logical concept of natural number, it would be largely a matter of routine to reconstruct the purely logical foundations of elementary arithmetic. The final step in Frege's philosophical program, combining a revised *Begriffsschrift* logic with the concept of natural number clarified in his *Grundlagen*, was completed with the publication in 1893 and 1903 of the two volumes of Frege's monumental *Grundgesetze*.

Between these three landmarks in mathematical logic, Frege needed to find and polish up for presentation a suitable concept of natural number. This is where things stood in Frege's logicist philosophy of arithmetic in 1884, when his second book, the *Grundlagen*, was published, constituting a vital second component in his three-part constructive pure logicism. The two works set the stage for Frege's *Grundgesetze*, in which basic laws of logic and arithmetic were formalized and theorems of elementary arithmetic logically derived. The two volumes of the third book were still nine years in the future.

Excluded from the *Grundlagen*, at least for the moment, were all the head-scratching *Begriffsschrift* formulas. Frege temporarily took leave of so unconventional and forbidding a symbolism to read in some of its more complexly branching and distinctly quantified variable-type reticulations. Frege intended his 1884 *Grundlagen* to be understandable by any intelligent philosophically competent reader as an informal fine-grained philosophical analysis of the concept of number, refreshingly without the syntactical complexities of his 1879 *Begriffsschrift*. If anyone with a strong logical or mathematical background was tempted to thumb through Frege's 1879 monograph, they would face considerable obstacles in its ungenerous sketchy prose explanations of what the author was trying to achieve. The *Grundlagen* had to stand on its own, a compact work in lucid prose. It would then have the further advantage of potentially attracting readers back to the earlier *Begriffsschrift* to give the logic a second look and offer it a second chance. It would then be seen in the light of Frege's purely logical concept of natural number developed specifically for an application of his *Begriffsschrift* as a general functional calculus of concepts. Frege's *Grundlagen* is not entirely independent of his *Begriffsschrift*, although the two can be read in isolation without understanding how they are meant to fit together. That is indeed the main problem. Frege intended the *Grundlagen* all along as providing the concept of natural number that *Begriffsschrift* logic could then parlay via freely available well-defined functions into all of elementary arithmetic, beginning with its basic laws and proceeding through the logical inferential superstructure supporting all deductively derivable arithmetical theorems.

The machinery of logic presented in Frege's *Begriffsschrift* in and of itself is incapable of establishing any truths about mathematical objects outside the logical principles Frege set forth. There must be input made to the logic, and in particular a concept of number must be introduced, if the logic's mill wheels are to have any grain to grind. It was precisely this analysis of the concept of natural number, beginning in Frege's *Grundlagen* for excellent reasons with the numbers 0 and 1, that Frege rightly understood as the next step in his blueprint for revealing the logical foundations of all of mathematics, starting with elementary arithmetic. It might be said, braving the unmanageable counterfactuals of history, that even if Frege's *Begriffsschrift* had astonished and awakened his contemporaries, if it had won every European medal in mathematics available to the most skilled, insightful, and revolutionary among those toiling in the mathematical vineyard at the time, there would still have been a definite need in the movement of Frege's thought for him to take the further step charted by the *Grundlagen* without *Begriffsschrift* symbolisms.

Frege's *Begriffsschrift* does not explain what natural numbers are, nor was it ever intended to offer any substantive analysis, just as we would not expect a second-order predicate-quantificational logic comparable to Frege's to attempt such implications today. There are no numbers as objects in the text to stand as predication subjects entering into inferential relations with other mathematical functions. The myth that Frege wrote his *Grundlagen* out of frustration over the ungenerous reception of his *Begriffsschrift* overlooks this indisputable fact. Without a concept of natural number, the *Begriffsschrift* had no subject matter to which its logical laws and inferential principles could be applied. To speak anachronistically of an analogy that would have been lost on Frege and his contemporaries, the *Begriffsschrift* without the *Grundlagen* is like a pocket calculator without a battery. Or, to improve the comparison for readers today, it is like a pocket calculator with a battery but nothing inputting numerical values by pressing function keys. It would remain inert, lifeless, awaiting application, empty, unused, potential but not actual. To frame a description crafted in terms Frege would have recognized and possibly endorsed, the *Begriffsschrift* without the *Grundlagen* is a concept-function without an argument-object, a rifle without a round, a lantern with an unlighted candle.

Frege's *Begriffsschrift* was not merely metaphorically but actually and literally a machine lacking the input feeding of raw material on which to ply its principles. It was like a function spread out over nearly one hundred pages with all its separate transparently clear principles and structurally beautiful logical laws, lacking an argument-object to accept as input and make into something complete. Neither the *Begriffsschrift* nor the *Grundlagen* could possibly accomplish by itself Frege's grand design to lay bare for the first time the deeply logical foundations of mathematics. Frege's logicism required an understanding both of the concept-function of natural number and of the deductive inferential framework of mathematical reasoning supporting its origins in pure logic and purely logical deduction of arithmetical theorems. It was only in tandem, function applied to argument, concept to logical structuring of concepts, that Frege's *Begriffsschrift* and *Grundlagen* could come together eventually in the *Grundgesetze* as Frege's logical–mathematical masterpiece. It was only there that the finishing touches were made to the first stages of pure, rigorous, non-psychologistic logicism in Frege's philosophy of arithmetic.

The project of the *Grundlagen* was to clarify the concept of natural number. Frege had the option of using or eschewing the two-dimensional logical syntax of his *Begriffsschrift*. He chose not to apply any significant formal apparatus or notation, partly, perhaps, although the evidence is thin and indirect, because he had been chastened by the reception of his *Begriffsschrift* and partly because in the three intervening years he may have convinced himself that there was strictly no need to use any abstract symbolism in order to explain the concept of natural number. He may have concluded also, as has been suggested, that there were sound philosophical reasons in the interests of pure logicism for not explicating the purely logical concept-function of natural number in *Begriffsschrift* notation.

If the *Begriffsschrift* and the *Grundlagen* were intended as stand-alone components independent of one another until combined in the *Grundgesetze*, then it is explicable also on methodological grounds why Frege would abstain from using *Begriffsschrift* logical notation in the *Grundlagen*. The clarification as to why *Begriffsschrift* notation goes underground in Frege's *Grundlagen* need have nothing whatever directly to do with the discomfiting reception of the *Begriffsschrift*, as unpleasant for Frege as it probably was. Having informally analyzed the concept of number in his *Grundlagen*, its exact meaning, sharply delimited first in philosophical terms, could then be taken over into *Begriffsschrift* logic to see what kind of axioms were best chosen to express minimal principles about numbers satisfying the concept, in intuitively true arithmetical predications. With that foundation the logic could inferentially support all the upper superstructure of mathematics in its arithmetical and even geometrical wings, in the rigorous non-psychologistic deductively valid inferentially gapless transparently surveyable derivation of all mathematical theorems from all and only true mathematical axioms.

Courage and Cost of Conviction

Frege could have enjoyed an uneventful, but no doubt less rocky and almost unrelievedly disappointing, professional career in mathematics, if he had drudged along working on additional theorems and making formal inter-connections between Gaussian arithmetical–geometrical correlations, devel-oping these in greater detail, with greater precision and a variety of proof methods. He could have cultivated that little corner of the mathematical garden that he had previously sown through his PhD dissertation and that had remained at the focus of his Habilitationsschrift. He chose instead to pursue the wild card of logicism in the philosophy of arithmetic, indomitable in his discovery and invention of a symbolism for a second-level general functional calculus as a quantified logic of concept-functions.[29]

First the *Begriffsschrift* and then the *Grundlagen* were in obvious ways a publishing and critical disappointment to Frege. The satisfaction is in writing the books, working out their contents, and seeing them in print. In the process of writing, Frege further perfected his ideas. That was what the activity of theoretization was all about for Frege in the practice of scientific philosophy. He published for the honest purpose of further improving his understanding of the topics he found it most vital to clarify by calling forth worthwhile usable intelligent, even if not always gratify-ingly informed, criticism. He knew, as did those around him, especially his Jena mathematics colleagues, that the work had not been well received by those in a position to know. He must have been mortified.

What he suffered was not a blow that came all at once, but death by a thousand cuts, to put it over-dramatically. It was not death, admittedly, and there were not nearly so many as a thousand cuts. It was a disappoint-ment, but not the demise either of Frege himself or of the defense of logicism that he was mounting. The thousand cuts were confined to about eight blunt reviews, most of which were barely one-page notices. They could only be counted in the dozens if we included Frege's disappointments as to the number, length, and depth of reviews that

---

[29] The secondary literature on the background to Frege's *Grundlagen* in relation to the *Begriffsschrift* and how Frege conceived of the connection between the two, in light of Stumpf's letter of 1882, is disappointingly thin. There is a useful study to be made of how Frege thought about the topic and style of the *Grundlagen* after the unfavorable reception of his *Begriffsschrift*. The emotional-impact story has frequently been told, but it is not the only or even necessarily the best explanation of why Frege withheld formal symbolism from his *Grundlagen*.

might have been written and published but never actually appeared. There were not many commentators up to the task. The lack of response or a positive reception was nevertheless sufficient reason for disappointment. Frege is known to have been chagrined, reflecting on the reviews and the silence in the absence of attention, lacking further substance to ponder, lacking sound criticism of his first two books. He wanted something he could use, something he could learn from, good reasons for questioning his previous analytic starting-place or constructive proposals. After having read their remarks, Frege was more disappointed in the reviewers than he was in what he had written and they had consented to review. Disappointments have a way of snowballing. It must have piled disappointment on disappointment for Frege that no students were curious enough to read his work. They did not line up outside his office to talk to him, to find out something about the controversy he may have inadvertently stirred up. They were not there to ask him to explain this tempest in a teacup involving a new logical symbolism for a general logic of concept-functions. They did not inquire about his work when he would still have been only too eager to chat about it day and night. Meta-disappointment is the disappointment that comes with a sense of intellectual loneliness, that there is no one who cares with whom to share an investigation's birth pangs.

Frege, on the other hand, seems never to have doubted the rightness of the conclusions for which he argued in his caustically or uncomprehendingly reviewed books. Russell's paradox later upset Frege's applecart irrevocably, but that was at first announced only in a private letter, and later in several of Russell's books, rather than in a review as such of Frege's *Grundgesetze*. If we are speaking of the early reviews, especially those of the *Begriffsschrift* and looking ahead to the icy reception of the *Grundlagen*, Frege never once seemed to have been properly evaluated for the literal contents of his writings. Schröder is singled out as reading Frege thoroughly, carefully, and mostly respectfully, if unsympathetically. As evidence that Frege remained steadfast to the logicism embodied in these three major books, the latter in two volumes, and his published and unpublished essays and lectures, Frege's *Begriffsschrift*, still identified under variants of that title, sometimes as foundations of mathematics, appeared on the Jena mathematics course calendar between 1910 and 1914. He did not give up on logicism as the only possible analysis of mathematical truth, although much later he was certainly interrupted in the furthering of his logical reconstructive enterprise.

If Frege in his privacy of conscience retained anything of his Lutheran education, he might have been amused sometimes to hold before his mind the image of Martin Luther defying the Catholic authorities at Worms in 1521, proclaiming "Here I stand and cannot do otherwise." Frege, at whatever moment or during whatever span of time he decided to dedicate himself to his *Begriffsschrift*, had made a similarly fateful turn and taken an analogously principled stand. His direction now was to extend and expand rather than abandon the development of rigorous non-psychologistic Platonic realist logicism. That the critics did not like it was regrettable but could not be helped. The work of logicism called him irresistibly onward toward the completion of a full-scale reduction of the basic laws of elementary arithmetic to a purely logical concept of natural number and the deductively valid logical inference structures of the arithmetic's theorems. The critics did not improve, but nor did they derail the pure logicism Frege had set in motion. The work had simply to go on during these intervening years, as Frege read the critical notices and advanced the first two main planks of his formal philosophical logicism proceeding from the *Begriffsschrift* to the *Grundlagen*.[30]

Something in Frege dictated a conviction and desire that he must go another way instead. He had to rebel against the obvious thing that he had known before lifting a pencil. He was assured that everything that had come before had been a preparation for the new work, and that this was where he could best hope to find the way toward his greatest achievement. He was motivated at these metaphorical cross-roads to leap out of the plane that he and his teachers had previously explored, climbing analogically into a higher third dimension of Kantian explanatory transcendence. Frege was determined to advance to the most abstract and universal principles of logic, the uncharted territory toward which all his earlier studies seemed

---

[30] Among numerous recent authoritative sources on the famous 1521 episode at Worms, see Roland H. Bainton, *Here I Stand: A Life of Martin Luther* (New York: Plume, 1995), especially pp. 55–102 and 116–36. The role of the printing press in the rise of the Reformation is explained by Diarmaid MacCulloch, *The Reformation* (New York: Penguin Books, 2004), Chapters 8 and 17. An imaginative psychoanalytic reconstruction of Luther's adolescent mind-set is offered by psychologist Erik H. Erikson, *Young Man Luther: A Study in Psychoanalysis and History* (Gloucester: Peter Smith Publishing, Inc., 1962). See Elizabeth Eisenstein, *The Printing Press as an Agent of Change: Communications and Cultural Transformations in Early Modern Europe* (Cambridge: Cambridge University Press, 1979).

irresistibly to gesture. This striving motivated him and absorbed his energies throughout his teaching career at Jena. Here I stand, Frege could say with the hero of the faith who defied Church authorities of the day, "*und kann nicht anders.*" By analogy, Frege set himself on principled grounds against the mathematical establishment that resisted his innovations. They were reluctant to accept the philosophical revolution in mathematical thought that Frege forged at no small difficulty and in extraordinary detail even when they were capable of grasping it. Now, having reached the age of thirty-six, Frege's stubborn independence of thought led to his being sidelined for most of his lifetime in his chosen profession. He received only morsels of praise and approval, mostly from professional colleagues in the Jena circle, awaiting, but in his relatively long lifetime never attaining, a more sympathetic judgment that would come only long after his death in the later history of mathematical logic and analytic philosophy.

The challenge in understanding Frege's life and the development of his thought in the productive period between 1879 and 1884, in the interval from his *Begriffsschrift* to the *Grundlagen*, is to grasp what Frege had actually achieved, rather than his ranking in the opinions of his immediate contemporaries about the value of his work. The logical, mathematical, and philosophical world of the late 1800s was unprepared to take Frege's measure. They did what parochial minds usually do when confronted with something vastly unknown and labor-intensive. They rejected it without sympathetic interpretation or solid objections. We know today that Frege had something important to contribute. He was, however, unable to attract an appreciative readership; critics either did not comprehend what Frege was proposing, or resented something about Frege's presentation of the project that they found offensive. Frege had reached the point of taking the next step toward logicism in his analysis of the concept of natural number. The proposal marked his most significant accomplishment of 1884, the publication in that year of his eventually widely admired *Grundlagen der Arithmetik*.[31]

---

[31] A useful overview of these topics and this formative period in Frege's mathematical and philosophical writing career is presented by Guillermo E. Rosado Haddock, *A Critical Introduction to the Philosophy of Gottlob Frege* (Aldershot: Ashgate Publishing, 2012), especially Chapters 1–3.

6

The Logical Foundations of Number in the *Grundlagen* (1884)

W HAT WAS FREGE'S celebrated analysis of the concept of number that he defended in his second major publication? He presented the *Grundlagen*'s topic of inquiry in the following commonsense terms in the book's Introduction:

> To the question, what the number one is, or what the sign 1 refers to, one most often receives the answer, "Well, now, a thing." And if one then thereupon calls attention to the fact that the proposition
> "The number one is a thing"
> is not a definition, because on the one side it has the definite article and on the other the indefinite, or that it only assigns the number one to the class of things, that it only says, the number one belongs to things, but not which thing it is, then one is invited perhaps to choose any thing whatsoever that one would like to name.[1]

Frege's demand for definition, his desire to know the essential necessary and sufficient conditions for the object under investigation, is reminiscent of Socrates' similar objective in Plato's dialogues. Socrates, on the other hand, never seems to have received such a dim reply to one of his demands for the essence of a concept to be defined, hearing only that the subject in question is a *thing*. Anyone who answers the question perfunctorily in that way does not really want to play along with Socrates or Frege.

Whether or not numbers are things, and the number 1 in particular is a thing in the sense of being an object or entity, was nevertheless one of the main disputed topics of Frege's *Grundlagen*. Here, in his opening remarks, Frege expressed the brutish opinion of the anonymous philosophically untutored woman, man, or mathematician in the street. Frege

---

[1] Frege, *Grundlagen*; translated by Dale Jacquette, *The Foundations of Arithmetic*, p. 11 (hereafter quoted in translation as *Foundations*).

too finally affirmed this apparently uninformative but controversial categorization of numbers. He presented the analysis only after he had
positioned himself to define the concept of number, and of the natural
number sequence, as the basis for all arithmetic and ultimately all
mathematics. The cardinality of any choice of objects possessing a certain
property is the number of entities in the extension of the predicate
representing the property.

The concept of natural number for Frege was the higher-order
property of being equinumerous (*gleichzahlig*) or one–one correlatable
(standing in a *beiderseits eindeutige Zuordnung*) with the extension of a
lower-order predicate. If there is nothing in the extension, as in that of
the predicate "non-self-identical," then we have an intuitive reduction of
the natural number o as the cardinality of sets equinumerous with the set
of all and only non-self-identicals. There are none of these, there is
nothing existent that is not self-identical, implying that there is exactly
one zero. The existence of o accordingly also introduces the natural
counting number 1. That is the kind of thing we are finally to understand
numbers as being. A natural number *is* a thing, Frege granted. It is
nevertheless an unexpectedly technical kind of thing that requires a
somewhat convoluted expression involving higher-order identities of
the cardinalities of the extensions of lower-order property-exemplifying
existent entities.[2]

Methodological Cards on the Table

To arrive at this analysis, after clearing the ground of alternative proposals under persistent criticism, Frege outlined three principles by which
he proposed to conduct his philosophical inquiry into the concept of
number. He presented these methodological rules as guiding the
Grundlagen inquiry throughout, and obviously to some appreciable
extent shaping when not predetermining its conclusions. He explained
it as follows:

As basic principles, in this investigation I have adhered to the following:

---

[2] The venerable resource is Charles Parsons, "Frege's Theory of Number," in *Philosophy in
America*, ed. Max Black (Ithaca: Cornell University Press, 1965), pp. 180–203. See note 42
below.

The psychological is to be sharply separated from the logical, the subjective from the objective;

The meaning of a word must be inquired after in propositional context, not in isolation;

The distinction between concept and object is to be kept in sight.

In order to comply with the first, I have used the word "idea" always in the psychological sense, and have distinguished ideas from concepts and objects.[3]

All three of Frege's methodological principles deserve detailed discussion. Together, they constitute Frege's starting-place and establish the framework within which he proposed to investigate the concept of natural number. They also constitute a compact expression of his philosophy of logic and meaning. In the book, Frege took all three of these substantive largely ideologically prejudicial, not to mention in one case inapplicable, methodological scruples entirely for granted.[4] He had to start somewhere. He started here, and forthrightly said so. We are reminded of Frege's students in 1910, as Carnap reports, none daring to raise a question, no sure or trembling hands to be seen rising into the stratosphere, in case the professor were ever to turn around. Here Frege explained, but made no effort to justify, the three methodological principles by which his inquiry was directed.

Of Kant, Time, and the River

Suffice it to say that, if Frege's first principle is observed, then only non-psychologistic logic and arithmetic are objective. Kant maintained something more subtle than simply the opposite of what Frege's principle was intended to exclude. Nor is it correct to say that, insofar as the philosophical foundations of arithmetic are concerned, Frege was the objectivist and Kant the subjectivist. Kant was not a subjectivist in the philosophy of mathematics, but rather a different kind of objectivist than Frege. The pure form of perception (*reine Form der Anschauung*) of Kant's Transcendental Aesthetic in the *Critique of Pure Reason* is as pure and devoid of empirical psychological contaminants as Frege's logic. Pure logic and time as a pure form of perception are alike untainted by ephemeral empirical consciousness. Kant's transcendental philosophical foundations of arithmetic should not be dismissed from a Fregean perspective as psychologistic just because Kant's starting-place is the

---

[3] Frege, *Foundations*, p. 17.   [4] *Ibid.*, pp. 16–18.

experience of time. Kant's Transcendental Aesthetic of the possibility of arithmetic and geometry grounded in the existence of time and space as pure forms of intuition is itself mind-independently objective. It was only the reasoning by which Kant claimed to discover the Transcendental Aesthetic that began with the experience of moving physical objects in space and time. The psychology of spatiotemporal experience was not important to Kant, once the examination of conscious thought content had suggested the possibility of perception. After that, it became a question of necessity for Kant, of what must be true in order for perception of physical things appearing in space in time to be possible.

Kant's transcendental reasoning in support of time as pure form of perception grounding the possibility of arithmetic has several advantages over Frege's reliance on mathematical intuition in support of logicism. Frege incongruously depended not only as Kant did on the existence of a psychological occurrence, but also on the exercise of a psychological faculty of mathematical intuition as the final arbiter of substantive truth commitments in logic and the philosophy of arithmetic. Frege had no other answer to give in endorsing a particular set of axioms over alternatives than his own psychological certainty about their truth. He trusted his psychological intuitions of abstract Platonic mathematical truths. He may have thought that there is no choice and that everyone does the same. There are differences notwithstanding in the way in which intuitions enter into symbolic logic and mathematical system-building.

Fregean intuition is as psychological as the moments of perception assumed as Kantian givens for purposes of transcendental reasoning. The difference is that Kant began with something experientially concrete from which a distinct pure formal basis for arithmetic and geometry was then derived by transcendental reasoning. Kant's method, unlike Frege's intuition, was not essentially psychological, and it was not the final word about basic mathematical truths, although it began by asking philosophical questions about a familiar psychological occurrence. Kant's methodology exhibited more of the explanatory virtues such as maximal transparency of inference and justification that Frege professed but did not always practice when he merely spelled out the dictates of his own admittedly remarkable mathematical intuitions. It is easier to get on board with Kant and then follow the process of argument for time and space as pure forms of intuition that are shown transcendentally to ground the possibility of arithmetic and geometry. We have nothing comparable in Frege's case. We know the results of his private exercise of mathematical intuition only by what he presented as considered truths in his writings and publications.

At some level the same is true of Kant. Kant, unlike Frege, took us from a starting-place that all perceivers share, in order to make progress toward understanding the philosophical foundations of arithmetic. Transcendental reasoning then took care of all the rest. We do not need, as in Frege's logicism, to share the same mathematical intuitions about such complex matters as the truth of logical and arithmetical axioms. We do not have much knowledge of the process that brought Frege to such conclusions as that the foundations of elementary arithmetic are purely logical rather than of the purely temporal form in Kant's metaphysics. Transcendental ground in Kant is something reasoning discovers to be a necessary condition without which something that is given to philosophical reflection would not be possible. With the exception of logical proofs in his *Begriffsschrift*, Frege, for all his scientific integrity, was more dogmatic about substantive philosophical truths than Kant. This quality can be seen already in Frege's three *Grundlagen* rules of inquiry. They may be good, understandable principles that we can also agree to follow, as though we were joining a sacred club. However, Frege offered no argument in their defense, leaving it up to the reader to judge. He promised only to guide his investigations by the partly procedural and partly substantive rules he had laid down. He did not try to disguise metaphysical commitments in what would be his analysis of the concept of natural number.

Logic and Psychology

What is reasoning if not at least an idealized psychological activity? If that is true, and logic is about reasoning, then how did Frege's logicism hope to avoid psychologism? Any idealization of reasoning activity must of necessity begin with the thinking patterns of living individual psychological subjects.

If it is not true, then we can have no justification for expecting a formal system of symbolic logic to make pure or applied practical modeling reconnection with everyday, scientific technical, and above all mathematical reasoning. Episodes of reasoning in the ordinary sense are mental events in which rules are, mostly subconsciously, applied to representations of ideas in thought. The rules and representations themselves do not always need to be deliberated upon, providing an escape route from vicious circularity or irrelevance for anti-psychologism, without denying psychology's importance in and for logic. There must be objectionable and non-objectionable incarnations of psychologism. These need to be distinguished and treated accordingly, both theoretically and polemically, with some being criticized and repudiated, as Frege did, whereas others can be dismissed as harmless, which Frege did not think it his business to adjudicate. Frege tarred them all with the same brush, in order to move the discussion beyond psychology on every front. Here is what he had to say:

As much now as mathematics must refuse to tolerate all assistance from the side of psychology, so little can it renounce its close connection with logic. To be sure, I concur with the view of those who hold that a sharp separation is impossible. Thus far one would admit, that every investigation into the validity of an inference or the justification of a definition must be logical. Such questions, however, are not at all to be eliminated from mathematics, for it is only by means of their answers that the necessary certainty is attainable.[5]

Frege's first and second methodological principles have had the most lasting influence on analytic philosophy. Logicism in Frege's philosophy stands in sharp opposition to psychologism, he was clear. He was relentless also in his criticism of efforts to understand mathematical concepts by reference to conditions and processes under which we happen to think about or learn something of them.

There is the greatest difference, he cogently believed, between how or why we come to recognize that the number 1 is odd, and what constitutes the meaning of the number sign numeral "1," or the concept of being an odd number, resulting in the true predication of the property of being odd to the number 1. He offered the analogy we have seen of what we might think about the North Sea and how it is that we may come to know something about that body of water. Since no sane person would imagine that the North Sea is itself something merely psychological, an entity occurring only immanently within our thoughts, Frege believed that it was similarly reckless to advance a theory of number according to which numbers were in any sense psychological, merely conceptual or mental existences.[6]

---

[5] *Ibid.*, p. 16.

[6] Brentano may have been the unspoken target of Frege's barbs. The psychologism allegedly implied by Brentano's intentional inexistence or immanent intentionality thesis of his 1874

The fact that we have a concept *of* number, if we do, a good or clear, accurate, and defensible concept, does not entail that number *is itself* only a concept. If number were itself a concept, according to Frege's understanding of the metaphysical difference between concepts and objects, then number would not be an object. It could not then be a *thing*, as even passersby in the street are prepared to confide philosophically in Frege. Hence number could not be an object or entity in the most general sense, because it would be incomplete and in need of an object to take as argument from an approved domain of existent entities. Number, like any function, would then be something unsaturated. It would stand in need of being completed by an object. What kind of object could possibly complete a number, what gaps are there in numbers to fill? We can raise the question on paper, but only unproductively wonder. The number 1 is already complete. There is nothing it needs to have added. It is an existent entity that serves as the argument-object of other true arithmetical predications. We may come to believe many different sorts of propositions about numbers, just as we might concerning the North Sea. That fact, Frege argued, does not make numbers themselves into creatures of thought, just as it does not infringe upon the North Sea's mind-independent objectivity.

Frege's concept of number, to be sure, was not the only approach to avoid the subjectivism of a psychologistic explanation of the concept of number. There are other possibilities also, including Kant's, which Frege hoped to supersede if he rightly understood Kant's purpose and strategy. If Frege rejected Kant it was presumably not on grounds of objectivity versus subjectivity, but for other reasons favoring pure logic over time as a pure form of perception at the philosophical foundations of arithmetic. Knowledge by experience of the mere possibility of perception as a starting-place for Kantian transcendental reasoning does not make the conclusion of the argument subjective or psychologistic. It was valid for Frege to strongly disapprove of Kant's psychological starting-place for discovering the philosophical foundations of arithmetic, even if Kant's method and conclusions were not psychological or psychologistic. Frege directed his criticisms against leading contenders for an analysis of the concept of number in order to clear the way for his theory as the best,

---

Psychologie vom empirischen Standpunkt could have earned him Frege's cross attention in this connection. Kreiser discusses Frege's rejection of psychologism in *Gottlob Frege*, §3.6.2, pp. 237–49.

most reasonable alternative. Frege's *Grundlagen* analysis of natural number and of the number 1 in particular unsurprisingly triumphed at the end of the book. Pure logic as the ground of arithmetic was even more psychology-free than time as a pure form of intuition. The form may have been pure, but it was the pure form of intuition in conscious moments of a psychological subject's experience of perception. The definition, despite Frege's endorsement, is subject to numerous objections, most of which did not occur to Frege or his contemporaries. The objections, just as much as Frege's definition of number, are essential to understanding the development of his thought at the time.

In his later writings, Frege reflected on the ongoing debate in which he was engaged with the German mathematician and philosopher David Hilbert at the time, concerning the nature of geometry and the exact requirements of its axiomatization.[7] Toward the end of his active academic career, Frege seems to have softened his previously exclusionary distinction between the philosophical foundations of arithmetic and geometry. The suggestion has been made, and no doubt deserves continued discussion, that later in life Frege changed his mind about the Kantian proto-intuitionistic basis for arithmetic, in effect bringing both geometry and arithmetic back into some sort of Kantian framework.[8] From the perspective of Frege's early detailed mathematical study of imaginary and complex numbers, it is difficult to understand how in the first place he could have ever agreed with Kant in taking seriously any basis for a hard and fast separation of arithmetic and geometry.

Contextual Semantic Holism

Frege's second methodological principle has also been positively received by many later analytic philosophers. Frege's idea was that we cannot properly understand the meaning of a word when it is considered out of a larger expressive context. One of his objections to ordinary colloquial language was that it harbors ambiguities and equivocations that surface when we compare different ways in which words that are alphabetically the same can be used grammatically to formulate different thoughts.

---

[7] Frege–Hilbert correspondence in Frege, *Philosophical and Mathematical Correspondence*, Letters IV [xv]/1–9, pp. 32–52. The "Prolegomena zur reinen Logik" section of Husserl's *Logische Untersuchungen I* (1900) in the first edition is dedicated to refuting psychologism.

[8] See Kenny, *Frege: An Introduction*, pp. 211–13.

The same term taken in one context of usage and regarded only orthographically as a particular string of letters chosen from the alphabet can mean something completely different from what it means in a different expressive context. This much is common sense, and we can easily supply examples to illustrate Frege's point from our knowledge of everyday English. The word "bank" can mean a financial institution or the edge of a body of water, such as the shore of the North Sea. Frege's principle by which we are to consider the meaning of terms contextually was expressly limited to "the context of a proposition," and as such has given rise to relatively conservative forms of semantic holism.

Strictly speaking, Frege's contextualism may not go far enough. We see this even from such an unimaginative and equally equivocal proposition as "I keep my money in the bank." This could mean either that I keep my money in a financial institution or that I keep it along the edge of a body of water, say, in a box buried in the sand, perhaps where I think no one else will find it. The same word capitalized serves nicely for the purposes of Frege's illustration also in German, where "*Bank*" can mean either again a financial institution or a bench on which to sit, or a narrow work surface. Ultimately, we may have no choice in following Frege's contextualist prescription when inquiring into the meaning of terms but to look at increasingly larger units of discourse and expression, potentially involving all language usage in its entirety. If this is an unavoidable result, as Frege also seemed to recognize later on further philosophical reflection, it does nothing to detract from his sensible prohibition against investigating the meanings of terms in total isolation from their occurrence in propositional context.

It is in part because of such defects in our everyday way of communicating in speech and writing that Frege was driven in his first book to expound the ideal language of the *Begriffsschrift*. Among its other virtues as a supposedly perfect vehicle for the expression of scientific thought, Frege's *Begriffsschrift* was meant especially to avoid ambiguity of expression, never permitting an orthographically identical term to represent different objects or abbreviate different concepts or functions. Colloquial language, with all its defects, is out of logic's control, and can only look to keeping its own extensional corners sharp. A philosophical objection to Frege's second ground rule is that it opens the door to a practically inapplicable regress of meaning contextualizations. A regress on Frege's second methodological principle appears to extend from words in sentences to whole propositions. This was initially as he intended. Then, however, it was already too late to forestall the avalanche of contextualizations. If not all sentences considered in isolation are any more propositionally determinate in meaning than the individual words they contain, then semantics must look holistically to the meanings of paragraphs, pages, and increasingly larger works to finally comprehend all of written and spoken world literature. It would be a terrific thing to be able to consult all that writing, but it seems an impractical way of establishing whether in a given sentence the word "bank" means the water's edge, a place of financial transactions, or both.[9]

Concept ≠ Object Distinction

Frege's third principle, in contrast with its predecessors, has not enjoyed quite the same widespread acceptance in later analytic philosophy. Frege's point requires additional explanation. Ordinarily, we might think of a concept as an object, or at least as an object of thought. We suppose it to be something, some *thing* we can think about, whereas Frege insisted that we ought to distinguish object and concept categorically. He declared his own intention of doing so as a principle of methodology throughout the *Grundlagen*.

What, exactly, did Frege mean by a concept (*Begriff*), and how was it supposed to be different from an object (*Gegenstand*)? Why can a concept not also be an object? Frege understood by a concept an unsaturated predication function. We obtain a concept in one way when we begin with a proposition such as "The moon is round" and subtract or abstract away from it the subject term, "the moon," leaving behind only the predication "is round." This particle, "is round," which we can also write as a function with a blank space as "_____ is round" or functionally as "Round(__) = v," is what Frege considered to be a concept, a concept-function. It is unsaturated. It needs to be filled-in with a subject term, any of which from the logic's reference domain will do, in order to complete

---

[9] What I facetiously call *semantic holism, out-of-control-ism*, is the unbridled generalization of Frege's methodological principle (2) insight that "the meaning of a word is to be inquired after in propositional context, not in isolation." The problem is knowing where to stop. Why should the holistic contextualization of words occurring in a proposition not include increasingly more comprehensive embeddings of the language that finally coincide with all linguistic expressions of thoughts?

the expression, producing a true or false predication of the property of being round to some singularly designated object. Being true or false means that the predication is referentially meaningful. Frege included singular designation by definite description as a kind of proper name. He did not distinguish logically and semantically, as Russell later did, between proper names and definite descriptions.

The category of a Fregean concept by intention corresponds exactly to that of a mathematical function. We similarly consider an algebraic expression such as $x + y = z$, and abstract away part of the equation to obtain the explicitly unsaturated addition function, $x + y = \_\_\_$, or $= (x + y (\_))$. The fact that structural similarities and logical isomorphisms obtain was for Frege an encouraging sign that concepts represented by predicates in language are correctly modeled on the formal symbolisms of an algebra of functions in elementary arithmetic. Later, as Frege revealed more details of the development of his philosophy of mathematics, he decided that concepts and functions, despite being incomplete and unsaturated, could after all be the objects of higher-order predications to which higher-order properties were attributed.[10]

Frege on Competing Analyses

In the book's Section I, OPINIONS OF SEVERAL WRITERS ON THE NATURE OF ARITHMETICAL PROPOSITIONS, and Section II, OPINIONS OF SEVERAL WRITERS ON THE CONCEPT OF NUMBER, occupying almost half of the work in its entirety, Frege assumed a polemical task like Hercules' cleaning of the Augean stables. He criticized other writers on the meaning of arithmetical theorems and the concept of number in order to replace their suggestions by a more adequate analysis of the concept of natural number.[11]

Frege believed that his definition avoided the defects of his competitors, in addition to delivering uniquely attractive formal consequences in

---

[10] Kevin C. Klement in *Frege and the Logic of Sense and Reference* (London: Routledge, 2011), especially pp. 134–45 and 146–48, emphasizes that Frege's logic is a second-order functional calculus, involving not only functions of objects that are not themselves functions, but also second-level functions, functions of functions, which are needed in Frege's *Grundlagen* logicist analysis of the concept of number.

[11] Frege, *Foundations*, pp. 33–61.

its favor. Frege's rhetorical expository method permitted him to approach his theory by a process of elimination as the best and possibly only viable choice that could imaginably hold its own against the torrent of his criticisms of other theorists. The final success of Frege's polemic depends on two things: (1) the extent to which Frege anticipated all relevant alternatives to his own solution to the analysis of the concept of natural number; and (2) the extent to which Frege's objections were (or were not) directed against the strongest versions of rival explanations of natural number, and were (or were not) successful as attempted refutations.

Frege was obviously not the first or only philosopher to propose an analysis of the concept of number. If anyone wondered why thinkers should not simply accept one of the earlier efforts at defining the category from the grocer's shelf, Frege could answer by briefly explaining their ideas and offering substantial reasons to reject these rivals as inferior to his preferred analysis. He looked to Mill, in his 1843 book *A System of Logic, Ratiocinative and Inductive*, as maintaining that arithmetical propositions are inductive truths like the high probabilities of any logically contingent natural science. As an empiricist, Mill argued that all truths are experiential, and considered the kinds of perceptions that could support the truth of logical and arithmetical laws as generalizations of thinking processes involving logical inference and mathematics treated more or less on a par. In a subsection of his *Grundlagen* titled "Are the Laws of Arithmetic Inductive Truths?," Frege criticized inductivism as providing nothing more than a percentage of subjective responses lacking the synthetic *a priori* necessity, as Kant maintained, of the most basic arithmetical truths. Frege could not have permitted Mill's explanation of the concept of number in a book that was widely read and highly regarded at the time to go unchallenged.[12] Mill was mostly known for his defense of utilitarianism and a compatibilist account of moral responsibility, conducted in empiricist terms that Frege was eager to reject as objectionably psychologistic whenever they were presupposed in the philosophy of logic and mathematics.[13]

---

[12] John Stuart Mill, *A System of Logic, Ratiocinative and Inductive* [1843], ed. J. M. Robson, in Mill, *Collected Works* (London: Routledge & Kegan Paul, 1973).

[13] The category of a "Fregean utilitarian" is developed by Aaron Zimmerman, *Moral Epistemology* (Abingdon: Routledge, 2010), pp. 174–82. There does not seem to be any direct evidence as to what Frege, with his right-leaning social–political tendencies, especially later in life, may have thought about Mill's agenda for the improvement of conditions for individuals by the convergence of his refined greatest good for the greatest number principle

Frege regarded laws of arithmetic attributing properties to numbers as invaluable clues about their metaphysics. He held that we can investigate the nature of number in keeping with his second methodological rule, namely that one must always consider the meaning of a word in the context of a complete thought or proposition. The intended application was the contexting of a name for a natural number in a theorem of arithmetic. The present instance made terms for number concepts the germinal ideas whose meaning was sought in the greater context of lawlike arithmetical principles. Natural numbers in Frege's logicism were the fundamental argument-objects of arithmetical concept-functions. Give him only numbers, and Frege believed that all of arithmetic and whatever was reducible to a mathematics of functions on natural numbers could be purely logically reconstructed. The unit of meaning for Frege in the philosophy of arithmetic was the entire proposition as an expression of a complete thought about the properties of numbers. Frege did not allow himself to evaluate the meaning of "number" or 0 or 1, $\frac{1}{2}$, $\frac{1}{4}$, π, i, $a + bi$, and so on, in semantic isolation from full truth-valuational propositions, the theorems of arithmetic, in which the relevant corresponding numerals and functors, equation and identity signs, and statements appear. Recommending without rehearsing this preparatory line of criticism, Frege confidently drew the following conclusion:

§9. The previous considerations make it probable that numerical formulas are derivable from the definitions of the individual numbers alone by means of some general laws, that these definitions neither assert observed facts nor presuppose them for their legitimacy. It is therefore essential to ascertain the nature of these laws.[14]

Against Mill's Inductivism

The first question for Frege was to understand the meaning of arithmetical laws. He believed that it was only from these axioms that the concepts of individual numbers mentioned in the axioms of arithmetic could be abstracted. The question then was whether any predecessors prepared the way for Frege's critical survey of the metaphysics of

with applied natural science in the service of improving the health and happiness of humanity.

[14] Frege, *Foundations*, p. 25.

arithmetical theorems. Frege was not especially generous about crediting any precursor as offering useful suggestions toward his distinctive analysis.

Basic laws, axioms, of arithmetic, he argued, cannot be merely inductive, empirical, or logically contingent. The interpretation was excluded by the argument that normative rules and regulations can never validly be derived from purely descriptive matter-of-fact propositions, and because logical reasoning in the derivation of arithmetical theorems from the laws of logic was marinated throughout in normative standards of correct inference. They have, moreover, a necessity about their truth that is unlike any possessed by laws of nature.

We appreciate the difference when we reflect on the modality of an arithmetical theorem, $1 + 1 = 2$, versus that of an applied mathematical rule of kinematics, $F = ma$. Nor shall we add to a body of arithmetic the "theorem" that $1 + 1 = 3$, even if it should turn out that a large majority of benighted human calculators statistically persist in making such fundamental errors against the norms of elementary arithmetic, at least until the practitioners of such false arithmetic perish, which must happen eventually if their math is no better than that. Their longevity will depend on how long they may have needed the right relation and how in the interests of survival they have tried to compensate for the deficiency. If Mill's thesis that arithmetical theorems are inductive truths is correct, then philosophy will need to consider such pronouncements as $1 + 1 = 3$ as potentially true if they are widely accepted, with no independent means of detecting and correcting even the intuitively most flagrant miscalculations.

Numbers as Properties of Physical Reality

The first extra-psychological explanation of number Frege critically evaluated and summarily rejected was posed in the book's next question:

Is number a property of external things?[15]

The issue is more complicated than Frege appreciated. Whether he knew it or not, with no one to represent, champion, develop, and defend an alternative view on the horizon, the suggestion that number is a

---

[15] *Ibid.*, p. 35.

property of physical entities has a firm foundation in Aristotle's *ousiology* or substance ontology.

Aristotle maintained that only individual physical entities exist independently of all other things as the ultimate phenomenal reality of individual things he calls primary substances. Definitions, or the secondary substances of things, exist secondarily only insofar as they supervene or are ontically dependent on the existence of the primary substances in which they inhere. Inherent mathematical properties among others define the species of individuals by categorizing them as belonging to one equinumerous extension of predicates rather than another. Triangles, it may be, or prime or imaginary numbers. Mathematical objects are understood as nominalizations of inherent mathematical properties in existent physical entities, or, as Frege preferred to say, external things.[16]

Frege was unhappy with this answer in its most general terms in part because he believed that properties were incomplete and unsaturated, requiring application to an object in order to be satisfied. Frege thought, in contrast, that a mathematical object was intuitively a kind of entity, something existing in and of itself, independently of whatever anyone happens to think about it. It was not logic's obligation to keep track of all potential intended objects of reference. Frege was nevertheless willing to entertain the proposition that number might be a property of physical objects. He was not unaware that numbers were sometimes spoken of adjectivally, as when we say that these cherries are twofold, dual, a pair, and the like, just as we say that cherries are red, round, either sweet or tart, that they are two, or that there are two of them turning with their stems on a table. Why, then, not treat number as similar to color, taste, shape, location, and the like? Frege continued as follows:

§21. We should at least try to assign to number its place among our concepts! In language, numbers appear most often in adjectival form and in attributive connection, similarly as the words hard or heavy or red, which designate the properties of external things. This suggests the question whether one must conceive of the individual numbers also in this way, and whether, correspondingly, the concept of number could be combined, say, with that of color.[17]

---

[16] See James Franklin, "Aristotelianism in the Philosophy of Mathematics," *Studia Neoaristotelica*, 8 (2011), pp. 3–15; and Jacquette, "Toward a Neoaristotelian Inherence Philosophy of Mathematical Entities," *Studia Neoaristotelica*, 11 (2014), pp. 159–204.

[17] Frege, *Foundations*, p. 35.

Let the number of cherries in the dish = 2. Then the number of cherries collectively has the property of being identical to the natural number 2. Needless to say, it is not the cherries' only property, because they also have the properties of being red, tart or sweet, weighing so much, and having a certain fingerprint DNA. No one imagines that the cherries themselves are identical to the inherent number 2, any more than that the cherries themselves are identical to the property of being red or to the property of being sweet or tart. The cherries have the property of being identical *in number* to the natural number 2, just as they have the property of being red *in color*, tart or sweet *in flavor*, weighing a certain amount represented by another arithmetical metric, and the like.

Frege mentioned Cantor in this connection. Frege further invoked the recently despised name of Schröder. Frege understood Schröder's algebraic approach to arithmetic as taking a psychologistic representational view of the concept of number in which a faculty of mind "abstracts" number from its perceptions of things. Frege took notice in this part of his survey of alternative concepts of the analysis of natural number as a property of things, objective or subjective, as the case may be. He went no distance toward a refutation or critical examination of the general category. He seems to have been oblivious to the neo-Aristotelian option of regarding numbers, among other mathematical formal dimensional entities, as nominalized properties inherent in physical objects. The objectivity of mathematical properties inhering in primary substances provided exactly the mind-independence of natural numbers among any individuation of things that Frege's scientific anti-psychologistic perspective sought to advance. Frege said nothing decisive to exclude a carefully crafted neo-Aristotelian ontology of numbers as inherent formal properties. It is hard in any case to deny that mathematical properties exist secondarily, and that they may be logically reducible to purely logical properties, as Frege's logicism was ultimately supposed to prove.

The Resurgent Subjectivity Question

Frege, in a swashbuckling assault on a selection among recent and contemporary explanations of the concept of number, proceeded on to the next as though he had thoroughly excluded all possible alternatives in each category. Thereafter, he considered numbers as entities that have properties, rather than as properties themselves. Eventually, Frege argued that a specifically second-level functional calculus, a logic requiring no more than second-level functions of lower first-level functions, was needed to represent all basic laws and inferential proof structures of the theorems of elementary arithmetic.

The concept of a property and of a second-level property of a property turns out to be essential to Frege's analysis of the concept of natural number. The meaning of "number" was considered by Frege in the context of its occurrence in predicate position in true or false sentences, which he referred to from the beginning and later thematized as *Gedanken* or propositions. The category came into play especially, in accordance with the second *Grundlagen* methodological principle, in unpacking the meaning of a predicate like "number" in the propositional context of theorems belonging to what is nowadays more often called a first-order arithmetic. Numbers supposedly can only be entities, objects rather than properties or concept-functions. But are they objective or subjective? Frege turned the discussion in this direction:

Is number something subjective?

His answer, unsurprisingly, in §26, was no. Frege mentioned Rudolf Lipschitz as brazenly guilty of this offense against commonsense intuitions concerning the objective ontology of number.[18] The inconclusive justification for Lipschitz's interpretation was that numbers are not themselves perceivable physical objects. If numbers are not properties but things that have properties, then, for those thinkers unlike Frege who want to avoid commitment to an imperceivable realm or supernatural order of transcendent mathematical entities, the only obvious alternative is to consider that numbers are cognitive, conceptual, psychological, and subjective. At least we know that psychological occurrences exist, and that they are not perceivable in quite the way we observe rocks, rivers, animal bodies, and distant stars.[19]

We supplement Frege's reasoning with the consideration that, if numbers were subjective, then every thinker who entertained a thought

---

[18] Rudolf Lipschitz (1832–1903) was a mathematician at the University of Bonn after 1864. His research was primarily in mathematical analysis and theoretical mechanics, although he also wrote an interesting book on political implications of the development of natural science for the state.

[19] An excellent place to begin is Paul Vincent Spade, "Ockham's Nominalist Metaphysics: Some Main Themes," in *The Cambridge Companion to Ockham*, ed. Paul Vincent Spade (Cambridge: Cambridge University Press, 1999), pp. 100–117.

about a number, as in accepting the true proposition that 3 is a prime number, must be thinking about a different number 3, namely, the number 3 that resides in each thinker's individual distributed subjective mental states. The breakdown of identity conditions for numbers as single entities bearing properties on the subjectivity hypothesis refutes the idea without closing the avenue to more ingenious and inventive variations on a fundamental subjectivist theme.

Further evidence against the proposal can already be found in the fact that there is widespread agreement in elementary mathematics concerning the properties of numbers that would not be expected in the perception of obviously subjective conditions such as the color of an object among normally sighted and color-blind or chromatically challenged perceivers, temperature registered on a baby's as compared with a weather-battered seaman's skin, the sharpness of pepper or saltiness experienced in tasting a dish, and others of the sensations we usually think of as subjective. A classroom of students all thinking in harmony with the teacher that 3 is a prime number does not seem remotely like the subjective experience of the same students as to whether a candy is too sweet or not sweet enough, or the bath water too hot, too cool, or just about right.

Numbers as Mid-Nineteenth-Century Sets

Frege next considered the question of whether number can be understood as a set. The progression in his slash-and-burn evaluation of competing answers to the question "What is a number?" had been to eliminate or at least skirt around the solution that makes number a property, and to dismiss at least the crude forms of psychologism, of which Frege was a sworn opponent on account of his first methodological principle. Number must be an object rather than a property, besides something objective rather than subjective. It can only be an abstract entity that transcends the physical spatiotemporal world, in something like the way, whatever that is, in which Plato's Ideas are supposed to exist in an unchanging realm of real abstract things, an *Ideenhimmel*, as it would be termed in common German philosophical practice and perhaps also by Frege. There is nowhere else to look, other than in such an abstract ideal world of Being as contrasted with the world of Becoming in the dynamic phenomenal order of space, time, and causal interaction, where at every ontic organizational level there is constant motion of material entities through a convergence of physical forces.

The concept of a set appeals to philosophers of mathematics as objectively Platonic and, in that specialized abstract sense, *realist*. A set is more obviously an object, while sets can have properties, such as the property of containing or not containing a certain object as a member, being of a certain size or cardinality, intersecting membership with or excluding that of another set, and indefinitely many useful qualities and relations in the logic of arithmetic. Sets are presumably mind-independent. Frege dutifully examined efforts to identify numbers with sets, and gave the following disappointing report:

Number as set §28. Some writers define number as a set, multiplicity or plurality. There is a difficulty that occurs in this connection, through which the concept excludes the numbers 0 and 1. These expressions are quite indeterminate: sometimes they approach more closely in meaning to "heap," "group," "aggregate" – whereby a spatial gathering is intended – sometimes they are used as almost similar in meaning to "number," only more indeterminate. An analysis of the concept of number, the point is, cannot be found in such an explanation.[20]

The argument that numbers cannot be sets because there are no corresponding sets for the numbers 0 and 1 is bound to seem unfounded from the standpoint of contemporary set theory and its metaphysics. In Frege's time, the most widely accepted theory of sets in the professional opinion of working mathematicians did not countenance a null set corresponding to the whole number 0 or a singleton set corresponding to the whole number 1. Sets in the accepted sense in mathematical parlance in Frege's day only got started with a minimum of two members, nothing less was a set in the plural of things. A first set could be intuitively associated with the whole number 2, which would still apparently leave 0 and 1 without a set-theoretical sponsor.[21]

It is worth reflecting on Frege's reasons for taking contemporary set-theoretical strictures at face value, rather than challenging them by asking, as mathematicians later would, why there could not be a null and a singleton set in a set-theoretical analysis of the concept of number. Since arithmetical functions were freely available to Frege, why not begin a set-theoretical definition of natural number with 2, moving on to 3, 4, etc., while proceeding also in the opposite direction by swinging the

---

[20] Frege, *Foundations*, p. 42.   [21] See Chapter 3 note 8.

function $-1(\_\_) = n$ backward to define $-1(2) = 1; -1(1) = 0; -1(0) = -1;$ $-1(-1) = -2;$ and so on? Here we encounter a second major oversight of Frege's critical analysis of alternative conceptions of number. He did not, first of all, take seriously the strongest neo-Aristotelian analysis of the concept of number as the nominalization of an inherent formal property, as in a building's numerically expressed height, which is the key to understanding the link between pure and applied mathematics. Secondly, he did not consider how he might have stretched the received concept of a set to include empty and unary sets of objects. If Frege had pushed further against these soft obstacles, as later set theory had no qualms in allowing, then his main objection to identifying natural numbers with sets would have fallen to the ground.

There are other discrepancies that argue contrarily against treating numbers as sets. A set essentially has zero or some definite number of members, but numbers do not have members. What members does zero have, or the numbers 1, 2, 3, ½, ¼, π, i, a + bi, etc.? There are sets that have exactly two members, because the number of members belonging to each of the sets is identical to the number 2 ($= 2$). That is a respectable use of the counting number 2, but not a promising opening bid in the effort to reduce numbers to sets. It implies contrariwise the necessity of applying pre-existent numbers to characterize the properties and especially the cardinalities of sets. We further speak naturally of an intersection or union of two sets, but not of numbers, for which a different vocabulary for sometimes corresponding arithmetical functions is conventionally reserved. What could it possibly mean to attempt making reference to the *intersection* of numbers 2 and 3, or the *union* of 1 and π, as we freely say in the case of sets? We cannot reasonably or even meaningfully assert that any member of a singleton set is identical to the set, because the singleton set of {Abraham Lincoln} ≠ Abraham Lincoln, Lincoln having been at one time a living flesh and blood person and not an abstract set.

Units, Unity, and Numbers

Frege turned next to Section III, OPINIONS ON UNITY AND ONE.[22] Having disposed of competing accounts of the meaning of mathematical theorems and the reference of number terms, Frege was

---

[22] Frege, *Foundations*, pp. 43–61.

left with a space to fill by providing an improved analysis. He wanted to present the concept of natural number as something objective in the sense of mind-independent and consequently non-subjective, as he required of all mathematical entities.

The first suggestion again involved thinking of number terms as expressing a *property* of objects, a general category of explanation he had supposedly already rejected. Since the possibility had previously been discounted in the most general case, we may wonder why Frege did not simply invoke the same argument in the specific case of the natural counting number 1. Instead, he asked "*Does the number word 'one' express a property of objects?*," answering that (§45) "Number is not abstracted from things in the same way as color, weight, and hardness, it is not in the same sense as these a property of things. The question still remains of what is something asserted by means of a number statement?"[23]

It is sometimes too easy to be unimpressed with the apparent flimsiness of Frege's command of basic critical reasoning skills. To say that number is not abstracted from things in the same way as color and other properties of individual physical things that Frege mentioned is not to say that number is not abstracted from things. It is only to observe that the two are different kinds of properties that in each case may require a different kind or mode of abstraction. Frege did not pause to ask whether color is abstracted from things in the same way as weight and hardness. The answer is presumably the same, namely that they too are not identically abstracted, given the essential category differences among these several kinds of properties. From that fact alone it would obviously be invalid to conclude that therefore color is not abstracted from things, or similarly for weight or hardness, height, as previously considered, or any other property actually belonging to an existent physical entity. Arithmetical properties are very different from color properties, and may need to be "abstracted" in different "ways" as each case requires. If they are among the properties inhering in individual physical things, however, then in principle they should be capable in every instance of being considered in the abstract, named in appropriate cases with number terms as precisely those formal properties of actually existent things.

Frege rejected as though through guilt by association the effort to analyze the number 1 in terms of the concept of unity. He appealed to the difference in the properties of 1 and unit. There can be any number of units, for starters, whereas there is only one number 1. That says enough in the most compressed wrapper to defeat the proposal on purely extensional grounds by tried and true frontal counterexample refutation. Frege thought he was standing on firm ground in taking a final parting shot at alternative explanations of the concept of number:

§45. There is a distinction to be made between one and unit. The word "one," as a proper name of an object of mathematical research, is incapable of plurality. It is therefore senseless to allow numbers to result from the combination of ones. The plus sign in 1 + 1 = 2 cannot refer to such a combination.[24]

True to *Grundlagen* methodological principle (2), authorizing inquiry into the meaning of a term only in the context of a proposition, Frege rejected any identification between the number 1 and the concept of unit, which grates grammatically in expression even when communicated in that unassuming composition. The plus sign + in the elementary arithmetic theorem 1 + 1 = 2, Frege insightfully observed, cannot combine two number 1s. Although it is certainly true that 1 unit + 1 unit = 2 units, it does not follow that 1 = one unit or that 2 = two units, and so on. The identities are empty analytically uninformative tautologies that say nothing about any particular arithmetical entities. There is only one number 1, only one number 2, and so on, whereas it appears that logically speaking there could be unlimitedly many units. Counterexamples among the properties not shared by numbers and units, except uninformatively as numbers of units, militate again against identifying numbers with units.

Frege's Logical Analysis of Number

Frege believed he had now swept the ground of other ways of explaining the concept of number. He was ready to fill the void his criticism had left in its wake by developing in a series of painstaking stages his own detailed logicist analysis of number. The analysis of basic arithmetical concepts in Frege's second book continued in Section IV, THE CONCEPT OF NUMBER, where Frege explained that the concept of number is arrived at only by first understanding the meaning of a numerical identity. He stated it plainly (§62): "*To acquire the concept of number one must establish the sense of a numerical identity.*"[25] The fact that Leibniz's Law is invoked

[24] *Ibid.*, p. 56.   [25] *Ibid.*, p. 66.

in Latin and discussed briefly indicates that by numerical identity Frege meant the exact sharing of distinguishing properties by the same object under two different names.[26] Frege continued as follows (§§68–69):

I thus define:
  The number that belongs to the concept F is the extension of the concept "equinumerous with the concept F." ...Now the proposition:
  The extension of the concept "equinumerous with the concept F" is identical with the extension of the concept "equinumerous to the concept G"
    is true always and only then, if the proposition
  "The same number belongs to the concept F as to the concept G"
is also true. Here there is therefore complete conformity.
  One indeed does not say that one number is more encompassing than another, in the sense in which the extension of one concept is more encompassing than that of another; but the case in which
    the extension of the concept "equinumerous with the concept F"
    would be more encompassing than
    the extension of the concept "equinumerous with the concept G"
  can also simply not occur; rather, if all concepts that are equinumerous with G are also equinumerous with F, then also conversely all concepts that are equinumerous with F are equinumerous with G. This "more encompassing" may naturally not be confused with "greater" as occurs with respect to numbers.[27]

There is much on which to reflect in Frege's analysis taken thus far. His biography is not the place to explore all philosophical aspects of his thinking in the detail they deserve. Anyone wanting to learn the historical facts surrounding the progression of his thought nevertheless requires familiarity with some major details of his logic and philosophy of arithmetic, since it was primarily with such questions that Frege was preoccupied.

What is disconcerting in Frege's exposition of the concept of number is his appeal to a property of *equinumerosity*. It appears to imply a one–one correlation between the memberships of two or more sets whose constituents are mapped onto themselves, or of a set with itself in the limiting case. If one–one correlating is implied, then the concept of 1 is presupposed rather than offered as the well-grounded conclusion of Frege's analysis. He sagely remarked, in the section denoted "*Completion and proof of our definition*, §70: Definitions prove themselves by their fruitfulness. Those that might just as well be set aside without opening a gap in a demonstration are to be discarded as altogether worthless."[28]

[26] *Ibid.*, p. 68.   [27] *Ibid.*, p. 71.   [28] *Ibid.*, p. 72.

Frege's statement of the virtues of a good definition seems reasonable enough. It prescribes a general methodological commitment to a draconian application of Ockham's razor advising against multiplying theoretical entities beyond explanatory necessity. Frege's attention was unmistakably focused on mathematical demonstration and whatever serves its requirements, while whatever falls beyond its cutting board was supposed to be, as he says, "utterly worthless." The analysis or definition of number would have to prove itself by its usefulness in mathematical derivations. It would otherwise have no meaningful applications, but would lack significance in the usual sense, and be worthy only of repudiation, as Frege harshly directed, before proceeding as follows:

> We consider the following example! If a waiter wants to be certain that he lays just as many knives as plates on a table, then he needs to count neither these nor those if he lays only one knife alongside to the right of each plate, so that every knife on the table is located alongside to the right of a plate. The plates and knives in this way are mutually univocally [one–one] correlated with one another and indeed by means of the identical spatial relationship. If in the proposition
> "a lies alongside to the right of A"
> we think of another object inserted for a and another for A, then the unaltered remaining part of the content constitutes the essence of the relation. Let us generalize this![29]

The circularity objection raised against the Humean instantiation of equinumerosity is supposed to be avoided by the existence of exhaustive correlations with no unpaired remainder in the dining-table parable, and without the benefit of any concept of natural number, let alone the specific counting number 1. There are one–one correlations, but their existence can be considered spatial, Frege ventured, and hence theoretically implicit rather than numerical. Otherwise we might as well object that the analysis of $1 = \mathrm{df}x$ is bound to be circular on the grounds that "x," whatever x turns out to be, is *one* term.

The correlative spatial arrangement of plates and knives on a table until all have been paired up is only an analogy for the abstract correlation that exists or does not exist independently of the concept of any number, independently of psychological judgment, deliberation or intent. Frege declared that

The relation-concept thus belongs like other simple concepts to pure logic. The special content of the relation is not under consideration, but rather the logical form alone. And whatever can be asserted of this, its truth is analytic and known *a priori*. This holds as much of relation-concepts as of the others.[30]

Frege here let slip an interesting admission. If the concept of relation is a concept of pure logic solely on the grounds that it is "like other simple concepts," if that is the criterion for what is to count as a purely logical concept, then Frege was presumably saying that simplicity alone is the mark of pure logic. This suggestion cannot be meant literally, if color concepts and other matters of direct sensation are considered simple, as they have been in phenomenalisms that are sympathetic also to some of Frege's metaphysical presuppositions, and if color and other basic sensation types are not purely logical. Frege's formalism expedited a purely logical reconstruction of the basic laws of elementary arithmetic, based on a purely logical concept of number. What made Frege's concept of number purely logical, if the category applies, and specifically a concept of natural number, remains a matter of heated contention between friendly and hostile admirers of Frege's analysis.

Equinumerosity and the Concept of Number

The key concept in Frege's logical analysis of natural number is equinumerosity. Literally it is the property of being same-numbered. Frege handled equinumerosity in the definition of number as implying one–one correlation, without presupposing the meaning or making a prior commitment to the existence of mathematical object 1 (one), and thus by a hair's breadth supposedly avoiding circularity in the analysis of the concept of natural number.

Although Frege did not have Wittgenstein's distinction between saying and showing at his theoretical disposal, he appealed to extant correlations like that of the plates and knives on the table as brute correlation facts. They have an existence outside of arithmetic functions independently of any reference to the mathematical object 1. Extant unthematized one–one correlations provide the basis for one–one projections of all and only the members of the extensions of relevant predicates. Equinumerosity defines natural number through the concept of cardinality. We could equally well

---

[30] *Ibid.*, p. 73.

speak of equicardinality in Frege's philosophy of arithmetic. The example of the plates and knives arranged as Frege described shows what theory without circularity cannot hope to say when it is true as a matter of fact that Cardinality$\{x \mid$ Knife$(x)\}$ = Cardinality$\{x \mid$ Plate$(x)\}$.

The truth-valued identity statement is all Frege needed to define the concept of number of Fs, as he said, things with property F, which could also be the property of being a knife or being a plate. It is the identical cardinality under the circumstances envisioned of the set of all knives and the set of all plates. From here it is but the short step Frege described that took him to the general concept of natural number. It is a fact to which reference can be made without explicitly mentioning any natural number that in Frege's *Grundlagen* analysis of the concept was supposed to avoid circularity. Cardinality for Frege was a property like any other. It was an unsaturated concept interpreted as a function with a preselection of argument-objects if its completion is to have truth-value.

Were Frege's analysis of the concept of natural number to require cardinality determinations of any specific natural number (1 in particular), then the definition would be circular, defining a concept in terms of itself. That would be the case if Frege had chosen to explain natural number in terms of specifically numbered cardinalities. He did not do so, and to appreciate how deftly he avoided circularity in the *Grundlagen* analysis of natural number, we should compare it with what seems to be the only alternative. It is true or it is false that there are exactly as many plates as knives, whatever that number is and without invoking the concept of any natural number. If it is true, then Frege can go on to say something insightful about the general concept of natural number, without presupposing a distinction between arithmetical and non-arithmetical values, and without completing the predication so as to guarantee a truth-value with any specific arithmetical value n.

The concept of a natural number n must already be established if the concept of a natural number is defined by reference to the cardinality of a predicate's extension in the model Frege wisely did not follow of specifying cardinalities of sets as identical to a specific natural number in Cardinality$\{x \mid$ Knife$(x)\}$ = n or Cardinality$\{x \mid$ Plate$(x)\}$ = n. If we need to know what presumably exclusively arithmetical values are or are not available for truth-satisfaction in these predications as identical to n, then we encounter the problem of distinguishing the extensions of the predicates Arithmetical(__) = v and Non-arithmetical(__) = v. That way lies vicious circularity for Frege's logicism. He dextrously avoided the trap. It is on the strength of the above truth-valued correlations, Frege ventured to say, whatever their n-valued cardinality, with as yet no analysis of number set forth, that the extensions in question are *equinumerous* or same-numbered.

The identity statement Cardinality$\{x \mid \text{Knife}(x)\}$ = Cardinality$\{x \mid \text{Plate}(x)\}$ is true or false without making reference to any self-defining concept of natural number or any particular natural number n. It is not a predicate extension's cardinality that was crucial for Frege's analysis, but the identity of at least two predicate extensions' cardinalities. He could not on pain of circularity ground the analysis in any specific natural number as the cardinality of this or that set. He thought that equinumerosity of the cardinality of at least two predicate extension sets would be sufficient to further define the concept of natural number without circularity. It was the identity of cardinalities rather than the identity of any cardinality with any natural number n that was meant to be Frege's circularity escape hatch. With that much turf gained, Frege took the next step by explaining what it meant to speak of a specific number of things having a certain property. It is the cardinality of a specific exclusive subdomain of existent objects in the extension of a particular predicate.

We are escorted thereby that much closer to the analysis of natural number as a purely logical concept. Frege completed the explanation of number in the following sequence of assertions and inferences (§72):

The number which belongs to the concept F is the extension of the concept "equinumerous to the concept F"

and added further that

the expression
 "n is a number"
is synonymous with the expression
 "There exists a concept such that n is the number which belongs to it."
    Thus, the concept of number is defined, apparently, to be sure, in terms of itself, but actually without any error, because "the number that belongs to the concept F" is already defined.[31]

Frege warded off a related potential circularity objection in the final sentence. It may look at first as though the concept of number is defined

---

by reference to the concept of number. Circularity is avoided, if Frege read the situation correctly, in a two-step definition. The concept "the number that belongs to the concept *F*" had already been defined, properly grounded in terms of its meaning that Frege identified as its sense-meaning or *Sinn*. It did not further depend on the concept of the specific number *n* that numerically identifies the cardinality of a given predicate's extension.

Critics uncomfortable with this shuffle on Frege's part might object to the idea of speaking of number at any preparatory level of analysis as presupposing the concept that is required to emerge only at the end and as a result of the process. It is no consolation to learn that the concept of "the number that belongs to the concept *F*" has already been defined as a preliminary step toward defining the concept of number. Any definition of the sort must assume an understanding of the general concept of number in order to understand the concept of the specific number that belongs to the extension of an arbitrary predicate representing an arbitrary property *F* as a possible value of *n*. If there is a more reassuring route out of circularity, Frege has not clearly marked the way.

The Julius Caesar Problem

In the course of refuting alternative analyses of the concept of number, in the frequently discussed Julius Caesar problem in the *Grundlagen*, Frege revealed the *métier* of his proposed definition. The Julius Caesar problem has received sufficient attention to merit detailed exposition as a specialized topic in interpreting Frege's 1884 treatise on the concept of natural number.[32]

Frege introduced the difficulty as a challenge to opponents in *Grundlagen* Section IV. The Julius Caesar problem was not a challenge for Frege's analysis of the concept of number, but rather an objection to some of the competing definitions that Frege chose to dispute. Having rejected as inapposite the locutions "*a falls under F*" and "*b falls under F*" (in §62), Frege developed a single line of argument over a series of passages worth quoting at length in order to appreciate their interconnection (§56):

---

[32] See Dummett, *Frege: Philosophy of Mathematics*, pp. 209–17; and Weiner, *Frege Explained*, pp. 61–65.

Every individual number is a self-subsistent object

Of course, we can by means of this and the previous definition say what is meant by

"The number 1 + 1 belongs to the concept *F*"

and then, in the course of using this, provide the sense of the expression

"The number 1 + 1 + 1 belongs to the concept *F*"

and so on; but we can – to give a crude example – never decide by means of our definitions whether Julius Caesar belongs to a number concept, whether this same well-known conqueror of Gaul is a number or not. We cannot furthermore prove by the aid of our attempted definitions that it must be the case that *a* = *b*, if the number *a* belongs to the concept *F*, and if the number *b* belongs to the same concept. The expression "*the* number which belongs to the concept *F*," would therefore not be justified and thereby it would be generally impossible to prove a numerical identity, because we simply cannot subsume a definite number. It is only an illusion that we have defined 0 and 1; in truth we have only fixed the sense of the idioms

"the number 0 belongs to"

"the number 1 belongs to";

but it is not permitted by this means to distinguish the 0 and 1 as self-subsistent recognizable objects.[33]

We understand that Julius Caesar is not a number. The question is the concept of number by which Caesar is excluded. Caesar belongs to a concept of unitary things, but is not for that reason a number, let alone the number 1. Belonging to a concept is therefore a hopeless analysis for the concept of number. Frege's observation seems more commonsensical and tractable than efforts at exposition in the secondary literature have sometimes assumed.[34]

Frege was at pains to criticize a competing definition of the concept of natural number with which he disagreed. The objection was supposed to be that on such an account one cannot exclude the absurdity that Caesar is a number. Merely knowing what it means for something to *belong* to the

---

[33] Frege, *Foundations*, pp. 62–63.

[34] Macbeth's characterization of the Julius Caesar problem is interesting in this respect. She expands on the idea of concept "realization" which was mentioned only briefly by Frege to account for the exclusion of historical individuals from Frege's analysis of numbers. See Macbeth, *Frege's Logic*, pp. 161–64.

extension of a predicate representing a property concept-function like F does not further say what things do or do not belong to the extension. Caesar does not belong to the concept of number, but why not? Without a good explanation of this exclusion from the arithmetical predicate's extension, we are not in a position to distinguish numbers from such undisputed non-numbers as the ancient Roman conqueror of Gaul. The further philosophical implication then is that we cannot yet know what numbers are, what kinds of things are numbers.

Caesar is welcome to belong to the extension of many predicates, including Man, Human being, Soldier, a Julian, Citizen of Rome, and so on. Some, but presumably not all, of these extensions will turn out to be equinumerous, in the sense that it will be true of them outside of arithmetic that their members stand in one–one plates–knives correlation with one another across their respective subdomains of entities with all those of identical cardinalities. Those facts alone, should they obtain, will not make any of the entities belonging to these extensions identical with any natural number or any other arithmetical or more generally mathematical entity. It is the instances of equinumerous correlation of objects belonging to a predicate's extension in Frege's analysis, rather than the objects denizened in the extensions of predicates themselves, according to the proposal, that are identified as numbers under the analysis to which Frege took exception in citing the Julius Caesar problem. Caesar, whatever his other virtues and worldly accomplishments, is strikingly not himself any particular equinumerosity or one–one correlation. He is instead something with which such a correlation might hold in concert with existent objects in the extensions of other predicates.

If this is the real difficulty of the Julius Caesar problem, then effectively distinguishing between arithmetical objects like 2 and non-arithmetical objects like Julius Caesar is only half the battle. The problem remains of explaining why $+1$(Julius Caesar) $= n$ or, more generally, $+1$ (Julius Caesar) $= v$ should not have a truth-value for at least some n or v given that Julius Caesar at one time existed just as for Frege numbers abstractly exist. If we distinguish sharply between arithmetical and non-arithmetical objects, as Frege may have believed he could, then as a practical matter we can choose to exclude non-arithmetical from arithmetical applications to an arithmetical function. Satisfying a logical prerequisite for the possibility of enforcing a distinction never in itself constitutes a good reason for doing so. The missing inferential cabinetry must explain what it is about non-arithmetical existent entities that makes them unsuitable as argument-objects for arithmetical functions. It would be interesting to know Frege's opinion as to why Caesar is excluded from $+1(\underline{\hspace{1em}}) = v$, beyond the undeniable fact that Caesar is non-arithmetical. Even if there is no true completion of the function with Caesar, it remains obscure why Frege did not blanketly pronounce all similar predications false, such that, for any v, $V(+1(\text{Julius Caesar}) = v) = $ the False. It would be interesting to know what Frege meant by the distinction between the arithmetical and the non-arithmetical.

What (Kind of Thing) Is a Number?

In his *Grundlagen* Frege was interested in the nature of mathematical objects, especially numbers. He was interested in the properties of certain numbers, such as the property of being prime, even, odd, rational, irrational, fractional, imaginary, complex, transcendental, and so on. These properties were themselves not objects for Frege, but concepts interpreted as functions. They are unsaturated in that they need to be filled by predication subject terms, proper names referring to complete existent abstract entities, in this case, particular numbers.

The relation between objects and concepts is symbiotic in Frege's philosophy of mathematics. We recognize particular objects by virtue of their properties. This is to say the concepts that truly apply to them. We learn about concepts as functions by studying the objects that possess the properties represented by the relevant predicates or concept-function terms. When object terms are inserted in a concept-functor's blanks, they complete or saturate the otherwise unsaturated predicational contexts. The satisfaction of concept-functions in the meantime provides identity conditions by which one object is distinguished from another. We can meaningfully say that Odd(1) is a true thought or proposition = the True and Even(1) is false = the False.

The ball is round. The ball is green. The number 3 is odd. The number 3 is prime. There are objects, whether physical or abstract, arithmetical or more generally mathematical, and these objects are said to have properties from a range of possibilities befitting their ontic status. We do not sensibly literally say that the ball is prime, and we do not sensibly literally say that the number 3 is green. What we do say about numbers, judging from the grammar of number terms as they are contexted where Frege bade us look for them in the axioms and theorems of elementary arithmetic, is that they are, as the imaginary person of untutored commonsense judgment in Frege's Introduction to the *Grundlagen* has it, "Well, anyway, a *thing.*" Numbers for Frege *are* indeed things to which properties are predicatively attached. The number 1 has a range of properties, to consider only the true things that might be said about that upright first counting number. It stands in countless logical–mathematical relations to every other number and every other mathematical entity of every other kind, just as every particle of matter in Newton's universe is subject to gravitational forces and therefore locked into causal interraction with every other physical particle in motion anywhere in what Newton calls the infinitely extended and infinitely divisible "System of the World."[35]

Frege's extraordinary insight was that identity statements express the fact that the number that belongs to the concept ____ = 2 + 3, the number that satisfies the context to produce a true proposition, was the same as the number that belongs to the concept-function ____ = 5. More generally, if we let "F" and "G" stand for any two concepts, then Frege would analyze the identity statement $F = G$ as "the number that belongs to the concept F is the same as the number that belongs to the concept G." This might not seem to represent much progress in defining the concept of number, because the word "number" still appears on both sides of the equivalence. To avoid the problem and refurbish the definition without lapsing into ultimate circularity, Frege appealed to the concept of one–one correlation – *beiderseits eindeutige Zuordnung.* The relation is literally that of mutual univocal correlation. An identity or numerical equation such as $F = G$ (for numerical concepts F and G) holds true, in Frege's final formulation of the definition, only in the case that there exists an exact one–one correlation between the objects in the

---

[35] Newton's "System of the World" is explained in his *Principia Mathematica Philosophiæ Naturalis*, I (Berkeley: University of California Press, 1999). See also Newton, *De Gravitatione et æquipondio fluidorum*, in Newton, *Philosophical Writings*, ed. Andrew Janiak (Cambridge: Cambridge University Press, 2004). For relevant philosophical sources related to Newton's "System of the World," see Jacquette, "Newton's Metaphysics of Space as God's Emanative Effect," *Physics in Perspective*, 16 (2014), pp. 344–70.

extension of predicate "*F*" and the objects in the extension of predicate "*G*." That is to say, it holds only in the case that the cardinalities of the extensions of predicates "*F*" and "*G*" are identical. Frege likened the one–one correlation of objects to the waiter setting a table by laying down exactly the same number of knives and plates, without knowing or needing to know, or care, how many there are of each, and without even thinking about numbers or making use of the word "number." It is the unattended fact implied by the possibility of a knife being set beside every plate every time a plate is set in place or conversely, without omission or duplication.[36]

The fact that one–one coordination of elements exists independently of subjective belief, opinion, or knowledge was an evident Fregean safeguard against psychologism in the theory of number, and a means to thwart the vicious circularity that might otherwise threaten to disable the analysis. We can heuristically put the distinction psychologistically for the moment, in terms that Frege would ultimately not approve, by saying that we do not need to know the number of objects in the extension of a concept, predicate, or reference domain of arguments for a corresponding function, in order for it to be true that the extensions of predicates representing properties *F* and *G* are equinumerous, capable in principle of being set into one–one correspondence like the waiter's plates and knives. If properties *F* and *G* have this mind-independent one–one correspondence, then the number of *F*s = the number of *G*s, and Frege is on his way to explaining the concept of number generally.

The meaning of a number word, applying Frege's principle (2) of contextualist meaning, is nothing other than to be in exact one–one or "mutual univocal" (*beiderseits eindeutige*) correlation (*Zuordnung*). Frege formulated the definition in this specific terminology, requiring that the expression "*n* is a number" means the same as the expression "there exists a concept such that *n* is the number that belongs to it." Recurrent concern about circularity in the definition is supposed to be calmed by the fact

---

[36] Frege invoked David Hume's one–one correlation principle as *beiderseits eindeutige Zuordnung* in *Foundations*, p. 66: "§63. Hume already mentions one such method: 'When two numbers are so combined that the one has always a unit answering to every unit of the other, we pronounce them equal.'" Difficulties in Frege's appeal to the Hume correlation principle, and in J. L. Austin's translation of Frege's *Zuordnung* principle in his English version of the *Grundlagen*, are discussed in Jacquette, "Translator's Introduction and Critical Commentary," in *Foundations*, pp. xxvi–xxx. Austin's version is presented in Frege, *The Foundations of Arithmetic/Die Grundlagen der Arithmetik* (Oxford: Basil Blackwell, 1953).

that the concept of "number which belongs to concept F" is independently defined in terms of Humean primitive uncounted plates-and-knives correlations, by which the definition or analysis is logically anchored.

Number in expressions concerning the number of Fs is simply the extension of the concept "$= F$," or "equal or identical to the concept F." The concept is defined in turn by Frege in terms of exact one–one or mutual univocal correlation of the extension of predicate "F" representing property F. It follows logically as a result that in Frege's series of definitions the concept of any natural number n, and hence of natural number in general, as Frege wanted to define it, is the concept of the extension of the concept-function "$= n$." Number was defined logically by Frege, rather than psychologically or psycho-logistically. Assuming equinumerosity and cardinality are purely logical, Frege has fulfilled logicism's brief. It is altogether a matter of identity. Like the pair-wise laying of plateware and silverware, it is in turn therefore exclusively the stepchild of abstract one–one mutual univocal correlations of the extensions of appropriate predicates. As such, for Frege it was refreshingly independent of human belief, opinion, knowledge, judgment, or attitude about the respective relationships obtaining.[37]

If the purpose and content of Frege's analysis of the concept of natural number still seems uncertain, we can break it down, as Frege did, into three stages.

- Natural numbers (0, 1, 2, 3, . . .), after some discussion of contrary possibilities, are concluded to be self-subsistent entities, complete self-satisfied objects rather than unsaturated concept-functions needing to be satisfied by the insertion of an argument-object.
- The sense of the fully contextual numerical equation or identity proposition "the number belonging to the concept F = the number belonging to the concept G" is then fixed. It is here that the principle of matching units one–one or in mutual univocal correlation is invoked. The idea is common coin in many related commonsense discussions, but Frege attributed it to the eighteenth-century British empiricist philosopher David Hume, and named it after Hume.
- Upon considering applications and criticizing alternative definitions, Frege arrived at his solution whereby the number belonging to the concept F (the number of Fs,

---

[37] Crispin Wright, *Frege's Conception of Numbers as Objects* (Aberdeen: Aberdeen University Press, 1983); and John MacFarlane, "Frege, Kant, and the Logic in Logicism," *The Philosophical Review*, 111 (2002), pp. 25–66.

of things that have the property of being F) is identified with the extension of the concept "equinumerous (*gleichzahlig*) to F."

The definition identifies the concept of a natural number n in the context $n = m$ with the extension of the concept of having a certain equinumerosity, where the equinumerosity in question is the identity "$= m$" of the cardinality of extensions of two or more predicates. The number belonging to the extension of F (the number of Fs, which in this case is the number of things that satisfy the concept ____ $= m$) = the extension of the concept term "having the same number of things in its extension as the extension of predicate 'F' ('____ $= m$')." Hume's pairing correlation principle is then invoked:

§63. Hume already mentions one such method: "When two numbers are so combined as that the one has always a unit answer to every unit of the other, we pronounce them equal." It appears in more recent times that the idea that the identity of numbers must be defined by means of a univocal correlation has found much approval among mathematicians. But it at once raises logical misgivings and difficulties, which we should not pass by without examination.[38]

Having surveyed the alternatives, despite the difficulties implicit in the analysis, Frege believed that he had arrived at a concept of number that excels against its competitors by virtue of its material adequacy, avoidance of the Julius Caesar problem, and satisfaction of the three methodological principles he took as guiding the inquiry from its inception, especially the first stricture against psychologism. If a critic did not approve of Frege's methodology or did not agree that Frege's analysis of the concept of number in the end meets the demands of these requirements, then it was known exactly where to look in seeing how and why Frege gravitated toward the analysis of the concept of natural number that he preferred on the basis of forthright criteria.

From Concept to Existence of Numbers

With his definition of number worked out in painstaking detail, Frege defined individual natural numbers. He began with 0, which he equated with the null extension of the concept "not being identical with itself." The rationale was that nothing fails to be identical with itself, so there must be 0 entities standing in equinumerosity relation with the self-non-identical

[38] Frege, *Foundations*, p. 66.

members of any other set. Next, he defined the number 1 in terms of the number 0, as the number that belongs to the concept "identical to 0," following from the definition of number and the consequence that there exists exactly one number identical to 0. Frege, with all the instruments he needed prepared for use by previous detailed discussion now at hand, was ready to move forward by examining the definition's implications:

§74. We can now move on to the definitions of the individual numbers. Because nothing falls under the concept "not identical with itself," I define: 0 is the number that belongs to the concept "not identical with itself".[39]

After this preamble, having taken the first step toward understanding 0 as a particular number falling under the general concept of natural number that has now been defined, Frege showed informally how to define all other natural numbers in the series. He did so by means of the concept-function "follows in a series" and "member of a series of natural numbers ending with n," for any particular number n. These definitions enabled Frege to proceed in the remaining sections of the book to explore the implications of his analysis of natural number for the category of infinite numbers and the distinction between finite and infinite numbers, numbers other than the natural numbers previously defined (0, 1, 2, 3, . . .), including fractions, irrational reals, infinitesimals in the calculus, imaginary numbers, and complex numbers that link real and imaginary numbers together in algebraic operations.

Frege did not enter into much detail about how the irrational real numbers like π and the square root of 2 are supposed to be defined. The method is well known through the work of the philosopher-mathematician Dedekind, who showed that exactly specifying upper and lower bounds among fractional rational reals arrayed in orderly sequence along a number line continuum, which has since come to be called performing a *Dedekind cut*, precisely defines specific irrational real numbers. Dedekind proved that irrational reals satisfy self-identity conditions just as much as do natural numbers, fractions, negative integers, fractions, and the like for starters. They can therefore be assumed alike to exist, referred to, named, counted, quantified over, and made the existent objects of true or false predications. What Frege said in this deliberately abbreviated exposition of the concept of natural number suffices to give not merely the flavor but a solid understanding of how his analysis of

---

[39] *Ibid.*, p. 76.

number terms and equations in numerical identity statements could be extended to provide all the numbers and kinds of numbers needed for the basic laws and theorems of elementary arithmetic.[40]

Having turned his opponents out of their homes where they might have thought themselves safe in the security of very different proposals for understanding the concept of number, Frege ended on this triumphant note of confidence in the anti-psychologism of his analysis of the concept of number. He gloried in the definition's demonstrated objectivity as against those who would try to make number into something conceptual, mental, subjective, encultured, invented, anthropomorphic, and relative to time and place in human history, or to the Kantian Transcendental Aesthetic of time as a pure form of perception implied in passing moments of experience, none of which the Platonist Frege thought philosophy should abide. Frege summarized the *Grundlagen*'s single-minded accomplishment in the following terms, as always available to thought yet independent of the vagaries and vagueries of each subject's thinking:

CONCLUSION §105. On this conception of numbers, it appears to me that the charm of the preoccupation with arithmetic and analysis is easily explained. One could indeed say, paraphrasing a famous dictum: The real object of reason is reason. We are concerned in arithmetic with objects that are not known to us as something foreign from without by the intermediary of the senses, but rather that are directly given to reason, which, as most closely its own, can be completely transparently seen.

And yet, or rather because of that, these objects are not subjective fantasies. There is nothing more objective than arithmetical laws.[41]

Frege closed the discussion on Platonic realist terms. He knew that doing so did not by itself make what he said true. He had certainly not proved in the *Grundlagen* that there is nothing more objective than logical laws as a basis for arithmetic. He maintained, but cannot be said to have argued, that this is true. He offered an analysis that did not overtly depend on psychological states. The definition was unburdened by the other criticisms with which he castigated opposition forces who wanted to go psychologistic or set-theoretical, speaking only of the objects that may belong to the extension of a predicate without preventing Julius Caesar from filling the bill himself as a natural number in that over-generous sense. Frege believed he had covered all the possibilities. The analysis was

[40] See Chapter 5 note 17.   [41] Frege, *Foundations*, p. 95.

watertight, and he had campaigned most effectively in support of excluding all choices for the philosophy of arithmetic other than embracing his purely logical analysis of the concept of natural number.

The Critical Reception of the *Grundlagen*

Frege's second book was harshly criticized. This time, the most painful attack was delivered by Georg Cantor, a thinker of considerable reputation working in areas very similar to Frege's and highly competent to judge the value of Frege's work. It was Cantor who rehabilitated the mathematics of infinite numbers and introduced transfinite cardinal numbers and ordinals, belonging to an ascending hierarchy of higher and higher orders of infinity, each demonstrably greater in cardinality than those on which they are based and in terms of which they are defined.[42]

At the risk of engaging in bean-counting, for whatever it may be worth, it can be noted that Frege's *Grundlagen* was mentioned in print exactly once by Dedekind, in 1893, and once by Peano, in 1895, not including Frege's own references to his work, in all the time from its publication in 1884 to 1903, when Russell's *The Principles of Mathematics* appeared in its first edition. The second volume of Frege's *Grundgesetze* was published in 1903 too, with a hasty correction in response to Russell's paradox query. The students at Jena were only reflecting the common lagtime in the mathematical and philosophical community by failing to appreciate what brilliance Frege in his own way had to offer. As for reviews, the *Grundlagen* was unsympathetically and briefly discussed by Hoppe, Laßwitz, and Cantor, and lightly, but in Frege's mind unforgivably, criticized by Husserl, in his 1891 book *Philosophie der Arithmetik: Psychologische und logische Untersuchungen* (*Philosophy of Arithmetic: Psychological and Logical Investigations*). Husserl's first major book was in turn brusquely unsympathetically reviewed by Frege three years later in 1894.[43]

---

[42] Cantor, "Review of *Grundlagen der Arithmetik*, by Gottlob Frege," *Deutsche Literaturzeitung*, 6 (1885), pp. 728–29. See Frege, "Reply to Cantor's Review of *Grundlagen der Arithmetik*," in Frege, *Collected Papers on Mathematics, Logic, and Philosophy*, ed. McGuinness (Oxford: Basil Blackwell, 1984), p. 122.

[43] See Chapter 4 note 28.

Cantor is someone whose good opinion Frege had desperately hoped to enlist in support of his project. Cantor could have been a champion and redeemer to encourage Frege in his work. Instead, as we have almost come to expect, the very opposite occurred. We find Frege in the *Grundlagen* paying special homage to Cantor's then recent work, and, also in the *Grundgesetze*, making provision within his analysis of number for Cantor's groundbreaking discoveries in transfinite set theory.[44] It has even been argued that references to set-theory concepts, which had not been included in the *Begriffsschrift*, appeared in Frege's writings for the first time in the *Grundlagen* exclusively for the sake of being able to accommodate Cantor's mathematics and thereby court his good will.[45] Set theory would always have been awkwardly out of place in the *Begriffsschrift*, Frege's pure logic that had yet to be applied in a reductive analysis of arithmetic.

The passage inspiring this incredible interpretation appears about three-quarters of the way through Frege's *Grundlagen*, where he inserted the following conciliatory note that nevertheless contains within it the seeds of a substantial criticism of Cantor's set theory:

§85. Quite recently G. Cantor in a remarkable text has introduced infinite numbers. I agree with him absolutely in his appraisal of the view that generally permits only finite numbers to be regarded as actual. Neither they nor fractions, irrational nor complex numbers are sensibly perceptible and spatial; and if one calls actual that which acts upon the senses, or at least has effects that can have sense perceptions as near or remote consequences, then of course none of these numbers is actual . . . While in this I agree, as I believe, with Cantor, I nevertheless depart from him somewhat in terminology. He refers to my number as "cardinal number," while his concept of number makes reference to an ordering.[46]

Frege suggested on philosophical grounds what for him is a very mild adjustment of Cantor's terminology. It is easy to speculate that this was the basis for Cantor's later unfavorable review. However, Cantor also importantly complained that it was unfortunate that Frege had taken extensions of concepts as the foundation of the number concept. Reportedly, Cantor

---

[44] Frege, *Foundations*, pp. 84–85. Note that "sequence" membership, akin to set membership, had already been introduced in §29 of the *Begriffsschrift*.

[45] What is true is that there is no mention in the *Begriffsschrift* of set theory's founder Cantor, whose mathematics made its first appearance only in Frege's *Grundlagen*, five years later. See also Joseph W. Dauben, "Georg Cantor and Pope Leo XIII: Mathematics, Theology, and the Infinite," *Journal of the History of Ideas*, 38 (1977), pp. 85–108.

[46] Frege, *Foundations*, p. 84.

in preparing his criticism did not even read Frege's book, or did so only cursorily, as Dummett maintains, before dismissing its project in highly prejudicial terms.[47] Frege was wounded once again by Cantor's rebuff. He persisted nonetheless in drawing his oar against the tide, continuing undeflated in the project represented by the publication of his logic and philosophy, despite an established alternating pattern of unpopularity, hostility, and disregard.

Russell's more positive appreciation for Frege's *Grundlagen* analysis of the concept of natural number was reflected in his 1919 book *Introduction to Mathematical Philosophy*. This readable discussion of basic concepts of number in a logical framework was written in prison during WWI, while the conscientious objector Russell was serving his sentence for having published an article calling for a negotiated end to the war to which the authorities had taken exception. There, in Chapter II, "The Definition of Number," Russell offered his tribute to Frege's philosophy of mathematics, in appreciative comments, the second of which was taken as one of the present book's two epigraphs. There is no doubt that Russell's enthusiastic appraisal of Frege's analysis of the concept of number in the *Grundlagen* went far toward popularizing Frege's philosophy of arithmetic, in the sense of making his name and ideas known to a wider public.[48]

Although Russell broke ranks with Frege over more fundamental matters, especially in the philosophy of language, concerning the Fregean doctrine of the sense of referring expressions and sentences, Russell seems to have never wavered substantially in his regard for Frege's logicist analysis of the concept of number. Russell's rift with Frege is exemplified by the latter's enfolding of definite descriptions into proper names, where Russell saw fit to exclude them as distinct categories of denoting terms and phrases. It remains pertinent, despite his

---

[47] Dummett, *Frege: Philosophy of Language*, p. 630: "Cantor's response to the *Grundlagen* was to publish a scathing review of it (one of only three the book received), a review which revealed that Cantor had not taken the trouble to read Frege's book with sufficient care to understand it."

[48] Russell's "discovery" of Frege was a mixed blessing for the German logician. Russell made a wider readership aware of Frege's important work in mathematical logic and the foundations of arithmetic, but at the same time Frege's system was condemned by Russell's paradox. Russell's dramatic departure from Frege's sense–reference distinction is highlighted in Russell, "On Denoting," *Mind*, 14 (1905), pp. 479–93. See Herbert Hochberg, "Russell's Attack on Frege's Theory of Meaning," *Philosophica*, 18 (1976), pp. 9–34.

unqualified acclamation, to question the extent to which Russell fully understood Frege's *Grundlagen* analysis of number.

Defects, Circularities, and Omissions

Fregean logicism failed for a number of reasons. Frege near the end of his life seems to have reconsidered the question of whether the foundations of mathematics might after all begin with geometry rather than arithmetic. His moment of doubt is sometimes described as a return to Kant, on the assumption that Frege never questioned Kant's grounding of geometry in space as pure form of intuition. Even at this late time of life after all his struggles with logicism, Frege did not seriously consider the prospects of understanding arithmetic or geometry as based on partly metaphysical or psychological rather than purely logical underpinnings.

If we set aside questions about the more ambitious features of Frege's logic, we might wonder whether in spite of these setbacks Frege's definition of the category of natural number might at least have survived the criticisms that in the meantime are usually thought to have brought down logicism as an ultimately unworkable philosophy of mathematics. Classical logicism as a whole did not live up to its promise, although some parts of its gallant efforts have stood the test of time. What of Frege's *Grundlagen* definition of the concept of natural number? Does the value of his 1884 book consist in the author's having put his finger on exactly what should be meant by the concept of natural number? Or was this effort also part of Frege's failed logicism?

The question is sure to continue to exercise the philosophical imaginations of readers for many years to come, as it has ever since the publication of Frege's treatise. Without committing ourselves to one side of the controversy or another, we indicate some of the problems that plague Frege's analysis of the concept of natural number. The difficulty to be highlighted has to do with the threat of circularity in the definition. We have seen that Frege was at pains to avoid circularity, and the reason why he needed and wanted to do so should be clear. A definition is uninformative and to that extent worthless if it revolves in a circle. For then, in order to understand and apply the definition, we must already understand the meaning of whatever it is the definition is supposed to define. Frege wrote in §106, summarizing his purpose, "It came therefore to this, to stipulate the sense of a numerical identity, to express it without making use of number words or the word 'number.' We discerned in the possibility of one–one or mutually univocally correlating an object falling under the concept F with an object falling under the concept G a recognition-judgment about numbers."[49]

Frege seems to have believed that despite appearances his analysis of the concept of natural number deftly avoided vicious explanatory circularity. In one sense, it certainly did. Frege independently defined the concept of "the number that belongs to a concept F" as the extension of the concept "equal to the concept F." Equality in turn was defined as the mutual univocal correlation of the extensions of the relevant concept-function terms. Frege managed in this way to express the sense of a numerical identity without making use of number words or symbols. If we look more closely at Frege's analyzed *concept* of mutual univocal correlation, which is supposed to be the key element of the definition that avoids an explicit occurrence of number proper names, we detect a deeper difficulty. Austin, as Frege's first English translator, did Frege a disservice in this regard, translating Frege's phrase "mutual univocal correlation" (*beiderseits eindeutige Zuordnung*) as "one–one correlation." If Frege had actually used the term "one–one correlation" he would have been guilty of a blatant circularity in defining the concept of natural number in such a way as to depend on a prior understanding of the concept of the natural number 1 or one upon mentioning in analyzing the concept the existence of a one–one relation. We have no understanding of the concept of "one–one" correlation that is independent of the concept of the number one, while "one" and "1" obviously name a natural counting number.

We would already have to understand the concept of a number, and in particular the natural number 1, in order to understand Frege's definition of the concept of a natural number. On the other hand, Austin's choice of translation is candidly revealing. One–one correlation, after all, is precisely what Frege was talking about. Frege could have said "*eins–eins Zuordnung*," even though the phrase does not appear conventionally in nontechnical German. In that case, he would have expressly used one of the natural number designating terms in a series of definitions by which he hoped to explicate the concept of natural number. The fact that he refrained from doing so appears significant. If what Frege intended by

---

[49] Frege, *Foundations*, p. 96.

"mutual univocal correlation" is nothing other than "one–one correlation," if that is the force and effect of his terminology, the real meaning behind the diverting substitution of language, then the circle in his string of definitions is only lightly papered over by the definitions he provided.

Consider again the person setting a table. What is the correlation that takes place when the table is set, when tango dance partners team up, or the like? We have *one* plate and, next to *it*, *one* knife. Otherwise we notify the *maître d'*. If a waiter were to place *two* or *zero* knives next to a plate, we would understand at once that a mistake had been made. Regardless of whether we know in advance how many plates and how many knives there are, we most certainly already know what it means for plates and knives to be put in the required specifically one–one correlation. Unfortunately for Frege, such knowledge involves the arithmetical object number 1 and what it means for things in the extensions of different properties, including the tableware, to be equinumerous with their individualizable existent members in one–one correlations. It is *one* knife and *one* plate to a customer at each place setting. This much must be understood in order for the correlation to obtain. If it does not, then we have no grounds for regarding the cardinality of the extensions of any choice of predicates as being identical, even in the simple arithmetical equation by which 2 + 3 = 5.

The extension of "2 + 3" in caveman arithmetic is | | | | | (| | [+] | | |), and the extension of "5," not coincidentally, is likewise | | | | . Are "2 + 3" and "5" merely one–one correlated? Or are they not rather differently symbolized numerically identical mathematical entities? They appear to be precisely one and the same thing, represented as two type-different tokens referring to the same natural counting number. If that is true in the case of numerical identities or simple arithmetical equations generally, then why speak of *correlation*, when the issue is the absolute or numerical *identity* of mathematical objects designated by two different numerical proper names? Objects are not usually said to be *correlated* with themselves. There may be a further circularity in Frege's series of definitions involving the concept of being *equal* or *identical* to a concept. We do not have a mere analogy whereby the extension of "2 + 3" is to the plates being set as the extension of "5" is to the knives, but rather a situation in the case of the equation 2 + 3 = 5, where both "2 + 3" and "5" are analogous simply to the plates being laid or simply to the knives, with no one–one or mutual univocal correlation involved between the extensions of these two isomorphic numerical concept-function extensions. Thus 2 + 3 and 5 are one and the same abstract entity traveling under different passports, not two different things, like knives and plates, whose extensions can be one–one correlated.

Even when the waiter sets the table with knives and plates in exact one–one Humean correlation, the fact that this is correctly done presupposes the concept of the natural number 1 (one). True, there is no need for the waiter in setting the table to *think* about the number one or the concept of number, or to *say* these number names out loud. The fact that the waiter does not need consciously to consider the number 1, or the concept of one, or one–one correspondence does not strengthen Frege's cause. Such facts must be totally irrelevant from the standpoint of his rebuke of psychologism and his insistence throughout, beginning with the first of his three fundamental methodological principles, that we must not confuse the psychological with the logical. To turn a Frege-style criticism against Frege's reasoning, what if the waiter started setting down $n + 1$ knives per plate every nth time a place was set? The first setting goes as expected, but thereafter only the plates preserve one–one correlation, and an extra knife is added for every new setting. Is there not a *correct* way for the silverware and plateware to be positioned that precludes this deviant ordering? Does the concept of correctly setting the plates and knives at table not presuppose the concept of number, and in particular a concept of the number 1 implied by the concept of the relation of one–one correspondence? It is unclear how the circularity is supposed to be avoided. If we are only talking contingently about what it is that the waiter happens to do, the action the waiter performs, rightly or wrongly, then anything whatsoever might occur with respect to pairings of numbers of knives with numbers of plates.

Non-one–one correlations lack relevance to Frege's attempt to ground the concept of number in pure logic, but it is not clear how they can be excluded without circularity. The waiter might even, *à la* Wittgenstein's recalcitrant calculators in *Philosophical Investigations* or *Remarks on the Foundations of Mathematics*, maintain with a straight face that the same order of n tableware and plateware setting is preserved throughout, whereas conventional counting would say that the waiter is laying n knives and m plates where $n \neq m$.[50] Uncritical reliance on the Humean

[50] Wittgenstein, *Philosophical Investigations* §§201, 214, and 226; and *Remarks on the Foundations of Mathematics* (Cambridge: MIT Press, 1978) §§36–41. See Saul A. Kripke, *Wittgenstein on Rules and Private Language: An Elementary Exposition* (Cambridge: Harvard University Press, 1982). Kripke is criticized by Colin McGinn, *Wittgenstein on Meaning: An*

principle of mutual univocal correlation is a methodological deficiency in Frege's *Grundlagen* analysis of the concept of natural number that Frege did not seem to anticipate.

If mutual univocal correlation is not merely another way of expressing one–one correlation, then it is powerless to explain Frege's concept of natural number. If the correlation in question is not one–one or if it is something other than one–one, either one–many or many–one, regardless of how it is described, then there can be no basis for identifying numbers falling under a predicate with the predicate's extension. If, on the other hand, mutual univocal correlation is just another way of talking about one–one correlation, as Austin's translation bluntly acknowledges, then there is after all a vicious circularity in Frege's definition of the concept of number. The circularity arises because the definition of natural number presupposes that we already understand the concept of the natural number 1 as implied by and involved in the one–one correlations presupposed by equinumerosity or identity of the cardinality of two or more predicates' extensions. As a further consequence of this horn of the dilemma for Frege's definition of the concept of natural number, it makes his definition of the number 1 as the extension of the concept "identical with the number that belongs to the concept 'identical to 0'" superfluous, since in that case the concept of the natural number 1 is already presupposed by one–one correlation and the definition of the concept of the natural number 0, of which there exists uniquely one abstract arithmetical entity.[51]

The same is true even if we interpret Frege's *beiderseits eindeutige Zuordnung*, *pace* Austin, more generally as *any* mutual univocal *n–n* correlation for any unspecified natural number *n* > 0. The definition in that event requires that we possess a prior understanding of the general concept of natural number, especially including 0. In order to avoid the overt impression of circularity in Frege's analysis of the concept of natural number, while still taking advantage of the meaning of his technical terminology, in the translation quoted throughout the convention of rendering Frege's phrase *beiderseits eindeutige Zuordnung* as "mutual univocal [one–one] correlation" is adopted. This is intended to

Interpretation and Evaluation (Oxford: Blackwell Publishers, 1984). Among Kripke's few supporters on Wittgenstein, see Kusch, *A Sceptical Guide to Meaning and Rules: Defending Kripke's Wittgenstein* (Montreal: McGill–Queen's University Press, 2006).
[51] See note 42 above.

convey a more literal reading of Frege's terminology, in which no number term as such explicitly occurs. We recognize all the while that there is an "*ein*" ["one"] embedded even within "*eindeutige*," just as there is effectively the equivalent "uni" in "univocal." Since the phrase "mutual univocal correlation" is as vague in English as it is in German, we compromise in the cited translations by adding in brackets Austin's sense of the real meaning of the term the explanation "[one–one]." We can say with confidence that, if Frege's correlation is not one–one, then it is never going to work.

The avoidance of a number term other than the particle "uni" in "univocal" or "univocally" in translating the key concept of Frege's analysis of natural number still, regrettably, is not tantamount to avoiding all definitional, analytic or explanatory circularity. Frege argued that the definition in its final form did not contain a circle because the concept "the number belonging to *F*" in terms of Hume's correlation principle is never specified. Even if we try to understand the necessary sort of correlation as itself being free of any particular number concepts, and read "mutual univocal correlation" as involving no properly named natural numbers, Frege's definition remains incomplete. Hume's correlation principle does not explain the meaning of "the number belonging to *F*," but only defines correlations between numbers belonging to like-numbered isomorphic concepts *F* and *G* of identical cardinality. It does not adequately define the concept "having the same number of things as *F*," unless we already know the meaning and extensional value, the *number* of objects falling under the concept of "the *number* belonging to the concept *G*," "having the same *number* of things as *G*," or, equivalently, the *number* of objects falling under the concept *G*. The whole series of definitions is ungrounded without this information, and the information presupposes the concept of natural number, being equinumerous, and hence in general the concept of natural number that is supposed to be defined, excluded from the concept's noncircular analysis.

There are further misgivings concerning circularity in Frege's analysis. It is troubling that Frege's concept of the *extension* of a predicate or concept term appears on both sides of the definition in Frege's final formulation of the analysis of the concept of a natural number. Frege admitted as much in the footnote near the end of §68 (translation note 88), when he said "I presuppose that one knows what the extension of a predicate is."[52] Knowing only in abstract informal terms what is meant by the extension of a predicate is not adequate for Frege's purposes. The definition works only if we also understand what is meant by the extensions of two or more predicates being equinumerous, for the sake of which we seem to require a prior grasp of the concept of natural number. It is the very thing to be defined that must enter into its own definition. If mutual univocal correlation means nothing other than one–one or n–n matching of items or correlations holding between the extensions of predicates for any $n \geq 0$, then we have no such concept of the extensions of two or more predicates being equinumerous that does not already presuppose an understanding and implicit, if not explicit, application of the concept of a natural number, and in particular of the natural number 1.

The Significance of the *Grundlagen* in Frege's Logicism and Beyond

It is appropriate in evaluating Frege's project to quote what Frege himself said about Kant immediately after criticizing Kant's philosophy of arithmetic. In *Grundlagen* §89, Frege wrote that, "In order not to incur the charge of nit-picking criticism against such an intellect, to whom we can only look up with thankful wonder, I think I am also obliged to emphasize my agreement, which far outweighs my misgivings."[53]

Offering an overall assessment of the achievements of Frege's second book, in order to comprehend why, despite its difficulties, it remains after one hundred and thirty years a vitally important contribution to the philosophy of mathematics, requires mention of what has been of enduring value in Frege's living legacy to contemporary analytic philosophy. As Frege remarked with respect to Kant, the fact that we are in overwhelming debt to a thinker of the past should not daunt us from thinking the same problems through for ourselves, nor from criticizing even the most notable efforts of the past. We do so not out of untested irreverence, but because we must know whether they survive our sharpest criticisms.

Frege's *Grundlagen*, whatever its other merits or defects, is an undoubted paradigm of how to proceed methodologically in the clarification of concepts. Even if Frege's definition of the concept of a natural

---

[52] Frege, *Foundations*, p. 102.   [53] *Ibid.*, p. 86.

number is judged to be ultimately unworkable, we remain in debt to him for his cultivation of an intellectual atmosphere in which the finest details of conceptual analysis were sought out and critically scrutinized. Ideas were to be clearly laid before us for inspection, and cogent arguments offered as to why one approach to a problem might be regarded as unsatisfactory and another preferred. That is one noble model of scientific philosophy. The idea of it alone could have exerted an impact on thinkers also in other fields who were not directly contributing to the foundations of logicism. This has also remarkably turned out to be the case. We owe an enormous debt to Frege, and to his *Grundlagen* in particular, for establishing a culture of clearcut philosophical analysis and uncompromisingly meticulous argumentation that has persisted identifiably through ideological shifts occurring within the Frege-founded practice of analytic philosophy.

If Frege went too far in his rejection of psychologism, he was still on the side of the angels when he espoused as a model for philosophy the defense of objective scientific truth in matters of conceptual clarification. He was right to oppose a supine subjectivism that encourages the bold to say whatever they want in doing philosophy, merely by articulating unargued-for opinions as though philosophy were a creative literary writing exercise. For Frege that was not philosophy, which he considered to be instead an effort to work scientifically toward objective truths. He managed in his second book and other investigations to make a strong case for a more systematic way of recognizing the purpose, methods, and starting-places of scientific philosophy. His example has impressed succeeding generations who look to Frege as setting a high standard of rigorous conceptual analysis and philosophical argument, as rigorous as any to be found in the best work in mathematics and the natural sciences, for which philosophy in its most admirable moments symbiotically helps set the standards.

In his quest for, and insistence on arriving at, a satisfactory definition of the concept of natural number, Frege reminds us philosophically of Socrates in Plato's dialogues. Socrates settled for nothing less than the necessary and sufficient conditions by which an abstract concept could be fully understood in its universality. We approve of Frege's insistence on exactly defining the general concept of natural number, rather than assuming that this is something we must already know. The polemical sections of the *Grundlagen*, where Frege criticized his predecessors and contemporaries, read in fact rather like an extended Socratic ἔλεγχος (*elenkhos*, or elenchus in English), with heavy emphasis on the counter-example component of Socrates' method. Nor is this the only parallelism between Frege and Plato that might be spotlighted. We should not overlook Frege's firm commitment to *Gedanken* as the mind-independent meanings of thoughts and concrete sentences in a language. Numbers for Frege were also not physical–empirical entities, nor were they subjective–psychological creations of thought. He considered them abstract rather than "conceptual" in the popular sense. He reasoned that they must be something knowable *a priori*, real existent objects grasped only by reason, as in Plato's distinction between the sensible and intelligible world and the philosopher's mission of grasping the eternal Forms. Frege considered thoughts or propositions and their objects of predication in the case of natural numbers and a wider family of mathematical objects to be Platonic entities that transcend the world of perception and experiential phenomena.

Frege grappled in his early writings with some of the most difficult questions in one of philosophy's most persistently contested fields. Like other masters of skilled technique, Frege made an intimidating chain of reasoning appear intelligible, natural, and effortless. We learn from Frege how criticism and conceptual analysis can effectively be prosecuted. We see at first hand how a formidable selection of philosophical problems can be put in order and dealt with systematically, with enviable patience, rigor, and systematic thoroughness, leading to fruitful solutions to interesting and otherwise intractable difficulties. In the process, especially in the *Grundlagen*, we additionally acquire an enormous amount of information about the concept of natural number, about how the idea of number can and should not be defined, and the importance of attaining the sharpest conceivable degree of clarity at the foundations of a body of knowledge before proceeding to add advantageous theoretical fixtures to its superstructure.

When we read Frege's *Grundlagen* today, with its carefully explicated logicist analysis of the concept of natural number, whether we know it or not, we are considering a chapter in a much longer and more detailed history that ultimately combines a theoretical and a personal tragedy. None of these facts, no matter how important they are to bear in mind as we study Frege's 1884 work on the concept of natural number, prevented its recognition as having inaugurated an important new method for the analysis of concepts, a method with far-reaching implications and a new way of doing philosophy. He triumphed in later professional judgment only many years after his death. He was annoyed but undeterred by the critical and publishing failure of what he regarded unfalteringly throughout his life as his main lasting contributions to mathematical logic and its philosophy. Today he prevails in the history of logic and analytic philosophy, despite a maelstrom of challenges and the ultimate failure of his purely logical arithmetic. He does so precisely because of what he was trying to accomplish and how and why he failed to do so. Frege's pure logicism did not fulfill its ostensive promise, but it remains philosophically instructive. The clarity, simplicity, and surveyability of Frege's mathematical intuitions make a powerful case for pure logicism. We learn from its failure why it was worthwhile for someone with Frege's talents to have undertaken the experiment.[54]

---

[54] An evaluation of the impact of Frege's *Grundlagen* in the history of logicism is offered by Demopoulos, *Logicism and its Philosophical Legacy* (Cambridge: Cambridge University Press, 2013). For another evaluation of the relative merits of Frege's treatises, see Dummett, *Frege: Philosophy of Mathematics*, pp. 1–4. Dummett considers the *Grundlagen* to be Frege's "masterpiece," whereas the present interpretation, despite Russell's paradox, favors the *Grundgesetze*.

7

Professional Advancement, Marriage, and the Quest for Objectivity in a Scientific Theory of Meaning (1885–1892)

REGE'S SECOND BOOK, like the first, was unkindly reviewed. This time the principal critics were Husserl and Cantor. Cantor was then, and remains today, the father of modern set theory and transfinite cardinalities, the mathematical rehabilitator of existent infinite sets, series, and ratios. These abstract entities had since the previous century been considered nothing more than convenient fictions and nominalizations of calculation devices lacking philosophical justification.

Infinitesimals in the calculus of derivative and integral mathematical analysis are infinite ratios that after Cantor could hold their heads high, ontically speaking, as existent mathematical entities rather than non-referential syntax configurations. Recognition and appreciation of Cantor's transfinite set theory, detached from his quirky efforts to use mathematics as a Kantian third critique or *Critique of Judgment* bridge to the mathematical sublimity of God, were building impressively in the mathematical community roughly at the time Frege's *Grundlagen* was published. Cantor was a thinker of considerable reputation working in areas somewhat similar to Frege's, currently enjoying greater prestige than Frege, and competent, if he chose to do so, to judge the value of Frege's work. Frege may have desperately desired a positive, discerning opinion of his *Grundlagen* analysis of the concept of natural number from Cantor, but was unfortunately not to receive one.[1]

---

[1] Cantor, "Review of *Grundlagen der Arithmetic*." See Chapter 6 note 42.

Promotion and Chapel Bells

Frege's personal life was significantly enriched during this period. We are offered a study in contrasts of Frege's outlook after the publication of the *Begriffsschrift* and his outlook after that of the *Grundlagen*, in an existence that, typically for Frege's star, combined the promise of happiness with the reality of disproportionate emotional pain.

First, however, after long delay and postponed gratification, there was joy and satisfaction in Frege's world. On 14 March 1887, three years after the *Grundlagen* had appeared, Frege married his lifetime and only known intimate partner, Margarete Katharina Sophia Anna Lieseberg. Frege was thirty-nine. Margarete was almost thirty-one. Her appearance has been lost to history; one searches in vain for a photograph of her.[2] Wedding Margarete was the blissful summit of Frege's later life. He had achieved enough academic recognition to earn an Associate Professor's respectable salary pursuing his logical–mathematical–philosophical objectives. He could look after his mother nearby in her old age, and could afford to have a family like normal law-abiding citizens who were not revolutionaries in the foundations of mathematical logic.

The tragedy, for those who can see ahead, was that, despite their differences in age, Margarete did not survive beyond June 1904. Four years after her death, in 1908, Frege took on a very young boy from destitute institutionalized parents to raise with his longtime housekeeper, Meta Arndt. Bynum, in a previously cited passage in this connection, needs updating with respect to several facts in this part of Frege's chronology. Bynum compounds several mistakes when he writes "Even in his personal life sorrow and frustration plagued him; for after he was married to Margarete Lieseberg (1856–1905) of Greve Mill [Grevesmühlen], the couple started a family only to see all the children die young. About 1900 they adopted a son Alfred; but Frege's wife died in 1905 and left him to raise the boy alone."

We know that what Bynum describes is not fact, because it is a matter of historical record that Margarete died four years before Alfred was taken on as Frege's ward. Alfred was indeed later adopted by Frege, but certainly not around 1900. Alfred was not born until 1903, to another family in financial distress. Alfred was not made Frege's ward until 1908, long after Margarete's death, and was not adopted by Frege as his legal

---

[2] Kreiser, *Gottlob Frege*, pp. 489–96.

son and heir until roughly the time of the boy's eighteenth birthday, around 1921–1922. Nor is it clear what young-dying children of Gottlob's and Margarete's Bynum could possibly have in mind. No birth or death registers or comparable historical traces, church records or the like, have surfaced to date for such progeny. Margarete, for her part, died 25 June 1904, and not in 1905 as Bynum states.[3]

Frege seems to have borne all of life's bare-fisted blows, of which he received more than his share, with calm and steady resolution. Perhaps his short time in the reservists and his admiration for Otto von Bismarck, the conservative Prussian Chancellor of Germany, and certain aspects of German militarism had instilled in him a soldier's grit and determination to hold his ground and advance the cause of pure logicism in spite of the odds. At least, he was prepared to do so when he strongly believed that what he was trying to accomplish was possible. He would stand with his chest to the foe until Russell's paradox bullet brought him down. With his large-plan objectives before him as lodestone to his compass at all times, Frege never faltered in working toward the main purpose he had set out to achieve in logic, philosophy of mathematics, and philosophy of language. That Frege's lifelong research after all these personal and professional struggles should have failed so dramatically and decisively, according to Frege's own demanding standards, was the great tragedy in his philosophical life. Even here there was an unexpected ironic twist in Frege's frustration over what he took to be his failed efforts to establish a beachhead for the purely logical foundations of arithmetic.

---

[3] The previously cited quotation is from Bynum, *Frege: Conceptual Notation*, p. 20. The amount of misinformation circulating about Frege's family life is startling. Richard L. Mendelsohn, *The Philosophy of Gottlob Frege* (Cambridge: Cambridge University Press, 2005), p. 1, writes as follows: "The known details of the personal side of Frege's life are few ... Our knowledge of the remainder of Frege's personal life is similarly impoverished. He married Margarete Lieseberg (1856–1904) in 1887. They had several children together, all of whom died at very early ages. Frege adopted a child, Alfred, and raised him as his own." Who were these imaginary children of Frege and Margarete? They must have died very young indeed, prior to being conceived. Part of the problem is that Mendelsohn takes most of his biographical data about Frege's life from Bynum. See Mendelsohn, p. 203, note 1. In his note 2, Mendelsohn remarks that there is a discrepancy that he goes no distance toward resolving: "Kreiser (2001) reports that Alfred was adopted after Margarete died; Beaney (1997) reports that the two had adopted Alfred shortly before her death." Why not look into the matter, and resolve the inconsistency? Kreiser gets his facts straight, and Beaney and Bynum in this instance do not. Alfred was not born until 1903, and Margarete died in 1904. Alfred was not in need of a foster home until he was six years old in the later days of 1908, and was not legally adopted by Frege until 1921–1922, when Alfred, contrary to Mendelsohn's attribution, was no longer a "child" and had already been "raised."

Margarete Katharina Sophia Anna Lieseberg

The future Margarete Frege was born 15 February 1856. She died in 1904, aged forty-eight, by which time she and Frege had lived together as man and wife for about seventeen years since their marriage in 1887. Frege outlived her by twenty-one years. Margarete's father, Heinrich Georg Johann Lieseberg, was an official attorney in Grevesmühlen, Mecklenburg. Her mother, Fanny Delling, was from Wismar. Margarete had two sisters, Frieda and Fanny. It would be marvelous to have more information about Margarete, how she and Frege met, what their courtship and matrimonial relationship were like. With a ruffling of skirts and bonnets, they make a distant impression of a German Jane Austen household. The unfortunate truth is that Margarete is mostly lost to history. What we know, in addition to basic facts about her family, is only that she married Frege in 1887, and that she died of a protracted undiagnosed illness after seventeen years of childless marriage in 1904. Much more is known about the widowed Gottlob's ward and later adopted son, Paul Otto Alfred Fuchs, generally known as Alfred.[4]

Importantly, on 1 April 1885, Frege's "revocable" (*widerrufliche*) Associate Professor's salary was increased by slightly more than 133%, from 300 Marks to 700 Marks yearly. This was the godsend Frege may have been waiting for, a change in fortune that would make it possible for him at last to begin a family. At thirty-nine it was not too late. He was in reasonably good health. He had a professional vocation. He was a published, if not particularly well-regarded, author. He was a person of cultivated interests, with mathematical and scientific accomplishments to his name. He was no longer the most eligible bachelor in Jena perhaps, if he had ever been that, but a suitable match for the right woman who could complete his happiness or at least help him to weather whatever further blows his turbulent academic life might send crashing his way. In the event, the groundwork for Frege's future disappointments was laid in this year, with no warning signs of approaching storms on the horizon.

Frege made an art of his patient forbearance against neglect and misunderstanding. He read the criticisms his books occasioned with a combination of amusement and disgust. He must have thought about them, deciding in the end that they were not right about his work in any way that mattered. He was patient through his climb up the mathematics

---

[4] Kreiser, "Alfred," in *Frege in Jena*, ed. Gabriel and Kienzler, pp. 68–83.

degrees ladder. He was patient about his first pathetic earnings as a *Privatdozent* and even Extraordinariat, with the fine trickle and eventual disappearance of students who never sustained serious interest in what he had to teach. He awaited the arrival of select minds who might have been devoted to his *Begriffsschrift* and his overall logicist program for the reduction of mathematics to logic. As the work took shape, and as Frege began to understand later in life what supplementary clarifications were going to be needed, he brought his sharply focused analytic attention to bear on the meaning of identity statements in elementary arithmetical equations, and therewith the categories of function, concept, and object. To explain the meaning of cognitively informative noniterative true identity statements, like those found in arithmetical equations and complete expressions of functional relations, of the general form $a = b$, rather than the iterative $a = a$ or $b = b$, Frege further distinguished between the direct and indirect sense and reference of singular referring expressions.

Frege's prospects for professional advancement at the University of Jena were all this time improving. Abbe was earning enough from his work at the Zeiss Corporation to waive his university salary of 1,500 Marks per year as Honorary Professor, whereupon he requested that the uncommitted funds thereby released be made available to Frege.[5] The usual paperwork passed up and down the line. The university *Kurator* applied for Frege's annual salary to be increased from 300 to 1,000 Marks, effective 1 April 1885. In the end, Frege's salary was boosted by 400 Marks to a total of 700 Marks by the Ministry of State Service. Apparently that compromise amount was considered sufficient, and left over part of the money for other worthy purposes. This increase in salary was no doubt celebrated by Frege and his family circle – one can imagine Frege holding the letter bearing the news in one hand and a wine glass in the other. In the summer semester of 1885, as was typical for this span of his career at Jena, Frege taught Analytical Mechanics with eleven participants, and Mathematical Exercises (Analytical Geometry of the Plane), with four students in attendance. Frege's classroom *Dozent* fees, in addition to his recently bolstered university salary, and despite his regular salary and promotion, amounted in this period to a miserable 27.50 Marks. In November 1885 Frege was made a member of the

[5] Kreiser, *Gottlob Frege*, p. 425.

Scientific Examination Commission (FPC) for candidates of the higher Magisterium for the remainder of that year and the next. He was charged, with others, to examine candidates' qualifications for a teaching degree, as a member of a committee on which Thomae and the anatomist Heinrich von Eggeling had hitherto served. These duties were rewarded with a modest honorarium known as *Sitzungsgeld*.[6]

Meanwhile, at the beginning of the summer semester of 1900, a collaborative report on mathematical and physical education (including astronomy) was written with the participation of Jena lecturers Abbe, Felix Auerbach, Frege, August Gutzmer, Otto Button, Rudolf Straubel, Thomae, Adolf Winkelmann, and Gustav Neuenhahn. The proceedings of the committee were printed by the Carl-Zeiss-Stiftung, as offering "advice for candidates of the higher Magisterium in mathematics and physics at the University of Jena." The booklet was made available to potential students free of charge.[7] On 1 April 1886, Frege was awarded a lectureship in mathematics and his revocable remuneration increased from 700 to 2,000 Marks a year.

The fact that he should have been promoted at the university, after the debacle of the *Begriffsschrift* and *Grundlagen*, was significant in itself. The university budget proposals in mathematics for 1886 and 1887 each noted 700 Marks for Frege, and this amount was listed also in the 1888, 1889, 1890, 1891, ..., 1897 budgets, indicating that Frege was paid 700 Marks from University accounts in each of those years.[8] In the spring of 1886, a Ministerial Fund for Scientific Purposes was established, thanks to the financial contributions of Abbe acting within the Grand Ducal Ministry. It was Abbe again who petitioned for Frege to be granted the lectureship in the institute's staple Analytical Mechanics course, and requested that, for as long as the budget remained insufficient for the institute to pay him a decent wage, Frege be awarded from the Ministerial Fund sufficient additional remuneration that his total contractual compensation amount to 2,000 Marks annually.[9]

Abbe's request was eventually granted. Frege was given a teaching assignment financed by the Ministerial Fund for Scientific Purposes, with a revocable remuneration of 1,300 Marks paid annually.[10] The 700 Marks remuneration from the University Fund, together with the 1,300 Marks

---

[6] *Ibid.*, pp. 425–27.   [7] *Ibid.*, p. 326 and Appendix 4.2, pp. 333–34.   [8] *Ibid.*, p. 427.
[9] *Ibid.*   [10] *Ibid.*, p. 429.

from the Ministerial fund, constituted the total annual income for Frege of 2,000 Marks Abbe had requested.[11] This munificent increase in his life's prospects, relatively speaking, left Frege still confined, according to Stelzner's estimate, to the bottom of the middle class, "far surpassed by other officials and the self-employed."[12] Nevertheless, it was the financial platform Frege needed in order to advance his scientific work on the foundations of mathematics, and for the first time to entertain realistically the prospect of marrying his long-courted Margarete. Without this foundation, Frege would also probably never have been able to print the second volume of the *Grundgesetze*, as he later chose, out of practical necessity, to do at his own expense. His publisher was unwilling to bring out the second part of the book on speculation at the press's own expense, given that the first volume had failed to achieve adequate sales. In the summer semester of 1886, Frege picked up another lecturing fee of 15 Marks.[13] Now at last the dribble of payment from his students did not really matter to his quality of life. His indifference to the rewards of teaching began thereafter adversely to affect his interaction with students.

In 1886 Frege's colleague Eucken wrote a positive review of Frege's then recent *Grundlagen*. He was the only scholar at Jena to publicly acknowledge Frege's second book or submit a review of it for publication. Eucken ventured in the notice primarily to explain the basics of the book for the observant and knowledgeable reader, for whom a careful examination of Frege's analysis of the concept of number was described as a well-rewarded effort. He supported Frege's rejection of psychologism in the conceptual foundations of arithmetic, and voiced his appreciation for the philosophical motivations and style of argument preserved throughout Frege's inquiry.[14] In the winter semester of 1886–1887, Frege began teaching the *Begriffsschrift*, albeit with zero participants.[15] Thanks to his other, more reliably enrolling, stock course in analytical geometry, Frege pocketed another 30 Marks in lecture fees despite this drought.

On the wave of these convergent successes, Frege now married his little-known, presumably long-betrothed, Margarete Lieseberg. The

---

[11] *Ibid.*, p. 432. See also Stelzner, "Ernst Abbe and Gottlob Frege," pp. 22–23.
[12] Stelzner, "Ernst Abbe and Gottlob Frege," p. 23.   [13] Kreiser, *Gottlob Frege*, p. 441.
[14] Rudolf Eucken, "Review of *Grundlagen der Arithmetik*, by G. Frege," *Philosophische Monatshefte*, 22 (1886), pp. 421–22.
[15] See Kratzsch, "Material zu Leben und Wirken Freges aus dem Besitz der Universitäts-Bibliothek Jena," p. 539; and Asser, Alexander, and Metzler, "Gottlob Frege – Persönlichkeit und Werk," pp. 13–14.

unpretentious ceremony took place on 14 March 1887, not in Jena, where the couple would reside, but in the bride's home of Grevesmühlen, Mecklenburg. It was roughly at this time that Frege's mother, Auguste, built in Jena the new duplex house that Frege and his bride would occupy, with Auguste living in close proximity. These events were probably coordinated, all brought into play as a consequence of Frege's promotion and increased university stipend, on which everything else seemed to depend. Perhaps at one time the thought was that Margarete would help care for Auguste as she aged, when in the event it was Margarete who needed help at home after becoming incurably ill.

How did Frege and Margarete meet? Margarete's mother's parents, the Dellings, lived in Wismar at one end of Bohrstraße, with the house of Frege's family virtually around the corner. The likelihood is therefore that Frege knew Margarete through family connections or as a result of her family visiting in the neighborhood in Wismar. It is conceivable that they knew each other even from childhood. It is also rumored that during this period in his life, around 1879, approximately the time when Frege published the *Begriffsschrift* and was appointed Associate Professor, he began making frequent hiking trips in the area around Wismar, and that on one of these excursions he may have met Margarete for the first time. Hiking may have also been a pretext for the two sweethearts to meet. We can more or less imagine what we like. The facts can be summarized as follows. They met, and thereafter they married. They did not have children of their own. Frege took care of a ward, young Alfred, whom Frege eventually adopted legally as his son and heir, four years after Margarete passed away. They enjoyed married life together for about seventeen years, and then Margarete was carried off by an unknown respiratory ailment. At some level they must have suited and complemented one another. More than this we do not know.[16]

On 7 January 1887, Frege moved to the new house built with his mother's proceeds from the sale of the girls' school in Wismar. Frege's house was substantial enough for him and his mother, initially, and then also his wife later in the year, to occupy the ground floor, while the floor above was rented after 1889 to the university professor philologist Rudolf Hirzel and his wife. This gives an idea of the size of the house built by Frege's mother. The Hirzels too had no children, and lived above the

---

[16] Kreiser, *Gottlob Frege*, pp. 489–96.

Frege household until 1913. Frege's mother passed away in 1898, having been relocated to the Catholic Sisters' Home, which was coincidentally situated at Carl-Zeiss-Straße 10, in Fulda. Margarete's own bad health by this time made it impossible for her to care for Frege's mother properly at home.

During the winter semester of 1887–1888, Frege attracted two participants to his course on the *Begriffsschrift*, as well as to his more straight-laced offerings on Abelian integrals, with four participants, from whom he collected 18 Marks compensation. The next season there would be no takers, and this tediously repeated pattern continues throughout the remainder of Frege's teaching career at Jena, until very near the end before his retirement. Typical of the scant interest in his work was the fact that Frege in the fall of 1890 conducted an advanced training course for teachers in secondary schools and teacher training institutes on the concept of number, to an audience of only two, probably mostly baffled, attendees.

When considering Frege's biography, while there is no dispute regarding the occurrence of certain events in his life, it would be invaluable to have some guidance as to the kind of weight to attribute to them. We know that in 1887 Frege married Margarete. What we do not know and cannot properly fathom is what importance marrying Margarete had for Frege. Was Margarete the center of his universe? Was he trying throughout his adult life to make himself worthy of Margarete? Was he pioneering discoveries in logic, mathematics, and philosophy as a means to an end, namely to gain at least the minimum salary he needed in order to be able to propose marriage to his beloved? Was earning her love the motor of his life, the flame of his intense activity? Or was Frege primarily so dedicated to uncovering the purely logical foundations of arithmetic that marrying Margarete amounted to just the acquisition of another accoutrement of the professional academic bourgeois? Did he marry because it was expected of a reputable man in the scientific professions, perhaps to maintain an air of respectability? Was marrying his affianced Margarete a secondary consideration, or the throbbing heartbeat of all that Frege tried to do, the source of all his ambition? Would it not be interesting to know?

The fact that Frege in his most commonly reproduced photograph from late in life looks to be a beaten man, supposedly defeated by the journal reviews of his books, should not be allowed without qualification to govern impressions of his personality. There is more than one way to read Frege's character from, and preconceptions about his character into, a black and white photograph without accompanying explanations. Frege at the time was enjoying the full-throttle sensation of grasping alone the significance of logic for arithmetic. He saw all these formal disciplines as one, linked together like macromolecules. The power of that vision sustained him through the seemingly endless dry spell in which virtually no one else seemed to understand what he was trying to achieve, let alone what he had already accomplished toward the estimable goal he had charted. Frege must have loved Margarete as he loved mathematics, as he loved his devoted mother, Auguste, as at an earlier age he was taught to love Jesus and God. Frege was an Associate Professor of mathematics at Jena, a published author, a responsible loving son, and now husband to a woman who for the moment remains historically a shadowy individual in Frege's private personal world. She was by definition the love of his life. She waited for him to establish himself, as everyone seemed to be waiting for something momentous to happen.

The problem was not that Frege was desolute of prospects, quite the contrary. The problem was that Frege had chosen a path that was slow to reward groundbreaking initiative. It is possible that Frege followed the pattern here as in other aspects of his life. He saw these several roles and activities fitting together into a single pattern where everything had its place. Because he perceived this and understood its significance, he thought it incumbent on him, with his skills, to do what few others could attempt. He had previously devoted the greatest part of his attention to moving forward in his career, striving to make his mark with definite attainments, degrees, titles, positions, publications, and lectures, especially in local scientific society meetings. Now he would partner with a woman he loved, whom he had come to know over the course of what may have been a long courtship, who understood his struggles at least in part, at least in rough outline, as he would appreciatively and sometimes heatedly explain things to her. He would be happy, fulfilled, in this as in other aspects of his life. Everything would complement everything else in all that a well-rounded modern human existence could reasonably be asked to provide. If it had taken a while to arrive at this height, so after all did most valuable things in life take time to materialize. One can only experience so many kinds of pleasures in a single lifetime anyway.

Gottlob and Margarete must have felt their virtue rewarded. Frege's life was about to take a magnificent turn for the better. If something like this attitude ruled his thoughts, then there would never have been any question of whether logic and philosophy or Margarete came first in Frege's life. There need have been no division of loyalties, only an effective management of impending practicalities held in harmonious balance, as in the work–romance economy of any creative person.

A Scientific Theory of Meaning

We turn now from Frege's personal life at the time to his preoccupations in logic and philosophy. Frege had been wounded but not defeated by the checkered pattern of indifference, misunderstanding, and rejection with which his first two books had been dismissed. During this period he began to formulate some of his most important statements concerning the nature of logic, outlining the basic distinctions by which his philosophy of language and his philosophical semantics are best known and most highly regarded. The three important essays Frege wrote during this time were "Funktion und Begriff" ("Function and Concept"), "Über Sinn und Bedeutung" ("On Sense and Reference"), and "Über Begriff und Gegenstand" ("On Concept and Object").[17]

The essays, especially "On Sense and Reference," not only exerted an enormous influence on subsequent philosophical theory of meaning, but also laid the groundwork for semantic analysis as a newly discovered continent. The philosophy of language has topped much of the scientific philosophical agenda after Frege. It took shape in his shadow in the later evolution of analytic philosophy. If Frege had done no more than publish this single essay, he would have earned a respected place in the history of philosophy. These discussions of function, concept, and object are among the most metaphysical essays in Frege's folio. Frege in the 1890s essays introduced many of the problems, methods, and distinctions of later analytic philosophy of language. In these three essays, written or presented for lecture or publication almost immediately after the appearance of his *Grundlagen*, Frege outlined the basic categories by which his philosophy of language and his philosophical semantics are primarily known today. We touch on these works to learn what Frege was thinking at the time, supposing these

[17] Frege, "Funktion und Begriff," lecture to the Jenaische Gesellschaft für Medizin und Naturwissenschaft, 9 January 1891; "Über Sinn und Bedeutung," *Zeitschrift für Philosophie und philosophische Kritik*, 100 (1892), pp. 25–50; and "Über Begriff und Gegenstand," *Vierteljahrsschrift für wissenschaftliche Philosophie*, 16 (1892), pp. 192–205.

essays in the context of all his writings to cast light on Frege's overall applied logical philosophy of mathematics. "Function and Concept" and "On Concept and Object" are discussed in detail in the remainder of this chapter, reserving the next chapter in its entirety for "On Sense and Reference."

If Frege was disillusioned because of the reception rather than the direction of his work, then what was it about the negative critical reception, first of the *Begriffsschrift* and later of the *Grundlagen*, that had evoked his disillusion? It was undoubtedly a one–two punch. Frege must have concluded that he could not please his readership or overcome its antipathy to his proposal no matter what he did. He might as well go back to the *Begriffsschrift* logic then, and dress it up in what became the two massive volumes of the *Grundgesetze*. Once he had gone that far, innate bulldog determination saw him the rest of the way through. For whatever reasons, Frege was surrounded by the uncomprehending, with whom he could not productively communicate. They had refused to learn his language. That was the situation Frege had put himself in by publishing his *Begriffsschrift* and *Grundlagen*. It was the result of what he had intentionally or unintentionally withheld from those first two books. He should have let readers in on the secret of what was happening and what would come next. He should have offered clues in plain prose as to why these two things, a general functional calculus or logic of concept-functions and an analysis of the concept-function of natural number, were prepared in these two books as though on a staging ground for a major operation to follow, in which their separate forces would combine. The application of the *Begriffsschrift* to the concept-function of natural number in the *Grundlagen* would eventually happen, but not until four years later, when the time was ripe, in the first volume of Frege's *Grundgesetze*.

First came the form, then the content, corresponding to the concept-function and its argument-object, respectively. Exemplifying the function (argument) = value structure, Frege seems by analogy to have implemented an isomorphic model for pure logicism in three distinct stages: *Begriffsschrift*(*Grundlagen*) = *Grundgesetze*. It is not quite literally correct to label Frege's functional calculus as the *Begriffsschrift* concept-function in the cartoon formula, because the *Grundgesetze* required modifications of the *Begriffsschrift*. Moreover, it was not the *Grundlagen* itself that was made the argument-object of a *Begriffsschrift* logic, but rather the concept-function of natural number defended in the *Grundlagen*. Frege's grand design was characterized in oversimplified terms to make a point, like the explanatory anthropological formula water + brains = boats. If expository need should arise, we can always start handing out distinct labels for *Begriffsschrift*-1, *Begriffsschrift*-2, etc., or *Begriffsschrift*-before-1893, *Begriffsschrift*-after-1893, and the like. The problem is that Frege spoke without any effort at qualification of *Begriffsschrift* generally in any of its improvement stages, any concept-writing or concept-script, including that of Peano, and sometimes of the book with that provocative title. There was always a logic of propositions, objects, and concept-functions intended by Frege in these usages, and it was generally some genidentical variant of the original system presented in his 1879 *Begriffsschrift*.

Whatever it was that may have disillusioned Frege after the publication of his *Begriffsschrift* and *Grundlagen*, he did not allow it to overpower his confidence and will to carry through. There must have been folders and folders of pages for the *Grundgesetze* that Frege had accumulated at his writing desk or sitting outside on the garden veranda. Material for the masterwork would have appeared in bits and spurts long before the *Grundlagen* made its fateful plunge after the *Begriffsschrift* into what seemed at first to be the dark arcana of historical obscurity. Regardless of how bad reviews and lack of notice may have made him feel, Frege's writing and publishing choices and the active pursuit of his philosophical agenda by any legitimate means, even digging into his own shallow purse to bring the last book in the series to light, can be understood as justified on rational philosophical grounds. It did not seriously matter what most of his peers thought. It was, philosophically speaking, their loss, if they could not grasp the importance of securely riveting down all of mathematics beginning with arithmetic to purely logical foundations. The truths of arithmetic were promised reconstruction in a purely logical order of inference chains representing the mathematical reasoning whereby theorems are validly deduced.

Most of all, as Frege may have tried to comfort his damaged ego, it was irrelevant, especially in the long run, what the journals said. They were daily newspapers of ideas, floating opinions that were usually not based on serious study; they were like witty café chatter after the opera. Their readership was mostly the contributors to the journals, who read their own articles in them. Frege's books would last, and certainly outlast their reviews, their reviewers, and also their author. The important thing was that his works would find a place on university library shelves, where someone could take them down as Frege would have done if they had already existed, discovering to his or her delight within their covers an unsung world of abstract structures. There, in the texts, as long as they were printed and distributed, the logical dependence of the basic laws of elementary arithmetic on purely logical principles and deductive logical inference structures would be visually stripped naked to the bone in *Begriffsschrift* logical formulas and transformation sequences, for anyone who needed or wanted to see it. Someone had to do the work. Someone needed to show that this could be done, that the relations in question were existent and their descriptions true, that the reduction of arithmetic to logic could be demonstrated. The purely logical derivations of arithmetical principles from purely logical concepts were supposed to be transparently laid bare, but only when the *Begriffsschrift* logic of concepts was applied to the *Grundlagen* concept of number. This would not happen until eight years later in the *Grundgesetze*.

Frege was uniquely positioned in his time to appreciate the purely logical foundations of elementary arithmetic. With his mathematical background in the correlations by which arithmetic and geometry, with enough ingenious mapping functions, are formally interdefinable, Frege could picture mathematics as an applied extension of pure logic. There was a commission waiting for someone who knew how to represent logical derivations in a visually edifying symbolism. That could only be Frege. We do him no injustice in supposing that the fruit of his discovery/invention and late-night hard work was already there calling someone or other to the task, him in particular, as it happened. Frege, on the contrary, would have likely seen in the appearance of destiny a further confirmation of his Platonic realism. The very idea that such a thing could be done was an eternal mind-independent truth, whereas making it happen was down to his mathematical imagination and indefatigability. Thereafter, the idea having taken hold, Frege was committed to the project and prepared to see it through.

The *Grundlagen* was not a detour or glitch along the way from the *Begriffsschrift* to the *Grundgesetze*. It was for Frege the essential second step in a three-part logical construction, a three-movement symphony. The beauty in Frege's logic lies in appreciating how internally complex the linkages of reasoning sometimes need to be in support of the truth even of some propositions that are considered so obvious as not to be worth remarking let alone proving in the course of arithmetical practice. The charm is not in the power or use of the conclusions that terminate proofs, but in the inferential proof structures themselves. Arithmetical derivations of theorems from axioms and *reductio* hypotheses can be fully understood, thoroughly examined, checked for soundness, and purged of flaws only if they are exhibited as holding transparently within an explicit deductively logical inference structure. The symbolic image of reasoning must mark a proof's progress from its starting-place through all the precise truth-preserving rule-governed transformations of syntax in the logical derivation of each chosen theorem. The definitions, basic rules, and inferences must be explicit and open to inspection and criticism. This includes unmistakably the ballroom dance of Frege's *Begriffsschrift, Grundlagen,* and *Grundgesetze.*

What do we understand about the outlook on the world of one who, as a trailblazing mathematician and philosopher, chose an unpopular path in a conservative field of study and had to carry on predominantly alone? We discover, as Frege did, that there is a price to be paid for iconoclasm in such established trades as mathematics. If we consider the greeting-card philosophy that everyone chooses their own way in life, then it must be that Frege wanted nothing more than to be a quietly achieving misunderstood nonconformist who would ultimately influence the future of logic, mathematics, and philosophy. Whether that was Frege's purpose or not, it was historically the result of his writings. He never stepped away from the complete three-stage project in logicism by which he gave over the concept of natural number in the *Grundlagen* to the logical apparatus of the *Begriffsschrift,* establishing logical foundations for basic laws of elementary arithmetic from these preliminaries in his *Grundgesetze.*

Reviews, Essays, and Lectures

In 1890–1892 Frege drafted a review (which remained unpublished in his lifetime) of Cantor's *Gesammelte Abhandlungen zur Lehre vom Transfiniten* (*Collected Handbooks on the Theory of Transfinite Numbers*).[18] Spurned by the journals in this format, Frege found an opportunity to criticize Cantor openly afterward in his 1894 review of Husserl's 1891 *Philosophie der Arithmetik.*[19]

---

[18] See Frege's *Nachlaß,* "Draft towards a Review of Cantor's *Gesammelte Abhandlungen zur Lehre vom Transfiniten,*" in Frege, *Posthumous Writings,* pp. 68–71.

[19] Frege, "Rezension von E. Husserl: *Philosophie der Arithmetik,*" *Zeitschrift für Philosophie und philosophische Kritik,* 103 (1894), pp. 313–32. Frege's criticisms of Cantor in the review appear on pp. 324–26.

Frege during this time maintained a brief but contentful correspondence about the concept of number with Walter C. G. Brix, a technical advisor to the government ed in Berlin and eventually in the patent office of the German Ministry of the Interior. It is not known how the correspondence began, or why Brix chose to write to Frege.[20] Presumably he had seen, and perhaps struggled with, one of Frege's books. Three letters from Brix to Frege and one from Frege to Brix are valuable in part because, in his only surviving letter to Brix, Frege mentioned a number of historically noteworthy essay projects that were ongoing in his writing at exactly that time. They were the essays that, along with his professional promotion and marriage to Margarete, were among the principal incidents of Frege's experience at the time in the early 1890s.

Frege's three classic essays mentioned in the letter to Brix, dating from the interval between the *Grundlagen* and *Grundgesetze I*, were at the time presumably finished products prepared for publication, although their exact point of origin can only be conjectured. Besides being promoted, moving house and helping his mother get settled on the woodsy outskirts of Jena, getting married in Mecklenberg, writing three of the most important essays in the history of philosophy, teaching for lecture-fee crumbs, but with a respectable salary at last, and corresponding with persons like Brix, Frege must be assumed to have been always working in the background on the logical exposition and formal *begriffsschriftliche* inferential demonstrations of elementary arithmetical theorems that appear in his *Grundgesetze* only a few years later.

The third book, published in the event as only the first part of what was meant to be a single complete treatise, did not materialize magically in 1893 when *Grundgesetze I* was released. Frege must have had the material under development for many years previous to publication. It would not be a reckless interpretation to suppose that Frege was working on the *Grundgesetze* as one single massive text in mathematical logic continuously from the time of the *Begriffsschrift* in 1879 and throughout the *Grundlagen* and its sorry aftermath in 1884 and beyond. The *Begriffsschrift* retreats temporarily, going underground in the *Grundlagen*. There Frege acquired

---

[20] Frege's correspondence with Walter C. G. Brix appears in the *Nachgelassene Schriften und wissenschaftler Briefwechsel*, ed. Hans Hermes, Friedrich Kambartel, and Friedrich Kaulbach (Hamburg: Felix Meiner Verlag, 1976–1983), Volume 2, iv/1–4, pp. 10–14. These letters are omitted from the selected English translation of Frege, *Philosophical and Mathematical Correspondence*.

a brilliantly conceived logical analysis of the concept of natural number. Resurfacing in the *Grundgesetze*, a modified *Begriffsschrift* symbolic logic was used again to formulate essential definitions and churn out the deductive inferential structures by which basic laws and theorems of elementary arithmetic are cemented to purely logical foundations.

Frege's publisher failed to shrewdly calculate that many people would wait to see what happened before buying the first volume of a proposed set of two works in mathematical logic. The idea of delaying production of the second half of a complete technical treatise was not unprecedented, but also unlikely to end in success. By dividing the book for publication into two parts, Frege's publisher added to Frege's commercial and critical woes. As an analogy, who would buy the first half of a dictionary, encompassing the letters A–M, in the hope and expectation that it would sell well enough to warrant production of the second, N–Z, half? Frege persevered despite the insulting marketplace and scholarly sociological reality. The purpose that drove his energies was what he expected to be the unparalleled value of producing unequivocal symbolic logical pictures of truth-dependences and deductive inferences whereby arithmetic would have been shown definitively to derive from purely logical concepts and syntax transformation principles. The object was to model mathematical reasoning more sensitively than in traditional Aristotelian–Victorian syllogistic term logic like Hamilton's, Boole's, Brentano's, Venn's, and others'. Frege would replace these old-fashioned relics with a modernized fully algebraic functional calculus with application to the concept of natural number. He would install a new logic featuring skeletal images of the most basic logical structures of mathematical reasoning.[21]

Frege announced to Brix, among other projects in progress or in press, a critical overview of efforts to explain the concept of number by Hermann von Helmholtz, Leopold Kronecker, and Dedekind, among others, and a critique of published articles by Benno Kerry. The pieces by Kerry concerned logical intuitions and their mental processing, against which Frege warned Brix of psychologism in the philosophy of logic. Brix thanked Frege

[21] See Benjamin S. Hawkins, "DeMorgan, Victorian Syllogistic and Relational Logic," *The Review of Modern Logic*, 5(2) (1995), pp. 131–66. Extensive background material to the logic currents of the time is collected by Dov M. Gabbay and John Woods, eds., *British Logic in the Nineteenth Century* (Amsterdam: Elsevier, 2008); and Raymond Flood, Adrian Rice, and Robin Wilson, *Mathematics in Victorian Britain* (Oxford: Oxford University Press, 2011), especially pp. 360–64.

for sending "Function and Concept," the *Begriffsschrift*, "On Sense and Reference," and "On Concept and Object."[22] These were the principal works of Frege's middle period after the publication of his *Begriffsschrift* and *Grundlagen*, and before the publication of the *Grundgesetze*. Frege's generosity toward Brix, offering him a treasure trove of recent writings, books, and offprints, probably testifies more eloquently to Frege's lonely desire for interaction about his work than to any particular professional connection he might have had or sought with Brix.

Meaning in a Scientific Semantics: Functions, Concepts, Objects, and Identity

The essay topics Frege mentioned to Brix were not optional add-ons that happened to interest him at the time. They were not side-trips into the philosophy of language like the occasional paper on electrodynamics written to satisfy a momentary curiosity or to see whether or not there were any interesting affinities with his main line of work. They were absolute necessities that Frege believed he must adequately address. He knew that he could be called on to explain the exact meaning of such constructions in his arithmetic as numerical equations and complete identity statements of function(argument) = value correlations. If for no other reason than his own satisfaction that he had taken nothing essential for granted, he had to explain aspects of meaning with the right independently justified distinctions for all obligatory expression types in his logicist arithmetic. That fact puts identity statements at the forefront in Frege's logicism.

Frege needed arithmetical functions in order to build the laws of elementary arithmetic from logically more basic foundations. He was not in awe of their power or especially aware of their potential danger. Functions have as their arguments input objects that are converted to output values when the function is applied to a permitted argument. Concept-functions must be clarified as to the argument-objects they can properly accept. The clarification involves identity statements in a complete input–output functional correlation structure. Concept-functions written as $+1(\underline{\ \ })$ and Red$(\underline{\ \ })$ conveniently abbreviate a choice among

---

[22] Frege, *Nachgelassene Schriften und wissenschaftlicher Briefwechsel*, Volume 2, *Briefwechsel*, p. 10.

input–output correlations that are unlimited in variety. A complete statement is to write schematically $+1(\_\_) = n$ as in $+1(1) = 2$ and Red $(\_\_) = v$ as in $\text{Red}(a) = $ the True. Identity is conspicuously an essential element in any statement of a concept or function that includes, as it must, an output value correlate as well as representing the input operation; $+1(\_\_)$ by itself is not a function, and nor is $\text{Red}(\_\_)$ by itself a concept or property. For all logic knows, there are no numbers and nothing is red. Thus $+1(\_\_)$ by itself is not a functional correlation of anything with anything, but only an arithmetical operation to be performed on unspecified input with no indication as to the resulting output.

Numbers conveyed by word of mouth are welcome to enter $+1(\_\_) = n$. Julius Caesar must be turned away, although there is no exclusionary sign on the door. Short of at least an implicit complete statement of the concept-function, there is no precluding the *arithmetical* truth that $+1$ (Julius Caesar) $= 1$, or, for the same price, that $+1$(Julius Caesar) $=$ Julius Caesar. What would be the harm even if an imperial arithmetic were to legislate that $+1$(Julius Caesar) $= 2$? It would follow then that $-1(3) = +1$ (Julius Caesar), and the like. Still no tremors are felt in the foundations of arithmetic. Caesar becomes not only a Roman god, but also a consort of numbers. Concept-functions are everywhere in the elementary arithmetical equations in which Frege's logicism traded. The identity sign is indispensable in the logical analysis of elementary arithmetic, even in writing $1 + 1 = 2$, a fact that was not lost on Frege. His contributions to meaning theory, especially on concepts as functions distinct from objects and on the meaning of identity statements, amount to a special case of the meaning conditions for any developed language. There is minimally the predication of a property to an existent entity. We can write Fa, but, since a might not exist, Frege insisted that, as a requirement of meaningful expression, we must know that $Fa = $ the True or $Fa = $ the False. We are thereby directed back to the meaning and truth-conditions of identity statements. True or false arithmetical equations are special cases of interest in the semantics of identity statements that allowed Frege to comment on the meaning of language generally.

The effort to understand identity took Frege further along the path toward his mature semantic theory. In explaining the cognitive import of noniterative identity statements, Frege was drawn to propose his fundamental distinction between sense (*Sinn*) and reference (*Bedeutung*). Frege appointed a special technical sense of the German word "*Bedeutung*" that also translates nontechnically simply as "meaning." He split the meaning components of singular referring terms into sense and reference. Every proper name, including every definite description for an existent entity, has a sense and a reference, among the meaning components that interested Frege, and another dimension of connotation, namely image or poetic psychological content, in which Frege evinced no appreciable theoretical interest. Frege advanced a parallel distinction with respect to the complex meanings of entire sentences, highlighting a different kind of sense and a more narrowly circumscribed reference domain than in the case of names, definite descriptions, and other singular referring expressions. Declarative sentences, if they refer at all, refer only exclusively to either the True or the False. In clarifying these concepts, Frege took another step toward philosophical difficulty. It happened as he tried to nail down the categories essential for a reduction of the basic laws of elementary arithmetic to a purely logical analysis of the concept of natural number and purely logical derivations of arithmetical theorems.

Function and Concept

Frege presented "Function and Concept" to the Jena Society for Medicine and Natural Science on 9 January 1891. He situated his talk in relation to two previous meetings of the Society, on 10 January 1879, when the *Begriffsschrift* was first published, and 27 January 1882, midway between the publication of the *Begriffsschrift* and that of the *Grundlagen*. His marvelous aplomb is shown in the fact that he showcased his vastly ignored, shunned, and misunderstood *Begriffsschrift* as an unshaken vibrant forward-moving research program. He implied that it was cutting-edge at the time, within the unknown field that he was simultaneously creating in the philosophical foundations of mathematics. He brushed aside the annoyance of competitors like the psychologistic Schröder doing good formal work on the wrong side of the fundamental divide between subjective and objective scientific investigations. He explained how the logic of concepts could be used to exhibit the logical structure of interesting specimens of arithmetical reasoning.

Frege had addressed the Society about *Begriffsschrift* logic on two previous occasions, nine and twelve years before. Could Frege expect anyone to have remembered his specialized notation after such a long time and acquired facility with it in the meantime? He took advantage of the occasion of a technical talk to explain the essentials of the *Begriffsschrift*. As concept-writing or concept-script, an ideography, a functional calculus or a logic of concepts, the identification of concepts with functions that Frege's *Begriffsschrift* assumed as contentful subject matter provided the stuff to which its logical expressive and inferential calculus was applied.

Members of the Society would likely have confronted this problem at meetings before, whenever mathematical lectures were presented. What did Frege do to communicate his ideas? The twenty-odd pages of "Function and Concept" contained not only ordinary mathematical expressions that it would have been challenging for even a mathematically gifted listener to the script of Frege's lecture to keep in mind and follow in oral delivery without a written text but also long sequences of expressions in Frege's hard-to-decipher *Begriffsschrift* notation. They were presented at a relatively elementary level, but would have been mostly unfamiliar to the participants at the Society's gathering on the January evening in question. Frege could not have simply fluttered his fingers over the pictograms, but would have needed to take time to explain their meaning. He must have provided his listeners with supporting written materials that have not survived. Since the talks were often published by the Society, Frege's lecture may have been printed prior to its presentation, and made available to those attending, either free or at nominal cost, judging from the practices of other learned societies at the time. This locally prepared and probably uncopyrighted visual aid would not have ranked among a speaker's publications. Frege may otherwise have glossed over some of the technicalities, confining himself to the most memorable distinctions and implications to be emphasized.

With admirable clarity, Frege presented what everyone should always have already known, namely that concepts are incomplete *ungesättigte* things. They are not just like functions; they are in truth nothing other than functions. They are concept-functions that need to be saturated. They need to have the open spaces of their corresponding concept-functor predicates or property terms filled in by the proper name of an argument-object that in the resulting predication is said to have the property. As we know from later in Frege's writings, proper names can be a constant or a definite description spelling out a reference-fixing part of the term's Fregean sense in an enumeration of an existent object's collectively distinguishing individuating properties. Frege began the lecture as follows:

> Rather a long time ago I had the honour of addressing this Society about the symbolic system that I entitled *Begriffsschrift*. Today I should like to throw light upon the subject from another side, and tell you about some supplementations and new conceptions, whose necessity has occurred to me since then. There can here be no question of setting forth my ideography [*Begriffsschrift*] in its entirety, but only of elucidating some fundamental ideas.[23]

Picking up more or less where he had left off nine years ago, Frege explained that the pursuit of *Begriffsschrift* logic in the interval had persuaded him of the need to reconsider and precisely define the concept of a mathematical function. This was no small achievement, despite concerning what is in some ways a relatively inconspicuous category of formal expression.

His concentrated close examination of otherwise neglected topics gave Frege's writings a distinctive lasting impact on logic, mathematics, their philosophical foundations, and the practice of analytic philosophy. It was his pretheoretical sense for what stood in need of greatest clarification and where an analysis of a concept might be found that made Frege's work in this period methodologically and ideologically more artfully self-conscious and to that extent more philosophically profound, not to mention mathematically better informed, than that of many of Frege's contemporaries. These trademarks of critical style eventually made Frege into a patriarchal figurehead of philosophical analysis as scientific thought began to emerge internationally later in the twentieth century, far away from its birthplace in Germany.

Single-Argument Functions

Frege in the Society lecture explained that "My starting-point is what is called a function in mathematics. The original reference of this word was not so wide as that which it has since obtained; it will be well to begin by dealing with this first usage, and only then consider the later extensions. I shall for the moment be speaking only of functions of a single argument."[24] Functions have arguments, and there is no limit to the number of arguments functions generally can take, each combination producing a

---

[23] Frege, "Function and Concept," *Philosophical Writings*, p. 21.   [24] *Ibid.*

determinate output. Single-argument concept-functions are sometimes called qualities, and concept-functions with two or more argument places are known as relations.

Arguments for functions in Frege's logic are existent objects to which the function applies. If we write Fa or $F(a)$, we express the fact that concept-function F is applied to argument-object a. The arguments of functions belong to the function's *domain* of values, any of which can be taken as input to the function, while the function's *range* includes the specific values that result when a concept-function is applied to any of the argument-objects in the concept-function's domain. If the function is $+1(\_\_) = n$, then the function's argument is anything that can be meaningfully inserted into the unsaturated context enclosed by parentheses as fodder fit for the function. Not every object in every referential semantic domain can be inserted into every function context or taken as the function's saturating argument-object: $+1(\text{red}) = n$, $+1(\text{Madelaine}) = n$, $+1(\text{Julius Caesar}) = n$, and $+1(\text{Brazil}) = n$ make no sense as arithmetic has come to be defined, although philosophers must wonder why not. Here $+1(\_\_) = n$ is a function whose arguments come from a domain of numbers, and whose range includes all the concept-functions's outputs correlated with each input argument-object.

What Frege meant by a concept is a function, whether in ordinary thought and language or in mathematics. It is neologistically what for emphasis is called a concept-function. Concept-functions in any subject matter are alike, even when superficial distinctions are observed, by virtue of being predicated of objects. The concept red or of something's being red is predicated of a sunset to obtain $\text{Red}(\text{sunset}) = v$, or, more colloquially, in the predication "The sunset is red." The sunset has the property mentioned, namely the quality of being red. Structurally, Frege was impressed by the comparison of syntactical forms between concepts and functions. When we think, write, or say $+1(\_\_) = n$, the application of a function to an argument is analogous to when we think, write, or say $\text{Red}(\_\_) = v$. The concept of plus-one, the successor function in Dedekind–Peano arithmetic, is nothing other than the concept-function $+1(\_\_) = n$. The function must be defined over the right range of output values correlated with the right domain of input values. The concept red is interpreted as the function $\text{Red}(\_\_) = v$, which is defined as true or referring to the True only in the case that the argument (existent object) to which the function is applied is red, and is otherwise false and refers to the False. Accordingly, we have perchance

$+1(1) = 2$ and Red(a) = the True or = the False, depending on intended object a's condition.

It is not the case that Frege hoped by means of this identification to explain the concept of red or arithmetical addition by 1. Attempting an analysis of the concept of red as the function Red($\_\_$) = v takes us no closer to understanding what red or the color red is supposed to mean. The same goes for addition. There is no good answer to the question as to the nature or mechanism of $+1$ other than exhibiting inputs to, and matching outputs from, the function. Frege chose the concept of red or addition by 1 only to illustrate. We have already seen the lengths to which Frege had to go in the *Grundlagen* in order to analyze the concept of natural number. The concept of red or being red might require still more heroic measures, should it be amenable to being defined analytically at all. There can in principle be irreducible functions, just as there are often said by non-Fregeans to be basic, primitive, indefinable concepts. If we accept Frege's interpretation of concepts as functions or concept-functions, then the explanation for the analytic irreducibility of some concept-functions is obvious.

A surprising amount can be accomplished in elementary arithmetic by means of single-argument concept-functions, provided we can avail ourselves freely of all the many different concept-functions we may need to reconstruct all the mathematics we want. With enough ingenuity, it may be possible to reduce all putatively multiple-argument concept-functions to single-argument concept-functions of more complex abstracted internal logical structure. It takes some doing, but Frege seems to have understood that formally the work could be outsourced. He relied for simplicity on single-argument place functors at the outset in his discussion, on the background assumption that functors with two or more argument spaces in the functional calculus are not strictly needed if we pack enough content into a single-argument functor's meaning. Compression by property abstraction enables Frege's logic to satisfy a larger number of conditions that are met at once by the instantiation of an internally complex function F, when $F = \lambda x[\ldots x \ldots]$ for a conveniently abbreviated property, with ellipses designating any internal logical complexity. The fact that an identity statement expresses a meaning equivalence of terms can also be formulated truth-functionally without identity in $\forall x[Fx \leftrightarrow \lambda y[\ldots y \ldots]x]$. It is any concept, property, or function symbolized in Frege's logic signified by the predicate "F." If abstraction names any property, then we should always be able to designate that property by an n-place single predicate "Fn." Whether it is possible to reduce all n-ary relational predications to unary single-argument-place functors is an interesting question that Frege did not try to answer.[25]

Mathematical Language and Its Philosophy

Frege may not have been the first to make explicit connections between mathematical functions and the properties or concepts involved generally in linguistic predications. The apple is red; the number 3 is prime or identical to 1 plus 2. In "Function and Concept" he brought mathematics into the fold as a coterie of languages, for which he explained the role of concept-functions in mathematical reasoning more emphatically and memorably than had any philosophical predecessor.

Frege first had a historical story to tell. He explained that functions are treated knowingly in the annals of mathematics when they are required for the expression of the laws of mathematical analysis, the differential and integral calculus. He observed that it was in such applications that laws were first introduced as holding generally for all functions. This, he proposed, was surely the place to sleuth out what the word "function" was originally intended to mean. Without citing or quoting offenders, Frege proceeded to indict nameless interlocutors who would have tried to explain the category of "function" with the clouded answer "A function of x was taken to be a mathematical expression containing x, a formula containing the letter x."[26]

Frege dismissed efforts to understand functions in these terms. He could not resist referring his audience to those polemical passages of the *Grundlagen* where he had ripped into a troika of theorists who had proposed contrary analyses of the concept of number: "This answer cannot satisfy us, for here no distinction is made between form and content, sign and thing signified; a mistake, admittedly, that is very often met with in mathematical works, even those of celebrated authors. I have already pointed out on a previous occasion the defects of the current formal theories in arithmetic."[27] At this point in the essay,

---

[25] Equivalences involving property abstraction are discussed in Jacquette, "Qualities, Relations, and Property Exemplification," *Axiomathes*, 23 (2013), pp. 381–99.
[26] *Ibid.*   [27] *Ibid.*, pp. 21–22.

Frege was referring in this connection not only to the *Grundlagen*, but also to a previous meeting of the Society.[28]

Identity and Function Values

Frege now brought the identity sign in the full expression of a function applied to an argument to center stage. If we write out the function F with one argument as "For all x, there exists a y, such that $Fx = y$," then the link between the function applied to an input argument object and its output value is generally expressed by means of the identity sign, $=$. An intended application is where $V(Fa) =$ the True or $=$ the False, or for short simply $Fa =$ the True or $Fa =$ the False, depending on whether or not object a in fact has or does not have the property symbolized as concept-function F.

The provision of a complete theory of functions was indispensable for Frege's effort to reduce the laws of elementary arithmetic to purely logical principles. Frege needed to be in possession of a correct explanation of identity in the identity relation as it enters into the correlation of a function's inputs with outputs. He had to ask "What is identity?" What is the identity relation or relational concept-function, and what, if anything, does the identity sign denote? We find Frege trying to work out exactly what was required for identity and the identity conditions for mathematical objects during the late 1880s and early 1890s. In all three of the landmark essays from this period that Frege wrote and published or presented to scientific meetings at the time, he attempts to explicate how identity relates the input and output of a mathematical concept-function, the ideal appliances by which all of mathematics is supposed to derive from purely logical foundations.

Frege reasonably insisted that we should never mistake the language by which a referent is represented for that which the language is intended to represent. Frege felt the need to stress repeatedly that the philosophical foundations of arithmetic must not confuse the language of functions with its meaning, effectively real functions with conventional functors. Functions are something objective. They exist because they are relational, and relations exist. If relations did not exist, then it would not be true to say that $+1(1) = 2$, because $+1(1)$ could then not truly be identity-related to 2. Frege prescribed a narrow path for his explanation of the

---

[28] Held on 17 July 1885.

meaning of mathematical concept-functions. Frege alerted his listeners in the following way: "So also here; a mere expression, the form for a content, cannot be the heart of the matter; only the content itself can be that."[29] These are important words of Frege's to recall when in about another ten years he reads Russell's cordial letter announcing the logical contradiction in the *Grundgesetze*.[30]

Frege had disagreeable words for the "celebrated authors" who failed to correctly understand the distinction of things and signs in mathematical languages. Those guilty of these philosophical felonies were generally more celebrated than he, undeservedly so for their inexplicable inability to keep symbol and symbolized straight. Frege's indignation at his neglect in the profession occasionally bubbled forth even in his scientific writing when he thought an opponent had it coming. The *Grundgesetze* Foreword is another *locus classicus*. Importantly, Frege denounced "the current formal theories in arithmetic ... [where we] have talk about signs that neither have nor are meant to have any content, but nevertheless properties are ascribed to them which are unintelligible except as belonging to the content of a sign."[31]

He seems clearly to have had Hilbert in mind. Hilbert was inclined to treat mathematical symbols insouciantly as meaningless syntactical tokens to be manipulated in rule-governed ways with paper and pencil and other means of calculation, more like a boardgame than a serious attempt to discover and describe the truth about an order of abstract objects and their ideal interrelations.[32] A sign, properly so-called, does not merely have syntactical form, Frege implied, but must possess meaning or semantic content. Some theories of functions treat signs as lacking

---

[29] Frege, "Function and Concept," p. 22.

[30] See Nicholas Griffin, "The Prehistory of Russell's Paradox," in *One Hundred Years of Russell's Paradox: Mathematics, Logic, Philosophy*, ed. Godehard Link and John L. Bell (Berlin: Walter de Gruyter, 2004), pp. 349–72.

[31] Frege, "Function and Concept," p. 22.

[32] The dispute occurred in a series of letters exchanged between Frege and Hilbert in 1899 on the meaning of mathematical signs, in Frege, *Philosophical and Mathematical Correspondence*, Letters IV [xv]/ 3–4, pp. 34–43. See Stewart Shapiro, "Categories, Structures and the Frege–Hilbert Controversy: The Status of Meta-Mathematics," *Philosophia Mathematica*, 13 (2005), pp. 61–77; Patricia A. Blanchette, "Frege and Hilbert on Consistency," *The Journal of Philosophy*, 93 (1996), pp. 317–36; and Blanchette, "Frege (1848–1925)," in *The Oxford Handbook of German Philosophy in the Nineteenth Century*, ed. Michael N. Forster and Kristen Gjesdal (Oxford: Oxford University Press, 2015), pp. 207–29.

content altogether, which for Frege meant that they would then fall outside the *Begriffsschrift* logic as nonsensical syntax jumbles.

A sign is a sign of something; a symbol symbolizes something. Otherwise, we have no business speaking of signs or symbols, but must speak of meaningless syntax strings as in an orthography of font types. Pure syntax, to the extent that it deserves to be called syntax, lacks any inherent representational capacity, being at the level only of an alphabet that does not even signify vocalization units. We use linguistic signs to mean something, as Frege knew, and the question is how to understand the internal logical structure of meaning itself, once we have clearcut instances of it in hand. Other questions are interesting, but not nearly as urgent for Frege, who saw them as belonging more to empirical psychology or cognitive studies, as is more antiseptically said today. He considered the psychology of sign usage to be largely irrelevant for logic and philosophical semantics.

Frege reinforced the distinction between sign and signified, railing against their confusion in the philosophy of mathematics. He was especially impatient about their obscured entanglements in efforts to define the concept of number, as he continued:

I must here combat the view that, e.g., $2 + 5$ and $3 + 4$ are equal but not the same. This view is grounded in the same confusion of form and content, sign and thing signified ... Difference of sign cannot by itself be a sufficient ground for difference of the thing signified. The only reason why in our case the matter is less obvious is that the reference of the numeral 7 is not anything perceptible to the senses. There is at present a very widespread tendency not to recognize as an object anything that cannot be perceived by means of the senses; this leads here to numerals' being taken to be numbers, the proper objects of our discussion; and then, I admit, 7 and $2 + 5$ would indeed be different. But such a conception is untenable, for we cannot speak of any arithmetical properties of number whatsoever without going back to what the signs stand for.[33]

Names in Frege's *Begriffsschrift* must refer to something existent, or they are not really signs. They may have sense but not reference, no referential meaning. Signs must designate existent objects if properties are to be meaningfully truly or falsely predicated of them. Lifeless syntax is a dead-end, as far as Frege was concerned. We are required in every case to consider what a sign in the context of a predication signifies, what a symbol symbolizes or represents. Without an interpretation of signs there is no deciding such properties of numbers as whether 7 is or is not

---

[33] Frege, "Function and Concept," p. 22.

the same number as 5 + 2. Number names are not meaningless tokens in a sometimes useful, primarily amusing game as Hilbert wanted to say, taking an easy way out of what appear to be intractable metaphysical difficulties. Mathematical identity statements, for Frege, even when they are trivially explicitly iterative, were packed with objective sense-meanings that have nothing to do with psychological attitude or accompanying phenomenology.

The difference for Frege between concept and object was more clearly explained in the essay that bears the name "On Concept and Object." In "Function and Concept," Frege staked out the distinction in the following way:

> I am concerned to show that the argument does not belong with the function, but goes together with the function to make up a complete whole; for the function by itself must be called incomplete, in need of supplementation, or "unsaturated." And in this respect functions differ fundamentally from numbers.[34]

Functions differ fundamentally from numbers because numbers are objects, and as such predicationally complete. They look complete in *Begriffsschrift* notation, if we allow object constants like "1," "2," and the like, or "a," "b," and so on, to symbolize numbers that as objects can have functions like $+1(\_\_) = n$ applied to them. Functors are visibly incomplete, with a gap marked by parentheses in this representation to indicate an insertion place. They are completed as predicative concept-function expressions applied to appropriate object-arguments in such elementary applications as $+1(1) = 2$ and $+1(2) = 3$. They are symbolized more abstractly by means of constant-functions and algebraic variables, by which numbers are symbolized again as objects in identity statements such as $+1(a) = b$ and $+1(b) = c$. If it seems too basic to repeat these points, we should recall that it is from such tiny seeds that all of mathematics is supposed to result when concept-functions of specific kinds are set upon the mathematical entities that basic applications of concept-functions to the natural numbers are able to deliver.

Again, Frege remarked in emphasis that "The two parts into which the mathematical expression is thus split up, the sign of the argument and the expression of the function, are dissimilar; for the argument is a number, a whole complete in itself, as the function is not."[35] Frege cautioned against confusing the output value of a concept-function with

---

[34] *Ibid.*, p. 24.   [35] *Ibid.*, pp. 24–25.

the concept-function itself. In his example of concept-function $2 + x - x$ or $2+(\_ - \_) = 2$, the concept-function is one thing, and the fact that the value of the concept-function is always 2 is something else again. The concept-function is not $= 2$. Rather, it is a concept-function that has 2 as its only truth-making value.

The concept-function Frege considered is inherently unsaturated, incomplete until it is given over to an object and a specific value is output from the concept-function's application to that specific input. If 2 is something complete and the concept-function that outputs 2 is something incomplete, then 2 cannot be identical to this or any other unsaturated concept-function. The input and output of an arithmetical concept-function, Frege maintained, can be represented geometrically, as we have known since the time of Descartes, on a two-dimensional grid with a horizontal and vertical axis to which a numerical metric is applied for each of two coordinates. The concept-function itself stands outside its propositional and graphic representations. It is the real concept-function relating existent things that underwrites mathematical truth, and only indirectly its applied utility in the exact natural sciences.

Concept-Functions

If any of this was particularly new to Frege's audience, it has become commonplace today. The rising popularity of discussions surrounding the topics of reference and identity is largely due to Frege's influence. Frege had a definite purpose in rehearsing basic facts about arithmetical functions as he prepared in his Göttingen dissertation to extend the geometrical representation of real numbers to unreal, imaginary, and complex numbers. Complex identity-preserving mappings are functions from arithmetic to geometry and back again. Frege's Göttingen dissertation remained on the periphery of his concerns also in writing now about concepts, functions, objects, and identity.

Frege deduced the important conclusion that identity of reference does not logically imply identity of the thoughts by which an identity of entity is expressed. He took as his criterion the fact that, in the sentence "The Evening Star is a planet with a shorter period of revolution than the Earth," the thought expressed is other than that expressed by the sentence "The Morning Star is a planet with a shorter period of revolution than the Earth." He argued as follows: "And yet both sentences must have the same reference; for it is just a matter of interchanging the words 'Evening Star' and 'Morning Star,' which have the same reference, i.e. are proper names of the same heavenly body."[36] Frege announced here for the first time a topic he took up at greater length in his most famous essay of 1892, "On Sense and Reference." He recognized a theoretical necessity rather than issued a decree when he stated that "We must distinguish between sense and reference."[37]

Taken together, Frege's early 1890s essays provide background needed to understand the meaning contents of arithmetical equations. Avoiding special pleading, Frege offered a semantics of predications most generally, identity predications after that, and arithmetical equations as the final point of interest. Frege described more precisely what he meant, and says he had meant all along in previous writings, by the category of a concept. It is a function. There are specialized arithmetical concept-functions. Concepts generally are functions, and every predication can be broken down into an object, complete in itself, and an incomplete, unsaturated component that is the concept-function. A concept-function is never complete in itself, but only when applied to any of the existent entity argument-objects in the concept-function's domain. Frege in "Function and Concept" unequivocally characterized concepts as functions:

Statements in general, just like equations or inequalities or expressions in [mathematical] Analysis [calculus], can be imagined to be split up into two parts; one complete in itself, and the other in need of supplementation, or "unsaturated." Thus, e.g., we split up the sentence
        "Caesar conquered Gaul"
into "Caesar" and "conquered Gaul." The second part is "unsaturated" – it contains an empty place; only when this place is filled up with a proper name, or with an expression that replaces a proper name, does a complete sense appear. Here too I give the name "function" to what this "unsaturated" part stands for. In this case the argument is Caesar.[38]

We can rewrite the expression in a manner more in keeping with Frege's use of *Begriffsschrift* notation in the form Conquered-Gaul (Caesar). The object taken as the concept-function's argument-object is Caesar, Frege explained, and the concept-function is the incomplete unsaturated context, the concept-function of having Conquered Gaul or satisfying the concept-function Conquered-Gaul($\_\_$) = v. More prosaically, it is the property of having conquered Gaul. According to Frege,

[36] *Ibid.*, p. 29.   [37] *Ibid.*   [38] *Ibid.*, p. 31.

we can do the same for all predications involving any concepts construed as concept-functions more or less like those encountered in mathematics.

Frege did not merely strike an analogy between predication of properties in attributions of concepts to objects and the structures of mathematical functions. He theorized that they are one and the same, traveling under different names in different kinds of languages. Mathematics for Frege was a special symbolic language. Since mathematics is a language, it is possible within its rules to express meaningful thoughts. If mathematics is a special language then its meaning and truth conditions must be subject to the general requirements of a universal semantics. Frege's logical semantic analysis recognized that predications of properties to existent entities are the most elementary meaningful constructions in any language, mathematics included, and that mathematical functions are but a special case of the predication of a property to an existent entity which unites meaning and truth requirements for all languages under a single theory of concept-functions.

Frege's purpose in the early-1890s essays was nothing less than to provide all that he thought he needed in a concept-functional philosophy of language in order to support the applications of primary interest to his logicism in explaining the meaning and truth or falsehood of arithmetical equations. Arithmetical concept-functions are saturated with numbers or other mathematical entities as argument-objects available in a general or specialized subdomain, as the correlation in its infinite wisdom may require. Insofar as the reference of arithmetical equations is concerned, there are only two possibilities, the True and the False. Frege explained, with immediate reference to the tricky case of imaginary numbers, "that the value of our function $x2 = 1$ is always one of the two truth-values."[39]

Identity of Thought versus Reference: The Julius Caesar Problem Redux

Frege explained that the implementation of the analysis of concepts as functions requires that concept-functions in the first place be given "sharp delimitation." This preliminary honing of a concept can involve enormous labor, as the pages of Frege's *Grundlagen* attest with respect to the concept-function of natural number, when we are entitled to predicate the property

---

[39] *Ibid.*, p. 30

of being a natural number to a candidate entity. The boundaries of concept-functions so construed must be clearly established, to the point where they allow no vagueness or ambiguity of extension in their exact definition. We must be able to know in particular what the symbol "+1 ($\oplus$)" or "$\oplus$ + 1" means, in Frege's example, if "1" symbolizes the abstract natural counting number 1, and "$\oplus$" symbolizes a physical entity such as the Sun.

In his *Grundlagen*, Frege made precisely the same point logically, using the illustration of Julius Caesar. Here he pursued the theme. Caesar or Sun, though existent objects in the logic's referential domain, are not appropriate choices of substituend as arguments completing syntactical arithmetical concept-functions. The completed application +1(Julius Caesar) = n, despite being a saturation of a concept-functor by an object term, is such that presumably, for any domain entity N, $V(+1(\text{Julius Caesar}) = N) \neq$ the True AND $V(+1(\text{Julius Caesar}) = N) \neq$ the False. A similar argument applies when the completing object is the Sun in +1($\oplus$) = n.

The interesting philosophical question is why Caesar or $\oplus$ cannot serve as an argument-object for arithmetical concept-functions. Frege tried to sharply define, if not justify, the exclusion. The domain of arithmetic is at stake if the boundary of arithmetical properties does not exclude predication to objects like Julius Caesar. The further challenge was to determine whether a plausible division can be maintained to partition the reference domain of objects that can meaningfully constitute arguments for particular kinds of functions from that of those which cannot. To do so we must exactly characterize the subdomain of objects that provide suitable arguments for the arithmetical function +1(__) = n.

What could be easier, it might be thought? We are talking about numbers. The Sun and Julius Caesar are not numbers. Even if they rub elbows with numbers in the logic's referential semantic domain, containing all and only the existent objects that can be properly named, referred to, and stand as predication subjects in true or false statements in a language, counted, quantified over, and the like, they are no more arguments for arithmetical functions than the number 1 would be for the concept-function Conquered-Gaul(__) = v. We merely stipulate that the arguments of the function +1(__) = n are all and only numbers. We include for this purpose all and only the integers, rationals, irrationals, all reals, in other words, imaginary, complex, and transcendental numbers, and whatever else mathematicians consider to be genuine numbers, as individual abstract referents. Those things alone can then have 1 added to them to produce a meaningful output value, represented symbolically as a relation between the application of a concept-function to its input argument and its output value denoted by the identity sign, =. The Sun and Julius Caesar are not admitted because they are not the right sort of object. They are excluded as non-numbers, and the problem is solved.

The difficulty is, unfortunately, not so easily avoided. The reason is that all the numbers we would like to include in the subdomain of legitimate arguments for the arithmetical function $+1(\_\_) = n$ are themselves the output of arithmetical functions. The relevant constructions, beginning with $+1(\_\_) = n$ itself, as a variation of the Dedekind–Peano successor function in the foundations of mathematics, are applied in the very first instance to natural number 0 or 1. Imagine that we have a simplified semantic domain for the Fregean functional calculus. The domain expands, although it never contracts constructively, as more objects are produced by applications of the successor function $+1(\_\_) = n$, or any other arithmetical function. The analogy is strained because abstract objects do not change over time. Sets do not grow or shrink in size, but are abstract, beyond space and time wherein alone alterations of properties can take place. The point is heuristic, intended to help explain Frege's intuitive suggestion about the role of functions in the mathematical order.

Let the domain of all existent objects for the logic relevant to function $F = +1(\_\_)$ at first be $D = \{1, \text{Julius Caesar}, \oplus\}$. Natural number 1, courtesy of Frege's *Grundlagen* analysis of the concept as that of an existent abstract mathematical entity, is chosen at some point with a positive result. The product is $+1(1) = 2$, as we need not be reminded, and the expanding domain under construction now is $D^* = \{1, \text{Julius Caesar}, \oplus, 2\}$. We are reminded that membership in $\{\}$ sets is unordered, so putting 2 at the end has no special significance. What we expect to happen next is that the function will draw from the expanded domain the argument 2, to instantiate $+1(2) = 3$ and $D^{**} = \{1, \text{Julius Caesar}, \oplus, 2, 3\}$, and so on. The question in this simplified model containing only two non-arithmetical objects is what, if anything, prevents the application of function $F = +1(\_\_) = n$ to Julius Caesar in $+1(\text{Julius Caesar}) = n$ or to the Sun $(\oplus)$ in $+1(\oplus) = n$. It is certainly not standard elementary arithmetic to permit adding 1 to Julius Caesar or to the Sun. If we cannot prevent the combination syntactically, then *Begriffsschrift* logic and the semantic integrity of its True–False dichotomy are exposed to absurdity.

There is something disconcertingly suspicious about the application model nonetheless. It seems to be engaged in self-perpetuating motion. We need the outputs of all relevant concept-functions in order to pre-determine the permissible inputs by which the needed outputs are produced. It is like designing a machine that must manufacture all its own parts. The objection did not come as news to Frege. It is important to understand Frege's reaction to the problem. He perceived the objection in all its implications as potentially undermining the philosophical foundations of mathematics with a vicious circularity. The criticism casts doubt on the free availability of concept-functions by which the domain of mathematical objects is supposed to be defined, those belonging to elementary arithmetic first, and then whatever can be built on them.

The problem is that we need to know (a) what values an arithmetical function produces, in order to know (b) what arguments the function can accept, in order (c) for the function to produce any values at all. Julius Caesar and the Sun are out, although we still do not know why. We have just learned that we cannot lean on our commonsense intuition that Julius Caesar and the Sun are not arithmetical objects, and as such cannot be among the arguments of the arithmetical successor function $+\mathrm{I}(\_\_) = n$. We do not know in advance what objects will or will not turn out to be values of the concept-function until all arguments have been taken into consideration. Hence we cannot restrict the concept-function's subdomain argument-object intake to all and only the objects belonging to the concept-function's output. We cannot simply exclude Caesar and the Sun as non-numbers, unless or until the set of all and only numbers has been constructively determined as the total outputs of all and only arithmetical functions. The total outputs of all and only arithmetical functions can in turn be established only when the totality of permissible argument-objects for all arithmetical concept-functions has already been fixed.

The puzzle regarding whether the Sun and Julius Caesar can enter an arithmetical function as input argument or output value amounts to the question "What is an arithmetical object?" That is the philosophical interest of the Julius Caesar problem, not a need in practice to prevent mathematicians from mixing up arithmetic with leaders of the Roman Empire. The concept-function is arrived at by definition or analysis of a number or related mathematical entity. The truth about constructivism in the philosophy of mathematics is that it is always *re*constructive. It

gains traction only after a branch of mathematics has already been established. Any way of connecting those objects afterward must then appear
historically as though by miracle, insofar as ground-up construction is
concerned. The process proceeds by appeal to an already-available mathematical foundation or origin arrived at by algorithmic syntax transformations. The sequences of arithmetical functions applied in Frege's case to
the natural number 1, to generate first the positive integers or natural
numbers and then all integers including 0 and the negative integers,
rationals, and irrationals, and graduating from the real number line to
the number plane where imaginary numbers, complex numbers, and other
rare exotica considered to be genuine numbers are exactly situated, have an
order of definition and construction. With the right concept-functions
completed by the right argument-objects, any additional subdomain of
mathematics should in principle be just as respectable as the natural
number 2 positioned precisely on the real number line between the natural
number 1 and the natural number 3.

Frege revealed in the lecture that in the intervening five years since the
publication of his first book he had distanced himself from calling the
horizontal stroke in *Begriffsschrift* notation the *Inhaltsstrich*. From now on
he simply wanted to call it "the horizontal." More significantly in this
context, Frege held that the horizontal was referentially meaningfully
applied not only to an equation like — 1+3 = 4, the reference of which
Frege said *is* = the True, and — 1+3 = 5, which Frege said *is* the False,
but also (this is the remarkable part) to the subpropositional construction — 4. Since a number like 4 is not a proposition, it does not bear a
Fregean truth-value. It can be neither true nor false, and its reference in
Fregean terms can be neither the True nor the False. At this point Frege
stepped in and lumped — 1+3 = 5 and — 4 together as being or referring
to the False. It is, for all Frege's endorsement, profoundly unsatisfying to
have — 4 be identified with or considered as referring to the False, when
it is unmistakably not the kind of thing to be either true or false, ≠ the
True and ≠ the False. This is conspicuous fudging. It is as much an illicit
use of the symbolism in Frege's example as it would be to write — ⊕
or — Julius Caesar. The objection is that for Frege only propositions
should be assertable, either by the vaguely psychologistic *Inhaltsstrich* of
long-gone *Begriffsschrift* days, or by the more neutral term *Horizontal*, the
horizontal stroke or bar. If Frege now allowed — 4 to be or to refer to the
False, then he would have no steady ground to stand on in opposing — ⊕

or — Julius Caesar. The natural number 4, the Sun ⊕, and Julius Caesar are all alike *objects*, complete entities, unlike concept-functions. The flat stroke ending in referring symbols for Sun or Caesar does not have any obvious sentential meaning. It is a syntactical expedient that Frege considered logically harmless, but not one that was consistent with what Frege had previously said concerning his logical notation.

The more interesting question is whether Frege was able to maintain tight control on the *Begriffsschrift* reference domain. Frege did not always seem to know what belongs or does not belong among the objects assumable as arguments in referentially meaningful completions of unsaturated concept-functions. Nor is there anything surprising in this. How could Frege be expected to know which of all logically possible candidates were existent entities belonging to the logic's domain and which were not? He was dogmatic as it is about most of these things in relation to the metaphysics of mathematics. When logically troublesome apparently saturated concept-function constructions involving existent entities as argument-objects appear well-formulated in *Begriffsschrift* symbolism, as in $+1$(Julius Caesar) $= n$, and there is no guidance as to what numerical n or more exceptional value v should or even could be output, then simple referential semantic domain membership or exclusion cannot suffice to prevent the introduction and spread of nonsense in Frege's *Begriffsschrift*. There are subdomains of appropriate application within the general referential semantic domain comprehending all and only existent entities. The challenge of the Julius Caesar problem is to find principled ways of dividing up the domain of existents into mathematical versus non-mathematical applications. Frege seemed justified in his intuitive confidence that this could be done without engendering a vicious definitional circularity.

Arithmetical Function Chaperones

This is not at all what Frege wanted. He craved philosophical understanding of the situation, even after the Julius Caesar problem had been intuitively forestalled. The question was whether there was anything to be done about the Julius Caesar problem within *Begriffsschrift* constraints. The objects were there in the domain of all and only existents. Why is it, then, that not every object in the domain could be made the argument-object of every concept-function? Although any object can be chosen as an argument-object completing any random concept-function, in a completed true or false assertion, existent entities like Caesar or the Sun cannot meaningfully be taken as argument-objects of specifically arithmetical concept-functions like the successor $+1(\_\_) = n$. Frege demanded to know why this should be true.

What seems an inescapable but unacknowledged problem for Frege's theory of concepts as functions is explaining the apparent fact that some concept-functions are arithmetical. With that status comes the exclusivity whereby arithmetical concept-functions do not accept any non-arithmetical argument-objects that concept-functions otherwise allow in completed true or false concept-function saturations. He continued as follows:

We thus need a special sign in order to be able to assert something. To this end I make use of a vertical stroke at the left end of the horizontal, so that, e.g., by writing

$$\vdash 2 + 3 = 5$$

we assert that $2 + 3$ equals 5. Thus here we are not just writing down a truth-value, as in

$$2 + 3 = 5,$$

but also at the same time saying that it is the True.[40]

The arithmetical sentence $2 + 3 = 5$ refers to the True. It is worth knowing in the meantime that Frege, prior to his 1892 essay, "On Sense and Reference," distinguished between the sense and reference of all singular referring expressions classified as proper names (*Eigennamen*).[41] Frege applied the same division of sense and reference also to the meanings of declarative sentences. The meaning of a declarative sentence is a function of the meanings of its meaningful components, according to Frege's *semantic compositionality* thesis. We determine the meanings of concept terms or functors, and of the proper names for input and output values of the functions applied to argument-objects. They are considered thus far only as individual terms. Terms are put together constructively to compose sentences, beginning with the simplest predication that object a is F or has property F.

---

[40] Frege, "Function and Concept," p. 34.

[41] See Francis Jeffry Pelletier and Bernard Linsky, "Russell vs. Frege on Definite Descriptions as Singular Terms," in *Russell vs. Meinong: The Legacy of "On Denoting,"* ed. Nicholas Griffin and Dale Jacquette (London: Routledge, 2009), pp. 40–64; and Simon Blackburn and Alan Code, "The Power of Russell's Criticism of Frege: 'On Denoting' pp. 48–50," *Analysis*, 38 (1978), pp. 65–77.

The meaning of the sentence Fa has two parts in Frege's sentential semantics. The sense of the sentence is a function of the sense of concept-functor "$F(\_\_)$" and the sense of proper name "a." If the sense of "$F(\_\_)$" is the abbreviated concept-function or property of being French, and "a" is Sigmund Freud, then "Fa" compositionally has the sense that Sigmund Freud is, or satisfies the concept of being, French. Such completion of the concept function results in a false sentence. We obtain a true sentence by choosing a = Descartes, or for example by making $F(\_\_)$ the property of being Austrian or a psychoanalyst. The point is to bring expressive meaning into convergence with prevalent facts in order to get a sense of what language can do. According to Frege, the reference of a meaningful sentence, that is, the second component in its bipartite Fregean analysis, is either the True, if the sentence is true, or the False, if the sentence is false. Assuming it to be false under the original assignment of meanings for that Fa, then, for Frege, $V(Fa)$ = the False. Everything is as it should be so far in Frege's *Begriffsschrift* logic and semantics.

Negation and Quantifier Duality

Frege advanced to the next irrevocable step previously introduced in his *Begriffsschrift*. Truth-functional propositional negation was represented by means of the short vertical line dangling from what Frege now in "Function and Concept" began to designate the horizontal. Truth-functional negation turned out to be an innocent-appearing and even inevitable, but ultimately dangerous, addition to the algebraization of logic, especially of a language of propositional truth-functional connectives.

It is Monday. It is not the case that it is Monday. The foregoing statements are a proposition and its negation. If the proposition is true, the negation is false; and the converse. Without Frege's hanging negation sign a proposition is affirmed; with one attached the proposition is negated or denied. What could be more natural? Before Frege, logic had nevertheless not admitted a truth-functional operation of propositional negation. It is nowhere to be found symbolically in Aristotle's syllogistic term logic, although he considered the force of internal and external negation combinations informally.[42]

---

[42] Aristotle informally considered negation of predicate-complement categorical forms in *De Interpretatione* 19b5–20b11 (in Chapter 10).

That something satisfies function F, as might be said in contemporary linear logic, $\exists x F x$, Frege expressed by means of propositional negation. He took universal quantification as logically primitive. He rightly defined quantifier duality with negation and the universal quantifier, symbolized by the dimple binding variable letter "a":

$$\vdash\!\!\!\curvearrowright\!\!\!\underset{\top}{\overset{a}{}}\, F\,(a)$$

Frege's remodeled *Begriffsschrift*, he reported in the lecture, now had first-level and second-level concept-functions. They were distinguished by a different style of concept-functor or concept-function symbol. Frege considered the equivalent of $f(F(1))$ as the logical structure that obtains when a function is integrated to an upper limit in calculus. What Frege presented by means of this suggestive distinction was a gesture toward something like Russell's fully generalized simple theory of types, rising to only two levels. Frege believed there was never any need, at least in any anticipated *Begriffsschrift* applications, to postulate >2 orders of functions.

Nor, understandably, did he anticipate their utility in forestalling paradoxical freely constructible functions in *Begriffsschrift* notation in order to avoid Russell's paradox. That problem would not darken Frege's horizon until 1902. After 1902, Frege must have looked back at this time before learning of Russell's paradox as his period of living in a fool's paradise with no awareness of the logical inconsistency lurking beneath the placid surface of his *Begriffsschrift* and *Grundgesetze*. After having explained the role of first- and second-level functions in *Begriffsschrift* formalization of a differential–integral equation, Frege speculated on the generalizability of the multiple level of functions. He appears to have believed, contrary to what Russell will later conclude about the need for an endless hierarchy of ordered syntax types in light of the paradox, that the distinction between first- and second-level concept-function predications in the logic should always suffice for analytical purposes in the foundations of mathematics. Frege drew the line at two levels of concept-function predications, decrying from the outset the approach taken in Russell's unceilinged type theory:

Now at this point people had particular second-level functions, but lacked the conception of what we have called second-level functions. By forming that, we make the next step forward. One might think that this would go on. But probably this last step is already not so rich in consequences as the earlier ones; for instead of

second-level functions one can deal, in further advances, with first-level functions –
as shall be shown elsewhere. But this does not banish from the world the difference
between first-level and second-level functions; for it is not made arbitrarily, but
founded deep in the nature of things.[43]

Frege hinted at a logical reduction of second-level to first-level functions. Such reductions can in fact be effected by allowing a function $F(x) = f(G(x))$, although it is not fully clear in the present context of Frege's lecture and published essay "Function and Concept" whether this is even roughly the kind of thing he had in mind. Frege redrew the limitation of his previous discussion to concept-functions of one argument-object, and extended his conclusions more generally. He ended the essay with these words of warning: "Again, instead of functions of two arguments we can deal with functions of a single but complex argument; but the distinction between functions of one and of two arguments still holds in all its sharpness."[44]

Does it though? Does the distinction between functions of one and two arguments "hold in all its sharpness" if multiple-argument functions can always be collapsed into extensionally equivalent single-argument functions with correspondingly more complex content and abstracted internal structure? The only place where the difference makes a difference, if Frege's brief remark is rightly understood, is in the syntax of one-argument-place or more-than-one-argument-place concept-functors. We can say that a is taller than b, relating those two objects by the taller-than relation. Or we can say that a has the property of being taller-than-b. The latter method packs in reference to b as part of a one-argument-place property attributed to a. Ungainly or not, the construction shows that the distinction between one- and multiple-argument concept-functions is not as sharp-edged as Frege assumed. It is only the *language* of *Begriffsschrift* logic that admits structurally different concept-functors. Frege attempted to draw a hard and fast distinction between qualities and relations only by flagrantly violating his sacred principle of never confusing a referent with its psychological designation, image, idea, presentation, or linguistic sign. What further reality did Frege speak of as "deep in the nature of things," if symbolic logic can always make relations go away in favor of custom-designed single-argument concept-functions?

---

[43] Frege, "Function and Concept," p. 41.   [44] *Ibid.*

Identity as a Logical Relation and Logic of Identity Statements

In "Function and Concept" Frege said somewhat carelessly that "The possibility of regarding the equality holding generally between values of functions as a [particular] equality, viz. an equality between ranges of values, is, I think, indemonstrable; it must be taken to be a fundamental law of logic."[45] Here Frege slipped a notch from his usually circumspect methodology. He knew that not everything "indemonstrable" is a fundamental law of logic. Falsehoods generally had better be indemonstrable, but they can certainly not be considered fundamental logical laws for that reason. The identity sign in $Fx = y$, just like that by which $a = a$ and $\forall x[x = x]$, all easily translated into Frege's *Begriffsschrift* logical notation, is no doubt connected with a very fundamental principle of some kind. The question is what, if anything, would make it a fundamental law specifically of *logic*? Frege did not even try definitively to address this philosophical question. There are good arguments for considering the principle as belonging instead to mathematics or metaphysics, to say nothing of cognitive science, regionally in the kind of reduction to psychologism that Frege wanted at all costs to avoid in the philosophy of logic and purely logical foundations of mathematics. The question is critical in understanding pure logicism in its first-step quest for a purely logical analysis of arithmetic.

What makes identity $=$ as it appears in concept-functions on Frege's analysis a purely *logical* relation? If "$3 + 2$" is as such an arithmetical expression, why isn't "$= 5$" also a purely arithmetical concept-function? How does *logic* insinuate itself into the *Begriffsschrift Formelsprache* by means of "$=$"? It does not seem to do so, despite numerous laws about the operation, in the case of "$+$." However, we may grant that $+1(\_\_) = n$ is a concept-function. Its use may be subject to logical principles.

That fact alone, however, does not make $+1(\_\_) = n$ itself a *logical* concept-function in Frege's arithmetic. Frege wanted to claim "$=$" for pure logic, making arithmetical identity statements a special case of function(argument) = value–object predications. Frege's pure logicism did not recognize any contenders beyond pure logic and arithmetic. If identity $=$ was needed in applications beyond arithmetic, then by a process of elimination for Frege it could only be purely logical. He proffered no argument for making logic more fundamental than arithmetic. We are meant to share

45 *Ibid.*, p. 26.

his sense that there is no cogent alternative. It is uncertainty about what is and what is not purely logical that eventually spells trouble for Frege's logicism. It threatens the truth and credibility of Frege's thesis that all of mathematics, beginning with the laws and theorems of elementary arithmetic, is reducible to *purely* logical concepts and relations. If we want to explore the idea that identity itself is a relational concept-function, then we must be able to write $=(a, b) =$ the True, or $V(=(a, b)) =$ the True, when it is true that $a = b$. This is not the end of things, because in that case we must also be able to write $=(=(a, b),$ the True$)$. Here, too, $=(=(a, b),$ the True$) =$ the True or $V(=(=(a, b),$ the True$)) =$ the True, and we appear to be launched upon an explanatorily insupportable, semantically top-heavy vicious infinite regress of truth-value identities involving endless iterations of Frege's content-judgment stroke $|$—, where p is accepted as true, in $|$— $|$— $|$— ... $|$— $|$— $|$— p. Should team Frege be concerned?

The philosophical difficulties of Frege's logicism are a by-product of his inability to clearly distinguish purely logical from extralogical considerations in the conceptual foundations of arithmetic. This is the significance of the Julius Caesar and Sun problem with respect to the vital subcategory of arithmetical versus non-arithmetical concept-functions. What was built by Frege relies heavily on surveyable concept-functions of sets, quantities, and referential subdomains of objects singled out from among the total domain of all and only existent objects to meet Frege's preconditions for reference and referentially meaningful predication. Frege's logicism provided purely logical foundations of arithmetic only if set, quantity, and finally number are purely logical. He gave the appearance of reducing arithmetic to logic only by incorporating arithmetical concept-functions into what was supposed to be pure logic. The objection is that effectively he adulterated pure logic with arithmetic and then derived arithmetic again from their admixture. Even that might be agreeable, had Frege only explained what he meant by "pure" logic. He cannot have had in mind the mere absence of empirical elements, since that with a mighty thud would admit all of mathematics as purely logical. That is where Frege wanted to end up, not where he wanted trivially to start out.

Consider that for Frege after the *Grundlagen* number *is* a "purely" logical concept, whatever that means, given Frege's free use of equinumerosity and other questionable factors and devices like Hume's one–one correlation principle, concerning which complaints have already been made. If we can transact these problems and agree with Frege that number is a purely logical concept, then surely quantity, set, cardinality, and equinumerosity, all of which are number-related theoretical entities among others, must be so also. Make number purely logical and a deluge of purely logical consequences is immediately implied.

That was, of course, what Frege wanted. The trouble is that Frege promoted a pure logicism without clarifying or arguing in support of an exact concept of pure logic. Frege answered these questions with the arithmetic manifestly objectified ultimately in his *Grundgesetze*. The implication is that, to know what pure logic means, you need to look at Frege's *Grundgesetze* and its predecessor texts. The further implication is that there could be no independent criterion of pure logic other than comparison with the text whose pure or impure logic is under scrutiny. There is no way of judging whether or not Frege's arithmetic was purely logical as advertised. That Frege's pure logic excluded psychological factors is understood. Now what of the meaning of identity statements including arithmetical equations as a special case of function(argument) = value expressions?

Concept and Object, Function and Argument

Similar challenges were taken up by Frege in his essay published the next year, 1892, "Über Begriff und Gegenstand" ("On Concept and Object"), which appeared in the *Vierteljahrsschrift für wissenschaftliche Philosophie* (*Quarterly for Scientific Philosophy*). "On Concept and Object" was shorter than "Function and Concept" by almost a third, and did not make use of any *Begriffsschrift* logical notation. Like the *Grundlagen*, it involved scarcely any but the simplest arithmetical numerical expressions and variables for object individuals and types, of the sort that any well-argued philosophical essay might contain.[46]

The occasion of the article was an invitation for Frege to defend his *Grundlagen* against pointed criticisms that had been raised in a series of essays in the same journal by Benno Kerry. Kerry was a philosopher with mathematical and semantic interests that in some ways complemented Frege's, from whom he was not so far distant. Kerry displayed what for

---

[46] An excellent general overview on this specific topic is offered by Eva Picardi, "Kerry und Frege über Begriff und Gegenstand," *History and Philosophy of Logic*, 15 (1994), pp. 9–32.

Frege was the same regrettable psychologistic inclination as he had detected among most of his past and present competitors for the correct analysis of the concept of natural number. He was especially on the alert against subjectivism in the company of those who approached his level of technical mathematical competence. The others, dabblers in mathematics, unless they had a reputation like Mill's, were not worth bothering about. Frege took the opportunity of setting the record straight about key aspects of his theory, introducing countercriticisms of Kerry in the following terms:

> This seems to me all the more necessary, because [Kerry's] opposition is at least partly based on a misunderstanding, which might be shared by others, of what I say about the concept [of number]; and because, even apart from this special occasion, the matter is important and difficult enough for a more thorough treatment than seemed to me suitable in my *Grundlagen*.[47]

Frege's purpose was not merely rhetorical. He answered Kerry's objections to his analysis of the concept of natural number by poking good-sized holes in Kerry's arguments. Frege punctured Kerry's reasoning not merely with destructive intent, but rather as an occasion to explain and positively defend his position once again in light of the misunderstandings he believed Kerry must have somehow inferred from the *Grundlagen* concerning Frege's concept of natural number. Frege adopted the standard trope that, if Kerry had so seriously misread and misjudged him, then others might do so too. Frege wanted his position to be clear, as a reasonable precondition for meaningful criticism. Objections like Kerry's, Frege believed, would then be seen unmistakably to be misdirected against views other than those which he had actually propounded in his *Grundlagen*.

Philosophers are sometimes called upon to make clarifications of this sort. The conclusions in difficult analyses are often subtle, and even very astute commentators can go afoul of intended meaning despite exercising

---

[47] Frege, "On Concept and Object," *Philosophical Writings*, p. 42. Frege refers to a "series of articles" by Benno Kerry (1859–1889) in the *Vierteljahrsschrift für wissenschaftliche Philosophie*. Frege does not name the articles by Kerry to which he is responding in "On Concept and Object," but they are presumably the eight essays published between 1885 and 1891, jointly titled, "Über Anschauung und ihre psychische Verarbeitung," *Vierteljahrsschrift für wissenschaftliche Philosophie*, 9 (1885), pp. 433–93; 10 (1886), pp. 419–67; 11 (1887), pp. 53–116 and 249–307; 13 (1889), pp. 71–124 and 392–419; 14 (1890), pp. 317–53; and 15 (1891), pp. 127–67. See Volcker Peckhaus, "Benno Kerry: Beiträge zu seiner Biographie," *History and Philosophy of Logic*, 15 (1994), pp. 1–8.

the best intentions, skillful charitable interpretation, and honest reaction to a thinker's expression of philosophical ideas. Frege found himself in that position in "On Concept and Object." He wanted to defend still more forcefully the distinction between concept and object along the lines he had previously outlined in "Function and Concept." He used the opportunity of being called on to respond publicly to Kerry's encounter with the *Grundlagen* concept–object division to put forward arguments reinforcing the distinction and emphasize its importance in the logic of predication.

The fundamental idea Frege advanced in the early 1890s essays preceding *Grundgesetze I* was that concepts are functions, even if not all functions function like all other concepts, and that functions and concepts are different from objects. No function is an object, in Frege's metaphysics, and no object is a function. Objects for Frege were inherently complete entities that satisfy identity conditions as particular things, whereas concept-functions were inherently incomplete or "unsaturated," *ungesättigt*. Concepts interpreted as functions need to be fulfilled, saturated, or satisfied by an object, and are consequently not complete objects. Predicational completeness or incompleteness can be thought of in Frege's terms as rather like an arithmetical function, typified by the successor $+1(\_\_) = n$.

Frege first explained that, among the variety of usages for the word "concept," psychological, logical, and confusions of the two, he confined his category to the logical, avoiding the psychological. Frege approached psychologism more with garlic and crucifix than with convincing arguments. He was surely right to reject crude forms of psychologism. However, he offered no opposition to refined psychologisms backed up by equally scrupulous empiricist and intuitionist methodologies in the philosophy of logic. The question for Frege was not how other writers should use the word "concept" or "function"; that was a matter about which he did not propose to legislate or proselytize. He maintained that, in order to understand his theory of functions properly in its sharp distinction between concept-functions and argument-objects, a critic needed to understand that functions and concepts were not subjective occurrent or dispositional psychological moments or their contents, but objective abstract logical entities. Frege made the following observation: "What I decided was to keep strictly to a purely logical use; the question whether this or that use is more appropriate is one that I should like to leave on one side, as of minor importance ... It seems to me that Kerry's misunderstanding results from his unintentionally confusing his own usage of the word 'concept' with mine. This readily gives rise to contradictions, for which my usage is not to blame."[48]

Frege complained that Kerry "contests" his "definition" of concept, going on to explain and remind the critic that it was never part of his purpose in the first place to *define* the concept-function of concept-function. Kerry made a reasonable assumption, given Frege's characterization of concepts as functions. If what Frege said is not a definition, perhaps it is the next best thing. The explication amounts on first encounter to a surprising, insightful identification or reduction rather than a mere analogy and comparison. Frege rightly insisted that not everything can be analyzed, suggesting, while not arguing, that this is actually true of the apparently all-embracing concept-function of concept-function. Invoking the Kantian analogy between analytic and synthetic chemistry, and the model also of conceptual or philosophical analysis of complex concept-functions into simpler concept-functions, he expected eventually to arrive at basic primitive concepts that are incapable of being further reduced in meaning.

Frege alighted then on his main contention against Kerry. He objected to Kerry's relativism: "Kerry wants to make out that the distinction between concept and object is not absolute."[49] Frege held fast to his distinction, making as he says the property of being a concept and the property of being an object mutually exclusive properties that never univocally apply to the same things. Frege provided a useful comparison by observing that the same man can be both son and father, provided he is not son and father to the same person. The analogy for the concept of concept in Frege's auxiliary analysis of the distinction in his general calculus of functions is that the same abstract entity can be both concept-function and argument-object, but never in the same sense or playing the same functional role, whenever it is made an object of thought. It is a concept-function when unsaturated, as a man might be son to another man. As an object it is no longer unsaturated, but must be understood as relevantly predicationally determinate, complete more generally when taken as an existent entity in its own right. When application is made,

[48] Frege, "On Concept and Object," p. 42.   [49] *Ibid.*, p. 43.

the concept-function is no longer unsaturated, as by analogy the same man, without offending logic or taxonomy, might be father to his own son.

Frege approached the disparity between concept-function and object-argument from both directions. He first develops a likeness:

> Let us fasten on this simile. If there were, or had been, beings that were fathers but could not be sons, such beings would obviously be quite different in kind from all men who are sons. Now it is something like this that happens here. The concept (as I understand the word) is predicative. On the other hand, a name of an object, a proper name, is quite incapable of being used as a grammatical predicate.[50]

Previously, Frege had argued that no function can be an object. Objects are complete, whereas concept-functions are incomplete, unsaturated, and in need of satisfaction by acceptance of an appropriate argument-object. Now the objection is turned around the other way. Frege remarked that no object can be a concept-function, because no object is predicative. No Fregean object needs to be completed by accepting an argument or being applied to another object. Frege insisted that it makes no sense to say that Alexander the Great, the individual ancient Macedonian belligerent entity himself, is not true of any other object, say, his father Philip II. Although Alexander the Great is not true of anything, many things are true of Alexander the Great, and many properties construed as concept-functions hold true of him. The sign of this is that they result in true completions, as when someone says truthfully that Ma, taking "a" as a proper name for Alexander and "M" as the property or concept-function of being Macedonian.

Frege called attention to a fundamental equivocation that is all too easily made when reason is not alert. It is the often-unobserved distinction in the fallacy of confusing the "is" of predication with the "is" of identity. The equivocation occurs in arithmetical equations and in the relation between a function applied to an input argument and its correlated output value, as in $Fx = y$. An analogous distinction is sometimes blurred in egregious gullible inference, as in the following "proof" for the existence of God: God by concept or definition is, in the predication sense, omnipotent, omniscient, and perfectly benevolent. Therefore, God is, in the sense of being or existing; which is to say that God $exists$. Such casuistry is clearly not correct, although a variation of precisely that kind of inference can be supported as deductively valid in a logic like Frege's *Begriffsschrift*, where only existent

[50] *Ibid.*

entities have such properties as being omnipotent. For anything to have a property for Frege, by definition it is necessary and sufficient for the object in question to exist. If he wants to avoid the conclusion that God exists because God ostensibly has properties, Frege must cut the argument off at its root. He must deny from the outset that it can meaningfully be said that God is omnipotent, omniscient, or the like, that these properties can truly be predicated of God, unless it has first been independently decided that God exists.

Frege's concern was somewhat different in "On Concept and Object." Here the issue is whether an object, contrary to the main argument in the section, could not after all have the individualizing property or *haecceity* (Latin, *haecceitas*) of being Alexander the Great. The distinction between the "is" of identity and that of property or concept-function predication, like the difference between the "is" of predication and existence, marks a powerful dissimilarity. Frege's perceptive analysis discriminates between saying that there exists something that is identical with the existent object Alexander the Great, that, effectively, $\exists x[x = a]$, and saying that Alexander the Great, as before, is Macedonian, Ma. There is a property of being identical to Alexander the Great. We can meaningfully say that something has this property. We can speak of the property of being identical to Alexander the Great, which, as an abstract entity or concept-function, is not the same thing at all as the flesh and blood conquerer of almost all the known world in his time.

The existent object that has the property or fulfills the concept-function of being identical to Alexander the Great is none other than Alexander the Great. This entitles the trivial truth to be written as a predication to Alexander the Great of the property of being identical to Alexander the Great, $\grave{O}x[x = a]a =$ the True, or $V(\grave{O}x[x = a]a) =$ the True. The completed context $\grave{O}x[x = a]a$ is meaningful, as would be $\grave{O}x$ $[x = a]\oplus$, although only $V(\grave{O}x[x = a]a) =$ the True, whereas $V(\grave{O}x[x = a]\oplus) =$ the False. The same is true whether "$\oplus$" represents the Sun, as in Frege's essay of 1891, "Function and Concept," or any existent object $\neq$ a. The Sun, like Julius Caesar and every existent entity $\neq a$, does not have the property or satisfy the concept-function of being identical to Alexander the Great $= a$, resulting in a completed predicational construction identical in reference to the True. If only Alexander the Great under any designation is identical to Alexander the Great, then any contrary identity statement must bear the Fregean truth-value the False.

Fregean Objects and Concept-Functions

Frege got down to cases with Kerry when he considered the details of Kerry's counterexample: "Kerry ... gives the following example: 'the concept "horse" is a concept easily attained,' and thinks that the concept 'horse' is an object, in fact one of the objects that fall under the concept 'concept easily attained'."[51] This is the kind of criticism many people have in mind as a response to Frege's claim that concepts are never objects. We make the concept "horse" into an object in the sense of intention, an intended object of reference and predication, just as we do any particular flesh and blood horse to which we may refer and truly or falsely predicate a property. We do so without ceremony when we say *of* the concept "horse" that it is a concept; that it is a concept zoologically subsumed by the concepts "mammal," "vertebrate," and so on; that it is comparatively easier to understand than some concepts of quantum mechanics; and many other things besides.

We work harder to master some concepts cognitively than we do with others. Kerry understood this empirical fact as a sign that concepts can stand as objects taken as arguments of other concepts in predications. The idea so expressed almost seems trivially obvious and unworthy of mention. Frege agreed with the facts of Kerry's case, but not with Kerry's interpretation for Frege's uncompromising knife-edge distinction between concept-function and argument-object. Frege good-naturedly concurred with Kerry's example, up to a point, by responding "Quite so; the three words 'the concept "horse"' do designate an object, but on that very account they do not designate a concept, as I am using the word. This is in full accord with the criterion I gave – that the singular definite article always indicates an object, whereas the indefinite article accompanies a concept-word."[52]

The concept that serves as object for other concept-functions, if Frege has seen the distinction clearly in Kerry's objection, is not "horse," which denotes the concept of horse or being a horse, but rather "the concept 'horse'." The latter, importantly, is an existent *object* in Frege's full sense of the word. Whereas "horse" in the sense of "being a horse" cannot be an object, "the concept 'horse'" is an object of such predications as "The concept 'horse' is a concept that it is easy to grasp," or "The concept 'horse' is a zoological rather than arithmetical or musicological genus."

To tread carefully, where one misplacement of quotations can convert meaningful and even true statements into nonsense, we can say that for Frege the concept "horse" is not an object, although "the concept 'horse'" is an object. It is a concept-function taken as argument-object for appropriate second-level predications of concept-functions to the concept-function "horse." These Frege permits, and must anyway admit, while insisting consistently throughout that the concept "horse," by itself, the property of being a horse, because it is unsaturated and incomplete, is not an (existent) *object*. Frege seems to be on firm ground in making these assertions. He replies to Kerry's criticism by reinforcing the distinction between concept-function and argument-object with commonsense illustrations as he proceeds. The difference after a fashion could not be greater, if Frege was right. It explained the compositionality of linguistic expression, for one thing, as though that were not enough. It offered insight into how it was that objects and concepts lock together, when an object was taken as a concept-function's argument. It accounted for the two principal semantic components of meaningful predications, sense and truth-value as referential meaning, referring, respectively, depending on the facts of the world, to the True and otherwise to the False. The same two-dimensional semantics of sense and reference explained the meaning of any predication and hence of any identity statement. The meaning and truth-conditions of arithmetical equations were thus assured.

Semantic Compositionality

The astonishing feature of language for Frege was its ability under a finite choice of distinct symbols to combine and recombine syntactically in endlessly expressive ways. Around these possibilities grammatical rules in the natural histories of languages have sprouted to impose a loose sort of order on permitted constructions. Within a formal symbolism's grammar and formation rules, algebraic structures permit both assembly and analysis of all possible constructions out of (a) all singular referring terms, Fregean proper names in the most general sense, including definite descriptions, designating individual existent entities in the logic's referential semantic domain, and (b) concept-functors, predicates and property abstractions. We put together object and property symbols to create within a linguistic framework an expressive token of a grammatically recognizable expressive type. The constructions of developed languages

are compositionally capable of expressing endlessly complicated meaningful constructions, each capable in principle of supporting Fregean
sense and reference.

The question is how the meaning of a grammatical construction of any
length within a language is related to its meaningful recombinants.
Frege's reply was the predictable, and to that degree disappointing,
answer that the sense–reference meaning of a linguistic whole is a *function*
of the sense–reference meanings of its meaningful parts. That such a
concept-function is available for the true predication of a property to
existent objects implies only that the meaning of the whole has something
or other to do with the meanings of its meaningful constituents. The
function offers co-extensional correlations without informative explanation. Frege's solution works only for those who agree at the explanatory
niveau (level) where it is sufficiently comforting to consider that there is a
never further explicated functional relation of some sort or other between
the sense and reference of "Fa" and the sense and reference of "a" and
the concept-function "F," such that Meaning(Fa) = $f($"F," "a"). As to
what meaning-function f is or how it works, Frege in the three early 1890s
essays had nothing enlightening to say.

Given the extraordinary, potentially infinitely comprehensive ramifying syntactical variations available in a developed language, there must be
many different specific relational functions serving as meaning determinants. The same is true when a language's concept-functions are introduced into the regimented formalism of an algebraic symbolic logic such
as Frege's *Begriffsschrift*. The lesson is the variety of predicational forms
available when considering the distinct ways in which the meaning of the
proposition Fa is concept-functionally related to the sense-meaning of
"F" and the sense and reference-meaning of "a", on the one hand, and on
the other to the meanings of the whole significantly more complex
expression $Fa \wedge Rab \wedge \neg Rba$, compositionally depending on the meanings of lexical components and logical constants, in this case "F," "a,"
"R," "b," "$\wedge$," and "$\neg$."

To say as Frege does only as an article of semantic faith that meaningful parts are functionally related to meaningful wholes tells us nothing
whatsoever about the number or kinds of part–whole semantic functions
needed even in a rigorously axiomatic–theorematic language such as
elementary arithmetic. What Frege's logic and semantics, despite these
limitations, provide is a previously unacknowledged universal model of

n-ary functions taking on the requisite number of existent entities in n argument places to produce a predication that refers either to the True or to the False. The truth-value reference of the declarative sentence is based on the meaning-senses and references of meaningful components in the predication, purporting in many applications to express a fact about the extant state of the world. It offers a general functional framework within which to consider part–whole meaning relations in a universal semantics. The part–whole semantic functional thesis is insensitive to the plurality of meaning functions that might be needed unpredeterminedly many rungs up along the logical–grammatical constructive linguistic *escalier* (staircase).

Speaking of Concepts

Frege recounted at length what he meant in response to Kerry's mis-aimed critique in the 1892 essay "On Concept and Object." He complained that "Kerry calls my criterion unsuitable; for surely, he says, in the sentence 'the concept that I am now talking about is an individual concept' the name composed of the first eight words stands for a concept; but he [Kerry] is not taking the word 'concept' in my sense, and it is not in what I have laid down that the contradiction lies. But nobody can require that my mode of expression shall agree with Kerry's."[53]

Frege admitted that ordinary language is strained trying to say, following his distinction, that the concept *horse* is not a concept. (Frege uses italics where Kerry prefers quotation marks.) After all, Frege notes, we say without confusion that the city of Berlin is a city, and that the Italian volcano Vesuvius is a volcano. Why should we not then say, by exact parity of grammatical form, that the concept *horse* is a concept? That it has the property of being a concept? Plato is willing to go so far in his acceptance of the theory of abstract eternal Forms as to declare that the concept *horse* is truthfully a horse. How else could the Idea of Horse explain that all horses are horses, if not by their shared horse-like similarities? Abstractly, it is precisely this acknowledgment that gives rise to the infinite-regress problem of Plato's Third Man. For then there must be a yet-higher-order concept HORSE by virtue of which flesh and blood horses and the first-order concept Horse are all horses, which in

[53] *Ibid.*, p. 46.

Plato's metaphysics can only be yet another Form or Idea of *horse*, and so on, in unending regress.

Kerry having been safely put in his place, Frege proceeded in the lecture to explain his distinction in more constructive terms. One cannot improve on the beauty and simplicity of Frege's own systematic analysis in this part of the essay. Here is what he wrote:

> We designate this [concept] object by prefixing the words "the concept"; e.g.:
> "The concept *man* is not empty."
> Here the first three words are to be regarded as a proper name, which can no more be used predicatively than "Berlin" or "Vesuvius." When we say "Jesus falls under the concept *man*," then, setting aside the copula, the predicate is:
> "someone falling under the concept *man*"
> and this means the same as:
> "a man."
> But the phrase
> "the concept *man*"
> is only part of this predicate.[54]

Frege's analysis seems perfectly sound. If he was right, then he had adequately defended a watertight distinction between concept-functions and argument-objects against Kerry's misinterpretive naysaying. He continued as follows:

> When I wrote my *Grundlagen der Arithmetik*, I had not yet made the distinction between sense and reference; and so, under the expression "a possible content of judgment," I was combining what I now designate by the distinctive words "thought" and "truth-value." Consequently, I no longer entirely approve of the explanation I then gave, as regards its wording; my view is, however, still essentially the same. We may say in brief, taking "subject" and "predicate" in the linguistic sense: A concept is the reference of a predicate; an object is something that can never be the whole reference of a predicate, but can be the reference of a subject.[55]
>
> Somebody may think that this is an artificially created difficulty; that there is no need at all to take account of such an unmanageable thing as what I call a concept; that one might, like Kerry, regard an object's falling under a concept as a relation, in which the same thing could occur now as object, now as concept. The words "object" and "concept" would then serve only to indicate the different positions in the relation. This may be done; but anybody who thinks the difficulty is avoided this way is very much mistaken; it is only shifted. For not all the parts of a thought can be complete; at least one must be "unsaturated" or predicative; otherwise they would not hold together.[56]

---

[54] *Ibid.*, pp. 46–47.   [55] *Ibid.*, pp. 47–48.   [56] *Ibid.*, p. 54.

Concept-Functions and Frege's Platonism

That Frege with all his sophisticated mathematical training should have gone back to the most basic principles of arithmetic, to the root-bottom foundations of mathematical reasoning, testifies to his philosopher's heart and critical scientific mind. The desire to understand not merely high-end applications but more especially the conceptual foundations of a subject like mathematics epitomizes a distinctively philosophical orientation. Frege added that "'Complete' and 'unsaturated' are of course only figures of speech; but all that I wish or am able to do here is to give hints."[57] Like Plato, Frege believed that he could intuit truths about an abstract order that transcends the world of phenomenal experience; and, like Plato again, he could only use myth, metaphor, analogy, and symbolism to convey his deepest insights about the nature of mathematical truth.

Frege was a Platonist with respect to the existence of propositions, thoughts or *Gedanken*, as the abstract meaning contents of meaningful sentences. He was also Platonist insofar as the existence of the natural counting number 1 properly logically rather than psychologically psychologistically analyzed was concerned. Among arithmetical functions, subdomains of argument-objects are of the right kind for Frege only if arithmetical objects belong to a subdomain that admits such object-arguments as the natural number 1 to the arithmetical successor function $+1(\_\_) = n$, but forcefully keeps Julius Caesar and the Sun $\oplus$ from serving as argument-objects. The arithmetical successor function can only be referentially meaningfully applied to arithmetical argument-objects. Numbers are welcome, Roman generals who cross the river Rubicon and giant burning spheres of hydrogen gas generally less so. Frege concluded the essay on this note of philosophical resignation in trying to understand the matters he has compassed by means of ordinary concepts and in everyday language. He remarked that everyday language is not always suited for topics of fine technical abstraction:

It may make it easier to come to an understanding if the reader compares my work *Funktion und Begriff* [(*Function and Object*), discussed previously in this chapter]. For over the question what it is that is called a function in [mathematical] Analysis [calculus], we come up against the same obstacle; and on thorough investigation it will be found that the obstacle is essential, and founded on the nature of our language;

[57] *Ibid.*, p. 55.

that we cannot avoid a certain inappropriateness of linguistic expression; and that there is nothing for it but to realize this and always take it into account.[58]

What is wanted is a hard and fast relevant criterion-supported distinction in principle between arithmetical and non-arithmetical objects to serve as arguments for Frege's arithmetical functions, taking $+1(\_\_) = n$ as elementary, essential, and exemplary. The trouble Frege appears almost, but not quite, to recognize is that this very distinction cannot be drawn without lapsing into an unsuspected vicious circularity. Frege allowed that some concepts cannot be analyzed, but are rather the basic conceptually primitive or analytically irreducible ideas from which more complex concept-functions are constructed. Any honest effort at philosophical analysis must admit the same. Such concept-functions are like the chemical elements into which chemical compounds can be analyzed, but that cannot themselves be further chemically analyzed, even if they can be further physically reduced.

This all seems correct. We must grant Frege that, if there was to be analysis of meaning, then not everything could be analyzed. There must be something basic into which the complex is analyzed, at which point analysis terminates. The question is what is truly elementary and what is complex. This is where things begin to get interesting. There is a choice between, on the one hand, taking the points in Euclidean geometry as basic, undefinable though characterizable, and defining line segments as the shortest distances between any two points in space, and, on the other, taking lines or line segments as basic, and defining a Euclidean point as the one and only intersection of any two Euclidean lines. It all seems relative, even if not particularly subjective, rather than objective. Frege was too much a realist to consider that a theory can simply suit its author's pique and choose whatever it wants as elementary. He declaimed explicitly against that attitude in the philosophy of mathematics, and said that our choice of distinctions must conform to the objective truth of a mind-independent mathematical reality. Plato in *Phaedrus* 265e similarly gave an abattoir metaphor-comparison of carving nature at the joints.

It was a noble stance, but in the end every theory must build upon what is believed with good reason to be objective truth. It was in this context that the question of what is objective and what is true slides slightly out of center focus where we may have thought it could clearly be seen and

[58] *Ibid.*

definitionally nailed down. If Frege was driven to propose that the concept of the limited range of arithmetical arguments of arithmetical functions was something basic, primitive, and unanalyzable, then his logicism and whatever might be salvaged from his philosophy of mathematics must deal with the implication that numbers, including perhaps exclusively the natural number 1, are basic, primitive, and unanalyzable, logically elemental.

Unswerving Motivations

The snake has its tail in its mouth. That is not so bad. A snake might have its own reasons for closing its body into a loop. The Dane walking the bog pulls himself out of the muck by his own bootstraps. Worse, he seems, unlike the snake, to violate the laws of terrestrial physics. There is a challenge to gravity in the comic illustration only if we insist that the walker make progress by tugging on both boots at once. People get unstuck every day pulling on their own bootstraps, one boot at a time. Although it is admittedly more tiresome than levitating, it has practicality, slow but steady reliability, and conformity with natural law all in its favor.

These metaphors do not begin to describe Frege's theoretical difficulties. Frege seems to have become caught in dependence on what Russell follows Henri Poincaré in calling an *impredicative* definition. The concept defines itself in terms of itself, in terms of the concept to be defined, with apparent circularity (snake) or in a daring act of lifting itself out of the definitional mire altogether (bootstraps). Frege attempted to avoid commitment to necessary and sufficient conditions while satisfying minimal theoretical needs by saying enough true things about the concept to convey an idea of a specifically arithmetical category that neatly includes numbers and leaves the Sun and Julius Caesar unequivocally on the outside. By Frege's own guidelines for admitting concept-functions to the logic, sharp-edged co-extensionality identity conditions must be satisfied from the ground up. The stipulation requires more than merely saying some true things about a concept-function to cognitively fix its sense or reference.

Insofar as Frege's understanding of the concept-function Arithmetical $(\_) = v$ was concerned, pure logicism's project of providing a purely logical analysis of specifically arithmetical truths was in dire straits. The limitations of what Frege was attempting might never have fully dawned, implying that Frege had no logically approved way to single out specifically arithmetical objects or concept-functions. If the choice Frege faced was to distinguish the arithmetical from the non-arithmetical in order to solve the Julius Caesar problem, and if Frege could do so only either by circular definition or concept-functional analysis (snake) or by avoiding necessary and sufficient conditions for the distinction (bootstraps), then the better alternative might be to have allowed $+1$(Julius Caesar) $= 1$ or $+1$(Julius Caesar) $=$ Julius Caesar, rather than attempting in vain to arrive at a non-impredicative way of excluding Julius Caesar from argument-object saturations of arithmetical concept-functions.

Frege may never have been totally convinced, or not until very late in life, if at all, perhaps when he was already in retirement at Bad Kleinen, that rigorous non-psychologistic logicism as he had originally conceived it was not moving forward. Perhaps he allowed himself to consider then that the purely logical reduction of arithmetic to which he had devoted so many years of toil, enduring his reviewers' rebuke and contemporaries' scornful silence, had in fact been virtually a waste of time and energy. The project was fated to fail. Everyone except Frege seemed to have sensed it almost from the beginning. When at last Frege clearly saw the limitations of pure logicism, or thought he could recognize them in the paradox explained by Russell involving the set of those sets that are not members of themselves, he remained stubbornly resolved on a purely logical analysis of the arithmetical for one reason only. He continued to accept as unqualifiedly true the basic logical laws that had supposedly landed him in contradiction.[59]

---

[59] Frege's reaction to Russell's paradox in relation to *Grundgesetze* Axiom V was proportionate to his powerful conviction that the unconditional extensionality principle for the identity conditions of concept-functions must after all be true. He thought that there could be no imaginable alternative, if there were to be properly defined distinct concept-functions. The inability to reconcile his philosophical and methodological scruples with any conditionalization of an extensional identity principle for concept-functions seems to have driven much of Frege's reasoning about the 1902 paradox without resolution to the end of his life. Frege, Foreword, *Grundgesetze I*, p. VII: "As far as I can see, a dispute can arise only concerning my basic law of value-ranges (V), which perhaps has not yet been explicitly formulated by logicians although one thinks in accordance with it if, e.g., one speaks of extensions of concepts." Frege, Afterword, *Grundgesetze II*, p. 253: "I have never concealed from myself that [my basic law (V)] is not as obvious as the others nor as obvious as must properly be required of a logical law. Indeed, I pointed out this very weakness in the foreword to the first volume, p. VII."

8

Sense, Reference, and Psychological Epiphenomena in Frege's Semantics (1892)

F REGE MENTIONED IN a passage quoted near the end of his 1892 reply to Kerry, "On Concept and Object," that at the time of writing his *Grundlagen*, and presumably for some time before, while still at work on the *Begriffsschrift*, he had not distinguished between sense and reference as components of the meaning of proper names and declarative sentences.[1] Frege proposed the distinction and explained its origins and application in the most frequently discussed of his essays dating from 1892, "Über Sinn und Bedeutung" ("On Sense and Reference").[2]

The essay is recognized today as essential reading in contemporary analytic philosophy of language. Its defenders assume it to provide adequate meaning conditions for proper names and predicative sentences. We are taught by Frege to think in terms of two particular main dimensions, or "levels" as he calls them, of sense and reference. A third level, the last Frege distinguishes, is the psychological associations and mental images and other related conscious content that sometimes accompany a subject's grasp of, or facility in expressing and recovering, a name's or sentence's sense. The third level is largely ignored by Frege as belonging to subjective rather than objective factors in a scientific theory of meaning.

A proper name refers to something because the sense of the name points to that individual alone as satisfying its meaning. Sense determines reference, and with that reassuring closure Frege is safe at home. When a proper name has no reference, that fact is also established in part by the name's Fregean sense. The sense of the fictional proper name "Sherlock

---

[1] Frege, "On Concept and Object," pp. 42–43.
[2] Frege, "On Sense and Reference," *Philosophical Writings*, p. 56.

Holmes," perhaps being a detective residing at 221B Baker Street in nineteenth-century London, together with the mind-independent state of the external world determines that the name does not refer to any existent entity. Frege relegates to the third level of meaning the "poetic coloring" of thought and language, the connotations of language use and associated mental images that he sharply disjoins from objective scientific semantics. He does not use the word, but for Frege the third level of meaning is semantically epiphenomenal.

Identity, Sense, and Reference

To introduce and motivate a distinction between sense and reference, Frege in "On Sense and Reference" asked of "equality" "in the sense of identity" "Is it a relation? A relation between objects, or between names or signs of objects?"[3] He justified his own prior conclusion that identity must be a relation holding between names or signs of objects by the following argument:

In my *Begriffsschrift* I assumed the latter. The reasons which seem to favour this are the following: $a = a$ and $a = b$ are obviously statements of differing cognitive value; $a = a$ holds *a priori* and, according to Kant, is to be labeled analytic, while statements of the form $a = b$ often contain very valuable extensions of our knowledge and cannot always be established *a priori*.[4]

At the very end of the essay, returning to the problem of how to understand the truth-value as opposed to cognitive significance of identity statements, Frege succinctly explained how the identity statements $a = a$ and $a = b$ can have the same truth value despite the fact that only the latter noniterative formulation is potentially informative. Saying "Let us now return to our starting point," he invites the reader to accompany him down his previous path of reasoning:

When we found "$a = a$" and "$a = b$" to have different cognitive values, the explanation is that for the purpose of knowledge, the sense of the sentence, viz., the thought expressed by it, is no less relevant than its reference, i.e. its truth value. If now $a = b$,

---

[3] Frege, "On Sense and Reference," p. 56. See also pp. 60–61.

[4] *Ibid.* See Frege, *Begriffsschrift*, §§8 and 20–21. Compare this with §8, p. 15; translated by Bynum in Frege, *Conceptual Notation*, p. 126: "Now, let ⊢ ($A ≡ B$) mean: *the symbol A and the symbol B have the same conceptual content, so that we can always replace A by B and vice versa.*" Note that Frege's *Begriffsschrift* symbol for object identity, "≡," is replaced in the *Grundgesetze* by the conventional identity sign, "=."

then indeed the reference of "*b*" is the same as that of "*a*," and hence the truth value of "*a* = *b*" differs from that of "*a* = *a*." In spite of this, the sense of "*b*" may differ from that of "*a*," and thereby the thought expressed in "*a* = *b*" differs from that of "*a* = *a*." In that case the two sentences do not have the same cognitive value. If we understand by "judgment" the advance from the thought to its truth value, as in the above paper, we can also say that the judgments are different.[5]

Frege in the passage above is committed to understanding identity as a relation of names, rather than things named. Were Frege's analysis of identity statements as expressing a relation of names correct, then we should need to observe an equivalent of the convention for distinguishing between reference to object *a* and reference to the object's name "*a*." Identity expressed as a relation among proper names, as Frege holds, implies that any noniterative identity must be written as the obviously logically false statement "*a*" = "*b*." These are not the same but different proper names. We can only truly sometimes write "____" ≠ "____," when tokens of distinct types complete identity relata places in an iterative nonidentity statement. The possibility is not enough to assist Frege's semantics of potentially cognitive informative noniterative identity statements. The fact that "2" ≠ "1 + 1" does nothing to explain the meaning or truth of the arithmetical and truth-value assignment $2 = 1 + 1$ ($V(+1(1) = 2)$ = the True).

There is a suggestion that, at least in the first 1893 volume of his *Grundgesetze*, and therefore in his relatively mature view of things, Frege adopted an *objectual* or object-relating, rather than *nominal* or names-relating, theory of identity. If so, then the relevance for understanding Frege's seminal essay "On Sense and Reference" would be obvious. It could only be interpreted as a false start in understanding the semantics of identity statements that Frege later abandoned. However, it is more likely that Frege's position in the *Grundgesetze* would have been prefigured one year earlier, in his essay "On Sense and Reference" of 1892, which is known independently not to be the case. Nor is it likely with his *Grundgesetze* still in draft that Frege would have changed his mind about such fundamental matters without leaving any clue in his writings of 1892–1893. Looking ahead to *Grundgesetze I* §7, in order to better interpret Frege's theory of meaning in "On Sense and Reference" or perhaps contrast it with a perspective gained from hindsight, we can note that Frege there wrote

---

[5] Frege, "On Sense and Reference," p. 78.

We have already used the equality-sign rather casually to form examples but it is necessary to stipulate something more precise regarding it.

$$\text{"}\Gamma = \Delta\text{"}$$

refers to the True, if Γ is the same as Δ; in all other cases it is to refer to the False.[6]

These meager comments do not present much evidence with which a conscientious interpreter could set to work. The attribution to Frege of an objectual theory of identity in the passage that commentators have wanted to build upon is nevertheless by no means a foregone conclusion. The purpose of Frege's remarks in *Grundgesetze I* §7 was above all, as he stated clearly, to explicate semantic truth-conditions for identity statements, especially arithmetical equations and functional relations generally, rather than thematize the metaphysics of identity.

The identity statement, "$\Gamma = \Delta$," Frege maintained, denotes the True just in the case that Γ and Δ are the same object, and otherwise denotes the False. As a definition of the identity relation, what Frege said is hardly informative. We are not told what Frege understood by Γ and Δ being or not being "the same" (object), where "identical" and "same," "identity" and "sameness," are evidently synonym pairs. We find ourselves just as much in the dark about what it means for Γ and Δ to be the same as we are about what it means for them to be identical, exchange these equivalent expressions for one another as we may. The highly pertinent and deeply penetrating question Frege posed in the opening paragraphs of "On Sense and Reference" remains unanswered, and hence every bit as relevant to the question of whether *Grundgesetze I* §7 is consistent or inconsistent with the nature of identity in the 1892 essay. If "$\Gamma = \Delta$" denotes the True if and only if Γ and Δ are the same, then we must further inquire what Γ and Δ are. If Γ and Δ are objects, in the plural, so to speak, then no identity statement "$\Gamma = \Delta$" can possibly denote the True. Different objects are never identical, no two things are ever one and the same.[7]

The only alternative from Frege's perspective, which is more thoroughly articulated in "On Sense and Reference," is to explain that Γ and Δ are identical if and only if "Γ" and "Δ" are co-referential distinct names

---

[6] Frege, *Grundgesetze der Arithmetik, begriffsschriftlich abgeleitet*, Band I (Jena: Hermann Pohle, 1893) §7; translated in Frege, *Basic Laws of Arithmetic*, p. 11.

[7] Wittgenstein, *Tractatus Logico-Philosophicus*, 5.5301: "That identity is not a relation between objects is obvious"; and 5.5303: "Roughly speaking: to say of *two* things that they are identical is nonsense, and to say of *one* thing that it is identical with itself is to say nothing."

referring to the same object. This is not a new idea but precisely what Frege maintained in "On Sense and Reference." At best, Frege's brief stipulation concerning the truth-conditions for identity statements in *Grundgesetze I* §7 is equivocal. It does not settle the philosophical question as to whether identity is a relation of or between objects or something else, such as names and other singular referring expressions. There is a parallel sense in which the relata of identity statements in Frege's "On Sense and Reference" are objectual rather than nominal.

The reason is that the proper names "Γ" and "Δ" appearing in a true identity statement "Γ = Δ" must refer to the same existent *object*. The compact mention of identity in Frege's *Grundgesetze I* §7 does not univocally represent an objectual account of the identity relation or identity relata in opposition to Frege's nominal analysis in "On Sense and Reference." There is no sign in the *Grundgesetze*, looking ahead to see whether it sheds light on the interpretation of "On Sense and Reference," that Frege in the space of one year changed his mind drastically on the topic of identity at any stage of his philosophical thinking. Had Frege altered his opinion on such a crucial matter, he would no doubt have signaled his break from previous thinking, as he did later in the Foreword to *Grundgesetze I*, explaining the relatively much less monumental changes he had found it necessary to introduce in the variable system for quantification after the *Begriffsschrift*, in order to adequately represent two-level arithmetical relations, and as he bothered to do even in explaining the trivial replacement of the *Inhaltsstrich* of the *Begriffsschrift* with the *Horizontal* of the *Grundgesetze*.

"On Sense and Reference" detailed a brilliant, lucid, and nuanced analysis. Frege at no point stepped away from his *Begriffsschrift* argument that identity cannot relate objects, so that it must therefore relate names. Frege was undoubtedly right to emphasize an important conceptual connection between identity and reference, although the connection is perhaps rather different than the one he proposed. Frege held that it was necessary to distinguish between the sense and reference of proper names in order to explain the fact that true noniterative identity statements of the form $a = b$, unlike necessarily true iterative identity statements of the form $a = a$ and $b = b$, which are implied definitionally by the reflexivity of identity, are potentially cognitively informative. We can learn from them and communicate something nontrivial by their means. To better understand Frege's philosophical attitude toward identity relations and statements, it is important to examine Frege's position critically within the framework of his sense–reference semantics. These primary objections are considered in order to better understand the meaning, strengths, and weaknesses of Frege's distinction by setting it against a systematic critique. The following conclusions are explained and defended.

(1) Frege's diagnosis of the cognitive import of nontrivial noniterative identity statements is incorrect. It goes beyond objective sense to involve only psychological opinion about the sense and reference of a proper name or proposition.

(2) The faulty analysis of the cognitive import potential of noniterative identity statements is replaceable by proper application of Frege's characterization of the distinction between a proper name's sense and reference. The relatum of a true identity statement, trivial or otherwise, is always an individual existent entity related by the identity relation reflexively to itself, always, only, and necessarily exclusively in every instance, rather than holding nominally, as Frege consistently maintained in 1892–1893, as a relation between different co-referential names for the same object.

(3) The further suggestion is that true nontrivial noniterative identity statements are merely expressed by means of different Fregean co-referential proper names for an identity relation that always relates an object in potentially informative ways reflexively to itself.

(4) Additionally, and potentially more controversially, contrary to Frege's expectations, proper names involved in true nontrivial noniterative identity statements relating an object to itself have not only the same reference-meaning but for the same reason also precisely the same Fregean sense-meaning. This conclusion requires detailed explanation and argument.

(5) The convergence of identical total Fregean sense-meaning in the case of co-referential proper names in noniterative identity statements does not preclude cognitive informativeness for any language using thinkers previously unaware that the proper names involved in the nontrivial noniterative expression of an identity self-relation are precisely the same in both sense and reference.

(6) An argument establishes the connection between identity and reference whereby no existent entity can intelligibly be named or otherwise referred to in the absence in principle of minimally adequate self-identity conditions. The proposed explanation implies that non-satisfaction of identity conditions disqualifies a putative subject of naming on account of its being nothing stable capable of being individually named in the first place.

(7) Finally, if these objections are correct, then Frege's division of the sense and reference of proper names and declarative sentences must be given a different motivation than the one Frege provided. His effort to justify the sense–reference distinction in a two-dimensional semantics of the sense and reference meanings of proper names and propositions does not exclude other less problematic ways of

understanding the potential cognitive informativeness of true nontrivial non-iterative identity statements.

When these successive phases of critical reflection on Frege's "On Sense and Reference" distinction between *Sinn* and *Bedeutung* are completed, an unobstructed view of the meaning and correctness or otherwise of Frege's most frequently discussed theory of designative content and reference is attained. The principles are vital to the explanation of meaning in Fregean philosophy of language, but they are not always properly explained, and Frege's argument in support of his two-dimensional semantics is inconclusive. There is much of philosophical value to be explored among the consequences of a modified Fregean sense–reference distinction that makes all identity self-identity. The analysis distinguishes between iterative cognitively uninformative and noniterative potentially cognitively informative identity statements as alternative linguistic expressions of the one and only self-identity relation holding reflexively between every existent entity and itself. If the Fregean senses of co-referential proper names and declarative senses converge, cognitive informativeness is explained as differential knowledge of the identical Fregean sense-meaning and reference of the relevant terms, names, or sentences.

The Meaning of Arithmetical Equations

Ultimately, Frege needed a theory of meaning that would be useful specifically in explicating two dimensions of identity predications. A word of clarification is in order. Frege's *Begriffsschrift* logical notation is also called (syntactically) two-dimensional in another graphic ideographic or spatial sense. His conditional formulas are not linear, but, more extensively than normal mathematical linear text, they occupy both dimensions of the space in which they are inscribed. That is Frege's spatially two-dimensional logical symbolism.

Frege's sense–reference analysis of two of the three dimensions of the meanings of proper names and propositions is also said to be (semantically) two-dimensional. Here the dimensions in question are not literally spatial, as in Frege's two-dimensional *Begriffsschrift* syntax, but involve two different semantic aspects of what Frege considered to be the complete objective meaning of a proper name broadly construed or proposition. The subjective phenomenological "third level" of connotation and associated subjective associations in passing moments of thoughts about objects named and predications affirmed are simply ignored by Frege as irrelevant to an objective scientific theory of meaning. He did not say that individual ephemeral consciousness does not exist, but rejected psychology in that personal empirical sense as inappropriate in objective scientific theoretical semantics. Frege's theory of meaning had to be adequate to explain the truth of identity statements in the full explication of any predication, for that was its purpose. The predications whose two-dimensional semantics Frege was especially eager to explain as informatively true were identity statements in arithmetical equations. These he construed on a model of function(argument) = some value or equally concept(object) = some value. The output value-objects that interested Frege are primarily numbers and the truth-values of equations in elementary arithmetical theorems. For Frege to be satisfied, the theory had to explain the truth and potential informativeness of such arithmetical equations as $1 + 1 = 2$, $+1(1) = 2$. It must be possible for identity statements in arithmetical equations in particular to be both true and potentially cognitively informative for Frege's pure logicism. They must be capable of expressing logically–mathematically discoverable truths about a Platonic order of real arithmetical entities and their objectively true predications of properties. The two-dimensional meaning of true potentially cognitively informative arithmetical equations is a priority for Frege's logicism.

   The two remaining semantic dimensions for names and sentences in Frege's theory of meaning are the axial values sense and reference, *Sinn* and *Bedeutung*. Frege develops a semantics of reference for proper names designating existent entities, truth-values and truth-conditions, and the cognitive values dependent on differences in sense. The latter are potentially informative in noniterative identity statements of the form $a = b$, and not for iterative identities of the reflexive form $a = a$. Noniterative identity statements are true if the proper names they contain refer to the same existent entity. They can nevertheless be different in epistemic value if they involve co-referential proper names with diverse Fregean senses. Frege believed that the distinction explained the use of the identity sign and invocation of an identity relation as holding in relevant instances with both semantic (reference to the True) and Fregean sense-related epistemic (potential cognitive informativeness) dimensions, wherever he needed noniterative identity statements to fulfill both roles. Frege's spatial two-dimensional graphic syntax in the *Begriffsschrift* $\neq$ Frege's two-dimensional semantic theory of meaning. Epistemic features of co-referential proper names with distinct Fregean senses became an essential element of Frege's overture to the future of analytic philosophy of language. The semantics, like Frege's logic, was perfectly general, if not universal, but was intended all along to provide a sense–reference semantics and truth-conditions for identity statements in arithmetical equations.

Frege's pure logicist philosophy of mathematics analyzed arithmetical basic laws and theorems as concepts and inferences of pure logic. Whether a syntax string has at least one semantic dimension of sense and reference distinguishes nonsense from meaningful thought and its expression. Sense is minimal, reference optional. Frege requires values for both semantic dimensions in fully or completely meaningful proper names and declarative sentences. What, then, is the sense of a word or sentence? What is its reference? How are these different and how are they related?

Frege held that a sentence, when it expresses or fails to express an existent state of affairs, refers respectively to the True or to the False. These are the only referential values of predications, and therefore of iterative or noniterative identity statements in particular, in the arithmetical applications that most interest Frege. Iterative identity statements necessarily refer to the True, as a consequence of the universal reflexivity of identity. Reference is entirely a matter of naming, whatever that is. Proper names refer to existent entities, and sentences refer to the True or the False. Fregean sense is more complex, both in the case of proper names and in that of declarative sentences. The Fregean sense-meaning of a proper name is a set of sufficiently distinguishing properties of the thing named. The Fregean sense-meaning of the proper name "Aristotle," with qualifications pending, could be considered the property of being the student of Plato and teacher of Alexander the Great. The only existent entity with exactly those properties should then be the referent of the proper name "Aristotle," which is naturally to say Aristotle himself, the once-living ancient Greek philosopher of whom those sense-meaning properties are true.

Fregean sentential sense-meaning is semantically compositional. The Fregean sense of a sentence is a function of the several meanings of the sentence's component names and of the identity conditions of its concept-functors. Proper names can refer only to existent entities, and concept-functors must satisfy co-extensionality identity conditions.

Frege relied on the category of co-extensionality in offering what in his *Grundlagen* he professed to be a purely logical analysis of the concept-function of natural number. Equinumerosity, by which the concept-function of natural number was defined by Frege, is the co-extensionality of the cardinalities of the extensions of all and only those predicates, which is to say all and only those concept-functors, belonging to the analysis of a natural number *analysandum*. Once the co-extensionality analysis has got started, it largely steers itself, especially through the natural numbers. The general concept-function of natural number is satisfied by any one–one correlated predicate extension memberships. Frege in the *Grundlagen* began with the cardinality of the extension of the predicate "non-self-identical," which, extension standing empty, he reasonably associates with the natural number zero, 0. The extension of the concept-function predicate "0" or "= 0," on the other hand, is not empty, but contains exactly one denizen, the one and only existent natural number 0. It is provable thereafter in Frege's arithmetic that $\exists x[x = 0 \land \forall y[y = 0 \leftrightarrow x = y]]$, $\exists x[x = 1 \land \forall y [y = 1 \leftrightarrow x = y]]$, and so on. The march of natural numbers is more conveniently expressed by the successor function applied to 0 once the concept of 0 has been defined and its existence established, as ... $S(S(S(0))) \ldots = \{0, 1, 2, 3, \ldots\}$ or simply as the set of natural real numbers.

The point is not to revisit the blueprint of the *Grundlagen*, but to appreciate the extent to which Frege depended on a satisfactory theory of sentence meaning generally, and in particular of functional identity statements and arithmetical equations. Equations are everywhere in arithmetic. Frege had no option but to explain their meaning. Without this background in mind, it is hard to understand and appreciate the argument of Frege's 1892 essay "On Sense and Reference." We may be tempted to think of Frege's excursion into semantics and the philosophy of language in this and related writings of the time as a sideline hobby interest, remotely suggested by his work in the philosophy of mathematics, perhaps, but reflecting another side of his philosophical pursuits. The truth is instead that Frege was driven to a two-dimensional sense–reference semantics of predications, a distinction he confided to several contemporaries he had not originally considered, in order to explain the meaning, truth, and informativeness of the identity statements which are abundant in logic and arithmetic.

Fregean sense supports cognitive informativeness or uninformativeness as epistemic values that are pendant on the sense-meanings of iterative or noniterative identity statements. Fregean sense touches the state of the world by playing its part in determining a referentially meaningful proposition's reference to the True or to the False. It prescribes truth-conditions for meaningful sentences in a mostly mind-independent world of truth-makers and truth-breakers. A referentially meaningful sentence's reference to the True rather than the False or the reverse is determined by the correspondence or non-correspondence of a sentence's composite sense-meaning with the extant state of the world that the sentence describes, as one among the existent facts, here the predication of a property to an existent entity, by which the world is constituted. Truth and the True constitute another duo partnership of meaning and metaphysics, of applied semantics and applied ontology blended insensibly into the formal and natural sciences. Along with the hypothesis model that pervaded Frege's work within and surrounding his writings, the nature of truth in a Fregean framework marks not only the dependence of philosophy on science, but also their fusion at exactly this juncture in Frege's thought where his theory of meaning was put to work.

Objectivity in Frege's Theory of Meaning

The general structure of Frege's philosophical semantics and the sense–reference distinction is frequently discussed. Against this understanding, Frege's theory can be tested by introducing an interesting complication. The idea is to depart from mainstream interpretations of Frege's distinction between sense and reference, and even in a way from Frege's own explicit application of the distinction, by defending a thesis concerning the objectivity of sense. It is an interpretation that appears to be necessitated by Frege's determination to avoid psychologism in a scientific theory of meaning.

Frege defined a proper name as any singular referring expression, including definite descriptions:

It is clear from the context that by "sign" and "name" I have here understood any designation representing a proper name, which thus has as its reference a definite object (this word taken in the widest range), but not a concept or a relation, which shall be discussed further in another article. The designation of a single object can also consist of several words or other signs. For brevity, let every such designation be called a proper name.[8]

He distinguished between the *customary* and *indirect reference* of proper names and sentences analyzed compositionally as a function of proper names and concept terms. He characterizes the indirect reference of a proper name or sentence as its meaning in an *oratio obliqua* context, which Frege identifies with the name's or sentence's customary sense. The customary reference of a proper name is the existent entity it names:

> In *indirect* speech, words are used *indirectly* or have their *indirect* reference. We distinguish accordingly the *customary* from the *indirect* reference of a word; and its *customary* sense from its *indirect* sense. The indirect reference of a word is accordingly its customary sense. Such exceptions must always be borne in mind if the mode of connexion between sign, sense, and reference in particular cases is to be correctly understood.[9]

What Frege means by the customary sense of a proper name is the set of properties possessed by the object designated by the name that are customarily associated with the object by contributing to the object's satisfaction of Leibnizian identity conditions. Frege does not have much to say about the concept of sense (*Sinn*), reserving most of his discussion for the complementary category of reference (*Bedeutung*). Fregean sense takes care of itself once naming has been explained, so more detail is not needed concerning sense. Naming, by contrast, is reference in its

---

[8] Frege, "On Sense and Reference," p. 57. See *inter alia* G. P. Baker and P. M. S. Hacker, *Frege: Logical Excavations* (Oxford: Basil Blackwell, 1984), pp. 63–76, 88, 200–202, and 280; Christian Thiel, *Sense and Reference in Frege's Logic* (Dordrecht: D. Reidel Publishing Company, 1968), pp. 118–41; Dummett, *The Interpretation of Frege's Philosophy* (Cambridge: Harvard University Press, 1981), pp. 323–42; Carl, *Frege's Theory of Sense and Reference*, pp. 96–99; Martin Hahn, "The Frege Puzzle One More Time," in *Frege: Sense and Reference One Hundred Years Later*, ed. John Biro and Petr Kotatko (Dordrecht: Kluwer Academic Publishers, 1995), pp. 169–83; Nathan Salmon, *Frege's Puzzle* (Atascadero: Ridgeview Publishing Company, 1986); and Klement, *Frege and the Logic of Sense and Reference*, pp. 8–19 and 32–37. Valuable discussions are offered by Richard G. Heck and Robert May, "Frege's Contribution to Philosophy of Language," in *The Oxford Handbook of Philosophy of Language* (Oxford: Oxford University Press, 2008), pp. 3–39; and Dummett, *The Interpretation of Frege's Philosophy*, pp. 36–55.

[9] Frege, "On Sense and Reference," p. 59. Also p. 58: "If words are used in the ordinary way, what one intends to speak of is their reference. It can also happen, however, that one wishes to talk about the words themselves or their senses. This happens, for instance, when the words of another are quoted. One's own words then first designate the words of the other speaker, and only the latter have their usual reference. We then have signs of signs."

simplest form, crucial to meaning arguably throughout any semantics. It is where Frege focuses the analysis of meaning in "On Sense and Reference." He implies, although he does not explicitly state, and in fact appears in some places to deny, that, while there can be subjective differences of opinion about the sense of a proper name, a name's sense as something objective belonging properly to the scope of a scientific semantics includes not merely some outstanding but all and only an object's numerically distinguishing properties.

Exact reference requires in principle nothing less than numerical identification of specific individual referents. Post-Fregean logicians must ask whether the intensionally most fine-grained identity conditions implied by reference to specific individual existent entities need not also be extended from the actual world we inhabit to any logically possible world. If we can meaningfully speak of such things, refer to and make true or false predications of properties to them, then generally adequate identity conditions needed for reference as applied narrowly from a modal perspective to the actual world will need to be even more fine-grained. To conflate a proper name's or proposition's sense with differences of opinion about its sense would be to allow what for Frege is a philosophically objectionable psychologism to intrude into the domain of a scientifically respectable theory of meaning. In an important footnote to "On Sense and Reference," virtually the only place where Frege had anything of substance to say about what was supposed to be the first semantic dimension of sense, he wrote the following:

In the case of an actual proper name such as "Aristotle" opinions as to the sense may differ. It might, for instance, be taken to be the following: the pupil of Plato and teacher of Alexander the Great. Anybody who does this will attach another sense to the sentence "Aristotle was born in Stagira" than will a man who takes as the sense of the name: the teacher of Alexander the Great who was born in Stagira. So long as reference remains the same, such variations of sense may be tolerated, although they are to be avoided in the theoretical structure of a demonstrative science and ought not to occur in a perfect language.[10]

There are at least two ways of understanding Frege's semantic dimension of sense-meaning, applied to proper names in the ordinary sense as opposed to definite descriptions. These can be referred to as

[10] *Ibid.*, p. 58 note *. See Roger White, "Wittgenstein on Identity," *Proceedings of the Aristotelian Society*, New Series, 78 (1977–1978), p. 163: "... by and large the fragmentary hints we find in Frege do not so much point in the direction of a coherent and sustained

"mainstream" and "objectivity of sense" readings. Roughly, the mainstream reading, which agrees in all points with the application Frege wanted to be able to make on the basis of the sense–reference distinction, is that proper names in the ordinary sense, like "Hesperus" and "Phosphorus," along with definite descriptions like "The first bright heavenly body seen in the evening" and "The last bright heavenly body seen in the morning," can have the same reference in a true identity statement, although different names should generally be expected at least potentially to have different Fregean senses. The mainstream interpretation implies in Frege's application that Reference("The Morning Star") = Reference("The Evening Star"), but Sense("The Morning Star") ≠ Sense("The Evening Star").

The mainstream interpretation of Frege's sense–reference distinction agrees perfectly with what Frege said in important passages of "On Sense and Reference." Unfortunately, the mainstream interpretation does not agree even imperfectly with what Frege said in other parts of the essay, where he speaks of *the* sense of a proper name, presumably as opposed to the variable subjective opinions concerning the name's sense briefly discussed in the second footnote, as the relevant object's complete set of all and only its numerically distinguishing properties. Moreover, there are good reasons independent of Frege's arguments for considering the Fregean sense of a proper name or proposition as objective rather than dependent on what particular subjects may or may not know or believe themselves to know about the referents of proper names included in their speech acts.

The objectivity of sense reading denies that proper names in the ordinary sense can have the same reference if they have different sense. Contrary to the mainstream interpretation, it maintains that, for any proper names n_1 and n_2, Sense("n_1") = Sense("n_2") if and only if Reference("n_1") = Reference("n_2"). To say noniteratively and therefore potentially informatively that the tallest Norwegian = the smartest Scandinavian, if true, is to refer to the same individual under two different descriptions that are commonly supposed to have very different

reflection on the notion of sense, as much as suggesting that Frege, having established the existence of senses in order to overcome the problems in a theory of meaning he would otherwise be unable to resolve, was content to allude to sense so as to put it to one side for the sake of his main concerns which as far as his reflections on meaning were concerned were almost all bound up with his other notion, the notion of reference."

Fregean senses. Asserting that Ågot = Anniken in comparison, especially for non-Scandinavian speakers, does not necessarily force any
semantic wedge between the Fregean senses of the two proper names.
To do so would be to allow Frege's third level of meaning, the subjective psychological aspects of thought and its connotative expressions
in language that are supposed to be irrelevant to scientific semantics, to
encroach into explanations of the objective non-psychologistic meaning
of linguistic expressions, including identity statements in arithmetical
equations.

Frege encouraged what has become the mainstream reading by
which proper names with the same reference can or even must have
different sense. This, as a matter of fact, seems to be the heart and
soul of Frege's solution to the problem posed at the outset in "On
Sense and Reference." The potential cognitive informativeness of
apparently nontrivial noniterative identity statements of the form a
$= b$ is explained as a difference in the sense-meanings of proper names
"a" and "b." Frege claimed that the truth of the cognitively informative identity "The Evening Star = The Morning Star" is accounted
for by these two proper names (partial definite descriptions) "The
Evening Star" and "The Morning Star" referring to the same heavenly body (Venus). The cognitive informativeness of the identity
statement is supposed to be explained by the two terms having
different senses. Frege also said in the above quotation that definite
descriptions are to be included without further ado as singular referring expressions in the class of proper names. It has therefore seemed
natural and even inevitable for generations of commentators to suppose that for Frege it must also be the case that the truth of "Hesperus =
Phosphorus" is likewise to be explained by virtue of these two proper
names referring to the same object in outer space, while the informativeness of the identity is explained by the two terms having different
senses.

How exactly this legerdemain is supposed to work is left largely
mysterious. It is one of the distinctions that readers must pretend to
understand in order to pretend to fully grasp Frege's argument in the
essay. It is this latter extrapolation of Frege's sense–reference analysis of
objective meaning that appears insupportable, as even Frege in a moment
of clear reflection seemed to agree, given the otherwise superficially
reasonable requirements of his semantic program.

Sense Determines Reference

It is true that Frege said something like the claim that proper names can have the same reference but different sense. It appears on critical examination that either he was wrong in doing so, being thereby in conflict with things he maintained elsewhere, or he was making a subtler point that has understandably been blurred by the vast majority of critics, even those most sympathetic to his philosophy. The problem has to do with Frege's *compositional* account of the sense especially of definite descriptions, and his subsumption of definite descriptions within the general category of proper names. Proper names in the ordinary sense are semantically indistinguishable from definite descriptions in that both are singular referring expressions. Frege was satisfied to lump them both together in one grammatical category as proper names in his technical sense, allowing proper names to subsume definite descriptions.

There remains an important difference between proper names in the ordinary sense and definite descriptions on Frege's semantic theory. The distinction might have inclined him to distinguish, as Russell later did, between the meaning conditions for the sense of proper names and those for the sense of definite descriptions.[11] Whereas the sense of definite descriptions is always compositional, even in the limiting most elementary case, being a function of the component senses of the terms by which they are composed in the description, the sense of a proper name in the ordinary sense is not always compositional. It is generally conventional, and is compositional only derivatively if at all. Thus, the descriptive proper name "The Evening Star" appears superficially to possess a different sense than "The Morning Star," despite their identity of reference. The first description refers to the evening, whereas the latter does not. The second description refers to the morning, whereas the former does not. In the case of "Hesperus" and "Phosphorus," the situation is different. Neither of these proper names in the ordinary sense is composed of any other relatively more atomic referring expressions with potentially different sense.

---

[11] Russell, "On Denoting." Russell, beginning in 1905, departed significantly from Frege in understanding the meaning of proper names in several respects. He distanced himself in the end from the concept of a Fregean *Sinn* in understanding the meaning of a logically proper name. See Pelletier and Linsky, "Russell vs. Frege."

The two non-descriptive names are more purely referring. They are referential in meaning without possessing an obviously associated Fregean sense. We might as well call the planet *a* and *b*, and try to ask with no further information whether the sense of "*a*" ≠ the sense of "*b*." Nor does it help to know that Hesperus = the Evening Star and Phosphorus = the Morning Star, if that is how it goes, if there is nothing in another language that encodes these meanings in the names "Hesperus" and "Phosphorus." It is on just such examples that philosophers like Mill rely in arguing that proper names in the ordinary sense have no essential semantic content other than reference, no connotation, and hence no meaning beyond their respective referential value or purely denotative labeling of things.[12]

Frege did not try to go this far. He wanted only to distance himself from including meaning factors in the third level of associated mental content. He did not deny their existence. That is important. He nevertheless found no place for transitory ideas in objective non-psychologistic semantics. He concluded that an associated mental image, connotation, and "poetic" but nonetheless real "coloring" may sometimes accompany a thought's reference to an intended object by means of a word's or sentence's sense, what the symbol is being used to express and the thinker trying to say. However, Frege did not believe that these accidental subjectively variable associations occur in any lawlike way. More significantly, Frege built sense into the account where Mill would have none in his purely referential semantics. Mill was impressed with such examples as the proper name "Dartmouth." He famously remarked that the name might continue to refer to a city that had once been at the opening of the river Dart, even if the river were to shift its banks and no longer take its

---

[12] Mill, *A System of Logic*, Volume VII, Book I, Chapter II, §5, p. 33: "Proper names are not connotative: they denote the individuals who are called by them; but they do not indicate or imply any attributes as belonging to those individuals. When we name a child by the name of Paul, or a dog by the name Caesar, these names are simply marks used to enable those individuals to be made the subjects of discourse. It may be said, indeed, that we must have had some reason for giving them those names rather than any others; and this is true; but the name, once given, is independent of the reason. A man may have been named John, because that was the name of his father; a town may have been named Dartmouth, because it is situated at the mouth of the Dart. But it is no part of the signification of the word John, that the father of the person so called bore the same name; nor even of the word Dartmouth, to be situated at the mouth of the Dart. If sand should choke up the mouth of the river, or an earthquake change its course, and remove it to a distance from the town, the name of the town would not necessarily be changed ... Proper names are attached to the objects themselves, and are not dependent on the continuance of any attribute of the object."

origin anywhere geographically near what might through tradition continue stubbornly to be called the city of Dartmouth.

Name users, regrettably for Mill's purely referential theory of meaning, are not so easily defeated in attaching sense to a proper name if they
so choose. They can do so without much ingenuity even under Mill's
thought-experiment guidelines. After the river's drastic meander, the
name can still be said to mean in more recent times, as it did originally,
the city *founded* at the mouth of the river Dart. If that were taken as the
past-tense sense of the proper name "Dartmouth" – and why should it
not be? – then its meaning would remain unchanged, no matter what
topographic course the river happened to chart for itself over time. Frege
found Mill's purely referential semantics unsatisfying because it offered
no explanation of a proper name's reference. To say that a name refers to
whatever object the name has as its reference is no explanation. The dull
implication then is that a proper name refers to its referent. Frege, by
distinguishing between a name's sense and reference, can explain the
name's reference to a specific object as the object to which the properties
included in the name's Fregean sense uniquely apply. How is this done?
What is needed in a name's or proposition's Fregean sense in order to
determine its reference? It is precisely at this juncture that mainstream
and objective interpretations of Frege's sense–reference distinction
collide.

If the sense of the proper name "Aristotle" is to be the student of Plato
and teacher of Alexander the Great, to have exactly those properties in
Frege's illustration, then on the usual historical assumptions the one and
only object that possesses the properties of being both the student of
Plato and the teacher of Alexander the Great, that existent entity from
Stagira in Macedon, raised in the court of Philip II where his father was
physician to the king, student at Plato's Academy outside of Athens for
twenty years, author of the *Nicomachean Ethics*, that person, that entity, is
referred to by the proper name "Aristotle." We ignore the fact, as Frege
does, that "Aristotle" in Greek means literally "the superior one," as
much as "Dartmouth" means "mouth of the river Dart." Otherwise,
Frege believed, there can be no account of how the name "Aristotle," that
exact choice and arrangement of letters from the alphabet, could possibly
refer to a particular ancient Greek philosopher. Mill, pressed on the same
question, could only say that "Aristotle" refers to Aristotle, without being
able to say anything substantive whatsoever as to how that named object

is referentially singled out from all other potential referents by the utterance or inscription of his purely designative proper name. It is a mapping of names onto named entities, although it should be argued that mappings by themselves outside of cardinality determinations are never explanatory.

If we allow that for Frege the cognitive content of the true nontrivial noniterative identity statement "Hesperus = Phosphorus," expressed in terms of ordinary proper names, like that of the true nontrivial noniterative identity statement "the Evening Star = the Morning Star," is to be explained by virtue of the two proper names having different sense, then we saddle Frege with an avoidable inconsistency in his lifelong struggle against psychologism in logic and theory of meaning. We conclude then not only that what Frege referred to in his revealing footnote was two thinkers or language users having different subjective opinions about the sense of an ordinary non-compositional proper name like "Aristotle," but also that their difference of opinion amounts to a difference in the objective sense of the name. Frege thereby became unduly burdened with a thesis he was at great pains throughout his philosophical writings to avoid. He staunchly rejected the psychologistic proposal that the proper name "Aristotle" could have one *sense* subjectively for one person and another sense subjectively for another person. He would allow nothing of the sort into the objective meaning conditions investigated by a scientific semantics.

The problem does not arise for compositional definite descriptions in the same way as it does for singular referring expressions. Frege somewhat unfortunately clustered these definite descriptions together in the same general category of proper names, since he thought that both alike had an objective basis for distinguishing their senses whenever their component proper names themselves had different objective senses or their component concept-functors satisfied different identity conditions. The Evening Star = The Morning Star = Phosphorus = Hesperus = Venus, etc., yet the sense of "The Evening Star" is supposed to be ≠ the sense of "The Morning Star," and somehow the sense of "Hesperus" is also supposed to be ≠ the sense of "Phosphorus." There are two different words in each pairing, all with the same reference. It looked to Frege as though they need not have the same sense. It was hoped thereby to create enough wiggle room for nontrivial noniterative identity statements in their two meaning dimensions to be both true and cognitively informative. One problem is that it is not clear whether the proper names "Hesperus" and "Phosphorus" have any Fregean sense at all, unless it is externally provided, as when the transcription whereby Hesperus = The Evening Star and Phosphorus = The Morning Star is offered. If we try to say that the sense of "Hesperus" ≠ the sense of "Phosphorus" on the strength of this descriptive identification, then we are making the reference of "Hesperus" into the sense of the proper name, as likewise in the case of the reference of "Phosphorus." The further problem then is that any ostensible difference in the senses of the proper names "Hesperus" and "Phosphorus" is based on extrinsically supplied information with no foundation in any apparent intrinsic difference among the supposedly distinct senses of the names. Consider that if the sense of "Hesperus" is = being The Evening Star, and if The Evening Star as a matter of astronomical fact = The Morning Star, then by transitivity of identity it follows that the sense of "Hesperus" is also = being The Morning Star. The sense of "Phosphorus" was nevertheless supposed to be = being The Morning Star, and the sense of "Hesperus" was supposed to be ≠ the sense of "Phosphorus." Frege's semantics of sense and reference is burdened with an inconsistency it cannot tolerate.

If the sense of a proper name determines and explains its reference, as Frege insisted, then we must ask after the implications of two proper names with different senses having the same reference. The tallest Norwegian might be identical = to the smartest Scandinavian, but the sense of "the tallest Norwegian" is supposedly ≠ the sense of "the smartest Scandinavian." We imagine lining up all the Norwegians, identifying the tallest one, then comparing the intellects of all Scandinavians, and identifying the smartest individual from that part of the world. The individual then turns out, once the sorting has been done, to be the same individual as the tallest Norwegian. With a standardized criterion of comparative smartness the cataloging could be undertaken with just the results the thought-experiment considers. The uniquely identifying properties of being tallest Norwegian and smartest Scandinavian have nothing obviously to do with each other.

The senses of the two descriptions look to be distinct. The reference of the definite description in the two predications is identical, where it happens that the tallest Norwegian is also the smartest Scandinavian. The distinction is complicated by the fact that the properties in question are not as limited as they may at first appear. To be Norwegian is to be Scandinavian, a human being, primate, mammal, vertebrate, renate, chordate, animal, living thing, existent entity, and many other things besides that are not mentioned in the definite description "the tallest Norwegian." How is it known in advance that the property of being the smartest Scandinavian is not also included? If to be the tallest Norwegian is to be identical to the person who is also the smartest Scandinavian, because materially it happens that something is the tallest Norwegian if and only if that thing is the smartest Scandinavian, then being the tallest Norwegian materially implies not only being a Scandinavian but also being the smartest Scandinavian. The necessary transitivity of identity in these instances cannot be overridden by Frege's doctrine assigning distinct sense to syntactically distinct co-referential proper names and declarative sentences.

Frege would not have had us suppose that we establish a difference in the senses of two co-referential ordinary proper names simply by virtue of the fact that different thinkers and speakers can be differently informed or have different opinions concerning their senses. To do so would be to embrace a pernicious semantic psychologism of precisely the sort that Frege was everywhere concerned to eliminate from the scientific theory of meaning, that he had to exclude without argument as a violation of a methodological principle in order to distinguish things from their ideas. Frege admitted in the revealing third-page footnote * on the sense of the proper name "Aristotle" in "On Sense and Reference" that we can have different opinions about the sense of a name. Making that common-sense allowance is nevertheless a far cry from asserting that the name itself actually has different senses for any and every misinformed or under-informed thinker or speaker of the name who comes along. If for Frege the same sense-non-compositional ordinary proper name "Aristotle" cannot have different senses for different speakers in an objective scientific semantics, in addition to their being entitled to entertain different opinions about the total sense of the word, then the same must be true when several co-referential sense-non-compositional ordinary proper names are connected together in a true nontrivial noniterative identity statement, such as "Hesperus = Phosphorus," or semantically even more thinly in a logic's basic syntax for the constant-term expression $a = b$.

The Complete Fregean Sense of a Name

Where good Fregeans cannot allow different senses belonging to the same ordinary co-referential proper names in a nontrivial noniterative identity statement, the only reasonable alternative seems to be that the sense of proper names must include all and only the properties actually belonging to the entity referred to by the name. That is to say that the sense-non-compositional Fregean sense of the ordinary proper name "Aristotle" must include the set of all and only the characterizing properties possessed by Aristotle.

The only other possibility is to pick and choose a proper subset from an object's complete individuating constitutive property set. But on what basis can that be done, and with what justification in such different cases among all the things that can be named? Selections can obviously be made. Every existent entity has an unmanageably large complement of defining properties, which finite minds can deal with only partially and symbolically. What are the consequences if we adopt the subset of total properties route in interpreting the semantics of *Sinn*? The approach, for all its initial appeal, lacks not only philosophical foundation but also methodological guidance, if in any instance we cannot objectively justify one choice of characterizing properties over another. The fact that a complete list of a designated object's properties as an abstract entity taken as a proper name's total objective sense is beyond cognitive reach fits appropriately with Frege's largely Platonistic outlook toward the extra-experiential referents of mathematical terms and expressions. It provides identity conditions for existent entities under all logically possible circumstances in which reference to them might be made.

The objective meanings of propositions define something like the category of Bernard Bolzano's *Sätze an sich*, expressed as functions of meaningful predicative sentences. Frege from the beginning spoke of such predications as "thoughts" or *Gedanken*, which he later thematized as in his (1918) essay with that title, "Der Gedanke."[13] Of the

---

[13] Frege, "Thoughts" ["Der Gedanke" 1918] in *Logical Investigations*, ed. Geach (Oxford: Basil Blackwell, 1977), pp. 1–30. Compare with Bernard Bolzano, *Theory of Science* [*Wissenschaftslehre. Versuch einer ausführlichen und größtentheils neuen Darstellung der Logik mit steter Rücksicht auf deren bisherige bearbeiter*, 1837] (Oxford: Oxford University Press, 2014), especially Volume One, Part I, §19, pp. 58–61; and C. S. Peirce, *Collected Papers of Charles Sanders Peirce*, ed. Charles Hartshorne, Paul Weiss, and Arthur W. Burks (Cambridge: Harvard University Press, 1931–1935), Volume 5, pp. 411–36.

unsurveyably large set of properties constituting the sense of a proper name for any existent entity, Frege rightly remarked "Comprehensive knowledge of the reference [of a proper name such as "Aristotle"] would require us to be able to say immediately whether any given sense belongs to it. To such knowledge we never attain."[14]

Nothing short of the complete set of all of Aristotle's distinguishing, identifying, and individuating properties will do in constituting the complete sense of the proper name "Aristotle," *if*, as Frege believed, the sense of a name was supposed to determine its *exact* reference. Frege concluded that, despite the many beliefs and opinions there might be about the sense of a proper name, there was a unified sense of a proper name. It was *the* sense of the name, its total sense or total list of distinguishing properties:

> In the light of this, one need have no scruples in speaking simply of *the* sense, whereas in the case of an idea one must, strictly speaking, add to whom it belongs and at what time. It might perhaps be said: Just as one man connects this idea, and another that idea, with the same word, so also one man can associate this sense and another that sense. But there still remains a difference in the mode of connexion. They are not prevented from grasping the same sense; but they cannot have the same idea. *Si duo idem faciunt, non est idem.* If two persons picture the same thing, each still has his own idea. It is indeed sometimes possible to establish differences in the ideas, or even in the sensations, of different men; but an exact comparison is not possible, because we cannot have both ideas together in the same consciousness.[15]

Mixed identity statements involving definite descriptions with proper names in the ordinary sense, or, more generally, sense-compositional and sense-non-compositional singular referring expressions, such as "The Evening Star = Hesperus" or "The Morning Star = Phosphorus," can also be said to involve different Fregean senses, unlike identity statements connecting only purely referential non-compositional singular referring expressions.

[14] Frege, "On Sense and Reference," p. 58.
[15] Frege, "On Concept and Object," p. 60. See p. 57: "Let *a, b, c* be the lines connecting the vertices of a triangle with the midpoints of the opposite sides. The point of intersection of *a* and *b* is then the same as the point of intersection of *b* and *c*. So we have different designations for the same point, and these names ('point of intersection of *a* and *b*,' 'point of intersection of *b* and *c*') likewise indicate the mode of presentation; and hence the statement contains actual knowledge ... In our example, accordingly, the reference of the expression 'the point of intersection of *a* and *b*' and 'the point of intersection of *b* and *c*' would be the same, but not their senses. The reference of 'evening star' would be the same as that of 'morning star,' but not the sense."

Although Frege did not volunteer his own considered judgment about such cases, it seems possible, and perhaps even natural from what he did say, to conclude that mixed identity statements of the sort in question might express a properly inclusive sense relation. They might convey the sense of the sense-compositional, typically descriptive, singular referring expression "The Evening Star" or "The Morning Star" as a proper subset of the complete set of properties constituting the sense of the sense-non-compositional, typically unqualifiedly nominal, singular referring expressions "Hesperus," "Phosphorus," and, unless we think the planet is actually a goddess, "Venus." The sense of "The Evening Star" is thereby included in the sense of, say, "Hesperus," as part of the complete sense with which the ordinary proper name is objectively freighted. The descriptive proper name "The Evening Star," unlike "The Morning Star," makes specific reference to the star being the first bright star to appear in a clear evening sky. The sense-non-compositional ordinary proper name "Hesperus" has this sense-component included in its complete set of the properties of the planet, along with such properties as being the last bright body to appear in a clear morning sky, and many others as well, which the sense-compositional definite description "The Morning Star" need not have, at least explicitly, as part of its customary Fregean sense.

We can diagram without further comment in Figures 8.1 and 8.2 the essential features of Frege's theory of the customary and indirect reference and customary sense of proper names for normal direct speech, or *oratio recta*, and indirect speech, *oratio obliqua*. Frege found that *oratio recta* contexts preserve truth-value when substitutions are made within them among co-referential proper names and materially equivalent declarative

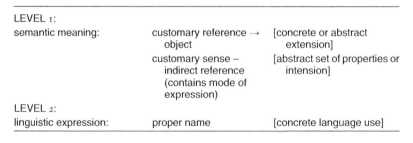

LEVEL 1:
semantic meaning: customary reference →   [concrete or abstract
                         object   extension]
                         customary sense –   [abstract set of properties or
                         indirect reference   intension]
                         (contains mode of
                         expression)
LEVEL 2:
linguistic expression: proper name   [concrete language use]

Figure 8.1   Frege's Sense–Reference Theory of Proper Names

LEVEL 1:		
semantic meaning:	customary reference → the True; the False	[abstract extension]
	customary sense – indirect reference	["content" of sentence (contains mode of expression) as function of sense of its component terms]
LEVEL 2:		
linguistic expression:	Sentence	[concrete language use]

Figure 8.2   Frege's Sense–Reference Theory of Sentence Meaning

sentences. *Oratio obliqua* contexts do not support the same uniform inter-substitutions *salva veritate*. They are different semantically, impervious to the exchange of co-referential proper names and materially equivalent along with his parallel treatment for the meaning of sentences in this way.[16]

[16] The model for these diagrams derives from Frege's famous explication of his parallel treatment of the meaning of proper names and sentences in his Letter VII [xix]/1 to Husserl, dating from 1891, in Frege, *Philosophical and Mathematical Correspondence*, ed. McGuinness (Oxford: Basil Blackwell, 1979), p. 63 (translating Frege's *"Bedeutung"* simply as "meaning"):

Proposition	Proper name	Concept word	
↓	↓	↓	↓
Sense	Sense	Sense	
of the	of the	of the	
Proposition	proper name	concept word	
(thought)			
↓	↓	↓	
Meaning	Meaning	(meaning) →	Object
of the	of the	(of the)	falling under
Proposition	proper name	(concept word)	the concept
(truth value)	(object)	((concept))	

Significantly, Frege adds, after presenting the diagram, as though to explain the parentheses surrounding the "meaning of the concept word (concept)," p. 63, "With a concept word it takes one more step to reach the object than with a proper name, and the last step may be missing – i.e., the concept may be empty – without the concept word's ceasing to be scientifically useful. I have drawn the last step from concept to object horizontally in order to indicate that it takes place at the same level, that objects and concepts have the same objectivity (see my *Foundations (Grundlagen)*, Section 47)." Frege's explanation of the *Bedeutung* or referential meaning of a concept word is an expression of his commitment to semantic referential extensionalism. He interprets the reference of a concept-function word

Problems in Frege's Identity Thesis

To conclude that the complete sense of a proper name can fall short of the totality of the named object's distinguishing identity-determining properties is to saddle Frege with a proposition he cannot possibly accept. He would then need to hold that the sense of a singular referring expression was a subjective matter of limited knowledge and differential opinion among individual thinkers and language users concerning an object's individuating properties. It is easy to suggest that in the case of "The Evening Star" the expression's sense is the singleton property included in the set {the first bright star to appear in the evening}, in contrast with that of "The Morning Star," whose sense might be understood instead as {the last bright star to appear in the morning}. Even this apparently modest proposal is problematic in Frege's efforts to achieve a scientific non-psychologistic theory of objective meaning, for at least the following three reasons.

(1) The "Evening" or "Morning" and "Star" components of the projected senses of the co-referential terms might at least be thought to be amenable to being easily read off directly from the expressions "The Evening Star" and "The Morning Star." The example turns out to have been propitiously chosen for that accidental feature. However, we must wonder whence the remaining essential components of the proposed distinct Fregean senses of the customary meanings of the two expressions are supposed to derive.

Proper names can often be misleading in this regard. We need look no further than the proper name for a world affairs administrative body called "The United Nations." How can the concepts "first," "bright," and "to appear" suddenly introduce themselves into the hypothetical senses of the terms "The Evening Star" and "The Morning Star"? They certainly cannot be read off directly from the syntax of the two names without a significant background of circumstantial etymological knowledge and a

purely extensionally in terms of existent objects possessing the property in the extension of the property-representing predicate. Frege's mention of empty concepts is puzzling, since he undoubtedly also recognizes the possibility of empty proper names and related putative singular referring expressions that do not refer to any existent entities. Frege not only fails to remark on the parallelism, which is crucial to understanding his reaction later to Russell's paradox of 1902, but provocatively he treats the meaning of predicates, concept-function words, or concept-functors as a special case, enclosing them alone of all other meaningful expressions in massive parentheses, apparently to indicate their distinct semantic status. Why he does this is unclear.

confident interpolation of specific content that the expressions themselves do not syntactically contain. There is, accordingly, no evident reason on the interpretation of Fregean sense criticized here why the sense of "The Evening Star" could or should not be instead {the dimmest star to appear on the evening of the winter solstice}, or, as another (fictional) example, {the star discovered by the astronomer Ms. Dolores Evening}. We might even imagine that these properties are actually true of the planet we call The Evening Star. Nor need defenders of the objective total property set interpretation of Fregean sense or *the* Fregean sense resort to the objection that, despite its bright appearance within our solar neighborhood at certain times of day on Earth, Venus = The Morning Star = The Evening Star is not a *star*.

(2) There is no way to read off the Fregean sense-meaning of many proper names from their syntax or orthography.

The Morning Star is also called Phosphorus, where the name "Phosphorus" might connote (falsely) a particular mineral composition or the burning yellow appearance of that substance when ignited. What "Phosphorus" clearly does not connote or convey is the property of being a star generally, let alone more particularly the last bright star to linger in the morning. If we freely stipulate that the sense of "Hesperus" = to be The Evening Star, and similarly for the sense of "Phosphorus" = to be The Morning Star, then we encounter the inconsistency already mentioned, whereby the transitivity of identity implies that the sense of "Hesperus" = the sense of "Phosphorus," on the grounds that something has the property of being the Evening Star if and only if it has the property of being the Morning Star.

Therewith all co-referential proper names acquire identical Fregean sense. Something similar applies for "Hesperus" as the equally sense-opaque alternative proper name of The Morning Star. The problem holds generally for virtually all proper names, notably in the case of Frege's own discussion of the sense of the hypothetically sense-impenetrable proper name "Aristotle" in the footnote to "On Sense and Reference," exceptions like "Harald Blue-Tooth," "Æthelred the Unready," and "Ivan the Terrible," some of which might even be ironically intended, notwithstanding.

(3) There is finally no adequate method of drawing the line by which a proper subset of the complete specification of a referent's properties is correctly distinguished

as *the* sense of a corresponding singular referring expression, proper name, or definite description.

Frege mentioned Aristotle's properties of being the student of Plato and teacher of Alexander the Great as at least partially constitutive of the sense-meaning of the name "Aristotle." He reasonably observed that different thinkers and language users might entertain different opinions about the proper name's sense. A certain language user might be of the opinion that the sense-meaning of the name "Aristotle" is {the student of Plato}, while another, not being aware that Aristotle studied with Plato, but believing another fact about the referent, might be of the contrary opinion that the sense of the name "Aristotle" was instead {the teacher of Alexander the Great}. It is precisely the kind of thinker-variable subjectivity that Frege elsewhere wants to avoid at all costs in an objective scientific theory of meaning.

The difference between the two language users, according to Frege, as undoubtedly he would have said, is the subjective truth that individually they associate the name "Aristotle" with one of two different properties of the name's referent, both of which belong to the complete total sense of the name "Aristotle." We touch but do not yet even scratch the surface of this vast body of Aristotle's distinguishing properties when we mention for expository purposes his being the student of Plato and teacher of Alexander the Great. Were it not so, then the differing opinions about the proper name's sense-meaning could not possibly qualify as opinions *of* or *about the* (common) *sense* of the proper name "Aristotle."

Frege inexplicably seemed willing also to accept a weaker version of the complete sense of a proper-name thesis, in order to uphold the cognitive informativeness of noniterative identity statements. He applied the sense–reference distinction against his better judgment in allowing different co-referential proper names to have different senses, rather than accounting for the differential informativeness of noniterative identity statements as the result of different lexical opinions and beliefs about the identical reference-determining sense-meanings of proper names "a" and "b," when it is true that $a = b$ but not everyone knows it.

Customary and Indirect Reference of Fregean Proper Names

If we say that name "a" is not identical to named entity a, "a" $\neq a$, then Frege maintains that "a" (mentioning the name occurring on the right-hand side of the nonidentity statement) refers to its customary referent, Aristotle, and "*a*" (mentioning the name *of* the name that appears on the left-hand side of the nonidentity statement) refers indirectly to the customary sense in this case of the proper name "Aristotle." This, we are reminded, *the* Fregean sense of the proper name "*a*" or "Aristotle," by the objective as opposed to the mainstream interpretation, needs to be the complete set of all of Aristotle's (individually distinguishing) properties, effectively Aristotle's *haecceity*.

Nor does Frege's distinction between concepts and objects avoid inconvenience by precluding the naming of properties, including the property of being a property. It is true that for Frege no concept can be an object, but it is not true that for Frege only objects can be named by ordinary non-descriptive proper names or patently descriptive definite descriptions. For Frege, concepts are unsaturated expressions, of the form "___ is F" or "$F(\_\_) = v$." He insisted that within the concept-function there is reference to a property, here, schematically, F, symbolized by predicate "F." In his exuberantly polemical reply to Kerry, in the 1892 essay published the same year, "On Concept and Object," discussed at length in the previous chapter, Frege explains that

In logical discussions one quite often needs to assert something about a concept, and to express this in the form usual for such assertions – viz. to make what is asserted of the concept into the content of the grammatical predicate. Consequently, one would expect that the reference of the grammatical subject would be the concept; but the concept as such cannot play this part, in view of its predicative nature; it must first be converted into an object [Frege refers in a note to his *Grundlagen der Arithmetik*, p. x], or, speaking more precisely, represented by an object. We designate this object by prefixing the words "the concept"; e.g.:
"The concept *man* is not empty."
Here the first three words are to be regarded as a proper name [Frege explains as follows in a note at this point: "I call anything a proper name if it is a sign for an object"], which can no more be used predicatively than "Berlin" or "Vesuvius." When we say "Jesus falls under the concept *man*," then, setting aside the copula, the predicate is:
"someone falling under the concept *man*"
and this means the same as:
"a man."
But the phrase
"the concept *man*"
is only part of this predicate.[17]

[17] Frege, "On Concept and Object," pp. 46–47.

Frege allowed properties to be respectably named. We might wonder what happens in that event to the disquotational theory of individual reference, the so-called "Fido"–Fido theory, as it is often called, when applied to properties, if the peculiar nonidentity of "a" $\neq a$ for properties ("F" $\neq F$, where F = the property of being a property or concept-function) is provable on the assumption that an existent entity is generally distinct from its proper name.[18] In application to the property of being a property, itself an object of unlimitedly many true and false predications, the non-objectual concept-function it embeds has the form "___ is a property" or "___ has the property of being a property." It is these unsaturated contexts in open sentences that for Frege constitute concepts (*Begriffe*) interpreted as functions, or for hyphenated emphasis concept-functions. As Frege defined things, concept-functions are rightly distinguished from objects (*Gegenstände*), but equally capable of being properly named, in association with their exactly specified extensions.

What Identity Assumes

What, then, do we learn when we learn that Hesperus = Phosphorus, or that The Evening Star = The Morning Star? What is the cognitive significance communicated by these noniterative identity statements? It is true, as Frege posited, that the names "Hesperus" and "Phosphorus" refer to the same object (Venus). It is also true, contrary to Frege's protestation, that the two names have the same sense-meaning, if by "sense" we mean, as Frege did, that they each possess the same set of distinguishing properties.

---

[18] The term "'Fido'–Fido theory of reference" originates with Gilbert Ryle, "Meaning and Necessity," *Philosophy*, 24 (1949), pp. 69–76. I use the expression to designate any theory that reduces meaning not merely to reference, but more specifically to purely formal disquotational referential meaning. As in Ryle, "'Fido'–Fido" has continued also to be used to characterize a strictly referential "correspondence," "eliminative," or disquotational theory of meaning. An informed insightful discussion of the topic appears in Gideon Makin, *The Metaphysicians of Meaning: Russell and Frege on Sense and Denotation* (London: Routledge, 2001), especially pp. 117–26. Makin writes, p. 117, "The slogan 'sense determines reference' is by now established as a fundamental and unchallenged truth which most writers on Frege would subscribe to – and I am no exception. But its precise meaning, as I will show, is controversial and in need of careful delineation." See Dummett, *Frege: Philosophy of Language*, pp. 93–97, 104–105, 227–29, 241–43, 589–90, and 679–80; and also Dummett, *The Interpretation of Frege's Philosophy*, especially pp. 95, 157, 245–46, 248–53, 362, 369–70, 441, 447, 461, 480, and 549.

The same is true even of "The Evening Star" and "The Morning Star." The distinguishing properties of the object referred to by these two definite descriptions are precisely the same. The Evening Star has the property of being the last bright star seen in the morning, just as The Morning Star also has the property of being the first bright star seen in the evening. We might not have known that the two names have the same sense or the same reference, which is one of the things we can come to learn in accepting the appropriate nontrivial identity statement as true. Psychology, if Frege is right, should not enter in. What if I have been praying and offering sacrifices to the Evening Star to destroy the Morning Star?

Fregean sense or *Sinn* meaning does not fully distinguish the meanings of the two names. There is supposed to be a residue. Despite Frege's contrary assertion concerning the identical reference and distinct senses of these two names for the same yellow planet in a nontrivial identity statement, the fully distinguishing sense-meanings of two co-referential proper names must always be identical. The two names have the same Fregean sense all along, a fact of which we are made aware when we learn that the two names have the same Fregean reference. What is of cognitive relevance in learning that The Evening Star = The Morning Star is rather a potentially subjectively psychological difference in a thinker's understanding the *connotations* of the names, of attaching differential coloring to the two names. It is, after all, only poetic to speak of the planet as the goddess Venus or star of the morning and evening. There is a semantic tag by which to fix a proper name's meaning, a prop for intention and memory in cognition. The difference in question understood as proposed nevertheless occurs only at the third level of subjective meaning and connotation in Frege's theory, implying the psychologism in theory of meaning that Frege disqualified from objective scientific semantics.

It is frequently but mistakenly said that Frege's theory of reference postulated only the two main divisions of sense and reference. We have also been guilty of a simplification up to this point in the diagrams of Frege's sense–reference analysis of the meaning of proper names and sentences. Although Frege regarded sense and reference alone as relevant to a "scientific" philosophical semantics, as the only objective factors in meaning, he recognized a total of three distinct aspects or "levels of difference" obtaining for names and sentences. In addition to the contributions of sense (*Sinn*) and reference (*Bedeutung*) to the objective meaning of an expression, Frege also noted the accompaniment of extra-semantic subjective elements of associated psychological image or idea (*Bild, Vorstellung*) as a third level of meaning. The critique of Frege's semantics invites a more expansive discussion on Frege's discounted third subjective level of meaning. Frege explained it thus:

> We can now recognize three levels of difference between words, expressions, or whole sentences. The difference may concern at most the ideas, or the sense but not the reference, or, finally, the reference as well. With respect to the first level, it is to be noted that, on account of the uncertain connexion of ideas with words, a difference may hold for one person, which another does not find. The difference between a translation and the original text should properly not overstep the first level. To the possible differences here belong also the colouring and shading which poetic eloquence seeks to give to the sense. Such colouring and shading are not objective, and must be evoked by each hearer or reader according to the hints of the poet or the speaker. Without some affinity in human ideas art would certainly be impossible; but it can never be exactly determined how far the intentions of the poet are realized.
>
> In what follows there will be no further discussion of ideas and experiences; they have been mentioned here only to ensure that the idea aroused in the hearer by a word shall not be confused with its sense or its reference.[19]

If we learn anything about Hesperus and Phosphorus, or The Evening Star and The Morning Star, when we learn that Hesperus = Phosphorus and that The Evening Star = The Morning Star, then in Frege's two-dimensional semantic–epistemic framework what we learn is that the terms that for us previously had at least different ideational connotations have not only the same reference but also the same sense. It is not, contrary to Frege's diagnosis of the situation, the case that we learn that terms with different senses have the same reference, because the two names on the present assumption have the same total object-distinguishing Fregean sense-meaning. Prior to learning the truth of the identity statement in which their respective alternative proper names appear we did not know that the two names were co–referential, that they therefore also unavoidably possessed the same total Fregean sense.

Cognitive informativeness is a psychological matter. Frege's abhorence of psychologism inclined him away even from considering psychological explanations of psychological phenomena. If I am surprised to learn that The Morning Star = The Evening Star, or that The Wolf of

---

[19] Frege, "On Sense and Reference," pp. 60–61.

Wall Street = my neighbor out at the lake, then my state of surprise is a psychological occurrence, and my potential surprise is a potential psychological occurrence. Why not give psychology its due, without overextending its welcome, in trying to understand specifically psychological aspects of our epistemic situation in thinking about what, for all we know, are the eternal unchanging purely logical foundations of logic and arithmetic, just as Frege would have them? A good place to begin this kind of psychological investigation of thinking about logic and mathematics is with the "intuitions" Frege invoked to explain how we judge an axiom set sound, its basic laws individually true. We are supposed to be able to recognize somehow that these selected axioms among all remaining alternatives are the right ones. Wired up differently, we might be astonished that two different sign tokens in two locations in an iterative identity statement $a = a$, one on the left and one on the right, might betoken the same object. Could we survive and even thrive with such a cognitive alteration? No doubt we could, as though wearing prism glasses, even if we cannot imagine ourselves with our way of thinking being called upon suddenly to use a similarly stultified symbolic convention for each inscription of a symbol type that is expected to have distinct reference.

Only if identity is always self-identity, capable of iterative or noniterative expression, could Frege have his cake and eat it too. He did not seem to recognize his situation as it has been assessed here. He did not size it up beyond knowing that identity was not a relation among a plurality of entities. He never made an attempt to accommodate the relation versus its expressive possibilities in his analysis of identity and the meaning of identity statements in "On Sense and Reference." He explained the distinction in the following way:

If words are used in the ordinary way, what one intends to speak of is their reference. It can also happen, however, that one wishes to talk about the words themselves or their sense. This happens, for instance, when the words of another are quoted. One's own words then first designate words of the other speaker, and only the latter have their usual reference. We then have signs of signs. In writing, the words are in this case enclosed in quotation marks.[20]

Frege did not follow the quotation-mark convention to indicate in $a = b$, as we continue now to do, that he meant to refer to proper names "a" and

---

[20] *Ibid.*, p. 58.

"b." If we were to write that the *signs* "a" and "b" were identical, "a" = "b," then the sentence would be false, even if it were true that $a = b$. It might be true that Mark Twain = Samuel Clemens, but the two names "Mark Twain" and "Samuel Clemens" are certainly not identical. They are not the same names, even if they are different names for the same person. The fact that they are not the same name but have the same reference is what makes the identity statement MT = SC potentially cognitively informative. If $a = b$ is a relation between proper names, as Frege assumed in the *Begriffsschrift* and afterward in "On Sense and Reference," continuing to do so also in the following year, 1893, in his *Grundgesetze*, then how can "a" and "b" be proper names for such distinct existent objects as Venus and the author of *Life on the Mississippi*, as opposed to "Venus" and "the author of *Life on the Mississippi*"? How can they be names for anything other than names, if true identity statements predicate relations holding only between proper names?

The Metaphysics of Self-Identity

Frege would have done better to follow the sympathetic suggestion of treating the metaphysics of identity as that of entity or intended object self-identity. It is by such lights a unique kind of relation, but not absolutely the only kind in its category. Frege patently cannot allow $2 + 5 = 7$ to describe a relation between the *signs* "$2 + 5$" and "7," for these are manifestly not the same sign, and not the same numerical proper name, as found in $2 + 5 = 2 + 5$ and $7 = 7$. If identity is always self-identity, then we can express identities in iterative and noniterative logical form, as need arises. We can allow, on purely syntactical sign-related grounds, somewhat but not quite as Frege proposed, that only noniterative identity statements are potentially cognitively informative.

When we write $a = b$, we are saying that there is one object that is called both "a" and "b." The identity relation itself is the self-identity of the object referred to alternatively as "a" or as "b." The noniterative expression of the identity relation can involve two different names for the same object. The identity relation itself, except in special circumstances where signs are said to be identical, different tokens of the same sign type, is not generally a relation between two different objects, as Frege rightly observed, but it is also not generally a relation between two names. The same is true despite the fact that two different names for the same object can be used to express the object's self-identity.

Frege illustrated the difference between sense and reference by means of a previously mentioned geometrical application:

> Let *a*, *b*, *c* be the lines connecting the vertices of a triangle with the midpoints of the opposite sides. The point of intersection of *a* and *b* is then the same as the point of intersection of *b* and *c*. So we have different designations for the same point, and these names ("point of intersection of *a* and *b*," "point of intersection of *b* and *c*") likewise indicate the mode of presentation; and hence the statement contains actual knowledge.[21]

The question that has been posed for Frege's distinction is not whether the intersection points designated are referentially the same geometrical object. They are definitely that. The question is whether or not "point of intersection of *a* and *b*" and "point of intersection of *b* and *c*" have or do not have the same Fregean sense. The first intuition is that they do not and could not have the same sense, because one refers to a line *a* joining two triangle vertices and not to *c*, while the other refers to *c* but not *a*. Their *sense* would seem to be different, as Frege's use of the sense–reference distinction for potentially cognitively informative noniterative identity statements in the sense–reference semantics of proper names, and Frege's thesis of sense-building semantic compositionality from the sense-meanings of proper names and concept-functor identity conditions to complex meaningful predications, seem clearly to imply.

Frege did not look to be relying on subjective differences in mere opinions concerning the sense-meaning of a proper name. When I happen to know that Aristotle was a student of Plato's, but have never heard that he was a teacher of Alexander the Great, whereas you know just the opposite, namely you know that Aristotle was a teacher of Alexander the Great, but have never heard that he was a student of Plato's, we are referring to the same ancient Greek philosopher, concerning whom our identifying characterizations do not entirely coincide and may not even overlap. If *for me* the sense of "Aristotle" is to have been a student of Plato, and *for you* the sense of the same name is teacher of Alexander, then our subjective associations will probably differ when we contemplate the name "Aristotle." This is another matter that Frege was normally careful to distinguish from *the* (complete) *sense* of a proper name. The confusion

---

[21] *Ibid.*, p. 57.

was not merely teetering on the precipice but had plunged full over into psychologism's infernal abyss.

Sense-meaning itself was objective for Frege. It was not dependent on the limited knowledge and erroneous opinions of particular speakers who may nevertheless use the same given proper name intelligibly in their communications, if only to falsely predicate properties of an intended object. Frege summed up his sense–reference distinction in the following terms:

> It is natural, now, to think of there being connected with a sign (name, combination of words, letter), besides that to which the sign refers, which may be called the reference of the sign, also what I should like to call the *sense* of the sign, wherein the mode of presentation is contained. In our example, accordingly, the reference of the expressions "the point of intersection of *a* and *b*" and "the point of intersection of *b* and *c*" would be the same, but not their senses. The reference of "Evening Star" would be the same as that of "Morning Star," but not the sense.[22]

The two cases, The Morning Star = The Evening Star and the intersection of lines *a* and *b* versus that of lines *b* and *c*, are not essentially different. They are alike in involving different terms designating the same existent object. We cannot know whether or not the pairs of proper names have the same or different sense-meaning unless or until we have a clearer understanding of what Frege meant by "sense."

Naturally, we do not expect anyone to be in command of all the facts that are true about Aristotle. That is a practical psychological and epistemic limitation that also does not affect the objective facts surrounding *the* sense of a proper name in a scientific semantics, and argues for the plausibility of Frege's distinguishing between sense-meaning and beliefs or opinions about sense-meaning. There is the objective sense-meaning of a proper name, Frege explained, which is essential to a scientific semantics, and there is a disorganized miscellany of knowledgeable and ignorant attitudes among proper-name users concerning any given proper name's Fregean sense. These are different things. We may want some grasp of a proper name's sense in order to use it referentially to designate a particular object in a mental or externally expressive act of intending to refer. We should never expect that for Frege the total sense-meaning of a proper name itself could differ erratically or haphazardly from thinker to thinker. Any such discrepancy is merely an artifact of our

---

[22] *Ibid.*

imperfect sub-omniscient memories and cognitive workspaces, for which there are pragmatic compensations that assure the exchange of linguistic information with relative dispatch among linguistically interactive intelligent beings, which exchange, for predictable reasons, is also not always perfect in execution.

Frege's Realism and the Complete Sense of a Proper Name

Above all, Frege distinguished between the *sense* of a proper name and *ideas* about the name's sense-meaning and the named object's properties. His firm insistence on this distinction is one of the ways in which Frege's metaphysical realism and arch anti-psychologism expressed itself in the semantic philosophy of "On Sense and Reference." It is Frege's Platonic realism talking when he speaks of *the* sense of a proper name, as opposed to passing occurrent psychological ideas, beliefs, and opinions about a proper name's sense. The suggestion is that Frege's realism demands that, if *the* sense of the proper name "Aristotle" excludes *any* constitutive property F that is true of Aristotle (a), in the predication Fa, then a possible pseudo-Aristotle or non-Aristotle (na) with all of a's properties *except* F will instead be the mis-targeted actual referent of the proper name "Aristotle." The proper name "Aristotle" refers then to na instead of a, and the fact that Fa and not Fna drops out is semantically irrelevant.

We assume that it is the ancient Greek philosopher a that is intended, and not a merely possible near-duplicate na. We suppose that $a \neq na$, but that a and na, if such a thing were possible, are otherwise identical *except* for the possession by a of the one constitutive property $F(\_\_)$ that is excluded from determining the sense of the respective proper name "a." The implication is not that "Aristotle" refers to a AND refers to na. Nor, heaven forbid, that $a = na$. The point is that, if the Fregean sense-meaning of a proper name is to determine the proper name's reference, then we should not exclude *any* property $F(\_\_)$ that belongs to the proper name's referent from its abstract unified ideal Fregean semantic sense-meaning, or what Frege speaks of as *the* proper name's sense. We cannot expect the identity conditions for reference to specific objects in a *Begriffsschrift* referential semantic domain to be any less exacting than Leibnizian intensional property-based identity conditions for individual objects. Fregean sense is the complete complement of a named object's distinguishing constitutive properties, namely, those that alone enter into the named object's intensional Leibnizian identity conditions.[23]

The Leibnizian identity principle is that $a = b$ if and only if any constitutive or identity-determining property of a is a constitutive identity-determining property of b, and conversely. Properties excluded from identity determinations prominently include properties that would imply the object's existence or nonexistence. How can we refer specifically to object a as a function of the referential aspect of the sense-meaning of proper name "a" if we do not have available *all* of the properties that are true of the proper name's referent, in the ideal (Frege's *the* or total) sense of the proper name? If the sense of the name "Aristotle" is going to be capable of determining its reference, then we must arm sense with all the properties needed to distinguish intended reference to a from accidental reference to na. For Fregean sense-meaning to have all it needs to exactly single out the referents of relevant proper names, Frege's concept of *the* (unified ideal total) sense of a proper name cannot exclude any constitutive distinguishing property that is true of the proper name's referent.

A semantic theory proposes what must be true in order for a proper name or declarative sentence to have reference as well as sense, and whether there is any interrelation between sense-meaning and reference, and if so what. Frege distinguished between sense and reference on the intuitive grounds that broadly fictional proper names and declarative sentences containing fictional proper names have sense-meaning but do not refer. Sense-meaning is no guarantee of reference, although reference failure is also determined by sense-meaning compared against the state or truth-making facts of the world. Frege argued as follows:

> To every expression belonging to a complete totality of signs, there should certainly correspond a definite sense; but natural languages often do not satisfy this condition, and one must be content if the same word has the same sense in the same context. It may perhaps be granted that every grammatically well-formed expression representing a proper name always has a sense. But this is not to say that to the sense there also corresponds a reference. The expression "the least rapidly convergent series" has a

[23] Jacquette, "Frege on Identity as a Relation of Names," *Metaphysica: International Journal for Ontology and Metaphysics*, 12 (2011), pp. 60–66, offers a formal counterexample, arguing that, contrary to Frege, identity cannot possibly be a relation among names, provided, which seems undeniable, especially by Frege, that there can be proper names *of* proper names, as also required for Frege's "second-level" functions of functions. See also Jacquette, "Intentionality on the Instalment Plan," *Philosophy*, 73 (1998), pp. 63–79.

sense but demonstrably has no reference, since for every given convergent series, another convergent, but less rapidly convergent, series can be found. In grasping a sense, one is not certainly assured of a reference.[24]

Frege drew an important distinction in this passage between the ideal relation of sense and reference in a perfect language, as opposed to the anything but ideal colloquial language in which we usually entertain and express propositional thoughts. Ideally, Frege's *Begriffsschrift* is the logic of those concept-function languages in which no proper name occurs unless it has reference as well as sense. Celebrated exceptions in ordinary discourse include "Pegasus," "Zeus," and "the least rapidly convergent series" or "the greatest prime number." Frege did not banish these terms from his *Begriffsschrift*, perhaps because they are syntactically indistinguishable from proper names with reference that refer to existent entities, or perhaps because they are needed under some designation in mathematical *reductio* proofs.

The third category involves putative proper names that are not clearly either existent entity referring or non-referring. There are no pre-set criteria for referring and non-referring names and sentences belonging to the third category. That fact contributes to the philosophical difficulties surrounding reference in practical applications. We gain a sense of the kinds of apparent names that do not clearly present themselves to judgment as referring or non-referring by considering putative names that could be real in legends buried away in the remote historical past, or in currently unproven and undisproven formal and natural scientific theories, as in cerebrally challenging excessively long complicated mathematical object terms and propositions. If legend, as opposed to accredited myth, states that for a time there was a surviving dinosaur in the ancient Hittite kingdom named Seymour, assuming no definite proof or disproof of a saurian's existence in the human era, then we today may never be in a position to say with good justification whether or not "Seymour" is a referring proper name like "Aristotle" or non-referring nominal invention like "Sherlock Holmes."

For Frege the applications of concern involve purported names and formulas that are ostensibly about arithmetical entities and truths. If we effect to name the even number greater than 2 that is not the sum of two (different) prime numbers something like "N," then, Goldbach's Conjecture being unproven and undisproven, we do not now and may

[24] Frege, "On Sense and Reference," p. 58.

never know whether "*N*" is a referring or non-referring term. It belongs, for the time being in mathematical judgment and possibly evermore, neither with referring proper names like "Aristotle" nor consigned to the semantic outerland of non-referring pseudo-names like "Sherlock Holmes." There is no choice for Frege's Platonic realism in the metaphysics of mathematics, supported by a classical bivalent truth-value semantics, except to interpret referential indeterminacy as epistemic. "*N*" either refers or does not refer. Picture Platonist Frege lowering his eyebrows and crossing his arms. We just do not happen to know which it is, given that relevant truths on which the semantic classification depends are at present epistemically undetermined. Mathematical realism, to its eternal credit, offers a consistent, if starkly dogmatic, stance.

The situation is not unusual. Knowing whether, and, if so, to what existent entity, a putative proper name refers when reference is not stipulative or definitional is usually an empirical matter; our knowledge is never perfect or complete. Gaps in knowledge as to the reference of some proper names in sociolinguistic circulation are expected, among numberless other unsolved empirical questions. There is a definite answer as to whether "*N*" refers or, as the realist suspects, does not refer. We just do not happen to know which it is, just as we do not happen to know whether or not molten gold flows in undersurface rivers on the planet Venus. That fact does not prevent problems like that of the reference or non-reference of "*N*" from posing theoretical difficulties for Frege's philosophical semantics. If we were omniscient, then perhaps we could classify "*N*" in the category with referring proper names or with non-referring pseudo-names, and there would be no indeterminacy in the theorems of arithmetic.

Intensional *Oratio Obliqua* Contexts

Frege tackled another semantic peculiarity of colloquial language applications in his *Begriffsschrift*, involving *oratio obliqua* indirect reference or quotation contexts, writing, in a previously plundered passage,

Accordingly, a word standing between quotation marks must not be taken as having its ordinary reference ... It is quite clear that in this way of speaking words do not have their customary reference but designate what is usually their sense. In order to have a short expression, we will say: In reported speech, words are used *indirectly* or have their *indirect* reference. We distinguish accordingly the *customary* from the *indirect* reference of a word; and its *customary* sense from its *indirect* sense. The indirect reference of a word is accordingly its customary sense. Such exceptions must always be borne in mind if the mode of connexion between sign, sense, and reference in particular cases is to be correctly understood.[25]

Frege responded to the semantics of quoted indirect discourse by introducing the terms "customary" sense and reference for what previously had simply been sense and reference. If I say "Aristotle is wise," attributing the property of being wise to Aristotle, then, simplifying, we can say that the customary sense of the proper name "Aristotle" is {student of Plato AND teacher of Alexander AND ...}, and the customary reference is the ancient Greek philosopher who was in fact the student of Plato and teacher of Alexander the Great. If I am quoted by quoter Q as having said "J said 'Aristotle is wise,'" then, in Q's use of the proper name "Aristotle," "Aristotle" no longer has its customary reference but instead acquires its indirect reference, which Frege called its customary sense. This further means that, when Q uses the expression in quoting J as having said that "Aristotle is wise," the reference of the proper name "Aristotle" is not Aristotle, but the customary sense of the proper name "Aristotle," which we say for simplicity's sake is to be {student of Plato AND teacher of Alexander}.

We must wonder whether this is what Q really means, whether this is a correct characterization of the sense of Q's use of the proper name "Aristotle" in quoting J as having said "Aristotle is wise." Why should Q not refer just as J does to the customary reference of "Aristotle," both in J's ascribing wisdom to the thinker and in Q's quoting the ascription of wisdom to precisely the same individual referred to alike and without qualification both in quotation and in quoted linguistic expression? Nor is it gratifyingly clear how quotation is even possible if proper names in the quoted expression inevitably have a different reference than they do when they are quoted. We should generally want and expect a quoted utterance to have the same meaning, sense, and reference as its quotation. Why should quoter Q not be able to correctly and accurately quote J without having the first idea as to what the customary sense of the proper name "Aristotle" is when embedded in the quotation context "J said _____," in order to produce a complete accurate quotation "J said 'Aristotle is wise'"? All Q should need to be able to do is pronounce the word "Aristotle" in such a manner that it is recognizable by and for others who know something more about Aristotle. They should only need to relate the information to their knowledge of quoted speaker J, who started all this trouble by uttering the apparently harmless sentence "Aristotle is wise."

We know why Frege wanted to distinguish between customary and indirect sense and reference for proper names occurring in quotation contexts. It was because these contexts do not support the intersubstitution of co-referential proper names like "$2 + 5$" and "7" or materially equivalent sentences *salva veritate*, preserving the truth of assumptions in the resulting inference. Certainly, $2 + 5 = 7$ or $V(+5(2) = 7) =$ the True, in Frege's logic and truth-conditional semantics. The objects related by identity in the true sentence for the $+5(\_) = n$ function with 2 as argument and 7 as value, "$2 + 5 = 7$," can be quoted in a variety of ways that do not support truth when these completed co-referential terms "$+5(2) = n$" and "7" are uniformly intersubstituted. Quotation makes a good beginning, although there is a wider family of related substitution failures that are collectively known as intensional referentially opaque *de dicto* contexts that Frege categorized as *oratio obliqua*. They are contrasted with purely extensional referentially transparent *de re* or *oratio recta* contexts, in which intersubstitutions of co-referential proper names and materially or logically equivalent sentences preserve truth-value, never transforming true sentences into false sentences or the reverse.

We shall provide a few examples of each, starting with substitution failure. Frege discussed this at length in the essay in connection with what are known after Russell as propositional attitude contexts. Frege spoke of judgments that do not support the intersubstitution of co-referential proper names *salva veritate*, that are intensional rather than purely extensional. If I truly judge that "7" is spelled s-e-v-e-n, it does not follow logically that I therefore judge truly that "$2 + 5$" is spelled s-e-v-e-n, even though no one disagrees that $2 + 5 = 7$. Here is what Frege wrote:

If our supposition that the reference of a sentence is its truth-value is correct, the latter must remain unchanged when a part of the sentence is replaced by an expression having the same reference. And this is in fact the case. Leibniz gives the definition: "*Eadem sunt, quae sibi mutuo substitui possunt, salva veritate.*" What else but the truth value could be found, that belongs quite generally to every sentence if the reference of its components is relevant, and remains unchanged by substitutions of the kind in question?[26]

[26] *Ibid.*, p. 64. Frege does not divulge his source for Leibniz's famous statement of the substitutivity of identicals. The passage appears in Gottfried Wilhelm Leibniz,

Frege was not quite a pure extensionalist. He was nevertheless actively earning his referential extensionalist wings with every new major philosophical publication. In "On Sense and Reference," he did not for the moment explicitly consider intensional referentially opaque *de dicto* contexts. He was nevertheless aware that there are such concept-functions and that substitutions into those contexts are not generally truth-preserving. This is still not at all to say that they are generally not truth-preserving. Some substitutions go through. That is never the point. The context is judged by the criterion of being intensional rather than purely extensional when the substitution of co-referential proper names or equivalent sentences *salva veritate* is prevented in at least one application.

Frege extended the range of contexts where customary reference breaks down into indirect reference identified as customary sense for a wide range of propositional attitude contexts. He remarked that "If one says 'It seems that …' one means 'It seems to me that …' or 'I think that …' We therefore have the same case again. The situation is similar in the case of expressions such as 'to be pleased,' 'to regret,' 'to approve,' 'to blame,' 'to hope,' 'to fear.'"[27] The fact that Frege exercised his energies over the logic of ordinary language, and did not merely retreat into *Begriffsschrift* notation, where propositional attitudes and quotation play virtually no part, is a sign of his commitment to identifying the common logic of reasoning, including, but not limited to, mathematics.

Frege distinguished the advantages of *Begriffsschrift* notation from the expressive resources of ordinary colloquial language. He understood that his notation nevertheless shared some of the defects that he hints may be the inherent birthright of every natural language. He separated what is presupposed by meaningful expression and what is literally contained in an expression's meaning. His persuasive example was that of the astronomer Johannes Kepler. Frege observed that, "If one therefore asserts 'Kepler died in misery,' there is a presupposition that the name 'Kepler' designates something; but it does not follow that the sense of the sentence

---

Mathematische Schriften [1850–1863] (Hildesheim: Georg Olms Verlag, 1971), Volume 7, p. 372. See also Dummett, *Frege: Philosophy of Language*, pp. 542–83.

[27] Frege, "On Sense and Reference," p. 67. A detailed treatment of colloquial analogues of logical expressions is given in "On Sense and Reference," pp. 66–67 and 73–76, where a comparison is made with Frege's *Begriffsschrift* as in these respects a more perfect language.

'Kepler died in misery' contains the thought that the name 'Kepler' designates something."[28] Frege then continued as follows:

If this were the case the negation would have to run not
> Kepler did not die in misery

but
> Kepler did not die in misery, or the name "Kepler" has no reference.

That the name "Kepler" designates something is just as much a presupposition for the assertion
> Kepler died in misery

as for the contrary assertion. Now languages have the fault of containing expressions which fail to designate an object (although their grammatical form seems to qualify them for that purpose) because the truth of some sentence is a prerequisite.[29]

The possibility of introducing into language terms like "Sherlock Holmes" that bear all the appearance of being proper names, but that, lacking reference, fail to satisfy the existence presupposition for the referential component of a proper name's meaning, is a defect of colloquial language that Frege's *Begriffsschrift* was designed to avoid. Frege noted with disapproval that not all mathematical languages manage to maintain this ontic standard, citing calculus or the language of mathematical analysis in particular as guilty of the offense.[30]

There is a confusion of presuppositions that Frege's *Begriffsschrift* was meant to clarify in a logically exact statement of relevant mathematical theorems. The other problem in colloquial language that Frege's *Begriffsschrift* was supposed to avoid is the annoyingly common use of tokens of syntactically indistinguishable proper-name types to refer to different entities. They are the source of all equivocation in reasoning. Frege blamed conceptual mayhem on the fact that, outside of his *Begriffsschrift*, words like "buck" can refer to both a dollar and a male deer. Frege complained as follows about the equivocations contained in Kepler's pronouncement:

This [failure to satisfy] arises from an imperfection of language, from which even the symbolic language of mathematical analysis is not altogether free; even there combinations of symbols can occur that seem to stand for something but have (at least so far)

---

[28] *Ibid.*, p. 69.   [29] *Ibid.*

[30] The instructive semantic antipodes of Frege's realism and referential extensionalism and Meinong's anti-realism and referential intensionalism in his *Gegenstandstheorie* or object theory in a breakaway wing of the Brentano school are discussed in Jacquette, *Alexius Meinong: The Shepherd of Non-Being* (Berlin: Springer-Verlag, 2015).

no reference, e.g. divergent infinite series. This can be avoided, e.g., by means of the special stipulation that divergent infinite series shall stand for the number o. A logically perfect language (*Begriffsschrift*) should satisfy the conditions, that every expression grammatically well constructed as a proper name out of signs already introduced shall in fact designate an object, and that no new sign shall be introduced as a proper name without being secured a reference. The logic books contain warnings against logical mistakes arising from the ambiguity of expressions. I regard it as no less pertinent a warning against apparent proper names having no reference.[31]

What Frege would not complain about is the fact that in colloquial language as in mathematics, even in pristine *Begriffsschrift* raiment, there is the possibility of there being more than one sign for the same intended object. This indulgence, which is rife in ordinary language, is something on which both Frege's *Begriffsschrift* and also his *Grundgesetze*, which was about to be published the very next year, vitally depended. Frege's logic and arithmetic needed this semantic opulence in order to be able to express the values of arithmetical functions in function(argument) = value form, as in $2 + 5 = 7$, where "$2 + 5$" and "7" are two different names for the same number. Multiple proper names for the same existent entity are required in order to build purely logical conceptual and inferential bridges from the principles of pure *Begriffsschrift* logic to the basic applied logical laws of elementary arithmetic.

That would be egregious substitution failure in a stupifyingly simple case. Frege responded to the problem by imposing the following distinction:

If somebody were to conclude: The reference of a sentence is not its truth value, for in that case it could always be replaced by another sentence of the same truth value; he would prove too much; one might just as well claim that the reference of "Morning Star" is not Venus, since one may not always say "Venus" in place of "Morning Star." One has the right to conclude only that the reference of a sentence is not *always* its truth value, and that "Morning Star" does not always stand for the planet Venus, viz. when the word has its indirect reference. An exception of such a kind occurs in the subordinate clause just considered which has a thought as its reference.[32]

The proposal was that a proper name appropriately grammatically contexted, the argument of a concept-function in colloquial expression, need not refer to its customary reference but could refer to its indirect reference, which Frege identified with the name's customary sense. Thus, when Q quotes S as saying "I sacrifice to The Morning Star,"

[31] Frege, "On Sense and Reference," p. 70.   [32] *Ibid.*, p. 67.

the Fregean proper name "The Morning Star" does not refer to Venus, and does not even for the same reason refer to The Morning Star. The *S*-quoting context that Q expresses, "The Morning Star," refers instead to the customary sense of the proper name "The Morning Star," which is the set of properties belonging ultimately to the named object designated in the customary reference of the name "The Morning Star," namely The Morning Star itself = the planet Venus.[33]

The Compositionality of Subordinate Clauses

If we ask after the implications of this redirection of the referential meaning of a statement from outside to within a quotation context, we discover in the above example that for Frege the referential component of "The Morning Star" is not The Morning Star but the sense of the proper name "The Morning Star." What does this reconfiguration of semantic intent accomplish for Frege? The unspoken principle on which Frege seemed to rely was that it is not only co-referential proper names that can ordinarily be substituted for one another *salva veritate*, but exclusively customary co-referential proper names. By changing the semantic status of quoted expressions, Frege removes them from consideration for intersubstitution on the basis of co-referentiality, where he assumes they can pose no threat to *Begriffsschrift* truth-value semantics.[34]

This much is an understandably shrewd move. Why, however, having made the reference of quoted proper names indirect rather than customary, did Frege further interpret the indirect reference of a quoted proper name as its customary sense? It seems implausible to attribute reference to a term's customary sense in quotation contexts, because the customary sense

---

[33] See Quine, "Reference and Modality," in Quine, *From a Logical Point of View* (Cambridge: Harvard University Press, 1961), pp. 139–59; Quine, *Word and Object* (Cambridge: MIT Press, 1960), especially pp. 144–51 and 271–76; and Quine, "Speaking of Objects," in Quine, *Ontological Relativity and Other Essays* (New York: Columbia University Press, 1969), p. 23; also pp. 2, 18–19, 32–34, and 45–46. Quine discusses the motto "No entity without identity" in *Theories and Things* (Cambridge: Harvard University Press, 1981), p. 102.

[34] Frege, "On Sense and Reference," pp. 78–79. The literature on *oratio obliqua* substitution failure contexts in Frege is enormous. Leonard Linsky seems to have been among the first to offer a detailed critical exposition of Frege's views exposing flaws in Frege's semantic theory. See Linsky, *Referring* (London: Routledge & Kegan Paul, 1967), pp. 31–35. An appreciative discussion of Linsky is given in Jacquette, "Intentionality on the Instalment Plan," pp. 69–75. See also Dummett, *The Interpretation of Frege's Philosophy*, Chapter 6, "Indexicality and *Oratio Obliqua*", pp. 83–147.

is a potentially infinite set of relevant identifying constitutive Leibnizian identity-determining properties.

Why conclude when S is being quoted by Q that S refers indirectly to the properties of The Morning Star rather than directly to The Morning Star? By Frege's own cherished distinction in "Function and Concept" and "On Concept and Object," the properties of The Morning Star in the customary sense (= indirect reference) of the proper name "The Morning Star" are unsaturated concept-functions. That is minimally to say that they are not Fregean objects.

Frege must consider that functions in the customary sense can somehow be designated as objects. In the quoted sentence, to speak of the two-argument-place function, having the property of being such that something sacrifices to it is attributed to the thinker or speaker and to The Morning Star. What such expanded reformulations reveal is that there is no escaping an intended object of customary reference in any part of Frege's analysis of meaning in "On Sense and Reference." Customary reference is pushed back by the semantic ploy, but never crowded out of the picture. Frege deals only obliquely with the general skeptical argument raised against his logic from this quarter. He argues, in two disconnected passages,

I reply that when we say "the Moon," we do not intend to speak of our idea of the Moon, nor are we satisfied with the sense alone, but we presuppose a reference. To assume that in the sentence "The Moon is smaller than the Earth" the idea of the Moon is in question, would be flatly to misunderstand the sense. If this is what the speaker wanted, he would use the phrase "my idea of the Moon." Now we can of course be mistaken in the presupposition, and such mistakes have indeed occurred. But the question whether the presupposition is perhaps always mistaken need not be answered here; in order to justify mention of the reference of a sign it is enough, at first, to point out our intention in speaking or thinking. (We must then add the reservation: provided such reference exists.)[35]

and

We are therefore driven into accepting the *truth-value* of a sentence as its reference. By the truth-value of a sentence I understand the circumstance that it is true or false. There are no further truth-values. For brevity I call the one the True, the other the False. Every declarative sentence concerned with the reference of its words is therefore to be regarded as a proper name, and its reference, if it has one, is either the True or the False. These two objects are recognized, if only implicitly, by everybody who judges something to be true – and so even by a sceptic.[36]

---

[35] Frege, "On Sense and Reference," pp. 61–62.   [36] *Ibid.*, p. 63.

Frege inadvertently provided conclusive reasoning as to why *the* total sense of a proper name must ideally be the complete abstract set of *all* the named object's Leibnizian identity-determining properties. It is the same full complement of constitutive properties as that needed to determine exact reference by fixing a referent's identity. It is only if we try critically to peel the mainstream and objective sense–reference semantics apart in detailing Frege's theory that his theory of meaning begins to look inadequately developed.

We might wonder how different the basic structure of Frege's philosophy of language would appear if he had made states of affairs the referents of sentences, in particular the truth-making and truth-breaking extant conditions of the world, rather than the extensionally bluntly convergent reified truth-value objects that he pulled out of a hat, the True and the False. What if the sentence "Object a has property F," Fa, were interpreted as referring to the state of affairs in which object a has property F? Then "a" in the sentence can refer to a, the function in the sentence; and $F(\_\_)$ can represent the concept-function F or the state of affairs of something such as a having or being F. There will then exist an exact correspondence of syntactical and semantic components. When what the sentence says agrees with the state of affairs that the sentence represents and to which it refers, the sentence can be said to merit the higher-order truth-value functional predication $V(Fa)$ = the True, rather than making as Frege preferred the reference of the sentence "Fa" identical to the True. Frege seemed to have most of the elements needed for a commonsense semantics of proper names and sentences in his grasp, which he then put together in counterintuitive ways. At the end of the essay, in the final paragraph, Frege concluded as follows:

Let us return to our starting point.

When we found "$a = a$" and "$a = b$" to have different cognitive values, the explanation is that for the purpose of knowledge, the sense of the sentence, viz., the thought expressed by it, is no less relevant than its reference, i.e. its truth value. If now $a = b$, then indeed the reference of "b" is the same as that of "a," and hence the truth value of "$a = b$" is the same as that of "$a = a$." In spite of this, the sense of "b" may differ from that of "a," and thereby the thought expressed in "$a = b$" differs from that of "$a = a$." In that case the two sentences do not have the same cognitive value. If we understand by "judgment" the advance from the thought to its truth value, as in the above paper, we can also say that the judgments are different.[37]

---

[37] *Ibid.*, p. 78.

The sense–reference distinction had now earned its keep in Frege's philosophy of arithmetic. It explained the meaning, truth-conditions, and cognitive informativeness potential of noniterative identity statements. Referentially speaking, noniterative identity statements possess the same truth modality as iterative identity statements. It is only in the possibility of proper names appearing in noniterative identity statements bearing different senses that we are thought able to explain how it can be informative to learn that $a = b$, while remaining unimpressed no matter how many times we are told that $a = a$, $b = b$, $c = c$, etc.

Frege's solution fails to distinguish what he himself calls *the* sense of "*a*" from *the* sense of "*b*," when $a = b$. If *the* ideal Fregean sense of proper name "*a*" is the set of all the properties needed for Leibnizian identity of indiscernibles and indiscernibility of identicals in application to referent object a, which is to say absolutely all of a's distinguishing, identifying, and individuating properties, then as argued the sense of proper name "*a*" cannot possibly be distinct from the sense of proper name "*b*" when $a = b$. The sense of proper name "*b*" in that event will also be the set of all and only the distinguishing properties needed for Leibnizian identity principles applied to individuate b from any simulacrum. That is to say, it will be the set of absolutely all of b's distinguishing properties. These constitutive properties of a and of b must themselves be precisely identical whenever it is true that $a = b$. How could it be otherwise if the Leibnizian indiscernibility of identicals that Frege explicitly accepted is true, if sense determines reference, and if reference is always to specific numerically identical existent entities? Differential sense is consequently hopeless in explaining the potential cognitive informativeness of a noniterative identity statement $a = b$. The most that the sense–reference distinction can offer Frege in accounting for the cognitive informativeness of noniterative identity statements is to say that noniterative identity statements are potentially cognitively informative because not all language users are aware of the fact that when $a = b$ the total sense and therefore the reference of "*a*" must be the same as the total sense and consequently the reference of "*b*."

The solution would probably be too psychologistic for Frege's blood. We are comforted by the fact that cognitive informativeness is, after all, a psychological phenomenon, for which we should not in principle be averse to accepting a psychological explanation. The solution in schematic form, moreover, does not require Frege's sense–reference distinction. The difference in syntax between distinct proper names "*a*" and "*b*" is enough on which to hang a difference in potential psychological attitude, such as knowing something perhaps about the thing named "a," but not previously having known that it was also named "b." The sense–reference distinction in "On Sense and Reference" did not deliver what Frege required of it. It did not explain cognitive informativeness as an objective feature of the fully distinguishing sense-meanings of proper names and sentences. At most, the essay traded implicitly on subjective differences in what linguistic agents believe to be true concerning the distinguishing properties of the existent entities referred to by proper names in their opinions about the names' referents. If there is a unified complete or ideal sense of a proper name that includes all of the constitutive properties in a named object's possession, something which is already needed for Leibnizian identity criterion purposes, then one cannot appeal to differences in the senses of proper name signs "a" and "b" to explain why it can be informative to learn that $a = b$, *the* Fregean senses of which in their totalities must be identical, as the objective interpretation holds against the mainstream.

Other than Frege's demonization of psychologism and, by implication, it often seems, also of psychology, there was no good reason in Frege's semantic philosophy in "On Sense and Reference" why he should not have allowed the possibility of the cognitive informativeness of noniterative identity statements like $a = b$ to be explained against different doxastic and epistemic backgrounds, and the different subjective attitudes, beliefs, and knowledge-base of different subjects with respect to the properties of a and the properties of b. Cognitive informativeness is a subjectively relative psychological phenomenon. What is cognitively informative for one thinker in acquiring an identity-related belief need not be cognitively informative for another. Frege could have appreciated that the strategy offers another opportunity in $a = b$ of relating *the* (total) sense-meaning of proper name "a" to *the* (identical total) sense-meaning of proper name "b."

Frege at the Flowering of Logicism

Frege was now forty-four. He was happily married, or at least we have no reason to suppose that his marriage was not a happy one. He had his mother, Auguste, with him also nearby in the Jena duplex she had arranged to have built. Frege had a position, a salary, and opportunities to enrich his mind with culture and further develop his knowledge and talents. He was poised at exactly the moment before an imminent flowering of his logicism.

The work had already gone on for years in preparation. He had dedicated his life to the study of mathematics and laying the groundwork needed in order to show visually to those with eyes to see the logical dependence of the basic laws of elementary arithmetic on the fundamental concepts and inference principles of pure logic.

The unfolding of Frege's logicism took place only in his *Grundgesetze*, where the logic of concepts expounded in the *Begriffsschrift*, after certain modifications, met the category of natural number analyzed as a purely logical concept-function in the *Grundlagen*. It was the key element in applying the general functional calculus to accomplish a reduction of elementary arithmetic to logic. Without having done this, Frege had not yet taken the final step. There awaited a long commotion of painstaking formal logical derivations in the spatially two-dimensional *Begriffsschrift* notation of Frege's own distinctive design, a slow grinding effort at proving theorems with minimal rules and patently purely logical deductively valid substitution and syntax transformation principles. That arduous task would be undertaken soon in the *Grundgesetze*.

Nothing whatsoever was permitted to be swept under the carpet, hidden behind an impenetrable exterior of proofs or concealed in their presuppositions. That was the main point of the *Begriffsschrift* and *Grundgesetze*. It was the purpose for which Frege's pure and applied logics had been designed. All mathematical reasoning was to be laid bare. The dependence of arithmetic on logic would be undeniable, inescapable, again for those with eyes to see. It would be necessary only to establish all the incremental links, like physicians for the first time in the history of medicine tracing out connecting tissues, bones, blood vessels, muscles, nerves, gland ducts, and secretion channels. The *Grundgesetze* in its final form would be like the great octavo anatomies of the Renaissance that were compiled after a similar process of dissection to that which Frege would perfect in the abstract order of mathematical foundations. He would do so not in order to explore the inner connectedness of a human cadaver's internal structures, but to uncover the logical architecture of elementary arithmetic. He would present the mathematical logic counterpart of Andreas Vesalius's 1543 *De humani corporis fabrica*. Every naked part would be exposed to examination.

The preliminary movements in Frege's logicist revolution had not been well received. That was regrettable, annoying. The main thing was for the pictures of logical dependences of arithmetical laws on purely logical concepts and inference structures to be completed. The reductions would have to be accomplished with basic laws logically formalized and essential theorems deductively proved. Understanding on the part of contemporaries was a luxury. Such understanding would be nice if it happened, provided it was not also a hindrance on the road to truth. It was unnecessary in any event for Frege's self-imposed self-directed undertaking. Acceptance and accolades might or might not come later. All that would only constitute more superfluous ephemeral fly-by-the-moment occurrent psychology for Frege to disregard. He was fixed in purpose on discovering and explicating eternal truths, not running for public office. How could anyone judge what he had done until the third and final movement of the symphony had been performed? The actual work, but for some polishing, had already been prepared in draft as Frege put the finishing touches to the three 1891–1892 published essays on the metaphysics of concepts as functions, the distinction between function and object, and the distinction between sense and reference in the newborn analytic philosophy of language. In these three milestone essays Frege was focused on a general theory of meaning that would have special implications for iterative and noniterative identity statements in the axioms and logically derived theorems containing arithmetical equations whose meaning Frege's logicism was required to explain. The project would not be complete until essential formal demonstrations in the logic of concepts had been published. Frege had not yet taken that final definitive step, but was poised on the brink of doing precisely that as the year turned 1893.[38]

---

[38] A valuable source is Carl, *Frege's Theory of Sense and Reference.* See his "Introduction," p. 2: "[Frege's theory of sense and reference] expounded for the first time and in the most accurate way in his famous essay 'On Sense and Reference' in 1892, can be regarded as a classic work when one considers the impact the theory has had on contemporary philosophy. The modern discussion of reference, the idea of a systematic theory of meaning and the analysis of nonextensional contexts of discourse – all these topics are treated by Frege in this essay in a new and original way, and the modern discussions in these areas, from Wittgenstein to Carnap, Davidson, Dummett and Kripke, are, in some way or other, strongly influenced by [Frege's] arguments." See also Harold W. Noonan, *Frege: A Critical Introduction* (Cambridge: Polity Press, 2001), pp. 168–230; and Jacquette, "Referential Analysis of Quotation," in *Semantic and Pragmatic Aspects of Quotation*, ed. Paul Saka (Berlin: Springer-Verlag, forthcoming).

9

Frege's Culminating Masterwork – *Grundgesetze der Arithmetik I* and *II* (1893/1903)

U P TO THIS point in his logical–arithmetical trail-blazing, Frege had been like the voice of Ishmael calling in the wilderness. There was no conspiracy of mathematicians and philosophers leagued against him, although it might have seemed that way sometimes. The deafening silence, dismissal without useful objections, and misunderstanding to which Frege's first two books were subjected were not the product of ill will, let alone of collective animosity toward the Jena Extraordinariat in mathematics from Wismar. Competent readers were honestly not understanding Frege. They persistently failed to understand his work, even with repeated experiments involving, first, a short book dense with foreign-looking symbolisms, and then an equally short book containing virtually no symbolisms and none of the novel constructions of the general functional calculus presented in the first book. The moments were individually and collectively incomprehensible. The fault could only be the author's. Frege was not succeeding with readers capable of understanding his work because of something he was doing, or not doing.

Publication History

Frege needed to better explain his broader aims to potential readers. This, for methodological or less sufficient personal reasons, he never brought himself to do until it was too late. His approach was like trying to interest buyers in the only chassis for an automobile available for purchase without engine or driveshaft, and then, five years later, trying to interest perhaps the same group of potential buyers, plus whatever new ones may have entered the market, in the sale of the only engine and driveshaft for an automobile independently of the now-scarce no-longer-manufactured proprietary chassis. Some extraordinarily insightful individuals might have seen how the parts could go together, but even then most astute consumers would have wanted to see the actual assembly of components and some trial runs of the working mechanism, before they would surrender their negotiables, assuming that they wanted a vehicle and not the equivalent value in scrap metal. We need add to the analogy only that, unlike in the case of our knowledge of automobiles, buyers for the first components, beginning with the chassis, were not told what could be done with these parts as they emerged from the factory and were put on sale one at a time, or what the completed mechanism was supposed to be capable of doing.

The needed explanations were not provided in Frege's two first major steps toward the concrete demonstration of logicism. At the earliest, they did not become available until at least the first of the two volumes of his *Grundgesetze* had appeared in print. Readers of Frege's *Begriffsschrift* and *Grundlagen* needed to understand what these two products of his impassioned brain were all about, what they were for, and how they were expected to fit together eventually to create something new. In and of themselves, even when taken together, the *Begriffsschrift* and *Grundlagen* were deliberately meant to stand alone, and for that very reason Frege might have deliberately chosen an incomplete exposition, being transparent in his logic about everything except his mathematical philosophical purposes. Frege, until *Grundgesetze I* appeared, was making everyone guess. With its publication he turned the key in the treasure house door and opened its halls for mathematicians to inspect the rich logical structures hidden below the analytic surface of even the most basic axioms and theorems of elementary arithmetic. It is the body of mathematical truth without its façade, where most mathematicians before Frege would never have thought to look.

Apparently, there was no one out there who had understood or cared what in Frege's mind must inevitably come next. Frege's readers in the *Begriffsschrift* and *Grundlagen* were given the key and taken to where they could stand before the door. Any genuinely curious thinker would have considered turning the key in the door. That is exactly what was to have been expected and exactly what Frege's stunningly obtuse readers did not attempt. They may have noticed that there was a key to something or other, and that there was a locked door, and that was where it ended. Frege had to do everything. He was able and keen to do so, one cautious step at a time. In the *Grundgesetze* he turned the *Grundlagen* key in the lock of the *Begriffsschrift* door. We know it opened the *Schatzkammer* of logical structures underlying arithmetic because Frege showed them explicitly as the structurally articulated pure logic of the axioms and deductive proofs of theorems in elementary arithmetic. For those who knew what they were looking at, each *Grundgesetze* proof was like an opened chest of gold and worked gemstones, for the sake of which Frege's readers would have benefited from more of his guidance.

Frege's logical symbolisms displayed inferential structures visually in *Begriffsschrift* syntax for all to bear witness. The unveiling sequentially of logical concept-functions and inference structures internal to elementary arithmetic was visited by Frege not at random, but according to his vision of what was most fundamental and of greatest utility in applied logical theory analysis and construction, namely theoretical reconstruction, as in, first and foremost, Frege's rigorous non-psychologistic logicism. The *Grundgesetze* was supposed to reflect a real ordering of abstract mathematical relations underwritten by a *Begriffsschrift* and *Grundgesetze* arithmetic of fully algebraic pure logic applied to the *Grundlagen* analysis of the concept-function of natural number.

One of the most fascinating aspects of Frege's biography, beyond the chronicle of documented moments around which historical narrative depends, is the question of whether he might not have better explained the sweeping ultimate purpose of his grand design in either of the first two books. Supposing in retrospect that he could have known how badly his ship would sail launched in such spare trim, would Frege have been justified in withholding this amplification from the first two books, if he had it all to do over again? Frege had reasons for presenting the parts of his logicism in and as three main separate installments. The third movement of Frege's concept-functional logical masterpiece, of necessity rather than desire, was divided into two volumes published over the space of ten years. Frege's publisher, Hermann Pohle, fronted the costs of the first volume of the *Grundgesetze* on speculation. Frege financed the second volume ten years later from his own resources. The negative spin is that in this unfortunate process even Frege's make-believe readers offered only *Grundgesetze I* were deprived of an overview of the completed project's purely logical bridgehold on elementary arithmetic. If we are being more positive, as Frege may have conceived of the admittedly imperfect arrangement, *Grundgesetze I* was anyway the published completion of the groundplan for a still more ambitious total reduction of all arithmetic to pure logic. Somehow or other he would make sure that the second volume joined the first.

Suggestions have already been vaunted that Frege may have preferred the two components of his large-scale project each at first to stand on its own merits. He may have wanted them to be exposed to criticism and survive the strongest objections on their own terms before being put to use, like a scientific hypothesis. On this view, they would have to endure testing individually before they could be relied on to effect something as momentous as Frege's pure logicism. This would mean that criticism must not be optimistically colored by the hopes, expectations, and wishful thinking of potential supporters or detractors, especially on the part of critics predisposed toward or against any type of logicism. It is a better experiment all around if the general functional calculus and analysis of the concept of natural number are floated in separate installments without advertising their final purpose, their destination in the logicist equation. A potential critic who agreed with the objectives of Frege's logicism, alerted to the importance of the *Begriffsschrift* and later the *Grundlagen* in that grand design, might want these component parts to succeed badly enough to overlook fatal flaws and defects in the logic and concept-function of natural number. The integrity of Frege's program of using *Begriffsschrift* logic in order to derive arithmetic inferentially from the purely logical concept of natural number in his *Grundlagen* would have also been compromised had he relied on the *Begriffsschrift* to formalize a supposedly purely logical concept of natural number. Frege's *Grundlagen*, logicians might be inclined to say today, is conducted in the informal *metalanguage* of the *Begriffsschrift*, where many essential explanations about *Begriffsschrift* principles and the logic's symbolism are also expressed without circular dependence on the formalism by virtue of standing outside its formation rules in order to refer to and ask and answer questions about objects and constructions within the logic. An excellent place to begin metalogical inquiry is to ask whether the logic's rules are themselves logically consistent.

Frege wanted to garner the sharpest critical judgment that publication in the scientific press could entice, in order to make sure before proceeding that he was entitled to advance. He was almost too close to the logic to assume this critical role himself, or anyway he had done whatever he thought he could in this regard and felt the need to have independent reactions to the proposal. It was not his fault if at this point useful objections had not appeared. He produced proofs after deciding what needed to be proved and in what he perceived to be their exact order of dependence, taking theorems as lemmata for the derivation of further theorems. With the 1893 publication of *Grundgesetze I*, Frege thought he had built upon a cleared field for the purely logical reconstruction of basic laws, namely the axioms and selected theorems of elementary arithmetic. No one had come forward to challenge the program in its main outline or in any of the details Frege had thus far attempted. No one seemed to know what he was trying to do, so no one cared whether he succeeded or not, or cared what it would mean. He professed to court useful objections, and his statements seem to have been sincere. He openly challenged imaginary critics to theorize a superior foundations of arithmetic, or, as he declared impossible, identify a logical contradiction lurking anywhere in his *Grundgesetze*.

Slouching toward the *Grundgesetze*

The disappointment Frege felt was not to do with his philosophy of logic and mathematics. It was over the misunderstanding and failure to collect significant objections of any practical advantage for the *Begriffsschrift*. The bookstall and critical reception was unfortunate, undeniably. Frege was chagrined. He nonetheless took away from the sullen experience at least the firm sense that no one had as yet torpedoed his large-scale objectives. He had not received a criticism able to obliterate or even disable either of the two main individual components of logicism that by this point in time he had presented for independent scrutiny to scientific and philosophical readers of the *Begriffsschrift* and *Grundlagen*.

Unfortunately, the two books by themselves did not tell a complete story. Frege made insufficient effort to explain how they were supposed to be related. For that and other reasons, the unpreparedness of the profession for Frege's efforts to systematize elementary arithmetic on purely logical foundations denied Frege the sympathetic readership that could have paved the way for his efforts to revolutionize the philosophy of mathematics. As things stood, Frege's publications were as much an embarrassment as proof of cutting-edge mathematical discovery and invention. His advocates at Jena and the academic committees that were mustered to decide about such things as salary increases as a reward for successful teaching and research performance must have considered Frege a problem case.

Frege took a gamble in publishing stand-alone volumes before bringing their distinct contributions together in the *Grundgesetze*, the final act toward which everything else was building. He took a gamble in withholding a more complete explanation of his purposes, the endgame for which the *Begriffsschrift* and *Grundlagen* were only the opening moves. As with all gambling, there was an element of risk, a chance of miscalculating, of bad luck pitting oneself against the odds, or of things going wrong. Frege proceeded more with the confidence of engaging a master's skill, like the first moves on a chessboard when an opponent does not know what strategy to expect. Frege followed his own bad advice with a strategy that was in some ways brilliant and methodologically sound if we are interpreting it correctly, but that failed to consider the problem of reader comprehension and uptake. If Frege had nothing as concrete evidence of his productivity to show his supervisors, then a practical implication was the peril of never finding regular employment in mathematics at Jena or anywhere else at university level, perhaps owing to disrecommendation or an inability to impress on account of his work record alone. That consequence would also have hardly been conducive to Frege's seeing through to completion his logicist reduction of elementary arithmetic to pure logic.

On the charitable interpretation by which Frege for methodological reasons did not want to risk packaging all of his logicism together, Frege had good reasons to go forward exactly as he did. He advanced neither recklessly nor timidly, but as an exercise in sound cautious scientific method. He deliberately avoided jeopardizing the whole for the sake of an untested part that could have been corrected before the entire machine was assembled. No doubt the true explanation would need to combine rational and emotional elements, to distinguish which as though they could be split apart in Frege's motivations would be neither competent historiography nor insightful armchair psychology.

There was certainly no public adulation for what he had done, however much of a hero he may have already been at the Freges' Wismar fireside. Nor, however, had any damning earthshaking criticisms emerged as yet in the scant mostly useless notices that had appeared. Publishing the books, meaning that he could hold the finished products in his hand and turn their pages, and read the rare reviews, was an invaluable part of the process. It afforded Frege the opportunity to stand back, reconsider everything, and settle more firmly in his mind how the reduction of arithmetic to logic should continue to progress. There was no sufficient justification in any-thing Frege read of these first stages of his project to induce him to step away in good conscience from the line of inquiry on which he had embarked. His *Begriffsschrift* and *Grundlagen* had been field-tested, and, with some dust shaken off, would be ready for the next and final phase of the main event, which was to be realized in the two volumes of the *Grundgesetze der Arithmetik*.

Imagine tearing in half a book like the *Oxford English Dictionary*, and publishing only the first part, A through M, to see whether there might eventually be enough interest to make it worthwhile to make the second part available. The N–Z part would follow only if the publisher were sufficiently encouraged, and if people seemed to like having a guide to the spelling and meanings of words in the first half of the alphabet, thinking they might be game years later to give the second half a try. That is roughly Frege's situation in bringing out *Grundgesetze I* in 1893, uncertain as to whether or when the completion of the treatise would be brought about with the appearance of *Grundgesetze II*. The division of *Grundgesetze I* and *II*, frustrating as it must have been for Frege, also afforded the project a useful breather. The arrangements with the publisher would not have taken Frege by surprise suddenly in 1893. He knew what to expect and had planned around the publication of the book in installments. He could make efficient use of the interval to stand back sagely for deeper reflection on the prospects of pure logicism. He was equipped in the cupboard with all of the unpub-lished second volume of the arithmetic to be tested then against what critics might say about the first part. As Frege always seemed to prefer, he alone would know what was coming next, keeping the rest of the arithmetic under wraps until such occasion should afford. He could also save up or scrounge in the meantime the money that he would probably need to publish *Grundgesetze II*.

That work had been accomplished and at the moment would exist only up his sleeve in manuscript. It was valuable time during which Frege undertook more refined work on the purely logical concept-functions and inferential theorem proof structures of elementary arithmetic. He iden-tified concepts with functions and distinguished concepts from objects. He developed a two-dimensional semantics of meaning for the sense and reference, semantic meaning and epistemic cognitive informativeness, of proper names to existent entities satisfying Leibnizian property-related identity conditions. These aspects he construed as the complete objective sense of a name in the numerical identity-determining properties of the named object. They are the properties that collectively are true of exactly one referent. The sense-meanings of sentences which Frege considered at this time are compositional functions of the sense of component meaningful terms in the sentence. Tautologies and contradictions aside, reference to reified truth-values, the True and the False, reaches beyond compositional sense by depending on the contingent facts of the world as truth-makers and truth-breakers establishing a sentence's truth-value.

The essays of the 1890s leading up to *Grundgesetze I* were the philosophical foundation for the 1893 first volume of Frege's arithmetic. Frege's writing and rewriting of the *Grundgesetze* must have coincided with his parallel work on the 1890s essays. The two works, the *Grundgesetze* and, tied with a ribbon, the three 1890s essays in theory of meaning, are best understood only when read as integral to one another, rather than as separate unrelated streams in Frege's thought. The latter interpretation encourages the image of Frege developing a formal rigorous and non-psychologistic purely logical arithmetic, and also, incidentally, as a side interest and further sign of his greatness, providing while he was at it a general semantics for the meaning of names and declarative sentences, laying the cornerstones of analytic philosophy of language. The contrary evaluation developed here is that we literally cannot understand *Grundgesetze* identity statements in elementary arithmetical equations without the 1890s essays, that they constitute a continuum of thinking about the absolute truth of the function(argument) = value identity statements in arithmetical equations, recognizing the need both for the formally exact syntactical structure in the *Grundgesetze* and for support by the unequivocal semantic meaning conditions in the 1890s essays.

Frege accepted the opportunity to publish the first volume of his *Grundgesetze* with as much apparent optimism as he had shown in bringing the *Begriffsschrift* and *Grundlagen* to the ideas marketplace. The basic publication facts surrounding Frege's *Grundgesetze I* and *II* are explained in virtually identical terms by all commentators. We read in Beaney, for example, that

Frege had great difficulty finding a publisher for the *Grundgesetze*. In the end, Hermann Pohle of Jena (who had published his lecture "Function and Concept") agreed to publish it in instalments, the publication of the second being conditional upon the favourable reception of the first ... The second volume, it seems, was brought out at Frege's own expense.[1]

Mendelsohn similarly observes that

> *Grundgesetze* was published in 1893 by Hermann Pohle, in Jena. Frege had had difficulty finding a publisher for the book, after the poor reception given to his other works. Pohle agreed to publish the work in two parts: if the first volume was received well, he would publish the second one. Unfortunately it was not received well, to the extent that it was acknowledged by anyone at all. Pohle refused to publish the second volume, and Frege paid for its publication out of his own pocket some ten years later.[2]

The publication history of *Grundgesetze I* and *II* explains Frege's division of the text into two volumes as an economic necessity. If Frege delayed publication of the second volume at his own expense until ten years later, the reasonable explanation is not that he felt so bad about the reception of *Grundgesetze I* that he was despondent about publishing the second volume until another ten years had passed, by which time, perhaps for independent reasons, his mood had changed. It is more likely that he could not afford to subvent the book's printing until such time. He may have been saving as much as he could, while the costs of printing continued to rise. It is not known, and may never be determined, what Frege paid to publish *Grundgesetze II*, or whether he ever recovered any of his expenses through sales. It is only human nature to wonder whether Frege and Margarete discussed the diversion of hard-earned money to his publication plans for *Grundgesetze II*, when there seemed to have been virtually no prior interest in *Grundgesetze I* even among the meager numbers of mathematicians and philosophers.

The Logical Foundations of Arithmetic

Frege's efforts to gain an appreciative readership for his philosophy of mathematics, the reductive conceptual analysis of the basic laws of elementary arithmetic reconstructed in terms of the principles of pure logic, reached in this ten-year span its philosophical dénouement. He would still be calling out in the wilderness, but now much more loudly, and with something more contentful, a complete message in modified *Begriffsschrift* logical notation to cast out onto the waves sealed in a bottle from the shore.

---

[1] Beaney, "Introduction" to Beaney, ed., *The Frege Reader*, p. 5, note 8.
[2] Mendelsohn, *The Philosophy of Gottlob Frege*, p. 4.

Frege's *Grundgesetze* was intended as an axiomatization of arithmetic involving more applied intuitive fundamental logical principles than were spread out over many pages in Frege's exposition of his *Begriffsschrift*. It was aimed at the same general purpose of providing a rigorous formalization of a logicist reduction of arithmetic to concept-functions and inference rules of pure logic for which the *Begriffsschrift* was only a preparatory stage. It was the first movement in a mathematical dialectic of three distinct moments, the last spanning ten years. The division of labor represented by the first and projected subsequent volume of his *Grundgesetze* was for Frege to advance the axioms of logic and number theory in the first volume, and thereafter to extend the analysis of basic concepts of arithmetic to real numbers and higher mathematics, including Cantor's transfinite cardinalities. Frege did not seek further academic promotion after this time, but concentrated on the completion of his rigorous non-psychologistic logicism. It was a decision made possible, given changes in his personal circumstances, only because Frege's work during those crucial years was directly funded by endowment of the Carl-Zeiss-Stiftung thanks to Abbe's beneficence. The Stiftung eventually paid half of Frege's total salary, doubling his university earnings.[3]

Grundgesetze I (1893)

The most important event of 1893 in Frege's history was undoubtedly the publication of the first volume of his *Grundgesetze*. The original manuscript for the book is in the possession of the University of Jena's library.[4] It shows, say those who have seen it, that Frege had already completed the entire book in 1893, but chose to publish it in two installments, separated, as we have seen, by ten long years, or rather had no option but to publish it in this way. When the second volume of the *Grundgesetze* finally appeared in 1903, it completed Frege's project to reconstruct the basic laws of elementary arithmetic on purely logical foundations.

The publication problem reflected a convergence of Frege's publisher's monetary concerns centering, first of all, on the poor sales and critical

---

[3] Kreiser, *Gottlob Frege*, pp. 57–66, 113, 365, 417–19, and 613, offers details on Abbe's association with the Carl-Zeiss-Stiftung (and also with Carl Zeiss) and on the financial support Frege received from it.

[4] Kratzsch, "Material zu Leben und Wirken Freges aus dem Besitz der Universitäts-Bibliothek Jena," pp. 537–38.

reception of the *Begriffsschrift*, to which the *Grundgesetze* was rightly perceived as the technical successor. The practical difficulties were heavily compounded by the exorbitant cost of setting Frege's two-dimensional *Begriffsschrift* notation formulas in type for a work of such daunting length. Almost all the symbolisms were one-off. The specialized lead-alloy metal type uniquely designed for Frege's book could not easily be used again. The fonts were labor-intensive to make and consequently expensive to produce. There were many such formulas already in the *Begriffsschrift*, almost seventy-five pages' worth. Now, in the *Grundgesetze*, there were eventually, in both volumes of the treatise considered altogether, more than four hundred and fifty pages of formal symbolic logical expressions. Each formula, between the inclusion and position of the negation-sign danglers and exact placement of dimples for quantifiers holding a variety of different styles of variable, was charged with highly significant minor graphic particularities that had to be exactly correctly duplicated in the printed book, or their logical purpose would be ruined, in some cases converted to incomprehensible illogical gibberish. The results needed to be checked several times to minimize printing errors. The misplacement or omission of a single added negation tab in Frege's notation, or a missing or mistyped variable or constant object symbol, could wreak logical havoc throughout the system. The description barely begins to cover the difficulties of publishing Frege's arithmetic.

To gaze even casually at Frege's 1893 *Grundgesetze I* is to encounter what musicians sometimes call a *black page*. It is in that instance a musical score that is jam-packed with tiny rapidly timed notes and grace-notes in every measure, all difficult to master and correctly play, in a densely temporally conceived composition that demands to be performed rapidly and with extraordinary precision. If we think of Frege as a composer, not of music but in symbolic logic, then we must regard his 1893 *Grundgesetze* as the first symphonic mathematical movement in his final grand orchestral operatic masterpiece. To take the musical analogy one step further, American humorist Mark Twain (1835–1910) is sometimes falsely credited with the quip of Edgar Wilson Nye (1850–1896), that "Wagner's music is better than it sounds."[5] A casual peruser of Frege's *Begriffsschrift* or *Grundgesetze* might similarly remark that Frege's logic is and may work better than it looks.

---

[5] See the *Autobiography of Mark Twain: The Complete and Authoritative Edition*, ed. Harriet E. Smith, Benjamin Griffin, and Victor Fisher (Berkeley: University of California Press, 2010), p. 566, entry 288.12–26 for the qualifying comment by the editors.

Frege's previous *Begriffsschrift* publisher, Verlag von Louis Nebert, in Halle, would not touch the *Grundgesetze*. The house had learned its lesson the hard way, and the editors were probably surprised that Frege still had not. Bynum describes the obstacles Frege encountered in trying to bring to the scientific public's attention the final stages of the visible exact formal graphic pictorial reduction of the basic laws of elementary arithmetic to the fundamental principles of logic. He states without qualification, in an extended passage worth quoting at length, that

[...] no publisher would risk printing Frege's book. The manuscript was very long and filled with two-dimensional displays of Frege's special notation. This made printing more difficult and more expensive than for a book in ordinary language or customary logic. Furthermore, Frege's earlier works had been coldly received, and there was no guarantee that the new volume would not receive similar treatment. It seemed a great financial risk to print Frege's book; and apparently no publishing house was willing to take that risk.

The problem was finally resolved, however, by a compromise: the publisher Hermann Pohle in Jena, who had printed Frege's lecture "On Function and Concept," agreed to print the book in two installments, the publication of the second part to be dependent upon a good reception of the first. So, in late 1893, the first volume of *The Basic Laws of Arithmetic* (*Grundgesetze*) appeared.

Frege had no great expectations, however; for it is evident in the Preface that he feared the worst. Here, obviously pessimistic, he seems to try hard to prod or persuade prospective readers to study his book. He tells of disappointment over the reception – or lack of it – of his earlier works; and he informs the reader that the appearance of Volume II will depend upon a good reception of Volume I. He describes unfavourable attitudes and trends of the day, working against the acceptance, or even the reading, of his book; and he challenges other scholars to do better or find something essentially wrong with his work. He criticizes "formalism" and viciously attacks psychologism, as if to provoke an answer. Finally, he asks for support from other mathematicians against the corrupting influence of the "psychological logicians."[6]

Frege may have hoped that *Grundgesetze I* would do well enough to partly subsidize the publication of *Grundgesetze II*. Certainly the first volume without the second would not answer Frege's need to have the complete system available in print. The irrefutable proof of logicism would be the logical analysis of the basic laws and theorems of elementary arithmetic in the *Grundgesetze*. With that basis in place and arithmetical functions free for the asking, reducing all of arithmetic to logic was not yet available, but its final outcome in Frege's logic was assured.

---

[6] Bynum, "Life and Work of Gottlob Frege," in *Frege: Conceptual Notation*, pp. 34–35.

Frege's logic had so many different logical axioms and inference rules let loose without proper supervision that a skeptic has less confidence than elementary arithmetic before the *Grundgesetze* inspires that the logic was not riddled with logical antinomy or less drastic but still disqualifying formal disadvantages. The biographical fact is that Frege at this time seems to have been untroubled by any such considerations. Frege mentioned in the troubled Foreword to *Grundgesetze I*, after lamenting the disappointing reception of previous writings, his optimism, despite all and prescient in the event, about contributing to what he hoped would be "a renaissance of logic."

Frege's work was ultimately to have that effect. From his standpoint in 1893, surrounded by incomprehension and impassive indifference as to whether or not arithmetic was an extension of pure logic and, if it were, what difference it would make, and by doubts concerning his chosen means of demonstrating the truth of logicism in the structure he had erected in his three books, there was not much prospect of improving the situation by publishing *Grundgesetze I*. In Frege's judgment, it was work that needed to be done in just those historical circumstances; it was a scientific obligation for someone with his skills to undertake. There was a further leap to be made in the evolution of mathematical knowledge. It fell to his lot to deduce arithmetic from logic where no one else was sufficiently capable or motivated. The project by then had taken on an independent life of its own, which may have contributed to its sense of inevitability. The appearance, in two volumes if necessary, of the knockdown visual proof that elementary arithmetic is purely logical had for Frege become a Kantian hypothetical if not categorical imperative.[7]

Frege's Lament in the Foreword to *Grundgesetze I*

Bynum's characterization paints an unnecessarily wretched picture of Frege. What is distressing is not so much the disappointing reception of his work. Other thinkers have endured as much and worse in the history of science and philosophy. The contention that Frege might have experienced despair is rather attributable to the fact that he so candidly bared his soul on these matters in the *Vorwort* (Foreword) to *Grundgesetze I*. The

---

[7] Kant, *The Groundwork to the Metaphysics of Morals* [1785] (Cambridge: Cambridge University Press, 2012), especially pp. 28–34. See Sally Sedwick, *Kant's Groundwork of the Metaphysics of Morals* (Cambridge: Cambridge University Press, 2008), pp. 94–107.

whole thing can easily strike a sour note, as though Frege, just as he was about to achieve the culmination of his reduction of arithmetic to logic, were now lamenting, whining, and complaining about the fact that he had not received what he considered due regard for his previous accomplishments, especially in the *Begriffsschrift*. Frege's lament appears in the Foreword to *Grundgesetze I*:

> As one can see, the years since the publication of my *Begriffsschrift* and *Grundlagen* have not passed in vain: they have seen the work mature. But the very thing which I regard as essential progress serves, as I cannot conceal from myself, as a major obstruction to the dissemination and influence of this book. Moreover, what I regard as not the least of its virtues, strict gaplessness of the chains of inferences, will earn it, I fear, scant appreciation.[8]

An air of self-defeat hangs over the Foreword to *Grundgesetze I*. Frege was publishing the book, obviously. He did not expect that it would be properly received, as he explained. He felt obliged to produce the book, nevertheless. Here it is, attached in what follows the book's Foreword, although he says he knows already that the reader was not going to like it. He must follow through the project that he had originally essayed and was then ready to present before an ungrateful incomprehending world. The Foreword intones a classic pearls-before-swine litany.

Frege blames the logic itself in some ways. His readership problems have stemmed from the fact that the symbolism makes too great a demand on average customers, however subtle and advanced their mathematical ability and education. There was no one to whom an interested student of Frege's texts could turn. It was all entirely new. Frege continues in spite of these obvious facts of the matter to express surprise and disappointment that the project has not caught on with more enthusiasm among mathematicians and philosophers, and especially among logicians. The logicians out there that Frege was trying to reach by means of his previous two books and now the new consummation of all that preceded it should have been among the first to embrace Frege's discoveries.

His astonishment over the fact that the world did not share his excitement is one of Frege's endearing qualities. It had taken a toll on his energies, he reports, and on his ability to sustain difficult work on the project. The

---

[8] Frege, *Grundgesetze I*, Foreword, p. x. More details on the manuscript copy of the *Grundgesetze* in the possession of the library of the University of Jena can be found in Kratzsch, "Material zu Leben und Wirken Freges aus dem Besitz der Universitäts-Bibliothek Jena," pp. 537–39.

lack of a warm reception for his logic had resulted in a psychological depression that diluted his ability to make progress toward a complete exposition of pure logicism in its first phase on the more regular work schedule he ideally preferred. He continues thus in the Foreword:

> With this, I arrive at a second reason for the delay: the despondency that at times overcame me as a result of the cool reception, or rather, the lack of reception, by mathematicians of the writings mentioned above, and the unfavourable scientific currents against which my book will have to struggle. The first impression alone can only be off-putting: strange signs, pages of nothing but alien formulae.[9]

The demands of gapless transparency in all derivations imply that certain logical relations must be depicted so that anyone can literally see the truth-value dependences by which the basic laws of elementary arithmetic are derived from purely logical concept-functions and applied in deductively licensed logical inference structures. It was an excessive demand even for most technical readers at the time.

The harsh but worldly realistic truth is that a book's positive first impression is often the only thing that gives it a prayer of finding knowledgeable readers to invest the necessary time and energy in a second impression. Frege should have known this. He expected nothing less of the authors he had reviewed. He should have understood it already in 1879 with the publication of the *Begriffsschrift*. Had he not shown it in advance to anyone in his circle? Did he delight in their misapprehension, squinting at the wiry formulas? That he was driven against its predictable impediments even to a competent mathematical audience to use *Begriffsschrift* notation means that there was something about the notation itself that trumped any considerations of convenience or popularity and their more prevalent contraries, even among professional logicians and mathematicians. Frege did not adopt *Begriffsschrift* symbolism out of a perverse desire to make his readers learn something complicated and completely unprecedented for no worthwhile purpose.

Critics of the caliber Frege yearned to attract would immediately imagine their own array of possible applications for which Frege's *Begriffsschrift* should have proven an invaluable tool. Would they not? *Begriffsschrift* symbolism was not optional for Frege's understanding of logicism and of what the reduction of arithmetic to pure logic needed in order to achieve success in a concrete demonstration of its truth. He was explicit that there

---

[9] Frege, *Grundgesetze I*, Foreword, p. xi.

was no other way in which the investigation could be conducted. He developed a general fully algebraic functional calculus or logic of concepts as the applied logical scaffolding for the derivation of arithmetic from pure logic. The importance of what he had achieved could be seen only in the notation of a *Begriffsschrift* like Frege's. A visual display of logical structure, Frege believed, could be achieved only by graphically exhibiting in two spatial dimensions the truth-value dependence relations between propositions. The propositions of interest are theorems of elementary arithmetic, for which identity statements of numerical equations are basic relational predications. The logical inference structures by which arithmetical theorems are deduced from their applied logically expressed arithmetical axioms undergird the system and then join ranks as further established truths in an amplification of mathematical knowledge.

Continuing in this spirit, in what could be a line from a Gothic novel written by Mary Shelley in 1818, Frege dips into his sparing intellectual autobiography to add the following words to the *Grundgesetze* Foreword lament:

Thus sometimes I concerned myself with other subjects. Yet as time passed, I simply could not contain these results of my thinking, which seemed to me valuable, locked up in my desk; and work expended always called for further work if it was not to be in vain. Thus the subject matter kept me captive.[10]

As Frege rarely revealed much about himself, the passage is priceless in affirming that the *Begriffsschrift*, *Grundlagen*, and *Grundgesetze* exerted a psychological compulsion on his thinking. The imperative that had obliged Frege to continue using *Begriffsschrift* notation in his *Grundgesetze*, while acknowledging that the concept-script symbolism was "off-putting," at least on "first impression," also drove him to further complete the enormous challenge he had no one to thank for but himself. In spite of bad press and rampant misunderstandings, the terrible silence that other philosophers spearheading new lines of thought had sometimes encountered from an impacted old guard, Frege inched forward.

Frege now obligingly made clear what had previously been attributed to his attitude about publishing his logical discoveries. He did not expect widespread interest or understanding. That once cherished desire had long since been extinguished. He submissively placed his faith more meekly now in the existence of a someday reader who would

[10] *Ibid.*

discover an "inner reward" in understanding what Frege had written in the pages of *Grundgesetze I* to follow. He appealed to the imaginary reader who might find the book sufficiently intrinsically interesting to spread the word by giving the new book "a thorough examination" in an intelligent review. It did not seem like too much to ask, but it was strange nevertheless to invite and request such a thing, especially in the book's front matter. Significantly, Frege indicated that his purpose had been to solicit worthwhile criticism, if only in "a critical assault," so long as it was "based on a thorough study." His *Grundgesetze* Foreword laments that

> All that is left for me is to hope that someone may from the outset have sufficient confidence in the work to anticipate that his inner reward will be repayment enough, and will then publicise the results of a thorough examination. It is not that only a complimentary review could satisfy me; quite the contrary! I would always prefer a critical assault based on a thorough study to praise that indulges in generalities without engaging the heart of the matter.[11]

It is possible to understand Frege's remarks as something other than signs of overwork or bitterness, complaints about the persistent disappointments he had faced in previous stages of the work about to unfold, if anyone could be bothered to turn its pages. Rather, Frege documented in the Foreword the objective state of the campaign to explain all of mathematics as an offshoot of an algebraic formal symbolic logic formalized in *Begriffsschrift* notation, together with the philosophically discriminating analysis of the concept of natural numbers in his *Grundlagen*. Frege may have thought it historically valuable to record these facts about the thin reception of his *Begriffsschrift*, and of his brand of logicism in its present state of development. There was no better place to situate such remarks than in the book's Foreword. The purpose of recording the information in the book's Foreword was questionable, aside from the propriety of Frege's wheeling out the sad background.

Frege next anticipated a potential source of misunderstanding and prejudice against his *Grundgesetze* before the Foreword had even finished. It was a hurdle he perceived in the metaphysics of imperceivable mathematical entities, beginning with numbers. Frege expanded on this as follows:

---

[11] *Ibid.*

Of further disadvantage for my book is a widespread tendency to accept only what can be sensed as being. What cannot be perceived with the senses one tries to disown, or at least to ignore. Now the objects of arithmetic, the numbers, are imperceptible; how to come to terms with this? Very simple! Declare the number-signs to be the numbers. In the signs, one then has something visible; and this, of course, is the main thing. To be sure, the signs have properties completely different from the numbers; but so what? Just credit them with the desired properties by so-called definitions. [Etc.].[12]

He cannot resist slinging a dialectical barb against those who reject an ontology of imperceivable abstracta, who out of misguided consistency try to make a virtue of necessity by interpreting numbers as signs, effectively confusing numbers with numerals. Frege's clear target is probably Hilbert's formalism, although it is possible that he is also jumbling up Husserl's views about the role of what Husserl called "inauthentic" perception of mathe-matical relations in the symbolic notations involved in the conduct of mathematical thinking beyond the authentic simplest perceivable differ-ences in numbers of things. Frege's review of Husserl's 1891 *Philosophie der Arithmetik* appeared in the year following *Grundgesetze I*, in 1894, and Frege would certainly have seen Husserl's book at least a year before 1893. Having dispensed with formalism or irrealism in the philosophy of mathematics, Frege turned as prescripted against the menace of psychologism. He expostulated on a well-worn theme in Fregean polemics:

This may suffice to put my logical standpoint into a clearer light by the contrast. The distance from psychological logic seems to me to be as wide as the sky, so much so that there is no prospect that my book will have an effect on it immediately. My impression is that the tree that I have planted has to heave an incredible load of stone to make space and light for itself. Still, I will not give up all hope that my book will eventually aid the overthrow of psychological logic.[13]

For all his pique directed against psychologism, Frege in this section of the *Grundgesetze* Foreword was unable to mention any practitioners of the dark art he so vehemently rejected other than its forthright defender Benno Erdmann. Frege mentioned in particular Erdmann's *Logik I*, published in 1892.[14] It was only slightly better than having no one at all

---

[12] *Ibid.*, p. xiii. The translation is accurate, but does not quite convey the fact that Frege is mocking the position of formalists like Hilbert who attempt to detach mathematical symbols from all entities as meaningless symbolic game tokens.

[13] *Ibid.*, *Grundgesetze I*, Foreword, p. xxv.

[14] Benno Erdmann (1851–1921), *Logik*, Volume 1, *Logische Elementarlehre* (Halle: Niemeyer, 1892), p. 311.

to cite as guilty of the psychologistic offense, for which Frege berated Erdmann tirelessly in the Foreword to the first volume of his *Grundgesetze*.

Later in the Foreword, Frege warmed up his critique of psychologism, explaining the philosophical errors that became inevitable in his judgment once the distinction had been clouded. The comparison brought to mind again was that analogized in the *Grundlagen* demarcating the North Sea from ideas about the North Sea, between a thing and our subjective occurrent psychological representations of the thing. Psychological contamination and psychologism were blamed for the difficult reception with which Frege's writings on the philosophy of arithmetic had hitherto been met. Even before quitting the Foreword, he called psychologism to account for the negative reception he appears to have been pessimistically convinced his *Grundgesetze* would be certain to receive as soon as it came into the reader's hands:

A proper appreciation of the distinction I draw, between a characteristic mark of a concept and a property of an object, can scarcely be hoped for from the prevailing logic either, for that seems to be contaminated with psychology through and through. If instead of the things themselves, one considers only their subjective images, their ideas, then naturally all finer-grained, objective distinctions are lost and others appear in their place that are logically completely worthless. Thus I come to speak about the obstacle to the influence of my book on the logicians. It is the ruinous incursion of psychology into logic. Decisive for the treatment of this science is how the logical laws are conceived, and this in turn connects with how one understands the word "true."

There is poor Erdmann again. He was criticized by Frege this time for daring to have "mixed up" the existence implication of "there is" with actuality.[15] Perhaps he did so. Perhaps Frege read Erdmann as carelessly as he read others once he whiffed psychologism on their book jackets. That

---

[15] Frege, *Grundgesetze I*, Foreword, pp. xiv–xv. Frege wrote, pp. xxiv–xxv, "Let us see further how subtler differences in the subject matter are smudged over by the psychological logicians. The point was already made in the case of characteristic mark and property. This is connected with the distinction I have emphasised between object and concept, as well as that between concepts of first and second level. Naturally, these differences are indiscernible by psychological logicians; for them everything is idea. For this reason, the proper conception of those judgements which we express in English by 'there is' also eludes them." See Hoppe, "Review of Frege's *Grundgesetze der Arithmetik I*," *Archives of Mathematics and Physics*, 2nd Series 13 (1895), Literary Report XLIX, p. 8; and Giuseppe Peano, "Dr. Gottlob Frege, *Grundgesetze der Arithmetik, begriffsschriftlich abgeleitet*, Erster Band, Jena, 1893, pag. XXXII + 254," *Rivista di matematica*, 5 (1895), pp. 122–28; reprinted in Peano, *Opere scelte* (Rome, 1958), Volume 2, pp. 187–95.

is not a question that needs to be decided here. The interesting issue that Frege raised is that of how to use the words "existence" and "actuality."

The problem boils down to whether or not these terms are synonymous. Frege argued that actuality $\neq$ existence, in the sense that $\neg\forall x[\text{Actual}(x) \leftrightarrow \text{Exists}(x)]$. The reason is that, although it would be natural to say that there *are* or that there *exist* two square roots of 4, it would be strained at best to say that the square roots of 4 are *actual*. To be actual seems to carry the implication of existing in space and time, from which 4 and its square roots are usually, and certainly by Fregean thought, to be excluded. Consider how odd it would be to say that the two square roots of 4 are *actualized*. It was the blatantly psychologistic Erdmann and Erdmann alone who was raked over the coals by Frege in the *Grundgesetze I* Foreword for this transgression.

One would think that if the problem were sufficiently prevalent in the philosophy of mathematics to call down Frege's wrath in his Foreword as one of the sources of detraction from his efforts to mount the platform of logicism, then there would have been more representatives exploring more varieties of ways in which numbers could be considered psychological entities, innate or willful encultured creatures of subjective thought. Even if there were other subjectivists in the philosophy of mathematics to be mentioned, Frege confined his annoyance to Erdmann.

Adding further credence to the historical assertion that Frege already had both parts of his *Grundgesetze* ready to publish in 1893 when *Grundgesetze I* appeared, Frege previewed what readers of that book could expect in the sequel. He delivered a reckless challenge daring readers of the first volume to try to accomplish the same purpose in a different way, which he predicted was certain to fail, or, hedging his bets, not to prosper as well. He declared that "no one will succeed" in proving to him that his "basic principles lead to manifestly false conclusions." It was nine years before Russell would take up Frege's challenge and attempt to demonstrate that Frege's logic suffered from exactly the defect Frege here lightly brushed aside:

[T]he whole of part II is really a test of my logical convictions. It is from the outset unlikely that such a construction could be built on an insecure, defective basis. But if anyone has different convictions, let him try to build a similar construction on them and he will find, I believe, that it does not work, or at least that it does not work so well. And I could only acknowledge it as a refutation if someone indeed showed that a better, more enduring building can be erected on different basic convictions, or if someone proved to me that my basic principles lead to manifestly false conclusions.

But no one will succeed in doing so. And so may this book, even if belatedly, contribute to a renaissance of logic. / Jena in July, 1893. G. Frege.[16]

So ended the Foreword to Frege's *Grundgesetze I*, transforming pathetic lament into defiance. It is in such moments of enthusiastic excess that hubris incites nemesis. For Frege, nemesis descended in the ominous form of Russell's paradox in Russell's polite *Brief* (letter) to Frege of 16 June 1902.

Frege said that one route to refutation of his constructive project in logic would be to show that his "basic principles lead to manifestly false conclusions." This was not new information for readers of works like Frege's *Grundgesetze*. Then, however, came the magnetic taunt "But no one will succeed in doing so." He proclaimed the ultimate enticement for mathematical logical gamesmanship; that is, he broached the issue of whether logical symbolisms were only like rule-following movements of chess pieces in a conceptual space, or something more. Who could resist such a challenge? Evidently Russell could not refrain from taking up Frege's challenge. Moreover, Frege revealed his own considered weak point concerning Axiom V, upon which Russell, unable to fluently read or work around *Begriffsschrift* notation, remarkably latched hold.

Parts of the *Grundgesetze I* Foreword, other commentators have previously observed, do not add up to an especially becoming testimony of Frege's personality. However anguished Frege may have felt about the prior neglect of his hard-won and decidedly more attention-deserving and praiseworthy functional calculus, it did not do him much credit to bemoan quite so frankly and publicly his fate at the bookshops and with reviewers, offending mathematical and philosophical colleagues writing for professional publications. Frege understood the culture of reviewing from the inside, as a frequent contributor of negatively critical, even cutting and contemptuous, commentary on other writers' books. By 1893 he had reviewed works of interest in his field by Heinrich Seeger, co-authors August von Gall and Eduard Winter, Thomae, Hoppe, Hermann Cohen, and Cantor, and in the following year he would publish his caustic review of Husserl's 1891 *Philosophie der Arithmetik*.

---

[16] On this note ends the Foreword lament to *Grundgesetze I*, whereafter Frege turns from bewailing the unenthusiastic reception of his *Begriffsschrift* and *Grundlagen* to tout the advantages of his applied arithmetical logic in the *Grundgesetze*.

Frege assumed the risk, perhaps without appreciating its full potential. Why, then, did he whimper about how unfairly his *Begriffsschrift* had been treated in the Foreword to *Grundgesetze I*? Was it to attract more scientific interest in his logical, mathematical, and philosophical work by soliciting a previously unbiased reader's sympathy? Frege, like any adult, must have known that the world does not work that way. People do not take up a large treatise of mathematics because they feel sorry for the author whose previous book people also did not want to read. Frege could not imaginably be saying in the Foreword to *Grundgesetze I*, unless all this hard work and punishing lack of reward had rattled his reasoning, the equivalent of "please accept or at least consider my theory because no one else has" or "please accept or at least consider my theory because it has been neglected or has suffered from having its content misrepresented by so many others in the past." Adding that he had received unfair treatment as an earnest author making headward strides, if only more persons knew it, in a difficult technical field, did not make things any better or his unintentional self-portrait any more flattering. It seems incautious to suggest that in these parts of the Foreword to *Grundgesetze I* Frege was having a nervous breakdown on the printed page. What, then, was he doing? What was happening?

The *Grundgesetze*'s Statement of Purpose

To answer this historical interpretive question, we turn to a more detailed exposition of Frege's mathematical and philosophical writings from those years. Frege, in parts of the *Grundgesetze* Foreword that are not dedicated to conveying his lament about the poor reception of his *Begriffsschrift*, explained his purpose in the following concise terms:

In this book one finds theorems on which arithmetic is based, proven using signs that collectively I call concept-script [*Begriffsschrift*] ... As may be seen, the investigation does not yet include the negative, rational, irrational and complex numbers, nor addition, multiplication, etc. ... External reasons have made me postpone both this and the treatment of other numbers, and mathematical operations, to a sequel whose publication will depend on the reception of this first volume. What I have offered here may suffice to give an idea of my method.[17]

---

[17] Frege, *Grundgesetze I*, Foreword, p. v.

It was always the first movement in a larger composition to which Frege consigned his accomplishments in his own estimation and as he presented them to the world. The aspiration was to achieve an uncompromising *gaplessness* (*Lückenlosigkeit*) in the chains of logical inferences by which the basic laws of elementary arithmetic and its superstructure of theorems were represented and derived. Frege contrived within his logic to bring to light each arithmetical axiom, on the basis of very simple foundational, and for that reason arguably purely logical, concepts and inference principles. Frege would display, like a study in human anatomy, each assumption, presupposition, hypothesis, and anything else on which the proof of an arithmetical theorem might rest. The deductive logical derivation of the basic laws of elementary arithmetic simultaneously was to provide the basis for assessing the epistemic and truth status of each logically grounded law.

The non-negotiable requirement for Frege's logicism was that without exception every logical linkage in the structure by which the axioms or basic rules of elementary arithmetic were configured must be explicitly represented. The linkages had to appear in an ascending logical architecture from purely logical concept-functions through applied logical inferences in Frege's general functional calculus introduced by the modified *Begriffsschrift* logic of concepts in the preliminary chapters of *Grundgesetze I*. Frege insisted that all such inferences must be open to view, with everything essential laid out in a surveyable logical expression. Frege explained what he thought he had achieved in using the logic to represent the reasoning offered in support of arithmetical theorems. Only if the proofs of true Fregean thoughts in elementary arithmetic could be examined and scrutinized with nothing concealed could the frequently heralded thesis that "arithmetic is merely logic further developed" be properly assessed.

Frege's goal was not only to facilitate an evaluation of logicism's title to truth, but in the process to define and reinforce a particular version of logicism. The ideal of being able to look into all the inferential joinery of the derivation of an arithmetical proof in Frege's *Begriffsschrift* logical reconstructions of elementary arithmetical theorems was not open in his mind to responsible dispute. He remarked that

Although it has already been announced many times that arithmetic is merely logic further developed, still this remains disputable as long as there occur transitions in the proofs which do not conform to acknowledged logical laws, but rather seem to rest on intuitive knowledge. Only when these transitions are analysed into simple logical steps can one be convinced that nothing but logic forms the basis. I have listed everything that can facilitate an assessment whether the chains of inferences are properly connected and the buttresses are solid. If anyone should believe that there is some fault, then he must be able to state precisely where, in his view, the error lies: with the basic laws, with the definitions, or with the rules or a specific application of them. If everything is considered to be in good order, one thereby knows precisely the grounds on which each individual theorem rests.[18]

Fatefully, Frege mentions what he takes to be the logic's Achilles' heel. Rousing the counterexampling spirit of Russell some eight or nine years later, Frege in the Foreword to *Grundgesetze I* now directed like-minded readers to the best place to look for a damaging objection. It was to be precisely the problem that Russell fastened onto and concerning which he formulated under its presumed authority what he took to be the logical contradiction that Frege had boastfully maintained could never be found. Frege continued as follows:

As far as I can see, a dispute can arise only concerning my basic law of value-ranges ([*Grundgesetze* Axiom] V), which perhaps has not yet been explicitly formulated by logicians although one thinks in accordance with it if, e.g., one speaks of extensions of concepts. I take it to be purely logical.[19]

Purely logical *Grundgesetze I* Axiom V might even be. It is essentially a law that authorized Frege's logic to define sets from the unambiguous extensions of each respective arithmetical concept-function. The axiom thereby established extensional identity conditions for concept-functions, and imposed requirements for the exact definition of concept-functions in the *Begriffsschrift*. It is the axiom's largesse that Russell believed permitted introduction to the logic by definition of the set of sets that are not members of themselves. The logic of *Grundgesetze I* teased, but did not quite do as Russell assumed. Russell made use of Frege's dangerous truth-functional propositional negation, asking thereafter, as an application of the propositional excluded middle, whether the set of those sets that are not members of themselves is or is not a member of itself. Having arrived supposedly at an explicit contradiction, Russell convinced Frege that the set of sets that are not members of themselves, according to *Grundgesetze I* Axiom V, is a member of itself if and only if it is not a member of itself.[20]

---

[18] *Ibid.*, p. vii.   [19] *Ibid.*
[20] Additional literature on Russell's paradox is referenced in notes to Chapter 11.

The putative trouble for Frege's *Grundgesetze* posed by Russell's paradox was prefigured by Frege's Foreword warning that, while some readers might find Axiom V to be of problematic status or category, he *took* it to be purely logical. Frege told his readers where to look for difficulties. Sure enough, that is where Russell believed he was able to find a paradox when he took up the challenge of Frege's Foreword for anyone to identify a contradiction in the *Grundgesetze*. What Frege presumably did not anticipate was that Axiom V of all things would support syntactical inconsistency within the arithmetic. He seems to be concerned about the basic law only and exclusively from the philosophical standpoint as to whether it should be considered *purely* logical. What matters is whether or not Axiom V supports the book's primary intention of visually showing that the basic laws of elementary arithmetic are reducible through gapless chains of fully transparent inferential linkages dependent on purely logical basic concept-functions and deductive inference principles.

Frege's parting comment in the above quotation appears out of character. He labored throughout the span of his *Grundlagen* to argue, convincingly or not, that the concept-function of natural number, properly analyzed, was *purely* logical. As to the purely or impurely logical or illogical, even extralogical status of the as-yet not fully gauged power of *Grundgesetze I* Axiom V, he said only, almost offhandedly, "I take it to be purely logical." One wonders, then, why Frege could not have been content in his *Grundlagen*, and in that sense without bothering to write the book, merely to have said that he takes the concept of natural number to be purely logical. Surely more solid backgrounding is required for *Grundgesetze I* Axiom V than Frege afforded. Frege knew better than most of his contemporaries that merely calling the proposition an *axiom* does nothing to relieve one from the obligation to establish its credentials formally and epistemically as a basic law of logic. Axiom V is the weak spot in *Grundgesetze I*. Frege sensed this clearly enough to call attention to his uncertainties about its category, thereby reinforcing the interpretation that he was interested throughout his publishing career in maximizing useful objections from outside critics. It was a major part of what made his philosophy scientific. He called upon antagonists to do their worst, even with respect to co-extensionality concept-function identity law V. He did not yet know exactly what threat to the logic's integrity the axiom presented. It would take Russell, after an interval of nine years, to drive the difficulty home.[21]

Frege did not imagine that there could be a satisfactory alternative to his *Grundgesetze*. He rejected Dedekind's efforts in his 1888 *Was sind und was sollen die Zahlen?* as objectionably but perhaps only heuristically psychologistic. Dedekind's reconstructions of arithmetical theorems were considered by Frege to lack all the painstaking rigor and effort required in order to discern purely logical structures linking together the most completely analyzed logical combinations of elementary concept-functions and propositions. If anyone thought that Dedekind had already accomplished the needed analysis, Frege was quick to disabuse supporters of that impression. Dedekind was doing something that ascended to greater heights than Frege's logicism, but only at the prohibitive cost of not adequately explaining the foundations of arithmetic on which everything in the analytic structure logically depended. Frege began his cautioning about what to expect within the pages of his *Grundgesetze* and immediately segued to a thorough trouncing of Dedekind's treatment of the concept of number:

My purpose demands some divergences from what is common in mathematics. Rigour of proof requires, as an inescapable consequence, an increase in length. Whoever fails to keep an eye on this will indeed be surprised how cumbersome our proofs often are of propositions into which he would suppose he had an immediate insight, through a single act of cognition. This will be especially striking if one compares Mr. Dedekind's essay, *Was sind und was sollen die Zahlen?* [the title can be translated as *What Are Numbers and What Are They Supposed to Do?*], the most thorough study I have seen in recent times concerning the foundations of arithmetic. It pursues, in much less space, the laws of arithmetic to a much higher level than here. This concision is achieved, of course, only because much is not in fact proven at all. Often, Mr. Dedekind merely states that a proof follows from such and such propositions; he uses dots, as in "$M(A, B, C \ldots)$"; nowhere in his essay do we find a list of the logical or other laws he takes as basic; and even if it were there, one would have no

---

[21] Again, Frege repeated the challenge to critics to try doing better. In *Grundgesetze I*, Foreword, he wrote, p. ix, "If someone takes a different view, he should try to develop a sound and usable symbolic exposition on that basis; he will find that it will not work . . . No doubt in language the point is not so transparent; but if one pays close attention, one finds that even here there is mention of a concept, rather than of a group, an aggregate or suchlike, whenever a statement of number is made; and even if exceptions sometimes occur, the group or the aggregate is always determined by a concept, i.e., by the properties an object must have in order to belong to the group, while what unites the group into a group, or makes the system into a system, the relations of the members to each other, has absolutely no bearing on the cardinal number."

chance to verify whether in fact no other laws were used, since, for this, the proofs would have to be not merely indicated but carried out gaplessly.[22]

With these preliminaries dispatched, Frege at last offered the explanation of his objective that was missing from either of his two previous books. It was, as he has been consistently interpreted here as saying, to assemble together and set in motion the general *Begriffsschrift* logic of concept-functions with the *Grundlagen* concept-function of natural number. Frege speaks interestingly of the *Grundgesetze* endeavoring to *confirm* the analysis of natural number proposed in the *Grundlagen*:

> I here carry out a project that I already had in mind at the time of my *Begriffsschrift* of the year 1879 and which I announced in my *Grundlagen der Arithmetik* of the year 1884. By this act I am to confirm the conception of cardinal number which I set forth in the latter book. The basis for my results is articulated there in §46, namely that a statement of number contains a predication about a concept; and the exposition here rests upon it.[23]

It was a curious confirmation, if it was any such thing at all, of the analysis of the concept-function of natural number in the *Grundlagen* that Frege now described in the Foreword to *Grundgesetze I*. It should come as no surprise that the *Grundgesetze* would be consistent with Frege's *Grundlagen* understanding of numbers. One imagines Frege saying instead that his *Grundgesetze* will apply and make use of the conceptual analysis of natural number in the *Grundlagen*.

Throughout the interval that had elapsed since the publication of his *Grundlagen* in 1884, during the intervening nine years, he had preserved for its new application the meticulous analysis of the concept of number that the previous book had advanced. He had not changed his mind. On the

---

[22] *Ibid.*, Foreword, pp. vii–viii. Also, p. viii, "Mr. Dedekind too is of the opinion that the theory of numbers is a part of logic; but his essay barely contributes to the confirmation of this opinion since his use of the expressions 'system,' 'a thing belongs to a thing' are neither customary in logic nor reducible to something acknowledged as logical. I do not say this as a complaint; his procedure may have been the most appropriate for his purpose; I say this only to cast a brighter light upon my own intentions by contrast." See also, p. xiii, contra Hilbert's (unmentioned) formalism, "On occasion, it seems that the number-signs are regarded like chess pieces, and the so-called definitions like rules of the game. In that case the sign designates nothing, but is rather the thing itself. One small detail is overlooked in all this, of course; namely that a thought is expressed by means of '$3^2 + 4^2 = 5^2$,' whereas a configuration of chess pieces says nothing. When one is content with such superficialities, there is surely no basis for a deeper understanding."

[23] *Ibid.*, Foreword, pp. viii–ix.

contrary, he was now ready to put his former, and to his satisfaction philosophically established, analysis of the concept-function of natural number together with a modified form of the *Begriffsschrift* logic of concept-functions. Their cooperation would accomplish the formal expression of basic laws and gapless logical derivation of the theorems of elementary arithmetic.

Frege provided a rare glimpse behind the scenes of the transitions by which his *Begriffsschrift* had been applied to produce the first of a projected two-volume logical treatise in the *Grundgesetze*:

> The reason why the implementation appears so late after the announcement is owing in part to internal changes within the concept-script which forced me to jettison a nearly completed handwritten work. This progress might be mentioned here briefly. The primitive signs used in my *Begriffsschrift* occur again here with one exception. Instead of the three parallel lines, I have chosen the usual equality-sign ["="], for I have convinced myself that in arithmetic it possesses just that reference that I too want to designate. Thus, I use the word "equal" with the same reference as "coinciding with" or "identical with," and this is also how the equality-sign is actually used in arithmetic. The objection to this which might be raised would rest on insufficiently distinguishing between sign and what is designated. No doubt, in the equation "22 = 2 + 2" the sign on the left is different from the one on the right; but both designate or refer to the same number.[24]

We are given yet another peek at what has been going on in Frege's publication preparations for the *Grundgesetze*. The revisions he discovered to be necessary for the successful reduction of arithmetic to logic required that he abandon "a nearly completed handwritten copy." It would be fascinating to know more. When and how exactly did Frege come upon the limitations of *Begriffsschrift* notation that dictated a new version of the text? How much time did it then take Frege to revise the book, and how extensive was the rethinking he did in picking up the logic

---

[24] *Ibid.*, p. ix. See p. x: "What was formerly the content-stroke reappears as the horizontal. These are consequences of a deep-reaching development in my logical views. Previously I distinguished two components in that whose external form is a declarative sentence: 1) acknowledgment of truth, 2) the content, which is acknowledged as true. The content I called judgeable content. This now splits for me into what I call thought and what I call truth-value. This is a consequence of the distinction between the sense and the reference of a sign. In this instance, the thought is the sense of a proposition and the truth-value is its reference. In addition, there is the acknowledgment that the truth-value is the True. For I distinguish two truth-values: the True and the False. I have justified this in more detail in my above mentioned essay *Über Sinn und Bedeutung*. Here, it might merely be mentioned that only in this way can indirect speech be accounted for correctly."

anew and recasting its principles to meet the requirements he had in the meantime decided were essential?

The changes Frege mentioned seem relatively trivial, even superficial. Three parallel short horizontal lines were replaced by the identity sign. Taken by itself, that kind of change could be made to an existing manuscript with a blue pencil in the time-honored way of evolution of terms subject to improvement by their vigilant authors. Interpreting "=" as Frege now proposed effectively implemented the explanation of *identity*, of the sense and reference especially as expressed in nontrivial noniterative identity statements examined in Frege's 1892 essay "On Sense and Reference." It is conceivable, though the facts are presumably lost to history, that Frege brokered the distinction between sense and reference in the course of composing and revising his *Grundgesetze*. The Foreword to *Grundgesetze I* suggests a direct connection. In applying his *Begriffsschrift* to the basic laws and theorems of elementary arithmetic, he may have encountered specific expressive and interpretive needs that pointed toward a distinct sense-meaning and identical reference of the identity-related values of arithmetical equations. It would make sense that he saw the need to examine the division still more closely in the famous offshoot essay of 1892, approximately one year before publishing *Grundgesetze I*. The important changes affecting the use of object and higher-level variables in quantificational expressions were not described in greater detail in the *Grundgesetze I* Foreword, but only later in the text, where they were made the star syntactical attraction in Frege's transition from the *Begriffsschrift* to the *Grundgesetze*.

A Formal Exposition of Frege's Applied Arithmetical Logic

Frege presents the applied arithmetical logic's primitive signs. He introduces terms for function-concepts and relations. The reference of a Fregean thought or proposition is given as the True and the False, depending on whether the thought is true or false. Frege explains the valuations by means of simple arithmetical examples:

§2. I say: the names "$2^2 = 4$" and "$3 > 2$" *refer to* the same truth-value, which I call for short *the True*. Likewise, for me, "$3^2 = 4$" and "$1 > 2$" *refer to* the same truth-value, which I call for short *the False*, exactly as the name "2w," and I call the True the reference of "$3 > 2$." I distinguish, however, the *reference* of a name from its *sense*. "$2[\times]2$" and "$2 + 2$" do not have the same *sense*, and nor do "$2^2 = 4$" and "$2 + 2 = 4$"

have the same *sense*. The sense of a name of a truth-value I call a *thought*. I say further that a name *expresses* its sense and *refers* to its reference.[25]

Frege deploys the distinction between sense and reference more or less exactly as he had introduced it in the previous year's published essay, "On Sense and Reference." The indispensability of the identity or "equals" relation in arithmetical equations and relations of concept-functions applied to input argument-objects and identical output values obliged Frege to consider identity relations expressed in identity statements.

The *Grundgesetze* in its effort to reduce elementary arithmetic to concept-functions and inference principles of pure logic led Frege to consider the meaning of identity, regarding the truth-conditions of identity statements and the possibility of cognitively informative nontrivial non-iterative identities. These are found everywhere in arithmetic, illustrated by the potentially illuminating identity equations $2(2) = 2 + 2 = 4$. They offer the possibility of referring in different ways to the same mathematical entity, despite the fact, supposedly, that the sense of "$2(2)$" $\neq$ the sense of "$2 + 2$" $\neq$ the sense of "4." We have already seen reason to question whether terms with the same reference can have different total sense, *the* Fregean sense, as opposed to a proper part of the term's sense, and as opposed to the endless variety of different opinions there can occur sub-jectively among thinkers and language users as to the total Fregean sense of a Fregean proper name. Frege appears to have been unaware of or uncon-cerned about these problems. He proceeded with unfaltering stride toward the application of the "On Sense and Reference" distinction here in his *Grundgesetze* when presenting his exposition of the basic elements of logic.

Frege next introduces a short dangling vertical sign marking proposi-tional negation. He showcases it here in a simplest case depending from the horizontal, belying the awful power of truth-functional negation as one of the principal innovations of his *Begriffsschrift*. The negation sign did away with the need for a special symbol by which to express that a given Fregean thought had the truth-value the False rather than the True. The negation sign, or rather the truth-function represented by the negation sign, simply toggles the truth-value referential meaning of a thought or proposition to which it is attached on and off from the True to the False, and from the False to the True. Truth-functional negation was

---

[25] *Ibid.*, p. 7.

a formalization option that Boole before Frege chose very deliberately not to employ, in order to avoid the chance of exposure to logical paradox that Frege was finally to summon down upon his *Grundgesetze* like a judgment from Russell. The logic's commitment to truth-functional propositional negation is unassumingly disclosed in the following casual remarks:

§6. We do not need a specific sign to declare a truth-value to be the False provided we have a sign by means of which every truth-value is transformed into its opposite, which is in any case indispensable. I now stipulate:
    The value of the function

$$\top\,\xi$$

is to be the False for every argument for which the value of the function is the True; and it is to be the True for all other arguments.[26]

Continuing with a topic delayed from Frege's *Begriffsschrift*, and handled more efficiently only later in the *Grundgesetze*, the logic does not only need individual formulas representing specific Fregean thoughts or propositions, but must also be equipped with logical deductive inference and syntax equivalence, implication, and transformation principles, which Frege now proceeded to collect. Without further detailed comment, Frege presented inference rules for proofs and derivations of Fregean thoughts from other Fregean thoughts. The principles authorize logical deductions of theorems from axioms and other theorems of arithmetic, defining the logic of *Grundgesetze* arithmetic in the following summary text and the diagram shown as Figure 9.1:

§47. We have been seeing how concepts and objects with which we will be occupied later can be designated with our signs. This would be of little significance, however, if one could not also calculate with them, if, without mixing in words, series of inferences could not be represented, proofs not be conducted. We have now become familiar with the basic laws and modes of inference that are going to be employed for this purpose. We will now derive laws from them for later use, in such a way that the method of calculating is illustrated at the same time. I will first summarise the basic laws and rules, and add some supplementary points.[27]

The basic laws of Frege's *Grundgesetze I*, like those of his *Begriffsschrift*, adopting Frege's symbolism for the moment, are as follows. (I) If *a*, then, if *b*, then *a*. (IIa) If every object in the logic's domain has property *f* (if concept or function *f* is true of every object), then it is

---

[26] *Ibid.*, p. 10.   [27] *Ibid.*, pp. 60–61.

Summary of the basic laws

$$\vdash \begin{matrix} a, \\ b \\ a \end{matrix} \quad \vdash \begin{matrix} a \\ a \end{matrix} \qquad \text{(I} \;\; (\S18)$$

$$\vdash \begin{matrix} f(a) \\ \mathfrak{a}\; f(\mathfrak{a}) \end{matrix} \quad \text{(IIa} \;\; (\S20) \qquad\qquad \vdash \begin{matrix} M_\beta(f(\beta)) \\ \mathfrak{f}\; M_\beta(\mathfrak{f}(\beta)) \end{matrix} \quad \text{(IIb} \;\; (\S25)$$

$$\vdash \begin{matrix} g\!\left(\mathfrak{f} \begin{matrix} f(a) \\ \mathfrak{f}(b) \end{matrix} \right) \\ g(a = b) \end{matrix} \quad \text{(III} \;\; (\S20) \qquad\qquad \vdash \begin{matrix} (\text{—}\, a) = (\text{—}\, b) \\ {}_\tau (\text{—}\, a) = (\, \tau\, b) \end{matrix} \quad \text{(IV} \;\; (\S18)$$

$$\vdash (\acute{\varepsilon}f(\varepsilon) = \acute{\alpha}g(\alpha)) = (\underset{a}{\smile}\; f(\mathfrak{a}) = g(\mathfrak{a})) \qquad \text{(V} \;\; (\S20)$$

$$\vdash a = \backslash\acute{\varepsilon}(a = \varepsilon) \qquad \text{(VI} \;\; (\S18)$$

Figure 9.1   Summary of the Basic Laws

true of any individually named or otherwise designated object. (IIb) If a second-level statement attributes every second-level property *f* to a certain Fregean thought, then the thought instantiates any chosen particular first-order property. (III) If identity *a* = *b* has property *g*, then, for any property *f*, object *a* has property *f* if object *b* has property *f* also has property *g*. Given the interchangability of *a* and *b* where *a* = *b*, Frege remarks that the principle is implied by Leibnizian indiscernibility of identicals. Basic law (IV) is double negation, at least in the direction conditionally from not-not-*b* to *b*. Law (V) is the notorious extensionality principle on which Russell's paradox is predicated, which will be discussed in further detail in Chapter 11. Law (VI) effectively guarantees that every object in the logic's referential semantic domain can be named with a singular designating term or expression. The rules for deductively valid logical derivations in the *Grundgesetze* are now presented by Frege in the compact list shown in Figure 9.2, immediately following the above list of the logic's basic laws.

Fine technicalities of Frege's proofs in his *Grundgesetze* are beyond the scope of biography, even as a life history of an eminent logician and mathematician. The issues are sufficiently complex to warrant dedicated monographs of their own, in which thorough and systematic critical

§48. *Summary of the rules*

1. *Fusion of horizontals*

If as argument of the function — ξ there occurs the value of this same function for some argument, then the horizontals may be fused.

The two parts of the horizontal line that are separated by the negation-stroke in '$\smile$ ξ' are horizontals in our sense.

The lower and the two parts of the upper horizontal stroke in '$\underset{\zeta}{\overset{}{\top}}$ ξ' are horizontals in our sense.

Finally, the two straight strokes which are adjoined to the concavity in '$\overset{}{\smile}$ $\varphi(\mathfrak{a})$' are horizontals in our sense.

2. *Permutation of subcomponents*

Subcomponents of the same proposition may be permuted with one another arbitrarily.

3. *Contraposition*

A subcomponent in a proposition may be permuted with a supercomponent provided one also inverts their truth-values.[f]

Transition-sign: ✕

4. *Fusion of equal subcomponents*

A subcomponent that occurs repeatedly in the same proposition only needs to be written once.

Figure 9.2   Summary of the Rules

reconsideration of Frege's demonstrations in the book can be made the subject of specific studies. The book would not have been an easy text to review.[28]

To give a flavor of what follows next in *Grundgesetze I*, and later in *Grundgesetze II*, namely proofs of the fundamental theorems of cardinal number, Frege instructively explains some of the formal transformations needed to effect a logical derivation. Here we are reminded of Frege's warning in the Foreword of *Grundgesetze I* to beware of relentless gapless formalizations of the book's logical proofs. He begins as follows:

§53. Concerning the proofs to follow I would emphasize that the commentaries that I regularly give in advance under the heading "analysis" are merely intended to serve the convenience of the reader; they could be omitted without compromising the force of the proof, which is to be sought under the heading "construction" only.

The rules that I cite in the analysis are listed above in §48 under their respective numbers. The laws derived above are collected in a special table at the end of the volume, together with the basic laws summarised in §47. In addition, the definitions of Section 1.2, and others, are also collected at the end of the volume.

---

[28] The reception of the *Grundgesetze* was as disheartening as that of any of Frege's previous books. It is sometimes said, by Dummett, for example, that there were only two reviews of Frege's *Grundgesetze*, but it appears instead that there were as many as at least four. See Kreiser, *Gottlob Frege*, pp. 271–75.

A. Proof of the proposition

$$\vdash\begin{array}{l} \mathfrak{n}u = \mathfrak{n}v \\ \ \ \llcorner\, u^\frown(v^\frown)q) \\ \ \ \ \ \llcorner\, v^\frown(u^\frown)\mathfrak{X}q) \end{array}'$$

a) Proof of the proposition

$$\vdash\begin{array}{l} w^\frown(v^\frown)(p\smile q)) \\ \ \ \llcorner\, w^\frown(u^\frown)p) \\ \ \ \ \ \llcorner\, u\,^\frown(v^\frown)q) \end{array}\quad,$$

§54. *Analysis*

According to definition (Z) the proposition

$$\vdash\begin{array}{l} \mathfrak{n}u = \mathfrak{n}v \\ \ \ \llcorner\, u^\frown(v^\frown)q) \\ \ \ \ \ \llcorner\, v^\frown(u^\frown)\mathfrak{X}q) \end{array}'\qquad\qquad(\alpha$$

is a consequence of

$$\vdash\begin{array}{l} \dot\varepsilon\left(\raise2pt\hbox{-}^q\!\!\!\!\!\prod\begin{array}{l}\varepsilon^\frown(u^\frown)q \\ \llcorner\, u^\frown(\varepsilon^\frown)\mathfrak{X}q)\end{array}\right) = \dot\varepsilon\left(\raise2pt\hbox{-}^q\!\!\!\!\!\prod\begin{array}{l}\varepsilon^\frown(v^\frown)q \\ \llcorner\, v^\frown(\varepsilon^\frown)\mathfrak{X}q)\end{array}\right) \\ \ \ \llcorner\, u^\frown(v^\frown)q) \\ \ \ \ \ \llcorner\, v^\frown(u^\frown)\mathfrak{X}q) \end{array}\quad,\qquad(\beta$$

This proposition is to be derived using (Va) and rule (5) from the proposition

$$\vdash\begin{array}{l}\left(\raise2pt\hbox{-}^q\!\!\!\!\!\prod\begin{array}{l}w^\frown(u^\frown)q) \\ \llcorner\, u^\frown(w^\frown)\mathfrak{X}q)\end{array}\right) = \left(\raise2pt\hbox{-}^q\!\!\!\!\!\prod\begin{array}{l}w^\frown(v^\frown)q) \\ \llcorner\, v^\frown(w^\frown)\mathfrak{X}q)\end{array}\right) \\ \ \ \llcorner\, u^\frown(v^\frown)q) \\ \ \ \ \ \llcorner\, v^\frown(u^\frown)\mathfrak{X}q) \end{array}\qquad,\qquad(\gamma$$

Figure 9.3   Proof of the Proposition

First we prove the proposition:
The cardinal number of a concept is equal to the cardinal number of a second concept, if a relation maps the first into the second, and if the converse of this relation maps the second into the first.[29]

See Figure 9.3.

Several pages of further subproofs are required in order for Frege to be satisfied that the theorem has been derived in every essential particular and with no fractures in any of its inference linkages. The proofs advance progressively from the baroque to the rococo. It takes patience and a definite knack for working with complex formal symbolisms to fully track Frege's moves. Everything is there. Everthing is open to inspection,

[29] Frege, *Grundgesetze I*, p. 70.

just as Frege promises. Anyone who wants can look at any of the basic laws, inference rules, and their application in the derivation of any of Frege's theorems in the book and see exactly what Frege is saying. The existence of the book with these logical pictures illustrating the applied logical derivations of the basic laws of elementary arithmetic on grounds of purely logical concepts concretely proves the truth of Frege's logicism. A reader can admire Frege's handiwork, and, more importantly, check up on his reasoning to see whether any logical errors have been made or any extralogical principles performing essential inferential duty are lurking hidden in the shadows. Frege warmly invites the timid reader to critically examine all derivations, on the bombastic assumption that no mistakes were there to be discovered.

The Critical Reception of Frege's *Grundgesetze*

There are generally considered to be three reviews of *Grundgesetze I*. The most important was undoubtedly Peano's. There were also reviews by Frege's Jena colleague in mathematics Hoppe, and by later colleague Carl Theodor Michaëlis, appearing as late as 1896. Not unusually in technical subjects, philosophy not excepted, book reviews can often appear three years and even more later than the published book under critique.[30]

Dummett summarizes Frege's publication predicament and the disheartening reception or lack thereof of his major writings in two passages of two different books on Frege's philosophy. First, he writes that

Frege was always, with reason, disappointed with the reception accorded his books: that of Volume I of *Grundgesetze* he found especially discouraging, and he consequently delayed publication of Volume II for ten years.[31]

Dummett's explanation is not incredible, but by the same token not obviously accurate. He implies that Frege deliberately chose to delay publication of *Grundgesetze II* for ten years because he had been discouraged, not only by the reception accorded his previous first two books, but also more recently by the reviews of *Grundgesetze I*. If that were true, then there would have been a lag time of at least several years before the earliest reviews of *Grundgesetze I* could have appeared, after which more time would be

---

[30] See Kreiser, *Gottlob Frege*, pp. 269–70.
[31] Dummett, *Frege: Philosophy of Language*, p. xxii.

needed for Frege to digest them and decide what if anything to do in response. Nor is it clear what Frege could have accomplished by delaying publication of *Grundgesetze II* by ten years, even if he were terribly chagrined by the critics' lukewarm-to-belligerent reactions to *Grundgesetze I*. Is the idea that it took him so long to get over his bad feeling about the reception of *Grundgesetze I*, and then, after that expiration of time, he thought he might just as well proceed with the second half of the project at his own expense? Dummett's interpretation in the passage is no more plausible than it appears to stand on documented fact.

The testimony of other Frege scholars is that it was the publisher's implacable understandably financially driven policy, rather than Frege's emotion-driven choice, to delay publication of *Grundgesetze II* by ten years. No doubt there was a reasonable length of time assigned to see how the book would do. When it became clear that the cost of producing *Grundgesetze I* was not going to be recovered in anyone then living's lifetime, and presumably only once Frege had exhausted alternative avenues of having the second volume published without having to dig into his own pockets, the decision was made to go forward with Frege's personal speculative investment perhaps seven or eight years later to begin the process of bringing forth *Grundgesetze II*. It appears more likely, as previously suggested, that Frege had the whole book in manu-script ready to publish in 1893, although he may have been making improvements all along. Contrary to Dummett's view, Frege's publisher would not hazard publication costs for the entire treatise in 1893 without a trial run of the book's first half. It happened against Frege's preferences and the better judgment of those who would not expect to be able to sell a book one half at a time over a decade's interlude. In a second publication, Dummett has the following to say:

This, too [Frege's *Grundgesetze*], received only a single [*sic*] review (by Peano). The neglect of what was to have been his chef d'œuvre finally embittered Frege, who had complained, in the preface, of the apparent ignorance of his work on the part of writers working in allied fields. The resulting bitterness shows in the style of Frege's controversial writing. Seldom has criticism of previous writers been more deadly than in his *Grundlagen*; but it is expressed with a lightness of touch and it is never unfair. In volume 2 of the *Grundgesetze* (1903), however, the attacks became heavyhanded and abusive – a means of getting back at the world that had ignored him.[32]

---

[32] Dummett, "Gottlob Frege," *Encyclopedia Britannica.*

Dummett is right that Peano's review was the most informed, detailed, and comprehensive. Since it has been observed that Hoppe and Michaëlis too published critical notices of *Grundgesetze I* when it appeared, it is inaccurate to describe Peano's as the exceptional single lone review. As to Dummett's interpretation that Frege in *Grundgesetze II* became "heavyhanded and abusive," especially as "a means of getting back at the world that had ignored him," there appears to be little solid evidence for such an insalubrious exaggeration, amounting almost to character assassination, even as a description of Frege's conjectured subjective response.

The idea in contrast is not to idealize, let alone idolize, Frege. There were reprehensible aspects of his character that have yet to emerge in his writings and later political attitudes, from which the present historical–philosophical narrative does not shrink. The purpose is rather to consider what can and cannot be responsibly learned about Frege's personality from sparse ambiguous evidence. It should not be too revolutionary to ask whether Frege had good reasons to complain about some of his rivals in the philosophy of mathematics, or for trying to make his points heard above his perception of ringing endorsements everywhere of sham inadequately grounded rigor and detested psychologism. Irrespective of whether he was epiphenomenally a colossal grouch and an academic scold, especially of younger colleagues in the field, if Frege can be understood as having had good reasons for the choices that are sometimes supposed to reflect his negative disposition, then we should consider that the explanation for some of Frege's later animus need not reflect a morally abhorrent character, but rather might invoke his passion for the truth. The charitable account of rational grounds for Frege's behavior is sought in every instance, and can generally be discovered without ingenious effort at reinvention of the facts.

The dismal reception accorded yet another book in Frege's heroic workstream might nevertheless be called the Frege curse. An indication that things were not going to change significantly for Frege in terms of the unpopularity of his writings appeared on the teaching front. Winter semester 1893–1894 at the University of Jena found Frege teaching Abelian Integrals (integrals as in calculus, but in the complex number plane) to three students, and lecturing on his *Begriffsschrift* to empty chairs, in the year immediately after publication of *Grundgesetze I*. Frege earned 30 Marks lecture fees, but only for the Abelian Integrals course.[33] Bynum fills in the details of what we know about the publication history of the two-volume *Grundgesetze I* and *II*, related in another way to the disappointing response to *Grundgesetze I*:

> The reception accorded *The Basic Laws of Arithmetic I* (*Grundgesetze I*) was another frustrating blow to Frege's hopes and plans. There were only two reviews [by Hoppe and Peano], both unfavorable; and except for these there was neither approval nor rejection from the scholarly world – just silence. As a result, the publisher refused to print Volume II; and Frege's grand project . . . was unfinished. As it turned out, Frege did not give up – he was just delayed. (He was determined to see his project through; so, finally, ten years after the appearance of Volume I, he paid for the publication of Volume II out of his own pocket).[34]

Bynum finds another commentator in Hoppe's unencouraging report on *Grundgesetze I* to set beside Peano's negative review. He overlooks Michaëlis, but doubles Dummett's inventory. Bynum seems to be submitting the above interpretation as a publication history of both volumes of Frege's *Grundgesetze*.

According to Bynum's account, *Grundgesetze I* did not go over well. The reviews were supposed to have been negative overall. In fairness, neither of the reviews was entirely that. No one as yet wanted to join Frege's army, but his objectives had become clearer. The publisher, even with glowing reports on the first volume, on consideration of its poor sales, would not have produced the second, at what can be assumed would have been great expense, on further speculation. Frege remained steadfast with respect to the goal of bringing out *Grundgesetze II*. He did so only ten years later in 1903, in all probability, because until then he could not afford it, and the text must have taken time to produce. We are largely in the dark here. There are no surviving records of the costs and of the payment agreement between Frege and Pohle's press. The invoice for the work could not have been insignificant, or there would have been no need for Frege's subvention. Light could be shed on the problem only if it were known what a press at roughly the same time in Germany charged an author for private printing of a technical text of a certain length bearing enough positive

---

[33] Kratzsch, "Material zu Leben und Wirken Freges aus dem Besitz der Universitäts-Bibliothek Jena," p. 540. Asser, Alexander, and Metzler, "Gottlob Frege – Persönlichkeit und Werk," pp. 13–14.

[34] Bynum, "On the Life and Work of Gottlob Frege," *Conceptual Notation*, pp. 37–38.

comparison to Frege's. The information for comparison may someday emerge.

Frege's new book, even more than his first two preparatory studies, did not seem to have another friend in the world. It was the same old story. Frege soldiered on because he was compelled to do so by his sense of the importance of the endeavor. He believed that there was no other way to accomplish the project's honorable purpose except by the difficult path he had chosen. It is a path, it has been emphasized, thorny and eccentric, that Frege entered upon for what can be seen retrospectively as very good reasons. Were it true that he was not getting things right, Frege could in principle have understood and accepted the project's defeat, but at this time no one had as yet come forward with a criticism to unhinge his confidence. What he seemed unable to abide was the fact that virtually no one shared his sense of the importance of showing that elementary arithmetic could be reconstructed from purely logical concept-functions within an applied purely logical deductive inferential framework. Why, he may have wondered, wasn't everyone in the mathematics world trying to do the same? The lament of the *Grundgesetze I* Foreword is Frege's lonesome voice seeking intellectual sodality. He must have felt with each new insult to each new published stage completed in carrying out his interconnected three-stage task in the articulation of pure logicism for the public to admire as though he were trying to teach spelling to baboons.[35]

If we are to believe Bynum's operatic saga of Frege's life, then Frege's first hopes to be dashed were that *Grundgesetze I* would realize enough sales for the publisher to venture printing also *Grundgesetze II*. It was the publisher who had split Frege's unified project in twain, and Frege was sufficiently eager to have any of the work in print under any circumstances to accept the compromise. Now Frege faced the unsavory prospect that the book was not going to sell well enough to warrant his publisher risking the second volume of the set, the first volume of which was already like trying to sell rosaries to Lutherans. Frege would need to

---

[35] I do not deny that with enough effort one might teach a baboon to spell. Certainly the famed chimp Washoe and other advanced primates, gorillas as well as chimpanzees, have been taught sign language and can express simple but sometimes surprisingly constructed circumstance-adapted thoughts by its means. The point is only that it would be difficult to train apes to spell, just as Frege found it difficult to lure readers into learning his *Begriffsschrift* or *Grundgesetze* logical symbolism, for the same underlying reason by comparison that apes and Frege's readers alike would not understand the point or purpose of the exertion.

front the production costs of *Grundgesetze II* out of his own resources, and, given the nature of the intricate demanding type-setting, the expense would not be light. Frege or Pohle may have given the book five years to show promise of paying for itself and its volume *II* partner. What happened is what any independent observer of events might have predicted.

It was a good question for Frege's publisher Pohle how to sell the first half of a logic treatise and make the second half available only later if things went well. It was a publishing strategy that must have made sense in a ledgerbook, but one that is hard to justify from a scientific philosophical standpoint for any consumer of this sort of literature, especially at the time when *Grundgesetze I* was published. Until Russell's paradox unhorsed Frege, Frege seems to have at least day-dreamed about a *Grundgesetze III*. He might have imagined that after his death the further demonstration of *begriffsschriftliche* reductions of advanced arithmetic and higher mathematics, possibly with Cantor's transfinite set theory also more fully in *Grundgesetze* harness, possibly including analytic geometry to spice things up philosophically in relation to Kant, would be carried out by the descendants of his pure logicism. He may have expected the route to be followed by traversing a course of research initiation and expansion in much the same way as Gauss's insight about the topological planting of imaginary and complex numbers in a plane orthogonal to the real number line had fostered a ripple effect of mathematical research and innovation, education, and training. Frege had imprinted on himself exactly that model, having followed a paper trail to its living source in Göttingen, through the heavy wooden doors at Jena and back again.

In the event, historically, none of these pleasant scenarios was realized. *Grundgesetze I* once again fell flat. It fared even worse, if Frege had not already visited those depths, than the mute avoidance surrounding his *Begriffsschrift* and *Grundlagen*. Frege still had admirers and supporters at Jena. He was relatively secure as an oddball fixture of mathematics in the faculty. Unexpectedly and in unexpected places, first in Germany, then in England and the English-speaking philosophical community in the UK, Australia, and North America, thanks to Russell's appreciative mentions of Frege's writings on the philosophical foundations of arithmetic and by extension all of mathematics, Frege's reputation for having achieved something outstanding in the history of logic, mathematics, and philosophy slowly began to intensify and proliferate, to exert an ever greater impact on the course of what under his impress was eventually to become contemporary analytic philosophy of language and mathematics.

Frege, Man of Sorrows

What was noteworthy was the postponement of recognition of the value of Frege's innovations. An explanation is needed for the lack of understanding of his motivations and his plans for the parts of his logicism that he later attempted to fit together. There were misunderstandings of his work for which it has been argued that Frege in those years was himself largely responsible. Frege was decades ahead of his time. He was in some ways the very definition of the thing, because he was introducing new ideas that would take at least that long to gain understanding and respect. Frege at this point would surely have been not only satisfied with but grateful for understanding alone. A research partner to complement Frege's strengths and weaknesses would have been too much to ask for.

Was the picture as bleak for Frege as Bynum colors the scene? Bynum further maintains that

Sorrow and frustration continued to plague Frege after the publication of Volume I of *The Basic Laws of Arithmetic*. The cold reception the book received was another exasperating blow. Although his new book was a monumental contribution to logic and mathematics, no one realized the fact. However, instead of marking a premature end to Frege's grand project, the poor reception of Volume I initiated a special effort on his part to tie up the loose ends and bring the project to a successful conclusion. Between 1894 and 1902 Frege wrote a torrent of papers – published and unpublished, working out details of his own position and attacking opposing views. Near the end of this period he completed the manuscript of Volume II of *The Basic Laws of Arithmetic* and arranged to publish it at his expense.[36]

To speak of Frege's sorrow and frustration in 1893 is perhaps to exaggerate the truth in order to make a point. The words lend a personal dimension to Frege the mathematician and philosopher. The question is whether it is the right aspect that helps us to better understand Frege's personality and intentions, or whether it is baseless surmise and pop-psychological projection, perhaps of how a commentator lacking Frege's extraordinary personality and abilities, living in very different social

---

[36] Bynum, "On the Life and Work of Gottlob Frege," *Conceptual Notation*, pp. 41–42.

circumstances, imagines that he or she might have felt in a similar situation.

The striking disanalogy is that Frege was no ordinary Associate Professor. His accomplishments and meteoric rise to academic rank testify to early recognition of his indomitable character as much as his mathematical abilities. At least it became such when appreciated at a later time than his own in the history of mathematics, seen from a more fashionable modern perspective. Without a proper understanding of Frege's objectives, it is impossible to correctly judge even as an act of divination how Frege would have felt about bad reviews, and whether he would have allowed such feelings, even had he felt them, to dictate his theoretical decision-making about the logical analysis of arithmetic and the philosophy of logic and mathematics. The same must obviously be true if Frege's publication choices are rationally explained as part of his program to broadcast his ideas like a fishing-net to snare useful objections. He caught only a few scrawny eels, none that were useful for his purposes, none he could keep. He was nonetheless methodologically obligated sincerely to try.

The woeful reception of *Grundgesetze I* is seen in full retrospect as a consequence of Frege's being so far in advance of his time that there were at first few readers and thinkers prepared to take on board his revolutionary reduction of elementary arithmetic to a fully algebraic logic. If this was any part of Frege's thinking at the time, he has been amply vindicated by the subsequent history of logic, mathematics, and analytic philosophy. It seems that for Frege, from his own perspective, the primary purpose was not to earn a place in the history of logic and mathematics, but to solve the problems, work out the skein of logical interconnections, and use the spatially two-dimensional graphic resources of his *Begriffsschrift* to show for those who could appreciate the accomplishment how the basic laws of elementary arithmetic could be derived from the fundamental principles of logic.

Grundgesetze II (1903)

Frege's *Grundgesetze I* reiterated and revised the basic logical principles of the general concept-functional calculus in his *Begriffsschrift*, incorporating and emphasizing the improvements Frege had discovered to be necessary in the intervening years. It set the stage for the full treatment of logicism previewed in the *Grundgesetze I* Foreword as forthcoming in

Grundgesetze II, and projected by Frege into at least a third volume, the phantom unwritten unpublished unattempted *Grundgesetze III*, a fictional name with a modicum of sense and no reference for a first inkling of a project, representing more smoke than substance.

The two parts of the book that were published over ten years always belonged together in Frege's mind. He seems to have conceptualized them as two artificially disconnected parts that had originally been intended to appear in print together. For this reason, it seems appropriate at this point to break slightly out of chronological sequence and make a few remarks about the contents of *Grundgesetze II*. All such observations deserve more thorough examination from the standpoint of Frege's technical mathematical accomplishments, the validity of his demonstrations, the exact extent to which he recovered the theorems of traditional arithmetic he sought to rebuild on purely logical foundations, and the philosophical significance of his actual achievements in the second volume of his *magnum opus*. Merely as a brief catalog of the aspirations of *Grundgesetze II*, the following divisions of the text should be mentioned. Frege gave precise formal definitions of advanced functions for Section III, on real numbers. The discussion included a critique of theories about the irrational reals and Cantor's theory of irrationals, as well as those of Eduard Heine and Thomae, the latter of whom was one of Frege's mathematics colleagues at Jena. Despite their philosophical antagonisms, he referred to the mathematician more familiarly in *Grundgesetze II* as Johannes or J. Thomae.[37]

More important biographically, not to mention historically in the march of logic, mathematics, and philosophy, is that *Grundgesetze II* in its Afterword (*Nachwort*) included Frege's first public mention of Russell's paradox and efforts to avoid the inconsistency it seemed to imply for Frege's efforts at reconstructing the basic laws of elementary arithmetic on purely logical stock. The Afterword to *Grundgesetze II* completed a set of matching bookends wherein Frege enclosed *Grundgesetze I* Foreword and *Grundgesetze II* Afterword, both of which contained more personally and philosophically soul-baring information than is found elsewhere among Frege's writings on symbolic logic and the logical foundations of arithmetic.

---

[37] Frege, *Grundgesetze II*, "III.1. Critique of theories concerning irrational numbers," pp. 69–243; "III.2.b) Cantor's theory of the irrational numbers, II," §§68–95, pp. 80–96; and "III.2.c) The theories of the irrationals of E. Heine and J. Thomae," §§96–137, pp. 96–139.

10

Academic and Personal Life, the Review of Husserl, and Mathematical and Philosophical Correspondence (1894–1902)

F REGE'S 1891–1892 WINTER semester teaching included his customary course on Abelian Integrals and another on his *Begriffsschrift*. There was one student attending the first-mentioned lectures, and no one occupying any classroom seats for the second. If the time machine conjured were actually available for bookings, one imagines scores of mathematicians and philosophers today flocking to fill the empty *Stühle* (seats) in Frege's *Hörraum* (lecture hall).[1] For his teaching services to university mathematics students at that time Frege earned an ungenerous 12 Marks. This was in addition, naturally, to his 700 Marks university stipend or salary, plus 1,300 Marks from the fund established by his *Schutzengel* (guardian angel) Abbe specifically to keep Frege financially buoyant with an income totaling 2,000 Marks so that he could continue to pursue his mathematical investigations.

During the summer semester of 1892, immediately prior to publishing *Grundgesetze I*, Frege again walked students through Analytical Mechanics, one of his staples throughout his teaching career at Jena, this time with four participants.[2] He additionally offered a course on Basic Arithmetical

---

[1] See Kreiser, *Gottlob Frege*, p. 282; Kratzsch, "Material zu Leben und Wirken Freges aus dem Besitz der Universitäts-Bibliothek Jena," p. 539; and Asser, Alexander, and Metzler, "Gottlob Frege – Persönlichkeit und Werk," pp. 13–14.

[2] Kreiser, *Gottlob Frege*, p. 282; and Kratzsch, "Material zu Leben und Wirken Freges aus dem Besitz der Universitäts-Bibliothek Jena," p. 540.

Concepts, in which he surely must have been airing an application of his *Begriffsschrift* to the basic laws and theorems of elementary arithmetic about to be published in *Grundgesetze I*. There were three participants, which must have been somewhat gratifying. It may have come as some small relief and reassurance to Frege, who may have been wondering during those difficult fiscal times at the university how many administrators were looking over his shoulder to determine his quantifiable value to students and faculty colleagues, or the value of his mathematical research. Frege also taught Mathematical Exercises, the *Übungen* course that was required of undergraduate mathematics majors to complement abstract theory with practica. The offering enticed two participants to Frege's podium, to follow his course concentrating on integrals with a complex variable. During that comparatively lucrative semester Frege scored a total of 48 Marks in lecture fees.[3]

Life Goes on and Work Continues

Far from being inactive during this period, Frege published and prepared numerous writings for later publication. Despite the watery reception of his *Begriffsschrift* and *Grundlagen*, Frege never abandoned the noble cause of giving concrete mathematical proof to the philosophical ideal of rigorous non-psychologistic logicism. In 1892, along with the previously mentioned essays which appeared during the year, Frege wrote, but did not publish, his critical review of Cantor's 1890 book *Zur Lehre vom Transfiniten: gesammelte Abhandlungen aus der* Zeitschrift für Philosophie und philosophische Kritik.[4] Frege also wrote during this time a substantial run of "Comments on Sense and Reference," again unpublished in his lifetime, that, as commentators George and Heck remark, "expands some of the themes in [Frege's 'On Sense and Reference'] and discusses the importance of the sense–reference distinction in connection with predicates."[5]

During 3–16 October 1892, Frege attended the Jena advanced training courses that were mandatory for teachers in secondary schools and

[3] Kratzsch, "Material zu Leben und Wirken Freges aus dem Besitz der Universitäts-Bibliothek Jena," p. 540.

[4] Frege's unpublished review of Cantor can be found in his *Posthumous Writings*, "Draft of a Review of Cantor's *Gesammelte Abhandlungen zur Lehre vom Transfiniten*," pp. 68–71.

[5] Alexander George and Richard Heck, "Frege, Gottlob," in *Routledge Encyclopedia of Philosophy*, ed. Edward Craig (London: Routledge, 1998), Volume 3, p. 776.

teacher training institutes, just as he had done in 1890.[6] He optimistically offered a course to instructors at this level in the program on his *Begriffsschrift*. One never knew when and where the thing might catch fire, or how and when someone influential might hear about the logic indirectly as a result of his explaining its primary purpose and general utility to advanced secondary school mathematics teachers. How could they come to understand that the general functional calculus was the basis of all mathematics, being simple, elegant, flexible, transparent, and in the right hands gapless in inferential reconstructions of arithmetical theorems, and *not* want students near the start of their mathematical education to become familiar with his *Begriffsschrift*? At the time, in the winter semester of 1892–1893, Frege offered Analytical Mechanics II to two student participants, and taught the *Begriffsschrift* again, this time with an astonishing four enrollees. It would be possible to chart Frege's slowly rising stock, correlated with and perhaps attributable to the publication of his new work in mathematical and philosophical logic. Frege pocketed 36 Marks in lecture fees.

It is imaginable that interest in Frege's logic was stirred by the impending publication of *Grundgesetze I*. Given that the proofs (*Druckfahnen*) were then being corrected, and that colleagues would have mentioned the impending release of Frege's new book, the event might have inspired more students than usual to attend a Frege *Begriffsschrift* lecture course. There was always something worthwhile for a serious mathematics student to learn from regimented syntax deployment, even if the formalism and its applications were outside one's own immediate field of competence. There was a potential for fruitful cross-fertilization of ideas that students quickly learn to seek out, especially in unlikely overlooked places. Several students might have clustered in Frege's lecture room, if only out of curiosity to see what the mysterious work of the enigmatic professor in their midst, who was seen occasionally in the faculty's chambers and hardly anywhere else, was all about.

The daily life of Frege, his teaching and writing, had fixed themselves into a firm pattern at this point, amounting to a comfortable set of expectancies, minor rewards, setbacks, disappointments, and misunderstandings of the purpose of his writing. That was everything that made up an academic's daily life in late-nineteenth-century Thüringen, Germany.

[6] See Kreiser, *Gottlob Frege*, Section 4.3, pp. 341–50.

Frege corresponded with Edward Knoch in two letters dated 28 June and 11 July 1893, almost immediately prior to the publication of *Grundgesetze I*. Their correspondence concerned the difficulties Knoch, professor of mathematics and physics at the boarding school Conradinum in Jenkau (nowadays known as Jankowo Gdańskie) near Danzig (Gdańsk), another Hanseatic city in modern-day Poland, was having understanding Frege's *Grundlagen*.[7] The *Grundlagen* was symbolically less imposing than the *Begriffsschrift*, and still less so than the soon-to-be-released first volume of the *Grundgesetze*. Frege knew that the greatest philosophical difficulties constituting obstacles to understanding often occurred at the starting-places of elementary subjects. Difficulties were planted like noxious weeds among the simplest apparently most obvious distinctions, concepts, principles, propositions, and theses – whatever might be taken for granted by thinkers unselfconsciously in an auto-destructive mode. Frege's correspondence with individuals interested in his work was generally helpful, generous, and friendly. He was grateful for every opportunity to survey the whole plan again, to consider essential details and explain them, as much for his own edification as for his correspondent's, readying himself for logicism's next decisive concluding phase. He had active contact with several mathematicians and philosophers scattered primarily across continental Europe and Great Britain.

In the year 1903 Frege published an important paper on the philosophy of geometry. Frege seemed to agree with Kant, at least for the sake of argument, that intuitions of space provide the conceptual foundation for geometry, despite being comfortable mapping arithmetic into geometry and the opposite, working with arithmetized analytic geometry. Ashamed of its empirical ancestry, geometry tries to detach itself from the fact that it is the perceiving of physical objects in space and time primarily by sight and touch to which the concepts of space systematized in geometry owe their ideational origins. By Frege's time it was well known that different logically coherent geometries could be axiomatized under different archetypes, which were effectively descriptive of different geometrical spaces, not all of which would include or be limited to the cognitively grand-parenting perceptual space of Euclid, Newton, and Kant.

Frege in this later paper reaffirmed his commitment to a quasi-Kantian account of geometry. He developed symbolic logical underfixtures for

---

[7] Frege, *Briefwechsel*, Letter XXIII, p. 36.

arithmetic to replace Kant's reliance on time as a pure form of intuition, while appearing to accept, or, for the time being, at least not to question, Kant's doctrine that space as a pure form of intuition was the complementary transcendental ground of the mind's ability to understand geometry. Once again, Frege's familiarity working in abstract topology and even high-school use of Cartesian coordinates in geometrical modelings of algebraic functions through his dissertation and Habilitation ought to have reinforced the interchangeability of arithmetical and geometrical values. Kant also should have known better in the first place. The mathematics of his own day, appropriately interpreted, could have taught him not to try to drive a hard wedge between arithmetic and geometry.

Frege's 1903 paper is worth close examination, not only for philosophical reasons, but in part also for historical reasons. It represents a return to topics that Frege had not publicly discussed since submitting his Habilitationsschrift.

In the winter semester of 1894–1895 Frege taught Analytical Geometry to six students, lectured on his *Begriffsschrift* to two, and collected the handsome sum of 72 Marks in lecture fees.

On a personal front, in 1896 Frege's mother moved out of the house whose roof she had shared for several years with Gottlob and Margarete, although the couple had separate living quarters from hers. Auguste was ill and could no longer take care of herself or be properly taken care of at home. She was given residence, despite her Lutheranism, at the Catholic Sisters' Home Fulda in Jena, located appropriately enough at Carl-Zeiss-Straße 10. There she stayed until her death two years later in 1898. In the same year of 1896 Frege was appointed honorary Ordinariat or *ordentlicher* (full) Professor in Jena. Abbe, again acting as Frege's *Schutzengel*, played a decisive behind-the-scenes role.[8] The paperwork for the virtually meaningless honorary title journeyed up and down the halls of the university and the Grand Ducal ministries' offices. On 9 May 1896, the State Government of the *Herzogtum Sachsen-Weimar* (Duchy of Sachse-Weimar) announced that Frege had been made an Honorary Full Professor of mathematics at the University of Jena. On 26 May, Frege officially accepted and graciously thanked the bureaucrats for the honor in a formal letter.

---

[8] Stelzner, "Ernst Abbe and Gottlob Frege," pp. 23–25.

Kreiser notes that the title "Honorary Professor" is no longer used in the German academic hierarchy for university faculty. In Frege's time it indicated a teacher and researcher at professor level, without the expected broad command of an entire field of study, engaged instead in a valuable but narrowly focused specialty. Receiving the honorary Ordinariat title changed virtually nothing for Frege, except to assure that his income flow from that time forward had a protected legal status at the university. It did not disqualify Frege from future consideration as a candidate for an ordinary and not just honorary Ordinariat. More significantly, it did not change Frege's position in the mathematics faculty at Jena from Extraordinariat to anything higher. He was still an Associate Professor, although it was evident that the administration had not altogether forgotten about him. The extra money for Frege that came with the honorary Ordinariat, which was now to be a more respectable total of 5,000 Marks per year, was funded by the Carl-Zeiss-Stiftung at Abbe's instigation and on his personal influential recommendation.[9]

Mendelsohn again notes that "Frege's unsalaried Honorary Professorship at Jena was made possible because he received a stipend from the Zeiss foundation."[10] Beaney concurs: "After publication of Volume I of the *Grundgesetze*, Frege was promoted to Honorary Ordinary Professor, which was unsalaried but without administrative duties. With a generous stipend that he also received from the Carl-Zeiss-Stiftung, this freed him more for research; and he was certainly productive in the decade or so that followed."[11] Also Bynum is in agreement: "The position of Honorary Ordinary Professor was unsalaried and slightly less prestigious than the position of Ordinary Professor, but it gave Frege more free time for research. He was able to accept this unsalaried position because he was offered the generous stipend of 3,000 Marks per year from the Carl-Zeiss-Stiftung, a foundation that gave hundreds of thousands of Marks to Jena University every year. It is most likely that Frege's friend Ernst Abbe was responsible for the generous grant to Frege."[12]

Bynum has most of his facts right. He misrepresents the case in saying that an honorary Ordinariat was "slightly less prestigious" than the position of Ordinariat. With the emphasis on "honorary," Frege's official rank at the University of Jena remained that of Extraordinariat, Associate

[9] *Ibid.*, p. 25.   [10] Mendelsohn, *The Philosophy of Gottlob Frege*, p. 2.
[11] Beaney, "Introduction" to Beaney, ed., *The Frege Reader*, p. 6.
[12] Bynum, "On the Life and Work of Gottlob Frege," p. 42.

Professor. He had not risen above the rank at Jena that by then he had held for nine years, and would continue to hold until his retirement. He remained an Associate Professor with a piece of paper stamped and impressed with seals and perhaps a colored ribbon that said in Latin, with greater pomp and elaboration, "Thanks." Beginning in the summer semester of 1896, Frege was listed in the personnel directory at the Universität Jena as an honorary *ordentlicher* Professor.[13] On 7 June 1896, Frege gave a lecture comparing his *Begriffsschrift* with Peano's arithmetic at a special meeting of the Society of Sciences in Leipzig (*Gesellschaft der Wissenschaften zu Leipzig*), which he published during the next year, 1897.[14]

Advances in Logic and Mathematics through the Mail-Slot

Despite Bynum's portrait of gloom, these years were among the most dynamic and industrious in Frege's reflection and research. Bynum, in apparent dispute with his overall assessment, gives the following grocery list:

In terms of pages of manuscript, this period was the most productive part of Frege's career. He corresponded with Ballue, Couturat, Hilbert, Husserl, Knoch, Mayer, Pasch, and Peano. He published (1) a crushing review of Husserl's *Philosophy of Arithmetic I*; (2) a damaging critique of Schröder's *Lectures on the Algebra of Logic*; (3) a lethal reply to Peano's review of *The Basic Laws of Arithmetic I*; (4) a thoughtful comparison of his own logic and Peano's; (5) a convincing refutation of Ballue's

---

[13] Kratzsch, "Material zu Leben und Wirken Freges aus dem Besitz der Universitäts-Bibliothek Jena," pp. 535–37.

[14] For a review of Frege's "On the *Begriffsschrift* of Mr. Peano and My Own" by Viktor Schlegel in 1899, see Kreiser, *Gottlob Frege*, pp. 270–71. There was an active exchange of correspondence with Peano that extended through 1896. Given the importance to Frege's project of the free application of arithmetical functions, and the role played by identity in the complete statement of any function(argument) = value format, it is easy to see how Frege might consider identity to have a prominent place conceptually in the purely logical foundations of elementary arithmetic. Although Peano's review of Frege's *Grundgesetze I* was largely negative, it was an important event for Frege to have attracted the attention of this prestigious critic. As Bynum, *Frege: Conceptual Notation*, p. 38, remarks, despite the negative impact of Peano's review of *Grundgesetze I*, "It initiated a fruitful exchange of letters between Frege and Peano, and in 1900 or 1901 led Bertrand Russell to read Frege's works, starting the chain of events which eventually led to a general recognition of Frege's achievements." Bynum, *ibid.*, p. 263, refers to P. H. Nidditch, "Peano and the Recognition of Frege," *Mind*, 72 (1963), pp. 103–110.

"formalist" definition of "whole number"; and (6) a witty, satirical attack upon Schubert's philosophy of arithmetic.

He prepared, but did not publish, (1) three large manuscripts in "conceptual notation" – two (301 and 210 pages respectively) on the theory of magnitude, and one (258 pages entirely in symbols) on irrational numbers; (2) an essay on logical mistakes in mathematics; (3) a paper on the establishment of his strict principles of definition; and (4) two articles which argue *ad absurdum* the "peppercorn standpoint" of Weierstrass, Kossak, and Biermann that numbers are aggregates of objects. Besides all this, Frege completed the manuscript of Volume II of *The Basic Laws of Arithmetic* [*Grundgesetze II*].[15]

Between 1894 or thereabouts and 1903, Bynum might also have mentioned, Frege engaged in lively correspondence with Peano, among others interested in his work. Peano (1858–1932) was professor of mathematics at the University of Turin, Italy. The best of his many known contributions to logic is the *Formulaire de mathématiques* (1895–1905), in which he developed the logical symbolism that, as mediated by Whitehead and Russell's *Principia Mathematica*, became the basis of the linear sentential logical symbolism of contemporary logic, modifications of which remain popular today, in contrast with Frege's spatially more two-dimensional ideographic *Begriffsschrift* logical pictographs.[16]

The surviving Frege–Peano correspondence consists of eight letters in French from Peano, one letter of Frege's in German, and one reply from Peano written in Italian. The first of these letters was printed in the *Rivista di matematica* (of which Peano was the editor), with three draft letters of Frege's. No other letters between the two thinkers with so much in common intellectually have been discovered. No further messages from Frege exist, at least among Peano's papers at the Fondo Peano or among the safeguarded copies of Frege's letters that escaped the destruction of the originals in the Münster university library by bombing during WWII.[17] With the exception of a genial postcard from Peano in the year 1903 (XIV/2), the surviving correspondence between the logical arithmeticians dates from 1894–1896, after Frege had already published

[15] Bynum, "On the Life and Work of Gottlob Frege," *Frege: Conceptual Notation*, p. 43.
[16] Frege, Letter XIV [xxxiv]/1 to Peano, *Philosophical and Mathematical Correspondence*, p. 108. Frege's *Begriffsschrift* logical notation is described as "more" spatially two-dimensional because no linear logic script is entirely one-dimensional. Even if formulas are normally confined to one line of text, the symbols, if they are to be read, must, like ordinary letters of the alphabet, have some height and not merely length. Frege's *Begriffsschrift* has much more height than other logical symbolisms.
[17] Frege, *Briefwechsel*, p. 175.

Grundgesetze I. At the time, Peano was still preparing his *Formulaire de mathématiques II* for publication.[18] Frege's exchange with Peano was friendly, light, and mutually respectful, although each felt constrained as opportunity presented itself to criticize the other in no uncertain terms, as was their wont. Frege had done so already in his *Begriffsschrift* and *Grundlagen*, and Peano in turn offered objections to Frege's logicism in his perceptive 1895 review of *Grundgesetze I* among other places.[19]

Political and Mathematical Activity

On 9 October 1896 Frege became a citizen of Jena. He acquired therewith local civil rights beyond those of persons merely resident in the city. Frege could now vote locally for the first time. He began to become politically active in a modest way, and in directions that would later suggest social sentiments that were out of keeping with some of the core values of enlightened liberal pluralism. The question arises because, after gaining his sanction, almost a decade later, Frege joined a conservative political movement called the *Nationalliberale Partei* (National-Liberal Party, NLP). It was a bourgeois "liberal" party in name only, favoring, at least in its extremist rhetoric, a perspective that is likely to strike genuinely liberal sensibilities as excessively rightwing and militaristic.

---

[18] Frege, Letter XIV [xxxiv]/1 to Peano, *Philosophical and Mathematical Correspondence*, pp. 108–109.

[19] Peano, "Dr. Gottlob Frege, *Grundgesetze der Arithmetik, begriffsschriftlich abgeleitet*, Erster Band, Jena, 1893, pag. XXXII + 254," *Rivista di matematica*, 5 (1895), pp. 122–28. See Victor Dudman, translator and commentator, "Peano's Review of Frege's *Grundgesetze*," *The Southern Journal of Philosophy*, 9 (1971), pp. 25–37. Frege similarly corresponded on 4 December 1894 with Xavier Léon (XXVI/1), *Briefwechsel*, pp. 145–46. Léon (1868–1935) was the founder and, until his death, first editorial secretary of the *Revue de Métaphysique et de Morale*. The magazine was started in 1893, and in Volume 2 (1894), pp. 317–28, contained an essay of interest to Frege by Eugène Ballue, titled "Le nombre entier: considéré comme fondement de l'analyse mathématique." Frege wrote a reply, and there was editorial correspondence between the two concerning Frege's submission. While it was not always easy for Frege to place his writings in German philosophical and mathematical journals, Léon offered him the pages of the *Revue* in which to publish future contributions without further formalities. This turned out to be a generous offer of which Frege never took advantage. See Frege, *Briefwechsel*, Letter to Léon, p. 145. At the beginning of 1895, Frege received further honors, being admitted to the prestigious Kaiserlich Leopoldinisch-Carolinische Deutsche Akademie der Naturforscher, and later, in 1906, to the Circolo Matematico di Palermo, in Sicily. The article by Ballue in the *Revue de Métaphysique et de Morale* sparked an exchange of correspondence with Frege in the period 1895–1897.

Relatively late, when compared with his colleagues, in 1897 Frege at last became a member of the German Mathematical Society. In the same year, he wrote the unpublished fragment "Logik." It was to be a lengthy, potentially book-length, philosophical treatise on assertion, thought, sense, and similar concepts auxiliary to his *Begriffsschrift*, *Grundlagen*, and *Grundgesetze*. The manuscript appears to have been the chief predecessor to Frege's 1918 essay "Der Gedanke" ("Thought"), presaging the journal publications of chapter-essays in 1918 and 1923 of Frege's projected later posthumous *Logische Untersuchungen*.[20] Frege here admits for the first time that "true" and "truth" are for him indefinable terms, being conceptually analytically primitive, fundamental, irreducible, and unanalyzable. In 1897, Frege also in those busy days, while no doubt refining *Grundgesetze II*, wrote a lecture comparing Peano's logic with his own, which he later published under the self-explanatory title "Über die Begriffsschrift des Herrn Peano und meine eigene." The scientific paper was Frege's direct wounded and resentful response to Peano's review of *Grundgesetze I*. Frege further wrote, but did not publish in this period, the self-assessing essay "Begründung meiner strengeren Grundsätze des Definierens" ("An Argument for My Stricter Canons of Definition").

In June 1898, Frege voted for the National Liberal candidates in parliamentary elections. On 14 June 1898, Kreiser reports, there appeared in the *Jenaische Zeitung* an election call for all members and sympathizers of the National Liberals to vote for the NLP candidate, Ernst Bassermann, in Reichstag elections to be held on 16 June. The activist call-to-arms at least at the voting place was signed by Frege, among numerous others.[21] The NLP seems to have advocated a social agenda with which Frege's native conservativism agreed. This meant for him a strong united Germany, under iron rule and with a strong army and a powerful fleet as a security guarantee for the further continuous achieval of economic-technical and cultural advancement in Germany. It stood as well for an increasingly intensified fight against social democracy

[20] See George and Heck, "Frege, Gottlob," p. 776.
[21] See Kreiser, *Gottlob Frege*, pp. 528–29. On 14 November 1903 the *Jenaische Zeitung* published again an election call that Frege co-signed. It was to determine the official list of candidates for the upcoming municipal elections, from a merger of various bourgeois parties. The call was reprinted on election day, 16 November 1903. See Kreiser, *ibid.*, pp. 544–47. For more information on Frege's political background, see Kreiser, *ibid.*, Section 6.7.1, pp. 526–47. At Christmas 1903 Frege was awarded the title of "Counselor." For a detailed discussion of the process that led to this award, see Kreiser, *ibid.*, Section 6.1.1, pp. 461–69.

as one of the party's most important domestic political opponents. Frege was right of center on the basic political controversies of the day, although he did not officially join the NLP until 1905, nine years after officially becoming a citizen of Jena. Abbe, on the other hand, was ideologically viscerally opposed to the NLP. He later risked government investigation by openly supporting officially besieged Social Democratic candidates.

On 17 September 1898, Heinrich Georg Johann Lieseberg, Frege's father-in-law, died. Less than a month later, on 16 October 1898, Frege's mother, Auguste, to whom he had been so closely attached, also passed away. With the death of Frege's mother a contract of 6 January 1893 came into effect, imposing financial responsibilities on Frege in consideration of his brother, Arnold. Frege was legally obligated to pay his brother from the time of the death of their mother a lifetime annuity of 1,250 Marks, to be rendered in quarterly installments of 312.50 Marks. He was to guarantee the pension for Arnold by assuming a mortgage registration on his inheritance of Auguste's Jena property.[22] This legal writ would cause Frege grief later when he retired from the University of Jena in 1918. He wanted to sell the house then and move to another in Bad Kleinen, Mecklenburg. He was required instead to divide the purchase price with Arnold, and was able to buy a retirement property only with financial assistance from his wealthy young acolyte Ludwig Wittgenstein. It was also at about this time that Frege wrote the unpublished 1898 essay manuscript "Logische Mängel in der Mathematik" ("Logical Defects in Mathematics").[23] In 1899–1901, Frege, along with Thomae, was made deputy treasurer of the German Mathematical Society.

In 1899, as Frege's wife, Margarete, sank further into a long-standing undiagnosed illness, it was decided that they must try to hire domestic help. The couple published in the *Jenaische Zeitung* under Margarete's name a want-ad that read "*Zum 1. April suche ich ein Mädchen mit guten Zeugnissen für Küche und Haus. Frau Professor Frege, Forstweg 29*" ("As of 1 April I am seeking a girl with good testimonials for kitchen and house. Mrs. Professor Frege, Forstweg 29"). It would have been improper, presumably, for the man of the house to advertise for a "*Mädchen*." In the event, they hired Fräulein Meta Arndt to fill the position. She was

---

[22] *Ibid.*, pp. 567–68.

[23] Dummett, *The Interpretation of Frege's Philosophy*, p. 606, argues that the essay was written some time between 1898 and 1902.

loyal to Frege beyond his death twenty-six years later. Meta was born on 3 November 1879 in Gorstendorf near Dargun (Mecklenburg-Schwerin). She worked devotedly for Frege, remained single all those years, and accompanied Frege and then Frege's ward Alfred in Frege's retirement move from Jena to the vicinity of Bad Kleinen. After Frege's death she lived off and on with Alfred in Postow.[24]

In 1899, Frege's annual university remuneration increased from 2,000 to 2,500 Marks due to seniority, upon satisfying twenty years of satisfactory university affiliation, for a total then of 7,500 Marks.[25] In the same year, Frege wrote a critical philosophical diatribe titled "Über die Zahlen des Herrn H. Schubert" ("On Mr. [Hermann] Schubert's Numbers"). P. T. Geach explains the purpose of the essay in the following terms:

Frege's work was almost wholly unappreciated during his lifetime; he rightly considered his colleagues at Jena incompetent to understand him, and said this in print, which cannot have made his relations with them happy. The choice of one Schubert to write an encyclopaedia article on Numbers provoked Frege into publishing a vitriolic tract on Schubert's unfitness for the task. He had, however, the comfort of contacts with Russell and Wittgenstein, who both retained a deep impression of his genius.[26]

[24] Kreiser, *Gottlob Frege*, p. 493.

[25] Frege was also the recipient during this time period and beyond, encompassing the years 1899–1906, of correspondence from Louis Couturat (1868–1915), who taught philosophy at the Universities of Toulouse and Caen as well as at the Collège de France in Paris. Couturat's best-known works were *La logique de Leibniz d'après des documents inédits* and *L'Algèbre de la logique*, the latter of which was translated into several languages. Couturat wrote to Frege in French. There are seven letters from Couturat to Frege, Letters II [vii]/1–7, whereas none of Frege's letters to Couturat has been preserved, assuming Frege answered. See Frege, *Briefwechsel*, p. 18. Couturat opened the correspondence to request Frege's participation at the *Congrès International de Philosophie* in Paris in 1900. The third letter (II [vii]/3) is dated after the Congress and answers questions Frege had posted, concerning the logic of Hugh MacColl. Letters II [vii]/4–5 continued the discussion and introduced the additional problem of the introduction of an international "auxiliary" language. In the last two letters Couturat discussed his further research plans, among which he included the popularization of Frege's studies. Frege's reply to Couturat's first letter of 1 July 1899 has not been preserved, but Couturat's letter of 8 July 1899, which was probably sent in reply to Frege's answer, indicates that Frege must have declined Couturat's invitation to the Congress of Philosophy in Paris, although he agreed to join the Congress committee. The exchange with Couturat demonstrates again Frege's reticence to travel to professional conferences.

[26] P. T. Geach, "Frege," in G. E. M. Anscombe and P. T. Geach, *Three Philosophers* (Oxford: Basil Blackwell, 1973), p. 129. For details on the copy of Frege's original manuscript in the possession of the library of the University of Jena, see Kratzsch, "Material zu Leben und Wirken Freges aus dem Besitz der Universitäts-Bibliothek Jena," pp. 537–39. See Kreiser, *Gottlob Frege*, pp. 271–72. In or around 1899, Frege also drafted the unpublished essay

Beginning in the summer semester of 1900, Frege, together with his colleagues, published advice for candidates of the higher Magisterium degree in mathematics and physics at the University of Jena. The booklet included collective words of wisdom from participating lecturers in mathematics, physics, and astronomy. The contributors, alphabetically, were Abbe, Felix Auerbach, the otherwise unknown O. Button, Frege, August Gutzmer, Rudolf Straubel, Thomae, and Adolf Winkelmann. It was published by the G. Neuenhahn Verlag in Jena, and printed with Carl-Zeiss-Stiftung funding. As an instrument company, the Zeiss Corporation was aware of the potential for profit from advances in pure and applied mathematics, in support of optical engineering and the natural sciences generally. The management, beginning with the founder, Carl Zeiss, understood that mathematical applications and the dedicated minds to make them needed encouragement and guidance in a difficult and popularly misunderstood subject. The furtherance of mathematical and scientific education was in the company's enlightened corporate interest. The booklet was made available to students and other interested persons free of charge.[27]

Frege's Review of Husserl 1891 (1894)

In 1894, Frege published a relatively harsh review of Husserl's 1891 *Philosophie der Arithmetik: Psychologische und logische Untersuchungen I* (*Philosophy of Arithmetic: Psychological and Logical Investigations*).[28]

Frege's complaints were directed primarily against Husserl's perceived psychologism. Frege raised three specific objections that he says are particularly problematic for a psychological approach to the concept of number. First of all, he asked how Husserl could explain the equality of

manuscript "Über Euklidische Geometrie" ("On Euclidean Geometry"). According to Dummett, *The Interpretation of Frege's Philosophy*, p. 607, the essay was written between 1899 and 1906.

[27] Kreiser, *Gottlob Frege*, p. 326. This item of "Advice" is printed in Kreiser, *ibid.*, Appendix 4.2, pp. 333–34.

[28] Dallas Willard's edition and translation of Husserl's *Philosophie der Arithmetik* includes Husserl's 1887 Universität Halle Habilitationsschrift, *Über den Begriff der Zahl* [*On the Concept of Number*], which was reproduced almost in its entirety in his *Philosophie der Arithmetik*. See Husserl, *Philosophie der Arithmetik: Psychologische und logische Untersuchungen* (Halle: Pfeffer Verlag, 1891); and its English translation by Willard, *Philosophy of Arithmetic: Psychological and Logical Investigations with Supplementary Texts from 1887–1901* (Dordrecht: Kluwer Academic Publishers, 2003).

a perceived unit [*Einheit*], to which Husserl supposedly attempts to reduce the number 1, with the distinctness of units that are said to compose 2, 3, and so on. Secondly, Frege in a scolding review complained that Husserl had no adequate account of the psychological origin and distinction between 0 and 1. Thirdly, Frege charged that Husserl's psychologistic explanation of arithmetic could not account for large numbers the conceiving of which surpasses any human cognitive capacity. The review rewards careful critical evaluation in the context of better understanding Frege's *Grundgesetze I*, especially the vehemence of his attitude against any suggestion of psychologism in the philosophy of arithmetic, while setting the stage historically for Frege's gratuitous long-term dialectical opposition to Husserl.

A taste of Frege's objections to Husserl's psychology of arithmetic is conveyed by a representative passage from the 1894 review. Frege wrote the following:

Thus we have a blurring [in Husserl's 1891 book] of the distinction between image and concept, between imagination and thought. Everything is transformed into something subjective. But just because the boundary between the subjective and objective is obliterated, what is subjective acquires in its turn the appearance of objectivity.[29]

As the paragraph continues onto the next page of the original review, Frege resorted to counterfactual supposition as to how Husserl could imaginably try to psychologize the definition of a basic geometrical relation. Frege continued undeterred, and, significantly without bothering to quote Husserl's actual words, freely attributed to the work under review a reprehensible form of psychologism especially prevalent in the field of technical definitions of mathematical *concepts*:

An example from elementary geometry may illustrate it [Husserl's way of judging the value of definitions]. The usual definition given there is: "A right angle is an angle equal to its adjacent angle." The author would probably comment on this as follows: "The idea (*Vorstellung*) of a right angle is a simple one; so it is a wholly mistaken procedure to try to define it …."[30]

[29] Frege, "Illustrative Extracts from Frege's Review of Husserl's *Philosophie der Artihmetik*," in *Philosophical Writings*, p. 79.

[30] *Ibid.* Another selection in translation appears in Beaney, ed., *The Frege Reader*, as "Review of E. G. Husserl, *Philosophie der Arithmetik* I (1894): Extract," pp. 224–26.

The subtext of Frege's criticisms of Husserl is Frege's refusal to consider a psychological account of any psychological aspect of mathematical conceptualization and practical use, despite the evident fact that these are eminently psychological phenomena. Husserl does not ask, as Frege did, "What *is* the natural number 1?" He rather asks "What could be the origin in thought of our concept of the natural number 1 as it evolves over time?"

Husserl reasonably proposes that there is an experiential origin for authentic intuitions supporting elementary arithmetical principles in the perception of small numbers of things. Authentic number and numerical operations provide the basis for the inauthentic intuitions that accompany mastery of complicated mathematical syntax and algorithms for calculating the values of an unlimited variety of dedicated arithmetical functions applied to appropriate arithmetical objects. Numbers were featured among other mathematical constructions of all kinds. It was no more than any empirically oriented philosopher might say. Husserl was as likely to have been impressed with his teacher Brentano's sometimes Aristotelian and sometimes British Enlightenment empiricism as he was with the immanent intentionality thesis in Brentano's *Psychologie vom empirischen Standpunkt* or the lectures on *Deskriptive Psychologie* that Husserl attended in Vienna in 1890–1891. To these there still clings a distinctive flavor of Brentano's immanent intentionality thesis in Brentano's British empiricist unwillingness to attribute real external existence to anything outside of immediate sense impressions. The attitude was latent in Brentano's unwillingness in *Psychologie* to distinguish *Inhalt* from *Gegenstand*.

Husserl endeavored to explain the psychology and logic of elementary arithmetic, exactly as the subtitle of his book announced. To repeat the original title in full, it is *Philosophie der Arithmetik: Psychologische und logische Untersuchungen*. The choice of wording alone suggests that, unlike Frege, Husserl prioritized psychological over logical factors in understanding the philosophical foundations of arithmetic. The fact that Husserl was interested in much the same knot of questions as Frege makes Husserl potentially either a well-met fellow-traveler or a philosophical rival of Frege's. Frege was all too easily disposed to see competitors rather than potential collaborators writing on related topics. Husserl in the end was neither of those things to Frege, although for a time the two thinkers, in some ways motivated by similar interests, enjoyed a convivial correspondence and a lively exchange of ideas.

Frege may not have liked Husserl's book because in its pages there was far too much Husserl and not enough Frege. Frege had to distance himself from what he perceived as Husserl's psychologism in the foundations of arithmetic. In doing so, he repeatedly lost sight of the fact that, unlike himself, Husserl was not trying to explain the basic concepts or otherwise establish the metaphysical foundations of arithmetic. He was not doing conceptual analysis and he was not doing ontology. Husserl thought the novelty of his approach was to apply Brentano's proto-phenomenological mode of descriptive psychology to the most irreducible structural components of arithmetical reasoning. It was thinking about arithmetic that interested Husserl at the time, rather than the mind-independent truths of elementary mathematics. That was his privilege as an independent philosophical investigator, although it evoked in Frege a strong disapproval of the Husserlian enterprise.

Correspondence with Husserl

Frege corresponded briefly with Husserl in 1891, following the publication of Husserl's *Philosophie der Arithmetik*. The relevant letters VII [xix]/1 and VII [xix]/2 in Frege's collected *Philosophical and Mathematical Correspondence* were traded when Husserl was working in Halle. Their contact resumed briefly again in 1906 in letters VII [xix]/3 through VII [xix]/4, during Husserl's time at Göttingen, where, we remember, Frege earned his PhD in 1873.[31] Husserl originally wrote to Frege presenting him with a copy of *Philosophie der Arithmetik*. He must have done so, knowing Frege's philosophical orientation, in the expectation of an appreciative reader and a productive interchange of ideas, possibly a collaboration. The break-off in correspondence during the intervening years is accounted for as the chill that followed Frege's publication of his chastening, often off-target critical evaluation of Husserl's book, condemning psychologism even where it did not actually exist.

Although we do not have the letter from Husserl to Frege that reinitiated their brief dialogue, judging from Frege's 1906 reply in letter VII [xix]/3, the occasion was once again Husserl sending Frege a recent publication. The essay, according to the editors of Frege's correspondence,

---

[31] Frege's correspondence with Husserl is collected in Frege, *Philosophical and Mathematical Correspondence*, Letters VII / 1–4, pp. 61–71.

was the fifth 1904 installment in a series of essays Husserl was publishing in the *Archiv für systematische Philosophie*, in this instance criticizing two of Brentano student Anton Marty's papers on subjectless sentences and the relation of grammar to logic and psychology.[32] On receiving a copy of Husserl's *Philosophie der Arithmetik* back in the 1890s, Frege had sent Husserl a copy of his *Begriffsschrift*, among the other writings mentioned in their communications. In Frege's 1891 letter to Husserl, he says "I thank you especially for your *Philosophie der Arithmetik*, in which you take notice of my own similar endeavours, perhaps more thoroughly than has been done up to now. I hope to find time soon to reply to your objections." Husserl had in fact discussed Frege's work, the *Grundlagen* in particular, more than that of any other philosopher. Husserl knew some of Frege's other works as well, as indicated by the underlining and scribbling of marginal comments in the monograph copies and offprints of some of Frege's publications later found in Husserl's estate. Husserl owned a complete collection of Frege's published writings from between 1891 and 1894. His copies of Frege's writings can be examined at the Husserl Archives in Leuven, Belgium.

The supply line for the interchange of philosophical ideas between Husserl and Frege broke off. Contact was resumed only years later, in response to Frege's series of articles on the foundations of geometry published between 1903 and 1906. The circumstantial evidence seems partially to confirm that Frege's 1894 review of Husserl was responsible for at least a temporary fracture in what had previously been the beginnings of a more convivial philosophical relationship. [33]

---

[32] See Frege, *Philosophical and Mathematical Correspondence*, Frege's letter to Husserl, note 1 for Letter VII [xix]/3, p. 66.

[33] It was once widely held that Husserl started out as a Brentanian psychologistic intentionalist in the philosophy of mathematics, from which he turned only after Frege's 1894 review of his *Philosophie der Arithmetik*. A classic statement of the interpretation is offered by David Woodruff Smith and Ronald McIntyre, *Husserl and Intentionality: A Study of Mind, Meaning, and Language* (Dordrecht: D. Reidel Publishing Company, 1982). For contrast, see Claire Ortiz Hill and Guillermo E. Rosado Haddock, *Husserl or Frege? Meaning, Objectivity, and Mathematics* (LaSalle: Open Court, 2003). Compare also Jitendranath N. Mohanty, "Husserl, Frege and the Overcoming of Psychologism," in *Philosophy and Science in Phenomenological Perspective*, ed. K. K. Cho (Dordrecht: Martinus Nijhoff, 1984), pp. 143–52; Mohanty, "Husserl and Frege: A New Look at Their Relationship," *Research in Phenomenology*, 4(1) (1974), pp. 51–62; and Mohanty, *Readings on Edmund Husserl's Logical Investigations* (The Hague: Martinus Nijhoff, 1977), pp. 22–32.

Husserl referred in his *Logische Untersuchungen* to the Introduction to Frege's *Grundgesetze I*, signifying his familiarity with Frege's progress. However, Husserl did not indicate having been influenced one way or another by Frege. At any rate, later, in 1936, Husserl wrote the following memorable lines to Scholz: "I never got to know personally G. Frege, and I no longer remember the occasion for our correspondence ... At the time he was generally regarded as an outsider who had a sharp mind but produced little or nothing, whether in mathematics or in philosophy."[34] There was much for Frege and Husserl to disagree about, beginning with the exact proper meaning of concept terms and the metaphysics of concepts in the philosophy of arithmetic. There were divisions of methodology and definition, and disagreements regarding the role of psychology and disciplined study of the subjective, that would keep Frege and Husserl inevitably apart. It might be said from a detached bird's eye view that the two thinkers disagreed in an interesting and potentially profitable way, but that for reasons of ego and temperament on both sides the possible mutual benefit was never realized.

In letter VII [xix]/1, Frege's criticism of Husserl's agreement with Schröder was dealt with in *Grundgesetze I*, §33, principles 2–3. There were methodological infractions that Frege saw being committed left and right, invalidating the reasoning behind the conclusions of those two philosophers concerning the true nature of arithmetic, and explaining exactly where and how they went wrong. He criticized the strategy he later called "piecemeal definition" as contrary to the "principle of completeness," and also the now so-called "context definitions" that in his judgment violated the "principle of simplicity." Husserl, to his credit, never promised to do more in his *Philosophie der Arithmetik* than explain some structural aspects of the cognitive psychology of arithmetical thinking. It is not as though Husserl assured the readers of his book that he would demystify the logic and metaphysics of arithmetical reasoning, while offering nothing in the course of the book but psychological reflections on how thinkers actually reason empirically in matters of arithmetical calculation. Whatever his other philosophical merits and defects, Husserl did nothing of such a blatant moral-epistemically discreditable kind. He wanted only to understand how the most basic *ideas* of arithmetic could have arisen from a philosophical anthropological

---

[34] Frege, *Philosophical and Mathematical Correspondence*, Letters VII [xix]/1–6, pp. 61.

standpoint in human thought and practice, and how it had been possible for mathematics to ascend far beyond the basic intuitive perceptual starting-place of arithmetical thinking in immediate sense impression perceptions of small numbers of things, like the buttons on a shirtfront.

Husserl wrote ingratiatingly, but not necessarily for that reason insincerely, in the second paragraph of his 1891 letter VII [xix]/2 to Frege

> First of all, allow me to acknowledge the large amount of stimulation and encouragement I derived from your *Foundations* (*Grundlagen der Arithmetik*). Of all the many writings I had before me as I worked on my book, I could not name another which I studied with nearly as much enjoyment as yours. Although I could not on the whole agree with your theories, I derived constant pleasure from the originality of mind, clarity, and, I should almost like to say, honesty of your investigations, in which nowhere is a point too far stretched or doubt held back. All vagueness in thought and word is alien to your book, and which everywhere tries to penetrate to ultimate foundations.[35]

Kreiser surprisingly jumps from this statement of Husserl's to the startling conclusion concerning Frege's off-topic 1891 discussion "Über das Trägheitsgesetz" ("On the Law of Inertia") that "discouragement had temporarily caused him [Frege] to deal with other issues. His contribution to discussion of the law of inertia from 1891 shows what topics he sought."[36]

Looking only at the record of Frege's writings during roughly this active time, just prior to the 1893 publication of *Grundgesetze I*, one sees that Frege also drafted "On the Concept of Number: A Criticism of Biermann" (unpublished), concerning the *Neue arithmetische Schatzkammer* (*New Arithmetical Treasure Chamber*) by Lorenz Biermann of 1667. It strikes one as inaccurate therefore to say that Frege at the time had turned away from the foundations of arithmetic. According to Dummett, Frege's discussion of Biermann was written between 1888 and 1890.[37] We also find among Frege's *Nachlaß* and short, mostly unpublished, writings from this time "On the Concept of Number: A Critical Examination of Kerry," and a draft of what was to become Frege's 1892 essay "On Concept and Object." Nor should we overlook the fact that *Grundgesetze I* was not made to appear overnight by Frege's waving a magic wand. It was the product of

---

[35] *Ibid.*, Letter VII [xix]/2 from Husserl to Frege, pp. 64–65.

[36] Kreiser, *Gottlob Frege*, p. 225, my translation. See Frege, "Über das Trägheitsgesetz," *Zeitschrift für Philosophie und philosophische Kritik*, 98 (1891), pp. 145–61.

[37] Dummett, *The Interpretation of Frege's Philosophy*, p. 606.

many years of hard work that must have been taking place also during the period within which Kreiser suggests Frege had abandoned his main interest in establishing the basic laws of arithmetic as an outgrowth of pure logic. The time needed for Frege to compose and finalize these new writings is incompatible with Kreiser's chronology.

Philosophy of Psychology of Arithmetic

Frege could be acknowledged to have demolished Husserl's psychologism only if Husserl's philosophy of arithmetic were psychologistic. What does it mean to be psychologistic, to accept a form of psychologism, in the foundations of arithmetic? That was what Frege perceived with almost maniacal fervor as a threat to the sanctity of deductively valid inference and objective realist logicist philosophical foundations for arithmetic. It would be a bad thing undoubtedly for a Platonic metaphysics of objectively mind-independent logical and mathematical entities like Frege's if psychologism were true, if mathematical entities were mere creatures of real-time occurrent thinking. Frege was right to rail against psychologism in the form he attributed to Husserl in the writings of some philosophers of mathematics at the time. Whether Frege was right to attribute that objectionable form of psychologism to Husserl is an important question that is not decided by Husserl's book and the content of Frege's review alone.

The question is, if Frege did not hit Husserl's weak point, why did Husserl thereafter back away from further psychology-based philosophical studies? Why did Husserl shudder at the implication that he had fallen victim to psychologism, and why did Husserl later bite the philosophical hand that had fed him by reproving Brentano as psychologistic in his metaphysics and epistemology? The game of deciding who was more psychologistic which was played in late-nineteenth- and early-twentieth-century German-language philosophy was a dull moment, ironically, of individual and collective psychology in this academic philosophical milieu. Frege could not have undermined Husserl's psychologism, if Husserl had never succumbed to psychologism in the first place, despite discussing philosophically some aspects of the psychology of arithmetical cognition. Frege flew off the handle at the mere mention of the psychology of arithmetic in Husserl, possibly because Husserl was a philosopher rather than a psychologist in the narrower scientific sense that was then only beginning to emerge, and a mathematician in his own right.

There can be psychological as well as logical investigations in the philosophy of arithmetic. Husserl did not imply or in any way declare by this ordering of types in his book's subtitle that he considered logic to be reducible to psychology. Nor for that matter did he commit himself to the reduction of arithmetic to logical foundations. Jacques Hadamard did no less in his marvelous short treatise *An Essay on the Psychology of Invention in the Mathematical Field* many years later in 1945 (Hadamard revised this text in 1949).[38] Closer to Frege's time, Henri Poincaré in 1908 developed similar insights about the psychology of mathematical thinking.[39] Like Husserl before him, Poincaré did so without venturing to explain mathematical objects themselves or mathematical relations as anything mental, conceptual, intuitive, intentional, or subjectively psychological.

There is a psychology of the human activity of doing mathematics, as Frege, pursuing his own example from the *Grundlagen*, should have been well positioned to agree. The same is true even if mathematics itself is something abstract and intrinsically non- and extra-psychological, an imperceivable order of Platonically real entities with objectively real distinguishing qualities participating in objectively real relations. It is hard to understand how Frege could have reviewed Husserl's *Philosophie der Arithmetik* with such small regard for Husserl's many signposts indicating that he was presenting ontically non-reductive psychological and logical investigations of thinking about the fundamental concepts of arithmetic. It was not as though Husserl evinced no understanding of the difference. He wanted to consider mathematical thinking as grounded in the structures disclosed by Brentano's philosophically legitimized empirical Aristotelian faculty of inner perception exercised by the active intellect. The end result was Husserl's phenomenology of arithmetical thinking. He did not consider reducing arithmetic to thought, but proposed to inner-empirically introspectively investigate the structures of thoughts about arithmetic, psychological occurrences as undoubtedly they are, in stereotypical episodes of arithmetical thinking.

---

[38] Jacques Hadamard, *An Essay on the Psychology of Invention in the Mathematical Field* (New York: Dover Publications, 1954).

[39] Henri Poincaré, "Mathematical Discovery," in Poincaré, *Science and Method* [1908] (London: T. Nelson and Sons, 1914), pp. 46–63.

By "concept" (*Begriff, Konzept, Idee, Vorstellung*), Husserl, contrary to Frege, definitely meant something psychological, as when we speak of *my* concept of Shakespeare's eponymous character Othello, say, as the victim of his own excessive pride, versus *your* concept of Othello as a man whose personality was flawed by irrational jealousy. Another critic could say that Othello is supposed to be both lethally prideful and jealous. What Frege means by "concept" in contrast is an abstract universal concept-function serving just as well in mathematics as for constructing meaningful predications generally. Frege and Husserl were bound to get into trouble as soon as they started talking about concepts without tracking these terminological discrepancies. Frege held that different thinkers could not share their contents of thought or propositional sense unless they shared the same concepts. Why, however, should two theatergoers have to share the same concept of Othello in order to understand that they interpret the character differently, that, quite the contrary, they come away from the drama with very different concepts of Othello? The situation could almost be described as though two different tragic characters were presented on the stage instead of one. When Husserl said that he wanted to explore the (psychological) concept of number, Frege could not help thinking that Husserl was trying to make abstract real existent numbers themselves into corresponding subjective psychological concepts. That would be reprehensible from Frege's perspective, but it was not at all what Husserl had actually proposed.

The interesting questions about arithmetic for Husserl were partly, in his sense, conceptual and partly epistemological. Like a latter-day nineteenth-century German Hume, Husserl investigated phenomenologically the experiential basis for the most fundamental arithmetical concepts he believed thought capable of discovering. It is revealing that he looked at the Dedekind relations more-than ($>$) and less-than ($<$) as primitive. Frege considered them concept-functions distinguishable in sense, and in their contribution to the compositional sense and reference that existed for the first time when an arithmetical concept-functor was completed by a Fregean proper name for an arithmetical object. It now had reference to the True or the False. The proper name must have reference or its failure to refer compositionally would prevent any sentence containing it from referring to the True or the False.

We perceive that there is one moon, or one dried fish on a ceramic plate. In mathematics, a symbolic language is developed to capture the nuances of relations between unities, beginning with the generation of natural numbers that go beyond any finite human being's capability to count, visualize, or hold in memory. If Husserl was right, then, at a stage roughly around 10, coincidentally the normal number of fingers plus thumbs, which are literally digits, available for field calculations, we begin to depend on mathematical symbolism if we are to make a worthwhile arithmetic available. Many people can memorize large tables of arithmetical functions and values. Memory was needed, but not concerning all the outputs of all the inputs to all arithmetical functions. There are practical limits that are always transcended by mathematical developments. As Descartes was perhaps the first, but not the only one, to observe, the mind does not imagistically distinguish between a chiliagon (a polygon with one thousand sides) and a figure with one more or one fewer sides than a chiliagon.[40]

Long before that point is reached, if Husserl in his *Philosophie der Arithmetik* is right, mathematical reasoning depends not on perceiving units and simple operations that can be performed on units to reflect addition and subtraction and suchlike elementary abstract functions, but on something more symbolically representative. We see a dish containing three colored glass marbles. We reach in physically and take one away, and we say that removing one marble is like subtracting 1 from 3. How many marbles are there? There are two. What, then, is 3 minus 1? Here we hope not to have Wittgenstein's intransigent student from his *Philosophical Investigations* and *Remarks on the Foundations of Mathematics* answering, with a straight face, something like 19. The answer gratifyingly comes in as 2, and we breathe a sigh of relief. We put the marble back in the dish with the other two, and the lesson continues.

This is learning mathematics by communication of mathematical concepts from adept to novice through virtually shared perceptions of illustrative elementary instantiations of the simplest numerical relations. Frequent disclaimers and clarifications are made. We have to start somewhere. Husserl sagely argued that we cognitively push this type of *authentic intuition* of the marbles-in-the-dish kind as far as it can go. Then, as a culture of individuals with an interest in knowing more about mathematics, taking advantage of its calculation methods for many purposes, mathematicians create complex symbolic languages for expressing

---

[40] Descartes, *Meditations on First Philosophy*, Meditation VI.

more complex mathematical concepts and relations that begin to take on a life of their own. We perceive these written on paper, and we learn how calculation algorithms are encoded and enacted in the symbolism.

When we conquer mechanical methods for finding integrals and deriving differentials in mathematical analysis or calculus, never mind where the initial values come from, the pencil fairly glides on the page like an Olympic ice skater, without giving a thought to the meaning of any of the formulas produced during the internalized rule-governed syntax transformations. The hand and eye rejoice in the exercise of their training, and consciousness for the time being can concentrate on other things. The mastery of higher mathematical languages beyond elementary arithmetic is also perceptual, but no longer of swirly-patterned marbles, aggies or cats' eyes, moved around from one bowl to another. It is the perception especially of the inscribed formal languages of mathematics themselves, the axioms, theorems, and proofs of mathematics in mathematical symbolisms as they appear written on the lecture-room chalkboard or printed page, sketched in the sand with a twig, and in the imaginations of those gifted with such a facility.

The puzzling thing in bringing Frege's lacerating review of Husserl's *Philosophie der Arithmetik* at exactly this time into focus is therefore why Frege should have been unreceptive to what Husserl had proposed in the first part of his treatise. Frege too wanted to ascend from basic concepts of arithmetic to the higher reaches of the discipline by means of the deductively valid logical derivations of theorems from arithmetical axioms, the basic laws of elementary arithmetic. Husserl referred to this capability with mathematical reasoning in theorem derivation as inauthentic perception of the mathematical through the syntax of its formal symbolism. He left the ontology of arithmetic untouched, and dealt with it circumspectly in the sense of investigating the most basic arithmetical concepts thought can search out in a descriptive psychological inquiry of the living concepts grasped and formulated in temporally streaming moments of consciousness. He followed much the same method as Brentano in the latter's imminent intentionality or intentional inexistence thesis, leaving open the question as to whether there are entities existing outside the contents of perceptions as their intended objects, which the descriptively psychological phenomenologically accessible contents of conscious experiences might then be assumed more or less adequately to represent. The difficulties accruing to an articulation and defense of the latter alternative explain in part why a representational philosophy of mind and epistemology was rejected by Husserl, who was otherwise satisfied speaking of the mind's presentations. The conditions for representation in conscious moments are not met if Husserl was right, making mirroring, picturing in the mind, imaging, and receiving impressions as replicas or facsimiles of an external world all alike theoretically unviable.

Inner sense exists, Husserl decided, but must be trained up for its work, just as the eye must be taught to look with proper discernment through a microscope or telescope lens, or to read with understanding Cantor's transfinite set theory notation, or for that matter Frege's *Begriffsschrift*. Superficially or symptomatically, what seems to have divided Frege from Husserl most on the foundations of arithmetic was the previously remarked difference in their understanding of the load-bearing word "concept." Frege had complained of this already in his reply to Kerry in "On Concept and Object." He did not seem to appreciate that most of the philosophical world used the word "concept" in roughly the same psychological sense as Kerry and Husserl, rather than referring, as Frege wanted, in every instance to an abstract concept-function. Abstract concept-functions in Frege's sense were not designated as "concepts" by the majority of philosophers, but described by means of the words "abstract function" or "universal," categories with which Platonists like Frege were by disposition comfortable.

As to the effect of Frege's critique of Husserl's 1891 book, Richard L. Mendelsohn writes, in *The Philosophy of Gottlob Frege*, that "Husserl abandoned his psychologism shortly thereafter, but he was none too generous in later life when he recalled Frege to be a man of little note who never amounted to much."[41] The anecdote seems to paraphrase what Husserl at one point wrote to Scholz, namely that he never knew Frege personally, but understood that he was considered an outsider who, as previously quoted, had achieved virtually nothing "in mathematics or in philosophy."[42] What did Husserl mean by describing Frege as an outsider? Was he referring to Frege's position at Jena, in the mathematical and philosophical scholarly communities at large internationally, or in the world history of science? These things are not reliably judged by contemporaries. There is after all a

---

[41] Mendelsohn, *The Philosophy of Gottlob Frege*, p. 3.
[42] Frege, *Philosophical and Mathematical Correspondence*, pp. 61.

subjective side to the study of mathematics and the philosophy of mathematics, and egos to bruise and ambitions to fuel or discourage. There is also a fallacy known as *post hoc, ergo propter hoc* that cautions against concluding that something happens because of an event when the event merely precedes the later occurrence in time. Early symptoms of a disease are not themselves the cause of the disease's later effects, and are at most a sign or symptom of the ailment's presence. If it is true, as Mendelsohn remarks, that Husserl rejected psychologism shortly after Frege's unfriendly 1894 review of Husserl's *Philosophie der Arithmetik*, it still does not follow logically that Husserl abandoned his psychologism because of Frege's review.

It is clear on reflection that Frege's criticisms of Husserl's alleged psychologism in his 1894 review of Husserl's 1891 book were misplaced. Husserl studied the scientific phenomenological psychology of arithmetic. Despite being interested in the psychology of psychological concepts or ephemeral ideas of arithmetical objects, relations, and theorems, Husserl did not try to explain arithmetical objects, relations, or theorems *as* psychological. Frege did not understand Husserl's purpose or strategy, as his review testifies. Frege lambasted Husserl for sins of philosophical analysis of which Husserl was patently not guilty. Frege promised in his explicit methodological rules in the *Grundlagen* not to confuse sign with thing signified. Nor should Frege have allowed himself, as he apparently lapsed in his criticism of Husserl, to confuse the psychological concept of something with the thing of which it is a concept. Husserl observed the distinction properly in his *Philosophie der Arithmetik*, whereas Frege in his review of Husserl did not, but mixed them up irresponsibly together in his critique. He persistently misinterpreted what Husserl said about arithmetical concepts as objects in the psychological sense, whereby it is possible that my concept of Othello ≠ your concept of Othello. He expected Husserl to share his analysis of arithmetical and predicable concepts generally as unsaturated abstract concept-functions, which is not how Husserl wanted to talk.

Merely to have planted the idea that the foundations of arithmetic might be psychological, that mathematics might have been invented rather than continually discovered and rediscovered, made Husserl guilty of complicity with psychologism in Frege's judgment. Call it what you will, dress it up as phenomenology, whatever that is supposed to mean, as Frege read Husserl, his phenomenological study counted among the most treacherous forms of psychologism in the philosophy of mathematics.

The egregious error had to be called out on the carpet for the good of all legitimate research undertaken in the philosophical foundations of arithmetic. His was a principled wrath aimed at any insidious psychologism, which in the 1894 review he directed against Husserl almost as deputizing for everyone who had ever committed this error.

The interesting implication as we probe Frege's personality on the basis of the few available fragments of information is that he summarily rejected collaboration with Husserl. His review made it all but impossible. From the break in their previous correspondence Husserl seemed to have understood that Frege was not his ideological companion but rather an opponent. That, in any case, is one reasonable interpretation of the historical facts. Frege chose to review Husserl's book as he did. The fact that he attacked Husserl for his supposedly objectionable psychologism speaks volumes as to the effect Frege's participation in academic life and the intellectual battles he had waged had had on his judgment at this still relatively early to middle part of his professional career.

It has been tempting for some commentators to read between the lines of Frege's review a reaction to the negative responses his own writings had received. Just as Dummett remarks that Cantor does not seem to have read Frege's *Grundlagen* with any care, so Dallas Willard, the English translator of Husserl's *Philosophie der Arithmetik*, has argued that Frege in reviewing Husserl does not seem to have read Husserl carefully enough to avoid obvious errors of interpretation in his published *Rezension*.[43] The incidents surrounding Frege's review of Husserl shed light not only on his philosophy of language and mathematics, but also on his personality and its development during the period. The charge of psychologism was frequently made in the late-nineteenth-century

---

[43] Dummett, "Introduction," in *Frege: Philosophy of Language*, p. xliii: "In *Grundlagen* Frege made complimentary references to Cantor, which Cantor repaid by writing a savage and quite uncomprehending review of the book which is reprinted in the collected writings of Cantor with regretful remarks by [Ernst] Zermelo, the editor, about the misunderstanding between the two great men. Frege wrote a brief reply, and retaliated by scoring points off Cantor in Volume II of *Grundgesetze*." See also Dallas Willard, "Translator's Introduction" to Edmund Husserl, *Philosophy of Arithmetic*, pp. xxvii–xxviii: "If Frege had studied the *Philosophy of Arithmetic* fairly and thoroughly, he could not have missed the point. He would never have said such things as that for Husserl 'Everything becomes presentation. The references of words are presentations' [here Willard is quoting from Frege, "Review of Dr. E. Husserl's *Philosophy of Arithmetic*," *Mind*, 81 (1972), pp. 321–37]. Husserl was, in fact, *never* guilty of 'Psychologism' with respect to numbers and their laws, nor in any sense in which he later rejected and refuted it in the 'Prolegomena' to the *Logical Investigations* or elsewhere."

German academic community. Frege's objections to Husserl's *Philosophie der Arithmetik* need to be understood in this larger intellectual sociological context. Husserl was not merely the passive recipient of Frege's animus, but in his book raised explanatory difficulties specifically and explicitly for Frege's pure logicism. It was a time when to criticize another philosopher sometimes called for vicious rhetorical retaliation over and above reconsideration of whether worthwhile improvements might be made, at least in the expression of one's ideas. They were like galleons at sea sidling up in close proximity, discharging their cannons at each other in a commotion of water, smoke, and gunpowder, not always striking their intended targets.

It is interesting that Frege published no *Rezension* in that explicit format after reviewing in 1894 Husserl's *Philosophie der Arithmetik*. Despite terminating his official evaluating activity, Frege certainly continued to critically discuss writings in the philosophy of mathematics by authors with whom he disagreed. Frege's review of Husserl one year after publishing *Grundgesetze I* definitively marked the end of his participation as a reviewer in professional and literary journals. Was this purely coincidental, or was there something about the review of Husserl that disinclined Frege thereafter to review other writers' books? Or was there something about that review that had the consequence that he would henceforth not be invited to review other writers' books?

Neither of these hypotheses seems verifiably correct. Frege was a man of forty-four in 1893, no longer a boy from Wismar. He was married, with a professional position and professional responsibilities. He understood the difficulties to be expected in offering the world new ideas. He was not embarrassed out of writing further book reviews. The opportunity may not have arisen owing to a lack of invitations arriving in his mailbox, perhaps as an indirect result of his abrasive tone in previous reviews. (However, we should note that such rough treatment was something he and his writings also suffered often enough on the other side as the brunt of unfriendly criticism.) Perhaps he was too busy. Perhaps he was chastened by a later realization that he had after all seriously misunderstood Husserl, and criticized the young man's new book in unfair terms on the basis of an inaccurate cursory reading and hasty misunderstanding of Husserl's purpose.[44]

---

[44] There appears to be no generally accepted explanation or recognition of interest in the question as to why Frege's *Rezension* of Husserl's *Philosophie der Arithmetik* was his last

Crossing Swords with Hilbert

During the sixty-seventh *Versammlung deutscher Naturforscher und Ärzte* (Assembly of German Natural Scientists and Physicians), in Lübeck, 16–20 September 1895, Frege gave a lecture on 17 September in the department of mathematics and astronomy. Frege's talk on this occasion became the basis for his previously mentioned 1897 published lecture "Über die Begriffsschrift des Herrn Peano und meine eigene" ("On the *Begriffsschrift* of Mr. Peano and My Own"). Frege's lecture and later published essay was occasioned by, and intended as a clarificatory polemical response to, Peano's review of *Grundgesetze I*. It is significant, in keeping with previous comments about Frege's use of the word "*Begriffsschrift*," that Frege spoke here of Peano as having a *Begriffsschrift*. It describes a generic logic of Fregean concept-functions by any other name, the truth-functionality of its propositional component and mixed multiple-quantifier logic that is in many ways Frege's *Begriffsschrift*'s fraternal twin. The logics were close enough in Frege's estimation to warrant a comparison in order to demonstrate the advantages of his *Begriffsschrift* over Peano's.

Kreiser remarks on Frege's conspicuous absence from national and international scientific congresses that many of his colleagues and contemporaries attended. Against the background of these absences, Frege's participation at the Lübeck meeting stands out.[45] It was to be a memorable and momentous gathering for Frege. There he met Hilbert, and the two philosophers of mathematics began a conversation on the role and value of symbols in mathematics, the truth or otherwise of mathematical axioms and theorems, and many other central topics in the philosophy of mathematics. The meeting initiated a stimulating exchange of correspondence in the period 1895–1903, most parts of which still exist and continue to reward careful study.[46]

Hilbert had assumed a chair in mathematics at Göttingen University in 1895. This brought him into Frege's orbit geographically and historically to the home where Frege had written and defended his dissertation twenty-two years previously in 1873. In the winter

---

review after what had previously been a steady progression of active, often take-no-prisoners, reviewing.

[45] Kreiser, *Gottlob Frege*, p. 253.

[46] Frege, *Philosophical and Mathematical Correspondence*, IV [xv]/1–9, pp. 32–52.

semester of 1898–1899 at Göttingen, Hilbert lectured on "Elements of Euclidean Geometry," which was later the basis for his influential text *Grundlagen der Geometrie*. Hilbert's book with that title was published in 1899 as the literary part of a Festschrift for the unveiling of the Gauss–Weber monument in Göttingen city. Frege was intrigued, and tried immediately to understand Hilbert's methodological reorientation.

The editors of Frege's *Philosophical and Mathematical Correspondence* explain the situation as follows:

Frege may have had advance knowledge of Hilbert's views through an edited transcript of Hilbert's lectures prepared by H. von Schaper. This transcript reached Frege through Heinrich Liebmann (the son of Otto Liebmann, Frege's colleague at Jena), who was at the time a lecturer in mathematics at Göttingen and who had heard Hilbert's lectures. However, it is not certain that the transcript reached Frege prior to the publication of the work. Frege's objections to Hilbert's use of certain terms led to a more extended controversy between them which is contained in letters 3 to 8. Letter 9, which follows the others after an interval of three years, adds little to the controversy.

The Frege–Hilbert controversy has been much studied and discussed by writers on the foundations of mathematics. Although Frege's logical objections were well taken, and although a correct understanding of the axiomatic method must begin with Frege, the dominant view, especially among mathematicians, is still the view expressed recently by H. Scholz: "... no one doubts nowadays that while Frege himself created much that was radically new on the basis of the classical conception of science, he was no longer able to grasp Hilbert's radical transformation of this conception of science, with the result that his critical remarks, though very acute in themselves and still worth reading today, must nevertheless be regarded as essentially beside the point." While H. [Hans] Freudenthal has tried to give a more balanced historical account, his study points nevertheless in the same direction. H. G. Steiner does more justice to Frege's arguments, but his verdict, too, is largely determined by the traditional interpretation of Hilbert's school. A contrary interpretation has been proposed by F. [Friedrich] Kambartel, who argues that Frege's objections can be construed almost in their entirety as a well-founded critique of Hilbert's ideas. In the fifth letter, Frege proposed to Hilbert that their correspondence be published, but Hilbert did not take up the suggestion. Frege later had the following comment on this:

"Mr Hilbert's Festschrift on the foundations of geometry prompted me to explain my divergent views to the author in writing; and this gave rise to a correspondence which, unfortunately, was soon broken off. Thinking that the questions it dealt with might be of general interest, I thought of a subsequent publication. However, Mr Hilbert is reluctant to give his consent to it since his own views have changed in the meantime. I regret this because reading the correspondence would have been the most convenient way of introducing someone into the state of the question, and it would have saved me the trouble of reformulating it ...."[47]

---

[47] *Ibid.*, quoted in Section IV editors' introduction on Hilbert, pp. 31–32.

The last sentence makes it clear that Frege decided to continue the controversy in the form of an essay which appeared in 1903 under the title "Über die Grundlagen der Geometrie" in two parts. Hilbert himself did not react to it. A. [Alwin] Korselt undertook the defense of Hilbert's position, and Frege replied to Korselt in a new series of articles entitled "Über die Grundlagen der Geometrie."[48]

In a letter dated 1 October 1895, Frege regretted that he and Hilbert had been interrupted in their conversation at the scientific meeting in Lübeck. Hilbert promptly and collegially replied. He considered Frege's letter of such importance that he wanted to bring Frege to the Göttingen mathematical society for discussion. He revealed that in 1885 he had presented the substance of Frege's *Grundlagen* in a colloquium over which he presided.[49]

The central argument of the essay reflects an ongoing debate in which Frege was engaged with Hilbert. Hilbert was the more renowned mathematician and philosopher of the two at the time. They quickly centered their discussion on problems concerning the nature of geometry and minimal requirements of axiomatization. The question before them as they corresponded by post across the geographical corridor of Germany was the truth-value status, if any, of mathematical axioms. They often focused on geometry. Both were interested in the question of whether the basic laws of a formal language are true, and what justification there might be for accepting one set of axioms over a rival choice as correctly expressing the system's relevant truths.

Hilbert is considered a *formalist* in the sense of holding that it did not make any difference as to truth-value what axiom set mathematicians approved. "Formalism" is a word coined for Hilbert's approach not by Hilbert, but by the Dutch intuitionist mathematician and philosopher of mathematics L. E. J. Brouwer. Truth was irrelevant to the meaning and utility of mathematical formulas. Any axioms were "true" in and of the formal mathematical system the axioms defined, and in any higher independent symbolism-transcending sense by virtue of being mathematical syntax game tokens they were neither true nor false. The attitude was easily mistaken as blasé indifference to the truth. It was not obviously anything else. The question divided philosophers and mathematicians. It agitated philosophically minded mathematicians expecting objective *a priori* logically necessary truths among the derivable theorems of any

---

[48] *Ibid.*, Section IV editors' introduction on Hilbert, p. 32.
[49] *Ibid.*, Letter IV [xv]/1 to Hilbert, 1 October 1895, pp. 32–34.

branch of mathematics. Hilbert was a relativist about mathematical truth, at least at his most cavalier. Frege's realism could not abide loose talk of truths. Presumably, Hilbert did not care. Frege wanted the axioms of logic and mathematics to reflect a commitment to their truth like that conferred on verified laws of physics in natural science. All alike were hypothetical, admittedly. They could reasonably be considered true unless or until they led judgment astray. Sooner or later mistakes would make themselves known.

It would be beside the point to say that Hilbert was cynical about mathematical truth. Rather, he found the concept immaterial to what happens in mathematics, especially in mathematical proofs. Frege, in contrast, was naïvely (technically rather than pejoratively speaking) realist about mathematical truth, supposing that mathematical theorems must be objectively necessarily true predications of properties to existent abstract entities. He held that the deductive validity of mathematical reasoning could be vouchsafed only if mathematical propositions, especially equations that entered into mathematical proofs as deductive derivations of theorems, have a univocal truth-value that can be grasped after educated reflection. More particularly, the axioms of mathematics were expected by Frege, but not, or only ambiguously so, by Hilbert, to possess truth-value and in particular to be true in the same semantic sense as any other true proposition. Frege interpreted the truth of any mathematical proposition as the validly derived mathematical theorem's sentential reference to the True. It was the job of symbolic logic to determine which mathematical expressions were true and to exhibit their inferential proofs.

Mathematical truth was not taken as lightly by Frege as it was by Hilbert. Hilbert was satisfied to suspend the expectation that there is truth in mathematics in any ultimate extra-systemic sense. He did not see what difference it made whether mathematical theorems were true or not. He was prepared to engage in discussions of theorems ignoring truth. He did not fully share Frege's sense of urgency about inquiring into these hairy metaphysical puzzles in pursuit of truth. Hilbert was content provided only that the mathematical syntax manipulation game was played according to explicit agreed-upon symbol transformation rules resulting in formally interesting structures. If the rule-governed changes and exchanges of symbols that assumptions supported resulted in other sentences according to the rules of the mathematical syntax manipulation game, then that was all there was to the rule-governed constructed sentence constituting a mathematical theorem.

The speed bump in Hilbert's formalism was its reliance on rule-governed syntax transformations in each distinct mathematical game. If we ask what rules these shall be, Hilbert's only consistent answer was to say that we can let all internally consistent rules be tried out, allowing those which have a special utility or whose structures attract the interest of mathematicians to prevail. The reply would be plainly disingenuous. Hilbert knew just as well as did Frege that mathematical rules do not crop up like random mutations to be passed along or mown down according to selection-pressured practices in the society of mathematicians. He understood, like Frege, that deductive validity was defined in terms of the modality of truth-values, to speak in Frege-friendly functional terms, of input and output, assumption and inference, by truth-preserving syntax transformation in a rule-governed mathematical game. Was this only truth *manqué*? Was it a play on the word? Or, in considering deductive validity, were we not referring, like Frege, to semantic absolutes, the True and the False?

Hilbert, much like Frege, despite their differences, wanted a metamathematical characterization of mathematical reasoning. He demanded that all steps of a proof be subjected to critical scrutiny to determine their legitimating connection to a correct conceptual starting-place and rigorous derivation protocol. The analogy of mathematics with games is strained if the point is supposed to be that nothing in mere game-playing is in any sonorous sense "legitimating" or "correct." The main difference in the interesting long-distance philosophical partnership–rivalry of these two thinkers is that Hilbert believed that mathematical signs have no meaning beyond the rules associated with their formal syntax shapes in a play of transformation moves, while Frege thought that mathematical signs stand for mathematical objects that truly have the properties they are rigorously demonstrated as possessing. Frege argued that there is such an existent abstract object as the natural number 1 represented in arithmetical languages by the numeral "1," among countless other ways, and that the number truly does have the properties ascribed to it by the principles of elementary arithmetic and the derivational superstructure of higher mathematics. It has the property of being odd, of being the successor of 0 and predecessor of 2, and the like. He considered these facts about numbers as objective choice-independent truths, which had been discovered and verified but not made true by mathematical proofs. Their truth-makers were abstract mind-independent states of affairs rather than the consequences of an indifferently chosen inferentially self-consistent but otherwise epistemically insupportable combination of game-like mathematical syntax transformation rules. The difficult question otherwise is why those rules and not another set, while there are choices, are thought to govern pure logic and arithmetic.

Frege wrote a diplomatic but in essence challenging letter to Hilbert, in which he and his Jena mathematics colleagues Thomae and Gutzmer asked to know more precisely what Hilbert understood by the highly loaded mathematical terms "axiom," "definition," and "explanation."[50] That was not an unreasonable request, for the letter continued to say that the co-authors found the concepts "blurred in an alarming manner" ("*in bedenklicher Weise verwischt*"), at the cost of the logical rigor of Hilbert's exposition. These were challenging accusations. The correspondence in this period between Frege and Hilbert lasted almost a year. Hilbert's answers to Frege's questions were short and seemed always to deal with other problems than the exact requests for clarification with which he had been confronted in previous co-authored letters from Jena. He liked to change the subject. Frege wanted to debate Hilbert and engage with him dialectically, as Hilbert kept wriggling out of his grip. Hilbert avowed in the final letter of the set that he would prepare a follow-up detailed reply, but that was probably never written and has anyway not survived.[51]

Complementary Aims of Frege's Philosophical Discourse

Frege's mathematical and philosophical writings, after the completion of his Habilitationsschrift in 1874, as he began to find his own philosophical path and voice, can be divided into two main categories, among indefinitely many other ways of characterizing them. Some of Frege's writings advanced the formal theory of his *Begriffsschrift* by stages as a positive constructive contribution to mathematical logic. Frege's other writings, including the *Grundlagen* and the essays and book reviews in which he reinforced his philosophy of mathematics, philosophy of language, and objective scientific

[50] *Ibid.*, Letter IV [xv]/3 to Hilbert, 27 December 1899, pp. 34–38.
[51] *Ibid.*, Letter IV [xv]/4 from Hilbert to Frege (excerpt by Frege), 29 December 1899, pp. 38–43.

semantics in his newly introduced sense, were polemical, highly argumentative, and even bombastic in their criticism of rival ideologies.

Frege's assessment of Husserl and, prominently, of the algebraist and philosopher of mathematics Schröder, among others, including Erdmann, not to mention his historical–philosophical judgment of Mill's inductivism in logic and understanding of the concept of number, made it clear that Frege had no hesitation about declaring that in the philosophy of arithmetic he did not suffer what he took to be fools gladly. The cause for hesitation and concern is that under the cold light of fair reconsideration, more than one hundred and twenty years later, it is not always evident that Frege correctly understood the philosophical subtleties of the arguments he attacked. In some instances, Frege appeared to be directing counter-objections along with his vented spleen against ideological and methodological strawmen.

The category of importance at this juncture for understanding Frege's *Grundgesetze* of 1893/1903 is that it combined the theoretical development of an application of *Begriffsschrift* logic with the *Grundlagen* concept of natural number. The purpose was to arrive at purely logical formulations of elementary arithmetical laws and deductively valid derivations of elementary arithmetical theorems. The constructive enterprise was spiced with a generous dash of rhetorical assaults on dialectical opponents in the philosophy of mathematics. In his crowning defense of logicism, Frege had ample opportunity to undermine other thinkers in the field with whom he disagreed, and took it. It turned out that he disagreed with nearly everyone, although he demonstrated more respect and patience toward some than he did toward others. It was Frege's militant opposition to psychologism that pervaded both the constructive and the polemical aspects of his efforts in the *Grundgesetze* to bring all the independently machined components together into a fully algebraic reduction of arithmetic to concepts and inference structures of pure logic.[52]

---

[52] For a detailed discussion of Frege's rejection of psychologism and in this connection also with Husserl, see Kreiser, *Gottlob Frege*, Section 3.6.2, pp. 237–49. The secondary literature on psychologism and anti–psychologism both generally and specifically in Frege's case is vast. See especially Baker and Hacker, "Frege's Anti-Psychologism," in *Perspectives on Psychologism*, ed. M. A. Notturno (Leiden: Brill Academic Publishers, 1989), pp. 75–127; B. C. Hopkins, "Husserl's Psychologism and Critique of Psychologism, Revisited," *Husserl Studies*, 22 (2006), pp. 91–119; and Gerald J. Massey, "Some Reflections on Psychologism," in *Phenomenology and the Formal Sciences*, ed. Thomas Seebohm, Dagfinn Føllesdal, and Jitendranath N. Mohanty (Dordrecht: Kluwer Academic Publishing, 1991), pp. 183–94.

11

The Crucible of Logicism
and the Crisis of Russell's
Paradox (1902–1904)

RUSSELL SENT FREGE his famous letter on or shortly after dating it 16 June 1902. The letter must have taken less than a week to reach Frege in Jena. Frege replied almost immediately to Russell in a letter of 22 June.[1] Frege presumably received Russell's dispatch at the university. He was not slow to react. Speed was rather of the essence. *Grundgesetze II*, as the often-told anecdote goes, had already been corrected in proof and was under early production work at the printer. They were making the pages to go into the book, which may have been virtually ready for the binder, for which materials and labor Frege was personally out of pocket. Frege was persuaded that Russell had discovered a formal contradiction in the purely logical concepts and inference principles by which the basic laws of elementary arithmetic were meant to be grounded and theorems deductively inferred. The system entire was supposed in the very near future to appear as the second of two at long last collected volumes of Frege's *Grundgesetze*.[2]

The Herald of Inconsistency

Of the six basic supposedly purely logical laws in *Grundgesetze* arithmetic, it was Axiom V (§20) that was to cause Frege embarrassment, regret and grief. The weakness in Frege's system that it was thought to represent, which was highlighted in Russell's letter, derailed indefinitely

---

[1] See Frege, *Philosophical and Mathematical Correspondence*, Letter XV [xxxvi]/2 for Russell's letter and Frege's response.
[2] An overview of the publication history and essentials for understanding Frege's purpose in *Grundgesetze I* is provided by Montgomery Furth in his "Introduction" to Frege, *The Basic Laws of Arithmetic: Exposition of the System* (Berkeley and Los Angeles: University of California Press, 1967), pp. v–lx.

449

the writing of what might have become *Grundgesetze III*, the third volume in the projected series. Russell's paradox, in lieu of a philosophically satisfactory solution, prevented Frege from undertaking further constructive efforts in mathematical logic. The later release of this third volume would have ameliorated to some extent the embarrassment of spreading out the publication of *Grundgesetze I* and *II* over a span of ten years, seen afterward from a more aerial perspective.[3] That Frege thought all along in terms of the history of his accomplishments, having identified the goals of a rigorous non-psychologistic logicism as part of the more or less permanent published archive of the progress of mathematics, stands out in some of what he wrote and in almost all of his professional decision-making, including choices among publication options. Axiom V was held to blame because it countenances a *begriffs-schriftliche* formulation of the vital component of Russell's paradox, an ultimately quantificationally ambiguous attempt to define the set of sets that are not members of themselves.

Russell's Paradox Letter

There was virtually no logical or mathematical formalism in Russell's paradox letter. Everything was presented in ordinary German, with a final single statement of the paradox offered for comparison and further clarification in Peano's linear logical notation. The letter reproduced below in sections for commentary appears in a translation approved by Russell in his lifetime, which has previously been published and frequently reprinted. Russell's communication consisted of three relatively short paragraphs. In the first, Russell politely paid respect to Frege as the author of *Grundgesetze I*, a work he considered invaluable to his own

---

[3] Dummett, *Frege: Philosophy of Language*, pp. 657–58. Dummett writes, p. 658, "... the final sub-section of section Z [of *Grundgesetze II*, Part, not *Band* or Volume, III] is entitled 'The Next Problem.' It is thus quite evident that Frege intended to issue a third volume [*Grundgesetze III*], completing the unfinished Part III. The only reason he can have had for thus leaving the task uncompleted was the belief that Russell's discovery entailed a revision of his formal system too extensive for him to have the heart to undertake it." With all the heart and energy in the world, Frege still might not have been able to make progress against Russell's paradox within the framework of his philosophical–methodological scruples from the starting-place of supposing that Russell's paradox is a genuine logical antinomy implying a logical contradiction.

thinking about the logical foundations of mathematics. He began with a decorous opening salutation:

Friday's Hill, Haslemere, 16 June 1902

Dear colleague,

I have known your *Basic Laws of Arithmetic* [*Grundgesetze I*] for a year and a half, but only now have I been able to find the time for the thorough study I intend to devote to your writings. I find myself in full accord with you on all main points, especially in your rejection of any psychological element in logic and in the value you attach to a conceptual notation for the foundations of mathematics and of formal logic, which, incidentally, can hardly be distinguished. On many questions of detail, I find discussions, distinctions and definitions in your writings for which one looks in vain in other logicians.[4]

Russell praised Frege's work without sycophancy, and gestured toward some of their common technical interests. That was a promising start. The preamble of Russell's missive must have come as a breath of fresh air to the applause-starved Frege, especially where *Grundgesetze I* was concerned. The first volume had now been available for almost a decade. Frege may have felt as though the book had yet to find a worthy reader, and in the end might never do so. Certainly until this point Frege's latest work had not attracted any serious criticism. Hume, long before Frege, had similarly complained when his 1739–1740 volume *A Treatise of Human Nature*, as he dejectedly remarked, "fell *dead-born from the Press.*"[5]

Here at last, and from the already distinguished young aristocratic thirty-year-old logician and philosopher Russell, was a glimmer of acceptance and understanding. Putting the works as they emerged from the press in library catalogs was an idea that was perhaps finally starting to pay dividends for Frege. Patience Frege had in abundance for his revolution in philosophy of mathematics to gain traction. A slow trickle of appreciation would be more delicious to him than a sudden brief blaze of interest followed by long-lasting disregard and neglect. Having respectfully stroked Frege's ego, Russell now nonchalantly sprang a logical objection:

---

[4] Russell, letter to Frege 16 June 1902, *ibid.*, Letter XV [xxxvi]/1, p. 130. See Griffin, "The Prehistory of Russell's Paradox," in *One Hundred Years of Russell's Paradox: Mathematics, Logic, Philosophy*, ed. Godehard Link and John L. Bell (Berlin: Walter de Gruyter, 2004), pp. 349–72.

[5] Hume, "My Own Life," in Ernest Campbell Mossner, *The Life of David Hume* (Austin: University of Texas Press, 1954), Appendix A, p. 612: "Never literary Attempt was more unfortunate than my Treatise of human Nature. It fell *dead-born from the Press*; without reaching such distinction as even to excite a Murmur among the Zealots."

I have encountered a difficulty only on one point. You assert (p. 17) that a function could also constitute the indefinite element. This is what I used to believe, but this view now seems to me dubious because of the following contradiction: Let w be the predicate of being a predicate which cannot be predicated of itself. Can w be predicated of itself? From either answer follows its contradictory. We must therefore conclude that w is not a predicate. Likewise, there is no class (as a whole) of those classes which, as wholes, are not members of themselves. From this I conclude that under certain circumstances a definable set does not form a whole.[6]

Frege must have seen the problem immediately. Russell's eagerness was thinly disguised. *Grundgesetze I* Axiom V appeared to permit the definition of sets by the well-formed *begriffsschriftliche* formalization of their extensions. Coherently describable extensions turned out to be the crux. Russell perceived that Frege's Axiom V permitted syntactical construction of the set of sets that are not members of themselves. Frege's principle was supposed to imply that Russell's set exists, after which an excluded-middle (actually noncontradiction) Russell paradox dilemma was alleged to imply logical inconsistency at the tips of both horns. Axiom V was blamed as all that was needed to generate the alleged antinomy. It was the extension of the output value of an Axiom V-authorized function-concept, consisting of the set of sets that were not members of themselves. Frege's *Grundgesetze* did not seem to be able to prevent the contradiction that resulted when it was asked whether or not R is a member of itself, from which there apparently logically follows the conclusion that the Russell set of sets that are not members of themselves is a member of itself if and only if it is not a member of the set of sets that are not members of themselves. Something seems to have gone drastically wrong in Frege's arithmetic. The issue of how to remedy the situation remained an unresolved problem that plagued Frege throughout his remaining days.

Russell remarked in the letter's second paragraph that he was currently at work on a book on the principles of mathematics. It was the book with precisely that title, *Principles of Mathematics*, which was published by Russell in its first edition in 1903. Russell mentioned that he expected to discuss Frege's philosophy of mathematics thoroughly in the book, and asked Frege especially for reprints of his philosophical essays, indicating

---

[6] Russell, letter to Frege 16 June 1902, in Frege, *Philosophical and Mathematical Correspondence*, Letter XV [xxxvi]/1, pp. 130–31. It is assumed throughout, as Russell and Frege seem to have done in theory and practice, that, when Russell says that predicate "F" ["w"] cannot be predicated of itself, he means that it cannot be *truly* predicated of itself.

that he already owned or was planning soon to buy Frege's books. Frege was alerted by the remark that Russell was likely to discuss Frege in a book to appear the following year, the same year as *Grundgesetze II*, which was now in production and slated to be published. Frege had to assume that Russell would explain the paradox he had discovered in *Grundgesetze I*, laying responsibility for the contradiction on a lack of existence restrictions on concept-function formulation, enshrined in the otherwise unfettered Axiom V.

Something had to be done. *Grundgesetze II* was already at the printers. Or, anyway, by this time in mid-summer 1902 Frege had most probably seen and corrected the book's galley proofs. Whatever was to be done, it would have to be done soon. In the third paragraph of his 16 June letter to Frege, Russell got back down to business, concluding that

On the fundamental questions where symbols fail, the exact treatment of logic has remained very backward; I find that yours is the best treatment I know in our time; and this is why I have allowed myself to express my deep respect for you. It is very much to be regretted that you did not get around to publishing the second volume of your *Basic Laws* [*Grundgesetze II*]; but I hope that this will still be done.

> Yours sincerely,
> Bertrand Russell

Then Russell added, in a final addendum,

The above contradiction can be expressed in Peano's notation as follows:

$$w = \text{cls} \cap x\, 3\, (x \sim \varepsilon x). \supset: w\, \varepsilon\, w. = .w \sim \varepsilon w.$$

I have written to Peano about this, but he still owes me a reply.[7]

Russell's letter contained two different formulations of the paradox that Frege's *Grundgesetze I* Axiom V was supposed to imply are logically equivalent. The first was presented in terms of predicates and self-non-predications, and the other as a problem more specifically for Peano's set theory. Russell's first informal restatement of the problem in the letter to Frege was predicational, while the formalization he gave as his parting comment written in Peano's logical notation was set-theoretical.

It was natural for Frege and Russell to move easily back and forth between these two ways of speaking of predicates as concept-functors and sets of existent entities in a concept-functor's or property-representing

---

[7] *Ibid.*, p. 131.

predicate's extensions. The two thinkers were freely conversant about the set of objects forthcoming as the output value of a concept-function, consisting of exactly those existent objects possessing the property that the predicate cognitively or linguistically represented as belonging to its extension. Russell was at least partly in agreement with Frege's way of looking at these things, as he explained in the first part of the letter's first paragraph. There Russell expressed not only agreement with but also anticipation of many of Frege's ideas concerning the nature of functions in logic generally and their applications in the logical foundations of arithmetic.

Frege, with *Grundgesetze II* about to appear in print containing the weakness Russell's letter had exposed, under the expectation that Russell would discuss the paradox in his impending study, *The Principles of Mathematics*, did not enjoy the same luxury of calm deliberation and disregard of the contradiction as Peano. In a letter to Philip E. B. Jourdain of 23 September 1902, Frege soothed the misery by spreading it around to include Peano too. "In a letter to me," he reported, "Mr Bertrand Russell called my attention to the fact that my fundamental law V is in need of restriction. But our correspondence on this point has not yet led to a satisfactory result. Incidentally, this difficulty is not peculiar to my conceptual notation but recurs in a similar way in Peano's."[8] Unlike Peano, Frege could not take a seat on the sidelines and wait to see how things would turn out. He had been thrust by circumstances into the molten center of logical controversy, and he was compelled to play a part in whatever consequences might follow.

The Fundamentals of Russell's Paradox

Russell's paradox was not indirectly injected into Frege's *Grundgesetze* like a foreign invading virus. The paradox was meant to show instead that contradiction permeated the logic of *Grundgesetze* arithmetic all along. The internal infection reputedly occurred in the form of a freely assumable Fregean concept-function, the extension of whose output value was made identical to that of a particular specifiable set.

Call it the Russell set R of sets that are not members of themselves. Where the set comes from is something we need not trouble ourselves

---

[8] *Ibid.* See Frege's letter to Philip E. B. Jourdain, Letter VII [xxi]/2, 23 September 1902, p. 73.

about for the moment, as long as it is the output of some concept-function applied to some existent entity in the logic's reference domain. The destined set in Russell's application turns out to be the putatively coherently describable set of those sets that are not members of themselves. If we ask of such a set whether or not it is a member of itself, as the logical principle of the excluded middle (noncontradiction) seems to demand, then we appear to be caught in a dilemma, the two developments of which together imply logical inconsistency. The basis for Russell's paradox dilemma in Frege's theory of sense–reference sentential meaning translated as the assumption that the reference of the proposition that the set of those sets that are not members of themselves is a member of itself is exclusively either the True or the False.

Russell was supposed to have shown that $V(R \in R)$ = the True AND V $(R \in R)$ = the False. The freely introduced function, identity-related to the Russell set R, was believed disastrously therefore to imply $R \in R \wedge R \notin R$. The argument, assuming set R by Frege's *Grundgesetze* Axiom V or for any other reason to exist, was that, as an existent entity in Frege's domain, R was subject to the excluded middle, p or not-p, $Fa \vee \neg Fa$, $R \in R \vee R \notin R$. We know how the Russell paradox dilemma was supposed to proceed after that. Purportedly, $R \in R \rightarrow R \notin R$, and conversely. The implications of Russell's set membership and non-membership predications were supposed to be proved by dilemma to be jointly logically contradictory.

Russell's Amiable Demolition

Frege understood that his *Grundgesetze* had been mortally wounded by Russell's paradox. He may have needed to read the final two paragraphs of Russell's letter several times for the significance of its innocent-appearing question to sink in. Russell, it seemed, had torpedoed Frege's *Grundgesetze* by showing that the structure was already riddled with leaking holes throughout and sunk without their knowing it, just as the second volume of Frege's treatise was about to appear in print. The two would go down together with a glub. Years later, as we shall see, Frege confided to Richard Hönigswald in dry-land civil engineering terms that the effect of Russell's letter was to bring the entire superstructure of the *Grundgesetze* arithmetic crashing down. Worse, part of Russell's note explained that he was also publishing a book in 1903, *The Principles of Mathematics*, in which, Russell mentioned, he expected to include a lengthy discussion of Frege's logicism in the philosophy of arithmetic.[9] That could and would probably mean that the paradox would soon be paraded in public outside of Russell's previously private communication.

Frege was spurred into action. He had to say something about the contradiction. We cannot have contradictions in classical logic, because in that semantic environment they trivialize valid inferences by making every inference without exception or distinction deductively valid. Is there an argument to prove that there is no greatest prime number in arithmetic? If the assumptions of a deductively circumspect proof are syntactically inconsistent, then classically the logic equally proves that there is after all a greatest prime number. Is there a deductively valid argument to establish that God exists? In an inconsistent formalism there is likewise, then, a deductively valid inference showing that God does not exist. Taken as background to arguments proffered under the aegis of a logic harboring syntactical inconsistencies, contradiction makes every argument unsound in the sense of depending on collectively false logically contradictory assumptions. If an argument begins with the proposition that red is a color, an inconsistent logic on the semantic strength of its contradictions is deprived of the ability to prove that the proposition that red is a color is true. These drawbacks are unacceptable to Frege's classical logic. After nine years of *Grundgesetze I* having been in print, the formalism was now paying an awful price for including truth-functional external propositional negation in a fully algebraized logic.

Frege had to take the sting out of any revelation Russell might make in his forthcoming book by acknowledging the problem in advance and making appropriate adjustments to prevent the paradox from arising in his *Grundgesetze*. He had to do this virtually any way he could. Whether Russell was about to go public with the paradox or not, appreciating its force as Frege believed himself to do, he would have been the last honest laborer in the scientific vineyard to try to conceal the difficulty and hope that it would go away. For once he could not afford to be ignored. He had to take the upper hand. The moment of conflict was complex. That was the fascination. Frege was genuinely interested in the truth. He was committed

[9] Russell, *The Principles of Mathematics* (New York: W. W. Norton & Co., 1903), Appendix A, "The Logical and Arithmetical Doctrines of Frege," pp. 501–522. The supplement, significantly, is followed immediately thereafter by Appendix B, "The Doctrine of Types," pp. 523–28.

to a philosophical version of the scientific hypothetical method. Ideas were to be clearly formulated and rigorously tested, or they could have no legitimate place in *das wissenschaftliche Denken*. He believed, was utterly convinced, that Russell's paradox implied a genuine logical antinomy. He fell for the argument hook, line, and sinker. He concluded that, without appropriate provision, the paradox revealed that all of his *Grundgesetze* arithmetic was contradictory throughout, trivializing all its logical inferences at the same time as rendering them unsound, and allowing no basis for distinguishing formally between logical truth and falsehood.

One imagines Frege in his armchair or seated outdoors, with the letter still held between his thumb and forefinger, his hand supported upturned on his knee. He may have continued to look at the page with Russell's question from time to time. He had just arrived at the decision to make instant emergency arrangements with his publisher, insofar as it might still be possible, in order to add some new supplementary text to *Grundgesetze II*. He sat up suddenly as though to do something. Then he calmed himself down, reassessed what might still be done, and selected from among those possibilities that which good reflective judgment counseled.

The scenario was considerably more fact than imagination. Frege had to try to do something in any case before the book sallied forth as the laughing stock of readers aware of Russell's paradox and the triumph over Frege's logicism of Russell's very different Peano-inspired logical arithmetic. It had to be done if it could be done, and it would have to be done quickly. If amendments could no longer be made, then some other arrangement would have to be undertaken in order for Frege to own up to the paradox and cobble together some kind of dressing to stanch the system's logical inferential hemorrhaging. The inference-trivializing inconsistencies had been present in and doing their foul work among the *Grundgesetze* logical axioms all along. There was always the possibility of letting the book go through as it was, waiting for Russell's *Principles* to be published, and then responding with a journal article, or perhaps another small book. That would be a kind of solution, but not one that Frege could have considered desirable. He would not have wanted to feud with Russell. He was pleased with the Englishman's attention, but he had been persuaded that the Russell paradox implied an intolerable logical antinomy in his *Grundgesetze*, and by inverted reasoning entailed the existence of the Russell paradox set on which the paradox dilemma was predicated.

As Frege complained in the *Grundgesetze I* Foreword lament, it was not as though the mathematical community's attention had at any time been intently focused on his work. Even Russell did not discover the paradox directly in Frege's *Grundgesetze*, whose *Begriffsschrift* logical notation Russell later admitted he could not read. Peano's formalism served as Russell's Rosetta Stone at the time for translating Frege's two-dimensional *Begriffsschrift* hieroglyphics into a logical demotic. There, to his gratification, he believed he had found an exact variant of Peano's paradox implied by permitted application of Frege's Axiom V. Indeed, the historical documentation is clear, Russell reasoned by analogy from Peano's logical arithmetic, which he could read, to look for the same underlying problem in Frege's *Grundgesetze*.[10]

This brought Frege to the second, and more difficult, point. He needed to have something definite to say. He had to decide in a race against the clock how to react and defend his logic and pure logicism against the glitch in *Grundgesetze* arithmetic represented by Russell's paradox. Frege's trouble was that he could conceive of no alternative foundations for arithmetic other than the purely logical concepts and inference principles to which his analysis aspired. They were the same basic laws he now believed Russell had proven to be logically inconsistent. Out of desperation, he clamped onto Axiom V a condition to restrict a revised extensionality principle, forestalling definition of the Russell set. He never satisfied himself philosophically that the basic logical law should not be unconditional. How else could concept-functions be properly introduced into any theoretical science, if not by the equivalent of the unconditional extensionality concept-function identity principle in *Grundgesetze* Axiom V? If the law were to be conditionalized, then it would have to appeal to a restraining concept, whereas the logical integrity of the arithmetic's identity conditions for concept-functions was precisely what Russell's paradox challenged. Frege could imagine doubting whether the basic law was after all purely logical, as he had previously somehow concluded. That the pretend axiom was logically false, however, that it necessitated outright syntactical contradiction in Frege's arithmetic, was a disaster. What could be wrong in requiring that

---

[10] See Nino Cocchiarella, "Whither Russell's Paradox of Predication?," in *Logic and Ontology*, ed. Milton K. Munitz (New York: New York University Press, 1973), pp. 133–58; and Hochberg, "Russell's Paradox, Russellian Relations, and the Problems of Predication and Impredicativity," *Minnesota Studies in the Philosophy of Science*, 12 (1989), pp. 63–87.

concept-function $F(\_\_) = G(\_\_)$ if and only if they have the same extension of existent entities respectively possessing property F and property G? Frege could not answer the question, but considered it an analytic problem that urgently needed to be solved.

Frege was not only under creative pressure, but also facing an impending book production deadline. The crucial moment was near. The book would be bound, packaged, and set on his publisher's shelves and in a few bookshop windows, advertised in a few specialized periodicals. Before such time it was not unthinkable, however additionally expensive, for Frege to submit further explanatory material to be typeset and included as the new last-minute concluding remarks of *Grundgesetze II*. This was precisely what Frege managed to do. He wrote an Afterword to *Grundgesetze II* that complemented the Foreword to *Grundgesetze I*. Frege appears originally not to have planned to write an Afterword. He was moved to do so only by the exigency of responding in some way as time permitted to the difficulty Russell had mentioned almost incidentally as an offhand query in the paradox letter's second paragraph and concluding remarks.

The *Grundgesetze II* Afterword contains its own handwringing lament, of a different sort than the *Grundgesetze I* Foreword. In the Foreword lament, Frege mourns his lack of astute readers, while in the Afterword lament he bewails the fact that he had found one, in the person of Russell.

Continuing Philosophical Exchange

Russell's note to Frege began a broken chain of professional correspondence that lasted for a total of ten years, from 1902 to 1912.[11] The correspondence is a treasure trove in which Frege and Russell discuss all the core concepts of Frege's philosophy of logic and arithmetic, including, but not limited to, his categories of object, concept-function,

---

[11] Frege, *Briefwechsel*, p. 200: "The correspondence includes ten letters from Frege to Russell, a draft of Frege's letter to Russell dated 13 November 1904, and eleven letters from Russell to Frege." The editor of Frege, *Philosophical and Mathematical Correspondence*, Brian McGuinness remarks, p. 130, that "All of Russell's letters to Frege were written in German. At least one letter, written in 1912, is now lost. [...] Of all of Frege's letters to Russell only the last [...] has survived in the original. Russell kept it in his possession, judging it to be purely personal ... The rest were sent to [Heinrich] Scholz and are now known only from photocopies."

class, sense and reference of proper names, and of sentences and sentential truth.[12]

The editors of Frege's *Philosophical and Mathematical Correspondence* explain the exchange of letters between Russell and Frege in the following terms:

Bertrand Russell (1872–1970) corresponded with Frege from 1902 to 1912, though most of the correspondence belongs to the years 1902–4. The correspondence opens with Russell's announcement of his discovery of what is now known as the Russell paradox, and most of it is concerned with various solutions proposed by Russell and rejected by Frege to that paradox. But the correspondence also touches on most of the central concepts in Frege's philosophy of language: sense and meaning, object and concept, truth and falsity, proposition, and class. Russell's discovery of the paradox came at a time when Frege's life's work was substantially complete: vol. II of his *Basic Laws* [*Grundgesetze*] was about to be published. Russell's major works were yet to come: at the time of the discovery he was preparing his *Principles of Mathematics* for publication.[13]

The focus especially of the early part of the Frege–Russell correspondence was unsurprisingly Russell's paradox. There was just the one thing, Russell casually remarked in his 16 June letter. He adroitly positioned himself to harpoon Frege against the *Begriffsschrift* free introduction of arithmetical functions, as sanctioned supposedly by *Grundgesetze I* Axiom V. There seemed to be a question having to do with predicates that cannot be predicated of themselves, that are consequently predicated of themselves if and only if they are not predicated of themselves. Russell explained that it appeared there could be such freely formulated predicates in Frege's *Grundgesetze*, thanks to Axiom V, implying that the entire system's attempted reduction of the basic laws of arithmetic to purely logical foundations was throughout logically-semantically compromised by contradiction.

More importantly, in Frege's *Grundgesetze* the paradox seemed to arise because of the virtually unconditional recognition of any concept-functions. Frege's concept-function largesse was attributable to the extensionality identity principle for functions that Axiom V in *Grundgesetze I*

---

[12] The reference is to Russell's then work-in-progress *The Principles of Mathematics*, which was published the following year, in 1903. Russell, letter to Frege 16 June 1902, in Frege, *Philosophical and Mathematical Correspondence*, Letter XV [xxxvi]/1, p. 131. The original German text is published in Frege, *Briefwechsel*, pp. 212–14.

[13] Editor's Introduction to XV Frege–Russell, in Frege, *Philosophical and Mathematical Correspondence*, p. 130.

formally acknowledged and codified. The *Begriffsschrift* and *Grundgesetze I* were endangered by no mere stovetop fire then, although it may have seemed like that to their hopeful supporters, but by an all-consuming conflagration. Frege, grasping its potential significance, took the paradox deadly seriously. As we know from his Afterword to *Grundgesetze II*, and the continuing correspondence with Russell primarily on this topic, Frege believed that a philosophically acceptable non-*ad hoc* solution to the paradox must finally be found in order for the constructive project of pure logicism to go forward. The solution was never found, and Frege's constructive project of pure logicism was stopped dead in its tracks.

Unfortunately, Frege never arrived at a sense of the full range of possible paradoxes, and in haste he was driven to seizing on the specifics of the Russell set. Frege and Russell tried out possible solutions for discussion in their exchange of letters, especially in the rest of 1902 and at the beginning of 1903. The solutions proposed in the correspondence were closely examined by Frege not only for their "technical" capability in forestalling the Russell paradox, but also on grounds of their philosophical justification or lack thereof, and the further implications they might have for metaphysics, especially in evaluating the prospects of one kind of solution as against its competitors.

What was not questioned on Frege's or Russell's part in any of this interchange was that there was a genuine paradox in Frege's logic that Russell had discovered and that somehow needed to be solved. The only question they considered in this highly directed spate of epistles was how the paradox might be forestalled. The object was to decide what must be done, what to do about it, and what advantages a given solution might have over available alternatives. Russell already had an answer worked out in his *Principles*, Appendix B. It was surely written before he directed his first note to Frege. He studied Frege's efforts and checked them against the exclusion of all diagonal self-non-applicational paradoxes that he believed had been achieved by enforcing a hierarchically ordered predicational type theory. Paradoxical syntax combinations generally denied the predication of a logical, semantic, or set-theoretical property to itself. Self-application, often labeled self-reference, was to blame. Universal type theory prevents self-applicational and self-non-applicational constructions from occurring in logic generally and therefore also in the logic of arithmetic. Cleansing logic of formal paradox comes at a price, but type theory was designed to preclude the entire family of paradoxes typified by several forms of Russell's paradox featuring the self-non-application of the set of sets that are not members of themselves.

Frege answered Russell's 16 June notice almost immediately in a letter dated 22 June 1902. At the beginning of his reply, Frege wrote in the same offhand collegial spirit as that with which Russell began his note: "Many thanks for your interesting letter of 16 June. I am glad you did agree with me in many things and intend to discuss my work in detail."[14] Frege was cordial, professional. Inside, as he copied out these words, he has often been supposed to have been experiencing a heroic suppression of panic. Frege got around to the point only later in the letter: "Your discovery of the contradiction has surprised me beyond words and, I should almost like to say, left me thunderstruck: because it has rocked the ground on which I meant to build arithmetic . . . Your discovery is at any rate a very remarkable one, and it may perhaps lead to a great advance in logic, undesirable as it may seem at first sight."[15] Frege would have similar words expressing his reaction to Russell's paradox in the Afterword to *Grundgesetze II*. The letter must have been written first, and parts of the Afterword seem rehearsed, tried out for fit in writing to Russell, as much of the Afterword seems personally addressed to the English colleague.

Frege declared that Russell's paradox had rocked the ground of his pure logicism. Frege's reference to Russell's paradox occasioning a great advance in logic was prophetic. It was no mere servility or empty adulation for the Cambridge philosopher on Frege's part. The search for similar paradoxes and the prospects of making any logic fully consistent, semantically and deductively complete, and compact had not exerted much impact on the history of mathematical logic before 16 June 1902. Hilbert, because of rather than despite his formalism, played a significant role in promoting these ideals as driving forces in foundational mathematical logic studies. It is not reckless to consider that, had it not been for Russell's epistolary announcement of a paradox in Frege's *Grundgesetze*, and its subsequent discussion in the logical and philosophical literature, the urge toward searching out the metalogical properties of formal systems of logic that characterized so much of twentieth-century mathematical investigations might never have gained quite the momentum or

[14] Frege, *Philosophical and Mathematical Correspondence*, Letter XV [xxxvi]/2 to Russell dated 22 June 1902, p. 132.
[15] *Ibid.*

attained quite the intensity that it did historically once Russell's 1902 argument had punctured Frege's logic. Russell's paradox, historically speaking, triggered an astonishing cascade of defining moments in the evolution of symbolic logic which was taking place over the course of these years.

Calling on Dummett's interpretation, we find Frege's response to Russell's letter reflected from another perspective:

Frege's immediate reaction, as shown in his first reply to Russell, which has been widely quoted, was consternation. By his second letter, he had recovered his composure. Even while he does not yet see how to avoid the paradox, he remains firmly convinced of the truth of his principal doctrines, and on the basis of them dismisses a number of tentative suggestions by Russell (who is casting around among a great many disparate ideas). Halfway through the correspondence, Frege hits on the modification of Axiom V which seems to him satisfactory. (Russell agrees that Frege's solution is probably correct, but by this time has formulated the vicious-circle principle, which of course continues to attract him, despite Frege's objections.)[16]

Dummett continues the history of events, also from Russell's standpoint, quoting from Russell's later written reflections on the discovery of his paradox and its impact on Frege's logicism:

Frege devoted nearly his entire career to a grand and beautiful project that combined philosophical and mathematical argument. He continued to push forward in spite of years of discouraging responses to his work. And when, after many years of work, Frege finally produced the work in which he believed he had brought his project to fruition, he was confronted with definitive failure. Some years after his discovery of the contradiction, Bertrand Russell wrote:

As I think about acts of integrity and grace, I realize that there is nothing in my knowledge to compare with Frege's dedication to truth. His entire life's work was on the verge of completion, much of his work had been ignored to the benefit of men infinitely less capable, his second volume was about to be published, and upon finding that his fundamental assumption was in error, he responded with intellectual pleasure clearly submerging any feelings of disappointment. It was almost superhuman and a telling indication of that of which men are capable if their dedication is to creative work and knowledge instead of cruder efforts to dominate and be known.[17]

Finally, Frege in his reply to Russell of 22 June 1902 announced the impending release of *Grundgesetze II*, about which Russell in his letter of only the previous week had expressed the hope that it be published some day: "The second volume of my *Basic Laws* [*Grundgesetze II*] is to appear

---

[16] Dummett, *Frege: Philosophy of Language*, p. xxii.   [17] *Ibid.*

shortly. I shall have to add to it an appendix where I will do justice to your discovery. If only I could find the right way of looking at it."[18]

It seems reasonable to infer that Frege, in his more or less immediate reply to Russell, did not yet have in hand a good idea as to how he might solve or avoid the paradox. Frege must have responded to Russell the day or a few days after he received Russell's note, and could hardly have been expected to have prepared a very creditable solution between the time he opened Russell's letter, dated 16 June, and 22 June, the day by which his first rejoinder was dated. Frege seems to have expected that there would be no problem in adding an appendix on the Russell paradox. He would have to find a good answer, and he did not yet know what it would be, but he would think of something. He tried to appear casual about the matter, taking aim at a pesky unexpected problem.

Frege did not dismiss Russell's paradox as non-threatening, or argue that he could detect an error in the reasoning by which Russell appeared to expose a logical antinomy in *Grundgesetze I*. The paradox, he felt, was real enough. It was, moreover, the kind of argument Frege admired. He did not pass off Russell's objection as involving nothing more than an appearance of contradiction, arising understandably in Russell's thinking from mistaken assumptions. Nor, equally significantly, did he try to take the paradox head-on. He never questioned the existence of the paradox as a logical antinomy, once he thought he understood Russell's paradox dilemma. This seems to have been primarily because he was convinced that the paradox was a genuine logical antinomy, and never openly questioned the presupposition that by *Grundgesetze I* logical Axiom V the Russell paradox set of all sets that are not members of themselves exists.

Frege at no point suggested that Russell may have been misled into crying paradox as a result of overlooking an important distinction in the home logic that would have made Russell's category of paradox construction impossible. Frege instead forthrightly acknowledged the problem. He expressed dismay, and indicated immediately his intention to add an appendix to the book in order to grapple with Russell's recently announced objection. It was not only the correct academic response to a theoretical and publishing nightmare in the making; more than that, Frege was genuinely intrigued by this challenge to the unconditional purely extensional concept-function identity principle

[18] Frege, letter to Russell, 22 June 1902, in Frege, *Philosophical and Mathematical Correspondence*, Letter XV [xxxvi]/2, p. 133.

in what Russell had unmasked as the arithmetic's treacherous logical Axiom V.

Russell wrote to Frege on 10 July 1902, following a fairly regular exchange of messages, telling him that "My book [*Principles of Mathematics*] is already in the press: I shall discuss your work in an appendix because it is now too late to talk about it in detail in the text. When I read your *Basic Laws* for the first time, I could not understand your conceptual notation. Unfortunately my book was already completed at the time."[19] This is puzzling, because, within the space of only a few days, Russell had switched tack from informing Frege that Frege's logicism would feature in *The Principles of Mathematics* to the disclaimer that there would be an appendix in his book too, discussing Frege, whose work Russell could no longer include "in detail in the text." All this makes it seem as though Russell's discovery of the paradox in Peano, and his ostensibly finding it also in Frege, occasioned a flurry of last-minute appendices both to Frege's *Grundgesetze* and to Russell's *Principles*. The afterthought on Frege to which Russell referred in his follow-up letter in the event consisted of twenty-two closely typeset pages and was titled "Appendix A: The Logical and Arithmetical Doctrines of Frege." Frege's Afterword to *Grundgesetze II*, in comparison, amounted to thirteen pages that were not so densely printed, featuring many space-consuming *begriffsschriftliche* logical formulas. The comparison is imperfect, because Russell's purpose in *Principles* Appendix A was to present in synopsis and criticize the much more extensive essential principles of Frege's logicism, whereas Frege had only to respond to Russell's guileless-seeming question about *Grundgesetze* logic in his 16 June 1902 letter.

Frege wrote the following at the beginning of his reply to Russell (XV [xxxvi]/16):

> In the meantime I have received your *Principles of Mathematics*, vol. I, for which I thank you very much. Although I have not yet got around to taking more than a casual look at it, it has aroused a lively interest in me, and I am anxious to gain a more thorough knowledge of its contents soon. I note with satisfaction that you have devoted a special appendix to my theories. This will contribute greatly to making them more widely known and, I hope, to the advancement of science.[20]

It is hard to read between Frege's lines. However controlled he might have been at the shock of receiving news of Russell's paradox, he

---

[19] Russell, letter to Frege 10 July 1902, in *ibid.*, Letter XV [xxxvi]/5, p. 138.
[20] Frege, letter to Russell, 21 May 1903, in *ibid.*, Letter XV [xxxvi]/16, pp. 156–58.

expressed nothing emotional, nothing betraying a nonscientific attitude. His prose projects only absorbing interest in what he believed Russell to have discovered. Frege was awakened by Russell to another aspect of the applied arithmetical logic of concepts. It was something he owned up to that he had not previously considered, as he now knew he should. There was something new and unexpected to learn about the finely interconnected core of logical relations from which he believed arithmetic derived.

The fact of Russell's paradox, as Frege believed it to be, once the dust had settled, was immediately of a piece for Frege with all other logical–mathematical challenges. It was these formal structural problems and what can be learned from them that had sustained Frege all along in his years of study on both sides of the lecture podium. Here the wonderful difference unexpectedly visited upon him at just that moment by the heralding of Russell's paradox happened spectacularly to imply the deductive triviality of his entire system of arithmetical logic. As in the case of a machine that had exploded, Frege must have wanted to know why this was happening in his arithmetic. It was interesting and potentially enormously instructive to consider these developments, as Frege reacted to unsolicited disclosure of Russell's paradox.

Frege's *saison d'enfer*

It was to become a season in hell for Frege. Everything had gone wrong, and there was scant time to set it right. Frege, indisputably, had called down the avenging fury of nemesis in his haughty *Grundgesetze I* Foreword. He boldly dared anyone to find a better reduction of arithmetical laws to another extralogical foundation, or in a different way to advance logical foundations of a different kind than his *Grundgesetze* presented. He then went still further in hazardously challenging readers at large, in the arrogant last paragraph of the Foreword, to demonstrate that his logical arithmetic nurtured any hidden logical contradictions.

It was precisely the latter provocation that Russell seems to have taken up in his letter of 16 June 1902. He caused in the process an enormous stir in Frege's life. Frege was suddenly thrown into precipitous damage control, by just a few crisp destructive lines written in German, as was all Russell's correspondence with Frege. The crisis was never resolved satisfactorily by Frege, and certainly not in terms of his own demanding standards. Russell's paradox in this regard marked a major philosophical milestone in Frege's life.

We can survey the whole received history of this dramatic episode in an evocative summary by Dummett:

While volume 2 of the *Grundgesetze* was at the printer's, he received on June 16, 1902, a letter from one of the few contemporaries who had read and admired his works – Bertrand Russell. The latter pointed out, modestly but correctly, the possibility of deriving a contradiction in Frege's logical system – the celebrated Russell paradox. The two exchanged many letters; and, before the book was published, Frege had devised a modification of one of his axioms intended to restore consistency to the system. This he explained in an appendix to the book. After Frege's death, it would be shown by a Polish logician, Stanisław Leśniewski, that Frege's modified axiom still leads to contradiction. Probably Frege never discovered this. Even a brief inspection, however, of the proofs of the theorems in volume 1 would have revealed that several crucial proofs would no longer go through, and this Frege must have found out.[21]

The chronology of what was where when might as well be accepted as it has come down to us in time-honored recitations of historical–philosophical folklore. Whether or not *Grundgesetze II* was actually at Pohle's printer on, speaking conservatively, 18–20 June 1902, when Frege would have received Russell's letter at the earliest, remains partly conjectural, unless or until a relevant previously unknown document turns up to settle the matter in one way or another.

If we are trying to understand the life of Frege as much as the paper trail he left behind, then we cannot avoid considering the question of the impact of Russell's paradox on Frege's psyche. How was he affected, especially in his professional work, from the time he received Russell's letter in mid-summer 1902? Adding an interpretive note to Frege's biography, Dummett dramatically caps off the episode with his sense of what communication about the paradox with Russell may have meant to Frege, and the impact it may have had on the balance of Frege's life and philosophical pursuits:

In any case, 1903 effectively marks the end of Frege's productive life. He never published the projected third volume of the *Grundgesetze*, and he took no part in the development of the subject, mathematical logic, that he had founded, though it had progressed considerably by the time of his death. He published a few polemical pieces; but, with the exception of three essays in the philosophy of logic produced after the end of the war, he did no further creative work. In 1912 he declined, in terms

---

[21] Dummett, "Gottlob Frege," *Encyclopedia Britannica*.

expressing deep depression, an invitation by Russell to address a mathematical congress in Cambridge.[22]

Previously, in *Frege: Philosophy of Language*, Dummett had written some words about the dampening effect of Russell's paradox on Frege's perspective on life and logicism. Stringing together selected scattered comments of Dummett's in this earlier source, we find him explaining the facts surrounding Frege's publication history in the woof and weave of an interpretation Dummett develops at greater length, from which quotations interrupted by my commentary follow:

> As the book was in the press, Frege received Russell's letter announcing his discovery of a contradiction in Frege's theory of classes. [. . .]
>
>   Frege's immediate reaction, as shown in his first reply to Russell, which has been widely quoted, was consternation. By his second letter, he had recovered his composure. Even while he does not yet see how to avoid the paradox, he remains firmly convinced of the truth of his principal doctrines, and on the basis of them dismisses a number of tentative suggestions by Russell (who is casting around among a great many disparate ideas). Halfway through the correspondence, Frege hits on the modification of Axiom V which seems to him satisfactory. (Russell agrees that Frege's solution is probably correct, but by this time has formulated the vicious-circle principle, which of course continues to attract him, despite Frege's objections).[23]

Not everyone will perceive the same "consternation" in Frege's immediate 22 June 1902 reply to Russell that Dummett claims to see, even scouring between the lines for concrete evidence. What is there to be seen instead in Frege's reply, and in his reactions to Russell's paradox with other correspondents, is something more like fascination and a desire to know more. Knowledge for the scientific mentality is always more a process than a finished product. Like the experimental scientist, although he sometimes comes across as dogmatic, Frege offered every part of his work pragmatically, in the best sense of the word, in the spirit of hypothesis leading the way toward open-ended truth. That is the best we mortals can do, even with the most finely honed high-powered intuition for abstract truths.

Frege wanted to inquire, in order to learn, not to sweep problems under the carpet. He needed to see in them the greatest potential for enlarging our understanding of the concepts and phenomena we regard as rewarding to study. Frege was always fully absorbed in the logical structures he discovered and articulated. Russell, in his brief note of 16

---

[22] *Ibid.*   [23] Dummett, *Frege: Philosophy of Language*, p. xl.

June, provided Frege's similarly scientific method in mathematical logic with a highly interesting logical–philosophical problem. Russell was exactly the kind of critic for which Frege had longed. Now that his perilous wish had been fulfilled, Frege had to think fast to decide what to do about it. Dummett recounts the essentials of the history of Frege's efforts in the Afterword to *Grundgesetze II* to circumvent Russell's paradox, by carrying out some modification in order to restrict applications of the original formulation of basic law V. It is transformed and reborn, at least in the book's Afterword, as V′. Dummett explains, in a series of remarks best appreciated sequentially:

Frege included an account of Russell's paradox, of his modification (Axiom V′) of the original Axiom V and of the way it avoids the paradox, together with some general objections to other lines of solution, as a hastily written appendix to Volume II. In 1930, five years after Frege's death, the Polish logician Leśniewski proved that Axiom V′, though it does not actually lead to a contradiction, yields the conclusion that there are no two distinct objects, and is thus manifestly absurd as a basis for the theory of classes, or for arithmetic in particular. In fact, in Frege's own system, though not in one based on standard predicate logic, it does yield a contradiction; for, since truth-values are objects, from the provable distinctness of the True and the False … it follows that there are at least two objects. There is no evidence that Frege ever discovered that Axiom V′ had this consequence: but the common assumption, that he remained satisfied with his solution, is almost certainly false. The second step, which anyone would take after weakening an axiom of a theory, is to check that the proofs he has given on the old basis still go through. The most cursory inspection shows that the proof of the basic theorem that every natural number has a successor breaks down when Axiom V is weakened to V′: since, as we shall see, it was essentially for the sake of being able to prove this theorem that classes were originally introduced into *Grundlagen*, this would be likely to be the first theorem the validity of whose proof under the weakened axiom Frege would have checked. It is thus probable that Frege very quickly came to realize the uselessness of his solution: since the terms in which he had posed the problem happened not to be those which would point towards a workable solution, he would be apt to conclude that no solution was to be found, and that his whole enterprise of reducing arithmetic to logic had collapsed.[24]

Dummett does not exaggerate the potential destruction of Frege's *Grundgesetze* arithmetic in the aftermath of Russell's paradox. Frege was also not deceived. He fully appreciated the implications, which he recounted in virtually identical terms. The question is how deep Frege may at first have assumed the problem to go, what the prospects for solutions might have been, and, most importantly, what alternatives, if

---

[24] *Ibid.*, pp. xl–xli.

any, there could possibly be, as the consequences of Russell's paradox made known in Frege's mind their logical system-shattering impact.

What was Peano saying about the whole calamity? So far there had been nothing but silence from the mathematician's office in Turin. Peano, like Frege, had taken advantage of academic opportunities that had been occasioned by the illness of more senior colleagues. That was a sad fact of university life. Peano and Frege, not to mention the entire history of mathematical logic, had an equal stake in coming to terms with Russell's paradox. If Peano had an answer to the presumed antinomy, he was not tipping his hand publicly or privately among colleagues through the mail in the mathematical airwaves of the time.

Dummett finds plausible confirmation for his explanation of the impact of Russell's paradox on Frege's work on the logical foundations of arithmetic after the publication of *Grundgesetze II* in 1903, the cut-off point in Dummett's understanding for Frege's productivity. The picture for Dummett begins to look like this:

This conjecture tallies very well with the known facts of Frege's subsequent career. In 1903, the year in which Volume II of *Grundgesetze* was published, Frege published two brief articles criticizing Hilbert's *Grundlagen der Geometrie*. After that, he published nothing of interest until 1918: he produced no constructive work at all, while even the polemic articles he wrote added nothing – save bitterness – to what he had done previously. In particular, *Grundgesetze* – still incomplete – was not continued. As a result, Frege did not participate in the second phase of the development of the subject which he himself had founded – mathematical logic and the study by its means of the foundations of mathematics ... It is known from a letter to Russell in 1912, refusing an invitation to address a congress of mathematicians in Cambridge, that he was at that time in a state of complete discouragement.[25]

Dummett does not delve into other factors in Frege's life during this time that may have played a part in explaining Frege's relaxed publishing agenda following the 1903 appearance of *Grundgesetze II* with its hurried Afterword on Russell's paradox. There could be no doubt that Russell's paradox had raised an interesting conundrum for Frege's *Grundgesetze*. The insuperable issue was rather whether there was anything face-saving to be done about it within the general framework of Frege's logical arithmetic. Dummett diagnoses the difficulty in Frege's *Grundgesetze I* Axiom V as that of allowing a "notion of classes."

[25] *Ibid.*, pp. xli–xlii.

Russell, in a later letter to Frege, as Dummett also observes, indicated that he had experienced an epiphany of sorts and come to the conclusion that classes were altogether superfluous (although another reasonable interpretation of Russell's remark in context is that a version of the paradox goes through even without supposing that there are sets or classes). If that is true, then it implies that Frege's logic may have been irrevocably ruined by the immoderate permissiveness of Axiom V under threat of a paradox that can equally be formulated by means of Fregean concept-object predications or Peano's or Cantor's sets or classes. That seems to have been Russell's understanding all along, for a paradox that is supposed to obtain in predicational and set-theoretical self-non-applications. Dummett adds that

> The idea of reducing arithmetic to logic had been wholly erroneous, the fundamental mistake lying in introducing the notion of classes, without which the reduction was impossible. The notion of classes, he now held, is a wholly spurious one, generated by a linguistic illusion. The discovery of the contradiction thus overthrew for Frege what he had regarded as his principal achievement, the derivation of arithmetic from logic. The probability that he discovered the inadequacy of his solution combines with the known facts – his abandonment of work in formal logic for good, of work in philosophical logic for fifteen years, and of work in foundations of mathematics for twenty years, his rejection of the theory of classes and of logicism when he did resume work on foundations, and his total discouragement in 1912 – to make this hypothesis virtually certain.[26]

Frege was stopped short in his intended forward motion. That is the undeniable fact that may admit of several explanations. Dummett does not hesitate to call the implications he believes are at play in his explication of Frege's philosophy. If Frege had not been hindered by Russell, the question naturally arises, why then did he not forge ahead with his original plans to pursue in *Grundgesetze III* the reduction of more advanced arithmetic to the applied logic he had developed in *Grundgesetze I* and *II*? Frege did not consign his *Grundgesetze* without further ado to the wastebin of discredited hypotheses. He also did not take the once-thriving system even a single step forward. The obstacle for Frege was finding a good justifiable way of forestalling Russell's paradox that would meet Frege's exceptionally high standards for inferentially gapless fully expressively transparent logical reconstructions of arithmetical proofs. He never found a way to do this to his own satisfaction.

---

[26] *Ibid.*, p. xxiv.

Frege wrote confidentially to Hönigswald many years later. He made no effort duplicitously to mask the facts in which he had long become enmeshed, but stated, in forthright recognition of the mathematical state of things, in a previously mentioned letter posted somewhere near the end of April and beginning of May 1925, only half a year before his death, that

It is hardly possible to examine all expressions which language puts at our disposal for their admissibility. The expression "the extension of F" seems naturalized by reason of its manifold employment and certified by science, so that one does not think it necessary to examine it more closely; but experience has shown how easily this can get one into a morass. I am among those who have suffered this fate, when I tried to place number theory on scientific foundations, I found such an expression very convenient. While I sometimes had slight doubts during the execution of the work, I paid no attention to them. And so it happened that after the completion of the *Grundgesetze* the whole edifice collapsed around me. Such an event should be a warning not only to oneself but also to others. We must set up a warning sign visible from afar: let no one imagine that he can transform a concept into an object.[27]

Frege almost appears to be making excuses for having overlooked the possibility of *Grundgesetze I* Axiom V being corrupted as Russell did for contradiction-revealing purposes. The construction of Russell's supposedly paradoxical set within the axiom scheme of *Grundgesetze* arithmetic was not a possibility for which the system's basic laws had been designed. What is unmistakable in Frege's matter-of-fact remarks to Hönigswald is that he considered the *Grundgesetze* to have "collapsed" around him as a result of the implications of Russell's paradox. He remarks on the vulnerability it exposed to the possibility of freely introducing paradoxical constructions into *Grundgesetze* arithmetic. The problem was real, tangible, and, ultimately, for Frege, inescapable with the honor of his original intentions still uncompromised.

Russell expressed the hope that the second volume of Frege's book would eventually appear, presumably not knowing it was already in press. It was one of those coincidences that dogged Frege's efforts to bring about a revolutionary age of mathematical logic. It begins to seem, and perhaps it began to seem so also to Frege, that things could finally advance in no other way, like the struggles of new life hatching in fits and starts from a stubbornly resistant leathery eggshell. An unmanageable counterfactual

---

[27] Frege, *Philosophical and Mathematical Correspondence*, Letter to Hönigswald V/2 [xvii/5], p. 55.

for Frege's life that may nonetheless be worth contemplating is how the history of logic would have played out if Russell had discovered his paradox and reported it to Frege nine years earlier in 1893 when *Grundgesetze I* was first put on sale. What creativity in Frege might Russell's paradox have awakened during those intervening years, if only he had known about the problem then?

That Frege was immediately impressed, that he was sincerely persuaded that Russell had uncovered contradictions in his *Grundgesetze*, is documented by the dating of their first exchange of letters. There in his reply dated only six days later Frege said right from the outset that he wanted to respond to Russell in an appendix to *Grundgesetze II*, which he informed Russell was then in press. He mentioned also that he did not yet know what he was going to say. Frege may have been slow to defend the logic because he was secretly pleased to have his book wrapped up in a controversy with someone like Russell. Now at last, he may have thought, an interesting discussion can finally get under way. It would call attention to the articulation and defense of pure logicism that he had labored so long to bring to just this stage of perfection. He might have been excited knowing that much would happen, that new truths were certain to be discovered along the way.

If his intention all along was to bait someone of Russell's calibre into productive dispute, then Frege would have had no reason to regret daring his readers to find a better analysis of arithmetic in its basic concept-functions, laws, and reasoning structures, or further daring the same readers to try their utmost to find logical contradictions anywhere in his *Grundgesetze*. He tweaked their noses by asserting that this was something they would never be able to do. Russell's paradox is important in Frege's biography not only because of the subsequent dampening effect it had on Frege's future work in mathematical logic, but also for its impact on his psychological certainty and his reliance on his previously trustworthy mathematical intuition. In the absence of metalogical proof to the contrary, which was unavailable at the time, there was no plan in mind for how such reassuring arguments rigorously demonstrating the syntactical consistency of Frege's logic might be made. For and prior to Frege, intuition was the only metalogic. Disagreements among metalogicians were no less inevitable then than today, now that metalogic has been formalized as a comparably regimented extension of the logic whose properties the metalogic is commissioned to investigate. Frege could only reluctantly relinquish pride in his hope that there would be no possibility within the inferentially gapless maximally transparent deductions of arithmetical logic for contradictions to hide.

Frege's *Grundgesetze* Afterword Response to Russell's Paradox

Frege addressed Russell's paradox in the Afterword to *Grundgesetze II*. He began with another lament. This time, it was about the sorrows of trying to develop and defend a formal system of logic. The complaint was in some ways the counterpart to his protests concerning the lack of capable readers and critical opponents for his *Begriffsschrift* and *Grundlagen* in the Foreword to *Grundgesetze I*. Now, in the quickly penned Afterword to *Grundgesetze II*, Frege acknowledged the problem of Russell's paradox that had come to his attention so recently and with such astounding impact on the program to reduce the axioms of elementary arithmetic to the concept-functions and inference structures of pure logic:

> Hardly anything more unwelcome can befall a scientific writer than to have one of the foundations of his edifice shaken after the work is finished.
> This is the position into which I was put by a letter from Mr. Bertrand Russell as the printing of this volume was nearing completion. The matter concerns my basic law (V). I have never concealed from myself that it is not as obvious as the others nor as obvious as must properly be required of a logical law. Indeed, I pointed out this very weakness in the foreword to the first volume, p. VII. I would gladly have dispensed with this foundation if I had known of some substitute for it. Even now, I do not see how arithmetic can be founded scientifically, how the numbers can be apprehended as logical objects and brought under consideration, if it is not – at least conditionally – permissible to pass from a concept to its extension. May I always speak of the extension of a concept, of a class? And if not, how are the exceptions to be recognised? These questions arise from Mr. Russell's communication.[28]

Frege elaborated on the litany of shocks and disappointments occasioned by Russell's recent paradox letter. He widened the implications of Russell's presumed antinomy for the logical foundations of mathematics more generally, including but not limited to *Grundgesetze* arithmetic:

> *Solatium miseris, socios habuisse malorum.* [Misery loves company, or, more literally, It is the solace of the wretched for companions to share evils.] This contradiction, if it is one, is on my side also; for everyone who has made use of extensions of concepts, classes, sets in their proofs is in the same position. What is at stake here is not my

---

[28] Frege, *Grundgesetze, Basic Laws of Arithmetic II*, p. 253.

approach to a foundation in particular, but rather the very possibility of any logical foundation of arithmetic.[29]

What was significant in the history of mathematical logic in those early adventure-filled days was that, in what followed next, Frege ran into considerable logical trouble trying to reconstruct the dilemma of Russell's paradox as a genuine logical antinomy, even informally in general conceptual terms. This should have been Frege's clue that perhaps there was something wrong with the definition of Russell's set and the paradox dilemma reasoning proposed to support the paradox.

Everyone had a stake in the problem whenever exact clearcut definitions of concept-functions were wanted. Formal theorists should have been galvanized to solve the contradiction posed by Russell's paradox as threatening the adequacy of any extensionality concept-function identity principle. Frege was agitated about the difficulty, but no one else besides Russell seemed to be troubled. The problem was universal. Frege had only dared to explicate an identity requirement for concept-functions, was only the first to have done this. It was as though Frege's logic were being punished for being more forthright about principles that other theoreticians had been assuming all along, concerning which they had avoided trouble only by failing to speak. Most of the world was thriving in ignorant bliss of the philosophical problems that tormented Frege.

Frege's Reconstruction of Russell's Paradox

For there to be a problem to announce, whether in a letter across the English Channel, or in the chastened Afterword to a treatise in logic after the problem had inopportunely made its presence known, there must be not merely an apparent paradox, but, in the context of Frege's arithmetic, a genuine logical antinomy. Russell explained his sense of paradox to Frege, but, for Frege to take the problem to heart, he needed to see for himself that a contradiction existed. He had to reconstruct Russell's paradox set and the dilemma based on it, so that the readers of his Afterword to *Grundgesetze II* would understand what all the fuss was about.[30]

---

[29] *Ibid.*

[30] See Russell, letter to Frege 16 June 1902, in Frege, *Philosophical and Mathematical Correspondence*, Letter XV [xxxvi]/1, pp. 130–31.

Frege waffled somewhat about the theoretical status of Axiom V, but eventually gave it his stamp of approval as a purely logical principle. He got things only partly right when he resumed as follows in the *Grundgesetze II* Afterword:

Mr. Russell has discovered a contradiction which may now be presented. Of the class of human beings no-one will want to claim that it is a human being. We have here a class that does not belong to itself. For I say that something belongs to a class when it falls under the concept whose extension is just that class. Let us now focus on the concept *class that does not belong to itself*. The extension of this concept, if it is permissible to speak of it, is accordingly the class of those classes that do not belong to themselves. We will call it the class K for short. Let us now ask whether this class K belongs to itself. Let us first assume that it does. If something belongs to a class, then it falls under the concept whose extension the class is. So if our class belongs to itself, then it is a class that does not belong to itself. Our first assumption leads to a contradiction with itself. But if, alternatively, we assume that our class K does not belong to itself, then it falls under the concept of which it is itself the extension, and thus does belong to itself. Thus again a contradiction![31]

Frege goes logically astray in inferring, on the basis of the assumption that K (Russell set R) is "the class of those classes that do not belong to themselves," that therefore "[I]f our class [K] belongs to itself, then it is a class that does not belong to itself." If Frege's K belongs to itself, it does not follow logically that K does not belong to itself. It does not follow that K does not belong to K, unless K is redefined as the class not only of *all* those classes that do not belong to themselves, but of *all and only* those. Compare throughout: It may be true that *all* Greeks are mortal, but it does not follow logically from the fact that *only* Greeks are mortal, contrary to which inference counterexamples are in plentiful supply.

We cannot be fully charitable to Frege in the long run, in his efforts to explain Russell's paradox, although we can be uncharitable in at least two different ways. We can say that Frege in defining K as the class of those classes that do not belong to themselves means *just* those classes, or he means simply *all* classes that do not belong to themselves. If he means, as we have first assumed, that K is simply all classes that do not belong to themselves, as Russell's paradox had previously been presented, beginning with the paradox letter, then the fact that K contains *all* classes that do not belong to themselves does not logically exclude the possibility that K also contains *other* classes, including itself. The situation logically is the

---

[31] Frege, *Grundgesetze II*, p. 253.

same as when the class of mortal beings includes all but not all and only Greeks.

When Frege concluded after these preliminaries that "Our first assumption leads to a contradiction with itself," his admission was false, logically insupportable. However understandable it may have been for Frege to have thought otherwise, there was no contradiction in the assumption that R or K is a member of itself. There would not be a contradiction but at most a false conditional, if assuming that the set of all sets that are not members of themselves is a member of itself implied that the set of all sets that are not members of themselves is not a member of itself. The implication holds only provided that the set of all sets that are not members of themselves is not also the set of just or all and only those sets. Ambiguity resulting from careless formulation makes dilemma reasoning from the definition of Russell's "paradox" set R to the contradiction $R \in R \leftrightarrow R \notin R$ deductively invalid.

When Frege tries to collect these results in the supposed derivation of Russell's paradox in *Grundgesetze* arithmetic, he proclaims "Thus again a contradiction!" The general conclusion is exuberant but manifestly false. The problem was not that Frege had misunderstood or somehow botched the reconstruction of Russell's paradox. The problem resided instead with Russell's original formulation. Frege can be faulted for not noticing where Russell's definition of set R went wrong. Frege did a relatively good job of recreating the essentials of the paradox dilemma, once the paradox set had been admitted to the logic. He did so unfortunately without noticing the logical flaw in the first conditional, rendering it false and therefore incapable of supporting paradox, even with a true conditional in the second dilemma horn. There was no paradox in validly deducing a false proposition from another false proposition. It must be true not only that if K is not a member of K, then K is a member of K, but also conversely that if K is a member of K, then K is not a member of K. The first conditional is provable, whereas the latter conditional, as we have seen, would not hold in Frege's logic of concepts, unless K were strengthened by being understood as speaking of "just" or "all and only" rather than merely "all" *those* sets that are not members of themselves.

Frege's *Grundgesetze* Afterword Solution to Russell's Paradox

Frege did not challenge the existence of the Russell set by any such paradox meta-dilemma. He intuited no *all* versus *all and only* equivocation in the description of the Russell set as the set of (those) sets that are not members of themselves. He accepted the existence of the set, and with it Russell's paradox as a genuine logical antinomy. He (mis)understood the paradox as posing a serious difficulty to be resolved if the *Grundgesetze* arithmetic were to be salvaged. This he proposed to do after the second volume's Afterword lament. He suggested and partially developed there a distinction on the basis of which Russell's paradox was supposed to be forestalled. Frege was never satisfied with his efforts in this direction, from the time he opened Russell's letter onward.

In place of Axiom V, Frege skirted Russell's paradox in a modified *Grundgesetze* by means of a stand-in substitute restricted concept-function identity principle V′. The revision of Axiom V in *Grundgesetze II* Afterword is presented in formal *begriffsschriftliche* terms, placing a condition on any instantiation of the extensionality principle. Frege remained buoyant and upbeat throughout the addition, once he had got the confessional lament already glossed off his chest. He explained as follows:

By transferring to value-ranges in general what we have already said of extensions of concepts, we arrive at the basic law

$$\vdash (\acute{\varepsilon}f(\varepsilon) = \acute{\alpha}g(\alpha)) = \overset{a}{\overbrace{\hspace{1cm}}} \begin{array}{l} f(\mathfrak{a}) = g(\mathfrak{a}) \\ \mathfrak{a} = \acute{\varepsilon}f(\varepsilon) \\ \mathfrak{a} = \acute{\alpha}\,g(\alpha) \end{array}$$

(V′

which has to take the place of (V) (I, §20) ... Let us convince ourselves that the contradiction arising earlier between the propositions (β) and (ε) is now avoided.[32]

Proposition β is the true conditional that if the Russell set is not a member of itself, then the Russell set is a member of itself, concerning which no criticism is raised. Proposition ε is the false conditional taken by Russell and Frege to be true, namely that if the Russell set is a member of itself, then it is not a member of itself. Frege noted that the contradiction supposedly arising between these two conditionals is avoided when the conditional Axiom V′ replaces the originally unconditional Axiom V.

The implication is not that the two conditionals are mutually contradictory. Frege's word here for *between* is the ubiquitous ambiguous "*zwischen.*" The German term can also mean *among*, in the sense of a

---

[32] *Ibid.*, p. 265.

contradiction supposedly occurring when the two conditionals are conjoined together to yield the contradictory equivalence that Russell set R is
a member of itself if and only if it is not a member of itself. This inference
previously permitted under unrestricted Axiom V Frege now claimed to
have blocked. He went to great lengths following the Afterword lament to
diagnose and expose what he took to be the exact cause of contradiction in
his previous commitment to Axiom V. He filled page after page reconstructing Russell's paradox within the *begriffsschriftliche Grundgesetze*
logical symbolism, further establishing that the paradox is otherwise
supposed to be deadly for the reductive logic of arithmetic that the
book was attempting to explicate.

Frege's method was to conditionalize the equivalent of the original
axiom as a restriction on its application. The relation in this revision,
following more contemporary logical notation than Frege's *Begriffsschrift*,
longwindedly stated that the identity or equality, as Frege also said, or,
equivalently, effectively, the logical equivalence, of the extension set of
objects with property F, the extension of predicate "F," given any true
predication Fa, with that of the extension set of property G, the extension
of predicate "G," given any true predication Ga, is itself identical to all
objects in the logic's domain having property F being identical to all
existent entities having property G (thus far, Frege's original unconditional Axiom V), *only when*, conditionalizing the original extensionality
principle in Axiom V now as V$'$, it is *not* the case that object a's *not* being
identical to the extension of G conditionally implies object a's being
identical to the extension of F.

The restriction does its job. It functions, unfortunately, in such a way
as to invite the classic objection that the solution is explanatorily *ad hoc*,
applying only to predetermined problem cases, without offering a more
general philosophical reason for accepting the limitation beyond a desire
to avoid contradiction. Frege in V$'$ was not merely logically implying but
explicitly stipulating that the new extensionality principle relates the
extensions of predicates in true predications of properties to the same
set of existent entities, conditionally upon it not being the case that, if the
object is not identical to the extension of predicate "G," then it is
identical to the extension of "F." That was transparently tantamount to
saying that the extensionality principle was true provided only that it did
not imply inconsistency or paradox. It was true, in other words, if and
only if it was not logically false. The restriction obstructed Russell's

paradox, but offered very little by way of general rationale or justification for the refinement other than the need to avoid contradiction. Russell's paradox failed for a much simpler reason that Frege did not notice, as a counterobjection explains.

Frege acknowledged that there were further issues involved in the measures he recommended for avoiding Russell's paradox in the newly attached Afterword. The need for qualification had arisen so unexpectedly that he had not been able to pursue all of these important logically and mathematically interesting implications. He knew that, if the solution to Russell's paradox were to be considered as succeeding at every relevant level, then it would be necessary to check through all of the proofs in his *Grundgesetze* that relied explicitly or implicitly on Axiom V from top to bottom, in a cascade of unsurveyed potential inferential ramifications, to make sure that they were still deductively valid once Axiom V had been replaced by V'. It was a task for the future, which Frege, with his publisher and printer breathing down his neck, had no time to undertake as the impromptu Afterword was being prepared to be set in type and added to the rest of the second volume of the book. Its production lag might have been holding up other publication projects in the Pohle queue. Frege mentioned some of the investigations remaining to be made, in light of the last-minute axiom *Ersetzung* (substitution), and concluded on what seems to be an optimistic note:

It would take us too far here to pursue the consequences of replacing (V) by (V') any further. One of course cannot but acknowledge that subcomponents must be added to many propositions; but one surely need not worry that this will raise essential obstacles for the conduct of proof. In any case, an inspection of all hitherto established propositions will be required.

This question may be viewed as the fundamental problem of arithmetic: how are we to apprehend logical objects, in particular, the numbers? What justifies us to acknowledge numbers as objects? Even if this problem is not solved to the extent that I thought it was when composing this volume, I do not doubt that the path to the solution is found.[33]

The fact that the restriction can be elegantly formalized in Frege's logic was not the issue. It did not settle myriad philosophical difficulties surrounding the approach. What was lacking was any penetrating insight into *why* it was that the excluded conditions were otherwise satisfied in the case of sets that are not members of themselves. Many sets, like the set

---

[33] *Ibid.*

of all train cars, the set of all and only train cars, and a large selection of other useful apparently unproblematic sets, are obviously logically harmlessly not members of themselves. Abstract sets are not train cars, and train cars, although they can belong to an abstract set, conversely are not themselves abstract sets.

Bynum continues his assessment of Frege's arriving at this chapter of his research program in an overview:

Frege did, indeed, essentially achieve a methodological ideal: the standard of rigour and formal correctness of *The Basic Laws of Arithmetic* [*Grundgesetze der Arithmetik*] had never been achieved before (even in the Conceptual Notation [*Begriffsschrift*]), and would remain unrivalled for nearly three decades.

Although Frege was satisfied with this rigorous, scientific form of Volume I, he was disappointed by its meager content. He was forced to publish, at first, only part of his work; and much of the initial instalment had to be devoted to an explanation of his improved "conceptual notation" . . . Even so, he believed that Volume I contained enough material to give the reader a good idea of his method and position; and he was firmly convinced that an honest reader would accede to all his arguments.

The only thing about which he expressed some reservation was his Basic Law V . . . Frege conceded that this is a principle "which logicians perhaps have not yet expressly enunciated"; but he nevertheless asserted, "I hold that this is a law of pure logic". He evidently believed that any objections to this could be met; for the final paragraph of the Preface rings with confidence:

It is *prima facie* improbable that such a structure could be erected on a base that was uncertain or defective . . . [34]

Frege in this period was admittedly beginning to sound less demanding than in the days of his idealistic youth. Why did he think it would suffice to say that he holds *Grundgesetze* Axiom V to be a law of pure logic? Was that not something that needed to be argued for at least as carefully as the analysis of the purely logical concept-function of natural number in his *Grundlagen*?

What, then, was the extent of Frege's elimination of such apparently harmless extension set membership inclusions and exclusions from full applicability of the extensionality principle in V'? Frege seems to have done little more in the *Grundgesetze II* Afterword than place a light bandage on a compound fracture. To speak more exactly, he seems to have thrown out the happy baby with the dirty bathwater for the sake of forestalling Russell's paradox. He must have known this himself at some level. He misguidedly perceived the paradox as a genuine antinomy to be

---

[34] Bynum, "On the Life and Work of Gottlob Frege," pp. 36–37.

solved, if his logicism were to avoid wretched doom, although he did not
know how to go about blocking the definition of Russell's paradox set or
derivation of the Russell paradox dilemma. As time passed, Frege became
increasingly convinced that he would not find an answer. It was a logical
puzzle that haunted Frege for the rest of his life.

What Frege Should Have Answered Russell

An informal argument has already been sketched to show that Russell's
paradox is subject to a meta-dilemma based on two different ways of
understanding the definition of the set of sets or of those sets that are not
members of themselves. The meaning of the definition's phrase "those
sets" can be disambiguated as meaning "all those sets" or as meaning
"just" or "all and only those sets." The meta-dilemma against Russell's
paradox is that in either case, for different reasons, following up on both
ambiguities, Russell's paradox logically does not validly go through in
Frege's arithmetic.

If Russell's paradox set R is impossible, then the concept-function by
which R is defined has no value extension and hence no reference in
Frege's arithmetic. If Russell's paradox set R does not exist, then Russell
cannot accuse Frege's *Grundgesetze I* Axiom V of permitting the Russell
set to imply syntactical inconsistencies in the logic. It can only do so in the
proof of a paradox, even hypothetically in either or both horns of a logical
dilemma, if it can possibly possess such properties as the property of
being a member of itself and the property of not being a member of itself.
Having a property is something that in Frege's logic and semantics can
only be truly *or* falsely meaningfully predicated of existent objects.
Logically, the two horns in the meta-dilemma are indicated in Russell-
style contemporary logical notation in these terms:

ALL versus ALL AND ONLY Russell Paradox Meta-Dilemma

> ALL: $\forall x[x \notin x \rightarrow x \in R]$
> ONLY: $\forall x[x \in R \rightarrow x \notin x]$
> ALL AND ONLY: $\forall x[x \notin x \leftrightarrow x \in R]$

The ALL formulation is evidently not strong enough to exclude the
possibility that $R \in R$. There is no logical contradiction in the conjunction
$\forall x[x \notin x \rightarrow x \in R] \wedge R \in R$. The conjunction reduces logically to R's being
a member of itself, $R \in R$. On the other hand, as we should expect, if we

consider ONLY or ALL AND ONLY definitions of set R, then from $R \in R$ it follows *modus tollendo tollens* that $R \notin R$. We get virtually for free the second conditional needed for Russell's paradox, namely, that $R \notin R \rightarrow R \in R$.

If by process of elimination we can only consider the definition of the Russell paradox set as the set of all and only (those) sets that are not members of themselves, then essential assumptions in the second horn of the Russell paradox meta-dilemma imply that the Russell paradox set does not exist. This means that the Russell set defined as all and only (those) sets that are not members of themselves, including all sets that are not members of themselves and excluding all others, is therefore incapable of supporting a genuine paradox in the sense of logical antinomy. It is the excluding of all other sets that makes for difficulty both in Russell's original paradox and in Frege's effort to recast Russell's statement of the professed contradiction. What happens, in the second uncharitable way of understanding Frege's reference to "all those" sets that are not members of themselves, if Russell through Frege is interpreted as meaning by class K just or all and only those, rather than merely all those classes that are not members of themselves? What happens if the definition of Frege's K and of the delegated Russell paradox set R is strengthened to what has been said would be needed, namely from *all* to *all and only* those classes that are not members of themselves?

There is a famous logic lesson illustrated by a fictional barbershop. It is only loosely designated a "paradox," and there is nothing essential about the practice of hairdressing. Many relational properties other than shaving customers would serve. The strongest conclusions forthcoming for the barber who by assumption shaves all and only those persons who do not shave themselves present more of an unobvious implication than a logical antinomy. The implication is that there can be no such barber. If the definition of Russell's paradox set similarly is too weak when "all (those) sets" is disambiguated as "all" and not all and only, when the Russell paradox set is defined like the barber as the set of "all and only" sets that are not members of themselves, the definition implies remarkably, as a consequence of Frege's *Grundgesetze I* logical Axiom V, that the Russell paradox set does not exist. The construction shows, unexpectedly perhaps, only that something innocent-seeming does not exist, without implying a logical antinomy of the form p and not-p. The barber "paradox," as Quine distinguishes these categories, is a merely potentially surprising result that may be philosophically rewarding to study with the tools of logic, but that poses no danger to the semantic integrity of any system of logical reasoning. The barber paradox, far from pinpointing a logical contradiction, reveals a theorem of predicate-quantificational logic. It is provable in Frege's general concept-functional *Begriffsschrift* that in a favorite illustration there exists no barber who shaves all and only those persons who do not shave themselves. It should be equally provable in Frege's logic and arithmetic, then, that there is no set of all and only those sets that are not members of themselves.[35]

The theorem is derived by asking a conspicuous self-referential question, "Who shaves the barber, if the barber shaves all and only those persons who do not shave themselves?" Does the barber shave himself? That cannot be, because the barber is defined as shaving *only* (and all) those persons who do *not* shave themselves. Then the barber does not shave himself. That also cannot be. The inference is again by definition, because the barber is defined as shaving *all* (and only) those persons who do not shave themselves. If the hypothetical barber does not shave himself, then he shaves himself. The barber shaves himself, that is to say, if and only if the barber does not shave himself, always on the assumption that the barber shaves *all and only* those persons who do *not* shave themselves.

The barber "paradox" does not establish that logic itself suffers from deep internal syntactical inconsistency. The implication is only that there can exist no barber who shaves all and only those persons who do not shave themselves. The proposition that there exists no barber who shaves all and only persons who do not shave themselves does not amount to a genuine paradox in the sense of a logical contradiction or antinomy. The consistency of logic is not threatened by the concept of a barber who shaves all and only those persons who do not shave themselves. There is no contradiction unless it can also be independently shown within pure logic that there is or must after all be such a barber. All we learn from the barber "paradox" is that there is no artist of the blade who shaves all and only those persons who do not shave themselves. We certainly do not learn that there both is and is not a barber who shaves all and only those persons who do not shave themselves, as a paradox in the sense of genuine logical

---

[35] A very different diagnosis of Frege's vulnerability to Russell's paradox and proposal for shoring up that deficiency is offered by John P. Burgess, *Fixing Frege* (Princeton: Princeton University Press, 2005).

antinomy would require. In both cases, there are no further ramifications for the logical integrity of any other logic-governed thoughts.

What we cannot reasonably expect to derive in pursuit of Russell's paradox is the first conditional required if the "paradox" is to constitute a logical antinomy. We cannot derive the converse of the second conditional, $R \in R \rightarrow R \notin R$, without accepting some highly disputable propositions. The first conditional, assuming that Russell set R is a member of itself and trying to deduce that therefore it is not a member of itself, is true *per impossibile* if and only if Russell paradox set R does not exist. This is a result of the barber paradox isomorphism on the definition of Russell set R as all and only (those) sets that are not members of themselves. We obtain the proposition only trivially on the insupportable ALL AND ONLY definition of R. If R is defined by ONLY or ALL AND ONLY, then R, like the barber of the parable, does not exist. If that is the case, then ALL, ONLY, and ALL AND ONLY formulations are literally meaningless in Frege's *Begriffsschrift*. They are not sanctioned as introduced under the auspices of *Grundgesetze I* Axiom V. We assume that nothing would cause Russell to step away from the ALL formulation, which means that the only alternative for him is ALL AND ONLY. He cannot rest content merely and exclusively with the ONLY interpretation. A single application in ALL AND ONLY, instantiating Russell set R for the universally bound variable x, produces the immediate contradiction $R \notin R \leftrightarrow R \in R$. This is to say nothing more logically ground-shaking than $Saa \leftrightarrow \neg Saa$, as a consequence of the harmless-seeming proposition $\exists x \forall y [Sxy \leftrightarrow \neg Syy]$, with the result only that $\forall a[[Saa \leftrightarrow \neg Saa] \rightarrow \neg \exists x[x = a]]$, $\neg \exists x \forall y [Sxy \leftrightarrow \neg Syy]$.

The implications for the ALL AND ONLY interpretation of the definition of Russell paradox set R are that (1) R does not exist; and (2) ALL AND ONLY is logically necessarily false, an anti-theorem, which it is easy to prove also in Frege's *Begriffsschrift* as the negation of the ALL AND ONLY formulation: $\neg \exists x[x \notin x \leftrightarrow x \in R]$. As in the barber "paradox," trouble brews when we ask self-applicationally who shaves the barber. The same kind of logical difficulty arises for the Russell "paradox" when we ask self-applicationally what if Russell set R itself is the set that is a member of itself if and only if it is not a member of itself? If the ALL AND ONLY definition of paradox Russell set R were permitted, then there would be an outright logical contradiction in the definition of R. Such internal inconsistency hardly makes for the logically interesting derivation of a contradiction from another explicit contradiction.

The original Russell set, literally speaking, both in Russell's paradox letter and in Frege's Afterword to *Grundgesetze II*, supposedly authorized by *Grundgesetze I* Axiom V, can be defined as $R = \{x \mid x \notin x\}$. In *Grundgesetze* symbolism, Russell's R, i.e., $\{x \mid x \notin x\}$, is written as $x'(\top(x \frown x))$. In Frege's symbolism, the expression $\{x \notin x\}$ is written as $\top x \frown x$. The Russell set $R =$

$$\backslash\!\!\underbrace{}_{a}\!\!\!\!\!-\!\!a \notin a \quad = \quad \backslash\!\!\underbrace{}_{a}\top\!\!-\!\!\in(a,a)$$

Frege, in the Afterword to *Grundgesetze II*, prefers to write more gothically, in his specially restricted variables toybox a term for a concept that does not fall under its own extension,

$$\top\!\!\!\underset{\mathfrak{g}}{\overset{\mathfrak{g}}{\lceil}}\!\!\begin{array}{l}\mathfrak{g}(\xi)\\ \grave{\varepsilon}(\!-\!\mathfrak{g}(\varepsilon)) = \xi\end{array}$$

This formula defines Russell set R merely as ALL Ra, the set of all (but not all and only) those sets that are not members of themselves. It is only existent sets that satisfy predication duality $\in$ and $\notin$ for set membership and set non-membership. Failing that, the Russell paradox cannot get off the ground. The Russell "paradox" set so defined enters Frege's logic in its ALL (but not ALL AND ONLY or Rao) form by means of the following *begriffsschriftliche* definition, authorized by Axiom V:

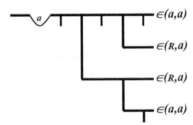

To define under an ALL AND ONLY interpretation that Russell set Rao is the set of all and only sets that are not members of themselves requires a more complicated additional clause to exclude sets that are members of themselves. Russell set Ra might otherwise be thought to be subsumed by this category, by virtue of including itself as the set of all but not all and only (those) sets that are not members of themselves.

The distinction between Ra and Rao analyses of Russell's equivocal characterization of the Russell paradox set is explicit in contemporary logical notation. We write for $Ra = \{x \mid x \notin x \wedge \forall y[y \notin y \rightarrow y \in x]\}$, and

$Rao = \{x \mid x \notin x \land \forall y[y \in x \rightarrow y \notin y]\}$. It is the ALL AND ONLY quantification of set non-membership in the Russell set that is then invoked, strengthened to avoid the possibility of including itself in the set of all (but not all and only) those sets that are not members of themselves. If R is all and only those sets that are not members of themselves, then $\neg \exists x[\in(x, R)]$, which for the extensionalists Frege and Russell, as previously concluded, implies in both cases that $\neg \exists x[x = R]$. The ALL AND ONLY interpretation of Russell set Rao, in contemporary logical notation, supports an inference that flatly undermines the existence presupposition of meaningful predications in Frege's and Russell's extensionalist referential semantics, $\neg \exists x[\in(x, Rao) \leftrightarrow \notin(x, x)]$.

Russell does not discover a paradox in the sense of a full-blooded logical antinomy in Frege's *Begriffsschrift* or *Grundgesetze*. At most he rediscovers a predicate-quantificational nonexistence theorem that is logically structurally precisely like the barber "paradox," both of which are provable as theorems in Frege's logic. Russell's discovery makes the following contribution to the *Begriffsschrift* cache of tautologies identified as theorems in the logic of quantity. It is proven *reductio ad absurdum* in *Begriffsschrift* for the closest proximity to Russell's self-non-applicational application:

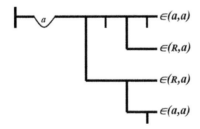

If for set-membership function "∈" we uniformly substitute "S" for "shaves," then we have exactly the Fregean functional calculus barber "paradox" theorem that there exists nothing that shaves all and only those persons who do not shave themselves. The logical inference structures for "shaves" or "is a member of" in the two cases is precisely the same. They are interchangeable within the same logical structure. The theorem is safely absorbed into Frege's logic along with all propositional and predicate-quantificational theorems, surprising or not, without visiting peril on the logical integrity of the logic itself of *Grundgesetze* arithmetic.

All Greeks are mortal, but unless all and only Greeks are mortal, there can be no deductively valid inference from the fact that the Persian Xerxes is mortal that therefore the Persian Xerxes is Greek. If, by "ALL" in defining Russell's ambiguous "paradox" set R, Russell means ALL AND ONLY (those) sets that are not members of themselves, then Russell's paradox, in an unknown act of suicide for his criticism, proves as a theorem of Frege's logic that the presumptive Russell paradox set does not exist. It is worth knowing that $\neg \exists x[\notin(x, x)] \wedge \forall y[y \in x \leftrightarrow y \notin y]$, just as it is worth knowing that we can prove as a logical theorem of Frege's general functional calculus or predicate-quantificational logic that there exists no barber who shaves all and only those persons who do not shave themselves. Russell's ALL AND ONLY set does not exist, and must be taken out of play for further consideration. It cannot be involved in any reasoning leading to genuine paradox in the sense of logical antinomy, where it would need to be meaningfully even if only falsely assumed to possess properties. It is useful to know that there exists no set of all and only those sets that are not members of themselves. That is where interest in Russell's paradox ends, with no cause for alarm at the prospect of contradiction spreading through the logical countryside.

In *Principles of Mathematics*, Appendix B, Russell himself proposed and discussed a controversial solution to the paradox, which also figures in his 1908 essay "Mathematical Logic as Based on the Theory of Types,"[36] his and Whitehead's *Principia Mathematica* and his *Introduction to Mathematical Philosophy*. It consisted of imposing type-orderings by which only predicates of higher-order type can take lower-order typed predictions as arguments. The idea was that the paradox was prevented if the logic prohibited construction of self-non-applicational predications. All equivalents of the set-theoretical definition of "paradox" set R are excluded in Russell's $R = \{S \mid \notin(S, S)\}$.

The problem in Russell's diagnosis is that the definition introduces R as the set of sets that are not members of themselves. That means that there is a property that can only be logically expressed as involving a certain property that is denied of the property itself. Self-non-application is plainly visible in the occurrence of the same predicate in both object

---

[36] Russell, *The Principles of Mathematics*, Appendix B, pp. 523–28; Russell, *Introduction to Mathematical Philosophy*, pp. 185–93; and Russell, "Mathematical Logic as Based on a Theory of Types," *American Journal of Mathematics*, 30 (1908), pp. 222–62.

and predicate position in the paradox definition. All the skyscraper construction we might try to build with a predicate used in predicating or denying the same predicate of itself is supposed to take place under the jurisdiction and with the implicit blessing of Frege's Axiom V. An interpretation of V that imposes set R rather than excluding it from the *Grundgesetze* seems to have its concept-function identity implications exactly reversed. The definition of R implies that the property of not being a member of itself is applied to itself, to that very set, whereas Russell's simple type theory forbids well-formed predications to an object of any property making explicit reference to the object itself by the same predicate appearing in a sentence in both object and predication place. $F(F)$ or $\neg F(F)$ are simplest cases of the type-theory lawbreakers declared non-formulas in *Principia*. Russell speaks of such constructions as *impredicative*, objectionable no matter when or why they appear.

As a final recommendation as to what Frege might have answered Russell, consider a possible Fregean reply to Russell's solution to the paradox. Russell's simple type theory forbids any term from truly or falsely applying to another term of the same type. If by virtue of this restriction we cannot meaningfully say that there is a set of sets that are not members of themselves, if to do so violates type-theory restrictions resulting in a self-non-application of the predication of a set's being a member of itself, then by virtue of the same prohibition we also cannot attribute meaning to many important relational self-predications.

It is not remarked in the literature, and may have escaped Russell's and Frege's notice, but Russell's type theory disallows self-applicational identity statements such as arithmetical equations as much as it disallows self-non-applicational "diagonal" constructions as referentially meaningless syntax combinations from the category of true or false predications. There could be no possibility for Frege willingly to accept Russell's type-theory solution to Russell's paradox if it excluded as improperly formulated true or false self-identity statements, typified by arithmetical equations. The implication would be embarrassing, to say the least, in a logical reconstruction of the principles of mathematics, where arithmetical equations are expected to be true or false. Frege certainly regarded them as referentially meaningful, considering them essential to a purely logical arithmetic.

Frege therefore missed another opportunity to argue against Russell's paradox and its motivation for type theory on behalf of the truth-values of arithmetical equations. Perhaps it sufficed for Frege to know that type theory was intuitively wrongheaded, as he began to regain trust in his intuitions. The argument is only that Frege would have been on solid ground to reject type theory already in Russell's 1903 *Principles* as depriving arithmetical equations and identity statements generally of referential true or false meaning, when a term is identity-relationally predicated of itself. For the sake of the true or false meaning of arithmetical equations and other identity statements, where identity is always self-identity, Frege could not accept Russell's type theory or its solution to the Russell paradox.[37]

Revealing Paradox Structure

A recent contemporary formulation of Russell's paradox gives the trick away. David Papineau, in *Philosophical Devices: Proofs, Probabilities, Possibilities, and Sets*, after a somewhat confusing explanation of the definition of Russell set R on a previous page, offers to explain:

1.9 Russell's Paradox
   First let us prove that R is a member of itself.

(a)   Assume R is *not* a member of itself.
(b)   But then, since R contains all sets that are *not* members of themselves, it is a member of itself.
(c)   So we have contradicted our assumption (a).
(d)   So "by reductio ad absurdum" we can conclude that (a) is false and R is a member of itself.

... Now we can similarly prove that R is not a member of itself.

(a′)   Assume R *is* a member of itself.
(b′)   But then, since R contains only sets that are not members of themselves, it is *not* a member of itself.
(c′)   So we have contradicted our assumption (a′).

---

[37] The concept derives from Henri Poincaré's *vicious-circle principle*. See Poincaré, 'Les mathématiques et la logique', *Revue de Métaphysique et de Morale*, 14 (1906), pp. 294–317; and Russell, "Mathematical Logic as Based on a Theory of Types." Wittgenstein in the *Tractatus Logico-Philosophicus* by implication defends Frege's *Grundgesetze* arithmetic from Russell's paradox as an equivocal syntax combination in which the same symbol is made to play two distinct predicational roles in order for the paradox to arise, contrary to picture theory of meaning requirements. See *Tractatus* 3.33–3.333.

(d') So "by reductio" we can conclude that (a') is false and R is *not* a member of itself.

We have now proved both (d) that R is a member of itself and (d') that R is not a member of itself. Something has gone badly wrong. This is Russell's paradox.[38]

It is indeed what is called Russell's paradox. Papineau is in step with official history. Like Frege in the *Grundgesetze II* Afterword, Papineau fails to reconstruct Russell's problem as a genuine paradox in the sense of logical antinomy. The sleight of hand occurs between (b), in one moment, in Papineau's derivation, where R is said to contain *all* (but not all and only) sets that are not members of themselves, and (b'), where R is said to contain *only* sets that are not members of themselves.

Where did the latter implication come from all of a sudden? Was only or all and only supposed to be implied by saying merely "all"? We have observed that Russell needs the ALL AND ONLY formulation of paradox Russell set R in order for the paradox to appear to gain altitude, whereupon the antinomy collapses when R is so defined as to logically imply its nonexistence. Neither Russell's original paradox statement, nor Frege's or Papineau's restatement, disambiguates the quantificationally equivocal definition of a set of (those but not just those) sets that are not members of themselves. Russell's paradox then appears to succeed only by smuggling an implicit *all and only* quantification into the difficult second paradox dilemma horn, under the guise of saying explicitly only "all." The *all and only* remains underground. There must be a juggling of quantifications in the paradox dilemma proof that Papineau instructively breaks up into its two main parts. The moment the *all and only* surfaces in unequivocally defining the Russell set, when logic owns up to the fact that the Russell set is quantificationally equivocal, every logician around the world would judge that the construction is nothing more interesting or dangerous to logic than the barber "paradox."

---

[38] David Papineau, in *Philosophical Devices: Proofs, Probabilities, Possibilities, and Sets* (Oxford: Oxford University Press, 2012), p. 11, after a somewhat equivocal explanation of the definition of the Russell set R on the previous page, maintains that "However, as Bertrand Russell first explained in 1901, the assumption that R exists generates an inconsistency. For we can prove both that R is a member of itself and that it is not." Papineau is correct as far as his comment goes, although he does not consider that the construction of Russell "paradox" set R for this reason can be proven by Frege's troubled *Grundgesetze I* Axiom V not to exist.

Papineau, of inferential necessity, follows in his exposition the ALL AND ONLY interpretation of Russell set R. In §1.8 Russell's Set, on the previous page, Papineau misreads his own use of set-theoretical notation, when he writes "According to the axiom of comprehension, there must be a set corresponding to this condition, namely, $R = \{x: x \text{ not-} \in x\}$. R will contain precisely those things that are not members of themselves." Actually, the formula Papineau mentions expresses only that R is the set of ALL sets that are not members of themselves, but *not* ALL AND ONLY those sets. It is always precisely at this juncture that the Russell paradox dilemma gets stuck in the mud. Papineau needs something more like, in his use of combined logical and set-theoretical notation, $R = \{x: x \in R \leftrightarrow x \text{ not-} \in x\}$. Without the equivalent, his definition of R above and his attempted use of R so interpreted in proving Russell's paradox provides only half, the easy part at that, of what is needed for logical antinomy. It commits Russell's fallacy of *saying* and limiting the explicit definition of the paradox set to an ALL Ra formulation in order to avoid obvious reduction to the nonexistent barber, while expecting ALL to have the logical force of ALL AND ONLY, Rao, in order to carry the inference (which, trivially, it does) that if $Rao \in Rao \rightarrow Rao \notin Rao$. Since Rao, just like the barber, by definition cannot exist, $Rao \in Rao$ and $Rao \notin Rao$ in Frege's semantics are referentially meaningless symbol strings that cannot enter into true or false predications or truth-functional relations.

Papineau understands that Russell at some level *needs* the ALL AND ONLY formulation of paradox Russell set R. For good reasons, he does not formalize the Russell set quantificational pledge in this way. He appeals instead to both the ALL and the ONLY parts to drive the paradox through in separate parts of the dilemma. This also commits Russell's fallacy, where ALL in the paradox dilemma is wrongly taken to imply or somehow serve with the same logical force as ALL AND ONLY. What Papineau does not notice is that the ALL AND ONLY formulation of paradox Russell set R as the equivalent of Rao, just like the barber, is already logically self-contradictory, implying that the Russell set does not exist. If the Russell set is nonexistent, then both for Frege and for Russell it can support no predication or inference leading to logical antinomy. It is a theorem of Frege's *Begriffsschrift* and *Grundgesetze* that there exists no "paradox" barber, just as there exists no ALL AND ONLY Russell "paradox" set Rao. The Russell paradox dilemma is deprived of anything existent on which to build a case for logical antinomy in Frege's *Grundgesetze*, or to justify type-theoretical restrictions on well-formed syntax combinations.[39]

[39] Another paradox challenges the existence presuppositionality of Frege's general functional calculus. If *a* does not exist, then, although *Fa* cannot be disallowed as a permissible construction on syntactical grounds, *Fa* will not have referential meaning. That is, for Frege on these assumptions, *Fa* ≠ the True AND *Fa* ≠ the False. It is nevertheless easy to pressure Frege into admitting that a certain putative predication involving identity properties and containing a non-referring or referentially empty singular term must be = the False AND by the above ≠ the False. The assumption in (1), as an instance of the existence-presuppositionality of Fregean logic, is that, if a first-level function(object) relation holds between any objects, then the objects in order to support properties must exist, E!. A truth-valuational function *V* is introduced in (1) and (2), to make the Fregean referential meaning of any Fregean *Gedanke* explicit. NF in (2) abbreviates a principle linking syntactical negation to the semantic falsehood of propositions. If the negation of a proposition is true, then the proposition itself is false. For present purposes, the argument does not need more than that. If we do not want to say that the truth-value of a proposition is false, then we should disallow even conditionally expressing that the negation of the proposition is true. Assumption (2) asserts that if the negation of a relational expression is true, T, which can be read as Frege's reified truth-value, the True, then the relational expression itself is false, or refers to the False, ⊥. Principle VE!, invoked in support of premise (3), restates Frege's presupposition that, if a putatively named object does not exist, then any effort syntactically to predicate properties of the object does not result in a meaningful proposition that is either true or false. As Frege would have it, the sentence in that case does not refer to the True or to the False. Assumption (3) states that, if an object does not exist, then any relational expression ostensibly referring to the object is not true, does not refer to the True, and is also not false, does not refer to the False. Assumption (1) might be derivable from (3), facilitating a compression of the inference below by exactly one step. An instance of an identity property is introduced as an =Property in assumption (4). If there are any identity properties, there is sure to be the identity property of being identical to a given named object *a*. Specifically, it is further and finally assumed in derivation step (5) that, whereas object *a* exists, object *b* does not exist. The contradiction that can be built on these assumptions and the previous section's definition of an identity property has a disarmingly simplified form, relying only on universal instantiation and classical propositional inference principles:

1. $\forall x, y, R[Rxy \rightarrow [E!x \land E!y]]$	E!
2. $\forall x, y, R[\neg Rxy \rightarrow V(Rxy) = \perp]$	NF
3. $\forall x, y, R[\neg E!x \rightarrow [V(Rxy) \neq T \land V(Rxy) \neq \perp]]$	VE!
4. $R1 = \lambda x[=a, x]\ (R1 = \lambda x[x = a])$	=Property
5. $E!a \land \neg E!b$	Stipulation
6. $a = b \rightarrow [E!a \land E!b]$	(1, 4)
7. $a \neq b$	(5, 6)
8. $a \neq b \rightarrow V(a = b) = \perp$	(2)
9. $V(a = b) = \perp$	(7, 8)
10. $\neg E!b \rightarrow [V(a = b) \neq T \land V(a = b) \neq \perp]$	(3)
11. $V(a = b) \neq \perp$	(5, 10)
12. $V(a = b) = \perp \land V(a = b) \neq \perp$	(9, 11)

The Aftermath of Russell's Paradox in Frege's Life and Logic

Post-Fregean–Russellian tradition in mathematical logic has been virtually unanimously agreed that Russell shot down Frege's balloon in his 16 June 1902 letter to the Jena logician. Carnap voices what has become the standard synopsis of the impact of Russell's paradox on Frege's logic:

> In addition, there was [Frege's] disappointment over Russell's discovery of the famous antinomy which occurs both in Frege's system and in Cantor's set theory. I do not remember that he [Frege] ever discussed in his lectures [of 1910–1914] the problem of this antinomy and the question of possible modifications of his system in order to eliminate it. But from the Appendix of the second volume it is clear that he was confident that a satisfactory way for overcoming the difficulty could be found. He did not share the pessimism with respect to the "foundation crisis" of mathematics sometimes expressed by other authors.[40]

What Frege referred to in his Afterword to *Grundgesetze II* was not the picture of dismay and sense of ruin that his overly dramatic introduction to this attachment has sometimes been thought to portray. Carnap came away from Frege's lectures in 1910 and 1914, seven to twelve years after the event of Russell's June 1902 paradox letter, having heard Frege continue undaunted in his muffled classroom exposition of the *Begriffsschrift*. Frege remarkably was undeterred only a few years later in advertising advanced lectures on *Begriffsschrift II*.

Hilbert, turning to one of Frege's contemporaries roughly at the time Russell's first correspondence reached Frege, responded to Frege's *Grundgesetze II* Afterword with marvelous disregard. Like Peano, he seemed not to be terribly impressed by Russell's paradox. He thanked Frege for sending him a copy of *Grundgesetze II*, including, of course, the

---

The contradiction collected in step (12) is semantic and in that sense metalogical. It highlights a syntactical inconsistency in any Fregean existence-presuppositional logic for the truth evaluations of a random noniterative identity statement $a = b$, when exclusively either ostensibly named object a or b does not exist. We can syntactically build referentially meaningless faux predications by putting together any name for something that exists with the putative proper name for something that does not exist as arguments of a relational function. The particular relation of identity illustrates a general problem for a Fregean theory of meaning and truth-conditions of relations and relation statements. The proof makes this explicit by quantifying over all relations in assumptions (1), (2), and (3), and introducing the specific identity property relation only in assumption (4). It is a paradox that Russell dare not raise, because it targets the existence presupposition for meaningful predications of properties exclusively in Frege's referential pure extensionalism that Russell, especially after 1905, fully accepts.

[40] Reck and Awodey, eds., *Frege's Lectures on Logic*, p. 19.

improvised Afterword. This caught Hilbert's attention. He flatly down-played Russell's paradox mentioned by Frege, potentially causing Frege even greater consternation at his sense of intellectual isolation. He was virtually alone now in his anxiety about the logical integrity of elementary arithmetic and the concept-functor co-extensionality of identical concept-functions. No one else seemed to care. Even Russell was not particularly interested in what Axiom V implied and how logic, mathematics, and every branch of science could manage without it, beyond supporting the logical contradiction he considered as justifying mathematical logic within a theory of types. If the principle were discovered implicitly at work, then Frege's scientific imperative required that he make the rule perspicuous. There was no other way for him to understand and critically assess a logical basic law's role in the definition of argument-objects and concept-functions and deductive inference.

Frege took the requirement for granted. He was the outsider again, crying in the wilderness. The vast majority of Frege's colleagues did not grasp with anything like his perception the logical gravity of the situation. They did not share his sense of the need to establish indomitable foundations for the basic laws of elementary arithmetic. Hilbert wrote as follows to Frege on 7 November 1903:

Dear Colleague, Many thanks for the second volume of your *Grundgesetze*, which I find very interesting. Your example at the end of the book (p. 253) was known to us here; I found other even more convincing contradictions as long as four or five years ago; they led me to the conviction that traditional logic is inadequate and that the theory of concept formation needs to be sharpened and refined. As I see it, the most important gap in the traditional structure of logic is the assumption made by all logicians and mathematicians up to now that a concept is already there if one can state of any object whether or not it falls under it. This does not seem adequate to me. What is decisive is the recognition that the axioms that define the concept are free from contradiction. I agree in general with your criticisms; except that you do not do full justice to Dedekind and especially to Cantor.[41]

There were many such paradoxes buzzing about Hilbert's mathematics workshop. He had heard of them, and might be amused by some of them, but he was not particularly exercised. Frege on the other hand was paralyzed. He saw no way out of the web of contradictions he believed Russell had exposed as spun for him out of the traitorous *Grundgesetze I*

---

[41] Hilbert, letter to Frege, *Philosophical and Mathematical Correspondence*, Letter IV [xv]/9, 7 November 1903, pp. 51–52.

Axiom V. Hilbert indicated in an offhand remark to Frege that the
paradoxes of which he was already aware have suggested to him that
"traditional logic is inadequate" and that "the theory of concept formation
needs to be sharpened and refined."

Frege, needless to say, could hardly agree with Hilbert more that
traditional logic was inadequate for the foundations of mathematics. He
had been not only saying this for years, but also working arduously to do
something about it to satisfy the need. Passive recognition of the obvious
in itself hardly lifted a hand toward providing a substitute for traditional
logic. It did nothing compared with Frege's labors to get logic and
arithmetic started moving in a more promising direction, once the
expressive and inferential inadequacies of syllogistic term logic in formalizing mathematical reasoning had been made known. Frege followed
a definite battleplan, the progress of which seemed to be lost on Hilbert,
even as he held Frege's treatise in his hands. Frege had been making
steady headway up to this point aiming at just the things Hilbert now
claimed needed to be done, that someone should try to do. Frege had not
been idly complaining about "the traditional logic," but working strenuously through all the difficulties and fine details of actually supplying a
replacement for syllogistic logic in the form of a general functional
calculus. Hilbert, despite acknowledging receipt of Frege's new book,
seemed entirely unaware of any of this.

Hilbert's reply must have been irritating to Frege. It appeared as
though Hilbert knew nothing of Frege's work taking shape over all
these years. He simply overlooked everything that Frege had been trying
to accomplish since before 1879, and the contribution he had been trying
to make, precisely in light of the limitations of "the traditional logic,"
about which Hilbert lightheartedly grumbled. Insult compounded injury
when Hilbert mentioned that something after all ought to be done about
the theory of concepts that Frege had all along tried to make the foundation of his philosophy. It needed to be sharpened and refined, yes, that
was the thing. If only someone were to set about doing something useful
in that direction. Hilbert's confidential expression of mild pique and
sudden realization of the logical situation must have seemed to Frege like
another confirmation that his contributions were being ignored.

The main disappointment, if it struck Frege that way, was that, unlike
Frege, Hilbert seems to have had no appreciation or sense of urgency
about the implications of self-non-applicational paradoxes, Russell's

included. He did not see it as something about which anything must be done. Hilbert appeared to regard purportedly paradoxical constructions in logic as little more than curiosities in the forward march of mathematics, which foundational studies anyway did nothing to promote. Mathematics was the thing, with a proven record of solid accomplishments. That could not be the case if mathematics had logically rotten foundations. *Ergo*, there was no need to worry as Frege constantly did about whether or not there was logically sound bedrock under mathematics. There must be. It was only a question of what the upgraded logic must look like. Logic in some countenance must make itself adequate to mathematical reasoning in the inferential derivation of theorems, not the other way around. Like many mathematicians, Hilbert believed that mathematics was not answerable to logic.

The final episode in the tragedy for Frege's lifework that unfolded beginning with his opening Russell's letter of 16 June 1902, the final irony, was that Frege's *Begriffsschrift* alone or as modified and applied in *Grundgesetze I* and *II* already had all the resources it needed just as it stood to defeat Russell's putative paradox. The paradox was based on a misunderstanding and misapplication of Frege's *Grundgesetze I* Axiom V. The fault was not surprising, given that Russell at the time did not fully understand Frege's logical symbolism. Russell's paradox can nevertheless be blocked in any notation. The paradox may have had no factual foundation in the principles of logic and meaning that Frege instituted in his treatise for the sake of discovering the purely logical foundations of basic laws and theorems of elementary arithmetic. The paradox nonetheless exerted a tremendous psychological effect on Frege. It influenced his work and life thereafter in widespread and mostly negative ways. If the Russell paradox meta-dilemma is correct, then there was never an objective basis for Frege to be psychologically swept along, concluding that the Russell paradox had credibly exposed syntactical inconsistency in the logical fabric of his *Grundgesetze*.

Unshaken Commitment to Logicism

Frege taught a course on his *Begriffsschrift* for the first time in the winter semester of 1879–1880. He offered it regularly every winter semester from 1884 until his retirement in 1918. In 1913, 1915, and 1917 the course was advertised as *Begriffsschrift II*. An interesting thing to know would be whether "*Begriffsschrift II*" referred to a more advanced treatment of Frege's *Begriffsschrift* than had normally been offered in the one-semester course. Frege would have found it wearisome repeatedly to pitch the same general functional calculus to a small coterie of perplexed Jena undergraduate students in mathematics.

Finding a way to accomplish this delicate balancing act of excluding paradox in a non-*ad hoc* philosophically principled way was a problem that preoccupied Frege for the remainder of his life, one he never resolved to his own satisfaction. Looking ahead, Frege may finally have been blindsided but not crushed or disheartened by Russell's paradox. He was unable to see what should be done. That was the truly insurmountable problem. He could no longer trust his mathematical intuitions. He could not even tell how far the damage extended, what other constructions might pose similar unforeseen logical hazards. He could not let go of his ambitions for his *Begriffsschrift* and *Grundlagen* in the *Grundgesetze*, yet he was dissatisfied with Russell's type-theory solution, as he was concerning any of the technical refinements with which he had tentatively experimented. Every time he wrote about the problem, even in the lament of the Afterword to *Grundgesetze II*, but already also in his immediate 22 June 1902 reply to Russell, and in correspondence with Philip Jourdain and others, Frege remained genuinely fascinated by the difficulty. He told Russell presciently that the problem was likely to lead to exciting advances. He may have been enthused partly because he understood that mathematical progress leading to the prevention of Russell's paradox would now be predicated on the naïve intuitive starting-place of his *Grundgesetze*. The arithmetic would have its moment in the history of mathematics no matter what, now that Russell had pegged it with a structurally interesting paradox.

As months and years rolled by, although Frege continued to teach the material to his students, he became increasingly unsure that an adequate non-*ad hoc* solution to Russell's paradox would ever be found. He needed a remedy to forestall all related kinds of logical antinomies. Where was such a thing to be identified? The fact that Russell's paradox took Frege by surprise reinforced the uncertainty as to what other unforeseen contradictions might be awaiting discovery. How could Frege anticipate all paradoxical constructions in his *Grundgesetze*, especially now that he had been disabused by Russell's paradox regarding the formerly presumed reliability of his intuitions? A solution justified on independent grounds was needed, one to stand on its own, as Frege wanted, a revision that did not disable the principles and proof strategies needed for the reconstruction of arithmetic and all of mathematics on purely logical foundations.

It was a tall theoretical order. Frege may at last have become discouraged. He may have cognitively worn himself out laying the foundations and proving the theorems of his *Grundgesetze*, all apparently to no avail. He could take no lasting comfort in Peano's also being in the same boat. If Peano did not appreciate the implications of the paradox and what needed to be done in the same way he himself did, that was his affair; similarly for Hilbert. Even if these theorists could put their heads in the sand like ostriches and pretend the problem would eventually go away, that could never exonerate Frege in his own mind of the self-imposed obligation not only to sweep logic clean of paradoxical constructions, but more vitally to understand the imperfections in his grasp of logic that had brought things to this crisis. His curiosity was aroused as to why Russell's putative paradox set could so briskly satisfy *Grundgesetze* comprehension principles and enter the logic's reference domain of existent entities. The paradox set was supposed to be an invited mischief-maker permitted by Frege's unrestricted Axiom V, a principle about which he had had reservations. Mendelsohn remarks that

Unlike Peano, to whom Russell had also communicated the paradox, Frege acknowledged it with his deep intellectual integrity and attempted to deal with it in an appendix – but to no avail, as he himself acknowledged. He was deeply shaken by this contradiction, which emerged from an axiom about which he had, as he said, always been somewhat doubtful. His life's work in a shambles, Frege's creative energies withered. The foundational paradoxes became a source of immense intellectual stimulation (as Frege himself had surmised in a letter to Russell) and his achievements were soon surpassed by the work of Ernst Zermelo and others.[42]

---

[42] Mendelsohn, *The Philosophy of Gottlob Frege*, p. 5. See Kurt Gödel, "Über formal unentscheidbare Sätze der *Principia Mathematica* und verwandter Systeme 1," *Monatshefte für Mathematik und Physik*, 38 (1931), pp. 173–98. The discussion of Gödel's impact on Fregean logicism (and Peano's and that of Whitehead and Russell, among other prominent formulations) is wide-ranging. Gödel's result was followed by generalizations from applied arithmetical logics to first-order logics by Alonzo Church and J. Barkley Rosser ganging up on logicism, against Frege, in particular, and also Russell. See Church, "An Unsolvable Problem of Elementary Number Theory," *Bulletin of the American Mathematical Society*, 41 (1935), pp. 345–63; Rosser, "Extensions of Some Theorems of Gödel and Church," *Journal of Symbolic Logic*, 1 (1936), pp. 87–91; and Geoffrey Hellman, "How to Gödel a Frege–Russell: Gödel's Incompleteness Theorems and Logicism," *Noûs*, 15 (1981), pp. 451–68. The nail in the coffin for Frege's efforts to escape Russell's paradox by conditionalizing the extensionality concept-function identity principle Axiom V in revised V' seems to have been

If Axiom V were restricted in order to forestall Russell's paradox, then it would remain guilty of other offenses. There should then be independent reasons for modifying V, implying general grounds for imposing an effective restriction other than logic's self-serving need to avoid Russell's paradox. This was another apparently solid wall against which Frege collided. Axiom V appeared otherwise intuitively true and perfectly acceptable, even and especially in its original unconditional form. Just looking at it carefully suffices to elicit agreement. If Frege's logical basic law was restricted solely to curtail Russell's paradox, then the distinction concerned only, and was based exclusively on, the desire to prevent a certain category of unwanted consequence, with no further attempt at independent justification. Frege's temporary solution was to propose an *ad hoc* restriction that he thought filtered out constructions like Russell's extension of a concept-function consisting of those sets that are not members of themselves. He believed on technical grounds that the revision worked, but he knew that it was philosophically unanchored, which is what rankled.

If Frege more than glanced at the second volume of Russell's *Principia Mathematica*, which he acknowledged having received to Russell in his last surviving letter to the Cambridge philosopher in 1912, if he gave it more consideration than Hilbert seems to have given *Grundgesetze II*, he would undoubtedly not have been relieved by Russell's infinitely ascending hierarchy of ordered syntax types, which Russell had explained already in Appendix B to *The Principles of Mathematics*. It would not have satisfied Frege. It would not have restored to him the intuitive feeling of rightness on philosophical grounds that he had previously felt concerning the arithmetic as a whole prior to reading Russell's paradox letter. Frege was desperate as he sailed out into open ocean without a compass or clear sense of the dangers that might be lurking in suddenly unfamiliar depths.

driven by Stanisław Leśniewski's demonstration that Frege's revised conditionalized axiom (V′) supports a contradiction other than Russell's. Leśniewski's proof was lost in original manuscript, and later reconstructed from memory by Bolesław Sobociński, "L'Analyse de l'antinomie russellienne par Leśniewski," *Methodos*, 1 (1949), pp. 99–104, 220–28, and 308–16; and 2 (1950), pp. 237–57. Geach offers a sleek version of Leśniewski's argument in "On Frege's Way Out," *Mind*, 65 (1956), pp. 408–409. See Robert Sternfeld, *Frege's Logical Theory* (Carbondale: Southern Illinois University Press, 1966), Appendix, "Subsequent Treatments of Frege's '*Nachwort*' Solution," pp. 163–68; and Dummett, *Frege: The Philosophy of Language*, pp. 656–57.

Importantly for this chapter in Frege's biography, it was only in the winter semester of 1902–1903 that Frege's *Begriffsschrift* lecture course was not advertised in the university listings. These offerings tended to be cyclically pre-set, although they could always be changed in the courses schedule under a number of unexpected contingencies. Frege read Russell's letter in mid-summer 1902. Breaking his established pattern since 1884, Frege canceled what in eight years had become his normal *Begriffsschrift* course for the 1902 winter lectures. It was also the only semester in mathematics at Jena after 1884 in which Frege did not hold any lecture or exercise course on a topic of logic ostensibly related to the foundations of arithmetic. Previously, from 1889 to 1901, excepting only the year 1897, the course catalogs of the summer semester at the mathematics faculty in Jena had regularly included Frege lecturing on the subject.[43]

The fact that Frege, excepting 1902–1903, did not back away from his *Begriffsschrift*, but later expanded the lectures to the defiantly titled *Begriffsschrift II*, suggests to some commentators that Frege kept faith with what we have styled the basic three-part *Begriffsschrift*(*Grundlagen*) = *Grundgesetze* model of logicism throughout the Russell paradox episode. Asser, Alexander, and Metzler reach much the same conclusion when they claim "This shows that Frege never lost confidence in the ideas of his *Begriffsschrift*, but the failure of his logicist program caused him to look for new ways of substantive justification of the concept of number. In which direction he did, we can only suspect after the present fragments."[44] There are always more explanations than strike judgment immediately as necessary. For a variety of logical–philosophical reasons and circumstantial causes, Frege was unable to fasten onto a formally satisfactory resolution of Russell's paradox that could be philosophically justified and integrated into the texture of his *Grundgesetze* with enough of its original framework intact.

What has entered the history of logic's hall of fame as Russell's paradox is no more a logical antinomy than is the barber "paradox." If Frege had responded in this way to Russell's announcement of a contradiction in his letter to Frege of 16 June 1902, Frege would not have needed at least the same kind of anxious lament as the 1903 Afterword to *Grundgesetze II*. More importantly, he could have upheld Axiom V without the restrictive

[43] Kreiser, *Gottlob Frege*, pp. 280–84.
[44] Asser, Alexander, and Metzler, "Gottlob Frege – Persönlichkeit und Werk," pp. 13–14.

conditionalization of co-existensionality identity conditions for concept-functions revised in V'. He could have sustained, at least for a time, all of his *Grundgesetze* arithmetic and the philosophical logicism it was meant to substantiate. He could have answered Russell's paradox instead of letting it freeze him in his tracks. He could have refuted Russell's type theory as a solution to the paradox compatible with the true or false referential meaningfulness of arithmetical equations and other identity statements. The question for continuing critical historical inquiry is whether there was any sound basis in the first place to suppose that Russell had found anything more than a superficial conundrum in Frege's *Grundgesetze*, easily dissolved by the Russell paradox meta-dilemma as of no greater moment for logic than the ontically deprived barber.

12

Personal Tragedy and a Philosophical Hiatus (1904–1917)

O N 25 JUNE 1904, Frege's wife, Margarete, died of an unspecified
protracted illness. Margarete Lieseberg Frege had been Gottlob's
companion for seventeen years. She was no doubt his Mecklenburg
sweetheart and fiancée for several years before that. Her parting may
have been interpreted by Frege in moments of ill humor as yet another
savage contradiction in what should have been a logically well-ordered
universe. He presumably did not want to lose her. After prolonged
illness, her death may also have seemed a blessing in relieving her of
further physical suffering. It is the kind of contradiction, among many,
that people not uncommonly experience in their lives outside the clois-
tered world of symbolic logic.

The combination of pressures impinging on Frege reached a sudden
cumulative crescendo. The hostile reception his published books had
almost unanimously received, the blow he suffered from Russell's artful
letter announcing a paradox existing right under Frege's own *Grundgesetze*
nose, and the need to find something responsible to say in a hurry in
response to Russell's paradox before the second volume could be published, followed the next year by Margarete's passing, seem to have con-
spired against Frege. His interest in writing faltered, understandably. The
vector sum of personal loss and professional disappointment must have
deprived him at least temporarily of the energy and will to resume his
former full-throttle logical–mathematical–philosophical pursuits. The
events of this cluster of years in Frege's life were to prove not his
immediate assassin, but the first cause of a profound weakening from
which he would never fully recover. Which is not to say that for the next
twenty-one years his life did not continue with pleasures and rewards as
well as difficulties of its own, as would likely affect many widowers in

Frege's emotional circumstances. Would Auguste have approved of his living with the thirty-plus (around half his age) housekeeper Meta Arndt after Margarete had departed? It is entirely possible that Auguste would have seen no harm in it. There must have been precedent galore for similar perfectly chaste contractual domestic arrangements even in provincial Wismar. Perhaps Gottlob could virtually do no wrong in Auguste's eyes. She might have accepted the situation gracefully; even had she not preceded Margarete in death, both women in Frege's life were no longer with him.[1]

Reflection and Reconsideration

Although Frege during the decade plus after Margarete's death and the announcement of Russell's paradox continued to occupy himself professionally, he seems to have recognized that the mathematical–philosophical project to which he had devoted so much energy in the past had foundational flaws that would require more rethinking to repair than he could personally expend. He taught, and satisfied his minimal administrative responsibilities at the university. He was drawing about two-fifths of his pay at the time from the Carl-Zeiss-Stiftung. It was an ideal situation in many ways. Frege was being paid by Zeiss for doing whatever mathematical work he wanted to do. Presumably, he submitted an occasional progress report that no one at the Stiftung would read, that not many there were capable of reading beyond the summary paragraph on the second page. The explanations of what he had been doing would be dutifully filed away in institutional archives, on the general principle that one does not give away good money for absolutely nothing.[2]

The hiatus in Frege's active pursuit of philosophical writing provided him with an opportunity to assess his achievements and setbacks, professionally and philosophically, during this coalescence of discouragements in his life. It was one of the longest distinguishable periods in his history, which was marked as though by far-spread canyon walls by his three major publications, the last in two parts separated by ten years. Because of his reclusion and inactivity at the time, his withdrawal under a

[1] Kreiser, *Gottlob Frege*, pp. 489–97.

[2] A useful source currently available only on library shelves is Felix Auerbach, *The Zeiss Works and the Carl Zeiss Foundation in Jena, Their Scientific, Technical and Sociological Development and Importance Popularly Described* (London: W. & G. Foyle, Ltd., 1927).

succession of disappointments and emotional blows, it was also the span of years in Frege's mortal existence concerning which there is the least information.

It is supposed to have been Frege's dark age, when he was philosophically inactive. He is portrayed by commentators on the history of this period as virtually sunk bewildered in an armchair for thirteen years, muttering to himself and cradling his graying head in his hands. Such an image of Frege is an unsupported distortion, as almost nothing could be further from the truth. What is true, as Frege himself remarked in different places, is that for a brief time after dealing with Russell's paradox and Margarete's death, among other forces apparently in league against him, he temporarily ran out of steam. The old drive that had moved him forward through his mathematical education and signature research and publication agenda was for the moment deflated. What was the point? Why was he bothering? These may have been among the self-doubts troubling his thoughts. Frege could also have simply held back on his research activities without consciously questioning the value of what he had been doing. He may never have lost faith in logicism, for the sake of which he would slow down until he began to feel his strength and motivation returning. He would start gradually and methodically again, with tasks he could more easily manage. He might engage in some light correspondence about his *Grundlagen*, or work up an essay about geometry in the *Begriffsschrift* for a meeting of the local mathematical society.[3]

There was still *Grundgesetze III* to consider. Vaporous though the specific content for such a continuing companion volume may have been even at the time, Frege knew that he had still only taken the first crucial steps in the logical analysis of even the most elementary theorems of arithmetic. He could think seriously about its design only at some later time, as his rigid sense of proper inquiry would allow, once he had dealt more satisfactorily with Russell's astonishing discovery. There was something in that beautifully corrosive compact statement of counterexample from which Frege thought he could learn important logical lessons. He had already started. He was only waiting for the light-haloed solution, the

---

[3] Dummett, *Frege: Philosophy of Language*, pp. 657–58. See also, for background, among others, Burge, "Gottlob Frege: Some Forms of Influence," in *The Oxford Handbook of the History of Analytic Philosophy*, ed. Michael Beaney (Oxford: Oxford University Press, 2013), Chapter 10, pp. 355–82.

brilliant insight, that always used to be revealed to him intuitively once he had fretted over a problem just long enough and just when he needed it.

Frege may have thought back to the Bible lessons from his youth at the Marienkirche in Wismar, recalling Matthew 13:4, about the seed that falleth on fallow and stony ground. He may have wondered morosely why the only seeds he was given to sow were always scattered on stones, where they never took root or bore fruit; where the birds came, as the Gospel says, and devoured them up.

Frege's private life was always very private, and he had virtually no public life outside of his work, research, and teaching. Given Frege's publication inactivity during those thirteen years, it is reasonable to suppose that the heart had at least temporarily gone out of his writing, as it seems to have done on virtually every front. It is unsurprising that there is nothing but a few interesting essays on geometry, no reviews as such after the 1894 review of Husserl's *Philosophie der Arithmetik*, and only sporadic correspondence and diary entries. Most of these are not especially scientifically or philosophically valuable, though often of biographical interest. Frege's strength and enthusiasm for logicism eventually began to return and reassert themselves in his thinking. Despite drawing a tight rein on publishing his work, Frege continued to labor at a considerable level of pitch. He no longer had a main project to which he devoted all his time and attention. *Grundgesetze III* was at least temporarily on hold. He pottered around, sometimes perfunctorily, in the interlude, trying to better understand and develop a non-*ad hoc* solution to Russell's paradox, writing on geometry, answering technical philosophical correspondence. He did not make much progress, and he definitely did not achieve the kind of success he would have demanded of himself under more favorable circumstances.[4]

We know that Frege placed a high value on his unpublished writings. The manuscripts of his *Nachlaß* or left-behinds were bequeathed and entrusted with all endearments to his by-then adopted son Alfred in a note appended to his will, in the expectation that the papers would eventually be published or archived.[5] This fact would be hard to reconcile with the assumption that Frege simply gave up interest in his work after Russell's paradox had capped the miserable misreception of all three

---

[4] See Chapter 11 note 3.
[5] Hans Hermes, Friedrich Kambartel, and Friedrich Kaulbach, "History of the Frege *Nachlaß* and the Basis for This Edition," in Frege, *Posthumous Writings*, pp. ix–x.

of his previous books, followed like divine wrath shortly thereafter by Margarete's death. Frege, weathering these assaults, did not see his homeless writings in logic and the philosophy of mathematics and language as worthless. What was more tragic in some ways was the fact that Frege began to look at his *Begriffsschrift, Grundlagen*, and the two volumes of *Grundgesetze* from a historical perspective, as unsuccessful or not entirely successful moments in a progressive dialectic that, despite false first steps, might at some later time deliver the rigorous non-psychologistic logicism that he had tried ineffectually to realize. Why his proposal met with widespread incomprehension and neglect continued to baffle and disgruntle.

The Paralyzing Grip of ἀπορία

What is undeniable is that Frege was fully convinced that Russell had discovered a genuine logical antinomy in his *Grundgesetze*. The problem of solving the paradox seems to have stymied Frege and wasted much of his diminishing energy going round and round, encountering the same difficulties in different forms, trying to break the grip of Russell's apparent contradiction on the logical integrity and semantic coherence of *Grundgesetze* arithmetic.

Frege was in the paralyzing grip of ἀπορία (*aporia*). The condition describes a state of puzzlement induced among philosophically minded thinkers when they are confronted with a polarity of choices that present themselves as comparably good or comparably bad, leaving the open-minded inquirer incapable of deciding in favor of one opposed side of a difficult question over the other. Philosophy is left not knowing what to say or where to begin. Thinkers as scrupulous methodologically as Frege interpret such standoffs as implying that none of the putative alternatives can be accepted and built upon, unless or until the puzzlement can be resolved. Frege could not see beyond the paralysis Russell's letter diffused through his thoughts about logic and arithmetic with the presumed derivation of intolerable contradiction. He was caught not just in any temporary, figure-this-out-in-a-week-or-so ἀπορία, but in a very constrictive one. He became, in fact, a living historical archetype of aporetic immobility, a casualty of the impact of Russell's paradox on his ability to move forward in his thinking about logic. He was and remains a classic illustration for all later philosophy, more locked into epistemic uncertainty than the scoundrel Meno, frozen in doubt and cognitive insecurity. Just as Socrates was reputed to have been able to waft about like anesthesia in his analytic interactions with disputants, so Russell here played the role for Frege of a mind-numbing Socratic dialectician.[6]

A Desultory Grinding of Wheels

Across the English Channel, equally convinced that the paradox was real, Russell was already establishing a different logical framework for logicism, building on more generalized provisions for avoiding the paradox set of sets that are not members of themselves. He developed type restrictions in a style of predication syntax that was not available to Frege.

Whitehead and Russell's *Principia Mathematica* in three volumes, published in 1910, 1912, and 1913 in the first edition, and 1925 and 1927 in the second, blocks self-non-applicational logical antinomies like Russell's paradox in Frege's *Grundgesetze*. The exclusion was achieved by syntax stratifications and logical formula formation rules enforced in a generalized theory of simple types.[7] Russell already had type theory fully in hand as a basis for a new approach to the foundations of arithmetic in his 1903 *Principles of Philosophy*. The work included first, as we have seen, an Appendix A, on "The Logical and Arithmetical Doctrines of Frege." Russell even then must have already known where he was going to take things next before he wrote his 16 June 1902 letter to Frege. The *Principles* Appendix A was followed by the only other appendix, Appendix B, "The Doctrine of Types."[8]

---

[6] A compact framework for discussion of Socrates' method is offered by Gregory Vlastos, "The Socratic Elenchus," *The Journal of Philosophy*, 79 (1982), pp. 711–14. See also (a different article with the same title) Vlastos, "The Socratic Elenchus," *Oxford Studies in Ancient Philosophy*, 1 (1983), pp. 27–58; and Plato, *Meno* 80a-b2.

[7] Alfred North Whitehead and Bertrand Russell, *Principia Mathematica* (Cambridge: Cambridge University Press, 1910–1913), first edition, Volume I (of 3), Introduction, Chapter II, "The Theory of Logical Types," pp. 37–65. On pp. viii–ix the authors acknowledge the study's "chief debt" to Frege, differing only where contradictions had been allowed to "creep into" Frege's logic, as they say, necessitating another kind of solution in the theory of logical types. Russell had discussed Frege at greater length in the first Appendix of *Principles of Mathematics* in 1903 and would do so in *Introduction to Mathematical Philosophy* (1919). *Principia Mathematica* acknowledges adoption of certain items of Frege's terminology, and stock concepts of propositional and predicate-quantificational logic that are usually paired with the same contribution attributed to Peano, who is credited on pp. 37, 149, and 356.

[8] See J. Roger Hindley, *Basic Simple Type Theory* (Cambridge: Cambridge University Press, 1997); and Peter B. Andrews, *An Introduction to Mathematical Logic and Type Theory: To Truth through Proof* (Berlin: Springer-Verlag, 2002), pp. 201–56.

Over the course of the years, as Frege mourned Margarete and the logical implosion of his *Grundgesetze* exposed by Russell's paradox remained unresolved before him, Russell was striding forward with his own logical reduction of mathematics. It was similar in many essential ways to Frege's, but its snazzier more mathematical-looking syntactical type theory preventing self-non-applications was advertised as avoiding the paradox Russell believed he had discovered in Frege. Frege was tied in knots over the paradox. Russell in the meantime was victoriously advancing new foundations for mathematics in symbolic logic. He went so much further, and already in his *Principles* had covered so much more of the territory in mathematics than Frege had attempted in his *Grundlagen* and *Grundgesetze*. Frege wanted only to completely understand the logic of the most elementary arithmetic, rather than to run a race toward a larger body of arithmetical conclusions. He thought that he could inch his way forward to reach advanced theorems only once he knew that his prior conclusions were unassailable. Whitehead and especially Russell cover their bets by anticipating inconsistency at the highest formal structural logical level at which logical or equivalently set-theoretical antinomy could arise in endlessly iterated predications. Ordered types are spoken of throughout the text of the *Principles*, and not merely in Appendix B devoted to their explication. Russell's Appendix B has the last word on a type-theoretical solution to the paradox just as Frege's Afterword to *Grundgesetze II* has with its prosthetic paradox-precluding conditionalization of Axiom V.[9]

Frege's publishing the addendum Afterword to *Grundgesetze II* could not have worked out better for Russell. Frege thereby acknowledged the problem and demonstrated that the best solution he could produce on the spot to Russell's paradox was a philosophically unjustified purely technical expedient. That allowed Russell to advance his and Whitehead's applied logical arithmetic in a different distinctive way, which was even preferable by some lights, appealing to a different infinitary mathematical kind of technical expedient in the simple theory of types. If Frege had not responded with his last-minute addition to the text, his own attitude would not have been written in stone, as now it was. It became part of the hardened historical record of the development of modern symbolic logic that Frege proposed a stopgap solution to the problem of Russell's

---

[9] Types had already been mentioned in Russell's *The Principles of Mathematics*, beginning with Chapter X, "The Contradiction," pp. 100–103. The theme is further examined in *Principles*, Appendix B.

paradox by effectively ruling exactly those self-non-applicational constructions out of court by an *ad hoc* restriction specifically designed to
block no other constructions. If such an expedient were valid, then why
not types? Russell could live with that answer and move his logicism
forward, whereas Frege philosophically could not.

Enormously to his credit, Frege under the circumstances would not
take another step. He would not compose so much as the first paragraph
of *Grundgesetze III*, unless or until the problem had been satisfactorily
solved. The paradox must be defeated, moreover, not merely by any
formally convenient expedient, as in the Afterword to *Grundgesetze II*,
but for good reasons and on philosophically respectable grounds. The
problem would have to be defeated by Frege's own sidereal standards, if
it were to be considered solvable in any sense at all by his lights. Among
other vital requirements, Frege would only advance in the direction of
Grundgesetze III in the next phase of logicism if he could arrive at non-*ad
hoc* independently justified concepts, distinctions, restrictions, and
restructurings of the whole framework of mathematical logic, implying
the exclusion of the Russell paradox set or disabling of the Russell
paradox dilemma.

The underlying trouble was that Frege's deepest logical investigations
offered no port of safety or escape. He could not begin to understand how
to correctly diagnose and solve the supposed logical antinomy entailed by
Russell's paradox. The crystal-clear world of intuitively penetrable symbolic logical relations had, after Russell's paradox letter to Frege, become
just as doubtful, uncertain, disappointing, and discouraging as all the
messy uncertain contingencies of physical, personal, and social relations.
It was just as bad as the kinds of things that psychologistic thinkers said
about logic and mathematics. The hard-grinding work of logic, Frege
discovered for the first time during this extended creative dry spell, is
after all no world of refuge away from the troubles of everyday life and
death. It could be just as parched, just as adverse and unproductive, and
just as mocking and inconsiderate of a thinker's sincere efforts to unlock
its secrets of formal structure as changing fortunes in the world of
practical affairs. It could reduce a rigorous reduction of arithmetic to
pure logic to the equivalent infantile disorder in which psychologism
found itself in the philosophy of mathematics.

Frege's reluctance, perhaps arising from sheer depletion of will, to
engage in the needed intensity of logical–mathematical–philosophical

inquiry at the time is not fully explained by singling out any particular external circumstance. One could invoke his wife's death in 1904, Russell's letter of mid-summer 1902, disappointing critical reviews of the books he had published in 1879, 1884, 1893, and 1903, or the lack of interest by students and of comprehension by colleagues insofar as his research was concerned. All of the circumstances in his life collectively contributed to everything that happened to Frege afterward, as they do in the case of every individual, regardless of how their life unfolds. Frege would not try to make further advances in mathematical logic until he had in hand a correct answer to Russell that was worthy of the problem. Frege would allow himself methodologically to appeal only to the kinds of arduously sharply and explicitly etched definitions of concepts and distinctions that he had required all along up to this deadlock. Anything else would be intellectual mush. He held himself to the same standards that he demanded of competitors in the workplace when they fell under his censorious review in one way or another. He had polemically criticized Mill, Schröder, Kerry, Husserl, Erdmann, and Thomae. He could even mention especially the first pages of the mathematician Dedekind's popular essay, based on his 1858 Zürich lecture, "Stetigkeit und irrationale Zahlen" ("Continuity and Irrational Numbers"). Frege could not let himself off the hook by which he had previously hung his ideological and methodological opponents. He could not admit that, if any expedient saved a system, then it was unobjectionable to rig up whatever kept contradiction outside the barricades. There were criteria of logical system-building to be explicated and their requirements had to be satisfied. A properly constructed logical arithmetic should not need splints and trusses to hold itself upright under any authorized application when later unexpected objections appear.

The further overriding tragedy of Frege's life was that he did not live to see a good solution to Russell's paradox emerge within the scaffolding of a revisited *Grundgesetze* arithmetic. He seemed to have understood that he would probably not have the difficulty rightly laid to rest during his remaining lifetime, and this may have diluted his energy further and prevented him from attacking the problem with a more seriously concerted effort at resolution. Given his increasing infirmity, the natural aging that afflicts mathematicians sooner or later, as it does anyone else, if they are lucky to live long enough, Frege was unable to contribute much more of his own input to the thought stream that was later to take shape around the concepts, methodology, and analytic attitude toward logic, mathematics, and philosophy that he had inaugurated, which he continues to sustain today by exemplary archetype. Joan Weiner describes this post-Russell paradox post-Margarete bereavement phase especially eloquently:

Frege published little more in the remaining twenty-two years of his life. Many have assumed that he succumbed to the discouragement that haunted him earlier in his career. The evidence, however, suggests otherwise. Frege worked for some time on finding a solution to Russell's paradox, but ultimately concluded that it could not be solved. His meager publication record is partly explicable by his having spent most of his efforts on the failed attempt to find a solution. Moreover, he did not abandon his intellectual work after concluding that his original project could not be carried out. For he had already come to this conclusion by 1918, a year in which he wrote, "In these difficult times I seek consolation in scientific work. I am trying to bring in the harvest of my life so it will not be lost" (Frege to Hugo Dingler, 17th November, 1918). The work to which he refers was begun in a series of papers titled "Logical Investigations." His aim was to provide a new, informal introduction to his conception of logic. Nor did he give up on his interest in the foundations of arithmetic. In another letter written after 1918, Frege wrote,

As you probably know, I have made many efforts to get clear about what we mean by the word "number." Perhaps you also know that these efforts seem to have been a complete failure. This has acted as a constant stimulus which would not let the question rest inside me. It continued to operate in me even though I had officially given up my efforts in the matter. And to my own surprise, this work, which went on in me independently of my will, suddenly cast a full light over the question. (Frege to Zsigmondy; undated, but after 1918)

In 1925, only three months before his death, Frege was corresponding with the editor of a monograph series about publishing a new account of the sources of our knowledge of arithmetic.[10]

Beaney adds to this picture a further element of Frege's personal day-to-day existence (although in the process Beaney unfortunately distorts some basic facts of Frege's history). He states in summary of this period of Frege's life that

In his last fifteen years at Jena, Frege published little, but the reason was as much personal grief as intellectual disappointment. His children by his wife, Margarete Lieseberg (born in 1856), had died young, and although they had adopted a son, Alfred, around 1900, his wife too died in 1905, leaving him to bring up the child without her. Bad health, also, was to plague him for the rest of his life. He did, however, have a significant influence on two more people, at the very start of their

---

[10] Weiner, *Frege Explained*, pp. 4–5.

philosophical careers, who were to play a major role in developing and transmitting his ideas. In 1911 he was visited by Wittgenstein, then a student of aeronautics, who had read about his views in Appendix A of Russell's *Principles of Mathematics*; and it was Frege who recommended that Wittgenstein go to Cambridge to study with Russell. From 1910 to 1914 several of Frege's lecture courses were attended by Carnap, who studied at Jena; and Carnap, like Wittgenstein, was quite explicit about the influence that Frege's work had on him.[11]

Beaney has many of his facts right, garbling other occurrences in Gottlob's and Margarete's personal life. He confuses the timetable for Margarete's death and Alfred Fuchs's later adoption in particular. The Freges did not jointly *adopt* Alfred in the legal sense of the word. Rather, Frege took on the then six-year-old boy as his *ward*, not "around" 1900, when Margarete was still alive, but in 1908, four years after Margarete's death in the last weeks of June 1904. Margarete may have known about Alfred, who was born on 30 July 1903. Efforts to place him in the Freges' home may already have been under way, with the process possibly subject to a delay occasioned by Margarete's declining health. It is also possible that Margarete knew nothing of Alfred. Alfred did not enter what was left of the Frege household as ward until years after Margarete's death, and was not adopted by Frege until roughly the time of Alfred's eighteenth birthday, which, according to the best sources, fell around 1921–1922.[12] Dummett, one regrets to report, gets his dates as badly mixed up as Beaney, when he writes "Though Frege was married, his wife died during World War I, leaving him no children of his own. There was an adopted son, Alfred, however, who became an engineer."[13] Margarete Frege had been dead for almost ten years when WWI broke out in Europe, and Alfred was not to be adopted as a Frege in legal surname for another seven years. The lad was aged only eleven when the guns of the Great War opened fire.

We must wonder where Alfred came from all of a sudden. Were we not in possession of the relevant background information, it would be something of a mystery. We may still question why Frege, a widowed man sixty years of age, would have taken home a six-year-old boy years after his wife, Margarete, had been carried away by ill health. Perhaps that was exactly why he wanted the boy in the house. If we do not expect such

[11] Beaney, "Introduction" to Beaney, ed., *The Frege Reader*, p. 8.
[12] Kreiser, *Gottlob Frege*, pp. 499–511; and Kreiser, "Alfred."
[13] Dummett, "Gottlob Frege," *Encyclopedia Britannica*.

behavior from the sour disappointed Frege that the history of philosophy has taught us to expect, then it may be the image of the embittered founder of modern logic that should be reconsidered. Taking Alfred under any contractual auspices of the state in exactly this period after Margarete had expired may have eased the burden of loneliness for Frege. He did not have to tend to all of the six-year-old's needs entirely by himself. He had the loyal assistance, and no doubt strong arm, of longtime housekeeper Meta Arndt, who was thirty-one years younger than Frege, and by all indications just as dedicated to raising Alfred. As resident in the home, she shared the implicit legacy of promise by which Frege agreed to care for and raise the boy in those later years. Meta would continue to tend house and after 1908 assumed also a motherly role for Alfred. It was not until Alfred had reached the age of maturity that Frege legally adopted the then young man as his son. Presumably, the decision was made so that Alfred could be legally named in Frege's will, to assure that the boy would inherit from Frege's estate without contest upon his death.[14]

Alfred's unfortunate parents are known. They were unable to care for the boy when Frege, perhaps through a church charity or local community service agency, resolved to take him in, both for the boy's good and to fill an empty place in Frege's house and emotional life, none of which in any case is to say that Frege did not treat Alfred as his son and call him his son all that time. It seems to have been a very loving relationship, perhaps the second or third most important in Frege's life.[15]

Meta stuck to Frege like glue. After Margarete's death she remained. When Frege moved to Bad Kleinen, Mecklenburg around 1918, after retiring in that year from the University of Jena, Meta was there. The idea was that they were going to share a house that Frege was having built in Pastow near Rostock. Frege did not live to see the building completed, but Meta, like Alfred, was bequeathed living rights in the Pastow house, where she spent the rest of her days. When Frege died she appealed for funding from the university as a widow would rather than the former Associate Professor's mere housekeeping employee. The trio of Gottlob, Meta, and six-year-old Alfred, a tornado in *Lederhosen*, all under one roof, constituted a surrogate family that must have satisfied different

---

[14] According to Kreiser, *Gottlob Frege*, p. 505, Alfred was already registering for classes at the Wismar Große Stadtschule as "Alfred Frege."

[15] Kreiser, "Alfred."

needs all around the dining table, with or without the further sanction of law or blood or conjugal connections. They enjoyed a normal happy life together.

Russell's Invitation to Cambridge

After more than seven years without contact had elapsed, Russell's now lost last letter to Frege of 16 March 1912 prompted Frege to re-establish contact on 9 June 1912 (XV/20 [xxxvi]/21). It was for the last time, as far as surviving documents testify.[16] Frege began by responding to a point of Russell's from an undiscovered letter that may no longer exist. Frege thanked Russell for the invitation to lecture at the Congress of Mathematicians in Cambridge noted above, begging Russell's indulgent understanding for his declining to attend.

Frege thanked Russell more especially – this was the second reason for his letter breaking the silence between the two men – for sending the second volume of *Principia Mathematica*, which Frege explained he had belatedly received and through which he had thus far only glanced, although he hoped noncommittally to "find time for a thorough study."[17] Another possibility preferred above these is that Frege was indifferent about the appearance of a new volume of Russell's *Principia* because the first book had already revealed Russell's commitment to a type-theory solution to the paradox. The artifice could in Frege's judgment have made whatever followed in Whitehead and Russell's mathematical logic of no more interest than Frege had been able to maintain in the long-term prospects of his *Grundgesetze* with its impromptu Afterword. Whatever Russell was doing in detail, whatever formal definitional and derivational clevernesses the book might contain, Frege knew beforehand from Russell's correspondence and *Principles of Mathematics* that type theory was not going to save the day by solving in a philosophically respectable way the deep logical problems that Frege believed were equally afflicting his *Grundgesetze* and Russell's *Principia*. Philosophically for Frege, for all its fine technical superstructure, Russell's *Principia Mathematica* was a complete nonstarter and a diversion of inquiry away from the main event.

---

[16] Frege, letter to Russell, *Philosophical and Mathematical Correspondence*, Letter XV/20 [xxxvi]/21), 9 June 1912, p. 170.
[17] Frege, *Briefwechsel*, p. 210.

Dummett superimposes a non-Fregean psychological interpretation on Frege's decision to turn down Russell's invitation to the Cambridge congress. It is not far-fetched, but at the same time it is not the only or necessarily the best explanation. Here is what Dummett imagines: "It is known from a letter to Russell in 1912, refusing an invitation to address a congress of mathematicians in Cambridge, that he was in that time in a state of complete discouragement."[18] The following is what Frege wrote to Russell:

Dear Colleague, For a long time now it has been weighing on my conscience that I have not yet replied to your letter of 16 March. I can well appreciate the great honor you did me by asking me to take part in the Mathematical Congress and to give a lecture there, and yet I cannot make up my mind to accept. I see that there are weighty reasons for my going to Cambridge, and yet I feel that there is something like an insuperable obstacle. And this is what makes it so difficult for me to answer your amiable letter. Please do not be angry at me for this. And now I must thank you cordially further for the pleasure you and your co-author gave me by sending me the second volume of your *Principia Mathematica*. Because I was away on a trip, the parcel sat for a few weeks at the local customs office without my knowing its contents. Other occupations and lack of strength have kept me till now from taking more than a casual look at the book; but I hope to find time for a more thorough study. Once more my cordial thanks! Yours sincerely, G. Frege.[19]

He is not Bertrand, Bertie, or even Russell, as he was to many others, but Frege's Dear Colleague. It was a somewhat formal, somewhat distancing conventional manner of address that might be used when writing to a total stranger in the profession with a question or requesting a copy of a publication, as was Frege's closing salutation. He reported "other occupations," which could have included the loss of Margarete and all the chaos that must have ensued at the beginning of this period in Frege's life during the summer of 1904.

One year after their burst of relatively productive exchange in November 1903 there was only silence between the two logician-philosophers, as far as one can tell from the preserved correspondence. The formal nature of the relations between them is emphasized by the first sentence of Frege's letter to Russell (XV/18 [xxxvi]/18) of 13 November 1904, where Frege began, conventionally this time, too, "Dear Colleague, Excuse me if, due to various distractions, I have only now got around to answering your letter of 24 May

---

[18] Dummett, *Frege: Philosophy of Language*, pp. xxiii–xxiv.
[19] Frege, letter to Russell, *Philosophical and Mathematical Correspondence*, Letter XV/20 [xxxvi]/21, 9 June 1912, p. 170.

of last year." Russell most probably would not have been aware of the "various distractions" to which Frege would have been subject during this timespan. He had not looked closely at his gratis copy of the first volume of Whitehead and Russell's *Principia Mathematica*, which would have arrived in 1910 or 1911, when he wrote to Russell again in 1912 on receiving the second volume.

He had been otherwise occupied, not feeling physically strong at sixty-five. He would not have been philosophically satisfied by the parts of Russell's logic that he could understand. Type theory as a preventative for Russell's paradox, whatever its formal elegance and sweeping ascent of logical syntax types, Frege would have found philosophically unjustified, an after-the-fact *ad hoc* fix for a problem that neither of them had as yet properly understood. One should deal with first things first. Logic cannot require prostheses, but must be pure and perfect from the ground up and everywhere within. Type theory gives this appearance only because it gets in at the beginning and builds a surrounding shell of permissible predication forms that proceeds upward without limit. Was it not also grating, beneath the formulaic congratulations, that Frege had had to wait ten years from the publication of the first volume for the second volume of his *Grundgesetze* to appear, and what's more had had to pay for the privilege, while Whitehead and Russell's companion works were popping out yearly, about as fast as they could check the proofs?

A Logically Disruptive Impasse

In addition to a subdued communication with other mathematicians, Frege during his publication dark ages wrote some important essays. These include "What is a Function?" (1904), "What May I Regard as the Result of My Work?" (1906) in fragmentary form, and other short pieces that testify to the fact that he had not suffered any sort of mental breakdown or sudden disability of his intellectual faculties.[20] He was still capable of excellent work, when he could bring himself to focus his critical attention on a particular concept-function that required more careful analysis. He was re-examining the foundation stones of what he considered by then to have been his failed reduction of arithmetic to

[20] See Hermes, Kambartel, and Kaulbach, "History of the Frege *Nachlaß* and the Basis for this Edition," in Frege, *Posthumous Writings*, pp. ix–xiii; and Kreiser, *Gottlob Frege*, pp. 564–66.

purely logical concepts and inference proof structures. He never doubted that the logic was correct. There might and perhaps there must have been something wrong, if anywhere, with the most basic informal concepts on which the logic was most deeply grounded, about which it would be important in any case to finally arrive at more definite clarity.

He did exclusively that, throughout this period and into the brief flourishing of publishing in philosophical logic he experienced in the interim 1918–1923 before his death. He wrote a paper criticizing Hilbert's approach to the philosophy of geometry. He worked additionally on essays in progress destined for journal pages. He drafted or refined much of this discussion during the publication dark ages, which can hardly be considered a time of philosophical inactivity. To write and to publish what is written before the ink is dry are obviously different things. Taken together, it hardly seems accurate to label the entire time-span 1904–1917 as being, in Dummett's excessive wording, "totally uncreative."[21]

Social Events and Academic Political Machinations

From at least 1905, Frege, having become a citizen of Jena, exercised his right to register as an official member of the National-Liberal Party (NLP), of which he had previously been supportive only as a signatory of declarations. The party appealed to Frege's desire for a strong Germany, with a powerful army and navy. The NLP, despite being "liberal," was staunchly anti-socialist.

The NLP pitted itself in particular against social democracy as its most important domestic political opponent.[22] Presumably the Social Democrats had more voting members than the NLP, and were therefore to be despised, whatever their platform. The NLP was a conservative political party, leaning perhaps slightly further right of center than many German citizens of the time might have preferred, and they may have marched occasionally in the streets of Jena, as any good political organization might. They did not seem to have constituted any sort of explicit hate group, although a frequently attested tendency toward xenophobia, anti-Semitism, Wagner, and *Bierstuben* was prevalent in much of German society in the nineteenth

---

[21] Dummett, "Frege, Gottlob," *Encyclopedia of Philosophy*, ed. Paul Edwards (New York: Macmillan, 1967), Volume III, p. 227.

[22] Kreiser, *Gottlob Frege*, p. 530, details Frege's involvement in the right-leaning NLP.

century. Frege, because of diary entries from his later years, has also been accused of this vulgar prejudice.[23] Anti-semitism and membership in the NLP were not a surprising combination. Frege seemed not to have had the moral perspective from which to counteract these common but philosophically inexcusable tendencies of his day. Philosophically he took little to no interest in practical philosophy or theoretical ethics. He comes across as boyishly naïve and unforesightful about social political events, as can be seen also in his correspondence with Wittgenstein in this later time frame about the onset of WWI.

It is tempting to foresee in the NLP a precursor of the *Nationalsozialistische Deutsche Arbeiterpartei* (NSDAP), the National Socialist German Workers' Party, or Nazi Party, that rose disastrously to

---

[23] Frege's anti-semitism should neither be explained away nor expanded into some kind of obsession. The evidence for Frege's attitude is primarily found in his unpublished diaries from 10 March through 9 May 1924. The typescript of the diaries had been prepared by Frege's adopted son Alfred in 1937–1938, and sent to Scholz, who was keeping and copying Frege's *Nachlaß* at the Münster University library. The location of the original diary from which Alfred made the transcription is unknown. The three entries dated 23–25 March concerning the concept of number can be found in Frege, *Nachgelassene Schriften.* The other parts of the diary express Frege's political and social attitudes, including his reactions to then-current events. See the annotated diary in Frege, "Gottlob Freges politisches Tagebuch," *Deutsche Zeitschrift für Philosophie*, 42 (1994), pp. 1057–98 (with an introduction by the editors on pp. 1057–66); and Frege, "Diary: Written by Professor Dr. Gottlob Frege in the Time from 10 March to 9 April 1924," *Inquiry*, 39 (1996), pp. 303–42 (with an introduction by the editors on pp. 303–308). Mendelsohn in introducing the English translation of Frege's diary sounds the theme of Frege the embittered, *ibid.*, p. 304: "Frege was quite old at the time of the writing of the diary. And there is reason to suspect that these later years were not easy for him. His life-project of reducing mathematics to logic lay in ruins, he was virtually unappreciated in his day, and he was surviving on a meager pension. Does the diary only record the words of an embittered old man?" In the Preface, Mendelsohn offers apologetic gestures regarding Frege's then-common but nonetheless embarrassing prejudices, *ibid.*, p. 305: "The views Frege expressed in the diary are far from original: they are the expression of an outlook that was shared by many in his day. What the diary shows more clearly than ever is how much Frege was a creature of his time, and how much more closely than we had previously been able to discern he was involved in and influenced by the philosophical activities of his time." Any historically responsible biography of Frege must acknowledge that, especially during his later years, after the disastrous defeat of Germany and the post-WWI humiliation of the Versailles Treaty, Frege became increasingly right-wing and anti-Semitic in his social–political outlook. The fact that Frege's attitudes were not uncommon in late-nineteenth and early-twentieth-century Europe, and Germany in particular, does not excuse them; nor do Frege's accomplishments in logic, mathematics, and philosophy exonerate him from his holding of morally indefensible attitudes. These are among the unpleasant facets that must be seen as a part of the complex montage of Frege's personality, regarding which he remains culpable for his uncritical assimilation of the prejudices of the culture surrounding him.

power in post-WWI Germany in the early 1930s. The party of Frege's choice, at least on paper, certainly opposed the kind of reform movements which the Nazis considered a sign of a culture's weakness. The NLP rejected philosophical principles like those supporting Mill's utilitarianism, which were aimed at improving life for the majority of people in an increasingly socialistic democratic framework. The virtues advocated by the NLP in opposition to social democracy were self-reliance, respect for and vigilant enforcement of the law, and the development of military muscle to further nationalistic interests in the long run. In this regard, however, the NLP was no more like the later Nazi party than many other political movements supporting bourgeois conservative values that have waxed and waned at various time in modern Europe. There was no suggestion that Frege's NLP advocated violence or military adventurism beyond resilient protection of national resources.[24]

In political outlook Frege was certainly no Mahatma Gandhi. From what little is known, especially from his diaries and limited political affiliations and activities, he was equally no Henry David Thoreau or Bertrand Russell. He was not a ruthless Niccolò Machiavelli hungry for power or a Friedrich Nietzsche unchecked by conventional morality striving for the greatest heights of human potential. In fact, he was far-right-leaning, crotchety, and hawkish. Frege's political life, where a yawning abyss takes the place of moral theory, was not obviously in sync with his philosophy. He did not interest himself in value theory or its practical application. Russell, as Frege's adversary and *de facto* publicist, in contrast, would become known more as a pacificist protestor and conscientious objector to England's involvement in WWI than as the founder of modern logicism in his *Principia Mathematica*. His name was associated with anti-war protest when he was jailed for six months in 1918 for publishing an article against which the government took offense. He gained attention for the kind of incident which, unlike derivations of theorems in mathematical logic, makes an impact in the newspapers and on the radio. By contrast, whatever he may have felt, especially as the war dragged on and its tragedy came into sharper focus, we have no record anywhere of Frege objecting to the atrocities of the first mechanized war in Europe, which brought to its soil so much senseless destruction. Frege warmly congratulated Wittgenstein on the latter's voluntary enlistment

---

[24] For more information on the political background of Frege, see Kreiser, *Gottlob Frege*, Section 6.7, pp. 526–47.

in the Austrian army in 1914. Frege was politically conservative, not only in ideology. He seemed as opposed to Russell in politics, all through the absurd prelude and horrific days of the war, as he had been regarding the question of what to do about Russell's paradox.

Abbe, who had been Frege's steadfast supporter, spokesperson, and champion both in the mathematics faculty and in his intercession on Frege's behalf with the Carl-Zeiss-Stiftung, died on 14 January 1905. On March 3, Frege signed an appeal calling on the local population to make donations and petition for government funding to erect a monument in Abbe's honor. Citizens of Jena were organized into a committee to identify an appropriate artist and financially and logistically realize the goal of building an *Ernst-Abbe-Denkmal*. Abbe was undoubtedly a talented and productive mathematician. It nevertheless speaks as much to the culture in Jena as a university town and site of the Zeiss Foundation that a recently deceased mathematician, of all professions, should merit a statue with an inscribed plaque, a monument or *Denkmal* in the most literal sense, for something as invisible in the world of public affairs as the strivings of theoretical mathematics.[25]

In March and April, following the winter semester of 1904–1905, Frege was prescribed a cure at a health resort. He went to the *Kur* in Köppelsdorf, near Sonnenberg in the Thüringen hill country.[26] Frege asked the university *Kurator* in writing on 27 April 1905 for permitted leave to continue a treatment he had already started. It was explained that the procedures previously administered had offered some immediate relief, but not yet effected a cure. Frege was suffering from nutritional disorders with severe nervous symptoms, and he complained that he was unable to take up his duties again immediately. Frege's attending physician, medical officer Dr. Otto Binswanger, confidentially informed the university *Kurator* of those facts of Frege's condition. Against the background of Frege's search for medical therapy it is easier to understand another factor contributing to the dry spell in Frege's logical–mathematical–philosophical productivity during the publication dark ages.[27] The request approved, "Frege thanked the *Kurator* in writing on 1 May 1905 for the rapid fulfillment of his request and the wishes expressed for his better health. The ministries were granted

---

[25] Kreiser, "Gottlob Frege: Ein Leben in Jena," in *Gottlob Frege – Werk und Wirkung*, ed. Gabriel und Dathe (Paderborn: Mentis, 2000), pp. 23–24; and Kreiser, *Gottlob Frege*, Section 6.6, pp. 519–26.
[26] Kreiser, *Gottlob Frege*, pp. 512–13.   [27] *Ibid.*

despite the already-started summer semester leave of absence."[28] He continued to suffer his annoying and sometimes debilitating symptoms, which were different in kind from those of Margarete, but alike in progressing without correct diagnosis or remedy. The way he can be seen struggling through his adversities shows him to have been a strong-willed, resourceful, patient, and forbearing man. Despite these virtues, he had braved more than enough storm fronts to weather in too short a time by the spring of 1905, and he badly needed replenishment.

In August 1913, Frege, whose nervous affliction was still debilitating eight years later, again requested medical leave, as he had previously in 1905.[29] The university *Kurator* at the time, Max Vollert, wrote the following on 18 August 1913:

> The Professor Dr. Frege asks for leave of absence for the upcoming winter semester. The now 64-year-old scholar, according to the testimony of his family physician Dr. Graf, is suffering from general nervous weakness, which forbids him from continuing teaching in the winter. Also, he still wants to bring some major scientific work to a conclusion. Frege has announced a four-hour lecture on mechanics and an audience about *Begriffsschrift* for the winter semester. His lectures are considered to be very difficult to follow, and usually attract only a few listeners. The philosophical faculty entertains no doubts as to the grant of the leave ... Neither do I.[30]

The supplementary request for leave was approved. Kreiser notes, in making reference to the *Kurator*'s letter of support for Frege's leave, that "It is not excluded that Frege began around this time also with the preparatory work for his *Logical Investigations*."[31] There is reason to believe that background inquiry and writing for those three famous final essays were undertaken as early as in the busy year 1906. Kreiser notes humorously Vollert's marginal comment pertaining to Frege's application for medical leave: "'I do not even understand the title,' evidently from the appropriate representative of the State Ministry of Altenburger [Thüringen or Thuringia], the word '*Begriffsschrift*' being underlined and marked on the application."[32] Vollert and the overseeing education ministry office join in frustration a distinguished lineage of readers who also did not understand what Frege was talking and writing about. During his semester leave Frege would have offered no lectures,

---

[28] *Ibid.*, p. 513, my translation.   [29] *Ibid.*   [30] *Ibid.*, pp. 513–14.   [31] *Ibid.*, p. 514.
[32] *Ibid.*, my translation.

although, according to other sources, he announced courses for the term on Analytical Mechanics I and *Begriffsschrift*.[33]

The year 1905 also witnessed academic political machinations directed against Frege. At the time, Robert Haußner occupied the Full Professorship of mathematics. The chair had been vacated on 1 October 1905 by previous appointee August Gutzmer, in order for the latter to accept an appointment at the University of Halle. Haußner's first move once he had secured his professorship was to dismiss Frege from collaboration on the mathematical seminar staff.[34] The full implications of the exclusion are not obvious. It was presumably undertaken as something more than a maneuver to preclude Frege from offering courses to advanced degree students at seminar level. It would certainly have been understood by colleagues and students as a public institutional embarrassment, as well as an insult to Frege. We can only assume that his enrollments and teaching had gotten that bad, and that the decision may have even come as a relief to Frege. Frege himself may have been beyond caring, chalking it up as another indignity suffered at the hands of the uncomprehending by whom he was surrounded.

Difficulties were beginning to pile up. Frege attended ever less to his official duties and concentrated more on his personal circumstances. Thomae, who was generally favorable toward or at least tolerant of Frege, commented on his effectiveness in recent times in a memorandum dated August 1906: "Now we may consider my colleague Frege here.[35] Unfortunately, I cannot deny that his [teaching] effectiveness has decreased lately. The reasons for this cannot be safely determined. Perhaps they are to be found in Frege's hypercritical tendencies." The *Kurator*, taking these circumstances as sympathetically as might be expected into account, acknowledged serious suffering in Frege's home life, by which he seems to have meant to include not only the bereavement occasioned by the death of his wife, Margarete, but also the loss of his friend and longtime colleague and supporter Abbe, within a relatively short time span.[36] The *Kurator* wrote on 2 October 1906 that "The Honorary Professor Dr. Frege has probably never been a good lecturer,

---

[33] *Ibid.*, pp. 284 and 513–14. Compare Kratzsch, "Material zu Leben und Wirken Freges aus dem Besitz der Universitäts-Bibliothek Jena," p. 543; and Asser, Alexander, and Metzler, "Gottlob Frege – Persönlichkeit und Werk," pp. 13–14.

[34] Kreiser, *Gottlob Frege*, p. 416.   [35] See for example the letter quoted in *ibid.*, pp. 385–86.

[36] *Ibid.*, p. 417.

hampered and bent down by heavy domestic suffering and hypercritical tendencies complicating the fulfillment of expectations for successful lively teaching effectiveness."[37]

It was Frege's hypercritical tendency that was blamed for his failures, cited as a character flaw of sorts; the better is the enemy of the good, as someone like Voltaire once said. This hypothetical perfectionist hypercritical tendency was annealed to the emotional strain Frege is known to have suffered. The double effect was to chase potential students away, and sometimes to freeze Frege into immobility even in pursuit of his offbeat plan of mathematical research. This phenomenon was witnessed most dramatically during this indefinitely extended period of Frege's drifting without anchor in the sea of symbolic logic he had created. As during his Habilitation defense, when Frege's reticence was first noted, as something mildly surprising to his Jena teachers, Frege needed and would consider it his prerogative to take whatever time was necessary to deal with worthwhile problems. The depth of Habilitation questions did not compare with Russell's, with exponential proportional effect on Frege's need to reflect on the challenge in his own way and in his own time. Frege contemplated the road blockaded ahead after Russell's paradox earthquake. He might have explained to Thomae and the university *Kurator* that the problem was actually that he had not been sufficiently hypercritical.

Alfred Fuchs, Logician's Ward

In 1908, Frege accepted the then six-year-old Paul Otto Alfred Fuchs, generally known as Alfred, as his ward. He brought him home to the care also of housekeeper Meta Arndt. There must have been agreement about this, an addition to the Frege household implying significantly more work. He would also be a valued lively companion to Frege and Meta. Weiner presents this accurate sketch of the basic facts surrounding Frege's wardship of Alfred:

Although Frege and his wife had had no children, after her death Frege took responsibility for bringing up a child. In 1908, six-year-old Alfred Fuchs's mother was seriously ill and his father had been committed to an asylum. No suitable guardian could be found among the relatives of his parents and the people who

---

[37] *Ibid.*, p. 418, my translation; see also p. 496.

knew Alfred in Gniebsdorf regarded him as incorrigible. At the suggestion of Frege's nephew, who was a pastor in Gniebsdorf, Frege became Alfred's guardian. Later, when Alfred came of age, Frege adopted him. Frege was, by all accounts, a kind and loving father. Alfred's school records indicate that he was well behaved and diligent. Alfred ultimately became a mechanical engineer.[38]

Alfred's reputation for incorrigibility adds a lively note to the bare sketch most commentators have penciled. Somehow, Frege and Frau Arndt over time must have managed to civilize the boy, showing him love and taking care of his needs in ways his parents had been unable to do. There may have been respects in which Alfred reminded Frege of Arnold, a basically good boy whose behavior was hinted at also having been sometimes less than exemplary.

From spring "Easter" term 1910 to spring term 1918, Alfred was enrolled as a student in the Stoyschen private secondary school. After 1915, the school was incorporated into the Jena secondary education system. Frege did not take the boy to the school that had formerly been the Pfeiffer Institute, where he had worked as a teacher of mathematics from 1882 to 1884, but opted for Stoyschen as better suited to Alfred.[39] "It is remarkable," Kreiser maintains, "that Frege made the choice to send his ward to the Stoysche School. This school followed the philosophical and pedagogical principles of its didactic founder Johann Friedrich Herbart (1776–1848)."[40] The teaching method emphasized the value of collective learning projects directed toward practical problem-solving,with quiet periods away from intense activities. The purpose was to encourage students to assimilate what had been learned before progressing to more advanced tasks. The perfectly reasonable idea was that some students needed more time than others to absorb what is often presented rapid-fire in pedagogies aimed at high-velocity ingestion of facts and techniques.

This may have seemed appropriate for Alfred with his reputed behavioral intransigence. The reason for choosing the Stoysche School, may, however, as Kreiser notes, have been Frege's caution. He did not wish to force Alfred on to an educational path for which he was not suited, especially when it remained to be seen whether he had the aptitude and application needed for eventual success in advanced study at a university. The School offered highly flexible preparation for a variety of different

---

[38] Weiner, *Frege Explained*, pp. 2–3.   [39] See Kreiser, *Gottlob Frege*, pp. 350–51.
[40] *Ibid.*, p. 502, my translation.

further career paths. Eventually Alfred decided on a career in mechanical engineering. Frege supported this decision, but it was Alfred's own choice, not something Frege in any way imposed on him.[41]

Depending on his program, performance, and preparation, Alfred could have been ready for university study by 1919, when Frege was already settled into the first year of retirement. Kreiser remarks that "Alfred has crossed over into the secondary school, because his name is not found among the former pupils of the school Carlo Alexandrinum in the Jena directory."[42] Like Frege, Alfred was educated in part at the Große Stadtschule Wismar. In the winter semester of 1923–1924, he enrolled at the Studium der Fachrichtung Maschinenbau an der Technischen Hochschule Berlin-Charlottenburg, in what at the time was a rural area but nowadays falls within the Berlin city limits. On 8 December 1928, Alfred took the Hauptprüfung (Main Exam). He received the degree of mechanical engineer (*Ingenieur für Maschinenbau*) on 12 July 1929. Frege would be dead in another year by the time Alfred journeyed to Berlin to undertake advanced technical training in 1924. The last that is known about him before his death outside of Paris in 1944 during WWII is that in 1937 he was living and practicing his trade in Braunschweig, in a building that was later completely destroyed by wartime fire-bombing, prior to relocating to Berlin-Schöneberg (Eisenacher Straße 90/91).[43]

Who was this six-year-old Alfred, and how did he come to live with Frege and Frege's housekeeper Meta? Alfred was born 30 July 1903 in Gniebsdorf bei Thalbürgel. Kreiser reports his death on 15 June 1944, whereas Mendelsohn says he died in 1945 in action during WWII.[44] Probably Kreiser's date is correct. Kreiser and other commentators provide the supplementary information, testified by his cousin Christian Frege from Bonn, that in WWII Alfred fell in Montesson,

---

[41] *Ibid.*, pp. 503–504.   [42] *Ibid.*, p. 504, my translation.

[43] *Ibid.*, pp. 506–508. Brian McGuinness, "History of Frege's Surviving Correspondence," in Frege, *Philosophical and Mathematical Correspondence*, p. xiv.

[44] Kreiser, *Gottlob Frege*, p. 508, my translation: "Concerning [Alfred's] life-path between this date [1929] and his death on 15 June 1944 in Montesson near Paris it is only known that in 1937 he was living in Braunschweig, on the third floor at Heinrichstraße 22, and then on the second floor at Altstadtring 1." Mendelsohn, *The Philosophy of Gottlob Frege*, p. 1, falsely reports that Alfred died in action during WWII in 1945. Montesson had been a factory and testing facility for advanced aeronautics ever since 1906.

near the Paris Torpedo Arsenal, where his engineering talents may have been in demand.[45]

Alfred's father was Karl Julius Alfred Fuchs, a small-scale farmer and mason or bricklayer. He was committed to an asylum (*Irrenanstalt*) in 1908, by which time Alfred's mother, Wilhelmine Lina Bauer, had already left him. She was born 19 May 1878 in Taupadel bei Eisenberg (Thüringen), and died 17 May 1910 in Apolda. Alfred had two sisters, Elsa Ella Toni Fuchs (1905–1990), and the short-lived Martha Anna Klara Fuchs (1905–1907). The family was Lutheran, which the odds favored sociologically in that part of Germany anyway at the time, but was also congenial to Frege's upbringing and early religious education in that faith. Alfred was not legally adopted by Frege until sometime between August 1921 and August 1922, unless there is a simple confusion in the recorded dates, although Frege had raised Alfred ever since the boy came under his care in 1908.[46]

The Parochial Chronicle of the Thalbürgel Parish that in 1908 entrusted Alfred's care to Frege and Frau Arndt included interesting details in a 1909 review of Alfred's family background. Karl Fuchs's father and grandfather had taken their own lives in despair over poor harvest prospects at the family farm. The sister of Karl Fuchs, Alfred's father, had drowned her two children in the thrall of mental disturbance. Karl Fuchs was a workaholic, striving to succeed where his father had failed, and constantly under stress. It is said that, if something prevented him from doing something, he would become excited and actually foam at the mouth in a trembling fit before he could bring himself to speak. His wife was pathetically limited and awkward, with increasingly serious heart trouble. With minimal assistance to be expected from Lina, Karl Fuchs was heavily overburdened, on top of his other obligations, by recent additions to the family, fueling discord in the household and leading to incidents of reported domestic violence. A petition for divorce by the abused woman failed because Lina did not adequately represent her cause at the district court. Finally she collapsed, causing Karl, who had already been on the brink for some time, to completely lose his mind,

---

[45] It is conceivable that Alfred, with his engineering skills, was employed at the Torpedo Arsenal in Montesson, a commune in the Yvelines district in the Île-de-France region. The fact that it would have been a prime strategic target for allied aerial assault at the time offers a plausible explanation of circumstances resulting in violent death.

[46] Kreiser, *Gottlob Frege*, pp. 499–500; and Kreiser, "Alfred," pp. 71–72 and 78–79.

whereupon he was taken to an asylum, and Lina was signed over to some kind of halfway house in Apolda. The children, Alfred aged five and a girl of three years, were first offered refuge in the parish rectory and then found permanent placements. The boy was turned over to Frege in Jena. Frege was no doubt on the short list for consideration because he was an uncle of the Thalbürgel Parish pastor. The girl was sent in the meantime to the children's home in Fraureuth near Werdau. The boy, the review continued, seemed quite spoiled, and the local peasants of the farming community where the Fuchses lived, in their peasant mentality, thought the boy was lost, hopeless educationally, and incorrigible in terms of his poor social conduct and lack of self-control. Once he had started to respond to the improved environment with Frege and Arndt, he soon came to be considered a good, tractable, and talented youngster, who after his transformation pleasantly surprised all those who had known him earlier.

Citing the Parish report, by Pastor Dr. Johannes Eberhard Burghard von Lüpke, who died in 1934, and was a great-nephew of Frege's mother, Kreiser continues as follows:

... Frege [has] assumed guardianship for the [Fuchs] siblings, not just for Alfred, but has taken only Alfred to live with himself. Whether it was right to separate the siblings is another question, the answer to which would certainly not have come easily to Frege. It would have been too much if, in addition to undertaking the responsibilities of guardianship for the two children, the 59-year old Frege had also had to raise both of them in his own home.

The local court, acting in its capacity as guardianship court, sought a guardian from among the circle of relatives and in-laws of Karl Fuchs and his wife, as prescribed by law, but no one suitable could be found. Even in those days an attempt was made to appoint, if possible, one and the same guardian for a group of siblings. The suggestion that this should be Frege almost certainly came from Pastor Dr. J. v. Lüpke. He had correctly recognized that adopting the two children might revitalize his uncle, and Frege himself undertook the guardianship as a duty which he tried to discharge to the very best of his ability. The farmers in Gniebsdorf were probably not the only ones to be amazed at how quickly he, together with his housekeeper, was able to get Alfred back on the right track. Alfred Frege did not lose contact completely with his sister Toni, but the relation was certainly not a close one. People in the village still recalled a visit Alfred Frege, a physically rather imposing man in a uniform of a naval officer, made to his sister, who had married in 1928, when she eventually moved back to Griebsdorf. She died in 1990.[47]

---

[47] Kreiser, *Gottlob Frege*, pp. 501–502, my translation.

There is reason to think that Alfred considered Meta Arndt his adoptive mother. She filled exactly that role faithfully for many years continuously in Frege's house. Before Frege's death in 1925, as the financial situation of Meta and Alfred deteriorated drastically, they had already given up the house outside of Jena that Frege's mother, Auguste, had built.[48] The property was purchased by mill owner John Hansen, while, most significantly, Meta and Alfred continued to live together thereafter in rental housing in Pastow near the city of Rostock, once the Jena house was no longer in Frege's possession. Frege, in the meantime, had begun building a house in Pastow, which he did not live to see completed. Legal right to live there for the remainder of their lives was bequeathed to Alfred and Meta. The building in which Meta had lived in Pastow after Frege had moved from Jena still existed for some time after Meta's death at the end of WWII. It was made available for war refugees in April 1945, and then from May onwards served as the seat of the local Soviet military headquarters.[49]

No "Highest Distinction" for Frege

Heinrich von Eggeling, shortly before leaving the post of *Kurator* of the University of Jena, in a note dated 6 May 1909 recommended Frege for the highest distinction (*Höchste Auszeichnung*). Apparently his successor, Max Vollert, questioned this, seeing no point in recommending Frege for any further distinction at that time, because his teaching activity "is without special advantage to the university" (*"für die Universität ohne besonderen Vorteil ist"*).[50] It was Grand-Ducal administrators who ultimately had responsibility for higher education in the Dukedom. They were given charge of periodic reviews of professors' teaching and research performance. Between Frege and the bureaucrats there stood Vollert, and that was just the trouble. Vollert was no stranger to mathematics. On the contrary, in addition to serving as university *Kurator* at the time, he was himself an accomplished mathematician. He could not simply let the paperwork cross his desk without offering his professional judgment as to Frege's mathematical qualifications.

---

[48] *Ibid.*, p. 630.   [49] Kreiser, "Alfred," p. 83.
[50] Vollert's damning pronouncement is cited by Kreiser, *Gottlob Frege*, p. 466.

Vollert's credentials were as impressive in this regard as those of anyone with a professorship in mathematics at Jena. He had been a classmate of Abbe's in mathematics, and was part of Abbe's web that was benefiting financially from Abbe's Carl-Zeiss-Stiftung connection. He was a prize-winning member of the Schaefer Mathematical Society, and he had worked for the government in administration of the *Materialfonds für wissenschaftliche Zwecke* (Material Funds for Scientific Purposes) in 1886. Through Abbe, beginning in 1889, he was, like Frege, partly salaried by the Carl-Zeiss-Stiftung.

Those who wonder at the magic of turning mathematics into Marks at an optics company in nineteenth-century Europe should consider not only the engineering but also the military applications of optical equipment in surveillance, reconnaissance, and logistics, making more accurate gunsights and periscopes, reducing glare and distortion of objects sighted through lenses, designing and rectifying maps, and countless other applications. There is no evidence that Frege or any of the other beneficiaries of Zeiss profits contributing to the advance of science were ever sat down and told to make a better optical gunsight. From what we know, they were supported in reasonable research interests of their own, as Frege seems to have been, the practical advantages of which, if any, could always be harvested later by others. The Stiftung seems to have functioned at the beginning of the twentieth century somewhat in the manner that hip corporations like Google in the information-technology-and-beyond industry have only lately rediscovered. Perhaps something similar was encultured in ancient Alexandria.

It should be recalled, when we read that Vollert could suggest no further distinction for Frege, that Frege and Vollert were partly intertwined by their shared friendship with Abbe and their dependence on Abbe's patronage. Friendship and the desire to please Abbe apparently had their limits. If the designation under consideration was meant to recognize someone as a distinguished mathematics teacher, professor of the year, as it were, then no one as *Kurator* at Jena could look the Grand Duke's education ministers in the eye and pat Frege on the back for any such award. His lectures were sparsely attended, there was no crowd of students signing on to work with him on *Begriffsschrift*-related projects, and there was no mass of highly qualified students marching forward from under his approving slight bend of the head to take their places in university mathematics departments in Germany and internationally. By no stretch of the imagination was he in any way an appropriate recipient for such an award.

If the "distinction" was supposed to have been at least in part for research, for acknowledged contributions to cutting-edge mathematics, then Frege was again not particularly comfortably situated. Needless to say, if Hilbert and Cantor did not fully appreciate what Frege was doing, then one could not expect even a mathematically trained administrator like Vollert to make responsible recommendations based on professional expertise. A skilled formal theorist generally sympathetic to Abbe's protégés might still be constrained to make better sense of Frege's by-default hermetic labor. He would be required to pass along his honest judgment to a paper-pushing career official functionary upstairs in Dukedom fiduciary circles. There the luxury of maintaining a university was sometimes in dispute, and its more esoterically engaged salaried employees could begin to look like prime fat to trim. It was Vollert's statutory duty to offer an opinion, and it was not his fault if Frege had squandered his opportunities to make a better career for himself at Jena.

It was a matter of credibility from Vollert's point of view. To meet his administrative obligations, he had to make a fair, correct, and factual report on the qualifications of faculty members when called upon for evaluation. His word on things had to be trusted up and down the administrative ladder. If Vollert declared Frege's work important, then he might be officially required to explain and defend it before govern-ment officials. Vollert might even in principle have been willing to do that, if only he had thought he could. As it was, Frege was flatly disrecommended in particular as a teacher, and his questionable produc-tivity and its lackluster-to-negative professional reception were weighed in the balance and found wanting during those dark dismal ages. Thirteen years had passed without further large-scale publications in mathematical logic issuing from Frege's atelier, at a time when he was also frequently, and increasingly more overtly, considered academically a teaching liability.

Frege continued a friendly antagonism in these years with his Jena mathematics colleague Thomae. In 1908, Frege published another of what Dummett calls his "polemical" pieces from this period, provoca-tively titled "Die Unmöglichkeit der Thomaeschen formalen Arithmetik aufs Neue nachgewiesen" ("Renewed Proof of the Impossibility of

Mr. Thomae's Formal Arithmetic").[51] A review of Frege's 1908 criticism of Thomae was published in 1911 by Carl Faerber, professor of mathematics in Berlin.[52] Four pages, it should be remarked, was not much space in which to prove a colleague's rival arithmetic logically impossible. In the world of succinct elegant mathematical demonstrations, however, such compact surgical criticism was fully precedented. We have seen the same efficiency of objection in Russell's three-paragraph 1902 paradox letter to Frege. A doleful four pages from Frege on Thomae would not be enough to prompt an unimaginative faculty or university administrator who was not specially informed to suggest any sort of academic distinction for Frege. He was barely treading water during these lean research and writing productivity years.

Mundane Truth-Makers

Frege's annual salary at the University of Jena increased in 1909 from 4,000 to 4,400 Marks.[53] Beyond the obvious fact that it was an exactly 10% rise, what did this mean for Frege and his workplace perception? It was a welcome boost, but probably did not reflect Frege's having especially pleased his academic overlords during this fifth year of his protracted publication lull. The supplement more likely represented an adjustment for inflation and the cost of living. It may have been extended university-wide to all employees, depending on their contracts and pay level. In Frege's case, at this time, he would have received 5% from the University of Jena and 5% from the Carl-Zeiss-Stiftung. Frege's payhike seems to have been obligatory, as did the matching increase he received from Zeiss.

Of interest in Frege's attaining exactly this salary increase at the time was that it showed again that, once Abbe had hooked Frege up with the Carl-Zeiss-Stiftung, Zeiss continued paying exactly half of Frege's salary even through his relatively unproductive years. The money was funneled from Zeiss to the university bursar and from the bursar to Frege, distributed as a regular single payment. Zeiss seems to have agreed to

[51] Frege, "Die Unmöglichkeit der Thomaeschen formalen Arithmetik aufs Neue nachgewiesen," *Jahresbericht der Deutschen Mathematiker-Vereinigung*, 17 (1908), pp. 52–55.

[52] Carl Faerber, "Referat von Prof. Faerber, Berlin," *Mitteilungen der Deutschen Mathematiker-Vereinigung*, 39 (1911), pp. 230–31.

[53] Kreiser, *Gottlob Frege*, p. 437.

double the university salary that Frege received coming directly from its funds, implying that in 1909 the university itself had bumped Frege's salary up by only 200 Marks, which was duly matched by Zeiss.[54]

The best tables of measures of relative worth for German currency within Frege's productivity dark ages are from 1913.[55] The reasons for this surfeit of data concerning 1913 are not entirely clear, but one possibility is the fact that both WWI and the much-studied Great Inflation in Germany began the next year in 1914. That coincidence has made economic events immediately preceding these occurrences of special historical significance. Consider the following as only a gesture toward understanding the comparative worth of Frege's 1909 salary increase. At the time, US $1 (1913) = 4.20 Marks (1913). The average commodities costs, independently of income, make US $1 (1913) = approximately US $24.30 (2015). Something that was needed, food items, say, that in the US cost $1 in 1913 would cost about $24.30 one hundred years plus change later in 2015. This means that the same amount of purchasing power of 1913 Marks in 2015 would be worth about 102.06 Marks if there were still German Marks in circulation today. Something that cost 4.20 Marks in 1913 would cost 102.06 imaginary 2015 Marks.

Frege's salary increase of 400 Marks in 1909 might be compared in purchasing power four years later in 1913. The calculation is attended by all the caveats qualifying any effort at economic retrodiction. Local economic circumstances can vary drastically even from one part of the same city to another and from household to household. Let that be enough warning, then, when it is suggested that, disregarding numerous other factors, together with the potential distortions of extrapolating backward from 1913 to 1909, an approximate valuation is reached in

---

[54] *Ibid.*, pp. 418–20. The investment of the Carl-Zeiss-Stiftung in the Universität Jena is indicated by the foundation's funding support for the building of the *Neues Hauptgebäude* (new main building) during Frege's tenure there, between 1906 and 1908.

[55] The assumptions are derived from the relative-worth-measuring utility available online at http://www.measuringworth.com/. I am unable independently to judge the accuracy of the information presented in such outlets. The calculations are intended only to provide a framework for looking into what Frege's salary and retirement pension would have been worth to him today in several currencies in terms of real buying power. It further suggests what such events as the Great German Inflation of 1919–1923 would have meant to him as a practical economic matter under conditions of limited fixed income unstable in its purchasing power, matched by proportionately outrageous pension payment increases valiantly trying to track the skyrocketing cost of living.

these equivalences of 400 Marks (1913) = US $95.29 (1913), and then, applying tables of relative worth conversion, = US $2,315.55 = €2,066.19 = £1,544.42 (2015). This is the roughly determined 1913 increase in purchasing power of Frege's 1909 salary enhancement, expressed in terms of its 2015 relative worth. Half of this came from the university and half from Zeiss. In 2015 purchasing power, the university had effectively spooned out about US $1,150 from its own resources for Frege. The picture is not much different for Frege from year to year until his retirement in 1918. These were nevertheless volatile economic times in Frege's Germany. The Bank Act of 1909 for the first time recognized bank notes as legal tender, paper money as such having been long in circulation. This set the stage for disastrous speculation unsupported by real assets. The policy was reversed in 1914, when in the summer of that year the German Great Inflation began to snowball. Frege was in retirement as of 1918 and became caught up in the turbulence.

Three years later, the pay pattern was repeated, when Frege's 1912 annual salary increased from 4,400 to 5,000 Marks. After 1911, a newly enhanced salary scale for the University of Jena came into effect. The provisions established, among other things, that the salaries for Honorary Ordinariat and Associate Professors were to be set at 5,000 Marks after 20 years of service. To this new minimum Frege's salary was also lifted by the same rising tide. Kreiser explains that

[Frege's] service time was calculated from 1 October 1879, so that the new regulation had to apply to him. The allowance for Frege in 1912 was to increase his salary by 600 Marks, to the total amount of 5,000 Marks. The increase was also known to have happened in that year, because in 1913 the amount appointed for Frege for the following year remained the same . . . Thus, Frege, after thirty-three years of service, was earning a salary that was equal to the starting salary of a Full Professor.[56]

To give yet another flavor of Frege's financial situation in relation to that of his colleagues in mathematics at Jena, Kreiser reports that, "From a review of the honorary positions occupied [in the Jena mathematics faculty], which summarizes [*Dozent* student fee earnings from] summer semester 1910 and winter semester 1910–1911, Frege is in last place with 163 Marks. Eucken's revenue amounted to 5,720 Marks, and J. Thomae 1,326 Marks."[57]

---

[56] Kreiser, *Gottlob Frege*, pp. 438–39, my translation.   [57] *Ibid.*, p. 422, my translation.

That comparison describes the hard facts about Frege's teaching at Jena in numerical grocery-store terms. Eucken was clearly top eliminator. Even Thomae managed to break four figures. He outperformed Frege, earning 8.14 times as much, while Eucken, the most popular by far, set a high standard in this term by earning 35.1 times more than Frege. These statistics did not bode well for Frege. These were his workplace competitors, if he cared about such things. In 1911, he still had another seven years of service to the University of Jena before he retired at age seventy in 1918. Seven academic years is a longer time than it seems when all the while Frege was shunned, perhaps even disrespected, by students, as he was by some of his colleagues. He was scorned by mathematicians who for the most part are remembered today only because they were at Jena with Frege. He was removed from seminar offerings, and there was no refuge from the storm at home in a wider scientific community that understood and appreciated his work. He was battered from pillar to post. Frege's superiors could suggest no distinction, and they had sound mathematical data supporting their frankly deprecatory assessment. Frege was paying a price for his individuality of outlook.

Wittgenstein's Visits (1911/1912)

In the Autumn of 1911, Wittgenstein paid his first visit to Frege in Jena. It was an important and energizing event for both thinkers, initiated by Wittgenstein's desire to meet Frege. Frege at sixty-three, recovering from the *volte-face* that Russell's paradox had inflicted on his official commitment to his *Grundgesetze*, still uncertain what to make of it all, and young Wittgenstein at the tender age of twenty-two, seem to have had an exultant meeting of minds. The event may have held more significance for Wittgenstein than it did for Frege. Wittgenstein was making a kind of pilgrimage, trying to touch base with someone whose work he genuinely respected as he transitioned from aeroflight engineering to philosophy and the philosophical foundations of mathematics. Moreover, in his isolation, Wittgenstein's visit was also an encouragement and pleasant diversion for senior logician Frege.[58]

---

[58] Kreiser, *Gottlob Frege*, pp. 487–88. Detail on the meetings is offered by McGuinness, *Wittgenstein: A Life: Young Ludwig 1889–1921* (Berkeley: University of California Press, 1988), pp. 73–84.

It has been suggested that the philosophical importance of the event for Wittgenstein was somewhat exaggerated in his memory of his first meeting with Frege, when he recalled the encounter in later years. It is difficult to put the sequence of events as they happened in proper chronological order. The time-honored story, which may well be true, was that Wittgenstein had read Frege and wanted to meet him in order to become his student at Jena. Frege in turn directed Wittgenstein to Russell at Cambridge, after which Frege mostly dropped out of the relatively well-known Russell–Wittgenstein dynamic. The skeptic nevertheless wonders whether it was exactly as described. Wittgenstein might have stumbled onto Frege's writings. He might have been more comfortable at the time with works on foundations of mathematics published in German. There was a wealth of such material. He went to Frege in Jena after properly written introductions, possibly arranged by a family or personal secretary. Frege knew, of course, who Wittgenstein was. He was a scion of one of Europe's wealthiest and most powerful iron and steel manufacturers. Wittgenstein's father was a man of high culture and enlightened politics, and, which Frege probably did not know, an adventurous man of rigid Austrian Biedermeier expectations for his children, up to his elbows in providing the metal for the first modern warfare that would engulf Europe only three years hence.[59]

Frege, with his right-wing leanings and membership since 1905 of the NLP, with its commitment to building up German military might, would not have been offended by whatever he may have thought this extremely well-cultured Austrian industrial prince, youngest of the Wittgensteins, may have represented of his family's commercial interests and their moral implications. Politicians decide to make war. They obtain the iron and steel and everything else they need from somewhere or other. The young man was interested in philosophy, although he did not seem to know very much about it. The usual things came up. He tried to talk like a Kantian. He had not really looked into it much. He had had a solid start on an engineering training, but he did not appear to have his heart in the work. Wittgenstein was already living in England, stationed in Manchester

[59] Ray Monk, *Ludwig Wittgenstein: The Duty of Genius* (Harmondsworth: Penguin Books, 1990), does not inquire into the meetings of Wittgenstein with Frege, which in many ways, despite their age difference, were defining moments for both philosophers. Monk begins with an early exchange of *Feldpostkarten* between Wittgenstein and Frege, who are said only to have met on at least two or three occasions before the outbreak of WWI.

working at the outdoor aerodynamics laboratory in the north of the kingdom flying big kites.[60] He had transcended the practical applications, and wanted to understand mathematics more generally, which for Frege must have been the really interesting thing about him. He had not properly embarked on anything yet, or built or proven anything, despite which he was already completely passionate about the subject. Still, he was possibly too intelligent, too fast, and too stampeding for Frege to take on as a student. How could he sustain the young man's respect, once Wittgenstein had understood the force of Russell's paradox and learned that Frege did not know how the problem could possibly be solved? The experience for Frege might have been like that of the early Pythagoreans when the first irrational length, the square root of 2, was discovered, throwing their harmonic whole-numbered arithmetically ordered model of the universe out of whack. Is that what Frege was encountering? Was it the irrational discovered in ancient Greek colonies surfacing like logical oblivion in the Bach-invoking music of Frege's *Grundgesetze*? Perhaps the young visitor already knew.

As for Wittgenstein, he would burn too bright. One could see it from a kilometer away. Frege would no longer know what to teach him. Why could he not have presented himself at Frege's office ten years ago, when Frege would have passed along what he thought back then was a worthwhile program to fully develop an applied arithmetical logic? He had had everything at his fingertips then: a methodology, a rationale, a philosophical endgame in sight, and brick-by-brick reconstructions of a powerful set of arithmetical theorems on purely logical foundations. There had been virtually no one else to talk to about it, although at least back then Frege had been sure of every part. How could Frege take Wittgenstein on as a student now? Was that what he really wanted, anyway? Why had he come? Was it just to see the relic, to paint a moment of history on his retinas before he took mathematical logic in totally new directions in pursuit of his own philosophical ideals? Indeed, in the course of time Wittgenstein did just that.

Frege, then, the campfire story continues, out of exasperation at his own inability to further Wittgenstein's advanced study in the philosophical foundations of mathematics, sent the ardent young thinker along

---

[60] Monk, *Ludwig Wittgenstein*, pp. 28–35.

to Russell, who was the acknowledged champion of the field.[61] It would be better for Wittgenstein to study with state-of-the-art paradox-makers than state-of-the-art paradox-targets and victims. Russell represented the best new philosophical thinking in the world of applied logical arithmetic. It may have been both exasperating and gratifying for Frege to learn of roughly his vision of logicism being carried out in England with an artifice of logical structuring that he could never philosophically accept. Russell was younger than Frege, but that could hardly be the explanation as to why Wittgenstein visited Frege in 1911, and then became Russell's student beginning later that same year. Frege was still six years from retirement, with a more than adequate span of time still stretching before him in which to supervise the dissertation of someone with Wittgenstein's intensity and drive, however much he may have needed to learn. Was Frege too shy? Was he perhaps intimidated by Wittgenstein, or just unwilling to take on any student who might potentially distract him from his brooding about the basic laws of logical arithmetic?

According to Wittgenstein's testimony, on the occasion Frege virtually danced around the room as he easily argued Wittgenstein down. It is not hard to tally up the reasons why Wittgenstein's wanting to visit Frege and the visit itself would have been stimulating to the founder of modern mathematical logic. "The visit of Wittgenstein was a great encouragement for Frege," Kreiser writes. "A young man on his own initiative had come to discuss with [Frege] logic and foundations of mathematics, philosophy of mathematics, and not merely in general terms, but with a knowledge of his major writings. This was something Frege had not previously experienced."[62] Geach, later a student of Wittgenstein's at Cambridge, put the essentials of Wittgenstein's 1911 visit to Frege in Jena in the following memorable terms, quoting extensively from Wittgenstein in an unnamed source for the relevant reminiscence:

Frege's work was almost wholly unappreciated during his lifetime; he rightly considered his colleagues at Jena incompetent to understand him, and said this in print, which cannot have made his relations with them happy ... He had, however, the comfort of contacts with Russell and Wittgenstein, who both retained a deep impression of his genius.

[61] See, among others, McGuinness, *Wittgenstein*, p. 73.
[62] Kreiser, *Gottlob Frege*, p. 577, my translation.

Wittgenstein's story of his relations with Frege was as follows. "I wrote to Frege, putting forward some objections to his theories, and waited anxiously for a reply. To my great pleasure, Frege wrote and asked me to come and see him. When I arrived I saw a row of boys' school caps and heard a noise of boys playing in the garden. Frege, I learned later, had had a sad married life – his children [*sic*] had died young [*sic*], and then his wife; he had an adopted son, to whom I believe he was a kind and good father. I was shown into Frege's study. Frege was a small neat man with a pointed beard, who bounced around the room as he talked. He absolutely wiped the floor with me, and I felt very depressed; but at the end he said 'You must come again,' so I cheered up. I had several discussions with him after that. Frege would never talk about anything but logic and mathematics; if I started on some other subject, he would say something polite and then plunge back into logic and mathematics. He once showed me an obituary on a colleague, who, it was said, never used a word without knowing what it meant; he expressed astonishment that a man should be praised for this! The last time I saw Frege, as we were waiting at the station for my train, I said to him 'Don't you ever find any difficulty in your theory that numbers are objects?' He replied 'Sometimes I seem to see a difficulty – but then again I don't see it.'"[63]

Wittgenstein says that Frege bounced around the room. Frege wiped the floor with him. Presumably the mopping occurred whenever Wittgenstein ventured onto another path that Frege had long since considered and of which he already knew the strengths and weaknesses. He was forearmed with counterarguments a callow Wittgenstein could not rebuff. Wittgenstein was impressed. Frege was delighted to have such a distinguished visitor.

In December 1912, it is believed, Wittgenstein made a second visit to Frege in Brunshaupten, at a Baltic seaside resort on the vast Ostsee inlet. Wittgenstein wrote a short note to Russell, dated 26 December, about having met with Frege again. Apparently, Wittgenstein asked Frege, as he did Russell at roughly the same time, whether he should consider becoming an airplane pilot or a philosopher.[64] There is no account from either participant at the 1912 rendezvous comparable to what we have of the first 1911 meeting between Frege and Wittgenstein, so we can only speculate what may have gone on in their discussion. Wittgenstein had been in Cambridge long enough to learn what he thought he could from Russell, and to see what he wanted to try to achieve in logic and philosophy. He would pursue a train of thought that had germinated in Cambridge, leading to something remarkable he had glimpsed there. He

---

[63] Geach, "Frege," pp. 130–31.
[64] See Russell, letter to Lady Ottoline Morrell, 27 November 1911. Cited in Monk, *Ludwig Wittgenstein*, p. 40; and McGuinness, *Wittgenstein*, p. 89.

carried his investigations forward thereafter in a partly self-carpentered cabin in Norway, perched on the wild fjord's rugged coast overlooking a fishing village. There he dictated notes on logic to distinguished visitors like G. E. Moore. After their electric meetings in 1911 and 1912 there continued a steady exchange of letters and postcards between Frege and Wittgenstein.

This was shortly before the start of WWI in August 1914. Wittgenstein voluntarily enlisted on the Austrian side and vanished into the fog of war, only to re-emerge later as an artillery officer and prisoner of the Italians in 1918. Frege would later claim, when for safe-keeping he was sent one of three copies of Wittgenstein's *Logisch-philosophische Abhandlung*, later to become the *Tractatus Logico-Philosophicus*, that he did not understand much of what Wittgenstein was trying to say. By the time Frege and Wittgenstein were able physically to speak with one another again, after the war had ended, they were in another sense philosophically so removed from one another that they were unable ever to talk productively again about the topics in logic Frege cared most about.

Correspondence with Wittgenstein

There was a relatively extensive 1913–1920 correspondence between Frege and Wittgenstein. The existence of the letters was long suspected, but they had been considered lost. Some, if not all, of Frege's messages to Wittgenstein were discovered by accident several decades past in a card-board box, tucked away on a publisher's shelf in Vienna. They were prepared for publication as recently as 1989, and consequently did not appear in the Frege *Briefwechsel*. The question of Wittgenstein's relation to Frege is equally significant in understanding the biographies of both these great logician-philosophers. There were altogether in the cache several hundred communications from family members, friends, and colleagues, all addressed to Wittgenstein during the period from 1913 to 1931, including a packet of twenty-four letters from Frege.[65]

There is an undated card from Wittgenstein to Frege in this assort-ment that places their logical and philosophical interests in bold relief against the background events of WWI and Wittgenstein's participation

---

[65] Frege, "Briefe an Ludwig Wittgenstein aus den Jahren 1914–1920," ed. Allan Janik, in *Wittgenstein in Focus – Im Brennpunkt: Wittgenstein*, ed. Brian McGuinness and Rudolf Haller, special issue, *Grazer Philosophische Studien*, 33/34 (1989), pp. 5–33.

in the war. The existence of another card was confirmed only by Frege's
reply to Wittgenstein of 11 October 1914, in which the previous note was
mentioned. Frege responded to Wittgenstein in the special military
Feldpostkarte of 10 November 1914. The right-leaning Frege congratulated Wittgenstein enthusiastically on enlisting for the war: "Dear Mr.
Wittgenstein! Thank you very much for your greeting cards. That you
have entered as a volunteer, I read with particular satisfaction and admire
the fact that despite this you can devote yourself still to doing science.
May it be granted to me to see you again healthy after the war, and
continue having conversations with you. Certainly we will thereby come
closer and at last understand one another."[66] Did Frege not know what
war was, or what would happen to young men like Wittgenstein in the
course of hostilities? The decision had clearly been made, so why should
Frege not commend the fellow's brave choice and wish him well in
the war?

Despite shared interests and Wittgenstein's profound respect for Frege,
bordering on Austrian Catholic reverence, it seemed that Wittgenstein and
Frege had palpable philosophical disagreements whenever they tried to
talk shop. Frege was one of the few thinkers for whom Wittgenstein had
genuine respect. It was known that he had learned long passages from
Frege's writings by heart. It is not surprising that Wittgenstein later
confessed that "The style of my sentences is very strongly influenced by
Frege. And if I wanted to, I could probably find this influence where none
would see him at first sight."[67] When Wittgenstein was trying to find a
publisher for his *Tractatus*, he turned to Frege again for advice after the
war's end.

Encountering the same difficulty as had Frege with *Grundgesetze II*,
Wittgenstein at first could find only the Viennese publishers Jahoda and
Siegel and Wilhelm Braumüller, as Kreiser tells the tale, who were willing
to take on the job on the condition, unacceptable to Wittgenstein, that he
pay for the treatise's paper and printing. Up against that brick wall,
Wittgenstein asked Frege to help him find a more suitable publisher.

---

[66] *Ibid.*, pp. 8–9.
[67] Wittgenstein, *Zettel* (Berkeley: University of California Press, 1970), §712. See Richard
McDonough, "A Note on Frege's and Russell's Influence on Wittgenstein's *Tractatus*,"
Russell: The Journal of the Bertrand Russell Archives, 14 (1994), pp. 39–46; and Reck,
"Wittgenstein's 'Great Debt' to Frege: Biographical Traces and Philosophical Themes," in
From Frege to Wittgenstein, ed. Reck, pp. 3–38.

The similarity in their publication experiences with texts in mathematical logic was eclipsed by the twisted difference that Wittgenstein in 1919 could have easily afforded to subsidize the publisher of his unconventional manuscript, but refused to do so, whereas Frege had had to scrape together his *Pfennige* in order to pay the publishing costs of *Grundgesetze II*. This, despite his limited means, Frege reconciled himself to doing. He probably felt obligated to assume the burden of his project, and was perhaps even grateful to have found a publisher and printer willing to undertake the work under any terms. Frege offered Wittgenstein an alliance with Bruno Bauch, the editor of the *Beiträge zur Philosophie des deutschen Idealismus* (*Contributions to the Philosophy of German Idealism*), where the three essays of Frege's *Logische Untersuchungen* would soon appear. This would be a respected publication outlet for Wittgenstein's *Tractatus*. The catch was that Wittgenstein was supposed to rewrite the book entirely in standard philosophical treatise format, with none of those irritating little numbers and stentorian pronouncements, but sequential arguments and good paragraph sense, just like everyone else was required to do in publishing their ideas in mathematics and philosophy.[68]

Frege's letters to Wittgenstein reflect the high regard in which Frege held the young man's thinking about logic, philosophy, and the foundations of mathematics. Their conviviality concealed the fact that Frege and Wittgenstein had arrived at very different, and in crucial ways diametrically opposed, views of logic in its relation to meaning, thought, and the world. The two independent-minded thinkers continued to derive pleasure from occasional interaction with each other. They had thought their way through to very strongly divergent conclusions in philosophical logic, theory of meaning, philosophy of language and mathematics, and metaphilosophical methodology.[69] There could be no question of collaboration. The communications uncovered in Vienna include, from Wittgenstein to Frege, eight letters, three regular cards, and four postcards, and, from Frege to Wittgenstein, two letters and one postcard, plus four letters, one letter-card, and one regular card from

---

[68] Frege, "Briefe an Ludwig Wittgenstein aus den Jahren 1914–1920," Letter 20 of 30 September 1919 and Letter 21 of 3 April 1920. In his missing reply between these messages Wittgenstein spoke frankly against refashioning what was to become the *Tractatus* into a conventional expository treatise.

[69] Frege, "Briefe an Ludwig Wittgenstein aus den Jahren 1914–1920," pp. 5–8.

Wittgenstein's sister Hermine to Frege. Scholz, acting as Frege's literary heir, in a letter dated 2 April 1936 requested of Wittgenstein copies of his correspondence with Frege. Wittgenstein was unwilling to comply. He answered on 9 April "I do possess a few cards and letters from Frege. They are, however, of purely personal content, not philosophical. For a collection of Frege's writings they have no value at all, but for me they have sentimental value. The thought of offering them to a public collection is repugnant to me."[70]

The second part of the correspondence between Frege and Wittgenstein began with 1915 Letter XLV/6, and from then on remained focused on Wittgenstein's logical–philosophical treatise where logic, in Wittgenstein's own previous phrase when describing it to Russell, was still simmering in the melting-pot. After Wittgenstein had been taken prisoner, his sister Hermine acted as delivery agent for his correspondence with Frege. She also assured that Frege received a manuscript copy of the *Tractatus*, under its original title, *Logisch-philosophische Abhandlung* (see Letter XLV/11). Wittgenstein requested an opinion of the book from Frege (Letter XLV/15), which Frege duly wrote (Letter XLV/18). Wittgenstein did not agree with the contents of Frege's assessment, and concluded that Frege, like most of the rest of the world, including especially the scientific philosophical community, would not understand the book, much as Frege in previous decades had been sorely misunderstood. Wittgenstein, disappointed at the prospect of becoming yet another logical–philosophical outcast, wrote to Russell on 19 August 1919 "I also sent my M.S. to Frege. He wrote to me a week ago and I did gather he does not understand a word of it all. So my only hope is to see you soon and explain all to you, for it is very hard not to be understood by a single sole! [*sic*, soul]."[71]

The correspondence between Frege and Wittgenstein that Wittgenstein had initiated continued nonetheless, although without much philosophical profit from Wittgenstein's point of view. Things had not improved by the time Wittgenstein wrote to Russell again on 6 October 1919: "I remain in correspondence with Frege. He does not understand a word of my work and I am already exhausted from sheer

---

[70] *Ibid.*, pp. 5–33.
[71] Wittgenstein, Letter R.37 to Russell from Cassino 19 August 1919, in Wittgenstein, *Letters to Russell, Keynes and Moore*, ed. G. H. von Wright (Oxford: Basil Blackwell, 1974), p. 71.

restatements."[72] The letters being exchanged between Frege and Wittgenstein at this time predated Frege's efforts to find Wittgenstein's text a home within the scientific journal citadels of German idealism. He could have done so only at a price that would have meant the desolation of everything Wittgenstein thought not only poetic but also philosophically essential about the striking expository style of his *Tractatus*. The work was supposed to be syntactically like a ladder whose rungs the reader would ascend, looking on the page somewhat like a work of *Konkrete Poesie* (concrete poetry). The literary style of the book was carefully chosen, or it might be said to have imposed itself on the composition process, to mimic this unique argumentive structure. How was any of that going to work, if the book were rewritten in its entirety to look like any other short treatise on subjects of logic, mathematics, metaphysics, meaning, and bonus associated topics of solipsism, the self or soul, causation and probability, freedom, philosophical methodology, and all the cluster of philosophical concepts on which Wittgenstein touched?[73]

An invitation to visit Wittgenstein on leave in Vienna from the front during the war was declined by Frege in another letter for reasons of health. Wittgenstein repeatedly tried to meet Frege's demands for greater clarification, until he felt he might have reached the point of diminishing returns trying to explain himself to the great but archetypically old-school German logician and philosopher. In a subsequent letter, Frege mused as follows: "I wonder if I am one of those who will understand your book? Without your *Beihilfe* [assistance] difficult."[74] Wittgenstein in the end gave up trying to help Frege understand, at about the same time that Frege arrived at his own conclusion that the two friends were never going to agree on an approach to main logical and philosophical topics. Wittgenstein despaired of being able to explain to Frege what he was expecting to achieve in the *Tractatus*.

Despite the fact that Wittgenstein credited "the great works of Frege" as among his main sources of inspiration in the *Tractatus*, Frege was unable to understand much of anything Wittgenstein presented therein.

---

[72] *Ibid.*

[73] The idea of the sentences of Wittgenstein's *Tractatus* stylistically mimicking the rungs of a ladder is explored by Marjorie Perloff, *Wittgenstein's Ladder: Poetic Language and the Strangeness of the Ordinary* (Chicago: University of Chicago Press, 1999).

[74] Frege, "Briefe an Ludwig Wittgenstein aus den Jahren 1914–1920," Letter 19 of 16 September 1919 to Wittgenstein.

Through all philosophical incongruities, the personal connection between the two men remarkably enough only strengthened over time. "The relationship between Frege and Wittgenstein," Schulte writes, "is one of the most spiritual father–son relationships in the history of philosophy":

> It is true that Frege was the most important philosophical influence on Wittgenstein, but on the other hand, one must not forget that Wittgenstein has never allowed more than a little bit of influence on his thinking. It is also true that Wittgenstein heavily criticized Frege. But strong criticism was Wittgenstein's normal way of expressing his respect for those he criticized. He also has the high assessment of Frege expressed in almost exuberant manner by his standards ... And just days before his death, he wrote the remark: "Frege's style of writing is sometimes great."[75]

Frege's honest puzzlement over Wittgenstein's aims in the *Tractatus* for once was not unique among logicians and philosophers. The Introduction to the work that Russell wrote for the 1922 translation provided ample evidence of Russell's considerable misunderstandings of his student's efforts to link anti-philosophy to logical and *a fortiori* ontic conditions of meaningful expression in any possible language. Russell seemed not to have fully grasped many of the details of Wittgenstein's text that were supposed to fit into the overall radically new conception of logic proffered to support the book's main *argumentum reductio ad absurdum*, namely that there can be no adequate discursive theory of discursive meaning.

Had the project succeeded, it would have left traditional eminently discursive philosophy behind. From Wittgenstein's perspective, having climbed the ladder's rungs to attain its highest viewpoint, there was literally nothing constructive for philosophy to do thereafter but disabuse philosophy's benighted practitioners of the fancy that there were profitable tasks for philosophy to undertake, meaningful questions to pose and try to answer. Wittgenstein's idea, to the extent Frege understood it, was too drastic. He said repeatedly that after the war he could not understand Wittgenstein, which was undoubtedly true. If Wittgenstein was right, if that could possibly be what he was trying to explain to Frege, then Frege's lifework in rebuilding arithmetic on purely logical concepts and inference principles would have been literal nonsense. That was not much improvement for Frege

---

[75] Joachim Schulte, "Frege und Wittgenstein," in *Gottlob Frege – Werk und Wirkung*, ed. Gabriel and Dathe, pp. 211–12.

over Russell's charge that his *Grundgesetze* was riddled with logical contradictions.[76]

Blue December

In December 1917 Frege was sixty-nine. He had been at Jena almost continuously for forty-three years and battled many storms on the home-front and in the public forum of mathematical opinion, painfully also within the fluttering paper leaves of logic and mathematics books and journals.

Next year at the end of term he would retire from Jena with the pension he had earned as Honorary Ordinary Professor of mathematics, effectively an *Extraordinariat* Associate Professor for his time of service. It had taken him years to build himself up to this point within the faculty and university salary system, and he had succeeded to the extent that he had only with the help of Zeiss. He had been grateful for their crumbs, as long as he was free to pursue single-mindedly in his own way the logical foundations of arithmetic. He paid for his independence with sluggish advancement and paltry pecuniary rewards, compared with what he could have achieved had he been merely a normal cut-and-dried mathematics professor, giving full attention to teaching students and publishing the occasional theorem in a well-respected center-of-line mathematics journal. Why could he not be more like Eucken, or more like Thomae? That was certainly not how Frege understood the opportunity he had been presented. He was determined to achieve something new, unprecedented, and lasting in the history of logic and philosophy.

The Zeiss foundation, in the meantime, would have probably been about as impressed with Frege's promise as the contemporary mathematical community seemed to have been, beginning with his colleagues at Jena and all the logicians he had managed to offend with his own acid criticisms, or who were frankly mystified by whatever it was he was trying to do. Zeiss had become Frege's lifeline, and Abbe had been Frege's lifeline to Zeiss. Now, as this chapter in Frege's biography narrowed to a close, Frege's mother, Auguste, his wife, Margarete, and Abbe had all in

---

[76] An interpretation of the continuity of anti-philosophy from Wittgenstein's early to later period is presented by Jacquette, *Wittgenstein's Thought in Transition* (West Lafayette: Purdue University Press, 1997). See Schopenhauer, *The World as Will and Representation*, Volume 2, p. 80.

fairly rapid succession passed away. Frege was mostly alone in logic, mathematics, and philosophy. At home at least he had Meta and Alfred. There was always something to talk about, decisions to make, disputes to settle, smiles to share around. Even Russell's gratifying notice of Frege's work came only with a noxious sting in its tail. Frege was defeated logically by a fault he could not identify somewhere deep within his logical system. The fact cruelly had to be discovered, moreover, by someone who, for all his international prestige as a philosopher of mathematics, could not even bluff his way through a first convincing command of *Begriffsschrift* symbolism.

The picture in Frege's case was arguably more complicated. Certainly he had health problems occasioned by anxieties and emotional turmoils. His ailments prevented his full participation at his former high-velocity level of writing and teaching. He had to cancel courses because of illness and withdraw to a spa. There were too many over-sized hailstones released at once precisely on him during too short a recuperation time. There was the enormous strain of preparing both volumes of his *Grundgesetze* with virtually no external encouragement, interrupted by the startling and inopportune appearance of Russell's paradox, couched in a friendly appreciative letter at first praising Frege's *Grundgesetze* before driving in the blade. Then came the loss of his mother, followed by the death of his wife and the death of his longtime supporter, personal friend, and intellectual intimate Abbe. These events could only be deflating. Seeing the *Grundgesetze* through to completion in its second volume in 1903 would have implied a sudden psychological release from the strain of years of concentrated cognitive labor that began building tension sometime before 1874.

The emotional and psychological release that would have occurred as the project was finally laid to rest and appeared in print, with Frege gritting his teeth for the usual round of incomprehension and abuse in published reviews, would have been one thing. What happened instead was that, just as the book was being made up for binding, distribution, and sale, Russell joined the party unexpectedly with his own surprising invitation, his scientifically philosophically motivated but no less exasperating brief paradox letter to Frege. Russell thereby occasioned for Frege another upheaval that took an enormous toll, along with all his other personal and professional troubles. The inescapable fact that rides roughshod over all other considerations in understanding Frege's frame of mind at the time is his cancellation of the very idea of a third volume, the putative *Grundgesetze III*. The next building block in Frege's logicism was presumably meant to focus on still more advanced topics surrounding the reduction of the basic laws of elementary arithmetic to the concept-functions and inference structures of pure logic, as Frege had once conceived its principles.

The death of Frege's mother, Auguste, and his wife, Margarete, added substantially to Frege's sudden evaporation of purpose, energy, and motivation for demanding mathematical and philosophical work. How could such a string of events have possibly done any less damage, even for a feisty, otherwise determined scrapper like Frege? His letter to Russell begging off an opportunity to speak about the foundations of mathematics at an upcoming Cambridge conference in 1912 was a telling sign, given Frege's official explanation as to why he would not attend. That he was recovering from a succession of emotional batterings was not to be denied, but need also not represent the best or most complete or convincing explanation for his decision, beyond what he said to Russell. Frege's reluctance can be understood as his not having arrived at a satisfactory resolution of Russell's paradox, fully grasping the implications he assumed it to have for the meta-foundations of mathematics, not knowing what to do about it or the exact sources from which it originated, and in the meantime having nothing in his own opinion worthwhile to say.

It is nevertheless an exaggeration to maintain, as Dummett does, that Frege did no worthwhile philosophical work during this time. There were significant published and unpublished essays and reviews written, and an active philosophical correspondence was maintained. Judging from outward signs there was undoubtedly a vigorous subterranean re-analysis of everything connected with the entire *Grundgesetze* arithmetic, from the day of its inception until Russell's three-paragraph note of mid-June 1902 apparently shot Frege's high-flying dirigible down in flames. Frege mentioned in correspondence with Russell and others that he had been heavily engaged in rethinking the basic laws of logicism. He was drawn and quartered by the fact that he could not find a good non-*ad hoc* solution to Russell's paradox. Worse, he could not find anything wrong with the starting-place he had first chosen for his *Grundgesetze* – other than its apparently sustaining a logical antinomy where he never expected to be so affronted, involving the concept-function of a set of non-self-membered sets.

It is also possible that Frege was not unable to do so, but simply did not want to publish much during this melancholy season. Despite continuing to think and write about logic and the philosophical foundations of arithmetic, albeit at diminished volume and speed during these years, he may have sought respite. He had endured more than enough psychological turmoil over his published thoughts to justify turning inward upon his own reflections about logic and arithmetic. He did not need to have more of his findings misunderstood and mistakenly criticized. It was not as though if he published another book the University of Jena would suddenly understand what a neglected jewel they had in their crown and reward and recompense Frege according to his just deserts. He knew, or thought for years before the paradox he knew, what he had achieved. It enabled him to stay floating despite negative reviews and dismal decades of neglect. He had long stopped caring about recognition or waiting for recognition to come during his lifetime. He was disappointed, no doubt shocked, by the Russell paradox, to be sure. He was ever hopeful, never totally deterred, nonetheless, even if for a time he experienced a contemplative downturn in publishing productivity. There was too much that was unquestionably right in his mind about the three books he had given the world, about the logical reductions in the basic plan of logicism they pictured.

The fact prevented Frege from taking the easy release afforded by a failed hypothesis, unless or until he could determine exactly how it had failed. As bad as things became, Frege could not simply walk away from his *Grundgesetze* anytime after 1902. He was humbled more than anything by the fact that he could plainly see with Russell that there was a contradiction, while at the same time he could find nothing within his arithmetic on which to fairly pin the blame. The basic logical laws of Frege's arithmetic had lost none of their lustre from Frege's perspective as in any sense intrinsically objectionable after 1902, despite the desperate search for something in the system that, with an accompanying explanation, might have been modified to preclude Russell's paradox. It was because Frege continued to believe in *Grundgesetze I* Axioms I–VI during the publication dark ages that he was prevented from simply turning his back on the original design for a rigorously derived non-psychologistic graphic–pictorial explication of logicism that would suffice as an undeniable concrete proof of its truth. He waited while regathering strength, hoping, but no longer expecting, somehow to make his next move in the international chess game in which Russell had stalemated, if not also checkmated, Frege's *Grundgesetze*.

He needed a rest, a distraction, something to take his mind temporarily away from what had become imponderable questions of mathematical logic, until he could return to them afresh. The boy Alfred, brought into the reduced Frege household four years after Margarete's death, to be raised by Frege and his steadfast live-in housekeeper Meta, must have provided unexpected laughter and a new set of responsibilities at this juncture in Frege's life. Bonds of emotional attachment were forged, and gentleness and love could blossom in Frege's heart again, under his now old man's gruff graying and bristly salt-and-pepper beard and moustachioed exterior. Always proving theorems, Frege proved in this instance what a good natural father he would have been to children of his own, judging from how ready he was to accept Alfred as an addition to his life.

Philosophically Active "Inactivity"

In 1914 Frege wrote the unpublished manuscript "Logic in Mathematics," which showed again that he was not fleeing altogether from the challenges of mathematical logic during the publication dark ages. The text seems to be Frege's sketches for lectures at the University of Jena given in the summer semester of that year, when Carnap attended the course and took notes that we have already combed for insights into Frege's logic and teaching persona, which were published as *Frege's Lectures on Logic*.[77]

What was going on in Frege's more personal life? Did Frege, like Russell across the channel, and so many others all over the world, regard the war as a bad thing? Frege's membership of the NLP suggests a jingoist advocacy of national resources for the military strengthening of Germany. There are terrible risks of oversimplification and fallacious inference here. Frege congratulated Wittgenstein in a *Feldpostkärtchen* for signing up on the Austrian side. Wittgenstein volunteered for service, perhaps with a young man's sense of the need to be part of such world-shaking events. He could have exempted himself from military duty, not

---

[77] Frege, "Logic in Mathematics," *Posthumous Writings*, pp. 203–50; and Carnap, *Frege's Lectures on Logic*.

least because of family connections, to avoid becoming cannon fodder like so many young men on all sides of the conflict in that generation, but also because he would have qualified, even had he been drafted, for a medical deferment.

As the war raged on, Frege penned other notices to Wittgenstein, who was probably stationed at the time in what is now Poland, serving on a gunboat patrolling the Vistula river that divides Kraków. He wrote, much as he did to Spieser, "I am glad that you still have time and energy left for scientific work. At the same time it is to me a sign of your well-being. I am also – apart from little things – doing well."[78] In 1916, Frege exuberantly proclaimed, in much the same voice, while pleading ill health when declining an invitation to visit Wittgenstein on leave in Vienna, catching up finally with Wittgenstein's notices,

Dear Mr. Wittgenstein! Thank you for your letter and your card. Your desire not to let the work of your mind be lost, I find very understandable and would like to be of service. But it is still doubtful to me whether I can come to Vienna. Thanks for your friendly invitation. Anyway, I hope that it may be granted to me in some way to carry on our scientific conversations, and we must indeed be approaching more closely that time.[79]

That was in April. By July, Frege was markedly less optimistic about his own progress. It was a time of fluttering postcards, a medium of postal exchange much favored by the military for ease of censorship, with everything short and written on the outside. The field-postcard still offered a chance to maintain contact with the world, which was important for upholding the morale of soldiers who often had neither the time nor the inclination to write anything of greater length than would fit on the back of a hand anyway. Postcards minimized the chance that enlisted men and officers might accidentally let slip anything of strategic value to untrustworthy civilians, who were also encouraged and sometimes permitted only to use postcards in writing to friends and loved ones in the armed services. Frege wrote the following:

Dear Mr. Wittgenstein! Thank you for your cards! I am glad that you are working scientifically. I cannot say the same of me. I do not know how it happens that I have nothing right at the present time ... I hope to carry on with you our scientific talks again in times of peace. Your G. Frege.[80]

[78] Frege, "Briefe an Ludwig Wittgenstein aus den Jahren 1914–1920," p. 10, my translation.
[79] *Ibid.*, p. 11, my translation.   [80] *Ibid.*

The lassitude was unchanged when Frege confided in Wittgenstein later, near the end of the same month of July 1916, still complaining of his slump:

Dear Mr. W! Many thanks for your cards! I am sorry that your earlier high spirits are missing from them. I very much hope that you regain these soon in the successful struggle for a great cause in a decisive world-historical context the likes of which there has never been. Right now I too lack enough strength and frame of mind for genuinely scientific work, but I am trying to occupy myself by working out a plan that I hope may be useful to the Fatherland after the war. Then I hope that we shall be able to resume our conversations so as to make progress on our mutual understanding and on logical questions.
With best wishes for your well-being,[81]

It is like this throughout most of their exchange. Frege bemoans his inability to get started with any oomph again in mathematical logic. Something has gone out of his once-sprightly, somewhat mischievous stride. He wished he could be doing more, and he looked forward to talking with Wittgenstein again about these scientific matters. Perhaps Frege hoped that, with Wittgenstein back in his study (Frege was not really expecting to travel so far away and over the mountains to Vienna), he would feel revitalized in his efforts to re-establish a rigorous non-psychologistic logicism, to get the train back on the tracks. The young man, with so many heterodox ideas in logic and philosophy, might see something obvious to him that Frege had overlooked. Having someone like Wittgenstein to talk things through with, someone who had studied with Russell and knew Frege's books and essays, who understood something of the formal structure of Russell's paradox in Frege's *Grundgesetze*, might be enough to rekindle the first exultant discussions that had begun in 1911 at Wittgenstein's initiative. The war could be blamed for interrupting their discussion, but of course young men must go off to war. The war would end and their philosophical interchange would resume.

Little did Frege know at the time how the war had changed Wittgenstein. More importantly, he was unaware just how far distant Wittgenstein's study of logic had taken him in an exceedingly unconventional anti-philosophical direction. Frege at the time had not yet seen even the fair hand-copied first-draft version of the *Tractatus* (*Abhandlung*) that eventually Wittgenstein, through the offices of the Red Cross and with his sister Hermine's help, would spirit out of the

---

[81] *Ibid.*, p. 12.

military prison at Cassino. There were three copies made and sent for safety, one copy going to Frege, another to Russell, and a third to Vienna architect Paul Englemann. Frege did not like and certainly did not understand most of what he eventually saw in Wittgenstein's text, as he unreservedly declared. He could help Wittgenstein publish the text, despite feeling embarrassed by it, perhaps, now that he had seen it, if Wittgenstein accepted what Frege may have known perfectly well was the insupportable condition that the *Abhandlung* text be mutilated to fit provincial conformist expectations of normal scientific discourse. It was an impossible demand.

There is a poetic view of the relationship that flourished between Frege and Wittgenstein after their initial meetings in 1911 and 1912, sustained by their frequent correspondence during the war. It was at one level a Goethean tragedy the two play out, radically minded, equally self-convinced thinkers on a collision course to crash philosophically, if not in their continued warm personal interactions. When the war was over in 1918, roughly marking the end also of Frege's publication dark years, Wittgenstein and Frege at last had the chance Frege had yearned for all through the war of talking together again. Still not careful about what he wished for, Frege's first contact with Wittgenstein as Europe wound down from its horrendous war was the inexplicable *Abhandlung* Wittgenstein had written, carried in his backpack through the conflict, and then sent forth for Frege's protection, consideration, approval, and publication counsel. Frege could not make sense of it; nor has he been alone as Wittgenstein's tract approaches its first century in print. When they were able to meet again to take up the scientific discussions for which Frege had longed, they could no longer meaningfully communicate philosophically.

Wittgenstein, his thought leading him in a very different direction, placed himself beyond the possibility of alliance with Frege or anyone else in any constructive scientifically modeled philosophical enterprise. That was not what he had concluded it was to be a philosopher. He rejected scientific philosophy in the general category of discursive philosophical theory-building, which in a way was the main point of the *Tractatus*, a model and method from which Frege would never back away. One wonders whether it occurred to Frege afterward that, if the war had not intervened, he and Wittgenstein might have saved a lot of wasted time by deciding four years earlier that there was not going to be enough common ground between them to entertain the possibility of Wittgenstein working progressively even in parallel lines with Frege's *Grundgesetze*. Or did the experience of war change Wittgenstein's philosophy in ways that put him out of reach of any scientific imprint of philosophical inquiry like Frege's and, for that matter, Russell's? Wittgenstein's *Abhandlung* manuscript in Frege's hands in 1919, one year after Frege's retirement, bewildered him considerably more than had Russell's 1902 paradox letter.

Frege's health, meanwhile, continued to get worse. He requested another medical leave of absence for the summer semester of 1917. He was not getting better, despite repeated treatments. His condition deteriorated progressively but not rapidly. How much longer he had remained to be seen. We know in retrospect that Frege lived another eight years. Again Vollert had to put in a word on Frege's behalf, writing to the state ministries in one of the most revealing satellite documents when patching together Frege's biography. Vollert explained the situation: "The now 69-year-old Counselor Professor Dr. Frege asks for [medical] leave on the basis of a certificate from the district physician Professor Dr. Giese. Because of his weakened health, [Frege] is unable to give lectures during the current summer semester. From the philosophical faculty, the request is approved. The lectures Frege gave, if they were ever actually given, always found at most only a few participants. I myself have no objections to the granting of the request."[82] The approval for Frege's leave of duties at Jena was made on 20 May 1917, and then, according to respective applications of 27 May 1917 and 23 July 1918, as Kreiser reports, extended also through the following two semesters.[83]

Frege was not in good physical health at that point. His age was catching up with him, although he had never been strong or especially active since his bout of virulent childhood illnesses growing up in Wismar. His execrable teaching was noted without moderating qualification or effort at softening. He was on the verge of retirement, if only his colleagues in mathematics could hold their breath a little longer. In the meantime, Frege was not doing the students any good even when he made enrollments. Why not offer him some dignity away from the classroom, as warranted by his medical condition? Better Frege drinking mineral waters and soaking in a heated mineral pool than boring and

---

[82] Kreiser, *Gottlob Frege*, p. 514, my translation.   [83] *Ibid.*

mystifying and possibly ruining the prospects of the mathematical faculty's most promising impressionable students.

Frege in 1917 was philosophically active to a more limited degree than before and proceeding at his own deliberate pace. He was undefeated with respect to the ultimate goals of pure logicism, working his way in slow motion by a different line of strategy toward an improved understanding of the fundamental concepts of logic in the aftermath of Russell's paradox. The new method was reflective rather than constructive. Frege was proceeding by means of a patient examination of the most elementary principles of reasoning that, previously unnoticed, may have incautiously led *Grundgesetze* arithmetic into the logical contradictions Russell had supposedly discovered. He did not live to complete the project, although the three-essay part he published later during his lifetime did not encounter the source of Russell's paradox or uncover any failings in the propositional fragment of *Begriffsschrift* to support a syntactical contradiction. Frege proceeded with his patient investigation of the most basic concepts of pure logic, after and despite the damage the Russell paradox was thought to have exposed as syntactical contradictions in *Grundgesetze* arithmetic.

13

The Late Essays in Philosophical Logic – the *Logische Untersuchungen* (1918–1923)

I N A FINAL burst of publishing activity in the last half-decade before his death, Frege produced some of his most interesting and admired contributions to the philosophy of logic. He brought to print in these years the previously mentioned essays "Thought," "Negation," and "Compound Thoughts." These works were intended by Frege to join forces in a book of several interconnected themes titled *Logische Untersuchungen* (*Logical Investigations*). The collection was not published as a single volume in Frege's lifetime, but only many years later by Frege scholars carrying out his design.[1]

The essays constituted an important chapter in the history of mathematical philosophy. There was almost nothing entirely new in any of the three late essays, compared with Frege's previously published books and essays, considered in light of their publication histories. Early drafts in some instances went back to the late 1890s, or were directly related to other written sources. These essays, among other writings unpublished in Frege's lifetime, are collected in his *Nachlaß*.[2] The arguments and analogies are worth critically examining, not only as intrinsically interesting, but as revealing some of the intricacies and continuities of Frege's thinking, his analytic logical–philosophical abilities, and a sustained

[1] All three of the essays now collected in Frege's *Philosophische Untersuchungen* were published in the journal *Beiträge zur Philosophie des deutschen Idealismus*. "Der Gedanke: Eine logische Untersuchung" (1, pp. 58–77) and "Die Verneinung" (1, pp. 143–57) were published in 1918, and "Gedankengefüge" was published in 1923 (3, pp. 36–51).

[2] The complete Frege *Nachlaß*, including correspondence, is collected in *Nachgelassene Schriften und wissenschaftlicher Briefwechsel*, with selections in Frege, *Philosophical and Mathematical Correspondence*. See the previously mentioned editors' introduction, "History of the Frege *Nachlaß* and the Basis for this Edition," pp. ix–xv.

interest in logic as he entered his final years. He was nothing if not still tenacious.

The content of these three essays, the fact that Frege at this late date made the effort to have them published, and his plans for using them in book format, probably intended for reworking as seamlessly interrelated chapters of a monograph, show above all that the events of the relatively recent past, though still not philosophically overcome by Frege, had not caused him to completely lose heart regarding his ability to make worthwhile contributions to the progress of a distinctively Fregean logic and a distinctively Fregean pure logicism.

Three Late Essays

The essays were separately published in the respected scientific–philosophical journal *Beiträge zur Philosophie des deutschen Idealismus* in 1918 and 1923. "Der Gedanke" ("Thought") and "Die Verneinung" ("Negation") appeared in the same year at the end of WWI, and "Gedankengefüge" ("Compound Thoughts") five years later, two years before Frege's death.[3] They attest to his philosophical cogency up through the age of seventy-five, or at least until his age when he wrote the final essays and prepared them for publication.

The essays were clearly meant to form a whole, the core of a projected integrated study. They were the first three chapters of a compact extended introduction to the study of symbolic logic. There was at least a fourth

---

[3] There existed previous correspondence between Frege and journal editor, Bauch. Bauch joined the philosophy faculty at the University of Jena in 1911, and was a co-founder of the German Philosophical Society in 1917. Bauch promised Frege direct publication access to the journal's pages for his writings and solicited contributions from Frege, allowing Frege to bypass the usual editorial screening and vetting for journal publication on the strength of his accomplishments. The correspondence between Bauch and Frege did not migrate into the *Philosophical and Mathematical Correspondence*, but appears in the original German edition of Frege, *Briefwechsel*, Letters III/1–4, pp. 1–8. Some correspondence appears to have been irrevocably destroyed in WWII. Frege may have welcomed the opportunity to have *carte blanche* to bring out some of his later writings, having been fed up with a career of editorial board misunderstandings and misjudgments of the value of his writings. The fact that Frege began the unpublished essay "Logical Generality" referring to an essay previously published in the same journal where the other *Logische Untersuchungen* appeared testifies to his confidence that the still unfinished essay would definitely find a home in the same journal in due course. It further supports the assumption that Frege's original plan for the *Logische Untersuchungen* included more than the three essays published together, all under Bauch's editorial management. See note 4 below.

uncompleted essay in draft dated from around 1923, on the naturally sub-sequent topic of quantification, titled "Logical Generality." It was evidently meant to be published as the sequel to "Compound Thoughts," to which it makes explicit reference as having appeared about five years earlier in the same journal as the others.[4] Another unfinished *Nachlaß* essay on "Number," judging from the few pages that exist, might have been a fifth possibility for inclusion in the *Logische Untersuchungen* on the grounds that it would be an appropriate successor in the series to the three completed essays, plus the fourth which was in progress but never completed. An essay it would be invaluable to see even in rough draft would have addressed the pressing problem of identity conditions for concept-functions. What is most con-spicuously missing from Frege's essay–chapter drafts and recorded plans for his *Logische Untersuchungen* is a discussion that would defend Frege's resur-rected general functional calculus against the bogey of Russell's paradox.[5]

Frege's three late core essays made several cross-references to one another as moments in a self-consciously developing unified philosophy of logic. The essays are admirable in their selection of topics and focus, taking each basic concept as an opportunity for expanded coverage of Frege's never-ending war on psychologism in logic and mathematics. They offer explana-tions of some of the most fundamental concepts, and, in the case specifically of "Negation," most revolutionary innovations in the history of logic. They are the kinds of remarks concerning his understanding of logical categories that Frege might have profitably offered the world before he unveiled his *Begriffsschrift* to a technically competent but uncomprehending readership. Frege might have written these essays at the beginning of his publishing career. Aside from new arguments and analogies, Frege's approach to the essentials of mathematical logic did not change essentially from start to finish, and this itself is significant in trying to understand Frege as a person, mathematician, and philosopher. If Frege had offered these three late essays at or near the start of his literary exploits, it might have prepared the way in his publication stream for a better appreciation of what his symbolic logic could then be understood as trying to achieve. If Frege had not wanted to proceed in quite this way, he might have reconsidered his choices shortly

---

[4] Frege, "Logical Generality," *Posthumous Writings*, p. 258, opens the essay draft with this explanation: "I published an article in this journal on compound thoughts, in which some space was devoted to hypothetical compound thoughts. It is natural to look for a way of making a transition from these to what in physics, in mathematics and in logic are called *laws*."

[5] Frege, "Number," *Posthumous Writings*, pp. 265–66.

after the dismal reception of his *Begriffsschrift* had registered as an undeniable fact.

Had Frege issued his *Logische Untersuchungen* much earlier, as an effort toward cultivating a proper public awareness of the philosophical background to his functional calculus, potential readers of Frege's *Begriffsschrift* would have better understood the purpose of formalizing a symbolic logic of concept-functions. They would have known something about why it was being offered, how the most basic parts of it were supposed to fit and work together, and why they should take notice.

There were no ideas in any of the three late essays that were new to Frege. There was nothing that had occurred to him suddenly in his senescence and semi-retirement, once the shelving of *Grundgesetze III* had left him free to ponder more intently what he was worrying about behind the curtains all those years. The picture of his plan for three essays and probably two successors was not necessitated by what little is known of their history. Reading backward from the *Logische Untersuchungen* to the *Begriffsschrift* in Frege's body of work, one sees that the general themes of Frege's later logical investigations were latent in his published work in logic and philosophy from the beginning. In retirement he published philosophical reflections on the most basic concepts of his *Begriffsschrift*, leading on the way, insofar as preserved documents indicate, at least to the *Grundlagen*. Frege's ideas in the three essays therefore would also not have been new to his, ahem, careful readers. The three late essays examined at greater length and in more detail some basic concepts of logic that are either largely taken for granted or hinted at only here and there in previous publications. Even an intellect of Frege's gauge, like that of any other type of thinker, takes some things for granted; maybe not as many as lesser thinkers do, but with no guarantee that that which has been presupposed is not after all among the rational structure's philosophically weakest and most vulnerable assumptions.

Frege's choice of topics and their sequence is revealing of his expressive syntactical constructivism. The essays were developed over time as though in dress rehearsal from two decades previously in unpublished writings. He began with *Gedanken*, which is literally to say thoughts, by which Frege meant propositions; which is further to say predications of properties, qualities, or relations, to existent entities. These constructions alone have truth-value in Frege's theory. They alone have referential meaning, referring to the True or the False, depending on their sense-meaning and the world's external truth-making or truth-breaking circumstances. All other constructions are referentially meaningless in Fregean propositional semantics, which, if they have Fregean sense, does not prevent them from being Fregean *Gedanken*. Like the referentially empty but not senseless proper name "Sherlock Holmes," the sentence "Sherlock Holmes is a detective" has Fregean sense without reference, without referring to the True or the False. The sense of the simplest predication is compositionally determined by the senses of the proper names of putative objects to which a concept-function is predicated. After that, it is up to truth-functions to produce referentially transparent compound thoughts, and to intensional operators to produce what for Frege were mostly logically uninteresting intensional or referentially opaque proposition-building contexts.

The difference is that, where Frege used the word "thought" in his early writings, in explaining the "*Horizontal*" or, as it was originally named, *Inhaltsstrich* as the extendable horizontal bar in *Begriffsschrift* notation indicating an assertible proposition or *Gedanke* following at the right, in 1918, thirty-nine years later, he devoted an entire essay to exploring the concept of thought and its expression in language, interpreted as the content of a sentence's propositional meaning in a third realm of being beyond the physical and abstract. It is effectively what the Fregean thought proposes, asserts, or says in a true or false predication of a property construed as a concept-function to a proper name for an existent argument-object. Frege clarified in a sentence or two in his early writings that what he meant by *thought* (*der Gedanke*) was not a real-time psychological occurrence. Thoughts belong instead to a third realm where their compositional sentential sense and reference, despite being mind-independent, are capable of undergoing change, particularly in contingent truth-value as real-time events unfold that are described in meaningful predications. The target case unmentioned by Frege seems to have been true or false sentences, especially about apparently open-ended future events like those Aristotle considered in *De Interpretatione* 9, 19a30–19b4, such as that, regardless of any intervening factors, it is eternally true or eternally false that there will be a sea battle tomorrow. Frege allowed that a proposition in the third ontic realm of mind-independent but change-supporting thoughts could transition from having no truth-value, the sea battle tomorrow not, at least yet, if ever, being an existent entity to which reference in Frege's logic would become possible, to making reference to the True or the False, as resulting truth-making and truth-breaking changing circumstances dictate.

In "Negation," Frege considered the truth-functional analysis of "not" as a concept-function on the truth-value of any and every Fregean thought. This advance marked the most progressive aspect of Frege's logic. The story of his intellectual development emphasizes truth-functional external propositional negation as setting Frege's fully algebraic general functional calculus apart from Boole and the stodgy pack of Aristotelian–Victorian syllogistic term logicians still trying to keep the old car running. Truth-functional negation distinguishes Frege's functional calculus as a fully algebraic logic of the kind still favored today in the inherited form of Frege's *Begriffsschrift* minus his *begriffsschriftliche* symbolism. The choice unfortunately led Frege into dangerous shoals.

Truth-functional negation and the material conditional, those two truth-functionally defined logical connectives in Frege's *Begriffsschrift*, together with related derivable truth-functions explained in the third logical investigation on "Compound Thoughts," were also not new ideas for Frege between 1918 and 1923. Allowing for all the lead-time needed for the essays to have been written, worked, and reworked prior to 1918, plus time for them to be set and corrected in proof, publication queues, and the like, much of it occurring during Frege's later publication dark ages, the work is believed to have commenced in some cases as early as 1906, with a fine-tuning of manuscripts that can be dated earlier still to the late 1890s in other cases.

The three late essays of his *Logische Untersuchungen* explain what Frege had always thought about these matters, rather than reporting new discoveries he had made since 1903. He offered guidance at last to some of his pivotal philosophical background. The topics were reasonably interpreted as being among those he had previously assumed his readers would agree with him in assuming without argument. It was almost as though in doing so Frege was revealing something too personal about himself that he could only describe from the perspective of old age and its reflective wisdom. He may equally have supposed that these were obvious concepts and categories that he would never have previously imagined any of his readers fit to turn the page would need to have explained. He was willing to go back over this terrain, more for his own sake moving in extreme slow-motion, making sure again of his starting-place in mathematical logic, while searching for clues to account for the vulnerability of *Grundgesetze* arithmetic to Russell's fiendish paradox.

There was another reason also, one that reflected an outlook characteristic of Fregean methodology. Considered from an energy economy standpoint, in this span of years, as Frege turned from seventy to seventy-five, retiring from the university at seventy in 1918, he did not need to publish anything. His main reason for writing after the first disappointments in the reception of his work was probably not the brass ring of academic promotion. He still had something worthwhile to say, despite all the setbacks his research program had suffered. One could retire from teaching any subject, including mathematics and philosophy, but one could not as easily retire from being a philosopher. Frege may have always wanted to explain in detailed and mostly nontechnical prose the basic concepts he considered vital to mathematical logic. He never had the leisure while funneling his efforts into the more demanding exposition and formal derivations of pure logicistic arithmetic to devote to these fundamental topics the close attention he finally decided they deserved.

The three late essays are important to consider, not only because of their intrinsic philosophical content, their message for logicians and philosophers today, but because of the light they shed on Frege's final thoughts and the continuation of logical–philosophical commitments he seemed to have held dear throughout his life. They give us a glimpse at the continuity and development of his philosophy in his final publications considered as his last confidences. That is the case even when they are not totally new compositions, even when they merely weave new arguments and analogies around beliefs Frege had implicitly presupposed, limiting himself from the beginning of his philosophical work to dropping occasional hints. Even when the essays merely tightened the laces in revisions of papers that had been drafted many years before, there is much to learn about Frege from this folio of essays and from the fact that he chose at this late date to publish them. He created a cognitive space in which to check his once-trusted mathematical intuition. As though Frege were learning to walk again, the hope may have been that he would gradually regain confidence in being able to perceive properly formulated mathematical truths. Selected writings unpublished in Frege's lifetime allow us to offer suggestions as to his state of mind in these winding-down years. Frege's unpublished papers collected in his *Nachlaß* sample the progression of his thought from the 1870s to 1924–1925.

Thoughts as Predications

In the three *Logische Untersuchungen* essays Frege crafted his distinctions, just as he had earlier done in his *Grundlagen*, without using *Begriffsschrift* symbolic notation. He relied entirely instead on ordinary intelligent talk about the components of logic and truth-functional relations, beginning with NOT and AND as logical connectives. The discussion was based on how Fregean thoughts in a third realm neither physical nor abstract as opposed to occurrent psychological ideas can be truth-functionally compounded in logical proposition-building operations. Frege worked forward from this intuitive starting-place to explain NOT and IF-THEN as basic truth-functional relations of the pictorial symbolism of his *Begriffsschrift* and *Grundgesetze*.

Psychological ideas cannot be truth-functionally compounded according to Frege. Ephemeral ideas as opposed to third-realm mind-independent objective thoughts or propositions are subjectively existent momentary psychological episodes that cannot serve as argument-objects for abstract truth-functions. Ideas do not hold still, is one way to put the objection. If we are speaking of the events of an individual's passing flickers of consciousness, then truth-functioning conjoining ideas does not make sense. If I think on one occasion that Jupiter is larger than Mars, and on another occasion that Mars is smaller than Earth, then I might have forgotten my thinking the first thought by the time I come around to thinking the second thought. There need be no moment of time at which I am thinking the conjunction of both thoughts. That kind of anomaly shows that conjunction is not a mind-dependent relation of psychological occurrences, but concerns something that does not reside like moments of subjective consciousness in physical time and space. Frege argued that we cannot truth-functionally conjoin or negate the existence of occurrent psychological ideas as a truth-functional operation. We can nevertheless acknowledge that some interesting ideas are ideas about Fregean thoughts that can be expressed in meaning content as a conjunction of the right choice of third-realm Fregean thoughts. If Fregean thoughts are not psychological occurrences, what then are they?

One, too easy, answer as to what Frege means by a "thought" is that it is whatever can appear at the end of a *begriffsschriftliche* "*Horizontal*" bar, or *Inhaltsstrich* in the terminology for his logical symbolism that Frege originally proposed. The question is what entitles a symbol to stand at the front of a content-stroke as an assertible proposition or thought. A thought for Frege is not an occurrent psychological episode, but rather the meaning contents or proposition expressed in certain kinds of possible events of consciousness, represented symbolically by means of colloquial or mathematical language. It is the potentially alterable possession of abstract truth or falsehood that an expression is used to express. As such, Fregean thoughts are in one sense similar to abstract entities, including numbers and logical–mathematical relations, all of which Frege interpreted as objectively mind-independent. Frege construed *Gedanken* as constituting a third metaphysical category, beyond the physical and the abstract. Thoughts were not mixed up with numbers in the Platonic realist ontic order, but nor were they physical spatiotemporal entities. They were obviously not physical. Nor were they abstract, if some thoughts could change their truth-values as the contingent events they describe unfold in real space and time.

Aristotle's *De Interpretatione* problem of the sea battle tomorrow was avoided by Frege's third realm category of thoughts, though one wonders at what cost. If it were eternally true that there will be a sea battle tomorrow then it could not be prevented no matter what the naval chain of command were to decide. If not, then nothing could be done to bring about the sea battle that eternal falsehood of the proposition precludes. Semantic determinism that otherwise squelches free will and moral responsibility as often conceived is circumvented in Frege's theory of thoughts. The finesse is achieved by positing a third non-physical and non-abstract realm of thoughts where some undergo changes of truth-value.

He could have avoided misconceptions about his semantics and ontology, the most basic elements of his metaphysics of logic in establishing its referential domain, if he had chosen a different unequivocally extrapsychological term for the relata of logical operations. He invited unnecessary confusions by calling the abstract arguments of truth-functions "thoughts," when they were meant to be the third-realm meaning contents of the epiphenomenal occurrent psychological thoughts that thinkers think, in moments of consciousness when third-realm Fregean thoughts are apprehended or entertained. The Fregean third-realm thought that there will be a sea battle tomorrow can change from having no reference to the True or the False to referring to one truth-value or the other, as real-time-and-space events on the sea develop.

The same is true for Frege's referential semantics of proper names. Prior to conception I can name my first child C_1 in the sense of assigning Fregean sense to the term "C_1." If the name sticks – and why would it not? – then, if and when my first child is born, the proper name "C_1" goes from having no reference but only thin Fregean sense, meaning little more than my projected first-born, to acquiring or revealing additional sense and transitioning at a particular moment of time from having no reference to referring to a temporally existing entity. Frege wanted a reference domain where he could park objects that were neither physical nor abstract, but capable of undergoing changes in their properties, notably truth-value, to which absolutely unalterable abstract entities like numbers were not considered subject.

Why numbers, unlike Fregean thoughts, should be immune from changes in properties was unexplained. Can we not meaningfully assert that the number 1 changes from not numbering any child of mine to numbering my children when C_1 is born? How is that supposed to be different from the Fregean thought "C_1 is my first-born" changing from having no truth-value reference to being true and referring to the True the instant that C_1 is born? Frege thought he needed a special order of existent non-physical objects capable of undergoing semantic change and brazenly posited a third realm. He did not create the realm. He was driven by philosophical reasoning to recognize its existence. He may in the process have opened the gates to treating all so-called abstract entities as third-realm existents capable of undergoing semantic change. That would collapse the abstract and third realms, leaving Frege with two ontic subdomains instead of three, namely the physical and the quasi-abstract of non-physical things, some of which change some of their properties over time.

Fregean thoughts are semantically distinguished from other kinds of elements in Frege's logic. They are different than proper names, including definite descriptions and concept-functions, including truth-functions and other more specifically arithmetical functions. Fregean thoughts alone among all these entities can have a truth-value, without which they are incapable of serving as the argument-objects of truth-functions. They refer, if they refer at all, to only one of two existent entities, the True or the False. To say, in a structurally basic application, that object a has property or function-concept F, Fa, also roughly in Frege's script, before truth-functions are applied, is to say something with sense, but not necessarily with reference. The elementary predication in particular compositionally for Frege has no reference to the True or the False if object a does not exist and proper name "a" has no individual reference. Fregean thoughts possessing truth-values are exclusively the arguments of truth-functions. In his *Begriffsschrift* and *Grundgesetze* Frege relied on two truth-functions, negation and the material conditional. He did not try to distinguish sharply between atomic and molecular thoughts. A negated thought is already the simplest type of compound thought, although Frege reserved the terminology specifically for combinations of more than one thought. The point is that for Frege, as in modern algebraic propositional logic generally, negation can take as its arguments any propositions of any internal truth-functional complexity. A negated conditional is manifestly not the simplest negation or the simplest conditional. The same is obviously true of the material conditional, whose two argument places can be occupied not only by the simplest Fregean thoughts, predications of the form Fa, but, again, like negation, by any Fregean thought of any internal truth-functional complexity.

Frege's chief concern in "Thought" was to argue that *Gedanken*, thoughts in his sense, are not psychological episodes. The latter he distinguished as *Ideen* (ideas), *Bilder* (images), and *Vorstellungen* (presentations). Thoughts themselves are not psychological, for Frege, although ideas of certain kinds are capable of expressing thoughts. Thoughts are third-realm meanings, with sense and reference reflected potentially in linguistic and, in principle, also artistic expression. We can think of Fregean thoughts as all the true or false predications of properties to existent objects that could possibly exist. If my wagon is red, then Red(my(wagon(a))) = the True (short for V(Red(my(wagon(a)))) = the True), and otherwise = the False. If it is false that my wagon is red, then it will be true instead that Not(red(my (wagon(a)))) = the True. "Thought" introduces, as Frege never previously took the opportunity to explain, the basic components of propositional truth-functional logic that underlie the *Begriffsschrift* theory of quantity in Frege's general functional calculus. Meanings are analyzed by reference to Frege's fully explicated algebraic logical structures. Analysis begins with any minimally predicational function(argument) = value identity statement. The structure of Red(my(wagon(a))) = the True implies My (wagon(a)) = the True, signifying that the object in question belongs to me as one of my possessions. Were object a not my wagon, then it need not be the case that my wagon is red, even if a is red. Wagon(a) is structurally here the most basic Fregean thought. If a is not a wagon, then questions of the ownership and color of object *a* do not arise. If *a* = 1, for example, then *a* is not in anyone's legal possession, just as it has no color.

The process of constructing and analyzing meanings gets started in Frege's logic as a task of clarification and logical synthesis of Fregean thoughts. The purpose of Frege's first essay of 1918 was to explain the fundamental units of meaning in the functional calculus, the argument-objects to which the truth-functions negation, conjunction, and material conditional are applied in order to produce compound thoughts. Next in natural order after "Compound Thoughts" was to have been a discussion of logical universality, the predicate-quantificational structure of the general functional calculus. As seen in Frege's *Nachlaß*, the essay was more than just begun, after which Frege did not live to see its further development through to completion.[6]

Against Psychologism in the Foundations of Logic

The first order of business for Frege, and the main anti-psychologistic purpose of "Thought," was to distinguish Fregean thoughts from the semantic ephemera of occurrent psychological ideas. Frege began with truth and truth-conditions for Fregean thoughts. He did not quite explain things in this way, but it appears natural to suppose that, if thoughts are truth-bearers, the things that uniquely of all other entities in the logic's domain can be true or false, if they alone are understood when referentially meaningful to designate the True or the False, then Fregean thoughts might best be explained through an understanding of the concept of truth. The opening sentence of the essay gestures suggestively in this direction, as though there might be other possibilities. "Just as 'beautiful' points the way for aesthetics and 'good' for ethics," Frege wrote, "so do words like 'true' for logic."[7] While soft-selling the proposal, Frege believed that there was no other value by which to understand what he elsewhere openly avowed as the "normative" nature of logic, taking as its value truth in its appointed sphere, rather than beauty, virtue, or the good.[8]

---

[6] The editors of Frege's *Posthumous Writings* in English translation remark in commenting on the five printed pages of "Logical Generality," that, having established the date of the manuscript, note 1, p. 258, "We may accept further that Frege intended to develop this fragment into a fourth part of this series of essays."

[7] Frege, "Thought," *Logical Investigations*, p. 1.

[8] Frege, "Logic" [1897], *Posthumous Writings*, p. 128.

Frege argued that ideas as pictures swept along in the conscious flow of subjective experience could not possibly be truth-value bearers, referring sometimes to the True and sometimes to the False. The problem, according to Frege, was that ideas could not stand in correct or incorrect correspondence to anything other than other ideas. We can compare two ideas, he allows, because they are both ideas. We cannot compare an idea with reality, precisely because they are ontically different kinds of things. He maintained that

A correspondence, moreover, can only be perfect if the corresponding things coincide and so are not just different things. It is supposed to be possible to test the genuineness of a banknote by comparing it stereoscopically with a genuine one. But it would be ridiculous to try to compare a gold piece stereoscopically with a twenty-mark note. It would only be possible to compare an idea with a thing if the thing were an idea too.[9]

Frege's analogy is striking; it delivers a certain rhetorical punch. Who can deny that we cannot compare a gold coin under the microscope with a 20 Mark note in order to establish that either one is authentic? We need a criterion of genuineness that applies only to currency of the purported same kind, the real thing to which we can look for characteristic similarities or dissimilarities in prospective counterfeits. The question is whether this is just like the situation involved in trying to compare an idea as a picture of reality with the reality it is intended to picture. Frege is not alone in holding that ideas can be compared only with other ideas. It is a staple of phenomenalism in perception theory to consider that all we as finite thinkers are ever privileged to compare with one another are percepts. We never have direct access to a mind-independent phenomenal reality beyond the pageant of perceptions in passing occurrent moments of consciousness. We can compare occurrent percepts with one another and with memories of an experience that are also ideas, but never with anything outside the orbit of ideas.

The proposal was straightforward. Frege was nevertheless concerned that the model of comparing one idea with another in the sense of psychological occurrences did not provide a sufficiently strong correspondence to constitute a criterion of truth. The fact that in Frege's example there existed a positive correspondence between markings on a

---

[9] Frege, "Thought," p. 3. Outstanding among the many commentaries on Frege's essay is an article by Gregory Currie, "Frege on Thoughts," *Mind*, 89 (1980), pp. 234–48. For an earlier philosophical rather than historical study, see John Perry, "Frege on Demonstratives," *The Philosophical Review*, 86 (1977), pp. 474–97.

metal coin and those on its equivalent in paper money did not determine whether either one was genuine, since there was nothing in principle to exclude both being phony. The microscopic comparison of two purported like-numbered units of money works only if one is known on independent grounds to be authentic, and only if the manufacture of money precludes the kinds of discrepancies that are likely to be detected under close examination of a counterfeit. We can no more determine truth in the sense of positive pictorial correspondence between an idea and reality than we can decide of a random coin and random bill which, if either, is genuine by comparing their external features. Wittgenstein would put forward much the same point later, years after Frege's death, in *Philosophical Investigations* §265, concerning criteria of correctness for naming a private sensation as an individual entity: "If the mental image of the [railroad] time-table could not be *tested* for correctness, how could it confirm the correctness of the first memory? (As if someone were to buy several copies of the morning paper to assure himself that what it said was true.)"[10] Comparing one idea with another idea similarly does not guarantee the access to the objective truth or falsehood of a proposition that Frege required. It was for the sake of this discrepancy that he would not accept the identification of a thought possessing semantic properties with an idea as a fleeting psychological occurrence. That consideration seems to rule out the possibility of understanding occurrent psychological ideas as truth-bearers by virtue of their not being capable of embodying a faithful pictorial depiction of the states of affairs they are supposed to represent.

The question for Frege throughout was the category or kind of thing subsuming truth-bearers. What kinds of things can or cannot have truth-value? He rejected the ephemeral ideas flitting through a thinking subject's consciousness as incapable of being true or false, at least insofar as one popular theory has it they are or are not correct images of a psychologically represented reality. We gain no advantage for truth, as with Wittgenstein's morning newspaper copies, in comparing one idea with another. Comparing an idea with the reality it may be thought to represent, even if attainable, would not allow us to see around the corners of our subjective representations of reality to compare them in direct representational confrontation with mind-independent reality itself.

---

[10] Wittgenstein, *Philosophical Investigations* §265.

Such imagined comparison could no more verify truth in the case of positive representational correspondences than even the most meticulous comparison of a coin with paper currency of the same denomination. Frege was directed for an answer to his first problem away from the lure of spatiotemporal psychological phenomena toward something mind-independent if not abstract. He continued as follows:

> I now return to the question: is a thought an idea? If other people can assent to the thought I express in the Pythagorean theorem just as I do, then it does not belong to the content of my consciousness, I am not its owner; yet I can, nevertheless, acknowledge it as true. However, if what is taken to be the content of the Pythagorean theorem by me and by somebody else is not the same thought at all, we should not really say "*the* Pythagorean theorem," but "*my* Pythagorean theorem," "*his* Pythagorean theorem," and these would be different, for the sense necessarily goes with the sentence.[11]

The crucial consideration for Frege was whether or not several thinkers could assent to the same thought expressed by the same sentence. This is normally expected of successful communication in any symbolic sign system, from colloquial street slang to Frege's *Begriffsschrift*. There must be something objective to serve as truth-bearer, if a thought correctly understood is not merely detained in the possession of any particular thinker or thinker's consciousness, but can be shared around as different thinkers collectively understand the meaning of a sentence and come, at least some of them, to share the opinion that the same sentence is true or is false in a social linguistic community. Frege's emphasis was on truth as the value of logic analogous to beauty and virtue or the good. Such facts Frege also took to prove that the meanings of sentences were objective, not privately subjectively owned by individual thinkers, each possessing his or her own meaning, like Wittgenstein's beetle in a box, described years afterward in *Philosophical Investigations* §293.

We do not typically speak of *my* Pythagorean theorem being true and *your* Pythagorean theorem being true, but rather of *the* Pythagorean theorem's truth. Frege rightly finds the idea of subjective truth-ownership preposterous, just as he would in the case of different thinkers possessing different number 3s when contemplating the truth of the Fregean thought that 3 is a prime number. He added the following:

> If every thought requires an owner and belongs to the contents of his consciousness, then the thought has this owner alone; and there is no science common to many on

[11] Frege, "Thought," p. 16.

which many could work, but perhaps I have my science, a totality of thoughts whose owner I am, and another person has his. Each of us is concerned with the contents of his own consciousness. No contradiction between the two sciences would then be possible, and it would really be idle to dispute about truth; as idle, indeed almost as ludicrous, as for two people to dispute about whether a hundred-mark note were genuine, where each meant the one he himself had in his pocket and understood the word "genuine" in his own particular sense. If someone takes thoughts to be ideas, what he then accepts as true is, on his own view, the content of consciousness, and does not properly concern other people at all. If he heard from me the opinion that a thought is not an idea he could not dispute it, for, indeed, it would not now concern him.

So the result seems to be: thoughts are neither things in the external world nor ideas.[12]

Frege's conclusion establishes a third-realm domain of thoughts as truth-value bearers in logic. Fregean thoughts as objective truth-bearers provide the objective subject matter, in the form of arguments to which all truth-functions, negation, conjunction, and the material conditional, apply, and by which the propositional understructures of logical inference are determined. They are independent of our ideas of them, existing, as Frege supposed, almost as though in the abstract, subject only in some instances to truth-value alterations. They consequently possess whatever truth-values belong to them independently of subjective thinking and opinion. Here was the objectivity that Frege sought all along for logic, that he presupposed must be true. It underwrote his frequent heated polemics against psychologism's wolves in sheep's clothing in the philosophical foundations of mathematics. There was a metaphysics of physical entities existing in space and time, from which, Frege assumed without argument in what was actually a matter of enormous controversy, ideas, passing moments of consciousness, and ephemeral psychological occurrences were excluded on account of their being something other than physical entities, not reducible in any case, insofar as he seems to have been concerned, to "things in the external world."

The Realm of Pure Thought

Although he did not immediately develop the suggestion, Frege clearly announced himself as an *externalist* of sorts in the philosophy of mind. Meaning is not contained within a thinker's episodic consciousness, but

[12] *Ibid.*, p. 17.

involves the thinker in an external relation to objective meanings, Fregean thoughts or propositions. Frege invoked a distinction he did not demonstrate or try to defend concerning the metaphysics of the psychological and the requirements of sense-meaning and reference. He planted his flag for another distinct ontic order specially postulated for Fregean thoughts as neither external perceivable physical objects nor internal mental objects or ideas. He drew the expected conclusion:

A third realm must be recognized. Anything belonging to this realm has it in common with ideas that it cannot be perceived by the senses, but has it in common with things that it does not need an owner so as to belong to the contents of his consciousness. Thus for example the thought we have expressed in the Pythagorean theorem is timelessly true, true independently of whether anyone takes it to be true. It needs no owner. It is not true only from the time when it is discovered; just as a planet, even before anyone saw it, was in interaction with other planets.[13]

That Fregean thoughts "need no owner" is a significant declaration. Frege made it clear that, as a consequence of their supreme objectivity, thoughts in his technical sense are mind-independent. To put the matter counterfactually, Fregean *Gedanken* would exist in the abstract, even if there never existed an intelligence capable of thinking them. Imagine that there are no psychological subjects who could entertain in real-time-and-space moments of consciousness the Fregean thoughts that are the third-realm contents of occurrent ideation, and we have still invoked a scenario in which there are Fregean thoughts that no one happens to be able to think. The Pythagorean theorem, to follow Frege's example, considered in itself as a mind-independent proposition, is a certified Fregean thought. It is not whatever is presented as the theorem to individual thinkers, all of whom understand the proposition and may happen to recognize its truth, but the referential meaning of the proper name in designating the theorem.

A pure thought for Frege was a thought that is not contaminated by psychology. Frege's category is similar to Kant's in his conceptual foundations of the metaphysics of morals. Kant analogously held that a purely moral motivation to act must not be diluted by consideration of psychological factors in pleasure or satisfaction of desire, whether of one's own or that of others.[14] A Fregean pure thought was likewise meant to be

[13] *Ibid.*, pp. 17–18.
[14] Kant, *Grundlegung zur Metaphysik der Sitten* (*Groundwork to the Metaphysics of Morals*). See the Königlich Preußische Akademie der Wissenschaften edition, Volume IV, pp. 393–97.

the meaningful sense content of a propositional (*Satzsinn*) psychological episode, abstracted from any of the contingencies of the psychological episode as an occurrence in real space and time. A Fregean pure thought, but for its propensity to change truth-value, is what contemporary philosophy characterizes as an abstract proposition that can be expressed in multiple languages and by mental events that are not themselves pure thoughts. They are only thoughts in the ordinary nontechnical, non-Fregean lived-through occurrent psychological or phenomenological sense. The further analogy is between Fregean thoughts as a third realm and their real-time psychological apprehendings or entertainings, on the one hand, and on the other the relation holding between abstract numbers and the concrete numerals, in particular arithmetical symbolisms, by which the numbers are denoted. Psychological episodes of entertaining and reasoning with and about pure thoughts are themselves necessarily impure, touched by logical contingency. They are limited by happenstance events in the accidental existences of psychologically advanced thinking subjects. The important distinction is that for Frege a pure thought was not a kind or category of thought in the sense of the thoughts we entertain and string together into inferences in episodic thinking. It was rather, by appeal to an incidental psychological criterion, the nearly abstract third-realm propositional contents of all such logically possible psychological apprehendings, regardless of whether or not they are ever experienced. Fregean thoughts transcend the subjectivity of all thinking understood in phenomenological terms as ontically Platonically independent of mind.

Frege now turns the tables on an interesting objection. It has to do with the thorny question of indexicals and demonstratives, the personal pronoun serving as illustration. Frege considers the following criticism:

[S]omeone perhaps objects: if I think I have no pain at the moment, does not the word "I" answer to something in the content of my consciousness? And is that not an idea? That may be so. A certain idea in my consciousness may be associated with the idea of the word "I." But then this is one idea among other ideas, and I am its owner as I am the owner of the other ideas. I have an idea of myself, but I am not identical with this idea. What is a content of my consciousness, my idea, should be sharply distinguished from what is an object of my thought. Therefore the thesis that only what belongs to the content of my consciousness can be the object of my awareness, of my thought, is false.[15]

---

[15] Frege, "Thought," p. 22.

The complaint is that the use of a personal pronoun in trying to express a truth in or about the thinker's psychological life, reflexively referring to the thinking subject, cannot be altogether mind-independent as an objective truth. It must instead make essential reference directly to the mind of the individual thinking subject, as grammarians and linguists say, *indexically*. The subject is effectively saying that something is true demonstratively of *this* thinking subject, which means for thinkers in our experience of herself or himself. Thought content, as has been argued on various grounds in philosophy during and since Frege's time, is apparently unintelligible if an attempt is made to understand it at a higher, more abstract and objective "third person" level that is supposed to be altogether independent of the contingencies of an individual think-er's lived-through moments of consciousness. Frege's reply is to draw a sharp distinction between ideas in particular and objects of a thinking subject's acquaintance more generally. He consciously or unconsciously repeats a battle cry of Berkeley's, namely that the subject of ideas cannot itself be an idea.[16] The point is persuasively made:

As the result of these last considerations I lay down the following: not everything that can be the object of my acquaintance is an idea. I, being owner of ideas, am not myself an idea. Nothing now stops me from acknowledging other men to be the owners of ideas, just as I am myself. And, once given the possibility, the probability is very great, so great that it is in my opinion no longer distinguishable from certainty. Would there be a science of history otherwise? Would not all moral theory, all law, otherwise collapse? What would be left of religion? The natural sciences too could only be assessed as fables like astrology and alchemy ... Not everything is an idea. Thus I can also acknowledge thoughts as independent of me; other men can grasp them just as much as I; I can acknowledge a science in which many can be engaged in research. We are not the owners of thoughts as we are owners of our ideas. We do not *have* a thought as we have, say, a sense-impression, but we also do not *see* a thought as we see, say, a star. So it is advisable to choose a special expression; the word "grasp" suggests itself for the purpose. To the grasping of thoughts there must then correspond a special mental capacity, the power of thinking.[17]

Frege said in the above, somewhat off-handedly, "Not everything is an idea. Thus I can also acknowledge thoughts as independent of me." The phrasing requires analysis. There are ideas about myself in which index-ical reference may be indispensable. Among the thoughts a thinking subject grasps, a correct theory of meaning "can *also* acknowledge

[16] Berkeley, *Three Dialogues Between Hylas and Philonous*, pp. 231–32.
[17] Frege, "Thought," pp. 24–25.

thoughts as independent" of the thinker. The implication seems to be that Frege wants to treat psychological experiences as ideational but not propositional. They are ostensibly about the individual thinking subject, but do not readily generalize to a level of objectivity beyond personal subjectivity. That would imply that there are no "I" or "me" Fregean thoughts or propositions. They would be categorically excluded from the subdomain of all and only Fregean *Gedanken*, thoughts or propositions possessing objective truth-value. This maneuver, whatever its theoretical virtues, is awkward in ways that Frege did not appear to appreciate.

If thoughts are truth-value bearers, the Fregean referential meaning of which is the objective True or the objective False, and if indexical references do not lend themselves to abstraction beyond the individual thinker's existence and psychological condition, then Frege cannot explain but is committing himself to setting aside the plain fact that it may be true or false that I am thirsty when I entertain or linguistically express the idea. Surely I can be honest or deceitful in expressing the thought that I am thirsty, perhaps even to myself. Grammatically, the fact that we have no hesitation in prefacing "I am thirsty" in appropriate contexts with a "that" clause – as when someone says "I can no longer conceal the fact *that* I am thirsty" – points toward the instantiation of a genuine proposition or Fregean thought. This is a problem Frege did not slow down to consider. Instead he plunged even more confidently ahead in the same unreconnoitered direction, maintaining that

In thinking we do not produce thoughts, we grasp them. For what I have called thoughts stand in the closest connexion with truth. What I acknowledge as true, I judge to be true quite apart from my acknowledging its truth or even thinking about it. That someone thinks it has nothing to do with the truth of a thought.[18]

Here is the rub. The problem prompts drastic action in Wittgenstein's *Tractatus* in response to the logical status of propositional attitudes. The framework of meaning theory assumptions Wittgenstein considers there makes proposition-building involving thinking subjects and their psychological states ostensibly directed at a proposition or Fregean thought unabashedly non-truth-functional, standing in violation of what Wittgenstein establishes as the *Tractatus*'s general form of proposition. The discrepancy moves Wittgenstein to argue on a lacerating interpretation of Ockham's razor that there exist no psychological subjects and hence

---

[18] Frege, "Thought," p. 25.

no propositional attitudes or any other kind of psychological attitude. These postulates are superfluous, Wittgenstein reasons. They are not needed to make sense of meaning, according to his hypothetical logical–metaphysical–semantic theory. Since they are not needed, they are eliminated from the ontology by Wittgenstein's hard use of Ockham's razor.[19]

Truth-Functional Negation

There are two kinds of negation, internal and external. Internal negation is at home in Aristotelian or Aristotelian–Victorian syllogistic term logic, including Boole's partial algebraization. Predicate complementation in term logic systems allows property F and internally negated or complementary property non-F to be predicated of a subject, and in particular of all objects satisfying a subject-term. External negation did not exist in symbolic logic until Frege invented a special sign for it, the perpendicular dangling tab in his *Begriffsschrift*. This simple idea is so widely understood today that we must remind ourselves that in a definite span of past time Frege needed to establish truth-value input–output correlations for negation as a truth-function reversing input values referentially from the True to the False, and from the False to the True.[20] It is in some ways the most beautiful miniature conceptual engineering in all of Frege's logic.

Differences between term logic internal negation in non-Fa, object a having property non-F, versus fully algebraic external propositional negation in such constructions as it is not-the-case that Fa, or $\neg Fa$, are explicit in the Aristotelian square of opposition. There the universal categorical A-sentence, "All S are P," is *not* the *contradictory* of the E-categorical sentence, "All S are non-P," in the square, but only its *contrary*. This means that not both A and E categoricals can be true, although, unlike contradictions, both can be false. Frege invented a truth-functional sign for negation as an operation on Fregean thoughts, reversing whatever truth-value they may have, and building on the explanations of the objective subject matter of logic from his first essay in this suite of three. When a Fregean thought is available, the first thing one can do with it is negate it, by denying that it is true or affirming that it

---

[19] Wittgenstein, *Tractatus Logico-Philosophicus* 5.54–5.5422.

[20] See Laurence R. Horn, *A Natural History of Negation* (Stanford: Center for the Study of Language and Information, 2001).

is false, thereby expressing the opposite of whatever propositional content the unnegated thought conveys.

The topic of negation arises naturally for Frege as a continuation of his concern in the essay "Thought" with the concept of truth as defining the value at which logic aims. It is what makes logic normative, according to Frege. He invokes an analogy with the concept of beauty that he says similarly drives aesthetics, and the concept of virtue or the good, by which ethics in moral philosophy is oriented. We unhesitatingly say that there are good and bad arguments, good and bad logical inferences, which we may also choose to call logical or illogical inferences, if we munificently consider them inferences at all when they logically fail so spectacularly. If a basic Fregean thought affirms the truth of the state of affairs the thought represents, then its negation denies its truth or equivalently affirms its falsehood. The concept of negation is considered so fundamental to logic today that it is hard to imagine the history of the subject proceding for thousands of years without a truth-functional propositional NOT serving the intuitive expectations of external negation. Needless to say, the word "not" and cognates in developed languages are used every day, but never as external truth-functional propositional negation in a symbolic logic. Until Frege's fully algebraized symbolic logic added to the horizontal content-stroke a short hanging vertical bar to *negate* the Fregean thought symbolized at the far-upper-right end of a *Begriffsschrift* logical formula, logicians never seemed to miss what previously they had never had to work with.

Truth-functional propositional negation was presented without much fanfare in Frege's 1874 *Begriffsschrift*. It took the stage with next to no philosophical declaration, as though there were nothing of much significance about negation that in symbolic logic as it had developed up to that point had not always been understood. This was marvelous naïvety or facetious aplomb. In his second important 1918 essay devoted to the topic, "Negation," Frege turned to the truth-functional operator he had first put in place more than forty years before for more detailed discussion. What could be simpler in logic than negation? There are predicative assertions expressible in the logic, for each of which there are also negations denying the assertions. What more could there possibly be to say about it? For Frege, understanding the most basic elements of logic was the primary point of the later essays. He considered the most basic facts more patiently than ever before, looking for clues and false leads. He searched most carefully where no trouble was suspected. Throughout his examination of truth-functional negation, Frege nowhere evinced a sense of how dangerous a truth-functional interpretation of colloquial negation can become. Nor did he pause to wonder why truth-functional negation had previously been cautiously resisted in symbolic logic. Frege offered some philosophical explanation alongside technical background to the first and most basic unary truth-function:

> A propositional question contains a demand that we should either acknowledge the truth of a thought, or reject it as false. In order that we may meet this demand correctly, two things are requisite: first, the wording of the question must enable us to recognize without any doubt the thought that is referred to; secondly, this thought must not belong to fiction. I always assume in what follows that these conditions are fulfilled. The answer to a question is an assertion based upon a judgement; this is so equally whether the answer is affirmative or negative.[21]

The role of truth in understanding the logic of Fregean thoughts was unmistakably emphasized by Frege as analogous to the concepts "good" in ethics and "beauty" in aesthetics. Fregean thoughts reformulated grammatically as questions "demand" of those capable of grasping their meaning that we accept as true or reject as false whatever referentially meaningful thoughts are presented for deliberation.

The Argument of Frege's Essay on Negation

Looking ahead to his treatment of compound thoughts in the third and final published essay, Frege considered how truth-functional compounding of thoughts can affect their ability to be "grasped by several people as one and the same thing." He referred in particular to a material conditional that is true as a whole compound Fregean thought, although at least one of its component Fregean thoughts is false. Logically, the conditional is false only when its antecedent or "if" component Fregean thought is true and its consequent or "then" component Fregean thought is false. The conditional remains true when its antecedent is false and when its consequent is indifferently either true or false.

Frege held that a material conditional, taking it as his test case, can be apprehended by several thinkers as a single entity satisfying specific truth-functional identity conditions. He further took this to show that

---

[21] Frege, "Thought," p. 31.

compound Fregean thoughts were not merely ideas flitting through moments of consciousness in which the mind grasps third-realm objective mind-independent Fregean thoughts. Frege marked a difference between, on the one hand, multiple thinkers being able to grasp a compound thought as a whole, despite its having false components, depending on the relevant truth-functions and truth-values of the Fregean thoughts that the truth-functions take as argument-objects, and on the other hand the inability of multiple thinkers to grasp the false component Fregean thoughts of true compound Fregean thoughts.

Why should this be? What difference between true and false Fregean thoughts accounts for Frege's conclusion that many thinkers can grasp the truth of a whole symbolic expression, even when it has false components, but cannot obviously do so with respect to the truth of any of the expression's false components? What light does the thesis shed on how Frege understood the epiphenomenal psychological grasping of the sense-meaning content of third-realm phenomena-transcending Fregean thought? Why cannot more than one thinker grasp the non-referential meaning of a false Fregean thought, when Frege did not try to maintain that grasping the Fregean sense of a false Fregean thought is impossible for a solitary thinking subject? Frege did not explain these distinctions as fully as he might. His argument, in which he offered a curious illustration of the general point he was trying to sustain, went as follows:

If a thought is true and is a complex of thoughts of which one is false, then the whole thought could be grasped by several people as one and the same thing, but the false component thought could not. Such a case may occur. E.g. it may be that the following assertion is justifiably made before a jury: "If the accused was in Rome at the time of the deed, he did not commit the murder"; and it may be false that the accused was in Rome at the time of the deed. In that case the jurymen could grasp the same thought when they heard the sentence "If the accused was in Rome at the time of the deed, he did not commit the murder," whereas each of them would associate a sense of his own with the *if*-clause. Is this possible? Can a thought that is present to all the jurymen as one and the same thing have a part that is not common to all of them? If the whole needs no owner, no part of it needs an owner.[22]

The answer is that a true Fregean thought is something definite. It is capable of being apprehended in occurrent psychological experience. If a Fregean thought is true, then it must positively correspond to its

---

[22] Frege, "Negation," *Logical Investigations*, p. 36.

appropriate truth-making state of affairs. A single truth-determining connection exists objectively in that affable case, to be grasped by more than one thinker. The definiteness of the state of affairs by which a true Fregean thought is made true makes it possible in turn for different thinkers to converge in their intentions on an identical Fregean thought. Thus is the first problem solved.

If a Fregean thought is false, however, then its referential meaning requirements are different. The thought could be false for any number of distinct reasons. Each thinker is free to entertain a different possible scenario under which the Fregean thought in question would be false, hence the lack of collective intentional convergence or communal grasping of "the" meaning of a false thought. If it is false that the accused in Frege's example was in Rome, then the accused might have been in Milan, Florence, Venice, Bologna, or for that matter anywhere else on Earth. Each individual thinker may then fasten onto a different possible state of affairs that makes the antecedent of the true conditional taken as a whole false, as in the counterfactual application Frege advanced. These are evidently different thoughts, undermining collective apprehension of the same false Fregean thought. Interpreting negation as the truth-functional output of falsehood from truth and its double, Frege drew the ontic conclusion that a false thought as nothing definite must therefore be nonexistent, on the background assumption, not explicitly articulated but everywhere accepted by Frege, that only definite determinate things exist. Frege went on to reason as follows:

> So a false thought is not a thought that has no being – not even if we take "being" to mean "not needing an owner." A false thought must be admitted, not indeed as true, but as sometimes indispensable: first, as the sense of an interrogative sentence; secondly, as part of a hypothetical thought-complex; thirdly, in negation. It must be possible to negate a false thought, and for this I need the thought; I cannot negate what is not there. And by negation I cannot transform something that needs me as its owner into something of which I am not the owner, and which can be grasped by several people as one and the same thing.[23]

The argument Frege has been developing at this juncture takes a brilliant unexpected turn. If negation as a truth-functional operation converts true Fregean thoughts into false Fregean thoughts, and conversely, and if only true, unlike false, Fregean thoughts can be grasped as

---

[23] *Ibid.*, p. 37.

definite existent things, then the same identity-condition-satisfying Fregean thought cannot simultaneously and for the same reasons be affirmed and negated, if, as Frege colorfully put it, I cannot *transform* something such as a negated thought that needs a particular objective truth-making state of affairs for whatever degree of definiteness it possesses. The accused person was imagined by me as not being in Rome because of his being in Milan instead, while he was imagined by you as being in London at the relevant time. If truth-functional negation is powerless to make something graspable into something ungraspable, and the reverse, then Fregean thoughts in particular should not be regarded as ideational in the first place. If Fregean thoughts are third-realm, mind-transcending and mind-independent, entities, then their being grasped or not grasped, and *a fortiori*, their being individually graspable or ungraspable, is as accidental to their nature as it is to a subject's experience.

More urgently, Frege argued that negation is not the destruction of a Fregean thought. It is instead the creation of a new and different thought with the opposite of the original thought's truth-value. He examined the question of whether the destruction of a Fregean thought occurs when the thought is truth-functionally negated, answering firmly in the negative:

> To the dissolution or destruction of the thought there must accordingly correspond a tearing apart of the words, such as happens, e.g., if a sentence written on paper is cut up with scissors, so that on each scrap of paper there stands the expression for part of a thought. These scraps can then be shuffled at will or carried away by the wind; the connexion is dissolved, the original order can no longer be recognized. Is this what happens when we negate a thought? No! The thought would undoubtedly survive even this execution of it in effigy. What we do is to insert the word "not," and, apart from this, leave the word-order unaltered. The original wording can still be recognized; the order may not be altered at will. Is this dissolution, separation? Quite the reverse! It results in a firmly-built structure.[24]

Truth-functional negation is logically well-behaved. To negate the Fregean thought that my wagon is red is not to obliterate that thought. The thought, as Frege picturesquely put it, continues to reside syntactically within its negation, as the persisting argument of that unary truth-function, without which the negation also could not exist. The obvious proof of this is just to see that the negation of the Fregean thought in

---

[24] *Ibid.*, p. 38.

question contains the original thought nested within the new syntactically expanded construction. There it serves as argument-object for truth-functional negation. The truth-functional relation is Not(red(my(wagon (a)))) = [referentially] the True if and only if Red(my(wagon(a)))) = [referentially] the False. Fregean thought cannot be obliterated, but must be preserved in order to provide the argument needed to complete truth-functional negation. Otherwise, there would be nothing to be negated, if the resulting negated thought were at the same stroke deprived of its distinguishing identity conditions. Negation is not Fregean thought-destroying, but Fregean thought-building, and consequently in the process explicitly thought-preserving. Frege succinctly explained it as follows:

> No non-thought is turned into a thought by negation, just as no thought is turned into a non-thought by negation. / A sentence with the word "not" in its predicate may, like any other, express a thought that can be made into the content of a question; and this, like any propositional question, leaves open our decision as to the answer.[25]

The same open-endedness in truth-value determination that Frege says is characteristic of implicitly question-presenting Fregean thoughts is further observed with respect to their truth-functional negations. If the Fregean thought, my wagon is red, as Frege liked to say, effectively asks to be affirmed or denied, then exactly the same applies with respect to the negation of the Fregean thought that it is not the case that my wagon is red, or that my wagon is not red. Shall the thought that my wagon is not red be accepted or rejected as true? The demand to know something's truth-value by which Frege explains the category of a Fregean *Gedanke* is unchanged in considering the thought's truth-functional negation. The parallelism reinforces Frege's suggestion that truth is logic's norm and ideal just like beauty in aesthetic philosophy and the good or virtue in ethics.

To such an extent was Frege convinced of the parity of Fregean thoughts and their negations that he claimed to have available no reliable way of distinguishing the two in practice. Surface grammar alone supplies no adequate criterion. That is clear when we consider the possibility of interpreting for once-living things the property of being dead as not being alive, or being alive as not being dead. If to be dead is just not to be alive, then the proposition that something is dead is an implicit negation of that thing's being alive, whereas if to be alive is just not to be dead, then the proposition that something is alive is an implicit negation of its being

---

[25] *Ibid.*, p. 39.

dead, at least among the once-living. If we ask which is intrinsically affirmative and which is intrinsically negative, the question appears impossible to answer univocally one way rather than the other without resorting to dogmatic stipulation. Frege illustrated the problem of distinguishing affirmation from negation between such properties, oversimplifying what are actually more complex matters of gender relations, as being a man (not a woman) and being a woman (not a man). He understood the grammatical equivalence of these appropriately matched negated or unnegated forms to imply that there is no determinate distinction between thoughts and their negations. Where they conflict, we are free to choose one as the negated form and the other as unnegated. It appears relative to culturally established linguistic practice in most instances, with nothing more solid than that, nothing carved in stone. Frege accordingly concluded that

A negation may occur anywhere in a sentence without making the thought indubitably negative. We see what tricky questions the expression "negative judgement (thought)" may lead to. The result may be endless disputes, carried on with the greatest subtlety, and nevertheless essentially sterile. Accordingly I am in favour of dropping the distinction between negative and affirmative judgements or thoughts until such time as we have a criterion enabling us to distinguish with certainty in any given case between a negative and an affirmative judgement. When we have such a criterion we shall also see what benefit may be expected from this distinction. For the present I still doubt whether this will be achieved. The criterion cannot be derived from language; for languages are unreliable on logical questions. It is indeed not the least of the logician's tasks to indicate the pitfalls laid by language in the way of the thinker.[26]

With no hard and fast distinction available for unnegated versus negated Fregean thoughts, Frege inclined toward treating them all as logically on a par. This was not merely a simplification of the complete algebraization of a general functional calculus to which Frege never ceased to aspire. It undermined any conceivable effort at attributing distinct metaphysical categories to Fregean thoughts as opposed to their negations. We cannot responsibly do so if we can never be entirely sure when a thought is negated or unnegated. We cannot in particular try to impose a further distinction whereby negated Fregean thoughts do not exist, or are "destroyed" by negation, whereas unnegated Fregean thoughts exist but are always at risk of being annihilated by negation.

[26] *Ibid.*, pp. 41–42.

Frege's third-realm *Gedanken* cannot be created or destroyed, but only grasped by thinking subjects in real time as some Fregean thoughts' truth-values change to reflect the changing circumstances the thoughts describe. Negated Fregean thoughts, when a difference is established, exist as truly and fully as unnegated Fregean thoughts.

These conclusions again were not new ideas in Frege. He had already argued for much the same theses in the less-than-two-page section on Negation in his 1897 unpublished *Nachlaß* essay "Logic." There he played virtually the same well-worked theme of the logical and philosophical unreliability of ordinary language grammatical conventions and distinctions, remarking that

> The prefix "un" is not always used to negate. There is hardly any difference in sense between "unhappy" and "miserable." Here we have a word which is the opposite of "happy," and yet is not its negation. For this reason the sentences "This man is not unhappy" and "This man is happy" do not have the same sense.[27]

Much later, in a July 1919 unpublished *Nachlaß* document, "Notes for Ludwig Darmstaedter," Frege continued unreservedly to maintain that "Negation does not belong to the act of judging, but is a constituent of a thought. The division of thoughts (judgements) into affirmative and negative is of no use to logic, and I doubt if it can be carried through."[28]

The argument further invalidates efforts to hold that the negations of Fregean thoughts are psychological, with a thinking subject denying their truth in a subjectively mind-dependent way. Frege disallowed this move by reaffirming with good reason that we can never be sure when we are dealing with a negated and when we are dealing with an unnegated thought. The implication is that there is probably no enforceable division between the two that would support a psychologistic categorization of negated Fregean thoughts to the exclusion of the non-psychologistic nature of unnegated Fregean thoughts. The fact that we can go back and forth between a Fregean thought and its negation, restoring the original Fregean thought as the negation of its negation, and so on repeatedly, argues that nothing in the truth-functional application of negation can destroy the base underlying Fregean thought or its negation that the function takes as argument. If negation destroyed a Fregean thought, then the identical thought would not survive to be negated again. It also

---

[27] Frege, "Logic," *Posthumous Writings*, p. 150.
[28] Frege, "Notes for Ludwig Darmstaedter," *Posthumous Writings*, p. 253.

seems to follow that a Fregean thought and its negation could never belong to opposed metaphysical categories, the one existent and the other nonexistent, objective and subjective, external and internal. One way or the other, a Fregean thought and its negation are ontically in it together. It is by means of this logical analysis of truth-functional negation that Frege links the second essay on "Negation" to the first essay "Thought." The two investigations jointly establish a domain of abstract mind-independent Fregean thoughts as the arguments of proposition-building truth-functions. We have the parts, and we know something already of what can be done to make more interesting complex meanings with them.

With the introduction of negation, Frege changed the history of mathematics by achieving for the first time a fully algebraic symbolic logic. We turn for minimal acknowledgment of the significance of this event to Frege's unpublished 1882 essay, reserved for his *Nachlaß*, "Boole's Logical Formula-Language and My Concept-Script." It is the shorter of two essays in which he compares *Begriffsschrift* algebraic logic to Boole's. He was aware, although he can be faulted for not sufficiently emphasizing the fact, that one of the innovations to which he could lay claim in surpassing Boole's partial algebraization of Aristotelian–Victorian syllogistic term logic was the decision to supplement, if not replace, a term logic's internal negation or predicate complementation with truth-functional propositional negation of Fregean thoughts. Frege presented the following list of what he took to be the principal differences between his *Begriffsschrift* and Boole's *Mathematical Analysis of Logic* and *Laws of Thought*. He concentrated in this part of his appraisal on the syntax of the two logical algebras:

I believe I have now adequately shown, that, as is proper, I divide the different tasks with which Boole burdens the one sign among several signs, without thereby increasing the total number of signs. The signs which I have also introduced elsewhere may be ignored in this context, since I am restricting myself to what corresponds to Boole's *secondary propositions*. As against his addition, subtraction, multiplication and equals sign, and his o and 1, we have:

1. The horizontal "content-stroke,"
2. The negation-stroke,
3. The vertical stroke that combines two content-strokes, the "conditional-stroke,"
4. The vertical judgement-stroke.[29]

---

[29] Frege, "Boole's Logical Formula-Language and my Concept-Script," *Posthumous Writings*, p. 52.

The negation-stroke, as Frege called it here (elsewhere he called it the sign for negation), makes all the difference between Frege and Boole. As a utility in its logical toolkit, *Begriffsschrift* truth-functional negation distinguishes the propositional logic subcomponent of Frege's functional calculus from any term logic that includes only the complementary property of being non-*F*. Boole has a clever way of defining material conditionals which he calls hypotheticals, by which he reconstructs in the term logic he formalizes a deductively valid inference of hypothetical syllogism. It is the deductively valid inference form: "If *p* then *q*, if *q* then *r*; therefore, if *p* then *r*." Boole does not thereby introduce an algebraic propositional logic in the contemporary sense of the word owing to Frege, without the equivalent of Frege's item 2, the negation-stroke. Boole manages within algebraic term logic constraints to advance a deductively valid reconstruction of hypothetical syllogism in a four-term Hamiltonian syllogistic term logic, a feat previously not attempted and unimaginable without Boole's analytic resources. The logic, lacking truth-functional negation as it did, did not approach Frege's in exact definition and expressive and inferential flexibility.

Frege seized the opportunity to interweave the first essay with the second, using truth-functional external propositional negation to prove that there is no fundamental metaphysical difference between negated and unnegated Fregean thoughts. He was equally well-positioned to maintain that there was no difference between negated and unnegated Fregean thoughts with respect to mind-dependence or mind-independence. Fregean thoughts, generally, even in what appear to be clearcut cases of negated and unnegated forms, needed to be treated alike, whatever that implied. Negations in the sense of negated thoughts were also third-realm entities for Frege. Minds do not do anything to Fregean thoughts in order to negate them. Their negations pre-exist alongside their unnegated forms in the third realm, never forgetting that Frege regarded the negated–unnegated thought distinction as superficial, conventional, and logically unfounded. Since Frege believed that he had already adequately demonstrated that thoughts were mind-independent, if there were no hard and fast distinctions between negated and unnegated thoughts, then the same must apply to whatever we choose to call their truth-functional negations.

If there are good reasons for thinking that any Fregean thought is mind-independent, then the effect of truth-functional negation is to imply that all thoughts must be mind-independent. There can be no exceptions, even if in these constructions it is possible to represent one Fregean thought's denial of the truth of another Fregean thought. The denial of the truth of a Fregean thought, understood as its truth-functional negation, is not explained by Frege as a psychological event, or something that the mind does in exercising judgment over a proposition's truth-value. It is not a matter of making up our minds that a proposition is false. The negation of a Fregean thought, according to Frege's "Negation," is as objective and mind-independent as Fregean thoughts were presumably shown to be in the first essay, "Thought." "Negation" continues the anti-psychologistic theme of "Thought," while adding further complications.

After this turning point, there can be no further opportunity for psychologism to intrude. In the third essay Frege passed directly to a consideration of "Compound Thoughts." Truth-functional proposi-tional negation, marked by the negation stroke or sign, reverses a Fregean thought's truth-value reference from the True to the False, and conversely. Frege explained briefly how the truth-function works. Then he returned to his constant bugbear, psychologism. Truth-func-tional propositional negation, if Frege's objections were correct, is to be congratulated for offering no port of entry for psychological ideas into philosophical logic. They did not come in with thoughts. They have not come in as their truth-functional negations. The defense is that many, if not all, Fregean thoughts can with equal justification be considered in logical form as alternatively negated or unnegated. Frege concluded that there exists no settled distinction to be developed theoretically, meta-physically, or psychologistically between the respective internal logical structures of predications exclusively as either essentially elementary or essentially negations of the elementary.[30]

Compound Thought-Building Truth-Functions

What would have been the third essay–chapter in Frege's *Logische Untersuchungen* was published as a self-standing essay in 1923 in the same journal as its predecessors. The editor, Bauch, was Frege's loyal friend on the masthead. It was to be Frege's last scientific publication,

---

[30] A provocative essay on Frege's topic is Nicholas Unwin's "*Quasi*-Realism, Negation and the Frege–Geach Problem," *The Philosophical Quarterly*, 49 (1999), pp. 337–52.

appearing two years before his death. We have already considered some of the possible reasons why it was not published until five years after the first two, with WWI ranking near the top of the list.

Frege explained compound thoughts expressed as the material conditional truth-function in the simplest applications involving two tokens of Fregean thoughts. He did so only indirectly. Truth-conditions for the conditional are not immediately intuitive. They are apt to be confusing for readers not already familiar with the definition as truth-dependence. Frege accordingly preferred, like many an introductory logic teacher, to begin with conjunction or logical multiplication in the AND connective. It is meant to be as intuitive as propositional negation NOT. Conjunction is interpreted as the truth-function in which both conjuncts need to be true in order for the conjunction as a whole to be true, which in every other instance is false. Once conjunction in combination with negation has been explained, Frege has all he needed to define the material conditional. He presented the conditional as the solitary truth-functional partner of negation in the *Begriffsschrift* propositional logical understructure. His purpose was to pictorially represent logical connectives for the sake of laying bare the purely logical foundations of elementary arithmetic. For that purpose he needed a truth-function that lends itself to graphic representation in which the truth of a thought depending on the truth of another thought is made visually perspicuous.

The material conditional is an if-then truth-functional construction with the desired pictorial virtues. It says intuitively that *if* Fregean thought p is true, then q is true, where it is also possible in the limiting case that $p = q$, or that p is true if and only if q is true. Truth-functional negation and the truth-functional material conditional enabled Frege to build compound Fregean thoughts to any required level of syntactical complexity. Negation and the conditional, once the latter has been defined by Frege in relation to conjunction and negation, $p \rightarrow q$ as truth-functionally equivalent to $\neg[p \wedge \neg q]$, are sufficient in the right combinations to express any of the remaining standard three truth-functions, including a return to conjunction, p and q ($p \wedge q$), inclusive disjunction, p or q ($p \vee q$), and biconditional or material equivalence, p if and only if q ($p \leftrightarrow q$).

Frege's essay on compound thoughts took logical constructions to the next level, at which every logical connection between Fregean thoughts as third-realm propositional meanings or Fregean sense-contents can be interdefined. Frege advanced systematically in the discussion from the basic truth-functional building blocks of logic. He began with truth-conditions, the truth and falsity that Fregean thoughts construed as implicit interrogatives require to have affirmed or denied as their referential meaning, designating the True or the False. He constructively showed how Fregean thoughts could be endlessly compounded in more complex expressions involving especially truth-functional negation and the conjunction first for heuristic reasons, thereafter reductively defining the gangly material conditional needed for logical pictorial purposes.

Although it is clear, especially looking backward, what Frege meant to accomplish by the distinction, his terminology for compound Fregean thoughts was somewhat confusing. If a compound Fregean thought is any construction resulting from the application of a truth-function to a Fregean thought or thoughts, then Frege ought to have included the negation of a thought as a compound thought. This he declined to do. If we look at the difference between negation, which in logic today is more likely to be called a *unary* truth-function or propositional operator, on the one hand, and the *binary* conjunction and material conditional truth-function of Frege's logic, on the other, they are distinct truth-functions and in that sense different ways of compounding thoughts. Frege evidently regarded compound thoughts narrowly as the compounding of two or more thoughts, excluding negation as a unary truth-function applying only to individual thoughts.

Another way to read Frege's references to compound thoughts is to consider his analysis as implicitly involving more than one token of a thought. Frege could not allow a negated Fregean thought to be categorized as even the most fundamental kind of compound thought, if, as he argued in "Negation," there is in the first place no essential proper distinction between negated and unnegated Fregean thoughts. The difference marks an interesting logical distinction, or lack thereof, and explains what otherwise appears as Frege's inapposite categorizations of truth-functions as negations or compound in defiance of the more unifying unary versus binary logical connectives. Frege opened this line of inquiry by remarking on the impressive semantic compositionality of languages. With a basic, possibly innate, grasp of grammatical attachments, we can construct and entertain entirely new symbolic expressions for Fregean thoughts that have never previously occurred to any thinking subject. Frege shared his sense of awe:

It is astonishing what language can do. With a few syllables it can express an incalculable number of thoughts, so that even a thought grasped by a terrestrial being for the very first time can be put into a form of words which will be understood by someone to whom the thought is entirely new. This would be impossible, were it not able to distinguish parts in the thought corresponding to the parts of a sentence, so that the structure of the sentence serves as an image of the structure of the thought. To be sure, we really talk figuratively when we transfer the relation of the whole and part to thoughts; yet the analogy is so ready to hand and so generally appropriate that we are hardly ever bothered by the hitches which occur from time to time.[31]

Semantic compositionality in Frege is the determination of meaning of larger units of expression as a function of the sense and reference meanings of component Fregean names and thoughts and identity conditions for admissible predicates. The concept was already at the center of his discussion in the preceding late essay on "Negation." An explicitly negated Fregean thought is a composite of a Fregean thought taken as argument-object to which the negation truth-function is applied. A negated Fregean thought becomes a compound of the original unnegated Fregean thought and negation truth-function. Negation builds something new and logically more complex from a Fregean thought, a concept that is essential to Frege's algebraization of logic in its application to the philosophical foundations of arithmetic.

Leaving negation out of account, Frege distinguished between two kinds of compound thoughts. The first category marks the effect of a truth-function on two Fregean thoughts. It is not clear in Frege's exposition whether he meant by this phrase always two different thoughts, or in some instances two different tokens of the same Fregean thought type. What he should have meant is certainly the latter, although it is easy to forget about iterative cases like $p \wedge p$ and $p \rightarrow p$, as they are only marginally useful in logical modeling and inference. The second kind of compound thought is the negation of a prior truth-function compounding Fregean thoughts, which is itself a structurally more complex compound thought. Although in his *Begriffsschrift* the two thought-compounding truth-functions are negation and the material conditional, in trying to explain the category of compound thoughts of first and second kinds, Frege begins with the friendlier conjunction p AND q. Conjunction is a first kind of compound thought under Frege's distinction when two thoughts or thought tokens are connected by means of a

[31] Frege, "Compound Thoughts," *Logical Investigations*, p. 55.

special truth-function, to create a Fregean compound thought of the first kind. A compound thought of the second kind is indicated in Frege's terminology when we negate a conjunction. Frege's insight is that a second compound thought, the negated conjunction, is as much a compounding of the two conjoined thoughts as their prior conjunction. Negating an elementary non-compound predication merely results in a negation, which in Frege's technical terminology is not a compound thought. This is an important part of what it means for Frege's *Begriffsschrift* to be algebraic. He stated the following:

> The negation of a compound of the first kind between one thought and another is itself a compound of the same two thoughts. I shall call it a compound thought of the second kind. Whenever a compound thought of the first kind out of two thoughts is false, the compound of the second kind out of them is true, and conversely. A compound of the second kind is false only if each compounded thought is true, and a compound of the second kind is true whenever at least one of the compounded thoughts is false. In all this it is assumed throughout that the thoughts do not belong to fiction. By presenting a compound thought of the second kind as true, I declare the compounded thoughts to be non-conjoinable.[32]

If the negation of a conjunction is true, then the compounded thoughts truth-functionally related by conjunction cannot both be true. In that sense they are not "conjoinable" in Frege's terminology. Truth-functionally, they cannot result in a true conjoint Fregean thought. Frege unsurprisingly interpreted these fundamental logical relations algebraically, as involving placeholders, like the alphabetical letters in arithmetical algebra, supporting the insertion and rule-governed *salva veritate* uniform intersubstitutions of logically equivalent terms symbolizing Fregean thoughts.

These ideas are so well-established today that it may seem trite to enter into further details. They are known thanks to the influence Frege eventually came to exert on the development of modern symbolic logic. In Frege's time, the concepts were new and revolutionary. Frege in any case may have been going over familiar ground in the most painstaking way in order to see whether he had made any conceptual gaffes along the way that might have made the logic vulnerable to logical antinomy in the form of Russell's paradox. He stated the following:

> The connective ["not [___ and ___]"] is the doubly unsaturated sense of this doubly unsaturated expression. By filling the gaps with expressions of thoughts, we form the

expression of a compound thought of the second kind. But we really should not talk of the compound thought as originating in this way, for it is a thought and a thought does not originate.[33]

Frege in the final sentence offered a valuable check against excessive explanatory reliance on reference to compound thoughts constructively, as though they were being built up from simpler elements over time in a process of assembly. This can be a useful metaphor for thinking about how thoughts are related to one another by truth-functional and logical inferential connections. We can imagine the syntax of logical expression manufactured by ideal machines on an assembly line. A compounding of Fregean thoughts is like following a recipe. *First*, take a Fregean thought, *then* conjoin it with another Fregean thought, *then* negate their conjunction. This is how we can proceed if we are writing down on paper the step-by-step logical operations of an algorithm. The image is strictly misleading. Fregean thoughts are not spatiotemporal physical entities. Something is not first done to them and then something else. Regardless of their internal compounded logical structure and how we heuristically depict their compounding as an event taking place in successive stages of operation, Fregean thoughts are unalterable in logical form. All that can change in some cases is their truth-value reflecting adjustments in truth-making and truth-breaking external world circumstances.

Working through other standard propositional logically compound thoughts, Frege arrives at combinations of conjunction with negation. Negation was applied to previously articulated compound thoughts of the first kind in order to arrive at compound thoughts of the second kind. Concerning this Frege made the following observations:

The connective in a compound thought of the fifth kind is the doubly incomplete sense of the doubly incomplete expression
    "(not ___) and (___)."
Here the compounded thoughts are not interchangeable, for
    "(not B) and A"
does not express the same as
    "(not A) and B."[34]

The material conditional or if-then construction, the workhorse along with truth-functional negation in Frege's *Begriffsschrift* propositional logic, does not make its appearance until about two-thirds of the way

[33] *Ibid.*, p. 61.   [34] *Ibid.*, p. 66.

through the essay. There the conditional is not taken as primitive structure, but explained as a particular compound Fregean thought involving
conjunction and negation attaching to simpler Fregean thoughts. The
material conditional is referred to by Frege, following Boole, as a
"hypothetical":

Instead of "compound thought of the sixth kind," I shall also speak of "hypothetical
compound thought," and I shall refer to the first and second components of a
hypothetical compound thought as "consequent" and "antecedent" respectively.
Thus, a hypothetical compound thought is true if its consequent is true; it is also
true if its antecedent is false, regardless of whether the consequent is true or false. The
consequent must always be a thought.[35]

Today, truth-functions are defined more conveniently for truth-value
input by means of truth-tables. Wittgenstein in his *Tractatus* did not invent
but popularized the matrix display by which each distinct truth-function is
uniquely specified. Truth-tables are definitions by possible cases of the
output truth-values of a compound thought as defined by its compounding
truth-functions taken as input in all combinations of the appropriate
number of compounded true or false Fregean thoughts. Frege did not
avail himself of the tabular device. He introduced logical interconnections
in ordinary prose. What he described nevertheless exactly coincides with
the contemporary standard truth-table definition of the material conditional, here, Frege's hypotheticals. In his *Begriffsschrift*, Frege was the first
to formally define the material conditional, as well as the other recognized
propositional truth-functions introduced as an aid toward understanding
the logical structures of compound Fregean thoughts. He could only have
been the first if the conditional was reductively defined by means of another
truth-function together with truth-functional negation, and if history is
right in judging that he was the first logician to have algebraized truth-
functional external propositional negation.

Frege took the opportunity to comment on the frailties of everyday
discourse for the purpose of the adequate expression of Fregean thoughts
generally in science and philosophy. That was one of his primary motivations for advancing beyond ordinary language toward an ideal formalized
symbolic logic that avoids the major defects of casual everyday thought
and discourse. A scientific language cannot allow ambiguous terms having more than one sense or reference. For the same reason logic must

---

[35] *Ibid.*, p. 68.

exclude or semantically work around empty terms with null reference wrongly presenting themselves as proper names or singular referring expressions and Fregean thoughts. "Sherlock Holmes" and "Sherlock Holmes is a detective" are stock-in-trade examples of a referentially empty pseudo-proper name and a grammatical sentence consequently possessing Fregean sense but no sentential reference to the True or the False. These are forbidden in the pure logic of the *Begriffsschrift*, which Frege designed specifically to overcome major defects of natural-language communication. Vernacular speech and writing evolve anthropologically and therefore in some ways accidentally, without being intended to address the more precisely dedicated needs of logic, mathematics, science, and philosophy. The same deficiencies are naturally not avoidable in every attempt to apply Frege's general functional calculus to everyday concepts, propositions and inferences. The relevant concepts usually need to be cleaned up, as Frege sanitized the concept-function of natural number in *Grundlagen*, before they can be applied in mathematical reasoning, for scientific and philosophical explanation.

Frege put together a chart exhibiting the six types of compound thoughts in his algebraic propositional logic, which is shown here as Figure 13.1, commenting as follows:[36]

Thus our six kinds of compound thought form a completed whole, whose primitive elements seem here to be the first kind of compound and negation. However acceptable to psychologists, this apparent pre-eminence of the first kind of compound over the others has no logical justification; for any one of the six kinds of compound thought can be taken as fundamental and can be used, together with negation, for deriving the others; so that, for logic, all six kinds have equal justification.[37]

Curiously, Frege resorted to negation and hypothetical or material conditional truth-functions to derive the other standard truth-functional connectives of his *Begriffsschrift*. He began with conjunction, as we have

I. A and B	II. not (A and B)
III. (not A) and (not B)	IV. not ((not A) and (not B))
V. (not A) and B	VI. not ((not A) and B).

Figure 13.1   Summary of the Six Compound Thoughts

[36] *Ibid.*, p. 73.   [37] *Ibid.*

conjectured, presumably because it is easier to understand its truth-functional compounding of Fregean thoughts. Connecting two or more Fregean thoughts by AND, after negation, is about the simplest and most nontechnically intuitive way of making a compound Fregean thought. It is vastly easier than it would be to begin with the material conditional and its counterintuitivities, as Frege has just explained and as every logic tutor knows.

Non-Truth-Functional Compound Thoughts

An obvious question is why Frege bothered with the material conditional. Negation and conjunction are formally able to accomplish in a different way everything of which negation and the material conditional are capable. We can understand why Frege followed this course, rather than pursuing any of the other possibilities he acknowledged, only if we remind ourselves of his graphic intentions in designing *Begriffsschrift* logic. The material conditional lends itself more naturally than conjunction to two–dimensional pictorial display of logical connections representing truth–value dependences. It does so especially where the truth–value of an asserted Fregean thought must be shown pictorially to depend on the truth–value of another Fregean thought token or type.

By placing the conditional thought below the horizontal content–stroke, attached by means of its characteristic right–angular hook, Frege literally shows that the truth of the thought appearing at the terminus of the relevant main horizontal is not simply true, but true only if the thought on which its truth conditionally depends is true. The construction logically guarantees that the conditional is also true when its dependent clause or antecedent at the end of the hook is true, regardless of the truth–value of the consequent lined up at the end of the main content–stroke, and when the consequent of the conditional in that position is true, regardless of the truth–value of the antecedent at the lower end of the dependent clause–marking graphic hook. Frege explained the truth–value interpretation of the material conditional or hypothetical informally in the third *Logische Untersuchungen* essay, "Compound Thoughts."

Frege then analyzed the generality of expression his system attains with the selection of negation and the hypothetical or material conditional as truth–functions. It is essential to his purpose that all other natural–language propositional connectives are reducible to these. Frege imposed, but did not try to argue for, a closure principle that would preclude the possibility of well-formed formulas in propositional logic being constructible in any other way. He maintained that a dependence relation holds, but did not try to prove any version of the reducibility claim. Undoubtedly, the oversight was because of the informal nature of the presentation to which he limited himself in these logical investigations. He recognized that to prove something as difficult as the assertion that no other truth-functions are needed in the expanding construction or reductive logical analysis of every type of compound thought would require more heavy-duty formal machinery, especially mathematical induction, than he could manageably bring into this nontechnical introduction to the basic principles of logic. He paused to remark that the closure he attributed to a formal language like the propositional logic of third-realm thoughts was unavailable in the natural sciences. Without delving into the deeper reasons for why the distinction exists, he continued as follows:

Compound thoughts of the first kind, and negation, are together adequate for the formation of all these compounds, and any other of our six kinds of compound can be chosen instead of the first. Now the question arises whether every compound thought is formed in this way. So far as mathematics is concerned, I am convinced that it includes no compound thoughts formed in any other way. It will scarcely be otherwise in physics, chemistry, and astronomy as well; but "in order that" clauses call for caution and seem to require more precise investigation. Here I shall leave this question open.[38]

Finally, Frege extolled an extensionality principle for compound thoughts. The stipulation was that compound thoughts "constructed," or, since they are abstract, perhaps, better, *analyzed*, by means of negation and another truth-function, such as the conditional, conjunction, or disjunction, should be considered *mathematical* in a precise sense. Frege meant by mathematical compound thoughts that the contexts in which thoughts are connected together are purely extensional, supporting the uniform intersubstitution of any co-referential terms or sentences always alike in truth-value *salva veritate*. They are to preserve the truth-value of the compound thought as a whole before and after intersubstitutions are made. The category was first described:

Compound thoughts thus formed with the aid of negation from compounds of the first kind seem, at all events, to merit a special title. They may be called mathematical

---

[38] *Ibid.*, pp. 76–77.

compound thoughts. This should not be taken to mean that there are compound thoughts of any other type. Mathematical compound thoughts seem to have something else in common; for if a true component of such a compound is replaced by another true thought, the resultant compound thought is true or false according to whether the original compound is true or false. The same holds if a false component of a mathematical compound thought is replaced by another false thought. I now want to say that two thoughts have the same truth-value if they are either both true or both false. I maintain, therefore, that the thought expressed by "A" has the same truth-value as that expressed by "B" if either "A and B" or else "(not A) and (not B)" expresses a true thought. Having established this, I can phrase my thesis in this way:

"If one component of a mathematical compound thought is replaced by another thought having the same truth-value, then the resultant compound thought has the same truth-value as the original."[39]

It is noteworthy logically and philosophically that Frege did not maintain that all compound thoughts are mathematical. He did not elaborate on the range of counterexamples among Fregean compound thoughts that should be considered non-mathematical. There are other types of combinations involving intensional rather than purely extensional Fregean thought-term intersubstitution contexts. They include, among others, reports of exact quotation and propositional attitude.[40]

Frege's Posthumous Writings

Frege, like most writers, prepared various texts that for different reasons were not published during his lifetime. Some were rejected repeatedly by journal editors, like the two essays comparing Frege's *Begriffsschrift* with Boole's logic. After a few attempts, Frege gave up trying to find those manuscripts a home. Others for reasons of waning of interest, distraction occasioned by more pressing projects, old age, and the like, were started but left unfinished at the time of Frege's death, along with first drafts later put to different uses, sketches for essays that were never completed, lecture materials, and letters.

The uncommitted writings were collected together by Frege as a modest scientific literary trust, which he bequeathed to his then recently adopted son Alfred. Frege knew that eventually the writings would be of

---

[39] *Ibid.*, p. 77.

[40] See Dummett, *Frege: Philosophy of Language*, especially pp. 186–92 and 264–94; Linsky, *Referring*, pp. 100 and 114–15; and Klement, *Frege and the Logic of Sense and Reference*, pp. 13, 75, and 126. On p. 158, Klement curiously argues that for Frege *oratio obliqua* contexts are not referentially opaque.

more interest than they were to his contemporaries. He placed confidence in the boy he had raised and then legally made his son to protect the relics. There were no further instructions. Alfred was told to keep them safe, but received no specific guidelines as to whether they should be published, sold, archived in a university library, or anything else. Alfred was asked only to prevent them from becoming lost. Frege might well have discussed the matter with Alfred beforehand, and perhaps did not rely merely on the content of the letter attached as a codicil to his will for the full understanding existing between them. It is doubtful that his leaving the materials to Alfred would have come as a complete surprise to the young man.

Having the papers archived or published by sale or donation would certainly have honored papa Gottlob's wishes to keep these desk-drawer writings from disappearing as though they had never existed, as though he had never grasped these Fregean thoughts. It might have been judged unseemly, fame-seeking even as his end approached, to leave behind a document urging his son after his anticipated death to find a publisher for his logical–philosophical left-behinds. He asked only that Alfred not let them vanish from history. Frege's brief note to his son consists of five sentences, discounting salutation and signature. The page in translation reads as follows:

Dear Alfred,
Do not despise the pieces I have written. Even if all is not gold, there is gold in them. I believe there are things here which will one day be prized much more highly than they are now. Take care that nothing gets lost. It is a large part of myself which I bequeath to you herewith.

                                                            Your loving father.[41]

The few lines manage to convey something vital about Frege's state of mind. There are three themes to be observed. Significantly, Frege opened with a request that Alfred not *despise* the unpublished writings he was bundling together. It was a rather guarded way to turn the materials over to his son that set a negative tone for the letter as a whole. Frege had become so conditioned this late in the day to expect the rejection of his ideas in his published works whenever they came to

---

[41] Frege's note naming his adopted son, Alfred, as his literary heir and executor of his unpublished writings in the letter to Alfred is reprinted from the editors' introduction, "History of the Frege *Nachlaß* and the Basis for this Edition," in Frege, *Posthumous Writings*, p. ix.

print that he found it natural to petition even his adopted son for patience and respite in not harshly judging these unpublished "pieces."

The second aspect of the letter concerned Frege's unyielding faith in the quality of his work. There was gold in the unpublished writings, he proudly maintained, allowing that not everything included was certain to be considered of value. The gold would need to be refined and separated from the dross. Someone sufficiently interested and capable of appreciating the importance of the Frege *Nachlaß* scraps, typescripts, and hand-written materials would come along. It was not vanity but Frege's sense of duty to the future of scientific philosophy that prompted him to ask that his unpublished and last thoughts not be burned or set out with the trash.

Third, Frege sealed the pact with Alfred by telling his son that with the transfer of these unpublished writings he is bequeathing "a large part of myself." His sense of self, self-identity, and self-image are bound up with his work. He continues to engage others in the expression of his thoughts, published or unpublished.

These are the three elements that in dialectical interaction shaped the entire course of Frege's personality as mathematician and philosopher: (a) his writings were mostly despised and misunderstood; (b) there was nevertheless pure gold in them, for those with eyes to discover their virtues; and (c) the unpublished writings were of enormous personal importance to Frege, representing a considerable part of himself and how he thought of himself, as in his remaining days he contemplated and wrote more unpublished pages about what he considered he had achieved.

This was Frege in a nutshell, Frege distilled. He was as under-appreciated in his work as he gradually became increasingly more unappreciated at his university job. Despite the world's disfavor, he believed his writings to be of importance, even those that hardly any journal would take on and present to the world. He never lost faith in the fundamental rightness of his methodology and its results, Russell's paradox notwithstanding. Having Bauch eager to publish his work only made Frege more cautious, since he could not in this case rely on the critical refereeing safety net that publication efforts at other journals would afford. He had weathered decades of neglect and misdirected criticism, followed by the numbing silence of even more sustained disregard. Frege, as some biographical commentators have popularly portrayed him at the time, was supposed to be a broken man. The image of Frege beaten down by

Russell's paradox, among other damaging factors that had mounted up after 1904, has become deeply ingrained in the contemporary philosophical imagination. Frege belied this image by the fact that he never renounced or relinquished the aims of his *Grundgesetze*. He continued in the *Logische Untersuchungen* to pursue by another route the same aims he had marked out for himself from the days preceding his Habilitationsschrift. Even the publication leftovers Frege bequeathed to Alfred, he said, presumably without exaggeration, were taken to represent a "large part" of himself. He identified himself with the work, with what he had done toward the founding of his signature brand of rigorous non-psychologistic logicism. He did not disown the enterprise, but neither did he ignore or try to bury away the problems it had encountered in Russell's paradox.

Frege at this late date had not turned his back on any of his life's work. As circumstances unfolded, he lacked time and energy to think his way back out of the paradox fly-bottle to regain the open air he had innocently breathed before receiving Russell's letter. The project was not scorned, and the ideals that guided Frege's explorations of logical concepts and structures continued to point the way forward, despite Russell's game-changing puzzle. Frege remained proud of and committed to the work, which he acknowledged as wrapping up a considerable part of his goals and ambitions, and of his self-image as thinker, logician, mathematician, and philosopher. He disavowed none of what he had done, while at the same time fully acknowledging that the project had been dealt a major upset by the discovery of what he continued to regard as a genuine paradox in his formal system implying rampant logical–syntactical antinomy. It was a problem for which Frege at this late date had yet to find an acceptable diagnosis, let alone solution.

Frege honestly did not know what to think about Russell's paradox. He nowhere admitted, as a totally trounced logician in this situation more likely would have done, that Russell's paradox proved that a properly adjusted *Grundgesetze* could not possibly succeed. He never granted in response that the whole idea of what he was attempting to achieve was wrong. He was stuck in a hard dilemma of indecision. He did not know where to begin. On the most penetrating reflection he could not abandon any of his previous starting-places. In particular, he could not in his own mind justify conditionalizing the extensional concept-function identity principle in Axiom V. He especially did not freely assent to awkwardly excluding a particular family of previously unexpected inconsistencies, as he did in the *Grundgesetze II* Afterword afterthought. Frege's indomitable spirit, despite having taken a severe battering, did not appear to have been conquered. He did not fully understand what Russell had discovered, and for that reason alone he was not yet in a position to abandon or further contribute to the cause of logicism he had advanced in his *Begriffsschrift*, *Grundlagen*, and *Grundgesetze*. He was literally frozen for a time in the grip of a splendid Socratic ἀπορία.

He confided to Alfred that there was gold in his unpublished writings. The affirmation does not scan like a concession of surrender and withdrawal from the contest. There was only so much that he could do, spanning seventy to seventy-five years of age in the period we are now considering late in his life. He knew that he would not last forever. When he died, his papers would be looked over. Alfred was a good boy, a responsible young man. Some things would need to be thrown away. The library at home would have to be cleared out. Professors collect a lot of paper. They know what to value, what to discard, and what to do with what remains. It is not usually much use to anyone else. Frege imagined his collected unpublished writings being sniffed over by an attorney or even his brother, Arnold, deemed of no commercial significance and deposited in the street or burned in the fireplace for more heat than light. If Thomae and Cantor did not understand his published books and articles, how could he expect to find sanctuary for his ideas once he was gone on the part of functionary officials or less accommodating relatives than Alfred? Frege wanted to avoid the outcome as a practical matter by enlisting Alfred's trustworthiness, safeguarding these last documents from thoughtless destruction. He appealed to his son's affection in administering the responsibility, signing off in the request as "Your loving father." Frege was indeed Alfred's loving father, and Alfred was Frege's loving son.

Frege's *Nachlaß* was saved by Alfred from immediate loss, but not, however, from the fire-bombing of Münster in an air raid on the city that took place on 25 March 1945. The resulting inferno engulfed parts of the university library and burned Frege's papers to cinders where they had been stored. Luckily, there existed elsewhere copies of many of the most important materials that had previously been prepared by the foresightful Heinrich Scholz (1884–1956). The harrowing story of Frege's *Nachlaß* is rivetingly told by the three editors of the 1979 translation of *Gottlob Frege: Posthumous Writings*, Hans Hermes, Friedrich Kambartel, and Friedrich Kaulbach, in their introductory "History of the Frege *Nachlaß* and the

Basis for this Edition."[42] It is difficult to determine from the book whether all of Frege's original *Nachlaß* handed over to Alfred at Frege's death is now contained in the edited and translated collection, or whether there once existed items that are known to have disappeared after Frege's death, of which no copies were made and of which the originals were irretrievably destroyed in the war. We know that this is true in the case of some of Frege's financial papers. Was everything of mathematical or philosophical interest saved? These events did not come to pass until twenty years after Frege's departure from the land of the living. The fate of his last writings remains of interest as something whose safekeeping custody he deliberately delegated as an expression of his attitude toward his lifework while he was still alive. Also, the editors of the *Posthumous Writings* use a bracketing device for some of the writings listed in the table of contents, suggesting that they might be additions to Alfred's original charge. The convention, unfortunately, is not explained, although the editors' standard use of brackets within individual edited texts in the volume is clear. The historically intriguing question is to know exactly what writings Frege intended to turn over to Alfred, that is, the complete inventory of "pieces" with nothing missing and without later insertions. The volume, together with its explanatory apparatus, is extremely useful, and there may no longer be a decisive way of establishing the collection's original contents.

The *Nachlaß* papers are a world unto themselves. There are brilliant analogies and gratifyingly lucid writing about some of the most challenging basic conceptual problems in logic and philosophy. The technical and philosophical implications of these remaining essays, notes, and fragments among Frege's output cannot be done justice here. Moreover, while it is reassuring to see that with but a few exceptions, one potentially important, Frege did not retract any of his previous philosophical conclusions, the *Nachlaß* materials for the most part also do nothing to advance Frege's logicism. Their greatest value is in better understanding some of the concepts Frege had already made extensive use of in his published works. We learn, for example, from such unpublished writings as the 1897 manuscript "Logic" that Frege at this early date already had a fully developed theory of mind-independent third-realm thoughts as distinguished from mind-dependent occurrent psychological ideas. The essay on this topic,

---

[42] *Ibid.*, pp. ix–xiii.

the central argument of which was nothing new in Frege's philosophy, did not appear in print until twenty-one years later in 1918, intended with its companion essay–chapters for inclusion in the *Logische Untersuchungen*.

Frege's "Notes for Ludwig Darmstaedter" of July 1919 gives us a rare glimpse of his autobiography. Darmstaedter was a German chemist and historian of natural science with whom Frege corresponded about a number of philosophical and pedagogical matters. Frege, in the course of explaining his intellectual orientation, sketched his reasons for taking a specific direction in mathematical logic in response to his perception of the appalling state of mathematics, and the need to introduce more rigor, precision, and a stronger conceptual foundation for the discipline. Frege wrote the following:

> I started out from mathematics. The most pressing need, it seemed to me, was to provide this science with a better foundation. I soon realized that number is not a heap, a series of things, nor a property of a heap either, but that in stating a number which we have arrived at as the result of counting we are making a statement about a concept. (Plato, *The Greater Hippias*.) The logical imperfections of language stood in the way of such investigations. I tried to overcome these obstacles with my concept-script. In this way I was led from mathematics to logic.[43]

Very shortly before his death in 1925, in the unpublished "Numbers and Arithmetic" (1924/1925), Frege entered another autobiographical mood, and almost seemed to continue seriatim from his notes for Darmstaedter:

> When I first set out to answer for myself the question of what is to be understood by numbers and arithmetic, I encountered – in an apparently predominant position – what was called formal arithmetic. The hallmark of formal arithmetic was the thesis "Numbers are numerals." How did people arrive at such a position? They felt incapable of answering the question on any rational view of what could be meant by it, they did not know how they ought to explain what is designated by the numeral "3" or the numeral "4," and then the cunning idea occurred to them of evading this question by saying "These numerical signs do not really designate anything: they are themselves the things that we are inquiring about." Quite a dodge, a degree of cunning amounting, one might almost say, to genius; it's only a shame that it makes the numerals, and so the numbers themselves, completely devoid of content and quite useless. How was it *possible* for people not to see this? Time and again the same cunning idea occurs to people and it's very possible that there are such people to be found even today. They usually begin by assuring us that they do not intend the numerals to designate anything – no, not anything at all. And yet, it seems, in some mysterious way some content or other must manage to insinuate itself into these quite empty signs, for otherwise they would be quite useless. That, then, is what formal

---

[43] Frege, "Notes for Ludwig Darmstaedter," p. 253.

arithmetic used to be. Is it now dead? Strictly speaking, it was never alive; all the same we cannot rule out attempts to resuscitate it.[44]

Once again, try as we might to bring the documents in Frege's writings, published or unpublished, into agreement with the depiction of his later years as a broken, defeated, embittered man, the picture is not borne out by the historical record. Frege was discouraged about the fact that other mathematicians did not share his sense of importance in bringing greater clarity to the foundations of their discipline. There was no doubt about that. He was certainly disappointed that he had been unable to rouse them from their state of complacency as to how arithmetic in particular was supposed to be grounded. He could not even get leading figures like Hilbert and Peano to take Russell's paradox as seriously as he regarded its implications for purely extensional identity conditions for concept-functions. His command of the situation polemically remained clear and penetrating. He had not to the very end given up on the ideals of his inquiry, even if recent gathering circumstances were now forcing him against his will and better judgment to finally abandon the quest.

Frege at Seventy-Five

Frege retired from the University of Jena in 1918. At the end of the university's summer semester in that year he sold and moved from the duplex house his mother had built, relocating from the university city of his first concentrated mathematical studies and later teaching and research career to the peaceful Mecklenburg village of Bad Kleinen. Frege's retirement home even in 2014 boasted a population of only about 3,700 persons. The retirement locale, opposite his boyhood home of Wismar, was not directly exposed to the raw climate of the Baltic Sea, but on the quiet more protected inland Schweriner Außensee. There Frege lived in retirement until his death seven years later in 1925.

With financial assistance from Wittgenstein, Frege moved to Bad Kleinen. He was building a house to share with Meta Arndt in Pastow near Rostock, where Alfred could enjoy frequent extended visits. Frege did not live to see the building completed. Arndt, as reward for many years' faithful service, was entitled to live out her life there according to the terms of Frege's will. Alfred was already in secondary school. Frege no longer had a position at the university, and at home there was an

---

[44] *Ibid.*, p. 275.

empty nest. His writing career was effectively over, but he had held up surprisingly well until this point. Seventy years in 1918, seventy-five in 1923, and still trading barbs with dialectical opponents, at least in his late unpublished manuscripts, up to that very moment.

The trail of correspondence between Frege and Wittgenstein discloses Wittgenstein's monetary support of Frege's retirement plans. There was supposed to have existed a letter from Wittgenstein to Frege of 25 March 1918. It was known of only by inference from Frege's reply of 9 April 1918, in which Frege thanked Wittgenstein for his generous donation.[45] Wittgenstein's munificence and the sale of his house in Jena enabled Frege to relocate to Bad Kleinen. The money from Wittgenstein seems to have been deposited for Frege at the local Jena Bank of Thuringia. Frege gratefully accepted Wittgenstein's support, which he acknowledged as having been offered from "the noblest impulse," appreciating the gift "with cordial thanks."

Frege's resettling in Bad Kleinen meant that Alfred had to change schools before his final secondary school year. It was at this point that Frege sent Alfred to the Große Stadtschule in Wismar, where Frege had been a student through Gymnasium from 1854 to 1869. For the 1918 term, just prior to his retirement, Frege additionally received a cost of living allowance of 750 Marks, and another one-time supplementary allowance of 600 Marks. He retired during the brief moment thereafter when the German currency was still relatively stable, on approximately 6,000 Marks a year.[46] All that was to change in the next few months, especially toward the end of the year, when inflation in the national economy hit an all-time high. Newsreels from the era show people literally pushing wheelbarrows full of devalued paper money in the street to buy a loaf of bread.[47]

---

[45] The existence of the letter from Wittgenstein dated 25 March 1918, arranging Wittgenstein's donation of retirement funding to Frege, can only be inferred from Frege's reply to Wittgenstein of 9 April 1918. See Kreiser, *Gottlob Frege*, p. 504. Wittgenstein generally preferred to donate support to artists and writers anonymously, as he did in the case of the poet Rainer Maria Rilke, painter Oskar Kokoschka, and others. See Monk, *Ludwig Wittgenstein*, pp. 108 and 110.

[46] Details in Kreiser, *Gottlob Frege*, pp. 439–40.

[47] See Gerald D. Feldman, *The Great Disorder: Politics, Economics, and Society in the German Inflation, 1914–1924* (Oxford: Oxford University Press, 1997); and Carl-Ludwig Holtfrerich, *The German Inflation 1914–1923* (Berlin: Walter de Gruyter, 1986).

In a *Kurator*'s memorandum of 20 December 1917, it was reported that Frege had been on medical leave for the previous one-and-one-quarter years. He petitioned to have his leave renewed until he reached the retirement age of seventy the following year. Frege's health never recovered its former vigor after the crashing blows of 1902–1904. It was noted that his lectures were, anyway, very rarely attended. Frege posted his request for leave on 10 May 1918, indicating that he had tried to take up his duties once again but was compelled to discontinue for reasons of health. He explained that it might even be necessary for him to leave Jena. Although he did not say so, departure from the university was considered in order to resume the hopeful but not yet successful cure he had taken in the nearby hill country. He frankly explained that he was trying to stretch things out until he could retire at the age of seventy after his birthday on 8 November 1918. Frege had effectively unofficially been in retirement since about 1916, with sporadic intermittent absences, already at the advanced age of sixty-eight. He gratefully waited out the retirement clock taking the waters at the spa.[48]

He also continued exchanging letters and field postcards with Wittgenstein. He engaged in a relatively active correspondence with Bruno Bauch, co-founder of the German Philosophical Society in 1917, Arthur Hoffmann, the other co-founder, Hugo Dingler, a German scientist and philosopher with interests in German idealism, with whom Frege also discussed matters of political economy, and, among others, Karl Zsigmondy, professor of mathematics at the Vienna Polytechnic.[49] It was during this time that Frege received one of three copies of Wittgenstein's *Abhandlung*, soon to become the *Tractatus*, and tried to make sense of some parts of the book, while nominally assisting Wittgenstein to find a publisher for the unclassifiable work.[50]

---

[48] Kreiser, *Gottlob Frege*, pp. 514–15.

[49] Frege engaged in an active philosophical correspondence at this time with Bauch, Arthur Hoffmann, Dingler, Karl Zsigmondy, Carnap, and others. For this period see Frege, *Briefwechsel*, some of the letters from which have been translated and printed in Frege, *Philosophical and Mathematical Correspondence*.

[50] Frege received Letter XLV/11 dated 24 December 1918 from Wittgenstein's sister Hermine, informing Frege that Wittgenstein had been taken prisoner, and that a copy of Wittgenstein's "work," the *Logisch-philosophische Abhandlung*, later *Tractatus Logico-Philosophicus*, had been sent from Italy to Frege for safekeeping. See Frege, *Briefwechsel*, p. 266. The communication is omitted from Frege, *Philosophical and Mathematical Correspondence*.

There was talk at Jena of awarding Frege a medal. It would have been the Knight's Cross, Division of the Order of the White Falcon or Order of the Saxe-Ernestine House. The honor would have been awarded on the occasion of Frege's seventieth birthday. It never happened. There was ample precedent for such an award, a frequent gesture of appreciation on the part of the university in recognition of a scholar's achievements and long years of service to the profession and its students. Vollert made inquiries in this direction, but the proposal predictably never materialized. The paperwork was passed along and stamped with seals in offices, this time through the government bureaucracies of Saxony-Meiningen, Saxon-Altenburg, and Saxe-Coburg Gotha, and examined by the appropriate Duke's state ministries, with the result that in the end the acknowledgment was not approved.[51]

An interesting fact is revealed in the surviving documentation, to the effect that Frege would be leaving his university-administered yearly Carl-Zeiss-Stiftung salary of 5,000 Marks. This was the amount of yearly retirement pension Frege began to receive after 1 October 1918, when he officially left the university. He was entitled at the time to receive a total of about 6,000 Marks of temporarily unwavering currency. By comparison, to show that Frege was not extraordinarily disadvantaged despite his questionable reputation and negligible benefit to students in the mathematics faculty at Jena, Thomae, who had been more conventionally active in research and popular as an instructor, retired on a pension of 7,000 Marks. Frege was also allocated cost of living allowances thereafter, and supplementary disbursements in several categories over the years of his retirement. Because of rising inflation in Germany after the end of WWI, and especially from 1919 onward, Frege's retirement package grew exponentially, rising to 12,233,100 Marks on 1 July 1923. By 1 November 1923, Frege's monthly pension had risen to 874 billion Marks. There was a tremendous amount of worthless paper notes in circulation. Adjustments downward were later made after currency and tax reform legislation had finally been enacted in December

---

[51] See Kreiser, *Gottlob Frege*, pp. 515–16.

1923, bringing Frege's retirement pension back down to relative numerical sanity.[52]

Frege's house in Jena sold in 1918 for what was deemed the reasonable price of 50,000 Marks. Frege did not receive all the money, because there was a dispute over the property as part of their mother's estate filed in the Wismar district court by Frege's brother, Arnold. After many years of minding his own business in Mecklenburg, he suddenly re-emerged in the story.[53] An equitable settlement was achieved, but the fact that Frege did not realize the total sale of the house his mother had built explains why his retirement to Bad Kleinen in the same year and making installment payments toward the building of a new house were made possible only by Wittgenstein's opportune financial assistance. Frege moved expediently when the way was clear. He was registered as a homeowner in Bad Kleinen from October 1919. He lived in temporary quarters for some of this intervening time in Jena. In summer 1918 his address was still given as Jena, Forstweg 29. For the winter semester of 1918–1919 and thereafter through 1919, after he had already moved to Bad Kleinen, he was recorded as residing temporarily at Kaiser-Wilhelm-Straße 24 (The Oil Mill), on a road that is now called August-Bebel-Straße. The house was an inn with rooms to rent, primarily patronized by students. By 1920, Frege and his address were no longer listed in the university course catalog.[54]

As 1923 closed, Frege was in continuing ill health. He had been jolted through some of the worst inflationary times any modern European nation has suffered. He had been in retirement in Bad Kleinen for five years, thanks in large part to Wittgenstein, and had begun to build a house in Pastow. He labored away during early retirement years on a proposal to reform electoral laws, a matter he had mentioned obliquely in an earlier letter to Wittgenstein.[55] Alfred was in the Wismar Große Stadtschule, and about

---

[52] Kreiser describes the financial implications for the 1919–1923 German inflation in *Gottlob Frege*, pp. 563–66. He writes, p. 563, my translation, "On 1 October 1923, Frege received 1,036,728 Billion Marks, which represented one twelfth of the value on that day of his yearly nominal pension of 6,000 Marks, calculated in gold. This amounted to 86 thousand million Marks, which by the 13th October had the exchange value of $21.50."

[53] Kreiser, *Gottlob Frege*, p. 627.   [54] *Ibid.*, p. 505.

[55] Frege in 1918 drafted and floated his extensive plan for "Suggestions for an Electoral Law," unpublished in his lifetime. He mentioned the proposal in his Letter III [ix]/15 to Dingler in Frege, *Philosophical and Mathematical Correspondence*, p. 30: "I am also concerned with matters that fall into the area of politics and political economy, as for example with proposals for an electoral law. But here I have the depressing feeling that my work will be in vain.

to matriculate for mechanical engineering courses in Berlin. Frege's lifework in mathematical logic and its philosophy remained under-appreciated. His was a name buried in the history of a discipline that had moved beyond him without understanding his involvement. He was still a living legend, but surpassed and disregarded even for what remain today some of the most valuable intellectual contributions to mathematical logic and the philosophical foundations of arithmetic in the nineteenth and twentieth centuries. Frege had but two years left to live, and he had just seen to press his final published logical investigation in the essay on "Compound Thoughts."

In the later three essays of the *Logische Untersuchungen*, Frege salvaged what he believed had survived the wreck of his *Grundgesetze* after Russell's paradox. He dusted them off and judged them capable of good service as he thought his way, together with the reader, back toward at least compound truth-functional logic, the truth-functional component of the general concept-functional calculus in his *Begriffsschrift*. The problem did not lie there. Not absolutely everything had been destroyed by Russell's paradox. Where exactly did the difficulty arise? If it was there, Frege would find it. If it was not, Frege would know. Frege explained the concept of a third-realm predicational or propositional content of thought. With propositions in hand, he described how to combine them truth-functionally in proposition-building negations, conjunctions, and the material conditional of his *Begriffsschrift*. Frege's writing of his *Logische Untersuchungen* proves that he had not given up on his original analytic and constructive philosophical platform for logicism. Frege must have been actively engaged in writing these papers for publication during his supposedly inactive slump or publication dark ages after 1904. Frege was rebuilding more carefully and cautiously than ever before. He was not idle nor, beyond the realm of an overactive historical imagination, was he stewing indulgently in annoyance or self-pity.

Nobody has time for this now. I have sent typewritten copies to representatives and other gentlemen, but have received only one reply – an affirmative one – from the president of the Farmers' Union, Dr Boehme. But there is no prospect that these proposals can ever be realized. Here I have of course stepped onto ground outside the field of my usual endeavors." It appears to have been this manuscript in progress that Frege also mentioned to Wittgenstein in his *Feldpostkarte* from about the same time. The proposal included background information, a short overview of the details of the plan, and advice for understanding the reforms, taking into account the political and constitutional debates of the time, with Frege's reactions. See Dathe, "Die Anfänge von Gottlob Freges wissenschaftlicher Laufbahn," p. 289.

14

The Twilight Years (1923–1925) and Frege's Enduring Legacy in Mathematical Logic and Philosophy

There is little cause for satisfaction with the state in which mathematics finds itself at present, if you have regard not to the outside, to the amount of it, but to the degree of perfection and clarity within. In this respect it leaves almost everything to be desired if you compare it with the ideal you may reasonably propose for this discipline, and when you consider that by its very nature it ought to be better fitted to approach its ideal than is any other discipline.

Frege, "Logical Defects in Mathematics" (unpublished, 1898–1899 or later, probably not after 1903; *Nachlaß*, p. 156)

THIS CHAPTER CLOSES the story of Frege's life. There is only sketchy information about the details of his death and how he spent his final moments. We know a great deal more about Socrates' passing than we do about Frege's. We know who Descartes's attending physician was when he died in 1650. Descartes was ushered from this world by a Dutchman, Dr. Johan Weulles, Queen Christina's personal physician in Stockholm, who may even have poisoned Descartes out of envy or religious antagonism. There seems in contrast to be no published information about the at-home circumstances in which Frege's life concluded.[1] Even the exact time and immediate cause of Frege's death do not

---

[1] Weulles (Johan van Wullen) was supposed to have been Descartes's intellectual enemy at Queen Christina's court in Stockholm where he was physician. He is sometimes rumored to have brought about Descartes's death by poisoning. There may also have been a religious, Lutheran (Weulles) versus Catholic (Descartes), conflict at work behind the scenes of Weulles's animosity toward Descartes. See Amir D. Aczel, *Descartes's Secret Notebook: A True Tale of Mathematics, Mysticism, and the Quest to Understand the Universe* (New York: Random House, 2005), pp. 195–97. Another popular but no less scholarly informed treatment

seem to be clearly known. Influenza or pulmonary inflammation is mentioned as likely, but without definite medical certification. His long-time battle with an unspecified digestive ailment may also have taken its toll.[2] The accumulation of prolonged weakening factors may have made Frege defenseless against lung infections his run-down body was no longer capable of resisting at his advanced stage of life. If so, it would have been a very common ending for the logician and philosopher, especially in the early part of the twentieth century in his part of Europe. Frege, surviving to almost seventy-seven, was in the tenth percentile of Germans dying of natural causes in the period 1915–1925. Average life expectancy for German men at the time was fifty-one.[3] Like most events of Frege's life, his death and funeral were a private affair. Hardly anything beyond the official public record after the event is known.

The Hour of Death

By 1924, Frege's financial reserves were practically exhausted. His income was far below the taxable amount. His pension or retirement pay in that year increased to 8,226 Marks. Kreiser reports that

The effect of the currency reform and the tax regulation associated with it at the end of 1923 on the pension calculation for Frege was that on 1 December 1923 his basic pension was calculated at 3,900 Marks, plus a 252 Mark residence allowance, thus 4,152 Marks yearly. His pension increased through four recalculations during the year 1924 to 8,226 Marks, and amounted on 1 April 1925 to 8,316 Marks, 7,458 Marks basic pension and 858 Mark residence allowance.[4]

is Russell Shorto, *Descartes' Bones: A Skeletal History of the Conflict Between Faith and Reason* (New York: Random House, 2008).

[2] See the death certificate reproduced in Kreiser, *Gottlob Frege*, pp. 624–25, which lists no cause of death. It was signed only by a certain A. Levermann on behalf of the Parish Council. Levermann was a local functionary who is not identified as a physician, although being a medical doctor would be part of an individual's legal name in Germany and would normally have been included on official documents of the kind. Nor does there seem to be evidence of any effort at discovering the exact cause of Frege's death having been made. It may not have been necessary or even usual in the year Frege died for a physician to pronounce the subject dead. He was plainly dead and there had plainly been no foul play. Kreiser does not locate or make mention of any physician's statement as to Frege's certification of death, citing only the report of the *Gemeindevorstand*.

[3] Average life expectancy for men in Germany in 1925 documented by the Statistisches Bundesamt Deutschland.

[4] Kreiser, *Gottlob Frege*, p. 564, my translation.

There is much that is not known and probably irrecoverable about Frege's fiscal condition at the time. The vast majority of Frege estate papers and the correspondence about the Jena house and other matters relating to Frege's capital in the last two years before his death were lost, without copies having been made. This conflagration also claimed the originals of Frege's scientific–philosophical *Nachlaß*. What is certain was that Frege's health and his material means of support in the two years preceding his death were both seriously depleted.

Toward the middle of July 1925 Frege's physical condition deteriorated rapidly. "Age-related weakness and stomach trouble began together to complete their work," Kreiser explains, interpolating the few known facts as he prefers. "Frege's physical condition in July 1925 threatened the worst to come. The drugs were no longer effective. The pain was alleviated only by means that at the same time put Frege into a sleep-like state. At this time he was receiving only liquid feeding, and less and less of it, leaving him malnourished."[5] The outcome could not have been in dispute. It was only a matter of a relatively short time. During the late middle of the night on 26 July 1925, Frege in his weakened condition died of natural causes, peacefully, one likes to think, in his retirement abode in Bad Kleinen.[6] He had presumably been mostly bedridden for some days. At the time, he was approximately four months away from his seventy-seventh birthday. He had been in weakened health for many years, and for a man of his age in early-twentieth-century Germany he can be said to have had a full life, with its usual rewards and some peculiar, mostly self-inflicted, pains. In Frege's lifespan he established virtually from scratch and immeasurably enriched the disciplines of mathematical logic and analytic philosophy that he personified in his adherence to a conscientiously scientific methodology.[7]

Frege's Funeral and Memorial

The funeral took place at 12:00 noon at the Old Cemetery in Wismar. Donations, as are sometimes solicited for memorial wreaths and suchlike, were specifically discouraged in accordance with Frege's wishes. He may have seen such gestures as a pointless waste of money or religious fetishism. Was there a religious service? It is likely, although we do not know. Frege's

[5] *Ibid.*, p. 624.   [6] *Ibid.*

[7] The most thorough recent source, emphasizing Frege's philosophy of language, is Matthias Schirn, ed., *Frege: Importance and Legacy* (Berlin: Walter de Gruyter, 1996).

obituary written by Alfred appeared in the *Mecklenburger Tageblatt*. It reads simply, in translation,

During the night of Saturday to Sunday dear God took from me my good, beloved father University-Professor Councillor Dr. Gottlob Frege in his 77th year of life.[8]

There follows a signature block in which Alfred identifies himself as the author of the notice and administrator of his father's funeral. It is interesting that it was not Arnold. Alfred gave the place and time for the burial service as Wednesday at the *alter Friedhof*. The Old Cemetery is known today as the East Cemetery or *Ostfriedhof*. A simple iron cross still marks the grave. It shows Frege's name and titles, which were legally parts of his name in Germany (Hofrat Dr. Gottlob Frege. Professor a. d. Universität Jena), and his dates of birth and death (the latter of which is incorrectly given as 28 July 1925, which was the date of the obituary in the *Mecklenburger Tageblatt*). There is nothing more. Alfred may have discussed the matter in preparation with Frege, because in the obituary notice he requested that there be no *Kranzspenden*, no donations for memorial wreaths. There was no mention of Frege's accomplishments in the brief notice, only of Alfred alone as surviving Frege in death. On 29 July 1925, Frege's body was transferred from Bad Kleinen to Wismar and buried in the Old Cemetery at a gravesite marked by grave stele number 360.

Ashes to ashes: Frege the mathematician might have appreciated having made a 360 degree return to stele 360, his mortal remains brought back to the sleepy Baltic harbor city of his birth and youth. He was interred in the family plot where his father had been buried approximately fifty-nine years earlier. It was the final resting place also of Frege's mother, Auguste, whose body was transferred from Jena, where she died, back to Wismar.[9] A bronze bust of Frege was placed more recently in the little sculpture park of the bomb-ruined Marienkirche in Wismar, where Frege and his family had been congregation members. Rather than the gravesite, the *Frege-Büste* is the main testimony of Frege's existence in his hometown. It was crafted by Karl-Heinz Appelt and mounted on a concrete plinth with an explanatory plexiglas plaque attached. It is not an immediately recognizable likeness, judging from the succession of photographs of Frege in circulation. There is something slightly wrong about the beard and elongation of the face. The image was presumably meant to reflect Frege around 1910, when the

---

[8] The original German wording of the announcement is given in Kreiser, *Gottlob Frege*, p. 629.
[9] *Ibid.*, p. 625.

mathematician was sixty-two years old. Another marker was affixed to the post-war building at Böttcherstraße 2, where Frege's place of birth once stood, to celebrate the "Frege Year" in 1998, the one hundred and fiftieth anniversary of his birth.

One should not undervalue these tangible remembrances, but Frege's real monument, the one that would surely have mattered to him the most, is not made of bronze or stone, but of paper and ink, and more recently computer inscriptions, the living legacy of his influential discoveries in logic, mathematics, and philosophy. It is embodied in the presence on library shelves of his writings, which he made every effort to publish, knowing that publication of his work was vital to the philosophical cause he served. Frege's influence is manifest in university curricula and logic and philosophy classrooms worldwide today, spilling over into a vast secondary literature on his thought and applications of his ideas.[10]

There was no death mask. It was the sort of thing that was becoming increasingly passé in the early twentieth century. It might not have been thought of, a token of Frege's importance that he might have discouraged anyway. The act of setting plaster over his face to preserve an exact image shortly after death, putting him in the same historical category as Napoleon, Goethe, and Beethoven, might have been thought to exaggerate Frege's significance. He was not a celebrity during his lifetime, even within the specialized narrow-interest field of mathematical logic and philosophy. There seems to have been no coffin photograph, or at least none that has survived in the public domain. At the time, personal cameras were not particularly common, and, just like with a death-mask-maker, having a photographer do professional work would cost

---

[10] The best gauge of the degree of interest in Frege's philosophy is indicated by the number of books and articles published in the last ten years. It would be a challenging effort to keep track of all the secondary literature on Frege. There has clearly been exponential growth in the Frege commentary, interpretation and criticism industry since Frege's death. Interest in his work has been more prominent since the 1970s, and dramatically more so beginning since about 1990. An electronic query made on 11 March 2015 while this book was in progress reveals that on *Scopus*, from 1960–1990 (thirty-one years) there were 79 entries on 'Frege', whereas in 1991–2015 (twenty-five years) there were 949 entries. *The Philosophers' Index* reports for these same periods 1960–1990: 655 entries, 1991–2015: 1,322 entries. *Web of Science* mentions 1960–1990: 395 entries, 1991–2015: 1,121. *Philpapers* 1960–1990: 589, 1991–2015: 999. *SpringerLink* (covering only Springer Verlag publications on Frege) 1960–1990: 71, 1991–2015: 135. Obviously, many essays during these periods will be mentioned multiple times by these listing sources, which, with the exception of *SpringerLink* are not exclusive in their bibliographic coverage.

money, of which Frege's survivors were soon to be in embarrassingly short supply. It is exceptional to think in historical terms when a loved one has died, especially when an individual like Frege has lived in relative obscurity, outside the course of world affairs. If Arnold came to pay his respects at the funeral, after his recent legal skirmishes with Gottlob over property inheritance, who else was there besides Alfred and Meta to view the body and bend the head for more than a couple of minutes passing through the Bad Kleinen house or later at the church?

Word of Frege's death began to spread, and was met with due solemnity at the University of Jena. On the day before Frege's burial, the Rector of the university, the lawyer Prof. Dr. Heinrich Gerland (1874–1944), announced at a meeting of the Senate, with fifty-one senators attending, that Gottlob Frege, along with Carl Cappeller (1842–1925), a professor of classical philology, had recently died. The dead were honored by the senators in session rising from their seats for a moment of silence. On the following day, that of Frege's funeral, the Rector officially shared in writing with the Thuringian Ministry of Education and Justice, Department of Public Education, in Weimar, the information that Frege was deceased.[11]

On the very day that Frege was laid in the ground, proving that bureaucracies can manage some events with efficiency, the University of Jena bursary acted promptly to terminate Frege's pension at the end of July 1925. Paperwork in the official archive indicates that the order was issued with dispatch exactly two days before the end of July, and no more than five days after Frege's death.[12] One assumes from the timetable that there was some budgetary impetus to prevent even another month's retirement payment beyond the letter of the law being issued to Frege's dependents. It was cut off at the tap as soon as possible after the former Jena Associate Honorary Ordinary Professor had been laid to rest and his pension obligation fulfilled. Frege might have admired the office's prompt rule-governed exactitude in the transaction. The effect of Frege's death was more than that Meta Arndt and Alfred Frege were suddenly bereft of the *liebevoller Vater*. Of even greater immediate material concern was that they were now without the reliable source of income that Frege had provided for their stitched-together family until his moment of departure.

---

[11] Kreiser, *Gottlob Frege*, p. 629.   [12] *Ibid.*, pp. 629–30.

Alfred and Meta

Alfred and Meta were disconnected from Frege's pension. When Frege died in 1925 there was virtually no appreciable estate on which they could live. There was property, but it was not immediately convertible to liquid assets. They would need to live somewhere. Frege must have anticipated the problems that were going to result from his weakened physical condition, but simply had no more to offer the housekeeper and his adopted son. They may have been hoping against hope that Frege would remain alive at least until the boy had finished his studies, so that they could keep drawing on Frege's university pension until then. Latterly, they may have banked, against the statistics, on him surviving the recent respiratory assault combined with chronic digestion problems, as he had probably survived several similar crises in the past. There was apparently nothing more by way of financial planning or distribution of wealth to be arranged. Frege did not die destitute, but he was unable to make provision for his immediate loved ones, once his pension had been decisively cut off *statim post mortem* only several days after his passing.[13]

It is interesting that there never seemed to be much question after Frege's death that Meta and Alfred would remain together at least until Alfred had finished his schooling. Perhaps it was all predetermined. Alfred would have a home to which he could return during this time with his adoptive father's faithful former housekeeper. He was supposed to be at school. He had transferred to Wismar when Frege retired from Jena and moved to Bad Kleinen. By 2 November 1925, Alfred, seeking relief from his and Meta's desperate circumstances, applied to the University of Jena Senate for a study grant so that he could continue his education. The grant petition protocol mentions also Meta Arndt. She was the "*Frau*," meaning woman rather than wife in the legal sense, for whom a higher level of economic support was requested. She was officially only Frege's housekeeper, and now sole guardian of Frege's legally adopted son. She hoped that the university would donate funding in support of the suddenly indigent dependents of their respected Honorary Ordinary Professor, and especially to provide financial assistance to continue Alfred's education. The Senate chair and members may have been sympathetic, but in the end they decided that they were not empowered to act in the matter. Educational assistance could not be

---

[13] *Ibid.*, pp. 565–70.

offered by the Jena University Senate merely on the grounds that
Alfred's adoptive father had been an Associate Professor there for many
years, but only by the academic foundation where Alfred was studying.
The application was worth a try, if only to apprise Frege's former
colleagues of his survivors' condition. The live-in housekeeper was not
mentioned as having any civil status other than that of being Frege's past
employee. She was a good housekeeper, and now she must find another
house to keep in order to maintain her livelihood. The bonds between
Gottlob, Meta, and Alfred were in truth more like matters of family than
ordinary contractual employment. It was revealing of her sense of desperation that Arndt thought it worthwhile to petition the university for
financial relief after Frege's death. It was the university, after all, from
which Gottlob's life-sustaining pension payments had previously flowed.
Now there was nothing. What were she and Alfred to do?

The fact seems obvious enough, and one imagines there could not have
been long deliberation about such a cut-and-dried jurisdictional matter
on the Senate floor. Subsequently, Frege's brother, Arnold, would also
petition to obtain a share of Frege's by-then dehydrated retirement
pension. That Alfred and Meta made their appeal to the university
indicates how dependent they felt on the institution where Frege had
given so many years of service. They may not have known at home that he
was considered disparagingly in the workplace by colleagues and the
higher administration. It was also testimony to how apprehensive they
must have felt, suddenly being thrown back on their own efforts, hoping
to be able to continue to receive some part of Frege's pension, or to be
awarded a special allowance. They looked first to Frege's former business, the faucet from which sustaining regular bank payments had previously flowed. Not knowing where else to turn, they were reduced first
to trying anything that might bring relief, and perhaps beginning to panic
about their situation. They may have been advised to petition the university first, so that others could not refuse them by saying they must try
this avenue before their request could be considered. While Frege was
still alive in 1918, shortly before his retirement, they had sold the house in
Jena built by Frege's mother, Auguste, to the mill owner John Hansen.
Meta and Alfred thereafter occupied rented accommodation in Pastow
near Rostock, when Alfred, who was already twenty-two years old in
1925, was not away at school. This was where Frege, with a generous
donation from young Wittgenstein just back from the war, was supposed

to have invested in building a house for them all to occupy together again. Almost anything else could happen, but not that. The house was completed only after Frege's death. It was not an asset to be converted into Marks to buy food and pay rent. Meta and Alfred were entitled by Frege's will to live in the Pastow house indefinitely, but when Frege died there was framing but as yet no habitable building.[14] How their other living expenses were met after Frege's death is not known. It would not have been out of the question for them to have appealed for and received assistance from the Lutheran parish to which they belonged, where the pastor, through whom the wardship of Alfred had been negotiated in 1908, was a distant relative of Frege's mother.[15]

On 26 November, Alfred turned over several letters and postcards addressed to Frege to the science historian Ludwig Darmstaedter for his autograph collection in the Prussian State Library. It appears that the letters had been pre-selected by Frege and set aside for this specific archival bequest. On 11 December 1925 Alfred's gratitude for the honor paid to his adoptive father Frege was communicated to members of the Jena Faculty of Mathematics and Natural Sciences. It was a courteous gesture, but it did not change the fact that Alfred and Meta were suddenly dangerously impoverished.[16]

Frege's lifework had come to an end. The work of understanding his life and his contributions to logic and philosophy had barely begun, and it was only long afterward that his output could be surveyed as a completed body of scientific discoveries. We begin by considering what can be known of Frege's character and personality from the facts of his biography, anecdotes, correspondence, and whatever clues were made known. The interpretive question is whether or not the disappointing reception of Frege's philosophy and the apparent conquering of his *Grundgesetze* by Russell's paradox, combined with the death of loved ones and professional dissatisfactions, brought him to his grave an embittered man. The legacy of Frege's *opera* in proper perspective within the evolutionary history of mathematical logic and analytic philosophy needs to be assessed in this history and at this juncture as the final tribute to Frege's accomplishments.

[14] *Ibid.*, p. 624. For details about Frege's estate, *ibid.*, pp. 565–67.
[15] The individual concerned was Pastor Dr. Johannes Eberhard Burghard von Lüpke. See Kreiser, *Gottlob Frege*, pp. 500–501.
[16] *Ibid.*, pp. 624–27.

The Apocryphal Return of Prodigal Son Frege to Kant

It is sometimes said that Frege in his last days, having expended all efforts to discover the source of Russell's paradox, unable in philosophical con-science to blame his unconditional extensionality principle as the root cause, rethought the possibility of returning to a quasi-Kantian proto-intuitionistic philosophy of arithmetic. By such a choice he would have acknowledged the advantage of working out a grounding of the basic concepts of arithmetic in the perception of objects occurring in and conditioned by time as a pure form of intuition, rather than as concepts of pure logic. That obviously would have constituted a drastic turnaround. Here is Dummett's frequently cited statement of this alleged shift in Frege's perspective on the philosophy of mathematics:

At the very end of Frege's life, he again started to work on the philosophy of mathematics, having arrived at the conclusion that one of the fundamental bases of his earlier work – the attempt to found arithmetic on logic – had been mistaken; but the work did not progress very far and was not published.[17]

If what Dummett says is true, why did Frege bother in his final publications to explain with such care the basic logical proposition-building operations of truth-functional negation, conjunction, and mate-rial conditional? Where is the evidence in any of these writings or in the *Nachlaß* of Frege's turning his back on pure logicism and gravitating toward a psychology of perception and Kantian transcendentalism invol-ving time as a pure form of intuition in the philosophy of arithmetic?

To offer such a possibility as historical interpretation is partly irre-sponsible conjecture. There is too little unequivocal evidence supporting Frege's abandonment of pure logicism at any time of his philosophical career right up to the end of his life. If it were true that Frege in his late maturity was ready to go back to Kant's transcendental aesthetics of time for his philosophy of arithmetic, then it would be hard to explain why he devoted his final publications and the *Nachlaß* which he so carefully entrusted to Alfred to the same topics in the philosophy of arithmetic seen in the same logical foundationalist perspective that he had always previously espoused. Where evidence does not rule, argument sometimes tries to make up for the shortage. The implied explanation for Frege's hypothetical change of heart concerning the logical foundations of

[17] Dummett, "Gottlob Frege," *Encyclopedia Britannica.*

arithmetic in favor of the Kantian thesis that time as a pure form of intuition explained the possibility of arithmetical truth is that Frege must have finally accepted Russell's paradox as irrevocably destroying the prospects of any philosophically respectable non-*ad hoc* restoration of logicism's advertised rigorous logically circumspect non-psychologistic grounding of elementary arithmetic. If there is a case to be made for the critical thesis that Frege near the end of his life changed his mind about the prospects of logicism, then there should be a more definite paper trail to the exact moment of Frege's imagined late-life Kantian epiphany.

Frege's last known writings support and do nothing to detract from the impression of his career-long unswerving commitment to logicism, from his earliest writings to the posthumous scientific literary texts he left behind in his *Nachlaß*. The popular philosophical narrative of Frege's last days questionably assumes that Frege had always agreed anyway with the conclusion of Kant's Transcendental Aesthetic in the first *Critique* that space as a pure form of intuition explains the foundations of geometry as one of two pure forms of intuition, as time did for Kant in the transcendental foundations of arithmetic, contrary to Frege's belief for all of his previous lifetime. The interpretation conjectures that near the end of his life Frege must have lost faith altogether in logicism, despite his attempt to patch up the logical axioms of *Grundgesetze I* in the *Grundgesetze II* Afterword. The reaction here for Frege was triggered like an electric jolt to the central nervous system by Russell's paradox letter of 16 June 1902. There should have been something comparable if Frege had turned against pure logicism in the philosophy of arithmetic in favor of Kant's metaphysics of mathematics, but the evidence for the claim that Frege accepted time as the ground of arithmetic in true Kantian spirit is thin and equivocal.

Anthony Kenny and others have argued that toward the end of his active writing career Frege abandoned the sharp distinction between the philosophical foundations of arithmetic and those of geometry. Kenny begins as follows, quoting as the source of his interpretation an unpublished *Nachlaß* item from very late in Frege's life, namely a small paper note thought to be from 1924–1925, the penultimate item included in the English translation of Frege's posthumous papers:

In the last year of his life Frege returned to the Kantian position which he had set out to refute at the beginning of *The Foundations of Arithmetic* [*Grundlagen*]: since arithmetic was *a priori*, but had turned out to be analytic, it must rest, like geometry, on intuition. In his last [*sic*] paper, "Numbers and Arithmetic," he talks with contempt of "kindergarten-numbers" – the numbers that give the answer to the question "How many," and to whose elucidation he had devoted the best years of his life. He once believed, he now tells us, that it was possible to conquer the entire number domain, continuing along a purely logical path from the kindergarten-numbers; but he has now seen the mistake in this:

The more I have thought the matter over, the more convinced I have become that arithmetic and geometry have developed on the same basis – a geometrical one in fact – so that mathematics in its entirety is really geometry. Only on this view does mathematics present itself as completely homogeneous in nature. Counting, which arose psychologically out of the demands of business life, has led the learned astray.[18]

What is clear from the unpublished manuscript, which is only two-and-a-third pages long in printed translation, is that Frege was making explicit a long-overdue recognition that arithmetic and geometry must be "completely homogeneous in nature." There is one unified mathematics, he now clearly understands, and it may have geometry at its foundation rather than arithmetic. Frege's pre-Habilitation background and teaching experience for years thereafter in mapping imaginary and complex numbers into a plane of values alongside the real number line conditioned him to regard the distinction between arithmetic and geometry as artificial, superficial. He became accustomed in all this mathematical conceptualization to going back and forth and back again from geometry to arithmetic with no logical barricade.

That he seems to have opted in this late unpublished manuscript for geometry over arithmetic is interesting. However, it does not prove what Kenny claims in his interpretation, namely that Frege made a late-life U-turn conversion back to Kantianism in the philosophy of mathematics. Frege's note would do so only if it could further be documented that Frege accepted Kant's Transcendental Aesthetic of the foundations of geometry as the pure form of intuition in perceiving physical objects distributed in space, as opposed to and in preference over logic. No one has thus far been able to prove that. For all we know, Frege was merely trying out ideas on paper in order to be able to remember the argument's conclusion, possibly for the purpose of refutation later on. Kenny's interpretation accordingly depends on the further highly questionable assumption that Frege, had he lived to pursue a unified model of the grounds of mathematics, would have

---

[18] Kenny, *Frege: An Introduction*, pp. 176–77. The quotation is from Frege, *Posthumous Writings*, p. 277.

regarded Kant's transcendental foundations of geometry as irreducible to logical concepts and inference structures.

Why would anything like that transpire? Why should Frege not consider that geometry, just as much as arithmetic, had purely logical foundations, especially given Frege's views up until this last-minute revelation that arithmetic had purely logical foundations, and that arithmetic and geometry with the right correlative functions at play were formally interconvertible? The inference Kenny superimposes on the quotation he proffers from Frege's *Nachlaß* essay on "Numbers and Arithmetic" is inconclusive for at least these reasons. Whether Frege himself traveled back down this route toward Kantianism in the philosophy of mathematics again depends on many factors, each of which is difficult to judge. The fact that Frege mentioned geometry but not Kant in this context is significant. If we assume all along, as one of the myths about Frege's presuppositions has it, that Frege distinguished sharply between arithmetic and geometry, then we must wonder what he made of his early conventional geometrical work involving imaginary and complex numbers when looking back on it years later. That he concentrated on arithmetic in the development of logicism is clear. Notably, there are no passages where he unequivocally declared that an alternative parallel kind of logicism could not be undertaken with the axioms of elementary geometry, just as he had attempted with the axioms of elementary arithmetic. The fact that these formal languages involved inferential structures of theorems logically deduced from alike axioms left only the task of explaining the most basic concepts in the axioms of geometry in purely logical terms, just as Frege believed he had done, albeit with some rough corners still to polish, in analyzing the concept-function of natural number on a supposedly purely logical basis, while reducing the basic laws of elementary arithmetic to principles of supposedly pure logic.

Frege at the height of his powers should have been more than equal to the challenge, favoring applied arithmetical or geometrical logic as his objective. He said nothing to preclude the venture. The project is stereotypically Fregean, even if Frege had reasons of his own for beginning his investigations with the logical foundations of arithmetic. Frege said nothing to disown logicism in the posthumously published pages on "Numbers and Arithmetic." If Frege did not reject logicism, whether directed toward arithmetic in the first instance or derivable from the parallel logical structures of an applied geometrical logic, then he did not embrace anything that could deservedly be called Kantianism in the philosophy of mathematics. He did not accept the idea of reducing the transcendental ground of all mathematics to space alongside time as one of two pure forms of intuition, as Kant too could not have sanctioned. A pure form of intuition is still a form. It is something formal, obviously, and therefore abstract, leaving Frege's third realm of *Gedanken* out of account. Frege offered no hint in his last writings that arriving at a unified ground for all of mathematics in the form of spatial perception would be the end of the story. He said nothing to indicate that he would have turned away from the hypothesis that geometry must also have an underlying purely logical rather than spatial substructure of which Kant was unaware.

Explanatory attractiveness in and of itself, even when illustrated by a charming Bible fable, does not always provide the most reliable guide to truth. It may pique and focus our interest, standing out from other merely logical possibilities by virtue of its appeal, wallowing all the while in abject falsehood. The evidence for supposing that Frege early in his philosophy accepted a clearcut distinction between geometry and arithmetic, and that later, near the end of his life, he accepted Kant's explanation of the transcendental grounds of the two distinct branches of mathematics, appears equivocal. The text and surrounding facts on which Kenny relies do not, on critical reflection, support the interpretation that Frege agreed with Kant in his late understanding of the grounding of arithmetic, abandoning pure logic in favor of Kant's transcendental aesthetics of time as pure form of intuition. Frege in any event did not return to Kant, if we rely, as Kenny does, on the *Nachlaß* pages titled "Numbers and Arithmetic." What Frege mentioned there cannot be considered a return to Kant, because Kant for his part would never have countenanced the reduction of arithmetic to geometry or vice versa. To do so would overthrow the supposedly independently established Transcendental Aesthetic in Kant's first *Critique* in its sharp-edged division between arithmetic and geometry, time and space.

Looking for signs in earlier writings that Frege started out distinguishing between the foundations of arithmetic as opposed to those of geometry, D. A. Gillies, in his 1982 study *Frege, Dedekind, and Peano on the Foundations of Arithmetic*, upholds a standard interpretation:

Although Frege attacks Kant on arithmetic, he defends him on geometry. Indeed he says, (1884) *Foundations of Arithmetic*, § 89, pp. 101e–102e [Austin translation]: "I have no wish to incur the reproach of picking petty quarrels with a genius to whom we must all look up with grateful awe; I feel bound, therefore, to call attention also to the extent of my agreement with him, which far exceeds any disagreement. To touch only upon what is immediately relevant, I consider KANT did great service in drawing the distinction between synthetic and analytic judgements. In calling the truths of geometry synthetic and a priori, he revealed their true nature. And this is still worth repeating, since even to-day it is often not recognized. If KANT was wrong about arithmetic, that does not seriously detract, in my opinion, from the value of his work. His point was, that there are such things as synthetic judgements a priori; whether they are to be found in geometry only, or in arithmetic as well, is of less importance."[19]

Some critics might find it an exaggeration to say that Frege distinguished sharply between arithmetic and geometry in the passage Gillies quotes. Frege was extraordinarily diplomatic about the sacred cow of German-language philosophy in his day, when in philosophical circles at the time for the most part the question was not whether philosophy should continue to adhere to Kant but which direction philosophy should choose in taking Kant into the future.

What Frege actually said is rather more cagey. He strongly commended Kant's philosophy of mathematics for recognizing the semantic–epistemic status of geometrical theorems as synthetic *a priori*. That is to say that they are not analytic in the sense that the predicate truly attributed to the subject can be found by analysis in breaking down the subject's component concepts. It is not contained in the subject's identity conditions, including the property represented by the predicate. Knowing that geometrical axioms are true does not depend on sensation or perception, when such truths are generally supposed to be mind-independent and extra-experiential. Frege allowed that the "true nature" of geometry, as Kant was the first to argue, is that it consists of synthetic *a priori* propositions, but for him they are interpreted as Fregean thoughts or *Gedanken*. Frege speaks appreciatively when he says that, even if Kant was wrong about arithmetic, it does not "detract from the value of his work."

Had Frege succeeded in reducing the basic laws of elementary arithmetic to the principles of pure logic, as he hoped and at first imagined he had accomplished, then geometry would follow compliantly along the same path in due course through the arithmetization of the geometrical coordinates for naming geometrical objects, axioms, definitions, and

---

[19] D. A. Gillies, *Frege, Dedekind, and Peano on the Foundations of Arithmetic* (Assen: Van Gorcum, 1982), p. 18.

logical inference rules underwriting deductive proofs of geometrical theorems. He did not broach the reduction of geometry to logic, perhaps because he thought he did not need to. What can at most be inferred from what Frege presented and from what he did not say about the relation between arithmetic and geometry in his *Begriffsschrift* and *Grundgesetze*, not to overlook his later essays on geometry, is that Frege concentrated on arithmetic and simply, and probably strategically, left geometry entirely, but perhaps only temporarily, out of consideration.[20]

Frege from the beginning had in mind arithmetical and geometrical applications of the general functional calculus. His discussion of the integration of *F*-functions by higher-level *f*-functions was abstracted from originally geometrical applications in the calculus. If Frege, as seems plausible, took it for granted that geometry must follow where arithmetic leads, then he may have chosen to plumb the logical foundations of arithmetic without mentioning geometry as the first main step in logicism's analytic and reconstructive program. The more interesting question would then be whether at any point in life Frege gave up hope in the prospects of logicism, of his *Begriffsschrift*, *Grundlagen*, and *Grundgesetze*. Perhaps he did so, subjectively, again with a dash of irony, psychologically, even if he would not have needed to abandon his attempt to establish the truth of pure logicism by its own successful instantiation. Merely placing geometry ahead of arithmetic for analytic purposes by itself would not imply Frege's abandoning logicism. There is no reason why Frege as a pure logicist should not have considered the purely logical foundations of geometry as taking precedence over the purely logical foundations of arithmetic in the philosophy of mathematics. That thought in those late days also would not imply Frege's return to Kant, if geometry has priority over arithmetic, but geometry, like arithmetic, has distinctive purely logical foundations.

The historical evidence for the interpretation of Frege as finding his way back home to Kant near the end of his life is slight and without exception equivocal. There is the dispirited report to Russell, declining the invitation to speak at Cambridge University on the foundations of

---

[20] Frege's unpublished papers on geometry are collected in his *Posthumous Writings*, namely "On Euclidean Geometry," pp. 167–69; "Notes on Hilbert's *Grundlagen der Geometrie*," pp. 170–73; and the 1924–1925 fragment "Numbers and Arithmetic," pp. 275–77. See Frege, *On the Foundations of Geometry and Formal Theories of Arithmetic* (New Haven: Yale University Press, 1971).

arithmetic. There are some other casual references in Frege's correspondence with colleagues elsewhere in the world to suggest that Frege may have abandoned logicism. That is only one side of things. The record additionally shows that Frege did not become completely inactive in philosophical logic in the period preceding his final two years. The facts are that Frege lost his mother, Auguste, and his wife, Margarete. Then his friend and mainstay Abbe died. With Frau Arndt's able help, he took on the nurturing of young Alfred, who was still a boy in short pants. His health was not good. He had to request sick leave several times, and on some occasions went to a *Kurbad* (spa) for a temporarily soothing health treatment. Frege pleaded health reasons even for not visiting Wittgenstein in Vienna, and nothing more need be read into his refusal of Russell's invitation to Cambridge.

If Frege in writing the 1924–1925 note on "Numbers and Arithmetic," so near the end of his life, meant to give up on the logical foundations of arithmetic in deference to those of geometry, he should have understood that, even under the best of circumstances, he could not, merely by virtue of prioritizing geometry over arithmetic in the philosophy of mathematics, literally return to Kant and the form of intuition of things in time as an alternative safe harbor. Prioritizing geometry over arithmetic, in Frege's final thoughts on the foundations of mathematics, supposing them to be such, rather than as previously the other way around, is not tantamount to automatically accepting Kant's transcendental grounds of geometry as space, the pure form of spatial intuition. Frege must still explain the formal structure of arithmetic as independent of the formal structure of time. There is no indication in any item of the *Nachlaß* that Frege had a plan of argument for this ambitious undertaking, nor that he ever gave up on the project of establishing purely logical foundations for mathematics, beginning as appropriate with arithmetic or geometry. There is no reason to think that Frege, late in life considering the prioritization of geometry over arithmetic, was attempting to avoid in the imagined turnaround the hard work of laying down purely logical foundations for geometry in the imagined turnaround, which would be analogous to what he had previously tried to provide for arithmetic. He may also have thought that looking at the logical foundations of mathematics from the standpoint of geometry rather than arithmetic might reveal something of interest and importance that had otherwise been overlooked about how things had invisibly gone so badly wrong in *Grundgesetze* arithmetic as to incur

Russell's paradox. The remarks are undeveloped, the comment only a fragment of thought on a fragment of paper.

Frege gave no signal indicating for those in the know that in his last years he had returned discomfited to Kant. He had persistently fled from psychologism. To the extent that he did so in response to Russell's paradox battering against *Begriffsschrift* and *Grundgesetze* fortress walls, Frege surrendered when there was, strictly speaking, no need for him even to blink. He allowed himself to tremble at the sound of an empty threat from a direction that never posed a danger to his logic and logicist philosophy of mathematics in the first place. The whole tightly interconnected package of object-argument and function-concept in predication, thought, meaning, identity, sense and reference, quantity, and truth-values, by which Frege had once wanted to explain every aspect of the formal reduction of the laws of elementary arithmetic to applied concepts of pure logic in a logical inference framework, was never actually in jeopardy.[21]

The Myth of Embitterment

To riff on and reverse the rhetorical opening of Marc Antony's funeral oration in Shakespeare's *Julius Caesar*, Act 3, Scene 2, we are not here to bury Frege, but to appraise and finally praise his life and sustained lifework of important accomplishments in mathematical logic and

---

[21] The narrative arc of the popular myth about Frege's lifelong dialogue with Kant and Kantianism in the philosophy of mathematics has him (i) adopting a first qualified Kantian concept of the pure form of intuition of space as the transcendental ground of geometry; (ii) rejecting Kant's account of the pure form of intuition of time as the distinct but parallel transcendental ground of arithmetic, and substituting an applied pure logic of concept-functions in its place; (iii) rejecting logicism when Russell's paradox proves insuperable on philosophically methodologically acceptable general principles; and (iv) returning to Kant a broken, defeated man with respect to the transcendental grounds of both geometry and arithmetic. The sequence cannot be recommended as describing Frege's philosophical journey compatibly with the fact that he never explicitly renounced logicism. Frege must have understood the problematic nature of the Kantian barrier-breaking mapping equivalences between arithmetical and geometrical theorems that would have united their foundations ineluctably in the final phase of logicism's reduction. Frege's relation to Kant is outlined in Chapters 3 and 5. See also Delbert Reed, *Origins of Analytic Philosophy: Kant and Frege* (London: Continuum Books, 2007); William Demopoulos, *Logicism and its Philosophical Legacy*; Peter Hylton, *Russell, Idealism, and the Emergence of Analytic Philosophy* (Oxford: Clarendon Press, 1993), especially pp. 167–203; and Sten Lindström, Erik Palmgren, Krister Segerberg, and Viggo Stoltenberg-Hansen, eds., *Logicism, Intuitionism, and Formalism: What Has Become of Them?* (Berlin: Springer-Verlag, 2009).

philosophy. We turn first to a question that may seem to tarnish the historical image of Frege's character and personality, in what we shall prejudicially call the myth of the embittered Frege.

It has become a staple of recent biographies of Frege to mention that the dull reception of Frege's writings, topped by Russell's paradox and upsetting events in his personal life, made Frege embittered. The bitter taste in Frege's mouth over difficulties in his work taken as established fact is then invoked to explain such things as Frege's later reluctance to attend mathematical and philosophical meetings, the falling off of correspondence with Russell after one surviving note of 1904 that is, significantly, from Russell to Frege with no archived reply, the palpable reduction of activity in his research agenda, and his desultory-to-nonexistent teaching efforts, as Frege's later years wore on and he became ever more unintelligible to students, as he began taking more frequent leaves of absence to recover his strength by immersion in curative waters.

Dummett sets the tone for what has become a litany of empathic commiseration over Frege's final years. He sounds the theme again of the persistently disappointing response to Frege's philosophy that is supposed to have contributed to making him an embittered man at the time of his death. "With the exceptions I have mentioned," Dummett remarks, "mathematicians and philosophers alike ignored him. This is far from the case now, of course: but in 1925 Frege died an embittered man, convinced both that he had been unjustly neglected, and that his life's work had been for the most part failure."[22] It is a refrain that has been repeated in many variations before and after Frege's death. The historical evidence for such an interpretation of Frege's character and personality nevertheless seems relatively slim. The portrait of Frege as embittered by the reception of his work makes a strong appeal for psychological projection and transference of the sort of emotion that a writer other than Frege, Dummett in this instance, imagines Frege might or must have felt. Frege himself would likely have disapproved of a subjective psychological explanation, in favor of accounting for the facts of his later professional life in terms of the considered reasoning that guided his decisions and inspired his actions. The explanatory charity required in understanding the personality of a thinker of Frege's stature also supports a nonconformist interpretation of his philosophical demeanor and general outlook on life in his golden years.

---

[22] Dummett, *Frege: Philosophy of Language*, p. xxv.

Rather than embittered, although there was probably a touch of bitterness, directed more at the University of Jena and its unpromising mathematics students than at the mathematical and philosophical world, Frege appears to have been more disgusted at the stupidity with which he was surrounded. A discouraging failure to understand the obvious was rampant among his contemporaries, who were either mathematically incapable of learning his notation or too lazy or unmotivated even to try. They might have done so if they had understood the payoff, but that was just the problem. Frege's two-dimensional functional calculus symbolism, the acme of graphic simplicity and transparency, appears even to have baffled Russell, who never fully gained facility with its pictorial representations of truth-functional negations and material conditional logical dependences. Frege released his *Begriffsschrift* as his first major publication. Whatever he succeeded in doing in the book, he failed to explain what he was trying to accomplish or why. He did not say clearly enough what the formal system in precisely this mode of presentation, the notation he had invented, was intended to achieve. Would he have taken the trouble to learn such a new notation if someone else had published the same or similar studies before he did? The answer, presumably, is yes, Frege would have done it. How hard could it be? Frege's logic was only new, not obscure. It was the pinnacle of lucidity, the very antithesis of obscurity. What was wrong with these supposed technical experts in the formal sciences? How could the brightest minds in mathematics and philosophy not have instantly recognized one of their own? It might have been enough to make many people bitter. The question is whether it did so in Frege's case.

Bitter or not, there is no reason to doubt that Frege at once and in different respects naïvely over-estimated and under-estimated his potential readership. He over-estimated the numbers that would be interested in the logical foundations of arithmetic under the best of circumstances. He committed the rookie mistake of assuming that what interested him would, without further preparation, automatically interest others. He failed to appreciate the need to motivate readers to master the general functional calculus when the whole thing was brand new and his potential readership unschooled. Frege was especially remiss when he withheld description of the applications that the logic was eventually supposed to have, the preparatory work for which had stretched out without a published roadmap over nine years. A charitable interpretation is that Frege was deliberate rather than naïve through many of his publication mis-adventures, leading up to June 1902, when Russell's calling card turned from honey to gall on Frege's tongue. We must suppose that the critical fiasco first of the *Begriffsschrift* and then of his *Grundlagen* contributed to making Frege bitter, if in fact he became an embittered man.

The case for the embittered Frege is made on the basis of a forced interpretation of only a few, palpably equivocal, historical facts. If the account were true, then Frege's bitterness would have been rooted in his own unrealistic expectations about the prospects of his immediate scientific and literary success. His bitterness, like most, one supposes, would need to be self-directed. It would be rooted as an early symptom in the self-destructive choices by which he presented his mathematical and philosophical ideas. We have argued on the contrary that Frege's publishing strategy defied popular acceptance for the greater scientific–philosophical good of having each component of the final product stand independently against criticism until they could be locked together in his *Grundgesetze*. Things did not work out as hoped in this regard for Frege. The fact that, on a charitable interpretation, he may have been proceeding rationally according to a strict methodology all along has implications for whether it is correct after these trials to consider Frege as having become embittered.

The historical evidence, judging from Frege's diaries and correspondence, scattered pinpoints of light where there are definite facts on which to build hypotheses, is insufficient to support the interpretation that the reception of Frege's work in mathematical logic and the philosophy of arithmetic, especially after Russell's paradox, made Frege into a resentful acrimonious curmudgeon up to the time of his death. All the known facts can be equally well explained by invoking Frege's understandable disgust, impatience, resignation, and frustration at himself for being unable to find a suitable solution to Russell's paradox. Frege may even have accepted many of these unalterable facts in his universe, with a grain of humor in his better moments, without the tempest resulting in embitterment.

We have only a popular pervasive philosophical–historical myth of Frege as a logician embittered by Russell's paradox and the miserable reception of his published writings. That the interpretation has some plausibility is no proof of its truth. Frege was not too embittered to assume wardship of Alfred in 1908. He was not too embittered to bounce around an astonished Wittgenstein in his study in 1911. He was not too embittered to write and publish the first three essays of his *Logische Untersuchungen* as late as 1918–1923. Here in particular he was also not too embittered to entrust the "gold" in his unpublished *Nachlaß* writings to Alfred, to be preserved for what he imagined to be a more appreciative posterity. It was a choice that would be hard to reconcile with the assumption that Frege had become so embittered as to give up entirely on the prospects of his ideal of logicism taking flight from the ashes of Russell's paradox. He laid the groundwork all over again in his *Logische Untersuchungen* for the general functional calculus, to see whether that part of the wreck could still float. He seems to have conceived of a further chapter on logical generality and probably another on the concept of number. Perhaps yet another chapter, unmentioned even in the *Nachlaß*, could have taken logicism beyond Russell's paradox by way of patient informal explication of co-extensionality identity conditions for logically permissible concept-functions.

Making a gallant effort in a technically difficult and historically groundbreaking undertaking, not being understood or appreciated, when, at least prior to Russell's paradox, Frege was satisfied that he was making steady progress toward a rigorous non-psychologistic logicism, would certainly disappoint, if not discourage. Disappointment and discouragement are often passing states of mind, after which a thinker's fighting spirit rallies. Long-lasting negative feelings resulting from theory-building confrontations with critics are overcome by rising to the occasion and refuting objections or refining the theory. Which of these descriptions best fits Frege, given the historical evidence? Frege was spelling out the purely logical foundations of the basic laws of elementary arithmetic. He was succeeding in his own mind, encountering no solid criticisms until summer 1902. Arriving in that situation after reading Russell's note was likely to disappoint and unsettle anyone trying to accomplish that kind of work. There is nevertheless no law of human psychology that says that anyone suffering a certain level of disappointment is certain or even likely to become bitter. Frege was more resilient than he is usually given credit for being in this chapter of his personal life and in the history of early mathematical logic and modern analytic philosophy. The fact that after June 1902 Frege continued to teach, write, and publish contributions to logicism argues for his not becoming so embittered as to turn away from his abiding philosophical passions.

Was he bitter or disgusted? What did it matter, provided there was something more to understand about the Russell set?

Mathematics, as Frege indicated in the unpublished remark taken as the epigraph for this chapter, which is estimated to have probably been written in 1898–1899, more than halfway through his life's journey, at about the age of forty-one, was in Frege's judgment in a disreputable state. He found it especially unconscionable for a discipline that was expected to set the standard for exact expression and necessary *a priori* proof of all its propositions to exist in a shameful unsystematized disarray of concepts, axioms, and theorems. It was like a clutter of medieval streets, in his judgment, badly in need of rational urban renewal. It was like a largely successful but theoretically unsupported practical culture of alchemical investigations before the systematizations of empirical discoveries about material substances in modern chemistry. Frege wanted to bring it all into respectable order. He meant to explicate the pre-existent purely logical structures by which basic mathematical concepts were ordered. Whereas Descartes expected to make mathematics the gold standard for all natural science and philosophical reasoning, Frege in contrast believed that mathematics as we find it is too disordered in its foundations and proof derivations to provide a positive role-model for any other discipline. Mathematics without proper philosophical foundations for Frege was mere syntactical technique, like a cookbook of recipes for obtaining results rather than a bastion of certain knowledge. Although it would be no trivial undertaking, mathematics must first set its own house in order, formally and philosophically. Frege believed strongly that better organization was needed. He considered candidly that he might be among the few persons capable of achieving the result. Frege as reformer of mathematics had in mind what in his time was resisted as an idiosyncratic project, insofar as the orthodox mathematicians who had to shoulder the weight Frege refused or was unable to lift at Jena were concerned. It was a noble ambition, one that, until Russell posted his paradox, Frege thought he had satisfied, no matter what other colleagues in the profession happened to believe.

Frege was old. He was ill. His teaching was pathetically below the faculty's standard. It was an embarrassment. The students had next to no interest in his logical foundations of arithmetic. They must have seen him in later years shuffling along the halls of the mathematics faculty as though he were already retired and was just wandering about aimlessly, returning to his former office out of confused senile force of habit.

His courses were largely unattended, even at the height of attention concerning logicism when *Grundgesetze I* and *II* were finally published. There was no one at Jena besides Abbe, who was working mostly at Zeiss on the mathematics of physical optics, to steer students toward Frege's courses. There was virtually no one until Russell outside of Jena to generate any external interest in Frege's work that might have percolated through professional channels, specialized journals, and conference discussions to awaken the curiosity of serious young mathematicians at the time. As far as we know, in all his fifty-one years of teaching mathematics at Jena, Frege did not manage to attract one graduate student specifically to work with him on *Begriffsschrift* or *Grundgesetze* topics. Carnap attended lectures, and there must have been some others, drifting in out of curiosity. We can hardly line a shelf with their transcripts of Frege's *Vorlesungen*. They attended in their negligible numbers primarily as advanced philosophical tourists, not dissertation or even master's degree students.

All of which is to say nothing at all about the merits of what Frege managed to accomplish in his writings or what he taught to the few students in attendance. The neglect and misdirected criticisms of his work, the facts about which are not in dispute, were among the main factors judged responsible for his becoming bitter, for those who believe that this increasingly became his predominant state of mind. Perhaps he did become somewhat bitter. More importantly, the affair of Russell's paradox left Frege lacking in cognitive confidence about some things he had previously taken for granted concerning the logical foundations of arithmetic. The unexpected turn of events affected his ability to do the technical work required if his logicism was going to prevail in some salvageable form over the logical antinomy that Russell and Frege alike steadfastly agreed Russell had discovered. He could no longer fully trust his previously infallible faculty of mathematical intuition. He was nevertheless genuinely fascinated, determined to fully understand the problem raised by the Russell set and paradox.

This is certainly how Russell remembered Frege's attitude upon learning of the paradox. Russell recalled Frege in two laudatory testimonials, the first in a letter to Jean van Heijenoort:

As I think about acts of integrity and grace, I realise that there is nothing in my knowledge to compare with Frege's dedication to truth. His entire life's work was on the verge of completion, much of his work had been ignored to the benefit of men infinitely less capable, his second volume was about to be published, and upon finding that his fundamental assumption was in error, he responded with intellectual pleasure clearly submerging any feelings of personal disappointment. It was almost superhuman and a telling indication of that of which men are capable if their dedication is to creative work and knowledge instead of cruder efforts to dominate and be known.[23]

He amplified this apparently heartfelt appreciation of Frege in remarks collected as Russell's *Last Philosophical Testament*:

With the beginning of the twentieth [century], I became aware of a man for whom I had and have the very highest respect although at the time he was practically unknown. This man is Frege. It is difficult to account for the fact that his work did not receive recognition. Dedekind had been justly acclaimed, but Frege on the very same topics was much more profound ... I read the introduction [to Frege's *Grundgesetze*] with passionate admiration, but I was repelled by the crabbed symbolism which he had invented and it was only after I had done the same work for myself that I was able to understand what he had written in the main text ... Frege thought, as I thought for a few months at the turn of the century, that the reduction of mathematics to logic had been definitively completed. But in June 1901 I came across a contradiction which proved that something was amiss. I wrote to Frege about it and he behaved with a noble candour which cannot be too highly praised.[24]

As the years passed and Frege dealt with more of life's hard knocks, he must have begun to think that he would never in his lifetime see the resolution of Russell's paradox in a remodeling of *Grundgesetze* arithmetic. The frustration for Frege was that after 1902 he did not know how to proceed. He did not know what he was supposed to have learned from the collision of Russell's paradox with an intuitively obvious extensionality principle for concept-function identity in the logical foundations of arithmetic. Frege believed that his *Grundgesetze* arithmetic hypothesis had technically failed. More aggravatingly, he did not understand why or what to do about it, and he despaired of his diminishing abilities to rethink it all through from what would have had to have been another fresh starting-place. Frege would need to proceed without a clue how to determine what the alternative starting-place should be. It was a task for another, younger thinker. After WWI had ended and Frege and Wittgenstein were reunited, it was clear that it would not be Wittgenstein who would take over the reins from Frege and

---

[23] Russell, letter to Jean van Heijenoort (Penrhyndeudraeth, 23 November 1962), quoted in van Heijenoort, *From Frege to Gödel: A Source Book in Mathematical Logic 1879–1931* (Cambridge: Harvard University Press, 1967), p. 127.

[24] Russell, *Last Philosophical Testament 1943–1968. The Collected Papers of Bertrand Russell* (London: Routledge, 1997), Volume 11, p. 107.

liberate rigorous non-psychologistic logicism from the Russell paradox morass.

We may optimistically imagine that we could remove the disappointment from the reception of Frege's work and end up with at least an even-keel Frege, rather than a miserable bitter Frege. This is not so clear. It presupposes that Frege was bitter, but offers no concrete evidence of the purported fact. Frege was not so embittered about life generally, despite his noted introversion, as to refrain from becoming an adoptive father. His assuming the role of guardian at the age of fifty, after his wife, Margarete, had already died, with six-year-old child Alfred as his run-amok ward, shows that Frege must have had another side to his personality than the sourful disappointed man of misery that historians of logicism are fond of portraying. Nor did such feelings, assuming Frege experienced them, prevent him from engaging in warm correspondence with a variety of appreciative thinkers who were interested in his work. Small though their numbers were, one was slowly complemented by another, often with Russell as the direct or indirect conduit. Frege, in other words, importantly, if he was embittered about the reception of his work, as rationally one might suppose he had every right to be, did not become misanthropic. This is the key fact. His actions testify that he was not embittered about everything in life. To say that Frege was embittered on the basis of his writings and surrounding documentation is top-heavy over-interpretation and psychological projection rather than responsible historiography.

Consider the facts. Neither Frege's mother nor his wife died suddenly. Nor did Frege when it was his turn. There was ample opportunity for psychological preparation in advance of these inevitabilities, and Frege as a young man had overcome his father's death many years before. It is what life offers everyone who is sufficiently fortunate as to live long enough to suffer its depradations. The loss of loved ones need not have made Frege specifically bitter. He took on Alfred to raise and love, and tried to build a surrogate family with the boy and Meta Arndt as house-hold companions. There is no replacing any person in a life of relationships, and presumably Frege had no thought of finding any substitute for Margarete. That Frege could not go back in time did not mean that he was unwilling to go forward with new persons at his side. The point is that Frege did not give up on the prospects of ordinary human happiness outside the walls of academia. After all, it appears that he succeeded better by far in attaining happiness at home. If Frege became bitter about logic and the failure of his *Grundgesetze*, especially after Russell's paradox, the effect was not so profound as to make him abandon his efforts to advance the cause of logicism in the philosophy of arithmetic. He was delayed and sidetracked, but he did not stop working on and thinking about the purely logical foundations of the basic laws of elementary arithmetic until physically he could no longer continue.

Frege lived the final twenty-three years of his life in the shadow of Russell's paradox. It appears that he did so needlessly. Frege had the resources to reduce the only promising part of the paradox dilemma to the logically noncontradictory barber. Here more than anywhere in Frege's life the previously invoked metaphor of the later Wittgenstein in *Philosophical Investigations* §309 aptly applies, where the purpose, as Wittgenstein explains his "aim in philosophy," is to show the fly the way out of the fly-bottle.

The way out of the Russell paradox fly-bottle should have been easy for Frege. The exasperating thing, even for historical biography, is to look back and see that the fly will not take what to others must seem to be the obvious exit. We watch it from outside the bottle, as we watch what happens to Frege in the wake of learning about Russell's paradox. We watch the fly try every escape route except the one that works. There is a solution; we can almost picture Frege making those moves and meeting the force of Russell's paradox head on, showing that there was no paradox, backing out of the fly-bottle step-by-step the way he came in, through the portal of existence requirements for the Russell paradox set function in Axiom V. It was precisely there that everything in Russell's imaginary logical antinomy came gyrating apart. Time and again Frege did not exploit any strategy remotely resembling the defensive metaparadox of undermining the Russell paradox aimed at his *Grundgesetze*. He was stuck buzzing against the sides of the blue–green glass bottle, a prisoner of his own supine acceptance of the Russell set as an existent entity. In the space between what we might otherwise have expected and even preferred Frege to do and what he actually chose to do there is to be found the fascinating person of Frege, his extraordinary intellect and moral and aesthetic character.

The decades since Frege's death witnessed a remarkable reversal of the assessment of the merits of his mathematical logic and philosophy. Despite what is widely perceived as the failure of his naïve form of rigorous non-psychologistic logicism and philosophy of arithmetic, Frege continues to exert a powerful influence on the development of "scientific" philosophy. Long after the fact, Frege's philosophy has gradually but forcefully come into its own. Frege has grown to be increasingly appreciated as the founder of modern algebraic symbolic logic and philosophical analysis. This is not belated guilty praise for an innovator who was under-appreciated in his own time, but a plain matter of historical fact. Dummett accordingly delivers the following panegyric:

Frege's work represents the beginning of modern logic because of his invention of the notation of quantifiers and variables ... By means of this notation he solved the problem that had baffled the logicians of the Middle Ages and prevented the further advance of logic ever since, viz., the analysis of sentences involving multiple generality. In him there also appeared the first clear separation between the formal characterization of logical laws and their semantic justification. His philosophical work is of an importance far more general than the area to which he principally applied it, the philosophy of mathematics: he initiated a revolution, in fact, as profound as that of René Descartes in the 17th century. Whereas Descartes had made epistemology the starting point for all philosophy, Frege gave this place to the theory of meaning or the philosophy of language. His work has been influential because he made the restricted part of philosophy in which he worked basic to all the rest. The effect was imparted in the first place, however, through the work of others, particularly that of Wittgenstein, who visited him in 1914 and who revered him. But, since John Austin's translation of the *Grundlagen* into English in 1950, the direct influence of Frege's writing among English-speaking philosophers has been very great. No one supposes that Frege said the last word on any topic; but there is scarcely a live question in contemporary philosophy of language for whose examination Frege's views do not form at least the best starting point.[25]

It is not a fine point to note that it is Frege's logic, now modified, streamlined, and formalized in linear rather than chunky two-dimensional expressions, that is today known as classical logic. It is the logic against which every innovative nonclassical logic continues to take its bearings by comparison and makes its conceptual point of departure. Frege's logic constitutes a weighty component of neophyte nonclassical logical structures. These systems often suggest changes in specific parts of

---

[25] Dummett, *Frege: Philosophy of Mathematics*, pp. 968–69; and Dummett, *Frege: Philosophy of Language*, pp. 665–84. For more information on and an assessment of Frege's achievements, see Beaney, "Introduction," *The Frege Reader*, ed. Beaney, pp. 10–14; and Irving H. Anellis, "Did *Principia Mathematica* Precipitate a 'Fregean Revolution'?," *Russell: The Journal of Bertrand Russell Studies*, 31 (2011), pp. 131–50.

a base classical logic that at bottom is always essentially structurally isomorphic to the general functional calculus of Frege's *Begriffsschrift*.

A Photographic *Lebenslauf* (1920)

[M]athematics and death never make a mistake. And if we don't see these solids [corresponding to the square root of –1 and "irrational formulas"] in our surface world, there is for them, there inevitably must be, a whole immense world there, beneath the surface.

Yevgeny Zamyatin, *We* (science fiction dystopia, 1921),
RECORD 18 "Logical Labyrinth," p. 98.

Frege's life, his character and personality, and the enduring value of his mathematical logic and philosophy, are eulogized by taking a final look at his portrait in a gallery of photographs. These are images made of Frege in his lifetime scattered over several years that have survived the ravages of time and two world wars. There are four frequently reproduced images of Frege that tell a story in themselves. We have seen three of them before, and we line them up now with a fourth from left to right for comparison to see Frege projected forward during his time.

The first we have seen shows Frege with the family in Wismar. Gottlob was gazing off distantly, as handsome, albeit recently sickly and introverted, a nineteenth-century German–Polish boy as one could hope to find anywhere on the Baltic. He was bored or melancholic, as befits a young person of extraordinary but as yet mostly untested and undeveloped ability. The second shows Frege upon graduation from Gymnasium at the Wismar Große Stadtschule. It is the one where he looks much like a young Charles Sanders Peirce at roughly the same age, but in a different year and on another continent. The third, from around 1880, shows Frege with Nietzsche-like tufted black hair and bushy soup-spoon-defying moustache, taken when he had recently been installed as Extraordinariat in the mathematics faculty at the Universität Jena.

Now we come to the fourth and last. It is a photograph of Frege at about seventy-two. It is reproduced on the dust-jacket cover of this book as on many other books about Frege and the analytic philosophical movement. The final photograph of Frege in the public domain is also perhaps the most famous and iconic. It shows Frege as an old man, his hair thinned and white, almost plastered tight against his head, the beard snowy and bristly. These carefully groomed sproutings handsomely frame the most prominent feature in the portrait, which is Frege's eyes. Frege looks directly at the viewer of the photograph. The retinas hold you and arrest your gaze. The left eye is foremost, almost cocked, the eyebrow arched above it in friendly curiosity, the forehead wrinkled above the eyebrow proceeding onto an expansive intelligent brow. Frege had not posed for the photograph so much as stopped whatever he was doing for the moment and allowed a photograph to be taken. The citation from Zamyatin provides Frege's caustic epitaph, complementing the camera's image.

Frege wanted the photo to show exactly who he was. He admired the truth of photography, the honest unfeigned direct causally effected correspondence of representation with reality. He had no other person to present to the instrument's lens than the one who left Wismar to seek his fortune in the turbulent world of mathematics and philosophy. Truth is all one, regardless of the mode of depicting a fact. Here the truth is exactly what Frege looked like around 1920, about five years before his death. He confronts the viewer of the photograph. The French word *regarde* best expresses the interaction. Frege did not know that he had approximately another five years to live, which was rather a long time under the circumstances. He knew what he had achieved and where, if not why, his lifework had failed. He knew that the fruit of his years of labor, the thought underlying all philosophical analysis and logical proofs of arithmetical theorems from their axioms, had barely begun to be understood. If it had not gone as well as it might, at least it had also gone better than he might have imagined at the outset. It had transformed him from a boy from Wismar to someone who had gained a place of prominence on the world stage in the permanent annals of mathematics, science, and philosophy. By then it must have seemed like a very long time ago.

When the last, *circa* 1920, photograph of Frege is examined in retrospect it is hard to see a defeated or embittered man, as one might, for example, in viewing daguerreotypes from late in Arthur Schopenhauer's life, with the philosopher seated at a table and mockingly emblematically fondling a pocket watch. He, unlike Frege, looks to all intents and purposes to be a bitter person, soured by years of disregard, and possibly having started out that way. Such a judgment is especially apt for Schopenhauer, who believed that a person's character was more fully revealed as the years passed but never changed over time. Frege now had a seventeen-year-old boy at home to raise, whom he took under his roof, and Meta Arndt took under her wing, just four years after Margarete Frege's succumbing to an unknown ailment. There was no obligation on Frege to bring Alfred into his home. He willingly offered the boy security and so much more, looking after a previously under-privileged six-year-old as though he were the boy's natural father. How bitter can you be with a child to look after running untrammeled through the house? There was laughter again in Frege's life. Where had the boy gone now? Did you hear what he said to the postman?

Frege completed the sum of his life's work. The finality is trivially but decisively marked by the moment of death. Frege remained remarkably faithful throughout to the ideas with which he began, in the assumptions that guided his thought and writing from his Jena Habilitation in 1874 through *Grundgesetze II* in 1903. Now he would try to write and publish what he should have explained at the beginning. His *Logische Untersuchungen* would announce his basic concepts as exceptionless simply expressed truths, before thrusting them symbolically out into the world, guilelessly expecting those in the know like himself to respond with understanding and appreciation. For all that, the world might have obliged him in just such a gratifying way. The community of mathematicians and philosophers unfortunately did not play along. They did not understand what Frege was trying to do, and things did not work out according to plan. Frege, despite repeated setbacks, does not look bitter in the late 1920 photograph. He appears severe, bemused, inquisitive, intelligent, cautious, crafty, and sly, as has been said before. He was seventy-two years old when the camera shutter dropped. He held himself obligingly slightly rigid as seconds of image-making exposure on the emulsion plate ticked away, or we should have had to remember him in his near-final incarnation only as a blur. With roughly five years still on the clock he appears to have had a fascinating intellectually and emotionally draining life.[26]

---

[26] The *c.* 1920 photograph of Frege two years after retirement belongs to the Universitätsarchiv Jena; there is also a copy in the Archiv für Kunst und Geschichte, Berlin.

References

Frege's Writings

I Original Publications, in Chronological Order

1873 – *Über eine geometrische Darstellung der imaginären Gebilde in der Ebene.* PhD Dissertation, University of Göttingen.

1874a – *Rechnungsmethoden, die sich auf eine Erweiterung des Größenbegriffes gründen.* Habilitationsschrift, University of Jena.

1874b – "Rezension von: H. Seeger, *Die Elemente der Arithmetik, für den Schulunterricht bearbeitet,*" *Jenaer Literaturzeitung,* 1(46), 722.

1879 – *Begriffsschrift, eine der arithmetischen nachgebildete Formelsprache des reinen Denkens.* Halle: L. Nebert. (Second edition, *Begriffsschrift und andere Aufsätze. Zweite Auflage, mit E. [Edmund] Husserls und H. [Heinrich] Scholz' Anmerkungen, herausgegeben von Ignacio Angelelli.* Darmstadt: Wissenschaftliche Buchgesellschaft, 1964.)

1884 – *Die Grundlagen der Arithmetik, eine logisch mathematische Untersuchung über den Begriff der Zahl.* Breslau: W. Koebner.

1885 – "Über formale Theorien der Arithmetik," *Sitzungsberichte der Jenaischen Gesellschaft für Medizin und Naturwissenschaft,* 19, 94–104.

1891a – *Funktion und Begriff.* Jena: Hermann Pohle, 1891.

1891b – "Über das Trägheitsgesetz," *Zeitschrift für Philosophie und philosophische Kritik,* 98, 145–61.

1892a – "Über Sinn und Bedeutung," *Zeitschrift für Philosophie und philosophische Kritik,* 100, 25–50.

1892b – "Über Begriff und Gegenstand," *Vierteljahrsschrift für wissenschaftliche Philosophie,* 16, 192–205.

1892c – "Rezension von: G. Cantor, *Zur Lehre vom Transfiniten,*" *Gesammelte Abhandlungen aus der Zeitschrift für Philosophie und philosophische Kritik,* 100, 269–72.

1893/1903 – *Grundgesetze der Arithmetik, begriffsschriftlich abgeleitet I, II.* Two volumes. Jena: Hermann Pohle.

1894 – "Rezension von: E. Husserl, *Philosophie der Arithmetik I,*" *Zeitschrift für Philosophie und philosophische Kritik,* 103, 313–32.

1895a – "Kritische Beleuchtung einiger Punkte in E. Schröders *Vorlesungen über die Algebra der Logik*," *Archiv für systematische Philosophie*, 1, 433–56.

1895b – "Le nombre entier," *Revue de Métaphysique et de Morale*, 3, 73–78.

1897 – "Über die Begriffsschrift des Herrn Peano und meine eigene," *Verhandlungen der Königlich Sächsischen Gesellschaft der Wissenschaften zu Leipzig*, 48, 362–68.

1899 – *Über die Zahlen des Herrn H. Schubert*. Jena: Hermann Pohle.

1903 – *Grundgesetze II*, see the entry dated 1893/1903 above.

1903/1906 – "Über die Grundlagen der Geometrie," *Jahresbericht der Deutschen Mathematiker-Vereinigung*, 12 (1903): 319–24, 368–75; 15 (1906): 293–309, 377–403, 423–30.

1904 – "Was ist eine Funktion?" In *Festschrift Ludwig Boltzmann gewidmet zum sechzigsten Geburtstage*. Leipzig: Verlag von Ambrosius Barth. 656–66

1906 – "Antwort auf die Ferienplauderei des Herrn Thomae," *Jahresbericht der Deutschen Mathematiker-Vereinigung*, 15, 586–90.

1908 – "Die Unmöglichkeit der Thomaeschen formalen Arithmetik aus Neue nachgewiesen," *Jahresbericht der Deutschen Mathematiker-Vereinigung*, 17, 52–55.

1918a – "Der Gedanke. Eine logische Untersuchung," *Beträge zur Philosophie des deutschen Idealismus*, 1, 58–77.

1918b – "Die Verneinung. Eine logische Untersuchung," *Beiträge zur Philosophie des deutschen Idealismus*, 1, 143–57.

1923 – "Gedankengefüge" ("Logische Untersuchungen – Dritter Teil: Gedankengefüge"), *Beiträge zur Philosophie des deutschen Idealismus*, 3, 36–51.

1969 – *Nachgelassene Schriften*. Ed. Hans Hermes, Friedrich Kambartel, and Friedrich Kaulbach. Hamburg: Felix Meiner.

1976 – *Wissenschaftlicher Briefwechsel*. Hamburg: Felix Meiner.

1989 – "Briefe an Ludwig Wittgenstein aus den Jahren 1914–1920." Ed. Allan Janik, with commentary by Christian Paul Berger. In *Wittgenstein in Focus – Im Brennpunkt: Wittgenstein*. Ed. Brian McGuinness and Rudolf Haller. Special issue, *Grazer Philosophische Studien*, 33/34, 5–33.

1994 – "Gottlob Freges politisches Tagebuch." Ed. Gottfried Gabriel and Wolfgang Kienzler, with an introduction and commentary. *Deutsche Zeitschrift für Philosophie*, 42, 1057–98 (editors' introduction 1057–66).

II English Translations of Frege's Writings

Translations from the Philosophical Writings of Gottlob Frege [BG]. Third edition. Trans. Max Black and P. T. Geach. Lanham: Rowman & Littlefield, 1980.

Collected Papers on Mathematics, Logic and Philosophy [CP]. Ed. Max Black, V. Dudman, P. T. Geach, H. Kaal, E.-H. W. Kluge, Brian McGuinness, and R. H. Stoothoff. Oxford: Basil Blackwell, 1984.

The Frege Reader [FR]. Ed. Michael Beaney. Oxford: Blackwell, 1997.

Über eine geometrische Darstellung der imaginären Gebilde in der Ebene [1873]. Translated as "On a Geometrical Representation of Imaginary Forms in the Plane" in [CP]: 1–55.

Rechnungsmethoden, die sich auf eine Erweiterung des Größenbegriffes gründen [1874]. Translated as "Methods of Calculation Based on an Extension of the Concept of Quantity" in [CP]: 56–92.

Begriffsschrift [1879]. Translated as "Begriffsschrift, a Formula Language, Modeled upon That of Arithmetic, for Pure Thought" by S. Bauer-Mengelberg. In *From Frege to Gödel: A Sourcebook in Mathematical Logic 1879–1931*. Ed. Jean van Heijenoort. Cambridge: Harvard University Press, 1967. 1–82. Translated as *Conceptual Notation and Related Articles* by Terrell W. Bynum. London: Oxford University Press, 1972.

Grundlagen [1884]. Translated as *The Foundations of Arithmetic: A Logico-Mathematical Enquiry into the Concept of Number* by J. L. Austin. Oxford: Blackwell, 1953 (second edition). Translated with an introduction and critical commentary as *The Foundations of Arithmetic: A Logico-Mathematical Investigation into the Concept of Number* by Dale Jacquette. New York: Pearson Longman, 2007.

"Über formale Theorien der Arithmetik" [1885]. Translated as "On Formal Theories of Arithmetic" in [CP]: 112–21.

"Erwiderung" [to Cantor 1885, *Deutsche Literaturzeitung*, 6(20), columns 728–29]. Translated as "Reply to Cantor's Review of *Grundlagen der Arithmetik*" in [CP]: 122.

"Funktion und Begriff" [1891]. Translated as "Function and Concept" in [CP]: 137–56; [BG]: 21–41; [FR]: 130–48.

"Über das Trägheitsgesetz" [1891]. Translated as "On the Law of Inertia" in [CP]: 123–36.

"Über Sinn und Bedeutung" [1892]. Translated as "On Sense and Meaning" in [CP]: 157–77. Translated as "On Sense and Reference" in [BG]: 56–78; [FR]: 151–71.

"Über Begriff und Gegenstand" [1892]. Translated as "On Concept and Object" in [CP]: 182–94; [BG]: 42–55; [FR]: 181–93.

"Rezension von: G. Cantor, *Zur Lehre vom Transfiniten*" [1892]. Translated as "Review of Georg Cantor, *Contributions to the Theory of the Transfinite*" in [CP]: 178–81.

Grundgesetze [1893/1903]. Edited and translated in part (Volume I plus Volume II Nachwort) as *The Basic Laws of Arithmetic: Exposition of the System* by Montgomery Furth. Berkeley: University of California Press, 1964. Edited and translated in its entirety as *Basic Laws of Arithmetic: Derived Using Concept-Script* by Philip A. Ebert and Marcus Rossberg with Crispin Wright. Oxford: Oxford University Press, 2013.

"Rezension von: E. Husserl, *Philosophie der Arithmetik*" [1894]. Translated as "Review of *Philosophie der Arithmetik* by Edmund Husserl" in [CP]: 195–209. Translated as "Illustrative Extracts from Frege's Review of Husserl's *Philosophy der Arithmetik*" in [BG]: 79–85; [FR]: 224–26 (extract). Translated as "Review of Dr. E. Husserl's *Philosophy of Arithmetic*" by E. W. Kluge, *Mind*, 81 (1972): 321–37.

"Kritische Beleuchtung einiger Punkte in E. Schröders *Vorlesungen über die Algebra der Logik*" [1895]. Translated as "A Critical Elucidation of Some Points in

E. Schröder, *Vorlesungen über die Algebra der Logik [Lectures on the Algebra of Logic]*" in [CP]: 210–28; [BG]: 86–106.

"Le nombre entier" [1895]. Translated as "Whole Numbers" in [CP]: 229–33.

"Über die Begriffsschrift des Herrn Peano und meine eigene" [1897]. Translated as "On Mr. Peano's Conceptual Notation and My Own" in [CP]: 234–48.

"Über die Zahlen des Herrn H. Schubert" [1899]. Translated as "On Mr. H. Schubert's Numbers" in [CP]: 249–72.

"Über die Grundlagen der Geometrie" [1903/1906]. Translated as "On the Foundations of Geometry" in [CP]: 273–340. Translated as *On the Foundations of Geometry and Formal Theories of Arithmetic* by E. W. Kluge. New Haven: Yale University Press, 1971.

"Was ist eine Funktion?" [1904]. Translated as "What is a Function?" in [CP]: 285–92.

"Antwort auf die Ferienplauderei des Herrn Thomae" [1906]. Translated as "Reply to Thomae's Holiday Causerie" in [CP]: 341–45.

"Die Unmöglichkeit der Thomaeschen formalen Arithmetik aufs Neue nachgewiesen" [1908]. Translated as "Renewed Proof of the Impossibility of Mr. Thomae's Formal Arithmetic" in [CP]: 346–50.

Logical Investigations [LI]. Translated by P. T. Geach (from Frege 1918a, b and 1923). New Haven: Yale University Press, 1977.

"Der Gedanke. Eine logische Untersuchung" [1918]. Translated as "Thoughts" in [CP]: 351–72; [LI]: 1–30. Translated as "Thought" in [FR]: 325–45.

"Die Verneinung. Eine logische Untersuchung" [1918]. Translated as "Negation" in [CP]: 373–89; [LI]: 31–53; [FR]: 346–61.

"Gedankengefüge" [1923]. Translated as "Compound Thoughts" in [CP]: 390–406; [LI]: 55–77.

"Gottlob Freges politisches Tagebuch" [1994]. Translated as "Diary: Written by Professor Dr. Gottlob Frege in the Time from 10 March to 9 April 1924" by Richard L. Mendelsohn, in *Inquiry* 39 (1996): 303–42 (editors' introduction by G. Gabriel and W. Kienzler, 303–8).

Nachgelassene Schriften [1969]. Translated as *Posthumous Writings* [PW] by Peter Long and Roger White. Oxford: Basil Blackwell, 1979.

"Boole's Logical Calculus and the Concept-Script" in [PW]: 9–46.

"Boole's Logical Formula-Language and My Concept-Script" in [PW]: 47–52.

"Draft towards a Review of Cantor's *Gesammelte Abhandlungen zur Lehre vom Transfiniten*" in [PW]: 68–71.

"Logic" in [PW]: 126–51.

"On Euclidean Geometry" in [PW]: 167–69.

"Notes on Hilbert's 'Grundlagen der Geometrie'" in [PW]: 170–3.

"Logic in Mathematics" in [PW]: 203–50.

"Notes for Ludwig Darmstaedter" in [PW]: 253–57.

"Logical Generality" in [PW]: 258–62.

"Number" in [PW]: 265–66.

"Numbers and Arithmetic" in [PW]: 275–77.

On the Foundations of Geometry and Formal Theories of Arithmetic. Trans. E. W. Kluge. New Haven: Yale University Press, 1971.
Wissenschaftlicher Briefwechsel [1976]. Translated as *Philosophical and Mathematical Correspondence* by Hans Kaal. Ed. Brian McGuinness. Chicago: University of Chicago Press, 1980.

Secondary Literature

Aczel, Amir D. *Descartes's Secret Notebook: A True Tale of Mathematics, Mysticism, and the Quest to Understand the Universe.* New York: Random House, 2005.
Albisetti, James C. *Schooling German Girls and Women.* Princeton: Princeton University Press, 1988.
Allwein, Gerard, and Jon Barwise, eds. *Logical Reasoning with Diagrams.* Oxford: Oxford University Press, 1996.
Andrews, Peter B. *An Introduction to Mathematical Logic and Type Theory: To Truth through Proof.* Second edition. Berlin: Springer-Verlag, 2002.
Anellis, Irving H. "Did *Principia Mathematica* Precipitate a 'Fregean Revolution'?," *Russell: The Journal of Bertrand Russell Studies,* 31 (2011): 131–50.
Aristotle. *The Complete Works of Aristotle.* Ed. Jonathan Barnes (Oxford Translation). Fifth printing with corrections, two volumes. Princeton: Princeton University Press, 1995.
Asser, Günter, David Alexander, and Helmut Metzler. "Gottlob Frege – Persönlichkeit und Werk." In *Begriffsschrift – Jenaer Frege-Konferenz.* Jena: Friedrich-Schiller-Universität, 1979. 6–32.
Auerbach, Felix. *The Zeiss Works and the Carl Zeiss Foundation in Jena, Their Scientific, Technical and Sociological Development and Importance Popularly Described.* Trans. Ralph Kanthack from the fifth German edition. London: W. & G. Foyle, Ltd., 1927.
Baedeker, Karl. *Northern Germany as Far as the Bavarian and Austrian Frontiers: Handbook for Travelers.* Revised edition. New York: Charles Scribner's Sons, 1910.
Bainton, Roland H. *Here I Stand: A Life of Martin Luther.* New York: Plume, 1995.
Baker, G. P., and P. M. S. Hacker. *Frege: Logical Excavations.* Oxford: Basil Blackwell, 1984.
——— "Frege's Anti-psychologism." In *Perspectives on Psychologism.* Ed. M. A. Notturno. Leiden: Brill Academic Publishers, 1989. 75–127.
Ballue, Eugène. "Le nombre entier: considéré comme fondement de l'analyse mathématique," *Revue de Métaphysique et de Morale,* 2 (1894): 317–28.
Balzac, Honoré de. *The Unknown Masterpiece and Gambara.* Trans. Richard Howard. Introduction by Arthur C. Danto. New York: New York Review Books, 2001.
Bauch, Bruno. "Lotzes *Logik* und ihre Bedeutung im deutschen Idealismus," *Beiträge zur Philosophie des deutschen Idealismus,* 1 (1918): 45–58.

Beaney, Michael. "Introduction." In *The Frege Reader*. Ed. Michael Beaney. Oxford: Blackwell, 1997. 1–46.

Berkeley, George. *A Treatise Concerning the Principles of Human Knowledge* [1710]. In *The Works of George Berkeley, Bishop of Cloyne*. Ed. A. A. Luce and T. E. Jessup. London: Thomas Nelson and Sons Ltd., 1948–1957, 9 volumes. Volume 1.

——— *Three Dialogues between Hylas and Philonous* [third edition, 1734]. In Berkeley, *Works*, Volume 2.

Bird, Otto A. *Syllogistic and Its Extensions*. Englewood Cliffs: Prentice-Hall, 1964.

Blackburn, Simon, and Alan Code. "The Power of Russell's Criticism of Frege: 'On Denoting' pp. 48–50," *Analysis*, 38(2) (1978): 65–77.

Blackwell, Kenneth, Nicholas Griffin, and Dale Jacquette, eds. *After "On Denoting": Themes from Russell and Meinong*. Hamilton: McMaster University for The Bertrand Russell Research Centre, 2007.

Blanchette, Patricia A. "Frege and Hilbert on Consistency," *The Journal of Philosophy*, 93 (1996): 317–36.

——— "Frege (1848–1925)." In *The Oxford Handbook of German Philosophy in the Nineteenth Century*. Ed. Michael N. Forster and Kristen Gjesdal. Oxford: Oxford University Press, 2015. 207–29.

Bolzano, Bernard. *Theory of Science [Wissenschaftslehre. Versuch einer ausführlichen und größtentheils neuen Darstellung der Logik mit steter Rücksicht auf deren bisherige Bearbeiter, 1837]*. Trans. Paul Rusnock and Rolf George. Oxford: Oxford University Press, 2014. Four volumes.

Boole, George. *The Mathematical Analysis of Logic: Being an Essay towards a Calculus of Deductive Reasoning* [1847], with a new introduction by John Slater. Bristol: Thoemmes Press, 1998.

——— *An Investigation of the Laws of Thought on Which Are Founded the Mathematical Theories of Logic and Probabilities* [1854]. New York: Dover Publications, 1958.

———*A Treatise on the Calculus of Finite Differences* [1860]. Fourth edition. Ed. J. F. Moulton. New York: Chelsea Publishing Company, 1872.

Bowie, Andrew. *Introduction to German Philosophy: From Kant to Habermas*. Oxford: Blackwell, 2003.

Boyer, Carl Benjamin. *The History of the Calculus and Its Conceptual Development*. New York: Dover Books, 1959.

Brentano, Franz. *Psychologie vom empirischen Standpunkt*. Leipzig: Duncker & Humblot, 1874.

Brouwer, L. E. J. "The Effect of Intuitionism on Classical Algebra of Logic," *Proceedings of the Royal Irish Academy*, 57 (1955): 113–16.

Burge, Tyler. *Truth, Thought, Reason: Essays on Frege*. Oxford: Oxford University Press, 2005.

——— "Gottlob Frege: Some Forms of Influence." In *The Oxford Handbook of the History of Analytic Philosophy*. Ed. Michael Beaney. Oxford: Oxford University Press, 2013. 355–82.

Burgess, John P. *Fixing Frege*. Princeton: Princeton University Press, 2005.

Burke, Edmund. *A Philosophical Enquiry into the Origin of Our Ideas of the Sublime and Beautiful* [1757]. Ed. with an introduction and notes by Adam Phillips. Oxford: Oxford University Press, 2008.

Bynum, Terrell Ward. "On the Life and Work of Gottlob Frege." In *Frege: Conceptual Notation and Related Articles*. Trans. Terrell Ward Bynum. Oxford: Oxford University Press, 1972. 1–54.

Cantor, Georg. "Review of *Grundlagen der Arithmetik*, by Gottlob Frege," *Deutsche Literaturzeitung* 6 (1885): 728–29.

——— "Beiträge zur Begründung der transfiniten Mengenlehre," *Mathematische Annalen*, 46(4) (1895): 481–512.

Carl, Wolfgang. *Frege's Theory of Sense and Reference: Its Origins and Scope*. Cambridge: Cambridge University Press, 1994.

Carnap, Rudolf. "Intellectual Autobiography." In *The Philosophy of Rudolf Carnap*. Ed. Paul Schilpp. LaSalle: Open Court, 1963.

——— *Frege's Lectures on Logic: Carnap's Student Notes 1910–1914*. Ed. Erich H. Reck and Steve Awodey. Introduction by Gottfried Gabriel. LaSalle: Open Court, 2004.

Church, Alonzo. "An Unsolvable Problem of Elementary Number Theory," *Bulletin of the American Mathematical Society*, 41(5) (1935): 332–33.

Chrudzimski, Arkadiusz. *Intentionalitätstheorie beim frühen Brentano*. Dordrecht: Kluwer Academic Publishers, 2001.

Cocchiarella, Nino. "Whither Russell's Paradox of Predication." In *Logic and Ontology*. Ed. Milton K. Munitz. New York: New York University Press, 1973. 133–58.

Corcoran, John. "Aristotle's Demonstrative Logic," *History and Philosophy of Logic*, 30 (2009): 1–20.

Currie, Gregory. "Frege on Thoughts," *Mind*, 89(354) (1980): 234–48.

Dauben, Joseph W. "Georg Cantor and Pope Leo XIII: Mathematics, Theology, and the Infinite," *Journal of the History of Ideas*, 38 (1977): 85–108.

de Maimieux, Joseph. *Pasigraphie, ou, Premiers élémens du nouvel art-science d'écrire et d'imprimer en une langue de manière à être lu et entendu dans toute autre langue sans traduction*. Paris: Bureau de la Pasigraphie, 1797.

Decker, Christine. *Wismar 1665: Eine Stadtgesellschaft im Spiegel des Türkensteuerregisters*. Berlin: LIT Verlag, 2006.

Demopoulos, William. "Frege, Hilbert and the Conceptual Structure of Model Theory," *History and Philosophy of Logic*, 15(2) (1994): 211–25.

——— ed. *Frege's Philosophy of Mathematics*. Cambridge: Harvard University Press, 1997.

——— *Logicism and Its Philosophical Legacy*. Cambridge: Cambridge University Press, 2013.

Dipert, Randall R. "The Life and Work of Ernst Schröder," *Modern Logic*, 1 (1990–1991): 117–39.

Dudman, Victor, translator and commentator. "Peano's Review of Frege's *Grundgesetze*," *The Southern Journal of Philosophy*, 9 (1971): 25–37.

Dummett, Michael. "Frege, Gottlob." In *Encyclopedia of Philosophy*. Ed. Paul Edwards. New York: Macmillan, 1967. Volume III, 225–37.

—— "Frege on the Consistency of Mathematical Theories." In *Studien zu Frege*. Ed. Matthias Schirn. Stuttgart-Bad Cannstatt: Frommann-Holzboog, 1975. 229–42.

—— *Frege: Philosophy of Language* [1973]. Second edition. Cambridge: Harvard University Press, 1981.

—— *The Interpretation of Frege's Philosophy*. Cambridge: Harvard University Press, 1981.

—— "Frege and Kant on Geometry," *Inquiry: An Interdisciplinary Journal of Philosophy*, 25(2) (1982): 233–54.

—— *Frege: Philosophy of Mathematics*. Cambridge: Harvard University Press, 1991.

—— "Gottlob Frege." In *Encyclopedia Britannica Online*. www.britannica.com/ biography/Gottlob-Frege

Edwards, Charles Henry Jr. *The Historical Development of the Calculus*. Berlin: Springer-Verlag, 1979.

Eisenstein, Elizabeth. *The Printing Press as an Agent of Change: Communications and Cultural Transformations in Early Modern Europe*. Cambridge: Cambridge University Press, 1979.

Erdmann, Benno. *Logik. Band I. Logische Elementarlehre*. Halle: Niemeyer, 1892.

Erikson, Erik H. *Young Man Luther: A Study in Psychoanalysis and History*. Gloucester: Peter Smith Publishing, Inc., 1962.

Eucken, Rudolf. "Review of *Grundlagen der Arithmetik*, by G. Frege," *Philosophische Monatshefte*, 22 (1886): 421–22.

Euclid. *The Elements of Euclid, with Dissertations*. Trans. James Williamson. Oxford: Clarendon Press, 1782.

Ewen, Wolfgang. *Carl Stumpf und Gottlob Frege*. Würzburg: Königshausen und Neumann, 2008.

Faerber, Carl. "Referat von Prof. Faerber, Berlin," *Mitteilungen der Deutschen Mathematiker-Vereinigung*, 39 (1911): 230–31.

Feldman, Gerald D. *The Great Disorder: Politics, Economics, and Society in the German Inflation, 1914–1924*. Oxford: Oxford University Press, 1997.

Flood, Raymond, Adrian Rice, and Robin Wilson, eds. *Mathematics in Victorian Britain*. Oxford: Oxford University Press, 2011.

Franklin, James. "Aristotelianism in the Philosophy of Mathematics," *Studia Neoaristotelica*, 8 (2011): 3–15.

Gabbay, Dov M., and John Woods, eds. *British Logic in the Nineteenth Century* (Handbook of the History of Logic, Volume 4). Amsterdam: Elsevier, 2008.

Gabriel, Gottfried. "Frege als Neukantianer," *Kant-Studien*, 77(1) (1986): 84–101.

—— "Leo Sachse, Herbart, Frege und die Grundlagen der Arithmetik." In *Frege in Jena: Beiträge zur Spurensicherung*. Ed. Gottfried Gabriel and Wolfgang Kienzler. Würzburg: Königshausen und Neumann, 1997. 53–67.

———— "Frege, Lotze, and the Continental Roots of Early Analytic Philosophy." In *From Frege to Wittgenstein: Perspectives on Early Analytic Philosophy*. Ed. Erich H. Reck. Oxford: Oxford University Press, 2002. 39–51.

Gabriel, Gottfried, and Wolfgang Kienzler, eds. *Frege in Jena: Beiträge zur Spurensicherung*. Würzburg: Königshausen und Neumann, 1997.

Gardner, Martin. *Logic Machines and Diagrams*. New York: McGraw-Hill, 1958.

Gauss, Carl Friedrich. *Disquisitiones Arithmeticae*. Leipzig: Gerhard Fleischer, 1801.

———— "Disquisitiones Generales circa Superficies Curvas," *Commentationes Societatis Regiae Scientiarum Gottingensis recentiores* 6 (1827): 99–146.

———— *Disquisitiones Generales circa Superficies Curvas*. Göttingen: Dieterich, 1928.

Geach, P. T. "On Frege's Way Out," *Mind*, 65 (1956): 408–9.

———— "Frege." In *Three Philosophers*. By G. E. M. Anscombe and P. T. Geach Oxford: Basil Blackwell, 1973. 127–62.

George, Alexander and Richard Heck. "Frege, Gottlob." In *Routledge Encyclopedia of Philosophy*. Ed. Edward Craig. London: Routledge, 1998. Volume 3, 765–78.

Giese, Gerd. "Frege und Wismar: Orte der Erinnerung." In *Gottlob Frege – ein Genius mit Wismarer Wurzeln: Leistung – Wirkung – Tradition*. Ed. Dieter Schott. Leipzig: Leipziger Universitätsverlag, 2012. 98–111.

Gillies, D. A. *Frege, Dedekind, and Peano on the Foundations of Arithmetic*. Assen: Van Gorcum, 1982.

Gödel, Kurt. "Über formal unentscheidbare Sätze der *Principia Mathematica* und verwandter Systeme 1," *Monatshefte für Mathematik und Physik*, 38 (1931): 173–98.

Griffin, Nicholas. "The Prehistory of Russell's Paradox." In *One Hundred Years of Russell's Paradox: Mathematics, Logic, Philosophy*. Ed. Godehard Link and John L. Bell. Berlin: Walter de Gruyter, 2004. 349–72.

Griffin, Nicholas, and Dale Jacquette, eds. *Russell vs. Meinong: The Legacy of "On Denoting."* London: Routledge, 2009.

Hadamard, Jacques. *An Essay on the Psychology of Invention in the Mathematical Field*. New York: Dover Publications, 1954.

Haddock, Guillermo E. Rosado. *A Critical Introduction to the Philosophy of Gottlob Frege*. Aldershot: Ashgate Publishing, 2012.

Hahn, Martin. "The Frege Puzzle One More Time." In *Frege: Sense and Reference One Hundred Years Later*. Ed. John Biro and Petr Kotatko. Dordrecht: Kluwer Academic Publishers, 1995. 169–83.

Hale, Bob. "Frege's Platonism," *The Philosophical Quarterly*, 34(136) (1984): 225–41.

Harreld, Donald, ed. *A Companion to the Hanseatic League*. Leiden: Brill Academic Publishers, 2015.

Hawkins, Benjamin S. "DeMorgan, Victorian Syllogistic and Relational Logic," *The Review of Modern Logic*, 5(2) (1995): 131–66.

Heblack, Torsten. "Wer war Leo Sachse? Ein historisch-biographischer Beitrag zur Frege-Forschung." In *Frege in Jena: Beiträge zur Spurensicherung*. Ed. Gottfried Gabriel and Wolfgang Kienzler. Würzburg: Königshausen und Neumann, 1997. 41–52.

Heck, Richard G., and Robert May. "Frege's Contribution to Philosophy of Language." In *The Oxford Handbook of Philosophy of Language*. Ed. Ernest Lepore and Barry C. Smith. Oxford: Oxford University Press, 2008.

Helfferich, Tryntje, ed. *The Thirty Years War: A Documentary History*. Indianapolis: Hackett Publishing, 2009.

Hellman, Geoffrey. "How to Gödel a Frege–Russell: Gödel's Incompleteness Theorems and Logicism," *Noûs*, 15 (1981): 451–68.

Hermes, Hans, Friedrich Kambartel, and Friedrich Kaulbach. "History of the Frege *Nachlaß* and the Basis for This Edition." In *Gottlob Frege, Posthumous Writings*. Ed. Hans Hermes, Friedrich Kambartel, and Friedrich Kaulbach. Oxford: Basil Blackwell, 1979.

Hill, Claire Ortiz, and Guillermo E. Rosado Haddock. *Husserl or Frege? Meaning, Objectivity, and Mathematics*. LaSalle: Open Court, 2003.

Hindley, J. Roger. *Basic Simple Type Theory*. Cambridge: Cambridge University Press, 1997.

Hochberg, Herbert. "Russell's Attack on Frege's Theory of Meaning," *Philosophica*, 18 (1976): 9–34.

——— "Russell's Paradox, Russellian Relations, and the Problems of Predication and Impredicativity," *Minnesota Studies in the Philosophy of Science*, 12 (1989): 63–87.

Holtfrerich, Carl-Ludwig. *The German Inflation 1914–1923*. Trans. Theo Balderston. Berlin: Walter de Gruyter, 1986.

Hopkins, Burt C. "Husserl's Psychologism and Critique of Psychologism, Revisited," *Husserl Studies*, 22 (2006): 91–119.

Hoppe, Ernst Reinhold Eduard. "Review of Frege's *Grundgesetze der Arithmetik I*," *Archives of Mathematics and Physics*, second series 13. Literary Report XLIX (1895): 8.

Horn, Laurence R. *A Natural History of Negation*. Stanford: Center for the Study of Language and Information, 2001.

Hume, David. *A Treatise of Human Nature* [1739–1740]. Second edition. Ed. Sir Lewis Amherst Selby-Bigge and revised by P. H. Nidditch. Oxford: Clarendon Press, 1978.

——— *Enquiry Concerning Human Understanding* [1748]. In Hume, David. *Enquiries Concerning Human Understanding and Concerning the Principles of Morals*. Third edition. Ed. Sir Lewis Amherst Selby-Bigge and revised by P. H. Nidditch. Oxford: Clarendon Press, 1975.

——— "My Own Life." In Mossner, Ernest Campbell. *The Life of David Hume*. Austin: University of Texas Press, 1954.

Husserl, Edmund. *Philosophie der Arithmetik: Psychologische und logische Untersuchungen*. Halle: Pfeffer Verlag, 1891.

——— *Philosophy of Arithmetic: Psychological and Logical Investigations with Supplementary Texts from 1887–1901*. Trans. Dallas Willard. Dordrecht: Kluwer Academic Publishers, 2003.

Hylton, Peter. *Russell, Idealism, and the Emergence of Analytic Philosophy*. Oxford: Clarendon Press, 1993.

Jacquette, Dale. *Wittgenstein's Thought in Transition*. West Lafayette: Purdue University Press, 1997.

———— "Intentionality on the Instalment Plan," *Philosophy*, 73 (1998): 63–79.

———— *On Boole*. Belmont: Wadsworth Publishing, 2002.

———— ed. *Philosophy, Psychology, and Psychologism: Critical and Historical Readings on the Psychological Turn in Philosophy*. Dordrecht: Kluwer Academic Publishers, 2003.

———— "Introduction: Psychologism the Philosophical Shibboleth." In *Philosophy, Psychology, and Psychologism: Critical and Historical Readings on the Psychological Turn in Philosophy*. Ed. Dale Jacquette. Dordrecht: Kluwer Academic Publishers, 2003. 1–19.

———— "Psychologism Revisited in Logic, Metaphysics, and Epistemology." In *Philosophy, Psychology, and Psychologism: Critical and Historical Readings on the Psychological Turn in Philosophy*. Ed. Dale Jacquette. Dordrecht: Kluwer Academic Publishers, 2003. 245–62.

———— "Frege on Identity as a Relation of Names," *Metaphysica: International Journal for Ontology and Metaphysics*, 12 (2011): 51–72.

———— "Thinking Outside the Square of Opposition Box." In *Around and beyond the Square of Opposition*. Ed. Jean-Yves Béziau and Dale Jacquette. Basel: Springer-Verlag, 2012. 73–92.

———— "Qualities, Relations, and Property Exemplification," *Axiomathes*, 23 (2013): 381–99.

———— "Newton's Metaphysics of Space as God's Emanative Effect," *Physics in Perspective*, 16 (2014): 344–70.

———— "Toward a Neoaristotelian Inherence Philosophy of Mathematical Entities," *Studia Neoaristotelica*, 11 (2014): 159–204.

———— *Alexius Meinong: The Shepherd of Non-Being*. Berlin: Springer-Verlag, 2015.

———— "Referential Analysis of Quotation." In *Semantic and Pragmatic Aspects of Quotation*. Ed. Paul Saka. Berlin: Springer-Verlag, forthcoming.

Kant, Immanuel. *Critique of Pure Reason* [1781/1787]. Trans. Paul Guyer and Allen W. Wood. Cambridge: Cambridge University Press, 1998.

———— *The Groundwork to the Metaphysics of Morals* [1785]. Trans. Mary Gregor and Jens Timmermann. Cambridge: Cambridge University Press, 2012.

Kanterian, Edward. "Review of *Carl Stumpf und Gottlob Frege*, by W. Ewen," *Philosophical Investigations*, 34 (3) (2011): 312–17.

———— *Frege: A Guide for the Perplexed*. London: Continuum, 2012.

Kenny, Anthony. *Frege: An Introduction to the Founder of Modern Analytic Philosophy*. London: Penguin Books Ltd., 1995.

Kerry, Benno. "Über Anschauung und ihre psychische Verarbeitung," *Vierteljahrsschrift für wissenschaftliche Philosophie*, 9 (1885): 433–93.

———— "Über Anschauung und ihre psychische Verarbeitung," *Vierteljahrsschrift für wissenschaftliche Philosophie*, 10 (1886): 419–67.

———— "Über Anschauung und ihre psychische Verarbeitung," *Vierteljahrsschrift für wissenschaftliche Philosophie*, 11 (1887): 53–116.

———— "Über Anschauung und ihre psychische Verarbeitung," *Vierteljahrsschrift für wissenschaftliche Philosophie*, 11 (1887): 249–307.

———— "Über Anschauung und ihre psychische Verarbeitung," *Vierteljahrsschrift für wissenschaftliche Philosophie*, 13 (1889): 71–124.

———— "Über Anschauung und ihre psychische Verarbeitung," *Vierteljahrsschrift für wissenschaftliche Philosophie*, 13 (1889): 392–419.

———— "Über Anschauung und ihre psychische Verarbeitung," *Vierteljahrsschrift für wissenschaftliche Philosophie*, 14 (1890): 317–53.

———— "Über Anschauung und ihre psychische Verarbeitung," *Vierteljahrsschrift für wissenschaftliche Philosophie*, 15 (1891): 127–67.

Klement, Kevin C. *Frege and the Logic of Sense and Reference*. Reprint edition. London: Routledge, 2011.

Kratzsch, Irmgard. "Material zu Leben und Wirken Freges aus dem Besitz der Universitäts-Bibliothek Jena." In *Begriffsschrift – Jenaer Frege-Konferenz*. Jena: Friedrich-Schiller-Universität, 1979. 534–46.

Kreiser, Lothar. "G. Frege 'Die Grundlagen der Arithmetik' – Werk und Geschichte." In *Frege Conference 1984: Proceedings of the International Conference Held at Schwerin (GDR), September 10–14, 1984*. Ed. Gerd Wechsung. Berlin: Akademie-Verlag, 1984. 13–27.

———— "Alfred." In *Frege in Jena: Beiträge zur Spurensicherung*. Ed. Gottfried Gabriel and Wolfgang Kienzler. Würzburg: Königshausen und Neumann, 1997. 68–83.

———— "Freges Universitätsstudium – Warum Jena?" In *Frege in Jena: Beiträge zur Spurensicherung*. Ed. Gottfried Gabriel and Wolfgang Kienzler. Würzburg: Königshausen und Neumann, 1997. 33–40.

———— "Gottlob Frege: Ein Leben in Jena." In *Gottlob Frege – Werk und Wirkung*. Ed. Gottfried Gabriel and Uwe Dathe. Paderborn: Mentis, 2000. 9–24.

———— *Gottlob Frege: Leben – Werk – Zeit*. Hamburg: Felix Meiner Verlag, 2001.

———— "Die Freges aus Wismar." In *Gottlob Frege – ein Genius mit Wismarer Wurzeln: Leistung – Wirkung – Tradition*. Ed. Dieter Schott. Leipzig: Leipziger Universitätsverlag, 2012. 69–97.

Kripke, Saul A. *Wittgenstein on Rules and Private Language: An Elementary Exposition*. Cambridge: Harvard University Press, 1982.

Kuehn, Manfred. *Kant: A Biography*. Cambridge: Cambridge University Press, 2001.

———— "Kant's Critical Philosophy and Its Reception – the First Five Years (1781–1786)." In *The Cambridge Companion to Kant and Modern Philosophy*. Ed. Paul Guyer. Cambridge: Cambridge University Press, 2006. 630–64.

Kusch, Martin. *Psychologism: A Case Study in the Sociology of Philosophical Knowledge*. London: Routledge, 1995.

———— *A Sceptical Guide to Meaning and Rules: Defending Kripke's Wittgenstein*. Montreal: McGill–Queen's University Press, 2006.

Landini, Gregory. *Frege's Notations: What They Are and How They Mean*. London: Palgrave-Macmillan, 2012.

Laßwitz, Kurd. "Rezension von *Begriffsschrift*," *Jenaer Literaturzeitung*, 6 (1879): 248–49.

Leibniz, Gottfried Wilhelm. *Mathematische Schriften* [1850–63]. Ed. C. J. Gerhardt. Hildesheim: Georg Olms Verlag, 1971.

Lindström, Sten, Erik Palmgren, Krister Segerberg, and Viggo Stoltenberg-Hansen, eds. *Logicism, Intuitionism, and Formalism: What Has Become of Them?* Berlin: Springer-Verlag, 2009.

Linsky, Leonard. *Referring*. London: Routledge & Kegan Paul, 1967.

Lotze, Hermann. *Grundzüge der Religionsphilosophie*. Leipzig: S. Hirzel, 1884.

Macbeth, Danielle. *Frege's Logic*. Cambridge: Harvard University Press, 2005.

MacCulloch, Diarmaid. *The Reformation*. New York: Penguin Books, 2004.

MacFarlane, John. "Frege, Kant, and the Logic in Logicism," *The Philosophical Review*, 111 (2002): 25–66.

Makin, Gideon. *The Metaphysicians of Meaning: Russell and Frege on Sense and Denotation*. London: Routledge, 2001.

——— "'On Denoting': Appearance and Reality." In *Russell vs. Meinong: The Legacy of "On Denoting."* Ed. Nicholas Griffin and Dale Jacquette. London: Routledge, 2009. 78–100.

Massey, Gerald J. "Some Reflections on Psychologism." In *Phenomenology and the Formal Sciences*. Ed. Thomas M. Seebohm, Dagfinn Føllesdal and Jitendranath N. Mohanty. Dordrecht: Kluwer Academic Publishing, 1991. 183–94.

McDonough, Richard. "A Note on Frege's and Russell's Influence on Wittgenstein's *Tractatus*," *Russell: The Journal of the Bertrand Russell Archives* 14 (1994): 39–46.

McGinn, Colin. *Wittgenstein on Meaning: An Interpretation and Evaluation*. Oxford: Basil Blackwell, 1984.

McGuinness, Brian. *Wittgenstein: A Life: Young Ludwig 1889–1921*. Berkeley: University of California Press, 1988.

McGuinness, Brian and Rudolf Haller, eds. *Wittgenstein in Focus – Im Brennpunkt: Wittgenstein*. Amsterdam: Rodopi, 1989.

Mendelsohn, Richard L. *The Philosophy of Gottlob Frege*. Cambridge: Cambridge University Press, 2005.

Milkov, Nikolay. "Frege in Context" [essay review of Gabriel and Kienzler, eds., *Frege in Jena* (1997)], *British Journal for the History of Philosophy*, 9 (2001): 557–70.

Mill, John Stuart. *A System of Logic, Ratiocinative and Inductive* [1843]. Ed. J. M. Robson [Mill, *Collected Works*. Volume VII]. London: Routledge & Kegan Paul, 1973.

Mohanty, Jitendranath N. "Husserl and Frege: A New Look at Their Relationship," *Research in Phenomenology*, 4(1) (1974): 51–62.

——— *Readings on Edmund Husserl's Logical Investigations*. The Hague: Martinus Nijhoff, 1977. 22–32.

——— "Husserl, Frege and the Overcoming of Psychologism." In *Philosophy and Science in Phenomenological Perspective*. Ed. K. K. Cho. Dordrecht: Martinus Nijhoff, 1984. 143–52.

Moktefi, Amirouche, and Sun-Joo Shin, eds. *Visual Reasoning with Diagrams*. Basel: Birkhäuser Verlag, 2013.

Monk, Ray. *Ludwig Wittgenstein: The Duty of Genius*. Harmondsworth: Penguin Books, 1990.

Nahin, Paul J. *An Imaginary Tale: The Story of $\sqrt{-1}$*. Princeton: Princeton University Press, 2010.

Newton, Isaac. *Principia Mathematica Philosophiæ Naturalis*. Trans. Bernard Cohen and Anne Whitman. Berkeley: University of California Press, 1999. Volume I.

——— *De Gravitatione et æquipondio fluidorum*. In Newton, Isaac. *Philosophical Writings*. Ed. Andrew Janiak. Trans. A. R. Hall and Marie Boas Hall. Cambridge: Cambridge University Press, 2004. 26–58.

Nidditch, Peter H. "Peano and the Recognition of Frege," *Mind*, 72 (1963): 103–10.

Noonan, Harold W. *Frege: A Critical Introduction*. Cambridge: Polity Press, 2001.

Papineau, David. *Philosophical Devices: Proofs, Probabilities, Possibilities, and Sets*. Oxford: Oxford University Press, 2012.

Parker, Philip M., ed. *Wismar: Webster's Timeline History, 1348–2007*. San Diego: ICON Group International, 2010.

Parsons, Charles. "Frege's Theory of Number." In *Philosophy in America*. Ed. Max Black. Ithaca: Cornell University Press, 1965. 180–203.

Peano, Giuseppe. "Dr. Gottlob Frege, *Grundgesetze der Arithmetik, begriffsschriftlich abgeleitet*, Erster Band, Jena, 1893, pag. XXXII + 254," *Rivista di matematica*, 5 (1895): 122–28.

——— *Opere scelte*. Rome: Edizioni Cremonese, 1959. Volume 2, 187–95.

Peckhaus, Volker. "Benno Kerry: Beiträge zu seiner Biographie," *History and Philosophy of Logic*, 15 (1994): 1–8.

——— "Schröder's Logic." In *The Rise of Modern Logic: From Leibniz to Frege*. Ed. Dov M. Gabbay and John Woods. Amsterdam: Elsevier, 1994. 557–609.

Peirce, Charles S. *Collected Papers of Charles Sanders Peirce*. Ed. Charles Hartshorne, Paul Weiss, and Arthur W. Burks. Cambridge: Harvard University Press, 1931–1935.

Pelletier, Francis Jeffry, and Bernard Linsky. "Russell vs. Frege on Definite Descriptions as Singular Terms." In *Russell vs. Meinong: The Legacy of "On Denoting."* Ed. Nicholas Griffin and Dale Jacquette. London: Routledge, 2009. 40–64.

Perloff, Marjorie, ed. *Wittgenstein's Ladder: Poetic Language and the Strangeness of the Ordinary*. Chicago: University of Chicago Press, 1999.

Perry, John. "Frege on Demonstratives," *The Philosophical Review*, 86 (4) (1977): 474–97.

Picardi, Eva. "Kerry und Frege über Begriff und Gegenstand," *History and Philosophy of Logic*, 15 (1994): 9–32.

Poincaré, Henri. "Les mathématiques et la logique," *Revue de Métaphysique et de Morale*, 14 (1906): 294–317.

——— "Mathematical Discovery." In Poincaré, Henri. *Science and Method* [1908]. Trans. Francis Maitland. London: T. Nelson and Sons, 1914. 46–63.

Posy, Carl J., ed. *Kant's Philosophy of Mathematics: Modern Essays.* Berlin: Springer-Verlag, 1982.

Potter, Michael. "Introduction." In *The Cambridge Companion to Frege.* Ed. Michael Potter and Tom Ricketts. Cambridge: Cambridge University Press, 2010. 1–31.

Pratt-Hartmann, Ian. "The Hamiltonian Syllogistic," *Journal of Logic, Language and Information,* 20 (4) (2011): 445–74.

Prescott, George. *History, Theory and Practice of the Electric Telegraph.* Boston: Ticknor and Fields, 1860.

Quine, Willard Van Orman. "On Frege's Way Out," *Mind,* 64 (1955): 145–59.

——— *Word and Object.* Cambridge: MIT Press, 1960.

——— "Reference and Modality." In Quine, Willard Van Orman. *From a Logical Point of View.* Cambridge: Harvard University Press, 1961. 139–59.

——— "Speaking of Objects." In Quine, Willard Van Orman. *Ontological Relativity and Other Essays.* New York: Columbia University Press, 1969.

——— "The Ways of Paradox." In Quine, Willard Van Orman. *The Ways of Paradox and Other Essays.* Revised and enlarged edition. Cambridge: Harvard University Press, 1976.

——— *Theories and Things.* Cambridge: Harvard University Press, 1981.

——— "Reply to Charles Parsons." In *The Philosophy of W. V. Quine.* Ed. Lewis Edwin Hahn and Paul Arthur Schilpp. LaSalle: Open Court, 1986. 396–403.

Reck, Erich H. "Wittgenstein's 'Great Debt' to Frege: Biographical Traces and Philosophical Themes." In *From Frege to Wittgenstein: Perspectives on Early Analytic Philosophy.* Ed. Erich H. Reck. Oxford: Oxford University Press, 2002. 3–38.

Reck, Erich H., and Steve Awodey, eds. *Frege's Lectures on Logic: Carnap's Student Notes 1910–1914.* Chicago: Open Court, 2004.

Reed, Delbert. *The Origins of Analytic Philosophy: Kant and Frege.* London: Continuum, 2007.

Resnik, Michael D. "The Frege–Hilbert Controversy," *Philosophy and Phenomenological Research,* 34 (1973): 386–403.

——— *Frege and the Philosophy of Mathematics.* Ithaca: Cornell University Press, 1980.

Rockmore, Tom. *In Kant's Wake: Philosophy in the Twentieth Century.* Oxford: Wiley-Blackwell, 2006.

Rosser, Barkley. "Extensions of Some Theorems of Gödel and Church," *Journal of Symbolic Logic,* 1 (1936): 87–91.

Russell, Bertrand. *The Principles of Mathematics.* New York: W. W. Norton & Company, 1903.

——— "On Denoting," *Mind,* 14 (1905): 479–93.

——— "Mathematical Logic as Based on a Theory of Types," *American Journal of Mathematics,* 30 (1908): 222–62.

——— *Introduction to Mathematical Philosophy.* New York: Simon and Schuster, 1919.

———— *Last Philosophical Testament 1943–1968. The Collected Papers of Bertrand Russell. Volume 11.* Ed. John G. Slater, with the assistance of Peter Köllner. London: Routledge, 1997.

Ryle, Gilbert. "Meaning and Necessity," *Philosophy*, 24 (1949): 69–76.

Salmon, Nathan. *Frege's Puzzle.* Atascadero: Ridgeview Publishing Company, 1986.

Santayana, George. *Lotze's System of Philosophy.* Bloomington: Indiana University Press, 1971.

Schildauer, Johannes. *The Hansa: History and Culture.* Trans. Katherine Vanovitch. Erfurt: Edition Leipzig, 1985.

Schildt, Franz. *Geschichte der Stadt Wismar bis zum Ende des 13. Jahrhunderts* [Wismar 1872]. Reprint edition. Charleston: Nabu Press, 2013.

Schirn, Matthias. *Frege: Importance and Legacy.* Berlin: Walter de Gruyter, 1996.

Schlote, Karl-Heinz, and Uwe Dathe. "Die Anfänge von Gottlob Freges wissenschaftlicher Laufbahn," *Historia Mathematica*, 21 (2) (1994): 185–95.

Schön, Karl. *Friedrich Schiller in Jena 1789–1799: Seine Lebens- und Schaffensjahre in Jena.* Munich: BookRix GmbH & Co., 2014.

Schott, Dieter, ed. *Gottlob Frege – ein Genius mit Wismarer Wurzeln: Leistung – Wirkung – Tradition.* Leipzig: Leipziger Universitätsverlag, 2012.

Schröder, Ernst. "Anzeige von Freges *Begriffsschrift*," *Zeitschrift für Mathematik und Physik*, 25 (1881): 81–94.

———— *Vorlesungen über die Algebra der Logik.* Three volumes. Leipzig: B. G. Taubner Verlag, 1890–1910.

Schulte, Joachim. "Frege und Wittgenstein." In *Gottlob Frege – Werk und Wirkung.* Ed. Gottfried Gabriel and Uwe Dathe. Paderborn: Mentis. 211–26.

Sedwick, Sally. *Kant's Groundwork of the Metaphysics of Morals.* Cambridge: Cambridge University Press, 2008.

Shabel, Lisa. *Mathematics in Kant's Critical Philosophy: Reflections on Mathematical Practice.* London: Routledge, 2011.

Shapiro, Stewart. "Categories, Structures, and the Frege–Hilbert Controversy: The Status of Meta-mathematics," *Philosophia Mathematica*, 13 (2005): 61–77.

Shorto, Russell. *Descartes' Bones: A Skeletal History of the Conflict between Faith and Reason.* New York: Random House, 2008.

Simons, Peter. "Judging Correctly: Brentano and the Reform of Elementary Logic." In *The Cambridge Companion to Brentano.* Ed. Dale Jacquette. Cambridge: Cambridge University Press, 2004. 45–65.

Sluga, Hans D. *Gottlob Frege* [1980]. London: Routledge, 1999.

———— "Gottlob Frege: The Early Years." In *Philosophy in History: Essays on the Historiography of Philosophy.* Ed. Richard Rorty, Jerome B. Schneewind, and Quentin Skinner. Cambridge: Cambridge University Press, 1984. 329–56.

Smith, David Woodruff, and Ronald McIntyre. *Husserl and Intentionality: A Study of Mind, Meaning, and Language.* Dordrecht: D. Reidel Publishing Company, 1982.

Sobociński, Bolesław. "L'Analyse de l'antinomie russellienne par Leśniewski," *Methodos*, 1 (1949): 99–104, 220–28, 308–16; 2 (1950): 237–57.

Spade, Paul Vincent. "Ockham's Nominalist Metaphysics: Some Main Themes." In *The Cambridge Companion to Ockham*. Ed. Paul Vincent Spade. Cambridge: Cambridge University Press, 1999. 100–17.

Standage, Tom. *The Victorian Internet: The Remarkable Story of the Telegraph and the Nineteenth Century's On-Line Pioneers*. Revised second edition. London: Bloomsbury, 2014.

Stelzner, Werner. "Ernst Abbe and Gottlob Frege." In *Frege in Jena: Beiträge zur Spurensicherung*. Ed. Gottfried Gabriel and Wolfgang Kienzler. Würzburg: Königshausen und Neumann, 1997. 5–32.

Sternfeld, Robert. *Frege's Logical Theory*. Carbondale: Southern Illinois University Press, 1966.

Struik, Dirk Jan. *A Source Book in Mathematics 1200–1800*. Cambridge: Harvard University Press, 1969.

Taylor, Brook. *Methodus incrementorum directa et inversa [Direct and Reverse Methods of Incrementation]*. London: William Innys, 1715.

Thiel, Christian. *Sense and Reference in Frege's Logic*. Dordrecht: D. Reidel Publishing Company, 1968.

Twain, Mark. *Autobiography of Mark Twain: The Complete and Authoritative Edition*. Ed. Harriet E. Smith, Benjamin Griffin, and Victor Fisher. Berkeley: University of California Press, 2010.

Unwin, Nicholas. "*Quasi*-Realism, Negation and the Frege–Geach Problem," *The Philosophical Quarterly*, 49 (1999): 337–52.

Venn, John. "Review of *Begriffsschrift*, by G. Frege," *Mind*, 5 (1880): 297.

Vikko, Risto. "The Reception of Frege's *Begriffsschrift*," *Historia Mathematica*, 25 (1998): 412–22.

Vlastos, Gregory. "The Socratic Elenchus," *The Journal of Philosophy*, 79(11) (1982): 711–14.

——— "The Socratic Elenchus," *Oxford Studies in Ancient Philosophy*, 1 (1983): 27–58.

Weber, Max. *Die Protestantische Ethik und der Geist des Kapitalismus*. [Original publication in *Archiv für Sozialwissenschaften und Sozialpolitik* 1904–1905.] Tübingen: J. C. B. Mohr, 1934.

Wedgwood, Cicely Veronica. *The Thirty-Years War* [1938]. New York: New York Review Books, 2005.

Wegner, Sven-Ake. *Eine kurze Einführung in Gottlob Freges Begriffsschrift*. Wuppertal: Bergische Universität, 1979.

Wehmeier, Kai. "Aspekte der Frege–Hilbert-Korrespondenz," *History and Philosophy of Logic*, 18 (1997): 201–9.

Weiner, Joan. *Frege Explained: From Arithmetic to Analytic Philosophy*. LaSalle: Open Court, 2004.

White, Roger. "Wittgenstein on Identity," *Proceedings of the Aristotelian Society*, 78 (1977–1978): 157–74.

Whitehead, Alfred North, and Bertrand Russell. *Principia Mathematica*. Three volumes. Cambridge: Cambridge University Press, 1910–1913 (first edition) and 1925 and 1927 (second edition).

Wilson, Mark. "Frege: The Royal Road from Geometry," *Noûs*, 26(2) (1992): 149–80.

Wilson, Peter Harnish. *The Thirty Years War: Europe's Tragedy*. Cambridge: Harvard University Press, 2009.

Winterbourne, Anthony T. *The Ideal and the Real: Kant's Theory of Space, Time, and Mathematical Constructions*. Bury St. Edmunds: Abramis Academic Publishing, 2007.

Wittgenstein, Ludwig. *Tractatus Logico-Philosophicus*. Ed. C. K. Ogden. London: Routledge & Kegan Paul, 1922.

———— *Zettel*. Trans. G. E. M. Anscombe. Ed. G. E. M. Anscombe and G. H. von Wright. Berkeley: University of California Press, 1970.

———— *Letters to Russell, Keynes and Moore*. Ed. G. H. von Wright. Oxford: Basil Blackwell, 1974.

———— *Remarks on the Foundations of Mathematics*. Ed. G. H. von Wright, R. Rhees, and G. E. M. Anscombe. Revised edition. Cambridge: MIT Press, 1978.

———— *Notebooks 1914–1916*. Second edition. Ed. G. H. von Wright and G. E. M. Anscombe, with an English translation by G. E. M. Anscombe. Chicago: University of Chicago Press, 1979.

———— *Philosophical Investigations* [1953]. Trans. G. E. M. Anscombe. Third edition. Oxford: Blackwell Publishing, 2001.

Wright, Crispin. *Frege's Conception of Numbers as Objects*. Aberdeen: Aberdeen University Press, 1983.

Zalta, Edward N. "Gottlob Frege." In *The Stanford Encyclopedia of Philosophy*. Ed. Edward N. Zalta. Stanford: Stanford University Press, 2012.

Zamyatin, Yevgeny. *We* [1921]. Trans. Clarence Brown. London: Penguin Books, 1993.

Zimmerman, Aaron. *Moral Epistemology*. Abingdon: Routledge, 2010.

Index